The Invisible Spirit

A LIFE OF POST-WAR SCOTLAND

1945–75

The Invisible Spirit

A LIFE OF POST-WAR SCOTLAND

1945–75

Kenneth Roy

BIRLINN

First published in 2013 by ICS Books
Institute of Contemporary Scotland

This second edition published in 2014 by
Birlinn Ltd
West Newington House
10 Newington Road
Edinburgh
EH9 1QS

British Library Cataloguing in Publication Data.
A catalogue record for this book is available from
the British Library.

ISBN 978-1-78027-246-7

Printed and bound by Gutenberg Press, Malta

Contents

Preface

This book was motivated by a curiosity about my own country. It was a belated attempt to give me an insight that I had always lacked – the knowledge of what was going on in Scotland in the early part of my life, when I was too young to understand or care. Before I wrote the book I was more familiar with Robert Burns's Ayrshire, the main figures of the Scottish Enlightenment and the clearances from the Highlands than I was with the events and influences of a later and not much documented Scotland – the one in which I was brought up.

I was born on 26 March 1945, six weeks before the end of the war in Europe. I am the same age as the baby who was wheeled in a pram through a crowded George Square in Glasgow on VE night – the starting point for the book – and who makes a brief appearance in the first chapter. Of course I have no memory of the night, but nor do I remember much else about the Scotland outside my circumscribed childhood. Edinburgh, a capital only 20 miles away, might have been a foreign city, so rarely (if ever) did my parents take me there.

Bonnybridge, the village of the Industrial Revolution in which I lived until I was 18 years old, was not as dull as it often seemed. It had an incidental role in a Scottish adventure, the removal of the Stone of Destiny from Westminster Abbey by Ian Hamilton's Christmas raiding party. When they got the stone back to Scotland they were unsure what to do with it. They brought it late one night to Bonnybridge and hid it in a place of safety under the floorboards of my Uncle George's office. George Bernard was a right-hand man of John Rollo, a local industrialist and patriot, whose St Andrew's Works was its temporary home. Rollo could keep a secret, and my uncle died without ever knowing that he had once sat above the Stone of Destiny, if not actually on it.

The stone was never mentioned in any of my classes at Greenhill Primary School, a few minutes' walk from St Andrew's Works; it meant nothing to me. But by 1953 it had been repossessed for the coronation of Elizabeth II – a disputed title. Not that I knew of this dispute, which again involved Ian Hamilton. One grey early summer morning we were marched out of the school gates to a wooden hut and sat in rows in front of a television set, the first I had ever seen, and instructed to watch grainy images from London, a faraway magical place.

So my first indelible memory is of a British occasion. I came to realise that I had been a child of this Britishness. It was a state of mind defined not only by a then unquestioned belief in the merits of a union of two nations but by instinctive socialist ideals. Few people in Bonnybridge had any illusions about their councillors, who wielded considerable power in the allocation of the new houses which rose in steep terraces above the village. But even the occasional abuses of power by the local Labour mafia failed to dislodge their loyalty to the party.

That party was never more British than under Mr Attlee, whose landslide victory a few months after my birth was loudly cheered. Bonnybridge approved also of such other pillars of Britishness as the National Health Service and the BBC. *Panorama* – the weekly 'window on the world' – was required viewing when television arrived in the village in the late 1950s. By then I was fitfully attending Denny High School and still learning nothing about modern Scottish history.

At the age of 25 I was editing my own theatre magazine, running my own theatre company and presenting a weekly arts programme on the BBC. I was barely interested in anything apart from this delightful but incestuous world; the larger affairs of the country were almost as elusive as they had been in my childhood. It was only when I joined the BBC full-time, working in news and current affairs, that I became painfully aware how little I knew of Scottish politics and society.

In 1975 I presented the BBC's television coverage of the arrival of North Sea oil. By then I had learned enough to see that event in symbolic terms. For me, it marked the end of the post-war era. That era was the subject matter of the formative years of my life; it is now the raw material for the next 500 pages.

Prestwick Airport
August 2013

A note about the style

I wanted to tell a story. The simplest way of doing so was chrono-logically: a chapter for each year. Although I considered adopting a thematic approach, I was never attracted by the idea. The sense of a story would have been lost.

I am unable to credit many of the journalists on whose work I have drawn. For much of the period covered by the book, bylines in the Scottish press were as rare as snakes in Iceland. Some of the journalism was of high quality – the evocation, for example, of Billy Graham preaching in the Kelvin Hall, which was no less admirable for being anonymous. I have supplied names where possible, but it was not often possible. Sometimes I employ short phrases in quotation without attribution; these are invariably from contemporary newspaper reports.

I have an aversion to the use of capitals in the titles of public and other offices. My ruthless policy is to use lower case except for titles where the importance of the office justifies capitals. There are few such titles.

1945

THE GUARD'S VAN

I

A sailor of the Royal Netherlands Navy was the star of the night in Glasgow. From the top of the Duke of Wellington's statue in Exchange Square he performed a burlesque of Hitler before addressing the crowd, thanking the Scots 'for the brave part you have played in the liberation of my country'. By midnight on VE Day they were still dancing the conga in front of the City Chambers and packing the air-raid shelters around George Square. 'Noise,' wrote an eye-witness, 'the sound of which had not been heard for six years. You could hear it half a mile away, solid and heart-warming.' The buses and trams ran late into the night, while bakers worked overtime to meet the demand for bread. It was 8 May 1945.

In George Square a way was cleared through the dense crowd for a woman pushing a grey utility pram. Only the civic fathers were missing; as a correspondent in the press complained: 'No dignitary appeared for us to hail with all the fervour that was pent-up within us. The loudspeakers were silent.' But little else was silent in Scotland that night, as the years of peace began with an explosion of patriotic high spirits.

From the lower Clyde came the hooting of ships riotously bedecked for the occasion. A pipe band paraded through Falkirk. On the steps of the Town Hall in Kilmarnock, Provost Carnie's call for three cheers for the allies was met with a thunderous response; the town bells which had not been heard since May 1939 were set ringing. A beacon lit on the summit of Craigie Hill was visible across a wide radius of Ayrshire. Earlier in the day the Sheriff Court in Stirling was adjourned, sparing the guilty the indignity of spending VE night in a cell. The bells of the Kirk of St John, Perth, began to peal immediately after Churchill's victory broadcast.

Such responses were repeated throughout the land in a national expression of joy – and overwhelming relief.

The following evening the BBC Scottish Orchestra performed the *Hallelujah Chorus* at a festival of thanksgiving in the Usher Hall. The address was given by Tom Johnston, the wartime Secretary of State for Scotland and perhaps the most respected Scotsman of his generation:

It was this unity of purpose that saved us, that took us from the brink of destruction and gave us the strength to achieve victory. It was the corporate all-in effort, each for all, that enabled us to match the hour, and to withstand – at one period entirely alone in the world – the organised fury of the fascist and Nazi powers of darkness. If we could only recapture part of that enthusiasm, elan and common purpose, recapture it for the much-needed reconstruction and betterment of our world – if only we could lift great social crusades like better housing and health from the arena of partisan strife, what magnificent achievements might yet be ours.

A week later in Dundee there was a sober postscript to the celebrations: the arrival of a German U-boat in the Tay. Its crew had been oblivious to the end of the war; only when the boat's broken wireless was repaired did the men learn that it had been all over for some days. A crowd of 1,000 gathered at King George Wharf to observe the rituals of surrender. A Royal Navy chief petty officer boarded her, ripped off the German naval flag and hoisted the white ensign; the boat was then inspected; small arms and ammunition were brought ashore. The crew had provisions for six more days.

With the restoration of normality, restrictions on street lighting were lifted and a weather forecast was published, the first for six years. A large depression between Ireland and the Azores was almost stationary; at the Springburn recording station the sunshine hours were recorded as nil. Three tons of empty bottles were collected from George Square, where the damage so displeased Councillor Jean Roberts, chairman of the parks committee, that she prohibited the square's use for open-air meetings for some time to come. It had been a good party. It looked like being a long hangover.

II

Among the VE Day babies a son was born in Paisley to Barbara Morrison and her husband, Flight Lieutenant W D Wallace. On the next day – a public holiday – Captain Aidan Duff, RAMC, the son of an Arbroath manse, married Rita Robertson in the first post-war wedding in Glasgow University Memorial Chapel. On the same day a notice in the press recorded the death of Captain James Barclay, 26, son of the provost of Stewarton, who was killed in action in the final hours of battle.

All that happened in the following weeks had the peculiar distinction of being 'the first' of the post-war era. The first house to be sold by auction was The Barony, Blairmore, with its 'undisturbed and wide views over Loch Long' (upset price: £1,500). The first reported road accident victim was six-year-old Nancy Crossan, whose life marked with sad precision the duration of the war. The first rare sighting was a greater spotted wood-pecker in the grounds of Castlemilk, a Glasgow estate which was soon to be converted into another form of estate less congenial to wildlife. An unknown actor called Stanley Baxter, of whom it was said that 'some variation in pace and intonation would improve his performance', appeared in one of the first stage productions, Unity Theatre's *Remembered for Ever*. The first out-burst from the ultra-censorious Free Church of Scotland opposed Glasgow Corporation's approval of 'secular concerts' on Sunday nights.

The first statistics were that 1,776 people in Scotland were suffering from pulmonary thrombosis and that the average height of the 13-year-old boy had risen 1.67 inches since 1930 despite the general privation. The first strikes were by 2,300 Shotts miners – who, having been warned by the government that they were breaking the Defence of the Realm Act, stayed out for a further six weeks – and 400 dockers in Aberdeen. In the first of two air disasters, 11 people, including five children and their mother, were killed when a Wellington bomber on a test flight over Lossiemouth developed engine trouble and crashed into a block of council houses; in the second, 17 American servicemen died when their Liberator aircraft, on a flight from Lancashire to Prestwick, crashed into Pildinny Hill near Ballantrae.

Incongruously, the first sign of acrimony in the letters columns of the Scottish press concerned the standards of Highland hospitality. 'A Traveller' complained of 'the very low standard of cooking and the continual repetition of the same dishes, the failure to attend to small details, the general attitude towards guests'. A E Towle, chairman of the Scottish division of the Hotels and Restaurants Association of Great Britain, replied that the rations allowed to hotels by the Ministry of Food failed to provide more than 25% of the meals with a main dish and that the rest had to be made up by unrationed foods which were difficult to obtain.

The Saltire Society, established in 1936 to improve the quality of life in Scotland, was likewise preoccupied with the state of tourism. In its first post-war report it pressed for 'the stimulation of a way of life which is the expression of our national character – and if that is not enough to attract the tourists, let us examine the cause of decay in our national character'. In the towns there was a need for restaurants which provided modestly priced meals in the evening – 'not limited to fish and chips' – and cooks should be taught how to make good coffee. 'We have a nostalgic regard,' said the report, 'for the type of hotel once common in Scotland where the proprietor was also host and his visitor's requirements received his personal care.'

For the majority there was no hope of imaginative cooking in personally supervised hotels. The first official edict brought a chill blast of reality as instructions were issued for the distribution of ration books: 'Bring your identity card and current ration book to the centre. Fill up the reference leaf, which is page four of the old ration book, and leave the reference leaf intact. The page must not be cut out. Every married woman and every woman who has been married at any time must write "Mrs" in front of her name at the top of the reference leaf, and every woman who has not been married must write "Miss". There will be no postal applications whatever.'

The first post-war General Assembly of the Church of Scotland opened in Edinburgh. Dithering on whether to admit women as elders, it remitted the question back to kirk sessions – a typical ploy of the national church when it found itself in a tight spot. J Strathearn McNab of Ayr said: 'In the Bible the clear view is that it is man's office to rule.' He was applauded when he asked the assembly 'not to listen to all those modern ideas about what the world is doing'. Sir James Simpson, Aberdeen, replied: 'The man from Ayr is going against the best interests of the church. He said that if I voted against him I was going against the will of God. I don't believe him.' The issue proved deeply divisive. One Kirk member wrote to the press: 'What do we hope to achieve by admitting women to the eldership? One of the main duties of the office is to assist in administering the communion, and this is a ceremony I have witnessed in many churches in the last half-century. Never have I failed to be struck by the quiet reverence and dignity with which it has been carried out; invariably it is impressive in its unobtrusiveness and equilibrium. How can we women improve it?' Charlotte Sweeney of Bearsden replied: 'With the desire not to offend many older and devoted women members, the church may alienate the large body of professional and business women who are working in a world where the campaign for equality is already largely won, as in medicine, law, the teaching profession and public representative bodies.' Women were finally admitted as elders – but not until 1966.

The first practical vision of what the new world might offer was articulated by Osborne Henry Mavor (who wrote his many plays using the pseudonym James Bridie). In 1943, with the help of his friend Tom Honeyman and others, Bridie had founded the Glasgow Citizens' Theatre, a wartime candle in the dark. He foresaw a 'commonwealth of theatres' in Scotland in which the Citizens' would play a major part, operating a 'true' repertory system offering the public a choice of three plays a week. Less inspiringly, Melville Dinwiddie, the BBC's Scottish regional director, announced plans for a new Scottish Home Service. Since the architect of these plans was a Church of Scotland minister, it was to be expected that a weekly religious service would come top of the list of forthcoming attractions. There would also be Scottish variety at least twice a week, special programmes by Sir Harry Lauder to mark his 70th birthday, a series by the comedian Harry Gordon entitled *Gordon's Gaieties*, outside broadcasts from seaside concert parties, a literary monthly (*Chapbook*), recitals of Gaelic songs (in English), Scottish dance music, and a weekly discussion series, *Talking About Scotland*, with Mavor, Sir Hector Hetherington, principal of Glasgow University, Augustus Muir, a Canadian-born author of Scottish parentage, and Sir William Darling, a former Lord Provost of Edinburgh. In a world hungry for enlightenment, Scottish news was relegated in Dinwiddie's prospectus to a five-minute bulletin on weekday evenings.

The second edition of *Poetry Scotland* appeared in June. It contained work by 26 writers including William Soutar, a considerable figure in the Scottish literary renaissance of the 1930s. The critics also singled out Edwin Muir, whose book *Scottish Journey* brought him a wider acclaim than his poetry; Ruthven Todd, editor of the works of William Blake, who was soon to emigrate to America; William Jeffrey, a poet in both Scots and English, to whom Christopher Grieve (Hugh MacDiarmid) once wrote a bitter letter complaining that Scotland was starving him; and George Bruce, who was to become a senior BBC producer and trenchant critic of the arts and literature. W S Graham's *The Children of Lanarkshire* earned particular notice as 'a striking poem'; Graham, of Bohemian temperament, had just moved to Cornwall, where he lived for many years in near-poverty, his work largely ignored in his native country.

The first post-war honours list brought a CBE for Agnes Mure Mackenzie for her services to Scottish history and scholarship. 'The most brilliant of living Scotswomen,' wrote Marion Lochhead, herself a fine poet. 'Of good Highland descent' – daughter of a Stornoway doctor – Mackenzie was described as 'a capable housewife who, in her own words, can do anything in a house except, perhaps, sweep the lum'. She told Lochhead that she adored Sir Walter Scott. 'If one could place her in any special period, it would be delightful to picture her in the late 18th century, the golden age of Scots society.' There was, however, little recognition of Scottish achievement in the first honorary graduation ceremony at Glasgow University, Sir Hector Hetherington giving thanks that the civilised world had 'passed safely, though with heavy cost, over a long, dark and dangerous road', before the award of honorary degrees to such functionaries as the canons of Canterbury and Bradford, the moderator of the General Assembly of the Presbyterian Church of England and the governor of New Hampshire. The same university published an order of merit for bursaries, with Gavin Dick of Hamilton Academy and Margaret Anderson of Ayr Academy first and second out of the elected hundred.

In the first criminal trial of more than passing interest, a jury at the High Court in Glasgow took only 10 minutes to acquit William Delaney, a 19-year-old soldier, of murdering his 17-year-old wife, but found him guilty of her culpable homicide. It added a rider that he had been provoked. In a statement to the police Delaney said he met the girl, Mary Maclean, in a Glasgow dance hall and when he got his papers for the army in July 1944 they ran away and were married. More than once he absented himself from his regiment without leave, returning to Glasgow to see her. She taunted him that she was in love with someone else, confessing adultery. One evening they went to the cinema together. 'We came home to her close and stood at the foot of the stairs. She started to kiss me, and a few minutes later she said she wished I was back in detention. She said I had better go home as all she wanted was a good time. I lost my head. I gripped her by the throat to frighten her and she fell down.'

Lord Moncrieff took an unusual view of the case. 'Here are these children, thinking they are grown-up enough to enjoy the privileges and face the duties of marriage. The man appears to be devoted. The woman appears to have been absorbed in pleasure, with a natural gift for teasing, unstable and irritable, often provoking, often forgiven.' He sent Delaney to prison for two years. The description of the accused as a child, the claims against the character of Mary Maclean as a mitigating factor, the exceptional leniency of the sentence – none of these curiosities of the case attracted any public comment.

III

The tensions and horrors of war spilled over into the peace. An angry crowd of 300 gathered in the mining village of Plean, Stirlingshire, demonstrating against the billeting of Italian prisoners of war at a local farm. The sequel was heard in Stirling Sheriff Court, where one of the prisoners got three months' hard labour for stabbing a young miner in the chest, while three local men were fined for breach of the peace. Although violent disturbances of this kind were rare, the treatment of prisoners of war, especially those who were working and living on the farms, was a source of contention and confusion.

William Young, president of the National Farmers' Union of Scotland, sought official clarification on whether farmers were allowed to feed them. He was informed that the giving of solid food by employers was an offence, that only soup and hot drinks were permissible, and that the feeding of prisoners was the responsibility of the War Office. This inflexible ruling did not prevent some prisoner workers from requesting food from farmers, and some farmers from offering it. At a branch meeting of the NFU in Forfar, a member complained that farmers were 'spoiling' the PoWs with extras.

Glasgow Corporation became the first local authority in Scotland to make use of prisoners of war in clearing sites for house-building. Sixty German soldiers, supervised by a British guard armed with loaded sten guns, began work at Pollok, to be followed by 400 others at Govan and Priesthill; they were paid 3s a week, the rate stipulated by the Geneva Convention. A German lieutenant who was employed as an interpreter revealed a little of his civilian life before the war: he had been the director of 11 cinemas, only one of which had survived the allied bombing. Journalists who visited the site reported that most of the prisoners were young and fit, that they were wielding picks and shovels and operating pneumatic drills, and that they had made 'good progress for a first day's work'. Councillor James McInnes of the housing committee said that as soon as British labour was available, the services of the prisoners would be dispensed with.

The shortage of labour delayed the demolition of air-raid shelters, which had been erected not only in streets and back-courts but in back gardens and basements; some accommodated as many as a hundred people. It was decided to leave the shelters in Princes Street Gardens in Edinburgh for the time being, but to plant flowers on their roofs. In Paisley there were demands for the work to be done by Italian and German PoWs.

At least one prisoner was in no position to assist with the reconstruction of Scotland. At a court martial in London in the summer of 1945 eight Germans stood trial for the murder of Sergeant-Major Feldweber Wolfgang Rosterg at a camp near Comrie. The camp known as Cultybraggan, set in 200 acres of Perthshire moorland, was Category 'A' – maximum security – and reserved for hardliners, the so-called 'Black Nazis', whose presence – 2,000 of them were held there at one stage – turned a peaceful backwater of rural Scotland into 'a little slice of Hitler's Germany'. The camp had a reputation for institutionalised bullying and intimidation, nothing less than slavish devotion to the führer being acceptable.

Within hours of Rosterg's arrival on 22 December 1944 he was a marked man. The officers suspected that he had helped the partisans in Russia and given information to the allies on bombing targets; there were unconfirmed suggestions that he had revealed details of his treachery in personal papers. Whatever the explanation, he was ordered to take part in a 'discussion' on his first evening at the camp. One of the accused asked him whether he was a National Socialist and Rosterg replied that he was emphatically not; that he had been 'about the world enough' not to believe in National Socialism any longer.

The following morning around 6.30 there was a mock trial. Rosterg stood with a rope round his neck as various allegations were put to him, and he was told that he must reply to each of them. He was then attacked with an iron bar. Shortly before 8am he was taken to another of the huts where one of his accusers told him that he had committed treason. 'I have only acted rightly,' Rosterg replied. He was told that if he had any honour he would hang himself. 'No,' said Rosterg, 'I cannot do that.' A rope was again put round his neck. As he was dragged 60 yards along a muddy asphalt path to his place of execution, he was viciously struck on the head, kicked and stamped on, until he went 'completely blank'. At first light, just before roll-call, they hanged him in the bath-house. By then he was probably already dead.

On the second day of the court martial the deputy judge-advocate gave an assurance to each witness that, although the press would be publishing an account of the trial, it would not publish the names of witnesses: 'You may fully and frankly tell your story to the court without any fear that your name will be broadcast in Germany or anywhere else.' But witnesses continued to be unnerved by the defiant mood in the dock. One man testified that when he complained to his comrades about what was being done to Rosterg because he held a certain point of view, the only reply was: 'You are just as bad a criminal as he is. If you think like that, you had better keep your mouth shut.' When he was asked to point out particular figures among the accused, one by one they sprang to their feet and, according to a journalist in the room, 'gazed at him with hard, unflinching eyes, one smiling sardonically'. One of the accused gave evidence that he went to see Rosterg's body because he 'wanted to see what such a monstrosity looked like'.

Rosterg's murder was committed in a camp under British authority. If the vigilance of those in charge was ever questioned, it was not reported. Three of the eight accused were acquitted. The others were hanged in Pentonville Prison, London, on 6 October 1945. Only one ever expressed any regret for his actions. In a single day all the remaining prisoners at Cultybraggan were transferred to other camps. The camp was never reopened and the buildings in which Rosterg was tortured and murdered were demolished.

In a second scandal that summer, the press – including some American correspondents – were given access to a Polish military detention centre at Inverkeithing. Lurid allegations about the conditions of the detainees had been published in *Pravda*, the official organ of Russian communism, which denounced the camp as 'the Polish Dachau' and claimed that it 'reeked of the blood of innocent people'. Stung by these accusations, the Polish Ministry of Information opened the centre for inspection. It was found that 53 prisoners were being held there, of whom 40 were awaiting trial.

The journalists spoke to a 23-year-old soldier, Josef Dobosiewicz, who had fought with the Second Canadian Army Corps in Holland. The journalists were so disturbed by what they heard that, at their formal meeting with the military authorities in the camp chapel, they requested that the young man should be brought from detention for questioning. Dobosiewicz spoke English with a Canadian accent. Asked if he had any complaints to make about the camp he replied: 'Yes, I have quite a lot, but I don't want to be put in chains.' 'What chains?' he was asked. He replied that one prisoner was shot while trying to escape and another who was captured was then kept in chains for two weeks. Dobosiewicz said he was being held by the Polish military authorities on suspicion of theft but that he was innocent of the charge. An officer instructed the guards to bring the chains for inspection. When they were produced, a British liaison officer said they were War Office standard issue – 'a stout leather body belt with handcuff attachments'. A guard volunteered that they were 'sometimes used when men made trouble'. The journalists challenged the authorities to explain the shooting. A colonel said that two men escaped and were pursued by guards, who shouted a warning to stop in accordance with Polish military law. One man did stop. The other was making for a wood. The guards fired; a bullet went through his heart.

A few weeks after the inspection, the source of *Pravda's* accusations, Dr Jago Dzinski, a former detainee at Inverkeithing, was set upon by a crowd of Polish soldiers and sailors outside the Cosmo Cinema in Glasgow where he had addressed a meeting. It was an inflammatory speech: when he claimed that the first people to make a pact with Hitler were the Pilsudski minority in Poland, members of the audience jumped to their feet, shaking their fists and pouring a stream of invective on the speaker. As soon as he emerged into the street, a crowd of about 100 rushed to close round him. 'You communist,' they shouted, 'we are not having any Russian propaganda here. You escaped from Inverkeithing, but you won't escape this time.' Dzinski, who was bundled by the police into a house, denounced his detractors as fascists.

IV

One May evening Flight Lieutenant William Reid knocked on the door of his mother's house in Baillieston, Glasgow. There were many homecomings in the late spring and early summer of 1945 but none more celebrated than the return of this Scottish hero.

Part of his extraordinary story was graphically described in the citation for the Victoria Cross he was awarded in December 1943 for 'most conspicuous bravery':

On the night of November 3rd, 1943, Flight Lieutenant Reid was pilot and captain of a Lancaster aircraft detailed to attack Dusseldorf. Shortly after crossing the Dutch coast, the pilot's windscreen was shattered by fire from a Messerschmitt 110. Owing to a failure in the heating circuit, the rear gunner's hands were too cold for him to open fire immediately or to operate his microphone and so give warning of danger; but after a brief delay he managed to return the Messerschmitt's fire and it was driven off.

During the fight with the Messerschmitt, Flight Lieutenant Reid was wounded in the head, shoulders and hands. The elevator trimming tabs of the aircraft were damaged and it became difficult to control. The rear turret, too, was badly damaged and the communications system and compasses were put out of action. Flight Lieutenant Reid ascertained that his crew were unscathed and, saying nothing about his own injuries, he continued his mission.

Soon afterwards, the Lancaster was attacked by a Focke Wulf 190. This time, the enemy's fire raked the bomber from stem to stern. The rear gunner replied with his only serviceable gun but the state of his turret made accurate aiming impossible. The navigator was killed and the wireless operator fatally injured. The mid-upper turret was hit and the oxygen system put out of action. Flight Lieutenant Reid was again wounded and the flight engineer, though hit in the forearm, supplied him with oxygen from a portable supply.

Flight Lieutenant Reid refused to be turned from his objective and Dusseldorf was reached some 50 minutes later. He had memorised his course to the target and had continued in such a normal manner that the bomb-aimer, who was cut off by the failure of the communications system, knew nothing of his captain's injuries or of the casualties to his comrades. Photographs show that, when the bombs were released, the aircraft was right over the centre of the target.

Steering by the pole star and the moon, Flight Lieutenant Reid then set course for home. He was growing weak from loss of blood. The emergency oxygen supply had given out. With the windscreen shattered, the cold was intense. He lapsed into semi-consciousness. The flight engineer, with some help from the bomb-aimer, kept the Lancaster in the air despite heavy anti-aircraft fire over the Dutch coast.

The North Sea crossing was accomplished. An airfield was sighted. The captain revived, resumed control and made ready to land. Ground mist partially obscured the runway lights. The captain was also much bothered by blood from his head wound getting into his eyes. But he made a safe landing although one leg of the damaged undercarriage collapsed when the load came on.

Wounded in two attacks, without oxygen, suffering severely from cold, his navigator dead, his wireless operator fatally wounded, his aircraft crippled and defenceless, Flight Lieutenant Reid showed superb courage and leadership in penetrating a further 200 miles into enemy territory to attack one of the most strongly defended targets in Germany, every additional mile increasing the hazards of the long and perilous journey home. His tenacity and devotion to duty were beyond praise.

He was 21 years old when this act of valour took place. After a spell in hospital he returned to active service, flying bombing sorties in France. He was engaged in one such mission when his plane came down near Rheims. Although the entire crew managed to bale out, only Reid – who landed heavily by parachute, breaking his arm in the fall – and the wireless operator survived. A German patrol detained them and they were escorted to Stalag Luft 3 in Southern Silesia and then, in bitterly cold weather, marched westward with 1,200 other British and American airmen to a camp south of Berlin. He was posted missing in July 1944 but was able to send a postcard to his mother to say that he had been captured.

Mrs Reid described with Scottish under-statement the scene on his homecoming. 'The door opened, and Willie shouted "Here I come, mother". It was a very pleasant surprise.' Reid VC visited his old school, Coatbridge Secondary, and announced that he had 'no definite plans for the future'. Demobilised in 1946, he resumed his studies at Glasgow University and later at the West of Scotland Agricultural College, became an agricultural adviser, and married Violet Gallagher, daughter of a Glasgow sports journalist. He died at the age of 79 on 28 November 2001 – 58 years after one of the bravest deeds of the war. In 2009 his VC was sold at auction for £384,000, the highest amount ever fetched for a VC awarded to a British serviceman.

V

If William Reid VC had no definite plans for the future that spring evening in 1945, some returning servicemen hurried home with pressing ambitions. Churchill called a general election for July, and many of the candidates were still in uniform. The free use of rank so irritated one Labour candidate, Adam McKinlay (Tom Johnston's parliamentary private secretary during the war), that he lodged an objection to his opponent's definition of himself as a lieutenant-commander in the RNVR, complaining that there was no indication of what he had been before the war.

McKinlay's legal challenge failed to halt the practice. There were few constituencies without at least one candidate professing his military credentials, and the newspapers were keen to play the patriotic card by promoting the cause of young men who had had 'a good war' (as it was usually called), a policy with the unhappy result of exposing any who had had no war to speak of, or no war at all. The references to Gordon Stott, Labour's candidate in Edinburgh West, were gratuitously unpleasant. It was acknowledged that he was 'well-known at Parliament House as an advocate', that he was a son of the manse, that he had been a brilliant student at Edinburgh University – but none of this counted. All that mattered was that, in 1941, Stott had been registered as a conscientious objector. The *Glasgow Herald* waited until the week of the poll before it aimed its poisoned arrow: 'Mr Stott, by reason of his attitude towards the war and his unwillingness to accept the responsibilities of military service, does not commend himself to the general body of electors.' It was nothing more than an offensive assumption on the newspaper's part, but it hurt.

For most of the candidates returning from active service, the experience of parliamentary electioneering was quite new. Some had never set eyes on their constituencies; some had never addressed a public meeting. They were as politically raw as they were physically brave. Among these remarkable people, the soldiers and airmen of the 1945 campaign in Scotland, many vanished into anonymity. But there were others who went on to make a mark politically or in other ways.

Major Iain Macleod came home with a war wound that left him in constant pain; his suffering would worsen as he developed a spinal condition. Macleod was fighting a seat, the Western Isles, so indifferent to the cause of the Unionist Party – the distinctive name of the Scottish Tories until 1965 – that there was no branch of the party on the islands. His father, Lewis-born but now a GP in Yorkshire, promptly overcame the difficulty by appointing himself chairman of the non-existent association.

In the most northern constituency in Britain, Major Joseph Grimond of the Liberal Party was attempting to unseat the Tory incumbent, Basil Neven-Spence. The north-east was another repository of Liberal hopes: Major Alastair Millar, who had entered Germany via Normandy with the 51st Division, was hailed in Banffshire as 'a young crusading stalwart convinced that the spirit of Liberalism is aglow'. His Unionist opponent, William Duthie, 'a fisher loon made good, much concerned during the war with the organisation of bread supplies', could not help sounding a little dull by comparison.

Three ambitious young journalists were among the Liberal candidates in seats ranging from distant prospect to downright unwinnable: Flying Officer Ian McColl ('bright and fluent') in Dunfermline, where a branch of the party had recently been established; Lieutenant John Junor in Kincardine and West Aberdeenshire; Flying Officer Ivor Davies in Aberdeen and Kincardineshire Central. Davies, wounded in the Burma campaign, had the help of his wife, who nursed the constituency until he was able to return.

Voters in Ross and Cromarty had the choice of two captains in the Cameron Highlanders: Labour's Angus Mackintosh and the Liberals' John MacLeod, who was introduced at meetings as the son of Duncan MacLeod of Skeabost. MacLeod, captured at St Valery in 1940 and held in a PoW camp until May 1945, was so out of touch with British affairs on his repatriation that for three weeks he did little else but read *The Times* in an attempt to catch up. 'Whichever candidate is returned,' wrote an observer of the campaign, 'Ross and Cromarty will be represented by a young man, a soldier, entering politics for the first time.'

A native of Islay, Lieutenant Alastair McNeill Weir, another of the ingénues, had the benefit of a strong political background; his father Lauchlan, Labour MP for East Stirling and Clackmannan until his death a few weeks before the outbreak of war, had been parliamentary private secretary to Ramsay MacDonald before turning against his leader with an excoriating biography. Lauchlan was the first Labour candidate to contest Argyll; his son now followed. Alastair, having served five years aboard a destroyer, suddenly found himself addressing the fishermen of Tarbert about the unpopularity of herring. The candidate had worked out that only three herring were consumed per person per year. He blamed social snobbery: the housewife in the flat would not cook herring or kippers becuse the neighbours would know what the family was having for tea.

A fellow socialist, Major William Ross, whose 'absence on military duty had prevented him from making himself known until his return from the Far East', was addressing crowded meetings in Ayr Town Hall. But where was Captain William Hughes? He too should have returned from the Far East. There was consternation in Perth Labour Party when the War Office sent word that it had lost touch with Hughes since he left Burma on a flight home. The candidate turned up in time to lodge his nomination papers and to declare in his opening speech: 'The people like controls.' His SNP opponent, Gunner J Blair Brown, had a simpler battlecry: 'Remember Bannockburn.'

In East Renfrewshire, with an electorate of 118,000 the biggest seat in Scotland, both the candidates were defined in the press as soldiers, suggesting some elusive social connection. Major Guy Lloyd (Unionist) was military commandant in Caen after the invasion of Normandy, while Corporal Daniel McArthur (Labour) had to obtain special leave from the Royal Engineers to fight the seat. Lloyd denounced Labourites as 'delegates of a fanatical and class-conscious group of political theorists' and their leaders as 'mere marionettes of an executive caucus, unelected, irresponsible'.

The fanatical, class-conscious group of political theorists in the capital included, in Edinburgh North, Sergeant Eustace George Willis and, in Leith, Corporal James Hoy, who, dismissed by one newspaper as 'a standard-pattern Labour man', drew a crowd of 1,000 to a local dance hall, as he campaigned on the bread-and-butter issues of housing and old age pensions. But it was an independent in Leith, John Cormack, a member of the Protestant Action Society, who received more notice than the mainstream candidates for his policy of sending 'all Poles maimed or not, and Southern Irishmen, back to their own lands'.

Was this the free world for which Major John Dallas, of the Royal Scots Fusiliers, had fought? The Labour candidate in Glasgow Shettleston held the Military Cross for his part in an attack on a German town. Attempting to force their way in by the only usable bridge, he and his men found the bridge blown to bits. In thick darkness and under heavy fire, he made a new plan enabling a temporary bridge to be laid, finally succeeding in entering the town.

The Tory in Glasgow Central, Colonel James Hutchison, was the most colourful of all the fighting men. As principal British liaison officer, he had played a big part in organising the French resistance, training and organising the Maquis (the bands of local guerillas). The 'Pimpernel of the Maquis' was so well-known to the Gestapo that he required plastic surgery in London to disguise his appearance before it was safe to drop him by parachute in Normandy. Throughout the election Hutchison carried a Union Jack made by the young French women of the Maquis from parachute silk. At one of his meetings he was so constantly interrupted that he lost control: 'I thought I was coming here to address a white audience. It seems I was wrong. There seem to be a great many here who are yellow.' A member of the audience objected that there were people present who had lost sons in the Battle of Britain and the candidate was calling them yellow.

But the candidate who stole the show was the Unionist in Glasgow Gorbals, one of the poorest constituencies in the country: a 22-year-old paratroop officer just back from the Persian Gulf. Lieutenant Ian Mactaggart ('of the housebuilding family') impressed the newspapers by his height – something over six feet – and was praised for 'his vigorous personality, his staunch championing of Mr Churchill, and his keen sense of the need for the raising of the conditions of life in crowded city areas'.

Mactaggart made an immediate impression in the Gorbals. At a public meeting he drew hoots and jeers when he claimed that 24s a week was enough for an unemployed man to live on; the meeting dissolved in uproar. But the resourceful candidate turned the situation to his advantage, informing the press that he intended to try to live on this amount himself. 'I shall give myself 24s and see whether I can last a week on it. I shall go round and try to get a room and see if I can feed myself.' A few days later the newspapers reported that he had started his seven-day experiment: 'He is not leaving Glasgow, but where and how he will live until next Wednesday has not been disclosed.' Suddenly no candidate in Scotland was receiving more notice than this well-to-do young Tory attempting to survive on a pittance.

He emerged looking fit and fresh-looking, apparently none the worse of his experience, but longing for a bath. He was still refusing to say where he had stayed: 'If you look at any close in Glasgow you will have an idea where I put up.' He continued to claim that it was possible to live on 24s a week 'without any considerable discomfort'. Closely questioned on how this was possible, Mactaggart admitted that he had been forced to give up his 30-a-day habit; the only cigarettes he had smoked were scrounged. He then produced an account of his household spending: rent of room, 10s; food, 9s 7d; church collection, 1d; postage stamps, 4s 3d; newspaper, 1d – total 24s. Asked how he managed on food which cost so little, he said it consisted mainly of cups of tea with bread, butter and jam. He treated himself to an egg one day, pie and chips another. But as the inquisition continued, the pie tasted more and more humble. He agreed that such items as laundry, insurance premiums, repairs to footwear and clothing could not be met out of a weekly income of 24s. Nor was it possible to go to the pictures. 'I entirely agree with all those who have written to the papers criticising me,' he confessed disarmingly.

The men fresh from battle moved and intrigued the newspapers. They made good copy, leaving more seasoned campaigners struggling to be noticed. Some were survivors of campaigns receding into history. A Glasgow Communist candidate, Peter Kerrigan, had fought with the International Brigade in Spain. Labour's William Earsman had gone to Russia on the outbreak of the 1917 revolution, becoming a major-general in the Red Army and a close friend of Trotsky. Labour's F W Pethick-Lawrence had once received a prison sentence for supporting a suffragette demonstration. Such characters were confined to the margins of the press coverage. It was a campaign dominated by the heroes of the hour.

VI

It was a very British election. But although the home rule question was not a dominant one, it did surface occasionally.

The nutritionist John Boyd Orr, standing as an independent for one of the two Scottish Universities seats, called in his election address for a 'measure of self-government' for Scotland. 'If the Scottish people had the power to develop the natural resources of our country for the benefit of our own people, we could put Scotland where it once was and where by the genius of the people it could still be – in the very forefront of the nations for the health, the character and the education of its people.'

Orr was one of the few candidates preaching the home rule message. Another was the Scottish National Party's Robert McIntyre, who campaigned in Motherwell on the slogan 'Scotland for the Scots' as he struggled to hold on to the seat he had won in a by-election in the last weeks of the war. When the 1,672 candidates fighting Scottish seats were canvassed for their opinion on home rule, only 116 replied. Seventy said they were prepared to support a bill giving that 'measure of self-government' proposed by John Boyd Orr; among them Major William Ross, Major Joseph Grimond, Lieutenant John Junor and three senior Labour figures, Arthur Woodburn, Joseph Westwood and Hector McNeil. Another outright supporter of 'a Scottish parliament for Scottish affairs' was the Labour candidate for North Lanarkshire, Peggy Herbison, school-teacher and daughter of a Shotts coal-miner.

A pre-war Secretary of State for Scotland, Walter Elliot, had represented Glasgow Kelvingrove since 1924. A Tory intellectual, an elegant writer, a close friend of O H Mavor, he faced a series of fractious meetings in the highly marginal constituency. At one of them, 'digging his hands deep in his jacket pocket', he dismissed the idea that 'bickering among Scotsmen' would cease if they were gathered into a parliament in Edinburgh. This, said Elliot, was pure fallacy; Scotsmen argued all over the world and the nearer they got to home the more bitter their arguments became. His candid assessment of the national character guaranteed Elliot a noisy reception wherever he went. A journalist reported that one of his campaign addresses was 'punctuated by catcalls from the back of the hall and retorts by his supporters'. When he said he had held Kelvingrove for a long time, a heckler joked sourly that he had been lucky. Elliot hit back: 'It is better to be born lucky than rich.'

His nationalist opponent, Christopher Grieve, rivalled him for frankness. An unashamed anglophobe, Grieve complained at a meeting in the Cosmo Cinema of an English 'invasion' of Scotland. As Hugh MacDiarmid he had already published his poetic masterpiece *A Drunk Man Looks at the Thistle*, yet the Scottish press still felt it necessary to explain who he was. He was described in one newspaper as 'a borderer from Langholm, a journalist as well as a poet, who found inspiration in the Shetlands'. Asked at one of his meetings what a poet was doing involving himself in politics, he invoked the Russian esotericist P D Ouspensky: 'There is nothing the powers-that-be fear so much as the individual thinker who cannot be brought to heel, for he is as potent as he is rare. In these circumstances a poet such as I cannot work in the seclusion of an ivory tower, but must descend into the open arena of public affairs and grapple with the powers of darkness.'

Although he could not claim to be a poet, James Maxton of the Independent Labour Party had something of the poet about him. The socialist pioneer, so revered that the Labour Party would not oppose him in Glasgow Bridgeton where he had been the MP for 23 years, celebrated his 60th birthday during the campaign. He had not been well. The press reported that his flowing, raven locks were greying. The one-man political institution was perhaps more than a little weary. Had he also made himself politically vulnerable? His Tory opponent reminded Bridgeton that the three-man ILP was the only party in the House of Commons 'that did nothing to help us defeat Germany … I ask the electors what they think of that'. The newspapers agreed that the fate of the small ILP parliamentary group – in the Glasgow seats of Shettleston and Camlachie as well as Bridgeton – might hang on public perceptions of the ILP's opposition to the war.

Lord Dunglass (Alec Douglas-Home), who had sat opposite Maxton in the pre-war House of Commons, was fighting to retain Lanark for the Tories, and bitterly resentful about 'the dirtiest campaign' he had ever fought. 'It is being said that I am a pro-Nazi, my name is being associated with The Link, and it is even being put about that while I was off ill I was off on some secret and discreditable mission. There is, of course, not a word of truth in these accusations.' The Link, established in 1939, was ostensibly a non-party body promoting Ango-German friendship, but its journal peddled pro-Nazi propaganda and its founder was interned for potentially endangering the safety of the realm. As a young MP Home had accompanied Chamberlain to Munich for the last meeting with Hitler; many years later he recalled 'the peculiar way in which Hitler walked – his arms hung low, almost to his knees, and swinging not alternately but in unison – and how animal it made him look'.

Home, though not a member of The Link, was further to the right than most candidates in Scotland. Sir John Anderson, Chancellor of the Exchequer and the National candidate for one of the Scottish Universities seats, was prepared to support nationalisation of water and electricity; Sir John Gilmour, the Unionist in East Stirling and Clackmannan, said that the government must have some control over the mining industry. Dunglass would have none of it. The newspapers noted that, as the campaign went on, he intensified his attack on state ownership. 'It must be condemned root and branch,' he said, 'because the same employer – the state – will own and run every aspect of our life.'

Nationalisation, however, was no more a central issue of the campaign than home rule. The dominant theme was the desperate need for housing – emotionally translated as 'homes for heroes'. Since the outbreak of war, 36,000 houses had been completed in Scotland, a further 3,300 partly completed, 75,000 houses damaged by enemy action had been repaired, but 100,000 more were urgently required to replace those unfit for habitation. The official target was set at half a million to be built within 10 to 12 years.

One of the first of Scotland's temporary (prefabricated) homes was opened in Glasgow in the final days of the campaign. 'The house looks very well,' reported one journalist. 'The walls of cement blocks are finished in pebble-dash with cream-coloured distemper. The roof of corrugated asbestos is low-pitched, and from any distance the cottage has a somewhat squat appearance. There is, however, no suggestion of flimsiness about it from the outside view.' From the coal fire in the living room, a duct system distributed heat to the other rooms. He found the kitchen 'well equipped with modern appliances' and was impressed by the fitted wardrobes in the bedrooms. Each house had a small garden with enough space at the back for a vegetable plot. The Ministry of Works undertook to supply 2,500 such houses in the city by the end of 1945, although under strict conditions. The families occupying them should not exceed 'four units' – man, wife, and two children.

VII

From the start of the campaign Scotland's overwhelmingly right-wing press misread the public's restless mood and the urgent desire for change. Was an election required at all? There was an honourable view that it should not have been called until the war in Japan was over. Other arguments for postponement were less credible. George McFarlane, the Unionist candidate for Glasgow Camlachie, said it was unfair that the women of Britain, who had put up with so much during the war, should have 'the extra burden' of a general election. The newspapers were sympathetic; one commentator wrote that 'housewives who have spent long hours in food queues are quite frank in stating that election speeches in the month of June is not their idea of rest and relaxation'. As for 'the menfolk', they could see no good reason for 'neglecting gardens or allotments, or missing their game of bowls' in order to attend election meetings.

There was no evidence of apathy. Attendances at meetings were huge, the issues fiercely debated, yet the newspapers continued to indulge in misrepresentation and wishful thinking. 'Election Outlook Clearer: Serious Conservative Reverse Thought Unlikely', reported the *Glasgow Herald* on 25 June. A few days later the same newspaper quoted the prediction of un-named 'electoral experts' that the Conservatives would win by 'a substantial working majority' over all other parties. By mid-July it would be 'a great surprise' if the Labour Party were 'thrust into office'. A great surprise to whom?

Lazy, self-serving assumptions were fuelled by personal adulation: the refusal to believe that Winston Churchill would be rejected by his people. Opinions to the contrary were greeted with incredulity. Sir Charles McAndrew, the Tory in Bute and North Ayrshire, said it amazed him to hear it said that though Churchill was unsurpassed as a war leader 'he would not be so good in peace'. A S L Young, the Scottish Unionist whip, said he had a feeling that 'the great majority of the electors have made up their mind to vote for the party led by Mr Churchill' and were not turning up at election meetings. W R Milligan, a future Senator of the College of Justice, standing for the Tories in Glasgow St Rollox, said that Churchill 'had the confidence of the whole world'. Peggy Herbison, speaking in her native Shotts, was one of the few dissenters, insisting that Churchill had not won the war – 'The glory should go to our boys who gave their lives' – while the son of a former Conservative Prime Minister, standing for Labour in Paisley, predicted that the election would turn on the forces' vote. 'I thought the soldier was beginning to think after the last war,' said Viscount Corvedale (Oliver Baldwin). 'I was one of them, but there were not enough. This time they are all thinking.' Corvedale believed that if 80% of these 'thinking soldiers' voted, there would be a surprising result. Few took him seriously.

Churchill came to Scotland in late June. Although the windows of the Conservative Club in Bothwell Street were smashed the night before his visit, the newspapers claimed that party rivalries vanished from the election scene as he paraded through Glasgow in a cream-coloured Renault touring car, standing upright, beaming, waving his hat, and occasionally giving the victory sign. Cries of 'God bless you', 'Good old Winnie', 'You're a man in a million' resounded through the city. Denied George Square by Councillor Jean Roberts, who was still sore about the VE Day damage, he addressed the crowd from an open-air platform in Blythswood Square.

He spoke of the roots of the housing problem – '500,000 young people in the army coming home to marry 500,000 young women and bring up 500,000 young children'. In Edinburgh, too, there was a tremendous reception as he arrived in Princes Street Gardens. When the loudspeakers packed up after the first verse of *God Save the King*, Churchill continued singing and 'the great crowd took up his lead and went on to the finish'. He started the journey back to England from the 'ghost' station of Balerno, seven miles from the city, which had been closed in 1943 but was reopened for the departure of the Prime Minister's special train. It had been a triumphant Scottish visit. He entered his private saloon, lit a cigar and settled down to read the newspapers, all of which were predicting his imminent triumph at the polls. Less than a month later he was gone.

One outstanding figure was largely missing from the campaign. Tom Johnston, who had started his career as a journalist, founding the socialist weekly *Forward* on an old printing press bequeathed him by a distant relative, had been an outstanding Secretary of State for Scotland (a post for which he steadfastly refused to draw a salary) in Churchill's wartime coalition. When the election was called, he announced his decision to stand down as an MP and decline the peerage offered by Churchill. He had, he said, spent 20 of the best years of his life trailing down to London: enough was enough. He had abandoned his dream of founding an evening paper in Scotland, mainly because he saw it as a project for a young man and he was no longer young – he was 63 when the war ended – but he looked forward to completing his *History of the Working Classes in Scotland* with a companion volume for the 20th century. He wrote in his autobiography, *Memories*: 'But just as I had retired from public life, voluntarily and in good array, and was preparing to engage myself in the writing and research work that I loved, did I not go and get myself inveigled in a series of public appointments which in cumulo tied me up for at least time and a half, and left me no leisure at all!' The first of these was the chairmanship of the North of Scotland Hydro Electric Board.

With Johnston's resignation from the cabinet, Churchill made an eccentric choice of successor. Johnston called the new Secretary of State, the Earl of Rosebery, 'an active restless enemy of all bureaucracy'. He said that if you wanted a thrill of excitement, equivalent to parachute jumping, 'you could always invite Lord Rosebery to motor you along Princes Street and make a circular dive through the traffic, and head for home again without a mishap'. Home for Rosebery was Dalmeny House.

There was much to be said in favour of the mad motorist. Rosebery was a fine patriot. In 1944 he had given £1,000 – part of his winnings on Ocean Swell in the Derby – to help found the Scottish Ancestry Research Council at Tom Johnston's instigation, in an effort to reverse the tide of emigration. He was, moreover, endearingly open. 'The Scottish Office,' he told Glasgow Press Club, 'was started by someone of the same name as myself. My father dragged it out of a garret in the Home Office when he was under secretary of state there. He said it was necessary that Scotland should have an office of its own. The minister did not agree with him, but my father fought for it and won it and I do not think that the minister, Sir William Harcourt, ever forgave him.' And he worked faithfully for his country as civil defence commissioner during the war, among many other offices official and voluntary.

But Lord Rosebery was not a MP; he was from another place in the Palace of Westminster. When Labour's Herbert Morrison came to Edinburgh and attacked the appointment, mocking Churchill for his apparent conclusion that there was no Scottish MP fit for the job, the earl's majestic progress along Princes Street was perhaps more erratic than usual. He said he objected to an Englishman 'who has never shown the slightest interest in Scotland coming up here on a vote-catching mission and making statements like that'. However, a certain amount of damage had been done.

VIII

Before the future of the nation could be decided, there was the long-anticipated first holiday of peacetime. The calling of the election for July had led to complaints that many voters would be disenfranchised. In order to avoid clashes with local trades holidays, it was decided that polling days would be staggered; on the first of them (12 July), only 13 of the 71 Scottish constituencies voted. Edinburgh was already on holiday; Glasgow was preparing to desert in droves.

Hotels and boarding houses on the Clyde Coast were crammed for Glasgow Fair Fortnight. In Ayr there had 'never been so many perambulators, with so many children and so much luggage' as on Fair Saturday 1945; 'pure murder' according to a railway official. In Rothesay the Pavilion was at last released from military occupation – 'de-requisitioned', as the ugly official jargon had it – for a twice-nightly summer show, and there were late dances three nights a week; motor boats resumed their trips round the bay; visitors flocked to Port Bannatyne. Both Rothesay and Dunoon reported queues for food. All the hotels and boarding houses in Edinburgh were full, and some holiday-makers in Portobello, the capital's unprepossessing resort, were forced to sleep out of doors on their first night.

Hour upon hour of torrential rain fell on Glasgow as enormous queues formed at Central Station. People waited eight hours for trains to Liverpool, London and Blackpool, huddling together in the shelter of doorways. By nine o'clock on Saturday night, the queue for Blackpool stretched out of the station down Hope Street. At midnight, when all the scheduled trains had gone, many hundreds were still waiting. There were rumours that specials might yet avoid an all-night camp-out. Sure enough, just after midnight a cheer went up from a distant platform: a train had been shunted in and would soon be bound for London. For the larger

Blackpool queue there was good news too: one more special would be on its way by 2am. But another front had opened up, as people started queuing for the early train to Aberdeen, due to leave at 5am.

After the wet start to the holiday there was the greater misery of a train crash. A London-bound express packed with Glasgow holidaymakers and servicemen, running at full speed after its descent of Beattock summit, hit a goods train at Ecclefechan station. The impact was violent. Six coaches were derailed as the passenger engine tore through the station, ripping up 50 yards of track, and the driver of the goods train jumped for his life. There were no miracles in the cabin of the express. Coal in the tender shot forward, inflicting fatal burns on the driver and fireman. When the first rescue workers arrived they were astonished that so many had survived. Some had serious injuries, including a broken spine, but only the two railway workers died; it seemed that the placing of a mail and luggage van in the first coach after the engine had saved many lives. A local farmer spoke of coming to the aid of a dazed, hysterical woman whose two-year-old child had been knocked from her arms and was nowhere to be seen. 'After a cup of tea she recovered a little, and her joy knew no bounds when her child was returned to her some time later.' The scene of the accident would have impressed the superstitious: it was only 10 miles from Gretna, where 227 soldiers were killed in the troop train disaster of May 1915, and where the London-Glasgow express was derailed in May 1944, killing three people.

Among the many scenes on station platforms that summer, of homecoming and exodus, prime ministerial farewells and lucky escapes, there was none more joyful than the one enacted at Glasgow Central Station on the day the count began. While ballot boxes, some of which had been stored in cells for several weeks, were finally opened all over the country, a party of 111 British evacuees returned after five years in Canada. Boys and girls who had left as small children came back looking bronzed, fit and grown-up, amazing their parents with their Canadian voices, relaxed air of self-confidence, and smart appearance. Boys shook hands with fathers who stared in wonder at their sports jackets and ties; tall, sophisticated girls threw their arms round mothers who barely recognised them.

Among the Scots was 15-year-old Margaret Ferguson of Glasgow, whose whole family turned out to welcome her home.

Margaret, speaking with a pronounced Canadian accent, told reporters she had had a wonderful time in Toronto, where she stayed with an aunt and uncle. Fourteen-year-old Frank McKechnie, also from Glasgow, 'brought tears to his mother's eyes when he stepped from the carriage'. Almost six feet tall, with cropped head and rimless glasses, he said he was pleased to be home before adding meaningfully that he wanted to go back to Canada 'as soon as possible'.

There was a second event of some interest on the day of the count: a speech to a summer school of the Workers' Educational Association by Robert Britton of Scottish Convention, a non-party group campaigning for home rule within the union. He produced one damning statistic after another: 600,000 people had left Scotland between the world wars; in 1940, 238,000 Scots were receiving poor relief; Scotland had the worst infant mortality rate in Western Europe owing to the 'downright poverty' of its people. He called it 'a tragic story of social and economic decline', and he might have added, if he had known what was happening on a station platform, that young men could not be blamed for wishing to leave Scotland forever.

IX

In the great landslide there were 15 Labour gains north of the border, not as many as might have been expected from so overwhelming an outcome in the country as a whole. Sergeant Willis took Edinburgh Central, while Corporal Hoy had a thumping majority in Leith, unseating the wartime minister for aircraft production. Lord Dunglass lost Lanark, a seat he had held since 1935, to a stationmaster, Tom Steele ('Vote Steele for strength'). The SNP surrendered Motherwell, which it had recently won. Peggy Herbison, who had J B Priestley supporting her at the final rally of her campaign, swept home in North Lanark by almost 10,000 votes. Walter Elliot, who might have been Secretary of State again, lost by 88 votes in Kelvingrove, where the Tories acknowledged that the service vote had gone heavily to Labour; Grieve, the poet, forfeited his deposit by a hefty margin. The facially re-arranged Colonel Hutchison held on in Glasgow Central, claiming that 'many forces electors somehow did not really know the issues at stake'. One of his opponents, Guy Aldred, the Independent Socialist, who got 300 votes, said: 'If I had been at the top of the poll I would have been inclined to demand a recount.'

Labour took both seats in Dundee. It held Greenock, where the eccentric Tory, Wing Commander Lord Malcolm Douglas-Hamilton, ignoring demands that he should discard the kilt, continued defiantly to play on his bagpipes such Scottish airs as *Bonnie Dundee* as he campaigned in the socialist enclave of Gibbshill, while his sister-in-law, Prunella Stack, organised a League of Health and Beauty in the town. The Tories were rewarded with second place ahead of the Liberal, who lost his deposit in a town where the party had a traditional following. The Liberal vote collapsed in Paisley too.

In Caithness and Sutherland, where 61 votes separated the three candidates, E L Gander-Dower, a pioneer of air transport, had the honour of being the only official Unionist to gain a seat in Scotland, finishing just ahead of Labour with the leader of the Liberal Party, Sir Archibald Sinclair, in third place. Sinclair never recovered from this blow.

Maxton and his ILP comrades were returned, defying suggestions that the electors would turn against them for their opposition to the war, and although the Scottish Roman Catholics had been instructed by their hierarchy not to vote for any Communist Party candidates because the ideology of the party undermined religion, Willie Gallagher retained West Fife.

Among the young hopefuls back from active service, Major Grimond came within 500 votes of unseating the Tory in Orkney and Shetland, Major Ross within 700 votes of making Ayr a Labour seat. The three journalists were rejected, although John Junor, a future editor of the *Sunday Express*, was only 600 votes short in Kincardine and West Aberdeenshire. Ian McColl made his way to the top of the Beaverbrook newspaper empire in Scotland, while Ivor Davies worked for the United Nations Association and espoused the cause of nuclear disarmament. Labour's Captain Hughes, the candidate who got mislaid on his way home, failed ever to enter the House of Commons but was reborn politically as Lord Hughes of Hawkhill. Lieutenant Iain Macleod abandoned the Western Isles, as any ambitious Tory would have done, and entered the Commons for an English constituency, rising to senior cabinet posts in the governments of Harold Macmillan and

Edward Heath. His early death, after he had been overlooked for the leadership of his party, robbed British politics of one of its ablest people.

Lieutenant Ian Mactaggart, who insisted that a man could live on 24s a week and then tried to prove it, enjoyed the life of a multi-millionaire property developer and baronet, promoting the Society for Individual Freedom; his daughter Fiona Mactaggart, a teacher and feminist, inherited some of his money, enough to make her one of Britain's wealthiest Labour MPs. In Banffshire, Liberalism was found not to be aglow after all, but the candidate, Alastair Millar, a Perthshire farmer, lived to fight another day. Of Major Dallas, who once captured a town by building a bridge into it but could not dislodge the ILP from Shettleston, of the SNP's Gunner Brown whose electors refused to remember Bannockburn, of Captain Mackintosh, Labour's candidate in Ross and Cromarty, and of Corporal McArthur, its man in East Renfrewshire, only the barest public trace remains. They disappeared from political life as abruptly as they entered it.

One of the new Labour MPs, Coatbridge's Jean Mann, soon to be known as the housewives' champion, had some difficulty booking a berth on the sleeper to London for the first day of the new parliament. There was a cancellation; she travelled first-class. 'I would have slept in the guard's van,' she said. How would Scotland travel – first-class or in the guard's van? We were about to find out.

1946

BREAD AND BUTTER

I

One Saturday night in July 1946 Mrs Ettinger, the owner of a baker's shop in Gorbals Street, Glasgow, made some of the first loaves to be produced in bread-rationed Britain. Rationing was the new government's strategy for dealing with the chronic shortage of basic foodstuffs, but Mrs Ettinger's customers were ill-prepared for it. When she opened her shop on Sunday morning she was struck by their 'dazed' condition. 'People are very surprised when they find how very little bread they are able to buy with their ration,' said Mrs Ettinger, 'and I fail to see how, for the number of units allowed, anyone is going to be able to purchase cakes.' There had been as much panic-buying as tight household budgets allowed. After a fortnight in rain-lashed English resorts, holidaymakers returned to Scotland weighed down by parcels of pre-rationed bread.

If cakes were out of the question, would there be any points left for biscuits? A Glasgow baker predicted that even the humble roll would be affected. Because of the restrictions on oatmeal and barley, there were fears for porridge and Scotch broth. All this was too much for the Scottish National Party, which issued a declaration that, 'so long as any oats are taken from Scotland to feed racehorses in England, it is outrageous that the people of Scotland should go short of their accustomed fare'.

Few areas of life were immune. The churches were worried about bread for holy communion, while hotels debated whether wedding cakes – on which there seemed to be no definite ruling – could be regarded as exempt. The great chieftain o' the puddin' race was another possible victim, prompting a question in parliament. Dr Edith Summerskill, parliamentary secretary at the Ministry of Food, gave an assurance that haggis would remain unrationed. 'I must point out,' she said, 'that this decision was not to prevent an uprising in Scotland, but because haggis contains the heart, lungs, and liver of a sheep, chopped up with suet, onion and oatmeal, while mealy puddings contain oatmeal and fat, and so rate as flour confectionery.' Alan Gomme-Duncan, the Tory MP for Perth, said he wished to 'congratulate the honourable lady on having given the first real definition of haggis'. The House erupted, as it sometimes did when the colonel made one of his amusing interventions. Back in Scotland, however, there was not much laughter. Police were called to one of the biggest bakers' shops in Glasgow to disperse a crowd of women protesting that, while some shops were selling rolls, teabread and cakes 'off the ration' this shop was not. Police quelled a second demonstration in Kirkcaldy.

The newspapers offered hints to housewives on how to spin out the bread units – BUs for short – and the *Glasgow Herald* published a recipe for barley meal scones requiring only half a pint of milk, 1 level teaspoon of salt, 1oz of margarine, and a little barley meal. It advised the frugally-minded to put the milk, salt and margarine into a pan and bring to the boil, stir in enough barley meal to make a workable dough, divide into two or three and roll out into large thin rounds the size of a soup plate, bake on a hot girdle till lightly browned underneath, turn over and bake quickly on the other side in the same way, and keep in a clean towel till required. The paper said the scones were best eaten hot.

II

In some ways the diet of the Scottish people in July 1946 was more restricted than it had been in July 1796, the month of Robert Burns's death. John Strawhorn, a local historian, gave a detailed account of what people were eating in Ayrshire in the late 18th century. There was very little butcher meat on the table. Breakfast was always porridge, followed by cheese or fish and oatmeal bannocks; from the equivalent breakfast in 1946 it might be necessary to cut out the porridge and the oatmeal bannocks. Dinner, taken at mid-day, consisted of two or three courses, including Scotch broth, a luxury a century and a half later. At the end of the working day in 1796 there was a supper of porridge or some other oatmeal dish, again not generally available in 1946. The oatmeal rationed in the middle of the 20th century was such a staple diet in the late 18th that Robert Burns carried it about with him in a pouch. When the poet left the family farm in Tarbolton to go to work in Irvine, he borrowed enough to keep him going until his father could send him a fresh supply from home.

A large gathering in Dumfries marked the 150th anniversary of his death. The Caledonian Society of Palestine sent a Galloway man, John Turnbull, all the way from Haifa. Several thousand delegates walked in procession to the Burns Mausoleum in St Michael's churchyard where wreaths were laid: 'From Burns lovers the world over'. John Clarke, president of the Burns Federation, delivered an address from the steps of the church. Burns, he said, brought back to Scotland the vernacular literature of the country; his frail body was 'the casket of the greatest heart that ever beat for human kind'; we need not moan about his poverty 'because without that poverty, almost from the cradle to the grave, the world would never have had his priceless works ... Burns learned in suffering what he taught in song'.

At a service in the church, the address was given by James Barr, a brawny character with the look of a farmer. He had been reared in the agricultural village of Fenwick on the edge of the Covenanting moors of Ayrshire. He was a scholar, a home ruler, a pacifist and a Labour MP – at one stage chairman of the parliamentary party, a role for which he was temperamentally ill-suited. He was more happily employed on a public platform, once reducing a huge crowd in Vienna to tears with the power of his oratory. In Dumfries Barr spoke passionately of how the poet had thrown off Calvinism with its unbending doctrine of election, its crude conceptions of eternal punishment. He quoted from Burns's letter to Robert Ainslie: 'I have every possible reverence for the much-talked-of world beyond the grave, and I wish what piety believes and virtue deserves may be all matter of fact.'

Burns fitted effortlessly into many Scottish self-stereotypes and was the object of a cult so uncritically reverential that Edwin Muir once mischievously suggested the demolition of his birthplace in Alloway as a contribution to modern Scottish literature. Yet, although a great deal was known about Burns's short life, some fairly basic questions about him continued to be fiercely disputed. Did he, for example, use English in his everyday conversation or did he speak in the vernacular that he employed in his work? There was no conclusive evidence either way; it is possible that he spoke English in some company and reverted to Scots in others. But there seemed to be no room for compromise in this debate. When the prolific novelist James Barke suggested heretically that Robert Burns was an English speaker, he received a critical mauling.

But that was the least of it. In his novel *The Wind that Shakes the Barley*, the first of five volumes of fictionalised biography, Barke speculated on Burns's early love affairs, including his relationship with Jean Gardner, a disciple of the Buchanite sect. Its leader, Elspeth, claimed a supernatural gift: anyone upon whom she breathed would be transported to heaven, including a parish minister in Irvine on whom she breathed with impressive effect. Did Burns go to bed with Jean Gardner? Did it matter? Barke's reasonable assumption – reasonable in the sense that it could not be disproved – that Burns may have lost his virginity with Jean, as he lost everything else in Irvine, including his wardrobe and savings, brought the fires of hell down on the author. The attacks were so vicious that his London literary agent felt obliged to come to his defence in letters to the press. It did no good. His assailants angrily persisted that earlier biographers had ignored the affair with Gardner 'for the sufficient reason that no evidence for it exists'.

In *The Life of Robert Burns* published five years later Catherine Carswell stated that Burns had been intoxicated by Gardner's combination of physical allure and religiosity and that they had a sexual liaison. Carswell's confidence would have been more convincing had she not got Elspeth Buchan's name wrong. Whatever the truth about Burns's sex life, it was all a long way from bread rationing. But it did distract the Scottish literary classes in the bleak summer of 1946.

III

So, though not to the same feverish degree, did a new play by George Scott-Moncrieff, *The Fiddler Calls the Tune*, at the Alhambra Theatre in Glasgow. Its author had spent his first years 'very happily' in Galloway before being moved south to Middlesex with his parents. Life for him there, he confessed later, was never as good as it had been before: he was always conscious of a difference of temperament between his own family and their southern neighbours. In London he wrote a pamphlet, *Balmorality*, denouncing such Scottish institutions as the Church of Scotland. T S Eliot encouraged him in thin times by giving him books to review for the literary magazine *Criterion*.

Convinced that things were happening in Scotland, he made his return in 1932 'prospectless and penniless, but full of high hopes in a cause'. He was 22, ready to man the barricades, but when he met the leaders of the nationalist movement he was taken aback by the spectacle of dour men in bowler hats. He and his wife Ann, a children's author, settled in a cottage in the hills near Peebles and he scraped a living from books, plays and verse. In 1939 he co-founded a joint Scottish-Irish quarterly, *New Alliance*, and sustained it through the war years, but he was the first to admit that the political renaissance he and others had hoped for had failed to materialise.

The Fiddler Calls the Tune was a timely work. The press hailed it as the depiction of a Scottish problem treated with understanding and insight – the conflict between the need for progress and the desire for continuity. The play took as its theme a row over a plan to introduce manufacturing industry into a glen, and the bitter opposition of the local people, who wanted nothing more than to 'keep their crofts and call their souls their own'. The play was well received. One critic wrote: 'There are no stage Scotsmen here, but real characters facing a real situation' and Scott-Moncrieff was praised as 'a Scots playwright with something to say, who says it well'. He had hit on an important question: who did call the tune in post-war Scotland?

The glens were traditionally resistant to change. Henry Grey Graham pointed out in his *Social Life of Scotland in the Eighteenth Century* that, when General Wade attempted to build roads, 'the Highlanders angrily grumbled at the change; complaining bitterly that the gravel wore away the unshod horses' hoofs, which hitherto had gone so lightly over the springy heather' and that they had opposed the planting of hedges, maintaining that 'hedges would harbour birds which would utterly devour their grain, and that they would prevent circulation of the air necessary to winnow the grain for the harvest'.

The modern parallel was the hydro scheme of the 1940s. On this occasion, the fierce resistance to improvement was neither inspired nor led by the ordinary people of the Highlands. When the bill to establish the North of Scotland Hydro Electric Board reached its third reading in the House of Commons in May 1943, a Welsh Liberal and Celtic scholar, Professor William Grufydd, declared: 'A deadlier method of destroying what remains of Highland life I cannot conceive. It is a method which will end for ever the life and civilisation of the Highlands and substitute for them not even the life and civilisation of the Connemara cabin; it will be the life and civilisation of the Dublin slum.' Grufydd's motives and credentials were a mystery; had the man ever been in Scotland? The bill survived, the board stumbled into existence, but the Luddites multiplied. Sir Alexander McKenzie Livingstone, a former MP for the Western Isles, said it would be 'a sorry reward to the Highland soldiers fighting abroad to find on their return that their homeland had been irreparably disfigured'. One newspaper correspondent claimed that Pitlochry would be 'practically obliterated' by the proposed Tummel Garry project.

The board did not enhance its own cause when, in the middle of the 1945 election campaign, it tactlessly launched an ambitious scheme to damn the waters of Loch Sloy and bore a tunnel through Ben Vorlich to provide electricity for the industrial lowlands. Why, its many critics demanded to know, was the board proposing to sell electricity for use in the south when its priority should be the people of the Highlands? The chairman, the Earl of Airlie, replied that, since it operated without subsidy, the board needed money in the bank before it tackled uneconomic projects (later it was to finance itself through loans). This explanation failed to silence the detractors. The *New Statesman* magazine was among the most articulate, implying that the hydro scheme was a plot to deny electricity to the Highlands. For once the left-wing weekly found itself in alliance with the Scottish lairds who, as Tom Johnston put it, 'saw amenity in the Highlands only along the barrel of a sporting rifle' and with the Celts who objected to the sale of water power at a profit.

The personality of the chairman was a hindrance. Unaccustomed to the rough and tumble of public controversy, Airlie reacted badly to criticism, particularly from his own kind. It was bad enough that the Earl of Haddington, speaking at the annual meeting of the Association of Rural Scotland, should describe the activities of the board chaired by his fellow peer as 'the greatest menace today to the scenery of Scotland'. But when Airlie's own son was blackballed for membership of the Perth hunt, the chairman decided that he and his family had suffered enough. He began the search for a more robust successor.

He found one easily enough in the former Secretary of State for Scotland. Johnston's determined leadership extended to a form of glorious larceny. Since timber for the workers' huts was almost impossible to get hold of, he cast his eye around the many disused war-time camps, some in excellent condition with baths and wash-houses. He decided that they should be transported whole to the sites of the new dams and power stations. The bureaucrats in London made sure that authority for such an audacious plan was frustratingly difficult to obtain. Johnston gave notice to 'whoever it may concern' that he was going ahead anyway. From one camp at Wig Bay, near Stranraer, he ordered accommodation for 3,000 men to be transported by road and rail to the Glen Affric scheme in Inverness-shire. No one arrested him.

The Highlands were not reduced to the life of a Dublin slum. Nor was Pitlochry obliterated. Instead it acquired such assets as a fish ladder, a trout laboratory at Faskally, and pleasure boats for the amusement of visitors, all at the instigation of the board. The great dams there and elsewhere were widely admired as feats of engineering. The board encouraged indigenous industries such as stone quarrying. In Orkney it conducted an early experiment in wind power. In every way the vision of an altruistic body promoting 'the economic and social welfare of the Highlands' was fulfilled. And, far from denying electricity to the people, the board connected 36,000 new customers in the Highlands in its first three years. Gradually the doubters and conspiracy theorists were silenced; Johnston was grateful to his supporters in the Scottish press, particularly Evan Barron, editor of the *Inverness Courier*, for supporting him. Without Johnston, however, the outcome might have been very different. Not for the first time and not for the last, Scotland owed him.

IV

Another case of the perennial conflict between progress and continuity, the theme brought to the stage in Scott-Moncrieff's play, was the opposition to the proposal for a road bridge across the Forth. J L Clyde, KC, counsel for the scheme's promoters, said it had 'inspired the hopes and won the support of all who looked forward to increased prosperity in Scotland'. Every local authority in Scotland endorsed the project. Only the Forth Conservancy Board opposed it – 'a small voice crying in the wilderness', said Clyde. The board argued that a bridge would be 'injurious to the interests of navigation' and that 'no new obstruction should be created which would in any way interfere with the passage of naval vessels to and from the port of Rosyth'. The fact that the Admiralty, having looked at the plan, had no objections to it failed to persuade the board to drop its challenge. A public inquiry was inescapable.

Clyde opened it by calling for 'a lifting of the Iron Curtain' over the Firth of Forth. 'In this modern world,' he said, 'contact with headquarters is more and more vital. Edinburgh will more and more become the centre of activity.' One of his first witnesses, Councillor John Sneddon of Kelty, agreed that the bridge would be a great service to Fife.

Clyde: 'I think you know that the main coal deposits in future will be in Fife and the Lothians?'

Sneddon: 'I think that is common knowledge now.'

Clyde: 'Do you look forward, therefore, to considerable industrial prosperity in the district?'

Sneddon: 'We have already made plans for that. An increase in population of 60,000 to 70,000.'

Clyde: 'Would the existence of a road bridge at Queensferry, with the increased traffic by road which that would involve, be an encouragement to the development of diversified industry in the county?'

Sneddon: 'There would be no doubt about that. From the employment point of view, such a development would be essential.'

It was not one of Clyde's tougher briefs: the objections of the Forth Conservancy Board were swept aside by a procession of supportive witnesses. But the resistance to hydro electricity and the opposition to better communications prompted awkward questions about the difficulty of making progress in Scotland. The Earl of Airlie, freed from the burdens of running the Hydro Board, fulminated in the House of Lords about the Attlee government's 'throttling hold on the people of Scotland' and predicted that a conflict was inevitable: 'We in the north are so bold and rash as to believe that the chaos in the country's affairs is largely due to the endeavour of the government to run everything from the centre, while the only hope of dealing with these complicated problems lies in decentralisation.' Inconveniently for this argument, both the hydro and bridge schemes had been obstructed mainly (though in the case of hydro not exclusively) from within Scotland. Rightly or wrongly, however, the nation's problems had come to be widely identified with an unacceptable degree of London dominance of Scottish affairs.

With the Civil Aviation Bill this resentment acquired a sharper focus. The government maintained that a separate Scottish corporation, running its own external services and managing the existing airports at Prestwick and Renfrew and the one being planned for Turnhouse, could not be justified. Several Scottish peers rose to cry of an injustice. Lord Tweedsmuir said: 'You will never develop the genius, energy and enterprise of a great country such as Scotland unless the Scots have full operational functions and full power of initiative.'

Prestwick, declared an international airport in April 1946 but seriously under-used, had become, said Tom Johnston, 'a byword for misunderstanding and ill-will between Scotland and England'. Among the passengers who did use it, there was almost universal praise. The first passenger to step off an airliner from Venezuela into the terminal building, businessman Henrique Masso, delivered a lyrical tribute: 'In the airports of North America, there is efficiency and cleanliness, but no artistry. In London there is neither artistry nor cleanliness, but a certain amount of efficiency. Here there is not merely efficiency and cleanliness, but culture and beauty. We have seen nothing like it elsewhere.'

Later that year a regular service to the Faroe Islands was introduced with a warning that, although the official flying time was three hours, the weather at the other end might disrupt the schedule ('The whole area suffers the disadvantage of almost continuous cloud.') These marginal additions to the airport's portfolio did little to ease the misunderstanding and ill-will between nations. Culture and beauty were getting Prestwick passengers nowhere fast, least of all to the Faroe Islands.

In November the government offered a concession. Lord Nathan, minister of civil aviation, came north to announce the setting up of the Scottish Advisory Council on Aviation 'with real responsibility in operating air services in Scotland'. The wording was significant: responsibility 'in', but not responsibility 'for'. It fooled the *Glasgow Herald*, which headed its report with the dubious claim that Scotland was now in charge of its own air services; the paper expressed confidence that the chairman of the council, Sir Patrick Dollan, a former journalist with a long background in Labour politics, would 'urge the special needs of the urban and rural communities with energy, eloquence and resolution'. Walter Elliot, recently restored to parliament, pointed out that the advice of Dollan's advisory council might or might not be accepted and that Scotland should be running its own show. Joseph Westwood, who had succeeded Rosebery as Secretary of State, attempted to lift Prestwick spirits with a feeble suggestion that 29 November 1940, the date on which the first American bomber landed there, would soon enter the school history books. (It didn't.)

For Scotland, 1946 was the year of advisory councils. The government's response to attacks on the centralised control of broadcasting was to set up a Scottish committee to advise the BBC on Scottish programmes. Several Labour members wanted more. Tommy Scollan, MP for West Renfrewshire, asked the minister, Herbert Morrison, if he had taken into consideration that there was 'an entirely different psychology in Scotland and that the people wanted to develop their own culture'; in the same debate Malcolm Macmillan (Western Isles) proposed a Scottish broadcasting corporation initiating its own programmes. Morrison replied that 'to break up the BBC into separate national undertakings would only result in damaging the whole system'. The Saltire Society maintained that if Scotland was to get only an advisory council, it should at least be appointed by the Secretary of State and not by the BBC. It sent a deputation to London, led by its chairman Robert Hurd and including the journalist Wilfred Taylor, to press this demand. Not much was done. London continued to call the shots, depriving Scotland of any meaningful autonomy.

What might Scotland have done in 1946 with its own broadcasting corporation? The Saltire Society, whose opinions on Scottish culture were always forcefully expressed, would have ended the routine broadcasting of church services: 'We do not know many who listen to them, except some invalids, and there could be special broadcasts for them.' It would have axed many of the more embarrassing variety programmes, which it dismissed as 'too dreadful for words', and encouraged a more intellectual approach to talks. And it would have abandoned news bulletins in

Gaelic, 'these dull effusions', which it claimed scarcely any Gaels listened to. M A MacCorquodale, of the Manse of Kinlochleven, thought otherwise: 'Why, I have known family worship in the Western Isles to be postponed at night until the news in Gaelic is over.'

Complaints of 'dull effusions' were not confined to Gaelic. There was a sour discussion in the press about the quality of the Scottish Orchestra, whose new Czech-born musical director, Walter Susskind, had fled Prague two days before the German invasion. The orchestra, almost half a century old yet still part-time, was compared unfavourably with visiting orchestras. Denis Wood, one of its players, wrote to the press to complain that admission charges for the regular concerts in Green's Playhouse (its Glasgow home, otherwise employed as a cinema) were too low, and that town councils were hiring the orchestra for much less than it was worth. In this case, unusually, no one recommended an advisory committee.

V

John Boyd Orr, founder of the Rowett Research Institute in Aberdeen and a world authority on the link between nutrition and health, was one of the few public figures big enough to rise above the prevailing culture. But Scotland was about to lose him.

In 1945 Orr was invited to become the first director-general of the Food and Agricultural Organisation (FAO) of the United Nations. An inspirational figure, a man in a hurry, he set about his mission – the feeding of the world's hungry, no less – with characteristic energy. One of his closest colleagues, a fellow Scot, Jean Ritchie, recalled that he would call the staff in Washington together and declare in rousing tones, 'Come on my lads and lassies, there's so much to do and we must all work even harder', and that all those in the room would be 'almost rising in their seats' in support.

Here, then, was a man of exceptional vision and influence. In his native Scotland, however, he was the talk of the trams only for his desire to go on simultaneously being the independent MP for the Scottish Universities, a seat he had won in a by-election in the spring of 1945 and held at the general election later that year. Orr checked with the Speaker of the House of Commons that this dual role would be in order; the Speaker gave his blessing. But he was soon being labelled the absentee member and criticised in letters to the press for his 'outrageous assumption' that he could do both jobs. His friend O H Mavor mounted a spirited defence. 'It shows,' he wrote, 'a painfully provincial attitude to badger him ... it is comforting to know that this nagging is confined to a small number of politically minded persons. Sir John was returned with the idea of making the voice of the liberal sciences heard in the councils of the nation. That the voice has spoken in the much greater councils of the world is hardly a matter for regret.' In the end Orr bowed to the 'painfully provincial' and stood down. He was succeeded by Walter Elliot, one of his first postgraduate students at the Rowett, who, as Secretary of State before the war, had introduced milk in the schools.

In a week of three by-elections in November 1946, Elliot had an overwhelming victory in the Scottish Universities seat, Major William Ross secured a handsome Labour victory in Kilmarnock, and Lady Grant of Monymusk became the Tory MP for South Aberdeen.

Priscilla Grant was 31 years old and a war widow. Still grieving over the death of her husband, she had stoically fought another of the Aberdeenshire seats in 1945, impressing journalists and party workers by going out of her way to canvass the opinions of the workers. Sixteen months later she was rewarded with a safe seat. In 1948 she re-married the son of John Buchan, the same Lord Tweedsmuir, author and explorer, who had had so much to say about the need to release Scotland's genius; together, in 1954, they piloted through parliament the Protection of Birds Act, a model for conservation law. A modest, cheerful woman, Lady Tweedsmuir was held in great affection, and when she died of cancer in 1978, at the age of 63, the parliamentary tributes to her were more heartfelt than most.

But the main political event of 1946 was not the resignation of Orr, the return of Elliot, or the introduction to parliamentary life of Willie Ross and Lady Tweedsmuir, considerable figures though all of them were. It was the death in July of James Maxton. The news was not unexpected; he had been ailing for some time. From his seaside home in Largs, where he had moved only four months earlier, he remained mentally alert until almost the end. Both Churchill and Attlee wrote to him regularly and his ILP colleague

John McGovern was with him on the final weekend. 'I had a greater love for Jimmy Maxton than for any other man I have met,' said McGovern on the day of his death. 'He had a perfect understanding of the loyalties and feelings and weaknesses of human beings. He never uttered a harsh word without afterwards having remorse of conscience. In my estimation he was too decent a human being for politics.'

Two thousand people attended his funeral service at Glasgow Crematorium, including (as the press quaintly noted) 'a few coloured people'. It was as politically ecumenical a gathering as was ever assembled in Scotland. The SNP – whose home rule cause Maxton espoused – were represented by Christopher Grieve and Oliver Brown; the Communists by Harry Pollitt and Harry McShane; Churchill by John Henderson, the Tory MP for Glasgow Cathcart; Lord Beaverbrook by Sandy Trotter of Express newspapers. Only 250 could be packed into the chapel; the rest stood outside in silence. Faintly, through the open doorway, the crowd heard the opening voluntary, *O Lovely Heart*, followed by the voices of the Orpheus Choir in *All Through the Night*. And then these lines from ancient Greece:

> *They told me, Heraclitus*
> *They told me you were dead*

Heraclitus, a pre-Socratic misanthropist of no known school of thought, who wandered the mountains nursing his contempt for the human race, is immortalised in a portrait by Paulus Moreelse as 'the weeping philosopher' wringing his hands over the state of the world. His name was an odd one to be invoked at the funeral of James Maxton, who believed in the potential of humanity, of socialism, of international brotherhood, who was surrounded by adoring friends, and whose revolutionary message was sauced with wit and laughter. What was Heraclitus, dead or alive, doing here? But as one journalist observed, it was 'an unorthodox service, impressive and moving'. Churchill sent a wreath of white heather, roses and carnations, inscribed 'In Memory and Respect', and Sir Hugh Roberton, founder and conductor of the Orpheus Choir, whose pacifism had persuaded the BBC that his choir was too subversive to be allowed on air during the war, delivered the oration:

> *He was a great man. He was more: he was a good man, a just man, a true man, a brave man, a man without malice … This man, whom we all loved, never sought to rule; he was content to serve. He was a man with*

no inferiority complex, neither had he any superiority complex. He was a justly proud man, knowing himself and knowing, furthermore, that neither he nor those about him were angels. It was the spirit of tolerance that made Maxton the great human being he was.

Born in Glasgow, Maxton received his early education in the Barrhead school where his father was headmaster. He graduated in arts from Glasgow University in 1906 with the aim of becoming a teacher himself. He did become a teacher, though not for long. He was no socialist in the early days; he voted for the Conservative candidate in a Glasgow rectorial election. Maxton was converted by listening to Philip Snowden at a lecture in Paisley, and promptly read as much socialist literature as he could lay his hands on. Although he was not an absolute pacifist – he once declared that he would have volunteered to serve in the International Brigade in the Spanish civil war if he had been able to find a doctor to allow it – he was a conscientious objector during the first world war. After a speech at Glasgow Green in which he called on Clydeside workers to strike, he went to prison for a year for sedition, was dismissed as a teacher, and found his dog stoned to death in an act of reprisal. He became a full-time organiser for the ILP, surviving on a diet which consisted mainly of black coffee and cigarettes, and in 1922 he entered parliament as the member for Bridgeton, a seat he held until the day he died.

This gaunt figure with the penetrating eyes, his long black hair theatrically bunched at the back, cut an arresting figure in the House of Commons, where he revelled in his reputation as 'the wildest of the wild men'. A year after his election he was suspended from the Commons for using the word 'murderers' to describe members of the government who had cut what he regarded as essential supplies of milk and food to the poor. He refused to withdraw ('I cannot apologise'), and after 40 minutes of sustained abuse appeared, according to his biographer Gilbert McAllister, 'on the point of physical collapse'. During the second war, he and McGovern, and the third ILP member from Glasgow, Campbell Stephen, demanded in vain to be recognised officially as His Majesty's Opposition for its stance as the chief if not only anti-war body in Westminster.

None of this quite explains his enduring appeal. Unlike his contemporary Tom Johnston he is not remembered for practical achievements; ever the rebel, he was neither a policy-maker nor a builder of useful schemes. His record as chairman of his party was far from impressive. He was a charismatic orator but a hopeless administrator. He alienated many in the ILP by his reluctance to consult the membership or his own executive on policy matters; under him the party declined into insignificance. Tom Johnston gave him credit for helping to change public opinion about so much needless suffering in the midst of plenty; but, on that score, John Boyd Orr did more of value without earning the gratitude of his fellow countrymen. Maxton was emotional, funny, lovable, eloquent. Alec Douglas-Home, asked many decades later to name a socialist worthy of his admiration, chose Maxton for his class and finesse as a speaker. There was something about him that appealed across party and particularly deeply to the Scots. He was, in Roberton's words, 'a great human being'. It was enough to guarantee him a place in the Scottish pantheon.

VI

In the month of James Maxton's death more than 12,000 people in Glasgow were suffering from infectious diseases. In the same month the National Health Services Bill was given a majority of 148 on its third reading in the Commons, the government hailing it as 'a measure of which parliament can be justly proud'. In that month a psychiatric clinic for ex-servicemen opened at the Southern General Hospital in Glasgow, a typical patient being described as a man 'returning to a position of responsibility in a trade handling rationed goods, who finds the complicated system of rationing and coupons too much for him, "cracks up", and becomes a sufferer from anxiety neurosis'. But psychiatric illness was still not greatly respected. Lord Cooper, the Lord Justice Clerk, said it went against the grain that there should exist a new defence of limited liabililty (diminished responsibility), allowing psychiatrists to 'under-rate the diabolical ingenuity of the real criminal'.

In the month of James Maxton's death two Perth families, including eight children, who had earlier been evicted from condemned property in the town and had been living in air-raid shelters in the South Inch ever since, were evicted for a second time. When the police ordered the occupants to leave, they refused; the police then confiscated their belongings and few pieces of furniture. In the same month James S C Reid, the Unionist MP for Hillhead, opposed the building of tall tenements in the proposed Scottish new towns, not on the grounds that they were socially undesirable or aesthetically offensive but because it would cost too much to instal lifts. He would go on to become an appeal judge in the House of Lords, deriving his title (Lord Reid of Drem) from the East Lothian village of his birth; among the many lavish tributes when he died in 1975, there was no mention of lifts for the poor.

On the day of James Maxton's funeral Sir Hartley Shawcross, the Attorney General, delivered the prosecution's closing speech at Nuremburg. He spoke of 10 million combatants 'killed in battles that ought never to have been' and 12 million men, women and children 'done to death, not in battle or in passion, but in the cold, calculated attempt to destroy nations and races'.

VII

Competitive sport, one of the palliatives of modern man but a long way from its ultimate fate as an addictive drug and source of popular hysteria, had resumed after six years in abeyance. Footballers earned a pittance compared with the fabulous sums paid to their successors. Professional golfers, even those who played regularly in tournaments, attached themselves to clubs, teaching and running the shop, without which they had no dependable source of income.

The attendance at the Open Championship, when it returned to St Andrews for the first time after the war, was so small that there was no need for the spectators to be roped off; they were free to follow the players, as they continued to do for many years until golf became just another form of mass entertainment.

One evening in 1946, between rounds of the Open qualifying, John Panton, an assistant professional in his native Pitlochry, did some practice putting on one of the greens of the New Course. He thought nothing of it. The next morning when he went to the clubhouse of the Royal and Ancient, he spotted a notice drawing competitors' attention to the rule that practice on the greens was forbidden until the qualifying had ended. The young man, anxious to be correct, at once told the championship committee of his inadvertent breach. He played his next round and scored well; he would have qualified easily; but as soon as he came off the 18th green he learned that he was out of the championship. Nine players who would have missed the cut made it because of Panton's disqualification. The committee, in an official statement, said it greatly appreciated his honesty.

A week later Jackie Paterson of Glasgow retained his World, Empire – there was still very much an empire – and British flyweight titles when he outpointed Joe Curran from Liverpool over 15 rounds at Hampden Park. A ring had been erected in the centre of the playing pitch, allowing most spectators a clear view of the action. The crowd of 53,000, a record for Scottish boxing, was lukewarm at the start, but as they saw Curran 'outboxed, outfought and outpunched' by a champion whose only serious trouble throughout the contest was a bad cut over his left eye, 'enthusiasm ran high'.

Of the two sporting Ps in July 1946 the disqualified Panton did better than the victorious Paterson. Paterson, who always struggled to make the eight-stone flyweight limit, could earn £100,000 from a single fight – boxing was one of the very few big money sports – and then lose it all on the dogs. He retired from competition in 1951 and emigrated to South Africa, where he worked as a lorry driver. At the age of 46 he was fatally stabbed in the throat during a drinking session. Joe Aitchison, a Scottish trainer, said that Paterson was the hardest hitter, pound for pound, that Scotland ever produced, 'a tremendous wee guy'. Panton, on the other hand, lived to the age of 92. He and his mercurial rival Eric Brown dominated Scottish golf for decades, but Panton was the more loved – for his equanimity in both victory and defeat and the impeccable sportsmanship for which he was noted from the start. The R and A, which had once regretfully disqualified him, made John Panton its honorary professional. He never won a major championship but, like James Maxton, was celebrated for reasons other than mere achievement.

1947

THE SHOW GOES ON

I

January 1947 was one of the coldest on record. The demand for electricity was so heavy that, in much of Scotland, the supply had to be disconnected for half an hour; gas, too, was in short supply. Travellers complained of unheated hotel bedrooms; restaurants pondered whether it was worth opening at all. Snow fell continuously. But at the Athenaeum Theatre in Glasgow the show went on: the first performance of a play by the daughter of a Scottish manse.

The set designer, Bet Low, an artist in her early twenties, recalled in old age how Glasgow felt that winter. On the strength of a few assorted jobs, she rented the front room of a flat in Sauchiehall Street, with nothing in it except a piano, a table, two chairs, and a huge mirror between two wooden shuttered windows. The floorboards were bare and there was no heating. She acquired a pull-out armchair bed, a sleeping bag, a small rug, and an electric ring and kettle for making tea. At night mice galloped round the room, so no food could be kept in it. She survived on hot dogs and coffee bought from a stall, and painted in a thick wartime coat, scarf and gloves.

She went out into the streets of the city, drawing people and places – Port Dundas with its coal puffer, grain mills and timber yards; Cowcaddens and Gorbals Cross, teeming with life, scarcely a car to be seen. People, she said, were never more friendly than they were then. 'Yet,' she wrote, 'the backdrop to everyone's life was the grim relentless black of the buildings. Black, black, soot-black Glasgow. As winter approached and chimneys smoked, fog turned to smog. Awful. People scurried about the streets, eyes streaming, handkerchiefs held over faces. White ones turned dirty umber in a minute.' She found companionship in the social circles of the left-wing Unity Theatre, mixing with Roddy McMillan, Russell Hunter and other young actors. It was there she first met Christopher Grieve, who was in the company of the artist Ian Hamilton Finlay. And then one day, 'unbelievably', the company's director, Robert Mitchell, who was always good with young people, keen to give them a start, offered her a commission to design and paint a set for a new play about tenement life, *Men Should Weep*. With Mitchell's rough stage plan, Bet Low went off to Unity to tell the resident designer, Tom Macdonald, expecting encouragement. 'He was thoroughly put out,' she wrote. 'Miffed. No help.' Perched on a ladder in a freezing workshop heated by a brazier at one end, she painted and stencilled the 18-foot-high flats.

The other struggling artist involved in this venture – the author – knew how the poor lived, if only as a sympathetic bystander. Her father had been the parish minister in Anderston, a district of wretched deprivation, and Ena Lamont – Ena Lamont Stewart as she was known after her brief marriage to Jack Stewart, a Scottish actor – believed that she unknowingly 'hoarded' sights and sounds from early childhood. She remembered ragged childen playing in the gutters, their tibias curved by rickets, and 'babies, barely visible above thick fringed shawls, mewing feebly and fruitlessly'. When she went to work as a receptionist in a Glasgow children's hospital she indulged in more blatant eavesdropping of the city's working class, carefully noting the 'marvellously rhythmic' speech with its capacity to express both humour and pathos. Out of these experiences of the 1930s her characters 'walked into' her plays as if she had known them long before they knew each other. Towards the end of her long life she liked to claim that the people in her head did the real work. Despite her association with Unity, which produced an earlier play, *Starched Aprons*, drawing directly on her hospital experiences, her writing was essentially observational rather than politically motivated. She was amused by her reputation as a communist. She preferred conversations with God.

The overnight reviews for *Men Should Weep* gave no clue to its ultimate status as a Scottish classic. The *Glasgow Herald* acknowledged that no aspect of the type of life depicted in the play had been left out – 'Everything is here, even the kitchen sink.' Stewart was credited with writing dialogue 'salty and full of the local idiom' and with a sense of humour, but a dominant dramatic theme was thought to be missing: 'Here is an excellent background against which little but the obvious and expected happens.'

Despite this lukewarm notice audiences loved the play. Robert Mitchell wrote to a friend that the opening night in London was greeted with cheering and whistling and that every performance since had had 'a big reception'. These happy auguries counted for nothing. Later in 1947 Unity had its grant cut off by the Arts Council of Great Britain. *Men Should Weep* received no further productions for 35 years and Ena Lamont Stewart disappeared into obscurity. In a National Theatre poll in 2000, her masterpiece was named one of the 100 greatest plays of the 20th century. But by then its elderly author had lost her memory and was unaware that she had ever written it.

II

Although *Men Should Weep* was almost a period play when it came to the stage, the living conditions of most Glaswegians had not markedly improved since the 1930s. More than half the houses in the city still had only one or two rooms. In the one-room houses, the 'single-ends', the kitchen was necessarily the heart of the home, the space not only for living and eating but for sleeping, the bed being set into a recess. Privacy was limited.

New towns, greenfield and clean, were promoted as a humane alternative to the insanitary confinement of city existence. The people of Glasgow were promised re-settlement, first to East Kilbride, 13 miles from Gorbals Cross, where Sir Patrick Dollan, chairman of the Development Corporation, outlined his vision of a town divided into four residential areas, each of 10,000 people, each with its own shops, schools and community centres. East Kilbride, he predicted, would attract industries of 'world significance'. For the health of the people, this vision could not be realised quickly enough. In the first eight months of the year 332 children under the age of two died in the city from gastro-enteritis.

The reasons for the outbreak were disputed. Dr Stuart Laidlaw, the medical officer of health, claimed that, if reasonable precautions had been taken, many of these deaths could have been prevented. He admitted that cases were occurring all over the city, but insisted that they were more prevalent in dirty conditions. 'Many people give little heed to the importance of proper refuse disposal or to the importance of keeping back-courts and closes clean and tidy. So long as parents fail to control the anti-social habits of their children and allow them to play with waste and garbage, so long will gastro-enteritis flourish.' Gavin McArthur, the director of housing, added that it was difficult to keep the dust down in back-courts where the surfaces were often broken. He quoted 'a particularly bad case' in which a council sweeper took two hours to clean a back-court; when it was inspected an hour later it was as bad as ever. He blamed the people for 'not taking a pride in their environment' – a comment presupposing that pride in such an environment could reasonably be expected in the first place.

Since the long, unusually cold winter had been succeeded by a long, unusually hot summer, drought was aggravating the problem. The council maintained that overnight, every night, it was hosing 60 miles of street and that, during the day, a squad of vehicles was constantly watering 300 miles of channels where the dust of the streets collected. The impression fostered by the officials was of a public-spirited local authority battling against a tide of filth largely of the citizens' own making. The citizens took a different view. Anderston and Sandyford Housing Association sent an open letter to Laidlaw: 'Is not the sharp rise in deaths of young children from gastro-enteritis contributed to by the inertia shown by officials of your department, rather more than by the habits of the children or the carelessness of a minority of tenants in the crowded tenements of the city?' The association pointed out that flies were attracted in large numbers to back-courts and basements where sewage flowing from choked drains was left unattended for weeks.

If the life of the inner-city tenements was squalid, that of the peripheral estates ('schemes') was no worse than bleak. Elizabeth Whitley, the young wife of a Church of Scotland minister, wrote to the press from Newark manse, Port Glasgow, evoking 'the dreich streets of the scheme, empty and dead, laying green country utterly waste'. In the Clyde area, where the setting was so 'supremely lovely', these schemes seemed to her 'a double desecration'; why, she demanded passionately, should the poor be expected to be grateful for 'the rawest and ugliest habitations'? But for the poor themselves, quality counted for less than supply. In the Lanarkshire village of New Stevenston people resorted to queuing all night on the doorstep of a house after the local authority announced that it had failed to locate the owner, who had gone to Australia, and that it proposed to offer the property for tenancy, initially rent-free. In Newton Stewart the shortage of houses was so acute that labourers working on a new development slept out of doors. Charles Oakley, regional controller of the Board of Trade in Scotland, told the British Association for the Advancement of Science that the key workers needed for the reconstruction of Scotland could not be persuaded to leave the Midlands because they had heard that housing conditions in Scotland were so poor. 'Their feelings can be understood,' said Oakley, 'if, to cap it all, they are called upon to live in lodgings in Scotland while their families go on living in the south.'

The desperate state of the housing stock was more than matched by the standard of the leisure facilities. The working-class man took his pleasure, such as it was, in pubs condemned at a meeting of Ayr licensing authority as mean and drab, their frosted-glass windows designed to keep anyone from seeing in. Henry Greer, a member of the authority, proposed a change in drinking conditions to make pubs 'happy places in the life of a community', where a man could meet his friends and have a pleasant evening. The reforms he envisaged did not begin to be glimpsed for quarter of a century.

Rural life was far from being an idyll by comparison. J B Frizzell, the education officer for Edinburgh, condemned the sanitation in country schools as revolting; a quarter of them still had dry closets and no running water. 'In some schools,' he told a summer school in Strathpeffer, 'water is as scarce as in the Sahara, and the idea of one towel to hundreds of children is a disgrace. No wonder the common skin troubles of childhood are spread.' Tuberculosis, unknown in the Highlands 70 years earlier, was now being taken there by 'railway trains and motor cars', according to the National Association for the Prevention of Tuberculosis, which defined it as a disease of cities and civilisation. Nor was rural Scotland spared the 1947 outbreak of infantile paralysis, whose youngest victim was a three-month-old child from Campbeltown.

These miseries were compounded by the economic crisis facing the country. The politicians gave notice that the people would have less of everything – less to eat, less to wear, less in their homes, less in their petrol tanks – and called repeatedly for self-sacrifice. When a firm in Maybole appeared to be mocking the restrictions, it found itself shopped in the Commons by Jean Mann, who asked the Board of Trade if it was aware that the firm had sold 1,250 tea-sets in a fortnight. 'I have received information,' the parliamentary secretary replied with a straight face, 'that large sales of pottery have taken place in Maybole and I am looking into the matter.' Making mischief out of this storm in a tea-set, Sir Thomas Moore, the Tory MP for Ayr Burghs, suggested that the firm had shown a spirit of enterprise. Opposition cheers were quashed by the minister. 'It shows a spirit of enterprise,' he agreed, 'but an unfortunate spirit of enterprise which I think we do not want to encourage in this country.'

In August the government introduced more severe measures still. Banning foreign travel for holidays was not expected to affect Prestwick Airport, most of whose transatlantic traffic consisted of emigrants and businessmen. The restrictions on car use – only 'essential purposes' qualified – were more serious, and motorists attending public functions were warned to expect police checks to establish that their journey was strictly necessary. 'This will mean the end of pleasure motoring,' said one car owner in a statement of the obvious. Numbers at public dinners and lunches ('luncheons') were limited to 100. The Guildry of Stirling and the Seven Incorporated Trades cancelled the dinners which normally followed their ancient ceremonies of Walking the Marches, and offered participants a drink instead. The King and Queen, with their daughters Elizabeth and Margaret, travelled through the night by train to Ballater, where the King inspected a guard of honour drawn up in front of the railway station, and then drove to Balmoral Castle on a journey which fell within the meaning of essential. A few days later the King was seen out on the royal moors of Deeside for the opening of the grouse-shooting season, 'enjoying the sport in brilliant weather'.

The weather was democratic. It was brilliant all over Scotland that summer. The only recorded break, a 45-minute downpour on the outskirts of Muir of Ord, was so remarkable that it merited a mention in the national press. On 14 August a morning haze in Glasgow reduced visibility to a few hundred yards and by mid-day the humidity was intense. Just before 3pm the temperature rose to 114 degrees in the sun. 'City dwellers perspired in conditions which were almost torrid,' a newspaper reported. 'Venturesome men' took to wearing alpaca jackets and drill suits. At the weekend the Clyde resort of Gourock was thronged with visitors holding picnic parties along the waterfront; extra buses had to be hired to take them home. At Prestwick there was an unusual sight, not a mirage in the heatwave, but an amphibious plane, the first of its kind to land in Britain, piloted by its owner, Boris Sergievski, all the way from New York. George MacLeod, the leader of the ecumenical community on Iona, gave thanks to God for a gift of Norwegian timber sufficient to roof the refectory of the abbey. The sun continued to shine. But attendance at public baths in Glasgow plunged by 90%, leaving few in the pools. There was a growing anxiety about catching polio.

III

It was a strange month in which to launch an international festival. Charles L Warr, Dean of the Thistle and Chapel Royal, minister of St Giles and a self-important eminence in Scottish life almost as inescapable as Sir Patrick Dollan, quoted a Highland proverb in justification of the project: 'The world will pass away, but music and love will last for ever.' He continued (in his sermon to the Edinburgh establishment): 'In the intellectual approach to religion Scotland has played a notable part, but for centuries we neglected the place of the arts and the emotions. Today, a new spirit is abroad. Scotland is awakening to the full significance of art and beauty.' It was the speech of a man unacquainted with the Glasgow slums.

Before the full significance of art and beauty could be appreciated, the preparations for the Enterprise Scotland exhibition – which was being organised in tandem with the new international festival – had to be observed. 'Scotland for ever! Alba gu brath!' exclaimed Sir Francis Grant as he despatched the fiery cross rallying Scots the world over to the launch of the Enterprise Scotland exhibition. At a ceremony on the esplanade of Edinburgh Castle, the pipes and drums of Scottish Command and the City Police entertained a large crowd. The fiery cross was lit and extinguished 'in traditional fashion' by dipping it in a brass bowl of goats' blood. The runners then fell in behind their leader, Duncan McNab Robertson of Maryhill Harriers, and at the sound of a pistol shot from Sir Steven Bilsland, chairman of the Scottish Council (Development and Industry), and the strains of *Blue Bonnets Over the Border*, the cavalcade set off at 'a smart trot' down the Royal Mile. Robertson took the cross as far as Peebles, where the runners stayed overnight before continuing into England. At some point it was discovered that the bloodstained charred stick had been waved upside down all the way from Edinburgh.

After these exciting preliminaries the exhibition itself could only be an anti-climax. Esmé Gordon, an Edinburgh architect, had brought together furniture and furnishings of Scottish inspiration and manufacture, including a tapestry based on a seascape by William Mactaggart which had been woven at the Marquis of Bute's workshop in Corstorphine. The 'latest in bath-time luxury' was revealed as a primrose-coloured bath, set on a grey-green terrazzo floor, with the taps positioned midway along the side 'so that the lucky inhabitant can make the necessary adjustments without unduly disturbing himself'. Gordon's model sitting room incorporated a small balcony library, his nursery had a blackboard 'already innocently chalked by the architect's own son', and the kitchen was fitted with machines 'to woo any woman to the domestic task'. The darker ironies of these displays, in a country riven by poverty and ill-health, passed without comment.

The two symbolic figures of the exhibition were a 25-feet-high model of St Andrew, 'scintillating in waves of aluminium and bronze foil to the point of suspension on the roof', and 'Jenny Weave', a sculpture whose hair floated 'upwards like Medusa's snakes, trailing clouds of textile glory'. Shipbuilding was celebrated with an 18-feet model of the Queen Elizabeth; mining by a three-ton lump of Midlothian coal rotating on its axis; woollens were displayed as tree foliage; Fair Isle tammies came dressed as sunflowers. There was no sign of the enterprising pottery firm from Maybole, and another Ayrshire industry, lace-making in the Irvine Valley, failed to secure participation; its trade association complained without success.

For artistic impression, neither the patron saint nor Jenny Weave equalled the impact of the moving hand, 'floating seemingly in space', which lit up one of the exhibition rooms in the Royal Scottish Museum. Its designer, Edwin Galligan, explained that it was intended to represent the hand of the Secretary of State, his thumb symbolising 'central control in London', the four fingers being the departments of Agriculture, Health, Housing and Education. There was no exploration of the satirical possibilities. Even the thumb caused no offence.

IV

In true Presbyterian style the first Edinburgh International Festival, around which Enterprise Scotland had been wrapped, was opened with a service in St Giles preceded by a procession of the worthies headed by Lord Provost Sir John Falconer and the town councillors, attired in vivid scarlet, down the High Street in the unremitting sunshine to which Scotland had become accustomed. Such was the weight of the occasion, four clergymen were required to conduct the subsequent devotions, Warr occupying centre-stage. While this ceremonial unfolded, there was an embarassing hitch. At Waverley Station an old single-deck corporation bus, loaded with members of the Old Vic Theatre Company, sat in the main carriageway for more than 30 minutes refusing to start. Shakespearean players, just off the London train, drifted aimlessly on to the platform and inquired of Hamish Maclellan, the kilted festival manager: 'How can we get a drink in Scotland on a Sunday? Is it necessary to have a passport?' Maclellan replied in an even voice: 'You just don't.'

Some objected to Edinburgh as the host city. Predictably one of the dissenters was the professional curmudgeon Christopher Grieve, who chose the opening of an exhibition of Celtic art to ridicule the capital's pretensions: 'Edinburgh has no justification for embarking on the present project because Edinburgh has never contributed anything to the two arts of music and drama. It is all a question of borrowing. We cannot live on borrowed goods.' Ian Finlay, assistant keeper of the Royal Scottish Museum, agreed that Edinburgh's claims were shallower than those of Glasgow, which was the home of the Scottish Orchestra, of the composer Francis George Scott, of the playwright James Bridie. All that Edinburgh had going for it, said Finlay, were romance and sentiment. He forgot to mention the good looks.

The native contribution was indeed slender: single performances by the Glasgow Orpheus Choir, the Scottish Orchestra, and the BBC Scottish Orchestra. Planting the roots of what would come to be known as the Festival Fringe, there were amateur productions by the Edinburgh district of the Scottish Community Drama Association, Edinburgh People's Theatre, a drama group attached to Edinburgh College of Art, and the Christine Orr Players, whose eponymous founder combined the talents of theatrical entrepreneur, BBC children's producer, script-writer and playwright. Robert Mitchell's Unity, despite the loss of its Arts Council grant, managed to bring to this unofficial festival – the edge of the authorised version, if not yet the Fringe – productions of *The Laird of Torwatletie* by Robert McLellan, one of the leading Scottish playwrights, and a Scots-dialect version of *The Lower Depths*. Gorki was hammered by the critics for 'moving along in the depths of human depression and misery'. It seemed that, whatever was required at the first Edinburgh International Festival, depression and misery were not. This was true more generally. Jessie Kesson's radio play about the life of a Highland croft, *This Wasted Day*, broadcast as the festival began, fell foul of the critics for its gloominess, its absence of 'richly diverting situations' and, most unforgivably, its 'sough of Celtic woe'.

No one captured the prevailing mood of spiritual uplift more than Sir James Fergusson of Kilkerran, historian, journalist and Ayrshire laird, who was soon to be Keeper of the Records of Scotland. Fergusson wrote that, in essence, the festival was not 'mere entertainment, a holiday distraction, but a solemn celebration, a worshipping of beauty in some of the loftiest forms that man has created. Quality is everything; and it is to welcome and applaud that standard that lovers of music and drama are converging upon Edinburgh from all over the world'. The *Glasgow Herald*, for which Fergusson worked at the time, volunteered in an editorial that beauty was a commodity 'that never has been and never can be rationed'. In this generous spirit the finest linen was brought to Edinburgh for the Festival Club in George Street and made its half-mile journey from Waverley Station under police escort. Within an hour or so of the club opening, 150 people had applied for membership. In the vestibule of the King's Theatre the same evening, a Chinese girl was heard gravely explaining to a fellow visitor that one could only buy matches in Edinburgh if one bought cigarettes at the same time. There was more cultural confusion on the first weekend when lovers of music and drama converging on the Festival Club discovered that it did not sell liquor on a Sunday ('You just don't') and that an unnerving Sabbath torpor had desended on the premises. A more awkward question, often asked, concerned Edinburgh's inability to support a symphony orchestra.

The 'borrowed goods', as Grieve had labelled them, were among the best. The Old Vic, the nearest thing to a national theatre in England, gave a certain lustre to the drama, the poor relation of the festival then as later. Trevor Howard, Petruchio in *The Taming of the Shrew*, was much praised. The company's producer, Ralph Richardson, even found time for a flying visit to Edinburgh, taking the dress rehearsal of *Richard II* before returning to London at once. His abrupt departure was reported rather coolly in the Scottish newspapers.

Where, though, was the nearest thing to a national theatre in Scotland? The Citizens', which might have adorned the first festival, was instead at home in the Gorbals. From there the distant sound of grapeshot could be heard as far away as George Street, Edinburgh. Bridie's *John Knox*, with John Laurie in the title role, had opened to mixed reviews. One of the kinder critics thought that Bridie had created 'a very human Knox – one who could play merrily with children'. There was a less flattering critique on the BBC's *Arts Review* from Moultrie Kelsall, who saw Knox as a judicial murderer driven by an obsession with the Calvinistic doctrine of election. 'If Mr Kelsall would like to see this nonsense in a play, I wish he would write it himself,' snarled Bridie in response, 'but first of all he should read, say, the *Confession of Faith* to inform himself of what Knox really thought about election.' This was terrific stuff, and it got better with the intervention of Grieve, who suggested that the Old Vic had spurned an opportunity to present the play in Edinburgh. He didn't blame them. He called the play 'a miserable fiasco, a scissors and paste job', in which Bridie had 'assembled the material but can do nothing with it. He has simply no idea. The thing peters out most ineptly'. Walter Elliot, the playwright's friend, had said that this was Bridie at the height of his powers, to which Grieve growled back: 'May I be fended from ever seeing him in one of his off-moments.'

Glasgow, as ever, was playing downtown New York to Edinburgh's Washington: all the good rows – the 'stairheid rammies' – were in the west. The politeness in the east could seem complacent, if not deadening. Moray McLaren, the Edinburgh-born novelist and biographer, of whom it was said that he was 'a romantic, a dreamer and a defender of lost causes, a man who brought style to living', who once travelled Scotland on a horse for the purposes of a book, who was married to the actress Lennox Milne, and whose plays included a re-working of *Hamlet* set convincingly in a Scottish mental asylum, was capable of better than a radio talk on 'the imperturbability of Edinburgh and its citizens through this artistic tumult'. It was the first hint of the caricature, fully developed later, of the people of Edinburgh as put-upon citizens detached from the allure of the festival. Ivor Brown, the critic and editor, in a talk in the Freemasons' Hall, visualised the city as 'one of the greatest stages in history', but there was always a slight doubt whether the many extras – the inhabitants – wholly appreciated the role of hosts which had been thrust upon them.

Edinburgh's idea of controversy that year generated heat rather than light. Although beauty had not been and could never be rationed – we had the *Glasgow Herald*'s word for that – the restrictions imposed by London's thumb forbade the floodlighting of the castle. Manny Shinwell, the Glaswegian minister of fuel and power, was the villain of the hour for failing to respond to the entreaties of Sir John Anderson (former Chancellor of the Exchequer) and Walter Elliot. A letter-writer claimed to have seen a hotel in Bournemouth 'floodlit from end to end', while the newspapers calculated it would require 'only' two and a half tons of fuel to give visitors 'one of the finest spectacles which any city in the world has to offer'. What, it was asked, was Shinwell thinking about? He may have been thinking about a strike of miners in Yorkshire while the country was, as he put it, 'hanging by a thread'. He may have been thinking about the sharp increase in the price of coal or the 16% rise in rail fares or the wretched condition of the poor in his native Glasgow. With all this in his mind, he may not have been thinking about the illumination of Edinburgh Castle. He finally conceded, though only to the extent of allowing floodlighting on specified days.

Lit or unlit, Edinburgh baked. Ivor Brown never forgot 'a sweltering morning during that first festival when I stood in the Old Town just below the Castle, looking the very model of a perspiring, rubber-neck tourist'. The stifling atmosphere failed to dissuade Eric Linklater, the novelist, from declaring at a Scottish PEN lunch that he had breathed in Edinburgh 'the sort of air that should have clothed all Britain after her historical triumph in 1945'. He called for 'war on all things dispirited' (it just wasn't Gorki's festival) 'since to be utterly dispirited in the name of realism was to deny the title of realist'. Another of the speakers, his fellow novelist Naomi Mitchison, had earlier fired off a letter from Carradale House (an address in Kintyre well-known to readers of newspaper correspondence columns) rejoicing over the government's plan to raise the tax on Hollywood film earnings ('There can be no more pleasing news than that the Americans are from now on keeping their films to themselves'). She was supported by Grieve, who attacked 'the phony Hollywood stuff' and said that Scotland should be 'getting back to its own roots'.

The opinions of the cinema-goers, if they were allowed to have any, seemed to count for little. Sir Patrick Dollan had promised 10 cinemas in the new town of East Kilbride, one large enough to seat 4,000 people. The Scots could not get enough of Hollywood. They went to the cinema more than any other race in Western Europe. If Mitchison and Grieve had their way, there would be precious little for them to see.

The final concert of the inaugural festival was given in the Usher Hall by the Glasgow Orpheus Choir. Its wartime proscription on account of the conductor's pacifist views had been forgiven if not forgotten. Leading his choir through *Auld Lang Syne*, an anthem often sung by patriots with a shaky command of the script, Sir Hugh Roberton moved the audience into linking hands 'in the traditional clasp'. Later, towards midnight, it was sung again in the Assembly Rooms to mark the end of a successful three weeks. Rudolf Bing, the festival director, pointed to the signatures of visitors from China, the United States, Switzerland and India in the visitors' book at the Festival Club as proof of the event's international pull. The Lord Provost declared that it had provided 'the spiritual tonic required after the strains of the war years and during the uneasy peace' and gave an assurance that plans were already being drawn up for next year.

V

The weather broke at last. One September evening a gale blew down the big top at Bertram Mills circus on Glasgow Green. Glasgow's medical officer of health welcomed the end of the heatwave, predicting that the onset of autumn would reduce the spread of the year's two curses, gasto-enteritis and infantile paralysis. Dr Laidlaw said the rain would wash away a great deal of the filth in the streets and that the cold would kill off the flies. He was right. But the change in the weather came too late for Nancy Riach, an outstanding Scottish athlete. By the age of 17

Nancy was the finest swimmer of her age Britain had ever produced; she had already won the 100 metres freestyle at the World Student Games in Paris and was regarded as a potential medal-winner at the 1948 Olympics. A trainee teacher at Hamilton Academy, she had been given special leave to prepare for the European Championships in Monaco. While competing there she developed a paralysis in her right arm, was taken to hospital, and died in her sleep. Her parents arrived at Nice Airport too late to see her alive; Mrs Riach collapsed on being told the news. Nancy's body was brought home to Airdrie, where a short service was held in the garden of the family house. Her life-long friend, Ruth Ritchie, sang her favourite hymn, *By cool Siloam's shady rill*. Crowds lined the route of the cortege to New Monkland Cemetery for two miles. The grief over Nancy's death, only a few weeks after her 20th birthday, was keenly felt all over Scotland.

1948

THREE CHEERS FOR THE OLD COUNTRY

I

At the start of the year Scotland was revealed as the only European country where the loss of its young women by emigration was greater than the number of its young men killed in the war. 'We have the remarkable position,' said J G Kyd, Registrar General, 'that in the age group 25 to 29 we have more young men in Scotland than we have young women.' He said it was too early to estimate the ultimate extent of post-war emigration, but the drift was clear: since 1945, 100,000 Scots, mostly in the 20 to 40 age range, of whom a disproportionate number were women, had gone to live in England. Kyd added that he did not recommend any restriction on people's freedom to leave – had it entered his head that this might be an option? – but that some 're-design' of Scotland was needed to give the young a reason to stay. For those who did stay the prospects of a long life were far from rosy. A boy born in Edinburgh in 1948 could expect to live until the age of 56, a girl to the age of 60. A boy born in Glasgow in 1948 would be dead by 1999, a girl by 2003.

Against this background of poor longevity it was scarcely surprising that the image of Scotland abroad was of a sick, impoverished nation. It was an impression reinforced by Sir William Darling, whose tactless remarks during a visit to America found their way into the *US Congressional Record*. The Tory MP talked of the old country, 'with its shillingsworth of meat a week, its declining standards of life'. Darling, a man who clearly enjoyed his food, was greeted with derision. 'I must say,' remarked Hector McNeil, minister of state for Scotland, 'that the honourable member does not look such a bad advertisement for our shillingsworth of meat.'

Darling had, however, merely confirmed the humiliating

stereotype of Scotland. Before he stumbled on American radio with his candid view of national privation, a food ship was on its way to the Clyde, laden with gifts for the poor people of Scotland from the prosperous folks of New England. This humanitarian mission was the idea of Alexander Duff, a native of Dundee living in the United States, who had impressed members of Boston Chamber of Commerce with his account of the starving natives back home. Duff told them that the Scots were so short of food that wealthy Bostonians should ship essential supplies to the needy. Another expat, Jeanette Paul, who had spent the war years in Clydebank, supported Duff with her tales of the 'rigorous life' in Scotland. Having listened to these distressing testimonies, the Chamber of Commerce was motivated to commission an Anchor Line ship, the MV Eucadia, to take 450 tons of food, clothing and medical supplies all the way to Yorkhill Quay in Glasgow.

Waiting for its arrival, on a wet day in early February, were Arthur Woodburn, the new Secretary of State for Scotland, Tom Johnston, chairman of the Scottish Tourist Board, and the City of Glasgow Police Pipe Band which played Scottish airs as the Eucadia docked. At a lunch hosted by Johnston and attended by many of Scotland's great and good, including Sir Harry Lauder and his sister Greta, the cinema magnate Sir Alexander King and Tom Honeyman from the Kelvingrove Art Gallery, the guest of honour was Michael Kelleher, president of Boston Chamber of Commerce, who explained that the supplies had been given in the spirit of a present from dear friends. 'Americans,' he said, 'have a high regard for the people of Scotland. This gift is made in the belief that if we don't try to do something for somebody else, we miss the whole point of living.' He told his Glasgow audience that, 100 years earlier, when the citizens of Boston sent food to Ireland to relieve the famine, his grandfather had been one of the recipients. Did anyone blink at this disconcerting parallel? The press gave no indication.

II

For the poor of Scotland there was the food ship. For the sick – who were often the same as the poor – the proceeds of street collections helped to support what passed for a health service in immediate post-war Britain. George Buchanan, Labour MP for Glasgow Gorbals, said that this form of charity should end and that the care of the sick was what he called 'a national job'. Buchanan – Geordie to political friend and foe alike – was a House of Commons character. One night in the smoking room he asked James Stuart, the Tory chief whip, how he managed with his home life. Stuart replied that his wife went to bed about 10.30pm whatever happened. 'Ye mean that?' Buchanan replied in awe. 'My God, Jimmy, ye're bloody lucky. I've seen me coming up the stairs at one o'clock in the morning fair frightened for ma life.' But his long parliamentary nights were convincingly accounted for. Buchanan was one of the ministers responsible to Aneurin Bevan for piloting the National Health Service Bill through parliament in the teeth of Conservative opposition.

If there was an interest group more hostile to the foundation of the NHS than the Conservative Party, it was the medical profession itself. The antipathy of doctors was general, no less pronounced north of the border despite the supposedly more humane sympathies of the Scots. The Royal Faculty of Physicians and Surgeons of Glasgow, representing senior figures in the profession, told the Prime Minister that the new service was 'not likely to operate in the best interests of the public and certain to impair seriously the ultimate quality of medical treatment'. Barely six months before it was due to come into operation, 700 doctors in the west of Scotland denounced the scheme as 'unacceptable in principle', mainly on the grounds that the payment of a basic salary by the state, no matter the figure agreed, would turn doctors into civil servants. Doctors in Perth described the powers conferred by the bill as dictatorial – 'as distasteful to the medical profession now as they were a year ago when the so-called negotiations began' – while J T McCutcheon, of the Glasgow division of the BMA, claimed that 'if the medical profession is twisted and deformed by legislation which smacks of totalitarianism, then it will lose its great traditions of service'.

An authority on totalitarianism was a patient in a Scottish hospital, a consumer of these great traditions of service. George Orwell, stricken by tuberculosis, had rented a remote cottage on Jura, as far away as possible from the distractions of London life, to write his dystopian masterpiece, *Nineteen Eighty-Four*, which he had been planning for many years. By the autumn of 1947 he was seriously ill; by December he had lost almost a stone and a half in weight; and a few days before Christmas he was finally re-admitted to Hairmyres Hospital in East Kilbride, where he had been treated for an earlier breakdown in his health. On this occasion he stayed for seven months.

Although cases of TB were multiplying – in Glasgow they had almost doubled since 1939 – victims of the disease were poorly served by the pre-NHS arrangements. A shortage of nurses left many TB beds empty. Hairmyres with its specialist unit was better staffed than most. A former patient wrote of it: '[It] was built in extensive grounds 580 feet above sea-level, with the idea of combining sanitorium treatment with facilities for training patients in outdoor work. There was a tree nursery, a market garden, pigs, poultry and a herd of Ayrshire cows, and for recreation, a putting green, croquet lawn and a football pitch. The theory was that rest in clean country air (whether sunlit or thick with falling snow) and a solid, balanced diet formed the best treatment for tuberculosis.' Smoking was encouraged as a way of treating the lungs.

The introverted Orwell found himself under the care of a temperamental opposite, a large, offensively jolly, heavy-drinking character named Bruce Dick, head of the thoracic surgical unit, who was given to slapping his patients' backs and exhorting them in a hearty manner. Orwell had a number of horrible experiences at Hairmyres, one of the procedures involving the pushing of a rod down his throat to examine his damaged lung. His friend David Astor said: 'It was a hideously painful thing, and very frightening. He spoke of this with a fair amount of horror.' There was a suggestion that the staff confiscated his typewriter in the interests of giving the patient the complete rest his frail body was deemed to require. This would have been a cruel punishment for any writer, but the rumour was never verified; Orwell did not refer to it.

On 5 July the National Health Service was born. More than 400 Scottish hospitals – 183 voluntary, 218 local authority, two nationally administered – passed into state ownership, the operational responsibility being devolved to five regional health boards. Until that day the GP was available free of charge only to patients who were insured, and the poor had access to consultant and specialist advice only through the outpatient departments of the voluntary hospitals. Clement Attlee said: 'We are seeking here not merely to provide services for those who are sick, but to make a healthy nation.' It should have been a proud day for Britain. Yet, although most doctors were now enrolled, their cooperation had been bought by financial inducement; in Scotland a stubborn one-in-five of all medical practitioners still refused to have anything to do with the National Health Service. On the same day comprehensive National Insurance and National Assistance schemes, abolishing the last remnants of the poor law and guaranteeing a uniform state pension, were introduced. It was, in Attlee's words, 'the most comprehensive system of social security ever introduced into any country'. The *Glasgow Herald* grudgingly acknowledged that Britain was now 'leading the world in progressive citizenship' but added that it was 'greatly to be questioned' whether the country could afford the reforms.

George Orwell, who was admitted to Hairmyres in the last months of the old system, left it as one of the first patients to be discharged from an NHS hospital. He returned to Jura, to his cottage at Barnhill, aware that he did not have long to live but determined to complete *Nineteen Eighty-Four*. As he wrote to a friend, Lydia Jackson, he 'had to finish the wretched book'. When the final draft was ready in November, he tried to recruit someone to come to Jura to type the manuscript. Although he was prepared to pay well above the going rate, no one could be found. His girlfriend Sonia Brownell said that 'George was perfectly aware that he could come to London and engage an efficient secretary, but as he saw things, leaving Jura was just not on'. For Sonia, leaving London was just not on either. Orwell was left with no alternative but to sit up in bed and type the 150,000-word manuscript himself. It exhausted him.

A memoir by a local woman, Mrs Nelson of Ardlussa, who knew Orwell by his real name, Eric Blair, gave a glimpse of this 'tall, gaunt, sad-looking man' for whose welfare she was constantly anxious. Mrs Nelson wondered how he would ever manage on his own. Living conditions on Jura were spartan even by the general standards of the time. Coal came by boat once a year. Lighting was by lamp and candles. Fresh food was scarce. There were no newspapers. Wireless reception was poor. Letters were delivered three times a week. Barnhill itself was miles from anywhere, reached by a rough road which deteriorated to a track. And he was gravely ill. He was dying. 'He knew that he had not very long to live,' wrote Mrs Nelson. 'On one occasion I thoughtlessly left a bottle of painkillers for toothache by his bed. I was in the garden when I remembered it and hurried in. I need not have worried.

Eric's concern was to have enough strength to finish the book.'

Orwell badly wanted Sonia Brownell's company. He lied to her that the house was 'fairly well appointed' and that the journey from London was not so formidable as it looked on paper. He promised her a room looking out to sea and a trip to the uninhabited bays on the west side of the island where the sand was beautiful and seals swam in the clear water. 'I do so want to have you here,' his letter ended. If there was a reply, it was never published. Sonia visited the island only once, after Orwell's death, was repelled by Barnhill's lack of comfort and amenities, and told friends that she could never have lived there.

Orwell left his cottage for the last time on a dark winter afternoon in December 1948. His car got stuck on the potholed road and he almost missed the ferry. 'I think it would be wiser to do as I first intended, when I took the place in 1946, & use it only for the summers,' he wrote afterwards. But there were no more summers on Jura. A month later he entered a sanitorium in the Cotswolds, marking the start of the final descent. One of his biographers, Jeffrey Meyers, believed that the effort of completing *Nineteen Eighty-Four* killed Orwell, and that 'the novel's vision of the future is correspondingly grim'. Meyers also believed that the fictional torture scenes in his last and greatest work were based on his medical treatment at Hairmyres.

III

The death in December 1947 of Stanley Baldwin, three-times Conservative prime minister, created a parliamentary vacancy in Paisley, the seat won for Labour by his son Oliver (Viscount Corvedale) in the 1945 landslide. Oliver, Eton-educated, an Irish Guardsman in the first world war, had rebelled against the political traditions of his family, declaring that he was a Marxist. Father and son agreed that the best way of coping with this split was simply not to discuss politics in the house, a strategy which seems to have worked amicably enough.

Oliver joined the Labour Party, served briefly as the member for Dudley (1929-31), and stayed with the party in opposition when Ramsay MacDonald formed his national government. But there was an issue far more sensitive than the divided political loyalties of the Baldwin family: Oliver was gay. The social conventions of the time made any acknowledgement of his sexuality impossible, and he fought the Paisley seat ostensibly as a single heterosexual, keeping his long-term partner John Boyle out of the picture. He gained immediate advancement as parliamentary secretary to the secretary of state for war, but there was little hope of further progress. The puritanical Attlee would not have allowed it, and Oliver was in any case destined for the House of Lords as soon as his father died and he inherited the hereditary title Earl Baldwin of Bewdley. Improbably he was then appointed governor of the Leeward Islands, a colonial territory in the Caribbean, scandalising Attlee by taking Boyle with him. His anti-colonialism made him a local hero of the islanders, who responded warmly when he supported their demands for greater autonomy. Politically and personally he was too hot for the British diplomatic service to handle, and he resigned in 1950 for the customary 'personal reasons'.

Baldwin's elevation led to a by-election. 'Keep your eye on Paisley', Benjamin Disraeli had written. The saying was wilfully misunderstood, not least in the town itself. It was passed off as if Disraeli had a high opinion of Paisley; that he considered it a place of outstanding curiosity or merit. Disraeli never came near Paisley and had nothing to say about it, good or bad. The famous quote was merely a whimsical reference in one of his novels, *Endymion*, whose eponymous anti-hero was a clever, greedy, ambitious politician sent on a reconnaissance to the provinces.

In Manchester Endymion met a mill-owner, Job Thornberry, whose wisdom and experience had given him an instinctive feeling for the restless mood of the workers. 'What you should do,' said Job, 'is to go to the Glasgow district; that city itself, and Paisley and Kilmarnock – keep your eye on Paisley. I am much mistaken if there will not soon be a state of things there which alone will break up the whole concern. It will burst it, sir, it will burst it.' Job Thornberry was alerting Endymion to the prospect that, if the revolution began, the fire would be lit in Paisley. Disraeli may have arrived at this fictional citadel of popular revolt by sticking a pin in a map of the industrial north and, faced with a choice between Paisley and Kilmarnock, casually selected Paisley. 'Keep your eye on Kilmarnock' would have had a certain alliterative flourish. But the honour went to Paisley, and was not only received seriously, but nurtured over the years.

Paisley was indeed worth keeping an eye on. It was every inch the town of the Industrial Revolution, not yet down on its luck, still grand enough to boast a number of gentlemen's clubs. Ten thousand people worked in the cotton thread mills. Many others were employed building machinery, dyeing cloth, making soap and marmalade, stirring cornflour. Its patterns gave it an international reputation; the villains in American crime novels were among the many smart people who sported a Paisley tie. The journalist William Hunter, a senior pupil at Paisley Grammar School in 1948, was pleased to be a buddy, the name given to the people lucky enough to have been born there. He came to think of the word itself – Paisley – as elegant and beautiful and wrote that his heart soared whenever he saw it.

If not revolutionary Paisley was at least honourably radical. From 1832 until 1924 it had an unbroken record of voting Liberal; Herbert Asquith, its member from 1920 to 1924, called it 'The maiden city of Liberalism', not that Paisley was ever a city. But in 1924 Asquith went down to defeat in a general election which reduced the party in the House of Commons to a rump. The Paisley Liberals were humiliated a second time in 1945, losing most of what remained of their support. But with Baldwin's enforced resignation the party went into the 1948 by-election hopeful that it could exploit the many difficulties facing the Attlee government.

IV

It seemed to have the perfect candidate in John MacCormick, a Glasgow solicitor who had become the leading campaigner for Scottish self-government within the UK. To understand MacCormick's growing influence in Scotland's political life, it is necessary to go back six years to a hot day in Edinburgh in June 1942, and the acrimonious annual conference of the National Party of Scotland, the original name of the SNP.

At the centre of the acrimony was Douglas Young, classical scholar, author and poet. Of his erudition there should have been no doubt. It was said that he could be found, aged two, in a small chair outside the family house in Merchiston, Edinburgh, reading aloud to passers-by from the book of Job. Part of his childhood was spent in Bengal, where he learned Urdu. At St Andrews University his fellow students – impressed by his great height, black beard and omniscience – nicknamed him God.

He was almost clever enough to be a deity. But many questioned his fitness to be chairman of the National Party of Scotland, the post for which he was standing. Early in the second world war he had gone to prison for 12 months as a conscientious objector, his stated principle being 'that the Scottish people through a democratic Scottish government should have control of whatever war effort the Scottish people wish to make'. Homer and Aeschylus, philosophers not often seen in Barlinnie Prison, accompanied him to his cell, while outside the jail, bagpipes played in his defence. Later he told his young student friend Ian Hamilton that he had enjoyed being in Barlinnie because it was the only time he had had no responsibilities.

By putting himself forward for the chairmanship against the incumbent William Power, a well-known journalist, Young immediately re-opened the split between two irreconcilable factions: those who believed that the party should close ranks behind the war effort and those who advocated a policy of detachment. When John MacCormick, the party secretary, attempted to make a speech in support of Power, most of it was drowned out in uproar. 'For the first time ever on a platform,' he wrote, 'I felt anger rising within me, and bitterness as well.' MacCormick was furious that Power, a man who had served the cause faithfully and well, was being abused by his own party and that the party itself had degenerated into a rabble.

When Young narrowly won the vote, and the new chairman asked the secretary for guidance about the next business, MacCormick voiced his disgust, resigned on the spot, and walked to the back of the hall, where he shouted above the din that anyone who felt the same should cross the road to the Rutland Hotel 'where future action could be considered'. Many leading figures in the party, including Power, joined him, leaving Douglas Young high and dry on the platform.

In his last book, published two years before his death, Young disposed of these melodramatic events in a few dry lines, converting himself to the third person for the purposes of the narrative and recording without comment that John MacCormick left to form 'a non-party pressure group called the Scottish Convention'.

Douglas Young's career as an academic in Scotland failed to

flourish. He lectured in classics for many years at the universities of Aberdeen and St Andrews but never secured a professorial chair in his own country. He was too controversial ever to be considered a safe pair of hands for promotion. Instead he emigrated to the United States, where he was professor of Greek at the University of North Carolina. He retired to his beloved Tayport, where he lived in a house named Makar's Bield (The Poet's Corner) and there he died in 1973, at the age of 59. His body was discovered with Homer open in front of it.

Since John MacCormick had done him no favours, Douglas Young could be forgiven for getting the name of MacCormick's new pressure group slightly wrong. There was no definite article about Scottish Convention, but it was definite about everything else. It would be open to members of all parties and none; it would examine Scotland's economic and social problems from a non-party point of view; it would not fight parliamentary elections; and it would agitate for a Scottish parliament. Within a few weeks of the impromptu gathering in the Rutland Hotel it had attracted more than 1,000 members and branches were being established in many parts of Scotland. But it was only when it was freed from the constraints of wartime that Scottish Convention gathered momentum. It held its first 'Scottish National Assembly' in Glasgow in March 1947.

MacCormick was a political itinerant. Having abandoned his first home in Maxton's ILP, and then dramatically quit the National Party, he had decamped to the Liberals and was their vice-chairman in Scotland. Now he sensed an opportunity in Paisley to create a political coalition for change. Several leading members of the Paisley Unionist Association who were also members of Scottish Convention started a campaign to persuade their colleagues not to put up a Tory candidate against him, and MacCormick was invited to address a joint meeting of the local Liberals and Unionists.

He had prepared a declaration ready to be signed:

We believe that the distinctive national traditions and characteristics of Scotland are of great value to the United Kingdom and to the world, and that they constitute a priceless heritage of the Scottish people. If the process of centralising the economic control of Scotland in Whitehall is allowed to continue that heritage will be lost and our national existence endangered. We therefore consider that a measure of devolution in the government of Scotland is a matter of urgency. We recognise that there are differing opinions as to the extent to which such a measure is immediately practicable, but we urge that all parties in Scotland should seek to reach agreement on this question and that it should not be made an issue of party politics.

According to MacCormick in his autobiography, published seven years after these events, the meeting approved his statement 'enthusiastically and unanimously' and he was promptly adopted as the 'National' candidate.

This was political naivety. Labour, which had selected Douglas Johnston, Solicitor General for Scotland, to fight the seat, leapt on the unlikely alliance. 'There is now no room for the Liberal Party,' said Robert White, chairman of Paisley Labour Party. 'The lamb has lain down with the lion. I have no doubt which will eat which.' The waywardness of MacCormick's political affiliations made him vulnerable to more personal attacks. John Taylor, Labour's Scottish secretary, borrowed from Disraeli with his joke that the National candidate was changing jerseys 'with such bewildering rapidity that Paisley finds it difficult to keep its eye on him'. Naomi Mitchison, in a letter to the press, made it clear that Scottish Convention – of which MacCormick was chairman – wished to disassociate itself from 'any support of [his] present political standpoint'. MacCormick himself had said publicly that he would be carrying 'no nationalist bombs' in his pocket when he went to Westminster, so putting paid to any hope of what SNP vote there might be in Paisley. How many more potential friends could the profligate candidate afford to lose? Then, to cap it all, the Scottish Liberals decided to take no part in the campaign being fought by their own vice-chairman.

'The by-election set-up is nothing more than a pitiful masquerade and an outrage to the political intelligence of the people of Paisley,' said Lady Glen-Coats, chairman of the party in Scotland, in a resignation statement. 'It deceives no one, and is the type of political pact with which I have not the slightest intention of being associated.' MacCormick protested that Glen-Coats 'failed to understand the position in Paisley' and that the pact had been 'widely welcomed by the general body of the electorate'. There was no evidence for this claim – it remained to be tested at the polls – and the Labour candidate, a fellow lawyer, gleefully seized on the ambiguity of MacCormick's position. What, Douglas Johnston wanted to know, did the label 'National' mean? Johnston provided his own answer: it was 'the last resort of the politically bankrupt who, without policy, ideas, ideals or guiding purpose, hide their political poverty behind a meaningless facade'. Labour's Jean Mann weighed in, mocking MacCormick at a public meeting. Was he animal, vegetable or mineral? she asked.

MacCormick could brush off the insults of political opponents, but not so easily the denunciation of Glen-Coats and Sir Archibald Sinclair, the former leader of the Liberal Party. He had thought or presumed he had their approval but stopped short of accusing them of bad faith. He believed they had acted hastily under the impression that he had sold himself to the Tories. But had he not done exactly that? This awkward possibility seemed not to have occurred to him, even when it gave him 'quiet pleasure' to share platforms with such well-known Scottish Tories and anti-home rulers as Walter Elliot and Lady Grant. Despite his feeling of 'disappointment' at the attitude of his party, the political innocent embarked on the campaign with undiminished enthusiasm. But the initial logic of the pact, with its emphasis on Scottish affairs, was quickly abandoned in favour of a more strident appeal to defend freedom. Paisley, said MacCormick, was 'the first place to have the opportunity of saying that it would not accept totalitarianism'. He predicted that the decision of the by-election would affect 'the whole future course of history'.

In February 1948, when John MacCormick made this ambitious prophecy, George Orwell was detained in Hairmyres Hospital, his vision of the totalitarian state – a state bearing no resemblance to the reforming Britain led by Clement Attlee – half-written. The outcome of the Paisley by-election did not affect the whole future course of history, although the publication of *Nineteen Eighty-Four* almost did, by profoundly influencing the thinking of late 20th-century man. The by-election was no more than a passing event, although one which generated great enthusiasm in Paisley. At one of MacCormick's public meetings the news of a message from Churchill 'broke in dramatic fashion', according to press reports. Churchill said it was fitting that Unionists and Liberals should come together 'in face of the grave situation into which the vacillations and perversities of this bigoted government have plunged the nation'. So another reason had been found for the pact – the mismanagement of the country, to add to Scottish devolution and the defence of freedom. MacCormick's reading of the letter was 'loudly cheered', said one report, 'creating an unmistakable atmosphere of excitement in the audience'.

A few days later, at his eve-of-poll meeting, all 1,500 seats in the Town Hall were filled 15 minutes before the start, and a crowd variously estimated at 1,000, 1,500 and 2,000 (the newspapers being notoriously bad at counting) stood outside, some hammering at the doors. The hall-keeper, noting the long queue around the building, said he had not seen such an overflow since the great days of Herbert Asquith. The excluded were finally pacified by the appearance of MacCormick's Tory supporters, Walter Elliot and Lady Grant, who delivered short addresses from the balcony. Inside the candidate was rapturously received, the singing of 'He's a jolly good fellow' breaking out as he arrived on the stage. 'It is a portent,' said Elliot. 'It shows that the political feeling of the people is deeply stirred.' MacCormick, in a final rallying call, summed up what had become for him the main issue of the by-election: 'Are you for freedom or against it?' He rose at the end and called for 'Three cheers for the old country and freedom'. The only doubt was which old country the candidate had in mind, but there was no doubting the messianic quality of the occasion.

On that momentous night two other events of interest took place. Four hundred miles from Paisley, Unity Theatre's production of Robert McLeish's melodrama of tenement life, *The Gorbals Story*, opened in London's West End. The cast had set off on the sleeper from Glasgow, spending their first day tramping the capital in search of lodgings. The critics were unanimous: the success or failure of the play would depend on the ability of the audience to follow the Glasgow accent. One of the actors, 23-year-old Russell Hunter, admitted there was a problem, but added: 'I don't mind what the critics say as long as they are honest about it. There's something about the play that seems to grip audiences.' By all accounts the first-night audience took kindly to *The Gorbals Story*. A glossary of Glaswegian colloquialisms was included in the programme to help southerners negotiate their way through the dialogue, and those who were still struggling with such gems as 'scunner', 'nyaff' and 'bumming your chat', generally found translators nearby. 'A good deal of *sotto voce* paraphrasing was going on in the stalls,' observed one critic. *The Gorbals Story* was still running in London months later, when the Paisley by-election which would affect the whole future course of history had become a distant memory.

The other event of note that night was in Paisley itself, in the

Central Hall, where a crowd of 800, with no overflow in the streets and no need for anyone to hammer at the doors, heard Sir Patrick Dollan – who else? – speak in support of the nigh-well-forgotten Labour candidate Douglas Johnston. There were few of the theatricals of the rival gathering in the Town Hall, and none of the rapture. Johnston, said one journalist, 'brought the method and the manner of Parliament House' to a speech supporting the Labour government's attempt to fashion 'an entirely new form of social democracy'.

In the receptions given to the two candidates, there was no hint of a result which would confound all expectations. MacCormick had predicted that if the turnout was 70% he would win. The turnout was 77%. It was not the first of the National candidate's predictions to be proved wrong, nor the last. Labour swept to victory with the largest vote the party had ever received in Paisley – 27,213 – more than 6,000 ahead of the joint ticket. The governor of the Leeward Islands sent a telegram: 'Hearty congratulations – well done, Paisley', and the *Glasgow Herald* was left to reflect gloomily that the voters had been seduced by full employment, cheap food, easier working conditions and shorter hours, taking themselves and the country 'one step nearer to the precipice'. John MacCormick said in the immediate aftermath of defeat that the pact should continue. He was wrong about that too. But he was not to be put down; and nor was Paisley, on which an eye continued to be kept, although it had not 'burst it' as Job Thornberry once believed it might.

V

The politically conscious citizens of Paisley were far exceeded in number by the film-goers, as many as 5,000 according to the press, who packed into Glasgow Central Station for the arrival of the British film actress Margaret Lockwood on a three-day visit to the city. Lockwood had recently starred in *The Wicked Lady*, a high-grossing melodrama about a nobleman's wife who becomes a highway robber for the hell of it, is mortally wounded, and dies alone. There was no danger of Miss Lockwood dying alone in Glasgow, where 14 policemen were required to escort her through the throng to the Central Hotel. Adoring fans snatched flowers from the bouquet presented to her as she stepped off the London train. Glasgow did these occasions very well.

Six years later there was an even bigger reception for Roy Rogers and his horse Trigger, both of whom were photographed climbing the stairs of the same hotel. It was rumoured that Trigger was stabled somewhere off the Parliamentary Road, not in the Central Hotel itself, and that Rogers had his white stetson glued to his head. Appearances in the film business were often deceptive; and seldom more deceptive, it seemed to Scots, than when Hollywood made one of its periodic attempts to raid Scotland for material.

Alan Gomme-Duncan, the aesthetically-minded Tory MP for Perth, was so upset by an import from America that he exposed it in advance to the House of Commons. 'There is a terrible Scots film on its way,' he told MPs. 'It is called *The Swordsman* and deals with the Highlands. This type of thing is indicative of the dangers there are if these films are not properly examined before they are put out to the public.' A tale of feuding clans, *The Swordsman* featured the families MacArden and Glowan, all of whom had clean collars and cleaner castles. One of the critics marvelled that Ellen Drew, who played the prettiest of the Glowans, never soiled her party frock and that, when she fell from her horse, the mud somehow failed to stick. The hero of the MacArden side (Larry Parks) was so tidy that he was 'evidently using his dirk as a safety razor', while various henchmen decorated the background in kilts which seemed to have been cut from travelling rugs. To the delight of the Scottish Tourist Board, if no one else, Scotland was depicted as a land of everlasting sunshine. A few years later (1954), when the Hollywood producer Arthur Freed came to Scotland in search of locations for a new musical, *Brigadoon*, he could find nothing 'Scottish enough' and decided to shoot the film in a Los Angeles studio, where the 'true' Scotland – the one of his imagination – could be re-created.

If the Americans felt it necessary to invent Scotland because the real thing fell short of expectations, the Scots themselves indulged in various forms of self-caricature which bore little resemblance to most people's existence. The young poet Maurice Lindsay, in a speech to the Royal Philosophical Society of Glasgow on the day after the Paisley by-election, bemoaned the 'artistically unjustifiable kailyardism' which he claimed was still prevalent despite the flowering of the 'Scottish renaissance' led by Hugh

MacDiarmid. Literally, the kailyard was a cabbage patch or small garden attached to a cottage. It became more widely known, and ridiculed, as a literary term evoking the excessive sentiment and lack of realism in the work of such writers as J M Barrie, J J Bell and S R Crockett, all of whom shared a taste for initials. After the second world war, the kailyard persisted not so much in literature as in the homespun newspapers and magazines turned out with astonishing success by D C Thomson, the firm which gave Dundee its journalism as others gave it jute and jam.

James Cameron, one of the greatest Scottish journalists, began his career working for the Thomson papers. He would assume the character of A Feckless Housewife, A Henpecked Husband, Wee Wully, The Saftest o' the Family, Always a Wallflower, A Bairn Without a Name, 'and kindred archetypes of the ridiculous, eccentric, or pathetic'. For a while he wrote under the pseudonym Percy the Poodle. Cameron was instructed that everything had to be communicated in paragraphs one sentence long 'and as far as possible in what was held to be the homely idiom of the Scottish working class', a bizarre construct of Doricisms as remote from the demotic speech of the Gorbals as ancient Greek. He was also responsible for commissioning illustrations for fictional stories, once producing the rough of a drawing of a young woman whose throat had been cut from ear to ear. The editor was horrified. Cameron agreed that perhaps the drawing was a bit strong. 'Strong, strong,' came the reply, 'it's no' a question o' strong. It's no' a bad scene. But for God's sake, boy – look at the lassie's skirt; it's awa' above her knees.' Cameron had the hemline lowered an inch or two and the revised work was approved. The gory depiction of a slit windipe had not been an issue.

If there was a greater curiosity than the content of Thomson's many best-selling daily and weekly titles, it was the arcane practices of the firm itself. H B (Harry) Boyne, a political journalist in London who was active in the National Union of Journalists, gave evidence to the Royal Commission on the Press which blew the lid on Thomson's singular customs. Employees returning from the second world war were required to undertake that they would not join a trade union. Newsagents who refused to open on Christmas Day, when their sole purpose would have been to sell Thomson papers, or who caused offence in any other way, could expect to have their supplies from the firm withdrawn. The inquiry heard the case of a woman, fined for careless driving in 1945, who was incorrectly alleged by a Thomson newspaper to have been driving while under the influence of drink. The woman, a complete abstainer, was awarded damages, after which the firm refused to accept property ads from her solicitors. Thomson, unrepentant as always, defended its 'absolute right to decide with whom we are prepared or not prepared to have business dealings'.

It extracted a spiteful revenge on Winston Churchill, once the local MP, who crossed Thomson in 1922 by daring to criticise it. Harry Boyne, a diligent researcher, checked the cuttings index and found only two references to Churchill by name between 1922 and 1945; during the war, when it was found necessary to refer to the guardian of Britain's freedom, he was described as the Prime Minister. Churchill's successor as the Dundee MP also incurred the firm's displeasure and, likewise, became *persona non grata*. The same policy of identifying wrongdoers by their office and not by their name applied to a chief constable and a senior council official. Emulating the wife of Tam O'Shanter in Burns's poem, the management nursed its wrath to keep it warm. It also believed in shrouding the members of the Thomson family in anonymity. Yet, despite these eccentricities, D C Thomson was the unrivalled triumph of Scottish journalism.

VI

In 1948 a scandal which had gripped Scotland 40 years earlier had its final denouement. On the night of 21 December 1908, in West Princes Street, Glasgow, Helen Lambie, the young servant of an 83-year-old woman named Marion Gilchrist, went out to buy the evening paper, as she did every evening, leaving her employer alone for about 10 minutes. In her absence a Mr Adams, who lived on the floor below, became alarmed by noises from Miss Gilchrist's flat. He ran upstairs to find out what was wrong, rang the bell, but got no answer. He was still standing at the door when Helen Lambie returned. She opened the door and went in, leaving Adams on the mat. A man appeared from the bedroom and, in Adams's words, walked 'quite coolly till he got past me, then went down quickly and banged the door at the foot of the close'. In the dining room, Marion Gilchrist lay battered to death. Adams had caught a glimpse of the murderer.

The police decided the motive was robbery: the dead woman kept a valuable collection of jewellery in her bedroom, although, disturbed as presumably he was, the murderer had taken only a brooch. Suspicion fell on a man who had been loitering at the corner of West Princes Street for weeks, perhaps with a view to establishing a pattern of comings and goings. He was fingered by the two witnesses at an ID parade which consisted mainly of off-duty policemen and someone who did not look in the least like an off-duty policeman. His name was Oscar Slater, who was born Oscar Leschziner.

Slater, a German Jew, had avoided compulsory military service in Germany by moving to London, where he made a living as a bookmaker. After a failed marriage he lived with a Frenchwoman, Mlle Antoine, variously describing himself as a dentist and as a dealer in precious stones. In 1906 he moved to Glasgow with Antoine and they lived together in a flat at 69 St George's Road. He had no known occupation, but gambled regularly in Glasgow night clubs. Where was the money to finance this lifestyle? His maid gave evidence at his trial that Antoine entertained men in London and Glasgow with Slater's agreement. The suggestions of prostitution and pimping proved irresistible to the Lord Advocate and the judge, both of whom emphasised Slater's low character, turning it into a trial of morality.

The jury took just over an hour to convict, although one of the 15 voted not guilty and five others went for the distinctively Scottish not proven verdict. Slater was sentenced to hang. More than 20,000 people, including the trial judge, signed a petition calling for the sentence to be commuted and, two days before the execution, it was.

Slater spent the next 19 years in Peterhead Prison. When he was released after sustained public agitation on his behalf, the Court of Criminal Appeal ruled that there had been misdirection by the judge and quashed his conviction. The Secretary of State for Scotland paid him compensation of £6,000 – equivalent to around £270,000 at the time of writing – and he retreated into obscurity, except for a brief period during the second world war when he was interned because of his German origin. In February 1948 Oscar Slater died at his home in Ayr at the age of 76, the victim of one of Britain's most notorious miscarriages of justice.

1949

ORDINARY CHAPS

I

On St Andrew's Day 1949 – not that the date had anything to do with it – it was announced in the House of Lords during the second reading of the Criminal Justice (Scotland) Bill that the sentence of drawing and quartering would soon be abolished in Scotland. Lord Morrison said it was a source of wonder that this gruesome penalty had ever existed in a highly civilised country such as Scotland – their lordships laughed – and added that he understood it had been introduced from England in 1707 – more laughter. Since 'the enlightened view' had come to pass, said Morrison, not only that the punishment should fit the crime but that the treatment should fit the offender, a number of other obsolete sanctions were being abolished. They were doing away with penal servitude and hard labour, and with corporal punishment in Peterhead, the toughest of Scotland's prisons, where Oscar Slater had once been incarcerated.

However, the harsh sentence of outlawry remained on the statute. A few days after Morrison's statement it was passed on Charles Shaw Bland, who had failed to appear at the High Court in Glasgow on three charges of housebreaking and a further charge of assaulting a woman with a jemmy. Outlawry put Bland outside the protection of the law and anyone giving him food or shelter, or any other form of assistance, would risk being charged with aiding and abetting. In olden days it was tantamount to a sentence of death – the court's way of saying, 'This man is wanted dead or alive'. Although the sentence now had more bark than bite, the fact that judges still occasionally imposed it revealed the limits of 'the enlightened view'.

In the Scottish press little was made of St Andrew's Day; events which took place on 30 November were reported without reference to the significance of the date. These events included the annual court of the Royal Scottish Corporation, one of the first of the mutual aid associations, founded in 1611 as the 'Scots Box', which entitled anyone who contributed regularly to the box to claim help in times of need. At a grand lunch in the Grosvenor House, London, a place where charity boxes were not much in evidence, the Earl of Rosebery was re-elected president and R G Menzies, replying to the toast, deplored the dropping of the word 'British' from the title of the Commonwealth. In Glasgow, at the annual dinner of the Saint Andrew Society, the toast 'Scotland Yet' was proposed by the Earl of Elgin, and another of the speakers, Commander T D Galbraith, the Tory MP for Pollok, later to be known as the first Lord Strathclyde, regretted the passing of hospitals, gas and electricity from municipal control. In Edinburgh the masonic Earl of Galloway was installed as grand master of the Grand Lodge of Scotland. In St Andrews the Duke of Hamilton, on his installation as chancellor of the town's university, said it would be an evil day for learning, for Scotland, and for the Commonwealth if university education became 'fettered to the needs of national industry and the export trade'. In this thicket of St Andrew's Day happenings, it was impossible to avoid tripping over the Scottish aristocracy, major or minor.

Signs of progress, other than the abolition of flogging in prison, were comparatively few on St Andrew's Day 1949. Alan Gomme-Duncan called in the House of Commons for a Scottish national theatre, a suggestion greeted with general indifference. Arthur Woodburn, the Secretary of State, promised 1,000 'aluminium bungalows' for people suffering from pulmonary TB. John McGovern, the MP for Shettleston, complained that people claiming benefits at the Ministry of National Insurance in Stockwell Street, Glasgow, were being rudely treated by staff. A fog descended on Glasgow, lying in patches on the river before spreading to outlying districts. The Burns and Laird steamer, the Royal Ulsterman, which was due to leave the Broomielaw for Belfast at 9pm, remained in her berth, and the 9.40am train from London St Pancras, due at 7.45pm, pulled into St Enoch at 10.45, a journey of 13 hours five minutes. On the Scottish Home Service, Moultrie R Kelsall spoke for an hour on such themes as 'ruthless industrial expansion in the Highlands', 'educating the mass at the expense of the individual', and 'the more regrettable excesses of trade unionism'. It did not seem odd that anyone should be allotted 60 minutes on the BBC to express reactionary views on anything that took his fancy. One critic commended Kelsall for his 'torrent of argument'.

II

A more cheerful St Andrew's Day event was the arrival at Prestwick Airport of the inaugural flight of the Scottish Mercury, a new service between the United States and Scotland. The plaided nationalist Wendy Wood was there to greet it. Out of the aircraft stepped J B Fry of the Thistle Guild of America, who declared: 'We have a firm belief in the ability of the Scots to build their own country under their own direction and leadership. But we don't know for sure what the Scots really want.'

What did the Scots really want?

Did they want to keep the idea of Scotland alive through, for example, the teaching of its history? Lord Cooper, Scotland's senior judge, thought not. 'Scotland is the only country in the world with an organised system of education which does so little to ensure that its youth are taught the story of their country's past,' he protested at the annual meeting of the Scots History Society. Cooper invited his fellow Scots to look at the leaving certificate examination, where they would find that the emphasis was laid on the teaching of English history, Greek history, Roman history, European history, and colonial history. The subject of Scottish history could be safely ignored and, said Cooper, it usually was. When Scotland's young people went to university, it was possible for them to graduate with first-class honours in history without any knowledge of Scottish history. Cooper gave the example of Edinburgh University, where Scottish history was bracketed with such subjects as the history of East Africa. 'There is a subject called British history,' he said, 'but so far as I can discover it consists of English history, with an occasional side glance at Scotland through English spectacles at times when Scotland crosses England's path.' Why, he wondered, was this educational policy allowed to prevail? It was calculated to 'condition the Scottish mind to turn instinctively towards London with the submission that the Moslem turns to Mecca'.

The process of assimilation threatened Scottish dialects, which were 'slowly dying out nowadays under the influence of the BBC and American films' according to the linguist Angus McIntosh. He launched a dialect survey encouraging local people, particularly in the west Highlands, to make recordings of folk stories. McIntosh believed this would serve the dual purpose of preserving dialect for study and keeping folklore alive. He said that Scots should celebrate the melody of a sentence spoken in Kilmarnock with the same sentence from the lips of someone living in East Lothian.

But if the teaching of Scottish history was discouraged, there was not much hope of local dialects being celebrated. More often the speaking of them was a punishable offence in Scotland's grim, disciplinarian schools with their rigid outlook and obsessive concentration on the acquisition of formal qualifications. As secretary of the Scottish Education Department, Sir William McKechnie, who died in 1947, was an early proselytiser of a more cheerful regime. Deploring the drab classrooms and the deadening curriculum, he developed the idea of 'sunshine schools' offering proper opportunities for physical education and recreation. 'Away with the lumber' was McKechnie's battlecry, but the lumber proved resistant. Margaret Kidd, QC, addressing the 1949 annual conference of the Educational Institute of Scotland, claimed that children were so driven to pass exams that, by the time they went to university, they were worn out.

She might have added that many were also chronically lacking in verbal confidence. G T Pringle, chief inspector of schools for the north of Scotland, told a conference in Aberdeen that, in oral interviews, Scottish youths compared unfavourably with their English counterparts, while another speaker at the conference, Dr J Minto Robertson, described lack of articulation as a national defect and called for a dedicated period to be allocated for speech training.

The teachers themselves bemoaned the lower qualifications being accepted for teachers, particularly of PE and music. A R Murison, headmaster of Marr College in Troon, asked rhetorically: 'What teacher, even if relieved of all the extraneous duties which have multiplied so alarmingly in recent years, can possibly do justice to classes of 45 and 40? What chance is there of giving the slightly backward pupil the individual education that he requires, what chance of revising with the irregular attender the lessons he has missed?'

The bleak physical environment did nothing to encourage

William McKechnie's challenging notion that education should be an enjoyable experience. Edinburgh's answer to the Gothic slum schools was to build prefabricated new ones, of pleasing appearance according to a press report, which could be taken down and re-erected on different sites as the need arose. 'Gone are the days of dingy walls, bad lighting and draughts,' claimed the report. But far from gone were the overcrowded classrooms and, within them, the ferocious teaching of a curriculum which packed a child's head with everything apart from the history of his own country.

III

Could, then, the native entrepreneur keep the idea of Scotland alive? There was not much sign of this innovative beast despite the establishment, in 1946, of the Scottish Council (Development and Industry) with the aim of stimulating economic regeneration.

The traditional industries were operating at full throttle. The recently nationalised Scottish pits produced half a million tons of coal a week, led by Lanarkshire (181,000 tons) and Fife and Clackmannan (156,000 tons each), with Lothian and Ayrshire not far behind. The productivity of the Harris tweed industry was equally impressive, the Western Isles exporting 4.5 million yards of cloth a year. Demand was so heavy that the weavers called a meeting in Stornoway to consider a proposal to introduce a utility tweed into their luxury market. Not a single hand was raised in favour.

A few industries based on newer technologies made a tentative appearance. In the Lanarkshire village of Carfin the Modern Telephone Company made telephones for inter-communication in factories and offices. The company admitted that home demand was relatively low and that most of the new-fangled products would be going abroad. The press found it necessary to add that the telephone had been 'invented by a Scot'.

Sir Andrew Murray, Lord Provost of Edinburgh, returned from a 12,000-mile promotional tour of America frustrated by Scotland's apathy: 'Time and again, I heard the desire expressed that there should be better links between Scotland and America. One ship a month is not enough. People want to come direct to the Clyde.'

Murray claimed to have detected a huge interest in the Edinburgh Festival, tourism and trade, but Scots in Detroit had told him of their disappointment when they bought goods thinking they were Scottish and finding that they had been made in the English Midlands.

An ardent nationalist, John M Rollo of the patriotic St Andrew's Works in Bonnybridge, articulated these frustrations in political terms. He wrote of the 'lonely furrow' he was ploughing: 'I have spent the last 30 years developing a new precision industry in Scotland and the past nine establishing a light precision industry in the Western Isles. I realise only too well the almost complete indifference under the present system of government to any developments unless they promise figures of employment which approach four-figure status.' Rollo was passionate in his belief that the problem of depopulation especially in rural areas would never be solved by the official reliance on attracting large inward investment. He failed to point out that this was the policy, not only of the Westminster government but of the Scottish Council (Development and Industry) set up by Scots themselves.

Rollo said it would be a duty of the Scottish parliament, for which he fervently campaigned, to encourage smaller, Scottish-born industries. His sentiments tapped into a more general discontent with the status quo which, by the end of the year, had found extraordinary expression. If the promotion of Scotland's distinctive identity could not safely be entrusted to the politicians, the educationalists and the men of business, perhaps the people of Scotland would have to take charge of their own destiny. They gave every sign of being interested in this possibility.

IV

Undaunted by his misadventure in Paisley, John MacCormick was soon back in non-party mode, imploring the Secretary of State for Scotland to offer some concession on home rule.

MacCormick was unimpressed by Arthur Woodburn, dismissing him as 'a typical party bureaucrat, efficient, uninspired and totally incapable of looking at anything except through the narrow eyes of party bias', and it is reasonable to assume that Woodburn was just as unimpressed by MacCormick and Scottish

Convention. He put it on record that he was 'yet to be convinced that there is any widespread demand in Scotland for such a measure' [legislative devolution], and that the Labour government had more urgent things to attend to, but promised a White Paper which would make 'certain recommendations with regard to Scottish affairs'. The recommendations amounted to nothing beyond a tinkering with the toothless Scottish Grand Committee. Convinced that Labour had no intention of delivering on home rule and that Arthur Woodburn was misrepresenting the mood of Scotland, MacCormick and his supporters redoubled their efforts. In April 1949, after two days of private discussion in Aberfoyle, the campaigners made their boldest move yet: they announced the launch of a Scottish covenant for public signature. This was its wording:

We, the people of Scotland who subscribe this engagement, declare our belief that reform in the constitution of our country is necessary to secure good government in accordance with our Scottish traditions and to promote the spiritual and economic welfare of our nation. We affirm that the desire for such reform is both deep and widespread through the whole community, transcending all political differences and sectional interests, and we undertake to continue united in purpose for its achievement. With that end in view we solemnly enter into this covenant whereby we pledge ourselves, in all loyalty to the Crown and within the framework of the United Kingdom, to do everything in our power to secure for Scotland a parliament with adequate legislative authority in Scottish affairs.

In the same adventurous spirit they decided to launch the covenant for public signature at a meeting in Edinburgh in the home of what was often called 'the nearest thing to a Scottish parliament' – the Assembly Hall of the Church of Scotland. On 29 October 1949, 1,200 delegates gathered in the debating chamber and John MacCormick called on Nevile Davidson, minister of Glasgow Cathedral, to say an opening prayer. No one in Scotland did this sort of occasion better than Davidson. His 'sonorous tones and unmatched eloquence' made a deep impression on John MacCormick, who wrote that the minister had given voice 'to the common purpose and united supplication of the people'. The assembly then broke into a rendering of *Scots Wha Hae* which set the tone for the rest of the day.

After much discussion MacCormick called on people who did not agree with the covenant to stand. A handful did. The first was Christopher Grieve, whose rabble-rousing had moved Donald

Boyd, a senior figure in the National Party, to issue a statement in February 1948 that, contrary to the extreme sentiments of Grieve, there was 'no hatred of England or English people in the mind of the average Scottish nationalist'. At the covenant meeting the unrepentant poet said he objected to the clause pledging loyalty to the Crown. 'I am a republican,' he declared, 'and I am out for complete independence for Scotland.' This was a jarring moment for John MacCormick, who was repelled by Grieve's anglophobia and regarded him as a liability to the home rule movement. But on a day of more or less warm unanimity Grieve's grandstanding had little effect; it was nothing if not predictable. Many influential Scots came to the rostrum to speak in favour of the covenant, including O H Mavor and John Cameron, Dean of the Faculty of Advocates. Mavor said that, for a great many years, Scottish artists had gone to London and made a living there, adding sardonically that 'pretty soon they become Englishmen, and very often a poor sort of Englishman they make'. Nevile Davidson remarked hopefully that the home rule issue 'completely transcended all political parties' and that the 'great steam-roller of centralisation in London' had to be reversed somehow.

Finally the scroll on which the covenant had been inscribed was produced for signature. MacCormick maintained that every person in the hall joined patiently in the queue. He exaggerated, though only slightly. The first to put his name to the document was the Duke of Montrose, followed by MacCormick, and one by one other leaders of Scottish society came up to add their names. It was an impressive spectacle. MacCormick called it 'one of the great occasions in the long history of our nation ... a turning-point in the life of our people from which there will never be any going back'. Half a century later, with the re-establishment of the Scottish parliament, he was proved right. But the following morning the *Glasgow Herald* offered a chilly view of the proceedings, giving more space to the response of Arthur Woodburn than to the meeting itself. Woodburn said: 'The alleged grievances reported in speeches were either trivialities or existed largely in the imagination of the speakers ... The development of a Scottish nationalist movement, even though it starts out with apparently innocuous generalisations, depends in the long run on becoming more and more anti-English and anti-British.' The Secretary of State had chosen to characterise the movement through the extreme personality of Grieve, who was indeed a handicap. It was left to the *Glasgow Herald* to heap its own derision on a meeting which 'did not contribute much in the way of realism to the debate' and in which 'emotions were not left aside'.

By Christmas the emotional Scots were signing in big numbers. John Cameron, addressing a covenant meeting in the Usher Hall in mid-December, was able to report that the number of signatories had risen from 200,000 to half a million in three weeks. He dealt with Woodburn's claim that the movement spoke for an insignificant minority of the people of Scotland, 'noisy but harmless'. Cameron wondered if the growing number of supporters suggested a noisy minority. 'It is true that we are just ordinary chaps,' he said. 'That is the most significant thing about us. But in a few short weeks, we have become a major political issue. Surely Scotland has as much right to self-govenment as the hundreds of millions of completely illiterate people who have got it. Why is it denied us?'

Cameron was stretching a point in describing himself, the Dean of the Faculty of Advocates, a future High Court judge, as an ordinary chap; just as Nigel Tranter, the chairman of the meeting, was no ordinary chap; nor W Ross McLean, KC, another of the chaps who spoke that day; nor MacCormick himself, who tended to sound, anyway in print, more like an Old Testament prophet than an ordinary chap. Nor could the Duke of Montrose, who opened a Scottish Convention Christmas bazaar in Glasgow, be considered by any stretch of the imagination an ordinary chap; nor his factor, the Liberal John Bannerman. The most remarkable fact about the movement was that it was inspired and led, not by ordinary chaps, but by some of the most influential chaps in Scotland. When Woodburn came close in the House of Commons to suggesting that MacCormick was in favour of blowing up parliament, a fatuous allegation, he showed how remote he had become from the reality of fast-unfolding events.

MacCormick ended the year with encouraging news for his supporters. New and larger headquarters were being opened in the centre of Glasgow. The towns to the fore in support of the covenant were named as Ayr, Arbroath and Stranraer. Of 95 town councils which had so far declared their position in response to a request to put public buildings at the disposal of Scottish Convention for the collection of signatures, three quarters (75) had agreed. An insignificant minority? It didn't feel like it.

V

In the closing days of 1949 Sir David Robertson, MP for Caithness and Sutherland, took up the case of the 100 islanders of Stroma, who had no access to medical services and whose passage to the mainland was often disturbed by storm. Two lighthouse keepers on Sule Skerry Rock, 40 miles off Cape Wrath, could not be reached for more than a week because of high seas. A brilliant academic, Dr A J Hird, 33, a specialist in diseases of the blood, was mourned by colleagues at Glasgow University after being killed in a fall while climbing Am Bodach, near Kinlochleven. The village of Luss, Loch Lomond, received 'electric current' for the first time when Lady Colquhoun of Rossdhu switched on the supply; her own house, the Rossdhu of her title, was also connected when she inserted the main fuse in the distribution board. Among those who welcomed the coming of electricity to the village was Mrs Cameron of Laurel Cottage; confined to bed, she said that electric light would help to make it easier for her to read. The otherwise myopic Arthur Woodburn announced the creation of 51 nature reserves extending from St Kilda to the Bass Rock. *Whisky Galore* was named film of the year. The Queen's Rooms Cinema, Aberdeen, was found not guilty at Stonehaven Sheriff Court of showing less than its minimum quota of British films, the sheriff ruling that the company had successfully proved that 'the character of the films available or their excessive cost' made it impossible to meet the quota.

It was reported that, 'despite the post-war temptations of easy spending', Scots maintained their reputation for thrift; Dundee, saving 14s 8d per head of population per week, was declared the thriftiest place in Britain, ahead of Aberdeen, which had to be content with second place. Hamish Henderson, a young Scottish poet, won the Somerset Maugham prize awarded by the Society of Authors with his book of poems, *Elegies for the Dead in Cyrenaica*, the prize carrying with it a condition that the winner should spend three months abroad; Henderson chose the Italian Tyrol to work on an English translation of *Letters from Prison* by Antonio Gramsci. Stirlingshire and Falkirk Water Board decreed that attendance at the annual inspection of the waterworks, a ritual notorious for its consumption of whisky, should be considered a duty of its members. Lerwick voted in a local plebiscite to remain 'wet' (allowing its licensed premises to stay in business). A Christmas tree appeared in George Square, Glasgow, for the first time. The Citizens' Theatre maintained its tradition of a 13-letter title for its Christmas pantomime, *The Tintock Cup*, in which Duncan Macrae appeared variously as the Empress Catherine of Russia, a South American dancer, and a Glasgow wife having 'a good fling', while James Gibson played a shop steward and Fulton Mackay a 'bewildered babe'. Severe gales and torrential rain made Christmas Day anything but seasonal. One farmer in the Crieff district, his livestock threatened by flooding of the Earn River, worked for many hours in the darkness before getting them to the safety of higher ground. The Scottish Post Office appealed to the public not to use telephones during the New Year holiday except in an emergency.

Surprisingly few lines were devoted to the achievement of John Boyd Orr in winning the Nobel peace prize. Despite his forbidding appearance, Orr could be fun. He loved Scottish dancing and a good joke. He was fond of the joke about the Scotsmen who were sent to Hell. 'Forgive us, God, we didna ken, we didna ken.' To which God replies: 'Well, ye ken noo.' He was known to his family as Popeye. He liked pandrops, of which he carried a bowl, and kind croquet, if such a version of the game existed. But he was often so distracted by work that he would knock the remains of his pipe into a waste paper basket and leave them smouldering, sometimes risking a house fire. The renowned nutritionist consumed orange and a vitamin pill in bed every morning, before sitting down to a hearty breakfast of bacon, eggs, and fried scones floating in grease. He had an unnerving habit on the telephone of not saying goodbye or indulging in any of the other conversational niceties. When he decided that the conversation had come to an end he would either hang up or say, 'That's all', and then hang up. Among the good causes to which he donated the proceeds of his Nobel prize was the world federal government, which never came to pass. He continued to write and travel in the interests of world peace, and lived to the age of 90.

1950

THE BRAVE WHO DIDN'T CRY

I

At 2.30pm on Thursday 7 September 1950 William McFarlane, of Football Row in the Ayrshire mining village of New Cumnock, went on duty with other members of the back shift. One of the last things he did before going to work was to write a letter to his wife's parents in Lancashire giving them the news that earlier in the day his wife had given birth to a fourth son. It was many months before the body of William McFarlane was recovered from the depths of Knockshinnoch Colliery.

All but a few of the 135 miners on the shift were overwhelmed by a freak of nature. A huge volume of liquid peat broke into the main coal seam, filling miles of underground workings, blocking escape routes. Seconds before the rush of sludge sealed their exit, six men scrambled to safety. The others found themselves entombed 700 feet beneath the surface – 116 packed in a roadway 45 yards long, the remaining 13, including William McFarlane, cut off from the main party.

Journalists arrived to find a crowd of 3,000 workers, relatives and volunteers at the pithead. A local reporter, Bill Aitken, stuffed his notebook into his raincoat pocket and joined 'a long line of helpers man-handling pit props, bales of hay, sheets of metal, small fir trees that appeared out of the dark as if by magic … anything that would plug the yawning chasm down which sludge continued to churn into the pit'.

In their underground prison the lives of the miners hung on chance. The mud could have engulfed them at any moment; the air quality was poor and deteriorating. But there was one thing going for them. A telephone was still functioning: not well, but enough to maintain contact with the outside world. This proved to be of practical as well as psychological value, enabling life-saving instructions to be given to the men. A way was found to reach them. But there would be no open passage to safety, for noxious gas filled 350 yards of the roadway which would have to be negotiated. Rescuers laboured for many hours with fans, sucking out gas and drawing in air as best they could. The odds against a successful outcome remained fairly long.

By Friday night no one had been rescued. An unpalatable fact had to be faced: if the miners were to come out in one piece they would do so only with the aid of oxygen masks and they would require training in their use. The hour demanded a hero, and it got one. David Park, a senior official with the National Coal Board, volunteered to go down the mine, becoming the first man to crawl through a hole which had been driven in the coal wall. Born in New Cumnock, a former miner himself, Park knew most of the trapped men personally. 'My mission was just a very small part of a magnificent rescue effort,' he recalled. 'Being a local man I felt it was the least I could do to go down among my friends, especially as I felt I could be of practical assistance.' He found them huddled in almost impenetrable darkness. The oversman, Andrew Houston, had done a tremendous job in stiffening morale. Every now and then the men would sing Burns songs and recite his poems ('A bit like a Burns supper – with no drink', as one of the survivors put it); there were a few jokes; even a little ribaldry. Park taught them how to use the oxygen masks and advised them to sit tight and do as little as possible, emphasising the importance of conserving their strength. He and Houston inspired confidence. But it was 30 hours since the start of the Thursday back shift. Would they finish the shift alive?

At the pithead the battle for survival at Knockshinnoch Colliery was being reported by journalists from many parts of the world, including representatives of the *New York Times* and *Life* magazine. They were fed by the women of New Cumnock, who would accept no payment. Round the clock the Salvation Army led prayers and poured urn after urn of tea, even after two of their members, young Arthur Morris and his fiancée Iris Wyllie, were killed in a road accident on their way home from the pit. Medical crews stood by, making do with snatches of sleep; the rescue teams now included men from the whole Scottish coalfield.

At 3.30pm on Saturday – 48 hours after the ordeal began – the first man was brought to the surface. The miners had agreed that the order should be: sick men, older men, married, unmarried.

Gilbert (Gibby) McAughtrie, 19, was so ill that he had to be carried all the way on a stretcher. This was a phenomenal feat in itself. Equipped with a mask containing half an hour's supply of oxygen, he was borne by his rescuers through the gas-filled area, then over a rough roadway, continuing up a mile-long gradient, at places rising as steeply as one-in-three, until the stretcher party finally reached the pithead. 'It's OK, dad,' were his first words to his father. 'They're singin' like linties down there.' There was muted cheering from the crowd as he was taken to the bath-house, which had been set up as a reception station, but as one reporter observed: 'The sense of uncertainty as to the fate of his companions imposed a general restraint.'

Two hours elapsed; nothing more to cheer. The crowd grew fearful until, at 5.50pm, the Earl of Balfour, chairman of the Scottish division of the NCB, announced that two of the older men had passed safely through the gas section to the fresh-air base underground. An hour later, four more. The Salvation Army promptly supplied cigarettes, food and tea to the rescued. But still there was no mood of celebration. 'The reception the men got when they came into view of their friends was calm and controlled and typical of the manner in which the relatives had maintained their night-and-day vigil,' wrote one correspondent. 'A wife would greet her husband with a quiet "Hello, John", and the men's responses were similar. Their rejoicing was obviously muted because of the families of the 13 men whose fate was still unknown.'

The last of the 116 in the main party reached the surface at 1.30am on Sunday. They were followed by David Park, who had stayed with them to the end. Then and only then did the people of New Cumnock return to their houses to sleep, for the first time in three nights in most cases. By the middle of the night the only lights left on in the village were those in the houses of the unlucky 13. Journalists who attended special services in the three local churches later that day marvelled at the stoicism of the community. But by Tuesday it was stretched beyond endurance. Sir Andrew Bryan, chief inspector of mines, announced that 'no false hopes could now be entertained' for the men still entombed. Yet, in appalling weather, hundreds of volunteers continued to work against the clock, shoring up the sides of the pit crater against encroaching mud, while relatives stood silently hour after hour in the drenching rain until all hope had gone. Sir Andrew Bryan described Knockshinnoch as 'one of the greatest rescue operations in the history of the mining industry'; Pathé News called it 'a truly remarkable story of how ordinary men worked tirelessly in a race against time and the forces of nature'.

II

Two years later the events of September 1950 inspired a feature film, *The Brave Don't Cry*, in which the heroes were played by a cast of Scottish actors including Ayrshire's own Jameson Clark. Its producer, John Grierson, was a Scot of exceptional skill and achievement, the father of the British documentary film movement and creator of the National Film Board of Canada. Born in Stirling – a town he always regarded fondly for its role in shaping the history of his country – he lied about his age (adding a year) to join the RNVR at the age of 17 and served in minesweepers during the first world war. Later, as a student at Glasgow University, he was much influenced by contact with the Red Clydesiders and might have entered politics. He said later that he chose to make his contribution to the socialist movement by producing films about the working man.

His critical reputation rests mainly on his documentary work, including *Drifters* (1929), a portrait of the herring industry, and *Night Mail* (1936), a lyrical evocation of the post crossing the border into Scotland overnight, but Grierson claimed that his favourite film was *The Brave Don't Cry*, a personal tribute to the mining community with whom he felt a close kinship. One of his admirers, the critic Ian Lockerbie, wrote of Grierson that he 'saw film as a new medium with an unparalleled power to educate the public about the important social issues of the day and thus to create in viewers a sense of involvement in the workings of their society'. Grierson himself defined his approach to his art as the 'creative treatment of actuality'.

III

Sir Harry Lauder, who died in 1950, personified another side of the national character. Even the name of his house in Strathaven –

Lauder Ha' – spoke to a folksiness which in Scotland was often called pawky. In obituaries he was hailed as a genius. 'No Scot but Barrie has mixed the grave and the gay in such effective proportions,' enthused one of his obituarists. 'Lauder, like Barrie, had the rare ability to lay his finger on that spot in the human heart where tears and laughter are interchangeable.'

Using a cromach as his prop he appeared on stage resplendent in tartan. His favourites – *Roamin' in the gloamin*, *A wee deoch an' doris*, *Keep right on to the end of the road* – were interspersed with rambling monologues, often of unashamed pathos, delivered in the fashion of homelies or mini-sermons. When he toured abroad audiences of Scottish expatriates lapped up his heady cocktail of nostalgic sentiment, all the more seductive for being far removed from the harsh realities of life in the old country. Yet, despite the elaborate artifice, the extreme thriftiness for which he was notorious and the revelling in his own immense fame and wealth, Lauder may have recognised the Scotland of New Cumnock, in which the brave didn't cry but got on with the serious business of life and death. He was not a Highlander. He was born in Portobello and began his working life as a miner before establishing himself as a genial turn at local concert parties.

A more credible representation of Scottish life was drawn by another former miner, Joe Corrie, from Bowhill in Fife, whose one-act plays formed the staple diet of the Scottish Community Drama Association's festival. At its peak in the late 1940s and early 1950s, 600 amateur teams took part in this annual ritual, including many groups associated with the mining industry. The quality varied from near-professional to rank bad. At the Glasgow drama festival in 1950, in which 27 teams competed over nine nights, the adjudicator, G Paterson Whyte, earned few marks for diplomacy. He said he could not help being struck by 'the deplorably low standard of performance'.

Productions of plays by Joe Corrie attracted particular derision for being set in the kitchen, a modest place seldom visited by Scotland's theatrical sophisticates, who preferred the light humour and cigar aroma of the drawing room. Corrie was so fixated on the kitchen, and the ordinary lives expressed within it, that he inspired a new genre known as the kitchen comedy. It was a term heavy with condescension, yet although he did turn out a prodigious number of pot-boilers in order to scratch a living, his best work, drawing on his experiences of the mining community, was convincing and moving. While Lauder indulged in pastiche and earned a fortune, Corrie occasionally flirted with documentary realism and remained poor.

Both were influenced, Lauder more obviously, by the tradition and culture of the music hall, the most potent creative force in Scotland. James Bridie's new play, *Mr Gillie*, a play said by the critics to concern the artist's place in the scheme of things, opened at the King's Theatre, Glasgow, in the winter of 1950. Bridie could not have found a home for his leading actor Alastair Sim, the Mr Gillie of the title, in his own theatre, since the Citizens' was still coining it in with the 1949 Christmas pantomime (*The Tintock Cup*) as far ahead as Easter of the following year.

As *Mr Gillie* went into rehearsal, the rival attractions in Glasgow included the comic Pete Martin in *Babes in the Wood* at the downmarket Queen's ('indigenous and uninhibited, idiomatic almost to the point of unintelligibility', sneered one critic); the comic Dave Willis in *Jack in the Beanstalk* at the posher Theatre Royal; the comics Harry Gordon and Alec Finlay in *Dick Whittington* at the Alhambra; the comic Jack Radcliffe and the tenor Robert Wilson in *Crackerjack* at the difficult-to-please Empire; and the comic Jack Anthony at the humble Pavilion. If there was a place for the artist in the scheme of things it was best in Scotland to be an artist who could tell jokes and carry off the part of a pantomime dame. Tom Honeyman returned from Benghazi declaring that he had seen a theatre there which beat anything in his own country; he spoke with some authority as a director of Bridie's Citizens', where no serious work could be staged for almost half a year.

Outside the extended pantomime season the Scots adored escapology – nubile girls emerging wondrously intact having been neatly sawn across the midriff; and they had a fondness for telepathy. Once Radcliffe and Wilson had deserted the Empire *Mr Gillie* was opposed across town by the act of Sidney and Lesley Piddington, in which a blindfolded Mrs Piddington received messages from her husband without any sign of word or gesture. The fact that this was a fairly accurate portrayal of a Scottish marriage seemed not to occur to the audience, who were reportedly mystified. The Piddingtons; the rough patter at the Queen's; the kitchen comedies of Joe Corrie; the cromach of Sir Harry Lauder – it was all escapology of one sort or another. But there was a lot of escaping to do, and most of it from a condition known loosely as real life.

IV

More than 2,000 couples a year escaped from their marriages, invariably without the assistance of telepathy. (Sixty years later, as this book was being written, the number had risen to 10,000.) The toll of dissolution was considered serious enough to attract the attention of the Church of Scotland, whose Glasgow Presbytery set up a panel to deal with the spiritual problems of divorced people seeking to re-marry in church. Before the second world war, such was the social stigma attached to the formal admission of marital collapse and the judgmental quality of the legal outcome, it had scarcely been an issue; in 1937, for example, only 642 couples were divorced in Scotland. Nevile Davidson, minister of Glasgow Cathedral, said the increase had been caused partly by the unsettled emotional conditions of wartime, but was also 'indicative of a much laxer attitude towards the responsibilities and obligations of marriage'. In Davidson's opinion the 'flight from domesticity' could only be arrested by plain speaking and an assertion of the high doctrine of Christian marriage. But the Church of Scotland's policy on re-marriage, permitting it to the 'injured' party but forbidding it to the 'guilty', did not bear close scrutiny, since – as Nevile Davidson himself acknowledged – the distinctions between 'injured' and 'guilty' drawn by a court of law were often blurred in reality.

Despite the desire of a growing number of Scots to end their marriages, there was no evidence of a decline in the popularity of the institution. P L McKinlay, Registrar General for Scotland, reported the unsurprising fact that, during the war, the marriage rate had been unusually high but that, less predictably, this trend had continued in the immediate post-war years. Between 1938 and 1945 the average age of brides fell from 26.7 to 25.9. McKinlay found that the risks attached to childbirth had diminished 'to an extraordinary extent' over the last decade, and that for both mother and child they were less in the second, third and fourth pregnancies than in the first. Between 1936 and 1941 the maternity mortality rate was 4.8 per 1,000 live births; between 1941 and 1945 it fell to 3.6; it continued to fall – to 0.9 in the third quarter of 1949.

However, the general health of the people remained poor. Surveys in Ayrshire and Stirlingshire showed that one in seven of the population received hospital treatment in a typical year and that, in both counties, 'a formidable proportion' of the patients left hospital still unwell. The link between social conditions and ill-health was more strongly established. Even in relatively affluent Ayr, 36% of the population were living in overcrowded conditions; the situation in Glasgow was considerably worse. Dr Stuart Laidlaw, the city's medical officer of health, reporting yet another increase in the number of cases of pulmonary tuberculosis, said the disease would never be brought under control until the people were adequately housed. In 1949, 1,093 people died of pulmonary TB in Glasgow, but only five from diphtheria, the lowest number ever recorded. In the same year the number of deaths in Glasgow of children under the age of one was a staggering 1,034.

Although life for many people in Scotland in the middle of the 20th century was hard, and for some extremely short, the leaders of the community often spoke in a severe moralising tone. The Church of Scotland's doctrinal stand on divorce was a model of Christian charity compared with the more extreme positions on questions of sexual morality. Two Roman Catholic priests rounded on the Ayrshire education committee for proposing to introduce sex education in schools; one condemned 'the rain of filthy liberalism' and 'the hyper-consciousness of sex led by a man called Freud', whose malign influence was felt as far as Saltcoats, while another deplored the 'awful corruption into which the Roman Empire had fallen, due entirely to sex education'. The other members of the committee listened to these outbursts before confirming their decision to ask Miss Annabella Duncan of the Alliance of Honour to give 'biological instruction' to pupils attending junior secondary schools, where children of lesser ability were taught, after a fashion.

A trial in the High Court was incidentally revealing of attitudes to abortion. A Glasgow doctor, Alexander Horace Walpole Marshall, stood trial charged with performing 'an illegal operation' – the official euphemism – on a girl aged 19. She testified that, 'accompanied by a man', she went to see Dr Marshall one Sunday in his consulting room in Skirving Street. She explained that she was going to have a child and was not married. He gave her an examination and confirmed that she was in the early stages of pregnancy. He told her to come back the following Friday. She asked about the bill, and they agreed £30. The following Friday the doctor gave her two injections and, some days later, two more injections. He then arranged for her to go into hospital. The girl admitted in cross-examination that she was a dreamer and had a tendency to imagine things. Dr Marshall's testimony was that, when she consulted him, he advised her to get married. She replied that this was not possible. He also suggested that she should go to hospital for the baby to be born and then to have it adopted. She said she would not do that either. A few days later the girl made an appointment to see him. When he examined her he found that the pregnancy had terminated. Faced with a choice between the girl's story (corroborated by 'the man') and the doctor's, the jury believed the doctor and took only 10 minutes to acquit.

In the same High Court Scotland's last outlaw, Charles Shaw Bland, who made a brief appearance in the last chapter, finally materialised in person. Between the first hearing of the case in his absence, and his capture by the police, the crime of outlawry had vanished from the statute, but penal servitude – a harsh form of imprisonment – was still available as a penalty. Bland, for his safeblowing exploits, got five years.

Penal servitude would soon go, but the so-called ultimate deterrent lingered into the 1960s. It did seem, however, that if you were convicted of murder, there was more chance of escaping the hangman, Albert Pierrepoint, if you committed the crime in Scotland. The sadistic Lord Goddard, Lord Chief Justice of England, giving evidence to the Royal Commission on Capital Punishment, said that too many reprieves were granted – he was referring here to Britain as a whole – and that the royal prerogative of mercy was exercised too freely. John Mann, a Scottish member of the commission, raised the question of the difference in applying the death sentence in Scotland owing to the defence of diminished responsibility north of the border, and asked deferentially if it was desirable that the laws of England and Scotland should be uniform in this important matter. Goddard responded that it was highly desirable, 'provided that the Scots will agree – for they are very jealous of their own law'. Mann said that, over a period of years – he was inexact about the number – in 590 cases of murder there had been only 23 executions in Scotland. 'Very low,' Goddard noted disapprovingly.

V

The pleasures of the innocent majority were not confined to the music halls; for men they extended to shabbily constructed terraces. The Scottish Football League consisted of two divisions – the A and the B – with 16 teams in each. At the start of the second half of the 20th century, which coincided with the start of the second half of the 1949-50 season, Hibernian led the A division followed by Rangers, Hearts ('the Jam Tarts'), Dundee, Celtic, St Mirren ('the Buddies'), East Fife, Motherwell, Partick Thistle ('the Jags'), Aberdeen ('the Dons'), Clyde ('the Bully Wee' – the origin of which was unclear), Falkirk ('the Bairns'), Raith Rovers, Stirling Albion, Third Lanark (the only club in either division which was not still alive in some form 60 years later) with the romantic Queen of the South at the bottom. Morton ('the Tun', from Greenock) headed the B division followed by Airdrieonians ('the Diamonds'), St Johnstone, Hamilton Academical, Kilmarnock (whose nickname 'Killie' won no prizes for imagination), the amateur Queen's Park ('the Spiders'), Forfar Athletic ('the Loons'), Dundee United ('the Tangerines'), Dunfermline ('the Pars'), Cowdenbeath, Stenhousemuir ('the Warriors'), Albion Rovers, Ayr United ('the Honest Men'), Arbroath ('the Red Lichties'), Dumbarton ('the Sons') with Alloa ('the Wasps') not carrying much sting as the worst team in Scotland. Rangers overtook Hibs at the last gasp to win the title; Stirling Albion and Queen of the South were relegated; Morton maintained their position at the top of the B division; and the Wasps continued to hold up the rest of Scotland for what was left of the season.

So ends this short sporting interlude.

VI

The organisers of the national covenant also had a taste for league tables. They named the small industrial town of Larbert as one of the places where support for a Scottish parliament was greatest; conveniently, Larbert happened to fall within the constituency of Arthur Woodburn, Secretary of State for Scotland and the politician most implacably opposed to the idea. John MacCormick and William Graham, the organising secretary, invited 18 student volunteers to address a press conference about their experiences of collecting signatures in Larbert and elsewhere.

As always, however, most of the talking was done by MacCormick. He quoted from the students' report that calls were made from house to house, and in the local iron foundries, over a period of three days. Six hours a day were devoted to the canvass, from which it was estimated that 85% agreed to sign, 10% wanted more time to think about it, and only 5% refused. The canvassers added that in working-class areas of the town, almost 100% of the people were behind the covenant, suggesting that the only resistance had come from the bigger houses of Larbert, of which there were few.

Stranraer came next: out of a voting population of 3,000, two-thirds had signed. There were honourable mentions for Inveraray, Tarbert, Ardrishaig, Girvan, and 'districts in Ross-shire'. The students denied suggestions of widespread duplication, disputing also that many people were signing with false names. They claimed that such unimpeachable citizens as ministers of religion and physicians were among the most enthusiastic signatories. MacCormick undertook that a card-index of supporters would be audited by a firm of chartered accountants. By that stage three quarters of a million people had signed: the size and complexity of the card-index was barely imaginable. The ever-hostile *Glasgow Herald* dismissed the notion of a door-to-door canvass as a reliable gauge of opinion; even if the covenant committee were to achieve its objective of two million signatories – 'and it may be doubted whether they will' – they could not legitimately claim that it was the duty of political parties to give effect to their proposals. The paper claimed that the campaign would obtain legitimacy only if a majority of the Scots MPs – 36 – were pledged to securing a parliament for Scotland and again it doubted whether this would ever be achieved.

Why, asked the *Glasgow Herald*, did the covenant committee not put up candidates of its own for parliament? John MacCormick's reply had the virtue of consistency: he repeated that the covenant was outside party politics, should remain so, and that home rule candidates did not in any way represent it. This explanation left him vulnerable to scorn from Christopher Grieve, who, exploiting MacCormick's Paisley episode, accused the covenant committee of being a cover for the Liberal Party.

VII

Grieve put up as an independent Scottish nationalist in Kelvingrove at the general election in February 1950, and polled 639 votes, a derisory result for the leader of the Scottish literary renaissance, although the four official SNP candidates managed only 9,708 votes in total. Another home ruler unattached to party, David Murray, 'ignited the contest' in the Western Isles, according to the press. His policy of 'Hearth and Home' included a demand for more consideration to be given to the 5,000 crofters of Lewis and Harris who were struggling to support their families. Murray received 425 votes and lost his deposit, a better result than Grieve's given the relative size of the two constituencies, if not quite a contest ignited.

The Liberals, keen advocates of a parliament in Edinburgh, had a dreadful election and were left with only two Scottish MPs, including an 'eloquent and persuasive young man', Jo Grimond, who unseated the Tory in Orkney and Shetland. The communists, much to the fore in MacCormick's covenant campaign, lost their only MP, Willie Gallacher, who wondered why the workers of West Fife had not seen that, in order to defeat the enemy, it was necessary to vote for his party. He promised to be back: 'We communists are tough people.' But that was the end of Gallacher and the start of another West Fife Willie, the anti-royalist Hamilton.

In an election dominated by national issues, there was not much hope of the covenant spirit finding political expression; all the nationalist candidates, and most of the devolutionist ones, did badly. The two unionist parties in Scotland both polled more than a million votes, Labour's 1,259,253 translating into 37 seats, the Unionists' 1,104,290 into 26. Among the Tory gains Lord Dunglass reclaimed Lanark, John S Maclay took West Renfrewshire and J L Clyde, KC, won Edinburgh West. To judge the core strength of the Tory vote, it was necessary to look no further than Glasgow, where the party held Cathcart, Hillhead, Pollok and Scotstoun and gained Govan and Kelvingrove: of the 15 seats in the city six were coloured blue.

It was not the most inspiring campaign, but in Scotland it had its moments. A hard-working Tory candidate, Betty Harvie Anderson, was delighted with the attendance of miners' wives at her open-air meetings in the forenoon (as morning was then more commonly known) in the working-class villages of Plean, Bannockburn, Cowie and Fallon in the Labour stronghold of West Stirlingshire. She insisted, however, on avoiding the use of loud-speakers after seven in the evening 'in order not to disturb children who may be sleeping'. All the candidates in West Stirlingshire regretted the absence of heckling, but the rude art had not been forgotten in Cupar, where John Strachey, the minister of food, had a groundnut thrown at him by angry farmers. Their aim was poor: it missed him and landed lamely on the press table.

The most wretched time was had by Arthur Woodburn. At a meeting in Partick Burgh Hall the Secretary of State was drowned out by nationalist demonstrators crying 'Judas, Judas', and as he drove away to catch the night train to London he was jeered. He fared no better at a meeting of Edinburgh University students a week later. When he addressed them as 'My dear friends' they roared with laughter. Asked why Labour was ignoring the wishes of all the Scots who had signed the covenant, and why the party proposed to deny Scotland a parliament of her own, he replied that the administration of Scotland was 'a practical operation which could not be settled without a ballot'.

Throughout Britain the poll was exceptionally heavy. In Springburn, Glasgow, there were long queues in the early evening as workers came off shifts. A voter in the Benula deer forest in Ross-shire walked 12 miles to vote, having been deprived of a postal vote on the obscure grounds that a sea arm failed to intervene between his home and the polling booth. In Orkney boats took voters from a number of the smaller islands to distant polling stations. Manny Shinwell wrote afterwards that the national poll – 84% – said more about the political awareness of the electorate than it did about a lacklustre campaign. The re-election of Jean Mann in Coatbridge and Airdrie gave Labour an overall majority. Attlee, who had addressed one of his biggest campaign rallies in the St Andrew's Hall, Glasgow, stayed in Downing Street but with a much-reduced majority.

Arthur Woodburn, whose obdurate handling of the home rule question had made him a liability, did not continue as Secretary of State. The more diplomatic Hector McNeil, MP for Greenock, succeeded him, accepting his oath of office in the Court of Session by calling it 'the greatest honour which could be bestowed on any Scotsman'. In his first speech to the House of Commons as Secretary of State, he promised that the government would 'fairly and generously' consider Scottish devolution. Peggy Herbison, able and likeable, was made an under secretary of state with a brief to tackle the greatest single problem in post-war Scotland – the shortage of decent housing. The new team at the Scottish Office was younger, livelier, and more in touch with the mood of the people. Or so it seemed.

But when the King delivered his speech at the opening of the new parliament, not a great deal had changed: there was no mention of Scottish devolution. During a Commons debate on the speech Alan Gomme-Duncan called for a royal commission to examine the relationship between Scotland and England and to look specifically at how much Scotland paid into the Treasury and how much it took out. In the Lords one of the Scottish peers, Lord Polwarth, said that a million people in Scotland had now signed the covenant – 'rather an impressive figure' – and he did not think the document could be lightly dimissed, yet the government was still content with 'a facade of control' in Edinburgh while the real power was exercised in London. Polwarth too wanted more information about Scotland's contribution to the exchequer.

Lady Glen-Coats, who had fallen out with John MacCormick so badly in Paisley, wrote an anguished letter to the press: 'Heaven forbid that we should indulge in a narrow nationalism, and I do not. I have travelled widely and I can say that never in any so-called civilised country have I seen worse conditions or a more deprived people than here in Scotland. We have to ask ourselves "Can this go on?" Let us leave England out of it. The question is: What are Scots going to do for themselves?' At the end of the year she was to receive an unexpected answer.

VIII

During the second world war there was a small mutiny in Paisley. 'The Battle of Britain was being fought,' wrote the mutineer, 'and the King and Queen were on a tour of Clydeside. We schoolkids were marshalled to show our loyalty by lining the streets and cheering. I refused. They were English royals. Nothing to do with me. Nothing could have more embarrassed my father yet he never reproached me.'

Ian Hamilton remembered his father as a very gentle man. Born into an age of Victorian splendour and certainty, John Harris Hamilton believed equally in Noah's Ark and the evolution of the species, took the greatness of the British empire for granted, loved the poetry of Kipling, and introduced his son to the speeches of Disraeli. For a while, young Ian went about the house shouting, 'Learn to aspire! Learn to aspire!' It was a Christian home, a British home. He loved and admired his father, a self-employed tailor who hated the work but maintained tradesmanlike standards and was angry if a button came off a jacket before it should. In later life Ian Hamilton tried to maintain the same exact standards as an advocate at the Scottish Bar. But the button had come off the conventionality of his life that mutinous day at Paisley Grammar School.

A decade after these events he was a member of John MacCormick's successful campaign team for the rectorship of Glasgow University, a group which also included James Halliday, president of the Nationalist Club, Bill Craig, president of the University Union, and Provan Murray, editor of the university magazine. MacCormick regarded Hamilton as 'perhaps most memorable of all', a brilliant and rebellious student whose magazine *Girn* was so critical of the establishment that the senate suppressed it. A close friendship developed. But when Hamilton declared one day, 'We must do something dramatic; something which will call the attention of the whole world to our movement', the leader of the national covenant reminded his young friend that it was a movement opposed to the use of violence. Hamilton agreed but told MacCormick that there might be something they could do which would hurt no one, yet make the government in London a laughing stock by exposing it to ridicule. He mentioned the possibility of returning the Stone of Destiny to Scotland. MacCormick did not demur and wondered if anything would come of the idea.

It was a stone of many noble bottoms and perhaps one noble head. For 400 years, if not time immemorial, the kings of Scotland had sat on it during their crowning. According to legend, it was the stone on which Jacob rested his head when he saw the vision of the angels ascending and descending the ladder; the same legend had it that the stone was brought to Scotland by Scota, daughter of Pharaoh, an ancestress of the Scottish royal line. Edward I, determined to deprive the Scots of this symbol of their independence and assert London's power, had it incorporated in the coronation chair in Westminster Abbey in 1296, and there it had been ever since, a festering source of patriotic resentment.

On Christmas Day – always the quietest of the year for news – the Scottish press was stirred from somnolence by a wildly improbable story from London: at 6am, a night watchman at Westminster Abbey, Andrew Hislop, had made his usual round of the premises and discovered that the stone was missing. It had been there at 5pm on Christmas Eve when the abbey was searched and locked, there being no watchnight service that year. It was seen again at midnight. But by the early morning it was gone. The police deduced that persons unknown – it would have taken more than one to accomplish the physically challenging feat of shifting three hundred-weight – must have concealed themselves behind one of the statues, of which there was no shortage, and removed the stone in the dead of night. They circulated a description of the occupants of a Ford Anglia saloon car – a woman in her mid-twenties with long dark hair, a long pointed nose, dark eyes and a fresh complexion and a man of about 29 of medium build and with a mop of uncombed hair. If this was intended to be a description of Ian Hamilton, the chief conspirator, and his female accomplice Kay Matheson, it succeeded in ageing both of them. Hamilton was 25, Matheson 22. It also gave the impression that Matheson travelled back to Scotland in company. She went alone.

On Boxing Day the papers were full of it. The *Daily Record* reported that the border had been closed and police blocks set up following the 'removal' – the *Record* avoided the use of the word 'theft' – and that the 'plot' had been planned and carried out by 'a raiding party'. The paper said that the Scottish National Party and Scottish Covention had 'promptly disowned any part in the scheme', although the reaction of Nigel Tranter, one of John MacCormick's supporters, came close to endorsement. 'We in the covenant movement stick to constitutional methods,' he said, 'but as an individual I would be the last to deplore initiative and enterprise shown by any person in Scotland – even if it is as misplaced as this is – if it will waken people up to the feeling in Scotland.'

The *Record* also quoted Hector McNeil's condemnation of the action as 'mean and atrocious', a point of view echoed more forcefully in the *Glasgow Herald*, whose leader was a model of editorial pomposity: 'The theft will be deplored by the great majority of Scots ... Pilfering from a church on Christmas Eve or

Christmas Day is not an achievement to be proud of and the fact that nationalist opinion of the extremist kind has made something of a fetish of the coronation stone in no way excuses the perpetuation of the theft.' It was, said the *Herald*, a case of childish misconduct or publicity-seeking vulgarity.

An un-named lawyer gave as his opinion that breaking into a place of worship and 'stealing therefrom' amounted to the crime of sacrilege under English law, for which a long term of imprisonment – perhaps 10 years – would be appropriate. Victor Warren, Lord Provost of Glasgow, from whom quotes could be rented free of charge, claimed that the theft 'struck at the very foundation of the freedom and religious tolerance of Great Britain' and was an act of disloyalty to the King and his Queen, 'a Scottish lady'. The establishment was, however, unexpectedly divided; the Earl of Mansfield said that if the stone was now back in Scotland, as seemed likely, it should stay there.

Ian Hamilton, having committed a second act of mutiny, did not go to prison; nor did his compatriots Kay Matheson, Gavin Vernon and Alan Stuart. None was ever charged. For a while the stone was kept in hiding in a basement under the office of George Bernard, a manager at John Rollo's St Andrew's Works in Bonnybridge. One spring day in 1951, in the final scene of this rattling yarn, Ian Hamilton and Bill Craig took it to the abbey where the Declaration of Arbroath had been signed by the lords, commoners and clergy of Scotland in 1320. It seemed the right place to leave it, and so they did – draped in a Saltire.

1951

DIRTY WORDS

I

The result from the Western Isles was the last to be declared in the 1951 general election, three days after the close of poll. Unsurprisingly Malcolm Macmillan held the seat for Labour and the SNP candidate, who polled 820 votes, lost his deposit. What made the result of some interest, other than its late delivery, was the unusual rebuke delivered by the returning officer to the crowd in Stornoway. 'The poll here was only 60%,' said Sheriff Robert Miller. 'If you look at the rest of the United Kingdom, you haven't much to be proud of.'

Miller himself had little to be proud of, having taken so long to organise the counting of a few thousand votes, but his comment found its way into the national newspapers, and the Outer Hebrides became a byword for electoral apathy as it was a byword for so much else. The preliminary results of the 1951 census showed that the number of Gaelic speakers in Scotland had dropped from 129,419 to 93,269 in a single decade, a decline so severe that John Bannerman, president of An Comunn Gaidhealach, made it a central theme of his speech at the opening of the 48th annual Mod in Edinburgh. Most of the remaining Gaelic speakers were concentrated in the outer isles of Lewis and Harris, but even in these strongholds the language was in trouble. Could Gaelic-medium education in mainland Scotland be its salvation? The annual meeting of An Comunn, which took place in the same week, approved a proposal by Raasay-born poet Sorley Maclean that Edinburgh Corporation should be asked to provide 'complete and adequate facilities for the teaching of Gaelic, at least in secondary schools', a suggestion which fell on deaf ears in the City Chambers.

The Mod itself gave a misleading impression of the state of

Gaeldom. A record crowd of more than 3,000 attended the main competitions. James Smith, a 22-year-old council clerk, won the gold medal for solo singing having been judged the most natural of the nine finalists. Another of the competitors, the Marquis of Graham, son and heir of the Duke of Montrose, appeared in the programme simply as 'Angus Graham, Arran' and impressed the adjudicator more for his kilted bulk than for his singing ability: 'It was almost as though a bit of one of the Cairngorms had come.'

The quality of the singing at the Mod was being questioned as never before. Neil Cameron, a speaker at the annual meeting, said that members of a Stornoway choir had told him that they had only a few words of Gaelic. 'We are getting a lot of people up here to sing Gaelic who have no idea what they are saying,' he complained. Alasdair Alpin MacGregor put it more bluntly. He called Gaelic singing crude, vulgar and ridiculous and said he had heard Mod gold medallists give an exhibition so bad that it made non-Gaels in the audience squirm. Alasdair Alpin MacGregor were, however, three of the dirtiest words in the Outer Hebrides. From the Butt of Lewis to the Sound of Harris there were probably none dirtier.

His latest book, *The Western Isles*, was considered so vile that Stornoway Town Council had asked the public library committee to ban it from the shelves. 'It has cast a slur on every innocent person belonging to the island of Lewis,' claimed Bailie W J Tolmin. Provost A J Mackenzie, condemning it as spiteful, said he could not reconcile such a 'frightful indictment' of the people with the hospitality the author had received in the islands. Another councillor said that Lewis people in Chicago 'wanted to know what the council were going to do about this book'. The only voice which rose in favour of freedom of speech in Stornoway public library was that of an ex-provost, who said the council was lowering its dignity in adopting 'the methods of the Spanish inquisition' by banning it.

The scandal of *The Western Isles* was still reverberating decades later. In 1975 John Lorne Campbell, in an article in the *Scots Magazine*, attacked the book as 'bitter, scatalogical and libellous', and in 1977 the broadcaster Derek Cooper reported that still no copy of it could be found in Stornoway public library. It seemed the ban was not only effective but permanent.

The sting in the book came in its tail. MacGregor, having devoted himself at length to the antiquity and folklore of the islands, took leave of his senses in the final chapters, laying waste the character of the natives. He found them dirty (alleging that they rarely took baths), lazy (not fully awake before noon), drunken (explaining their late start to the day), and cruel to their dogs. The women were old before their time because of the heavy burdens they were forced to carry by their indolent husbands, even in pregnancy. The youths were as dilatory as their elders, lounging in groups at street corners and misbehaving on the few buses. The refuse was put out anywhere and anyhow, and it was not unusual to see in the gutter of a Stornoway street a sheep's head newly decapitated. The shops were kept in a shocking condition with bluebottles all over the food. The main refuse dump on Lewis was 'one of the most unsightly spots in the world'. Tourists were received with indifference if not outright hostility. Telephone kiosks were vandalised, graveyards desecrated. The Highland schottische was danced with 'terrific abandon' – even this was a fault in MacGregor's jaundiced eyes – and the coming of picture houses had only been made possible by the easy money provided by the welfare state. Sexual life began early and often within the family. Inbreeding and illegitimacy were rife. Funerals were usually accompanied by fights ('to the effusion of blood') and wife-beating was commonplace. In Roman Catholic South Uist, where the main purpose of life (according to MacGregor) was to have as many offspring as possible, eight or 10 children and their parents inhabited corrugated iron sheds by the roadside. Then there was the ominous silence of the Sabbath: also very bad news.

II

The book sold well in many parts of the world. In the Outer Hebrides it had the status of an underground publication, passed subversively from reader to reader.

Why Alasdair Alpin MacGregor, an experienced writer, suddenly chose to blacken the name of the islanders is more interesting than the book itself. Until then he had specialised in nostalgic representations of the Highlands and islands, the sort written for the tourist and expat markets by people wearing rose-tinted spectacles and living a safe distance from Lochmaddy pier, in MacGregor's case Cheyne Row, Chelsea. He had a taste for archaic words, some hilarious to the modern ear, and used them in a quaint fashion which invited caricature. His fellow author Compton Mackenzie found the temptation irresistible, satirising MacGregor as a character in one of his novels, where he appeared thinly disguised as Hamish Hamilton Mackay. In *The Book of Barra* Mackenzie stepped up the attack on MacGregor's 'nebulous 20th-century impressionism'.

MacGregor quoted this phrase with approval in his preface to *The Western Isles* without making it clear that it was a personal attack on himself. He went on: ' … .it is because I so heartily agree with [Mackenzie] that I have included in the latter chapters of this volume a great deal of matter which, though by no means complimentary to the islanders, is true.' Poor MacGregor, wounded by the ridicule heaped on him by Compton Mackenzie, had finally decided to tell it like it was, or how he imagined it was. He then set about this self-appointed mission with unrestrained venom.

By the end the reader was left to wonder why, what with bluebottles in the shops and decapitated sheep-heads in the gutters, Lewis was not afflicted by some modern plague sufficient to see off most of the drunks and loiterers in a few gratifying weeks of pestilence. As an atheist MacGregor was the last person who should have made a life's work out of the Highlands and islands; his perception of the culture was neither instinctive nor sympathetic and it was riddled with contradictions. He had to acknowledge that, based on academic results, the people of the Western Isles were per head of population the brightest in the kingdom, yet still claimed to detect coarseness and ignorance in everything he saw around him.

An example of MacGregor's myopia was his account of an entrepreneur's attempt to revive the alginate industry in South Uist. The businessman was un-named, but the author gave the impression of some well-meaning outsider driven to despair by the natives. They would rather help to build the aerodrome at Benbecula than pick seaweed off the shore. Once the aerodrome was up and running there was still a reluctance to cooperate. MacGregor insisted there was work for hundreds, yet only 56 of the islanders showed any interest in picking seaweed off the shore for half a crown an hour, and many of them were unreliable; absenteeism was routine, there was no sense of responsibility to the employer.

Nothing in this rant suggested an understanding of the local temperament or of the long history of subjugation and abuse which helped to shape it. It was Farquhar Gillanders, a Wester Ross man, who said that to the people of the Highlands and islands any preoccupation with economics was a dismal one. A people betrayed by the collapse of a clan-based structure of social organisation, who had seen the best of their country given over to sheep, who had been abandoned on thin and precarious croft land, at first with no security of tenure, always vulnerable to the failure of crop, was not a people likely to respond well to the new industrialism in which they were paid a piecework rate for the amount of seaweed they managed to collect off their own shore.

The spirituality of the islands, the recognition that the past and the hereafter were always more natural than the present, MacGregor would never have understood. More surprising was his failure to grasp the significance of place and continuity, expressed through the long campaign for crofting rights and the desire for self-dependence.

In 1953, from the endowment of Herbert Ross, a whisky magnate, Lord Malcolm Douglas-Hamilton set up the Highland Fund to stimulate small-scale enterprises and appointed the patriotic John Rollo, the man who had secreted the Stone of Destiny in his Bonnybridge factory, to administer it. The fund gave loans on the basis of the character of the people applying for them and on that basis alone. Lewis was first in the queue, followed by Harris and Sutherland. The Highland Fund granted loans totalling £417,000 in 12 years, and most of the little projects it helped to start or develop were successful; the bad debts amounted to only 1.8% of the large sums advanced. If Alasdair Alpin MacGregor was taken aback by this result, there is no record that he had the generosity of spirit to admit it.

One important fact he did get almost right. He forecast (and eagerly anticipated) the demise of the Gaelic language. By 2001 the number of its speakers had further declined to 58,652, bringing Gaelic close to the point at which linguists would be inclined to declare it no longer viable. Encouraged by such initiatives as the printing of official notices in Gaelic and English, first recommended by Compton Mackenzie but dismissed as 'utter nonsense' by MacGregor, and by the teaching of Gaelic in mainland schools as Sorley Maclean had proposed, it stubbornly refused to die.

III

'Who can deliver Britain's armies from the palsied hands of balding war secretary John Strachey?' asked another of the Scottish caricaturists, John Junor, Liberal candidate for Dundee West. Junor left unanswered the question of how many armies Britain possessed in 1951 and the relevance, if any, of the Labour candidate's absence of hair. Junor himself was a tall, well-built man with a florid complexion. He remained red in the face throughout his life. Yet he did not drink excessively as many journalists did, and he seemed to be well enough most of the time. It is possible that he was red in the face because he was so full of righteous indignation, or pretended to be. 'Palsied hands' was early Junor, but would become characteristic of his prose. Later in his career he would conjure up a fictional character named Alice, who would pass the sick bag in response to the latest scandal or hypocrisy. Alice was a hard-working girl.

'Junor will be in, Strachey out, glory, glory hallelujah' was Junor's way of predicting the result of the contest in Dundee West. He assured the reporter from *The Bulletin* that his campaign meeting in a fine new aluminium primary school was so crowded that 'I had to go round the back, climb up on a ledge, and put my head in through the window'. A heckler brandishing some notes asked him: 'What's your policy?' Junor replied: 'I've got a policy all right, and it's not written on wee bits of paper.' He said he would like to help the cause of home rule by putting forward a private member's bill for a Scottish parliament.

He achieved the highest Liberal vote in Britain but failed to oust Strachey by 600 votes. It was Junor's last attempt to become an MP. By the age of 35 he had abandoned politics and was installed as editor of the *Sunday Express* for the next 32 years. Its rigid formula which left little room for flexibility or innovation looked dull, but it worked a treat with readers, all four million of them. Junor was a keen talent spotter. When a young Alan Watkins, later a distinguished political commentator, told his mentor at the London School of Economics that he had been offered a job by the editor of the *Sunday Express*, Professor Robson replied: 'No one could possibly be called John Junor.' He assumed it was a pen-name.

He was factually wrong about John Junor, whose real name it

was, however improbably. But the professor's instincts were correct. Junor resorted to the partial disguise of initials, 'JJ' appearing under his column of weekly commentary on current affairs, and he enjoyed for professional purposes an alternative self-created personality as the 'Sage of Auchtermuchty'. He was born in the Maryhill district of Glasgow and had no association with Auchtermuchty other than as a place he passed through in his car on his way to play golf at St Andrews. He did not claim ever to have stopped in Auchtermuchty to dispense sage-like advice; it was merely a convenient symbol for his newspaper column. He thought of Ecclefechan before settling on Auchtermuchty as his personal Brigadoon, a place which would contrast 'the old normality' as he saw it – decency, old-fashioned virtues – against the ugliness of the outside world. Auchtermuchty conjured up for Junor cobbled streets and village clocks which stopped long ago. In the end the illusion was all too convincing. Jean Rook, a *Daily Express* columnist, wrote in her autobiography that the 'dour little Highland village' (as she thought of it) was a product of John Junor's imagination.

If Auchtermuchty was unchanging, the same could not be said of its sage. He ceased to believe in a Scottish parliament and came to think of the Scots as 'a bunch of whingeing third-raters'. He believed that most of the best, himself included of course, had left their native land. He lived near Walton Health golf course in the Surrey stockbroker belt, a destination which brought to mind O H Mavor's observation that the Scots who went to England became more English than the English themselves. Junor coined a number of phrases well-known in his time, including 'Only poufs drink rosé'. A man known for his thrift, he always ordered the house wine in restaurants. White or red, it made no difference. But never rosé.

IV

Mavor, who worked only in his native Scotland and remained faithful to its interests, died in January 1951 at the age of 63. Alan Watkins' mentor would have been intrigued by Mavor, who wrote plays under two pseudonyms, the second of which was James Bridie. His first pen-name was Mary Henderson, the surname borrowed from his grandfather, a Dundee sea captain, whose daughter was Mary Ann Henderson. In the first production of Mary Henderson's *The Sunlight Sonata* by the Scottish National Players in 1926, the author took a curtain call unconvincingly dressed as a woman. Mavor called the play 'as Scots as Freuchie' – a Fife village not far from Auchermuchty. It concerned the Devil – a favourite Bridie character – and the Seven Deadly Sins, visiting themselves upon a party of Glaswegians picknicking by Loch Lomond.

Mavor, whose father Henry was a notable engineer, was brought up in middle-class Glasgow, a neglected place in Scottish literature. He trained as a doctor in the medical faculty of Glasgow University where he lingered longer than was usual, producing some memorable numbers of the university magazine (*GUM*) and 'talking and talking, talking and talking' with such friends as the future MP Walter Elliot. After service in the first world war – he was twice a soldier, returning as a major in the RAMC in the second – he became a consultant for a while. But he virtually abandoned medicine for the theatre as play followed play – *The Anatomist, Tobias and the Angel, A Sleeping Clergyman, Mr Bolfry, Dr Angelus, Daphne Laureola, Mr Gillie*, among many others.

The obituaries were warm and generous but realistic about Bridie's failings as a dramatist. He was labelled a careless genius for writing brilliant first acts, fairly good second acts, and poor to awful third acts. The essential problem was a restless mind; ever fascinated by the possibilities of the next idea, he lost interest in the one on which he happened to be working. An entertainer rather than a preacher, he came closest to expressing a moral philosophy in Raphael's advice to Sara in *Tobias and the Angel* that she must not be impatient with the common man. Mavor the uncommon man was so painfully diffident, such a slow talker, that he made a poor broadcaster and public speaker. Many years after his death his friend Ivor Brown wrote of him in *Scottish Theatre*: 'I can see him now with the eyes glinting behind his spectacles, the cigarette ash dropping on his coat, his murmured, fanciful, whimsical thoughts tumbling out amid the smoke and over a glass. He was clever, he was kind, he was unpredictable. He might be suddenly silent, but when he spoke one had to listen even though it strained one's ears to hear him. He was a master of the quiet and so often wasted word. He needed a Boswell.'

The *Glasgow Herald* rightly said that his death in the full flush of his creative powers was a serious loss to the Scottish theatre, which until he came along had been hard pressed to find native dramatists capable of producing material worthy of the skills of Scotland's many fine actors. His legacy as an entrepreneur – as founder of the Glasgow Citizens' Theatre and chairman of the Scottish Committee of the Arts Council – was more ambiguous. He did little to encourage some of the promising writers who had emerged through the left-wing Unity Theatre, crushing Ena Lamont Stewart's hopes of advancement with a few ill-chosen words.

He died of a brain haemorrhage. His funeral at the Western Necropolis in Glasgow, after a service in the University Chapel, was conducted by his minister cousin, Ivan Mavor, and the pall-bearers included his son Ronald (a second son had been killed in the second world war), Tom Honeyman, Alastair Sim and John Casson, director of the Citizens'. John MacCormick, who had been loyally supported by Mavor through his travails in Paisley, was there along with Hector Hetherington, Andrew Dewar Gibb, Eric Linklater, Moray McLaren, Robert Kemp, Gordon Gildard and James Crampsey from the BBC, and a host of other prominent Scots. Mavor, who had insisted that Scots ought to work in Scotland and who led by example, was much missed; in important ways, as a man who combined writing with a commitment to public life, he was never quite replaced. Sixty years later his many plays, so popular at the time, are rarely produced.

V

Had he lived, Mavor might have joined John Boyd Orr as an honorary office-bearer of the Scottish Covenant Association, founded in the autumn of 1951 to campaign for a government-conducted plebiscite on home rule. The cast of characters was almost identical to that of Scottish Convention which had instigated the unofficial plebiscite. Ian Hamilton was appointed organising secretary, John MacCormick convener, Nigel Tranter and Councillor Robert (Bertie) Gray vice-conveners. Gray was a figure of some intrigue – a monumental sculptor who had repaired the Stone of Destiny before it was despatched to Arbroath, then cast doubt on its authenticity by declaring that he had confused it with one of two replicas he had made.

There should have been a third vice-convener, Sir George Ogilvie Forbes of Aberdeenshire, a former member of the diplomatic service. He turned down the honour. 'I am 60 and I hope not yet gaga,' he told the association's inaugural meeting. 'But I belong to a rapidly disappearing class – what some might call the decadent class. Our movement will never make any progress until we can convince the working class – and a laird is hardly a suitable chap for that.' He gave a second and more disturbing reason for his decision – his religion. 'There has been a great deal of criticism that there are too many Roman Catholics at the head of our affairs,' he said. 'I appreciate the point of view of the critics.'

Others were not so appreciative. A few weeks earlier, in a speech of welcome to Gordon Gray, the new Roman Catholic Archbishop of St Andrews and Edinburgh, Agnellus Andrew spoke frankly of 'the psychological barrier' between Catholics and non-Catholics in Scotland. While acknowledging that life for Catholics was easier than it had been for their ancestors, people of his faith were familiar with an atmosphere which was at once difficult to define but easy to sense – an atmosphere of misunderstanding and mistrust.

Bigotry, prejudice and old hatreds died hard. Could these barriers of prejudice finally be broken down? Not yet, it seemed. Soon a diplomat was to declare that even his name on the letterhead of the Scottish Covenant Association would damage the home rule cause.

VI

The Bulletin, edited by the erudite J M Reid, noted with disappointment the invisibility of Scottish affairs from the 1951 general election. Both the Tories and Labour were promising a royal commission on the subject, and the Tories proposed two new ministers in an enlarged Scottish Office – a minister of state and a third joint under secretary of state. No doubt, the paper said, the covenant leaders were right not to make their cause a party matter. 'But what is still needed is some means of impressing on the big parties that the wish for self-government is something which Scots are not going to forget in a hurry.'

The paper had no ideas to offer on what those means might be, but a few in the nationalist community had ideas of their own. Oliver Brown of the *Scots Independent* wrote that, in the absence of palatable candidates, the only way for Scots to vote was to write 'Freedom for Scotland' across their ballot papers. Wendy Wood, founder of the Scottish Patriots, went further. She refused to pay National Insurance contributions, describing this as 'non-violent non-cooperation as a means of pressing for self-government'. The sheriff at Fort William was unimpressed and fined her £15. She refused to pay and, in the middle of the general election campaign, was committed to Duke Street Prison in the east end of Glasgow for 60 days.

It was a grim establishment with a gruesome history. The last woman to be hanged in Scotland, Susan Newell, went to her death at Duke Street in 1923 for the murder of a paper boy whose body she wheeled in a pram through the streets of the town. When her plea of insanity failed and she climbed on the gallows, she refused the traditional white hood. Duke Street had also detained suffragettes and political activists, including a minister's wife, Helen Crawford, who was sentenced to 10 days' imprisonment in 1914 for smashing windows. She refused to cooperate in having her fingerprints and photograph taken, had her sentence increased, and went on hunger strike. She was finally released on a doctor's recommendation.

In 1946 Duke Street's harsh regime was softened by the arrival of Scotland's only female prison governor, the Hon Victoria Bruce, sister of Lord Balfour of Burleigh. Bruce, a woman of humanitarian ideals, introduced educational classes and instruction in such improving activities as country dancing; the cells were now called rooms. What she thought of her new admission in October 1951 has not been recorded, but when R E Muirhead, one of the leaders of the home rule movement, wrote to Bruce asking that Wood should be allowed out of prison for two hours to deliver a speech which had been arranged before her imprisonment, the governor declined. The Scottish Home Department made it clear that Wood would be released from Duke Street if, and only if, she paid the outstanding fine.

Eight days passed. By the ninth day a group of sympathisers had finally raised £15. Muirhead turned up in a taxi, entered the prison, and emerged with Wood after 40 minutes. There was a sad coda to this episode when, a month later, Victoria Bruce died suddenly at the age of 53. Some of her former inmates continued to refer to her as 'our beloved governor', though Wendy Wood may not have been among them.

VII

By a quirk of Britain's electoral system Labour polled more votes than the Conservatives in the 1951 general election yet the Conservatives gained a small majority of the seats in the House of Commons. The Scottish newspapers were grudging in their praise of the outgoing government, *The Bulletin* being typical in its acknowledgement of 'the blessings of the Welfare State, a health service, cradle-to-grave insurance, better pensions for the aged, and so on'. The 'so on' it left unexplained before going on to pose the question: 'But what else have they to boast about?' By the paper's own admission the Attlee government had brought into being a revolution in social welfare, but it was still not enough; in some mysterious way the Labour Party should have accomplished more. Only later, considerably later, was the 1945-51 government recognised as a great reforming administration and Clement Attlee accorded the honourable place in history which his achievements merited. He came to be hailed by a Conservative Prime Minister, Margaret Thatcher, as 'a patriot, a serious man, a man of substance and no show'. But at the time of his departure, in the late autumn of 1951, he was not much lamented.

As soon as the count was declared in Moray and Nairn, the constituency he had represented for 28 years, James Stuart began a 570-mile journey by car to London. He was summoned at once to Chartwell, the country house of Winston Churchill, who was assembling the first Conservative government of the post-war era. Stuart wrote that, when the Prime Minister offered him a seat in the cabinet as Secretary of State for Scotland, he replied 'I will only let you down' and that Churchill then took his arm and said, 'No, you won't'. After lunch Stuart was handed a sheet with some names on it: a possible ministerial team at the Scottish Office, including a nomination for the new post of minister of state which had been created in response to the demands for home rule of one sort or another. Stuart did not like the look of the list and asked if he could have Lord Home (formerly Lord Dunglass) as minister of state. Churchill agreed.

And so, within a few days of the election, Scotland woke up to an administration in Edinburgh headed by the son of the 17th Earl of Moray, who would in due course inherit the title Viscount Stuart of Findhorn, assisted by the 14th Earl of Home, who would in due course renounce his hereditary peerage to become plain Sir Alec. It was a clean sweep for the Old Etonians, leaving a more obvious contender for Secretary of State, Walter Elliot, out in the cold, a man whose moment had come – and clearly gone.

Not long after his appointment, James Stuart was greeted outside the Palace of Westminster by his old friend George Buchanan, the former Labour MP for Glasgow Gorbals, who had quit politics to be chairman of the Public Assistance Board.

'I never thought ye were such a bloody fool, Jimmy,' Buchanan began.

'I'm sorry, Geordie, but what I have done wrong?'

'Och,' he said, 'to take on that job at the Scottish Office. Ye'll never make a bloody thing oot o' that.'

Stuart, who claimed that he had never wanted the job, continued to do the bloody thing long after George Buchanan was dead. In his autobiography he devoted only five pages to his six years as Secretary of State, citing as his proudest achievement the announcement of the building of the Forth Road Bridge. He had, however, wanted a toll of 5s, which would still have been cheaper than the 7s 6d it cost to cross from North to South Queensferry in the ferry. The toll eventually agreed was half a crown – the hourly rate for the back-breaking work of picking seaweed off a South Uist shore.

1952

BY THE GRACE OF GOD

I

On 4 February 1952 almost 1,100 people, most of them Scots, boarded an emigrant ship in Glasgow. It was its first voyage since the 27-year-old liner, built at the Fairfield yard in Govan, was bought and refurbished by the New Zealand government, renamed Captain Cook, and put into service 'for the use of settlers'. New Zealand was so hungry for new blood that everyone on board travelled free at the country's expense. Its chief immigration officer announced that New Zealand had vacancies for 30,000 migrants, skilled and unskilled, but that because of a desperate housing shortage, single people had priority over families. A ship full of ambitious young people made the trip from Glasgow to Wellington, via the Panama Canal, in 33 days. Long before it docked there was the unexpected death of a monarch, the arrival home from Africa of a new monarch, a disputed title, a period of national mourning, and the dawn of what the newspapers called a new age.

II

In the week of Captain Cook's departure, two Scottish intellectuals examined the unsatisfactory state of their country. J D Mackie, the historian, was critical of the narrow thrust of Scottish education, its emphasis on obtaining qualifications at the expense of education for its true purpose, which he defined as 'teaching people what is worth having in life and giving them the moral courage to go and get it'. His fellow Glasgow University professor, the lawyer Andrew Dewar Gibb, saw the national problem in more political terms, outlining his vision of a constitution for 'a new Scotland'. He proposed a Scottish parliament with power to raise its own taxes, supported by an elected second chamber.

Dewar Gibb had travelled a long way since he contested Hamilton and Greenock as a Unionist in two successive general elections in the 1920s. By 1936 he was chairman of the National Party, and in 1950 he published a book deploring the anglicisation of Scots law since the union of 1707, pointing out that the court of ultimate appeal in the House of Lords possessed not a single representative of one of the partners in that union – Scotland.

Ian Hamilton, a student in Gibb's Scots law class at Glasgow, remembered him as a fabulous creature, 'his great domed head shining above the podium'. He would begin by referring to 'a recent case' and then quote something from 1883. 'He was the first true eccentric I had met and he fascinated me,' Hamilton wrote. Generous in large things, he was mean in all things small. 'Put the stopper back on the decanter, Alison,' he instructed one of his daughters. 'Whisky's a spirit and it will evaporate.' The thought of keeping whisky long enough for it to evaporate left Hamilton awestruck.

The real meanness of spirit in Scottish life never evaporated, but lingered at the bottom of the glass. As the emigrants sailed to a new life thousands of miles away, small minds continued to do their worst. Whithorn Town Council revoked the licence of the Kingsway Cinema which allowed it to open on Sunday evenings. A council spokesman said that the films had been largely patronised by outsiders and that it was a pity to see 'the good name of Whithorn smeared by such people'. In the same censorious vein the Free Church of Scotland attacked the proposed visit of Princess Elizabeth and her husband, the Duke of Edinburgh, to a Buddhist temple in Ceylon: 'No intelligent Buddhist could regard the visit as other than curiosity.' Curiosity was never satisfied. The royal tour came to an abrupt end in Kenya.

The formal announcement from Buckingham Palace on 6 February consisted of 21 words: 'The King, who retired to rest last night in his usual health, passed peacefully away in his sleep early this morning.' His 'usual health' was wretched; he had been suffering from lung cancer after too many cigarettes, encouraged in the habit by his misguided doctors, just as the tubercular George Orwell had been advised that smoking would be good for him. Yet the death of this painfully shy, difficult, reluctant monarch, who had come to the throne at a moment of national crisis, was a shock to his subjects. The court did not deem it necessary to give the time of death – 'early this morning' covered a range of possibilities – but immediately after the first broadcast at 11.16am, radio listeners – 'mainly housewives' – rushed into the streets to spread the word, gathering anxiously around the stalls of newspaper vendors. In Dundee so many phone calls were made in the hour after the announcement that the exchange overloaded, blowing fuses.

The immediate Scottish reaction hinted at a national unanimity of grief. Theatres, cinemas and ballrooms in Glasgow closed their doors. Children in some towns were sent home early from school. The managements of the posher hotels decreed that their orchestras would be silent until after the funeral. A match between the Royal Caledonian Curling Club and a team of touring Americans was called off. Office-bearers of the Grand Lodge of Scotland – the King had been grand master mason in 1936 – wore black crepe over their regalia and, said the Earl of Galloway, would continue to do so for three months. A salute of 56 guns, one for each year of the King's life, was fired at Edinburgh Castle.

Attempts to maintain a semblance of normality were regarded as disloyal. When the curtain rose on the Kintyre drama festival in Campbeltown on the night of his death two office-bearers of the local branch of the Scottish Community Drama Association, including Sheriff J Aikman Smith, resigned in protest. On the same night the Royal Philosophical Society of Glasgow, 'after observing a silence', proceeded with its weekly lecture. A strike of 5,000 Clydeside shipbuilding and engineering apprentices, in support of their campaign for a wage increase of £1 a week, went ahead regardless. A few nights later the Scottish Orchestra not only gave its weekend concert in the St Andrew's Hall in Glasgow, but saw no reason to depart from its advertised programme. After the national anthem and 'a reverent silence', it embarked lustily on the overture of Berlioz's *Carnaval Romain*, an exuberant choice for so solemn an occasion. 'Was there nothing in the orchestra's repertoire which could more appropriately have opened the concert?' asked one critic. 'Quite incredible,' wrote another. 'The *Eroica Symphony* or the *Enigma Variations* could have been substituted.' It was also business as usual in Scottish football, 65,000 spectators turning up for a midweek game at Ibrox Stadium. Sir Patrick Dollan, chairman of the Scottish Fuel Efficiency Commitee, pronounced it scandalous that such fixtures should be played 'at a time of national mourning and fuel shortages'. In the same week 24,000 people attended the first three days of the Scottish Dairy Show, squandering more of Dollan's precious fuel.

The people who insisted on going to football matches or dairy shows, when such patriots as the Earl of Galloway were draping themselves in black crepe, may have been the same people who dressed irreverently in the streets. An anonymous reader wrote to the press: 'I was dismayed and distressed to find so many of the male population of Glasgow going about in coloured ties on Thursday. Family mourning is one thing and must be guided by the wishes of each family, but public mourning should be respected.'

Nevertheless an awkward question presented itself and, despite the etiquette of public mourning, it refused to go away. Would the young woman proclaimed Queen Elizabeth II be known in Scotland as Queen Elizabeth I? Or would the anglicisation of Scotland deplored by Andrew Dewar Gibb extend to the title of the new monarch? Within 24 hours of her father's death John MacCormick sent a telegram to the Prime Minister, the Secretary of State for Scotland, and miscellaneous Scottish dignitaries. He put it this way: 'Do you, on holding a position representative of the people of Scotland, acquiesce to the proclamation of Her Majesty Queen Elizabeth's title as Elizabeth II, such proclamation implicitly declaring that the United Kingdom of Great Britain and Northern Ireland should be held no longer to exist, that Scotland should be treated as having been annexed to, and submerged in, England, and that international treaties should be used as scraps of paper?' It was a big question, if essentially a rhetorical one, moving Sir Patrick Dollan to fresh heights of patriotic fury: 'When I read about people getting disturbed about such things as the numerals after the Queen's name, I begin to think that we are going daft. It does not mean a rap compared with the fact that we are getting seven million tons of coal a year less than we had in 1939 to keep the country's industries going.' When Dollan came into a room, the fuel shortage was never far behind.

The telegram divided Scotland. Gordon Baker of St Fillans, in a letter to the press, summed up one point of view: 'The sending of this telegram at such a time, when the royal family and the Queen have been plunged into such depths of mourning, is one of the most despicable acts conceivable, and I am sure that all loyal Scots will agree with me.' Not all did. Two 'loyal Scotswomen' (unnamed) wrote to the same newspaper: 'We had hoped that, as she is the sovereign of wider lands than Queen Elizabeth of England ever dreamed of, we would have been able to honour our young princess as Elizabeth the First of Great Britain and the British Commonwealth and Empire, as she truly is.'

MacCormick had touched a sensitive nerve, and the maladroit handling of the case by the Queen's advisers did nothing to appease Scottish sentiment. When his telegram was imperiously ignored he returned to the offensive, declaring that Elizabeth's courtiers had 'demonstrated that, in their eyes, the United Kingdom of Great Britain is synonymous with the no-longer-existing Kingdom of England'. It was an opinion shared by some of Scotland's civic leaders, all of whom were obliged to read a proclamation of the accession. At least two refused to do so in the required style. Robert Curran, the provost of Alva, omitted the words 'the Second' from the designation, and C Stewart Black, his counterpart in Paisley, adopted the same policy. Black said it would have been impossible for him to pronounce the words he had omitted. 'They would have stuck in my throat,' he said. 'I would have hated myself for the rest of my life if I had used them.' He survived a vote of censure by his fellow councillors.

True to form the *Glasgow Herald* dismissed these symbolic acts of rebellion, accusing the Scottish Covenant Association of making political capital out of the Queen's title. The paper maintained that any title other than the one proclaimed 'would only lead to confusion'. As issued by the Court of Session, it read: 'Elizabeth the Second, by the Grace of God, of Great Britain, Ireland, and the British Dominion beyond the Seas, Queen, Defender of the Faith.' On this grandiloquent note, the matter rested for the time being.

III

In the 10 days before the funeral, as most flags hung at half mast, a number of events passed without incurring the wrath of Sir Patrick Dollan. Anne Redpath became the first woman painter to be admitted to the Royal Scottish Academy (Phyllis Bone, the only previous female member, was a sculptor). An application to the Traffic Commissioners for extra bus tours to Loch Lomond was opposed by a member who claimed that he had seen the loch so often on such tours that Ben Lomond had begun to nod to him.

Smaller deaths were briefly noted: a former provost of Troon, Walter Donald, who fought in the Boer War and was present at the relief of Mafeking; Elizabeth Mackintosh, a year younger than the King when she died at the age of 55, who wrote under the pseudonyms Gordon Daviot and Josephine Tey and whose best-known work, *Richard of Bordeaux*, enjoyed a successful run with John Gielgud in the title role. Glasgow housing committee approved a scheme for a 'self-contained satellite township' at Drumchapel, with its own commercial and shopping centre, its own schools, baths and libraries, serving a population of 30,000.

The police were as busy as ever. Mario Macelli, 27, described as a 'servant' of Mr P Harris, 200 Nithsdale Road, Pollokshields, was assaulted when he surprised two intruders in his employer's home. The incident was of marginal interest for demonstrating that in Nithsdale Road, Pollokshields, people still employed servants in 1952. In a poorer part of the city (Carntyne Road), someone pulled the steel grille from a side window of St Bernadette's Roman Catholic Church, smashed the glass, poured petrol into the holy premises, then flung a lighted match inside.

The BBC, which had been criticised for its excessive gloom in the week before the funeral, exhibited signs of nervousness. From the point of view of its Scottish customers the King could not have died at a less opportune moment, one month before the Kirk O' Shotts transmitter was due to introduce the miracle of television to viewers north of the border. 'Efforts will be made to bring at least part of the television broadcast of the King's funeral procession to Scotland, but no guarantee can be given that these attempts will be successful,' the corporation announced twitchily.

In the event television did more than bring a great state occasion to Scotland; it asserted at the same time the ultimate Britishness of the day. The pictures of the funeral were projected on a wall of Glasgow City Chambers while 10,000 people took part in a memorial service in George Square; the band of the Highland Light Infantry (the City of Glasgow regiment) played the Dead March from *Saul*. 'The stillness was impressive,' wrote one journalist, 'and traffic stopped when buglers sounded the Last Post to signal the start of a two-minute silence, which was broken only by the sound of ships' sirens honouring the occasion in their own way. The city was hushed until the reveille sounded.' Tram and bus drivers had been instructed to stop their vehicles for the duration of the silence; the public took their cue from this gesture.

Most pubs in Glasgow respected the ruling of their trade association that they should not open until evening. Joseph Kelly was an exception. He allowed the punters into his pub in Glebe Street to see the funeral on a TV set which had been placed on the counter, but no drink was served. The only jarring note was 'the first TV housebreaking'. While William Raphael of Corsock Street sat in a darkened room watching the funeral with his son, an opportunistic burglar threw open a window and attempted to enter the house. Raphael's son jumped to the window, and the intruder fell back in shock – landing on his accomplice. It was a very Glasgow moment.

In Edinburgh some shops in Princes Street lowered their blinds while others were draped in black and purple. At 2pm a cannon was fired from the half-moon battery at the castle and, 'as the last wisp of smoke faded from the cannon-mouth', the life of the capital was stilled. Pedestrians on the north side of Princes Street stopped as one, turned to face the castle, doffed their hats. Hidden from public view on the roof of a building, a squad of workers rose stiffly to attention. The tramcars, their power cut off, stopped abruptly, their passengers standing silent and still. A reporter noted that 'the only movement was that of the flags flapping lazily at half-mast, the relentless crawl of the hands of the North British Hotel tower clock, and the drifting smoke of the chimneys. Faintly, from the distance, came the chime of a steeple. A harsh command, another round of gunfire, and Edinburgh sprang to life again'.

The memorial service in St Giles brought the ornaments of the Scottish establishment together under a familiar roof: the judges of the Court of Session, the members of the Royal Scottish Academy, the senate of Edinburgh University, the high constables of Holyroodhouse, the Royal Company of Archers (the Queen's Bodyguard for Scotland). The only ornament missing was the one with pride of place on the shelf: Charles L Warr, minister of St Giles and Dean of the Thistle and Chapel Royal, had been summoned to Windsor for the day. At Edinburgh University, 4,000 students attended an open-air service in the old quad.

Scenes like this were repeated all over Scotland. The crowd for the public memorial service in Greenock Town Hall was so vast that the service had to be relayed to overspills in the lesser hall, the Mid Kirk and Cathcart Square. In Perth most shops closed for three hours. The bell of the steeple at Forfar, where the King was the last surviving freeman of the burgh, tolled for 15 minutes before the silence. Another bell sounded on Iona, ancient burial ground of Scottish kings. In Inverness Old High Church, where every seat was taken, worshippers stood in the aisles. Fishermen around the Scottish coast observed the two-minute silence for the man who had been master of their fleet. Lighthouses did the same. And in St Andrews, members of the Royal and Ancient Golf Club, headed by Sir George Cunningham, the club captain, walked to church carrying a silver club and balls, including the ball which the King had presented to the club when he became captain in 1930. No doubt George would have appreciated this gesture, but it was a game that frustrated him. His inability to master it made him so angry that when the Duke of Windsor met someone from Britain after the abdication, his first question was whether his brother still got cross playing golf.

Anywhere there was a signal, television was sought out and watched communally. Crowds in Edinburgh and Glasgow gathered inside dealers' shops and round the windows, declaring the reception 'crystal clear'. It was not so clear in Stranraer – 50% strength at best – but excellent in Denny, where a set had been installed in the gymnasium of the High School.

The day was such a triumph that, soon afterwards, it was considered safe to restore the Stone of Destiny to the coronation chair in Westminster Abbey from which it had been removed on Christmas Day 1950. Alan Gomme-Duncan asked the Prime Minister if he was aware that 'among a very considerable body of Her Majesty's most loyal Scottish subjects there will be profound disappointment at this decision'. Gomme-Duncan told Churchill that, between coronations, it should be kept in Edinburgh. The political correspondent of the *Glasgow Herald* wrote: 'The fact that a coronation is to take place next year evidently made it desirable that the stone should be restored to its traditional resting-place as long as possible in advance, so that the public might have time to forget its sensational misadventures.' Despite awkward questions in the House of Commons about who had consulted whom before the decision was made, there was no great storm of public protest. Had some of the heat gone out of the home rule campaign? The Scots had seen for themselves the flickering images of a united kingdom. Many liked what they saw.

IV

The Elizabethan age began on the evening of the funeral with an address which startled the douce patriots of the Saltire Society. Sheriff R H Maconochie, QC, told them that he was a profound believer in corporal punishment and that borstals were soft. He added a recollection from his own youth: 'When I was in a public school in England I was thrashed every night – my crime was being Scots – and it did me a world of good.'

A H Stevenson, a probation officer in Ayrshire, unearthed figures from the 1940s, when judicial corporal punishment was still allowed in Scotland, showing that in Glasgow in 1940, 55 children under the age of 11 were birched of whom 35 made further appearances on criminal charges. Stevenson's point that birching was no cure for juvenile delinquency did not pass without challenge. J G Littlejohn, a Wigtownshire headmaster, told a teachers' meeting in Stranraer that when children were allowed to play in the streets and see gangster films, it was scarcely surprising that they snatched handbags and slashed other children with razor blades. He argued for a greater use of corporal punishment in Scotland's overcrowded classrooms.

The usual answer to the chronic shortage of properly qualified teachers was to employ unqualified ones. In Scotland in 1952 there were more than 1,000 uncertificated teachers. Wigtownshire education committee produced its own remedy for the malaise: it asked the Scottish Education Department for permission to allow children to leave school as soon as they reached the age of 15. 'The majority of children over 14 do not want any further education,' said a spokesman for the committee. 'If there were 12 leaving dates a year, employers would be assisted and there is a great demand for youths at present.' The enlightened views of Professor J D Mackie on the true purpose of education had failed to penetrate Wigtownshire, which preferred the early parole of the inmates into the local labour market.

The brightest went on to the Scottish universities, of which there were only four in 1952: Glasgow, Edinburgh, St Andrews and Aberdeen. The behaviour of students was the despair of Sheriff Maconochie, whose knighthood in 1955 confirmed that being thrashed every night for being Scottish was no impediment to progress in life. A quiet scientist, Alexander Fleming, had the misfortune to be elected rector of Edinburgh University and rose in the McEwan Hall to deliver a rectorial address on the subject 'Success'. A journalist covering this riotous occasion reported: 'Every sentence of Sir Alexander's address was greeted with loud cheers, hoots, the stamping of feet … He was constrained on several occasions to leave out parts of the prepared address and also to condense a number of passages. It was with obvious relief that he sat down at the end of the address to a tumultuous ovation.' Earlier, just before a procession of dignitaries filed in, squashed tomatoes were hurled from the galleries, dried peas projected by shooter, while balloons, bubbles and paper darts floated about the hall, all this to the accompaniment of whistles and trumpets. Fleming said afterwards that he had been subjected to an ordeal, but added tactfully that it had been a minor one. There were two arrests for disorderly conduct.

Fleming, who could occasionally be heard above the din, chose as his theme the importance of luck in the achievement of success. He gave penicillin as an example – 'sheer fortune' he called it. He described how an unwanted blue mould – a penicillium – came from somewhere and contaminated one of his culture plates of bacteria. This often happened, but on this occasion the mould appeared to be dissolving the material. He made some investigations and the more he investigated the more interesting it became. He discovered that the mould made a powerful and non-poisonous antiseptic, and he named it penicillin. It was an extraordinary chance. 'If my mind when I saw it had been occupied with other things I would have missed it. I might have been too busy to bother about chance happenings. I might have been in a bad temper. My chief might have insisted that it was not worthwhile pursuing this strange path. Then I would probably have thrown away the culture and thought no more about it. Had I done so, I would not have been giving this rectorial address, so my selection as rector really depended on my being in a good temper on a morning in September 1928. Fate ordained that everything happened and penicillin was born.'

Another Scottish scientist who believed in the importance of luck – 'the happy accident' – was James Black. A brilliant pupil of Beath High School in Cowdenbeath, Black won a scholarship to St Andrews University at the age of 15. Without it he would never have gone on to higher education; his father, a mining engineer, had funded James's three older brothers, a financial burden for the family, and there was no money left for the fourth child. Black studied medicine at the medical faculty in Dundee, but decided not to become a medical practitioner. 'I found the way patients were treated was unacceptable,' he said. 'Not cruelly or sadistically, but insensitively. They were just classes – a heart, a liver or a lung.' Intrigued by a textbook, *The Living Body*, he developed an interest in physiology. That was the first of the happy accidents.

In 1952 Black was working on the physiology of circulation in the veterinary school of Glasgow University when there was an unhappy accident which changed the course of his life. His father, who had already suffered one heart attack, died of a second attack 24 hours after a car crash. 'A trivial accident,' he recalled, 'but physiologically it wasn't trivial. I'm thinking of stress. In the living body the sympathetic nerves are there to help us through emergencies. So it was natural to imagine that something which you need to get through emergencies can't do bad things to you. That's true if you're healthy. But if you are putting this emergency system into a heart with damaged blood vessels, it is different. What I wanted to do was to protect the heart from adrenaline.'

His father's sudden death motivated Black, but it was one of the happy accidents that gave him the scientific inspiration. Reading Raymond Ahlqvist's *Pharmacology and Medicine*, he stumbled on the vital clue to his eventual development of the beta-blocking drug propranolol. Black took his ideas to ICI Pharmaceuticals and, in 1964, propranolol was hailed as a breakthrough in the treatment of heart disease. It became the world's best-selling drug and made the pharmaceutical companies a fortune, although Black himself profited very little from it. Modest, publicity-shy, temperamentally difficult, he was horrified to receive the Nobel prize for medicine, sensing that he would henceforth be regarded as an important person with something to say. When he was asked towards the end of his life how he would look back on his achievements he replied that he was 'struggling with problems inside my head most of the time, not out there regarding myself'.

V

For those who would never enjoy the privilege of firing dried peas into the McEwan Hall, or encounter unexpected success in a blue mould, or be blessed with James Black's ability to grasp the happy accidents, Captain Cook offered an escape route: it would soon be back, scooping up another batch of Scottish migrants. For some of the rest there was the prospect of a job on one of the new assembly lines. The press reported that with 'characteristic American hustle' two US-based companies were expanding after only a year in the Vale of Leven. Westclox were increasing their production of alarm clocks, while Burroughs were building a second factory to make more of their adding machines.

Journalists who visited the plants at Bonhill wrote of being fascinated by the process. At Westclox 500 employees – of whom 300 were women – worked on various stages of manufacture and assembly. 'From a bewildering number of toothed wheels, spindles, and many other parts, the clocks are gradually built up on the assembly line,' noted one report. 'The balance wheels are inserted and the clocks come to life. When the faces and hands are added there is an animated cartoon look about the process as the clocks are carried along by the conveyor belt.' The press deputation moved to the neighbouring plant of Burroughs, employing 1,000, and marvelled at the 1,800 parts required to make an adding machine or calculator. 'The latter term,' said the same report, 'is a better description of the machine made in the Vale of Leven, because it is capable of adding, subtracting, dividing, multiplying, and taking percentages, some in pounds, shillings and pence, some in dollars and cents, others in francs, marks and rupees.' Other factories on the industrial estate made elastic products and spectacle lenses, the total workforce of around 2,000 being drawn from the fragile industrial towns of Dumbarton, Renton, Alexandria and Balloch.

The pitfalls of the branch factory economy were not lost on George Middleton, general secretary of the Scottish Trades Union Congress, of whom Keith Aitken, the biographer of the STUC, wrote that he had 'a grin like a deflated football'. Middleton complained that unemployment in Scotland (around 3%) was consistently twice as high as it was south of the border. The difference was between low and very low, but Middleton shrewdly assessed the vulnerability of economic prosperity fuelled by inward investment. While the Vale of Leven expanded, a clothing factory in the Bridgeton district of Glasgow folded, moving Middleton to assert that employers who had been assisted to move to Scotland had some moral obligation to make a better fist of it.

Middleton himself was born among the inner-city slums of Glasgow (Townhead) and was heavily influenced by the mass unemployment he had experienced in the pre-war years and by his own participation in the hunger marches of the 1920s and 1930s.

He was ever the realist. 'Not uncommonly for one schooled in the Scottish communist tradition,' wrote Aitken, 'Middleton's idealism was underpinned by a robust practical belief in the need to focus on attainable rather than distant objectives.' In 1952, only three years into the job, his considerable influence on post-war Scottish life had only begun to be felt. He came to be known as 'the ugliest looking man ever to appear on television' and delighted in repeating the insult.

VI

The far from comely general secretary of the STUC was not invited to grace Scottish screens on the opening night of television in Scotland. None of the faces on 14 March 1952 had any known connection to hunger marches. First there was Big Ben, which bonged repeatedly in a patriotic manner, and then, as the *Daily Record* put it, 'a man with earphones over his head raised his hand and pointed to the far corner of the room'.

In the far corner sat the elegant figure of Mary Malcolm, who was not only the wife of a baronet (rejoicing in the name Sir Basil Bartlett) but boasted a kinship with the old Argyll family of Malcolm of Poltalloch. Malcolm introduced Alastair Macintyre, the chief TV announcer for Scotland, who introduced James Stuart, Secretary of State for Scotland, who said it had fallen to him to 'play a prominent part in a historic event, one which will be recounted in many houses in years to come'. Stuart was concerned that the new medium would interfere with children's homework and that it would give the telegenic personality an undue influence. Perhaps he was thinking about discrimination against George Middleton.

There was no show without Warr. The Dean of the Thistle and Chapel Royal intoned a prayer giving thanks to God for the wisdom of scientists. The Kirk was almost as well represented as the Scottish aristocracy: apart from Warr there was the equally ubiquitous Melville Dinwoodie, Scottish regional director of the

BBC; Ronald Selby Wright (known in irreverent company as Ronald Seldom Right); and Professor John Baillie, principal of New College, Edinburgh, which turned out ministers as efficiently as Westclox turned out alarm clocks.

After the formalities members of the Royal Scottish Country Dance Society gave a display hailed by the *Daily Record* as a brilliant touch, the paper adding that the whole experience was 'awe-inspiring ... there was something uncanny about it all'. The *Glasgow Herald* agreed that the ceremony 'had the requisite gravity and air of occasion', but felt that there might have been more shots of the audience. Later in the evening *In the News* assembled the first-ever Scottish current affairs discussion panel on television, including three MPs: the roguish Robert Boothby, the sardonic Hector McNeil, and the bluff Sir William Darling. Alastair Sim followed with 'a droll monologue about nothing at all', according to one listener. A news bulletin (sound only) and the national anthem concluded the day's transmissions at the decent hour of 10.30pm.

'To the new television viewer, unless he be completely without awe, the first appearance of an animated picture on his screen is a moment for wonderment,' said the *Glasgow Herald*. 'What appears is of secondary importance. In the early stages, the new viewer's interests are catholic: he is willing to watch anything.' But the number of catholic viewers in March 1952 was severely limited. Kirk O'Shotts, set on high ground, gave the new mast a reasonable range, though insufficient to reach the northern or western isles where the new amenity might have been appreciated during the long winters. In Aberdeen reception was 'poor, with heavy fading', in Kelso there were complaints of interference, but in Oban patients and nurses enjoyed a perfect signal from the county sanitorium 350 feet above sea level.

As with the King's funeral a month earlier, most of the viewing was communal. Forty-five minutes before the broadcast a long queue formed outside Parkhead Public Hall, where six TV sets had been installed, but only 300 people could be accommodated inside, necessitating a change of audience every half hour. This shuttle policy was adopted elsewhere in Glasgow with mixed success. At the Coupar Institute in Govan appeals to move were ignored.

Initially the Scots' attitude to television was a mixture of curiosity and native caution. The day before the launch the Post Office reported that, although 40,000 sets had been bought in

Scotland, only 1,641 TV licences had been issued. Edinburgh with 514, Glasgow with 211 and Dumfries with 134 headed a miserly league table in which Aberdeen, Biggar, Hawick and Stranraer had three licences each, Dumbarton and Helensburgh two, and Cupar, Campbeltown, Girvan, Lerwick and Lochgilphead one each. Tom Oswald, an Edinburgh Labour MP, said he resented an article in a London evening newspaper which suggested that the Scots were mean. 'Why,' he asked, 'should Scots who have bought sets be blamed for waiting until the service is available before taking out licences?' By the time of the opening ceremony 24 hours later the number of licences had risen to 2,730. The organiser of one of the public showings said it was his impression that Scots generally were wary of investing in the medium until they had seen it working.

The sense of an electronic miracle was conveyed by a reporter who visited Studio 1 of Broadcasting House in Edinburgh shortly before the broadcast. He found himself 'deep in a tangle of cables, half-opened packing cases, shrouded grand pianos, and television sets ... Panels of lights were winking fitfully and there was a mysterious high-pitched hum in the air'. The *Glasgow Herald* predicted that the arrival of television might come to be seen as a 'notable enough milestone on the road travelled by Scottish social history'. It got that about right.

VII

The God-fearing island of Skye was in no mood for milestones in Scottish social history. Far from being ready for John Logie Baird's box of tricks it was still struggling with the earlier invention of William Caxton. The churches were united in their condemnation of the proposed supply of Sunday newspapers. A statement read: 'We deny that there is any great demand for them in the isle of Skye, for there is no scarcity of newspapers in our island. They come in huge bundles six days a week, and it is quite unnecessary to augment their numbers by Sunday newspapers in order to instruct the people in national and international affairs. The Lord will visit this form of sin with suitable punishment.'

But it was not only in the Presbyterian strongholds that the early weeks of the Elizabethan era had the flavour of a crusade.

While Lady Bartlett prepared to introduce television to Scotland, Glasgow Corporation appointed a special committee to draw up a moral code for the city. 'At the beginning of the new Queen's reign,' said the civic leaders, 'citizens young and old are invited to join in a campaign to renew respect for ourselves, respect for others, and respect for God. The precepts of the moral code will include personal cleanliness of body and mind, honour, honesty at home, work and play, and respect for others in family life, employment and community.'

VIII

The moral code came too late for one young Glasgow citizen. Later the same week James Smith, a 21-year-old labourer, was found guilty at the High Court of stabbing a man to death at a dance in the Hibernian Hall – 'this curious evening's entertainment' as the presiding judge, Lord Cooper, described it. The accused claimed that the victim, Martin Malone, fell on top of him, that they both had knives, and that during the brawl, as Smith struggled to free himself, he accidentally stabbed Malone. 'I've done a daft thing,' he admitted. Smith's special plea of self-defence did not impress Cooper, who wondered how the accused could simultaneously claim to have stabbed Malone in self-defence and by accident. Not surprisingly, when Cooper challenged Smith on this point, Smith said he did not understand what the judge meant.

The curiosity was not confined to the evening's entertainment; it extended to the trial itself. It emerged almost in passing, during the questioning of a police witness, that a second knife had been found in the hall. This discovery could have been vital to the defence, potentially supporting Smith's story, yet the second knife was neither examined nor lodged as a production at the trial nor made available to the defence. Smith's counsel justifiably called this 'disgraceful'. The judge's uneasiness was transparent in his summing-up, in which he suggested to the jury that there might have been an element of provocation, in which case a verdict of culpable homicide would be appropriate. But, after an hour and 40 minutes, the jury convicted Smith of murder and Cooper was obliged to impose the death penalty.

Smith lodged an appeal, for which there were ample grounds, but the apparent miscarriage of justice was never corrected. The Secretary of State for Scotland refused to commute the sentence and on Easter Saturday 1952, while thousands of Glaswegians flocked to the Clyde coast in fine holiday weather, James Smith, who was not bright enough to know the difference between self-defence and an accident, was hanged in Barlinnie Prison.

1953

EVERY MAN FOR HIMSELF

I

The last day of January 1953, a Saturday, was a day from hell. In many parts of Scotland it started bright, if cold and windy, with no hint of the storm to come or of the devastation it would bring. By evening Holland had suffered its worst flooding since the 15th century and in the UK more than 500 people were dead. The disaster which had appeared from nowhere hit Scotland hard. Twenty-seven drifters of the Scottish herring fleet, most from east coast ports, were driven ashore in Loch Broom, many of them a total loss. Two of the crew of the Islay lifeboat lost their lives while they searched for a missing Fleetwood trawler. Twenty-two ships were missing or in danger in North Sea gales. In the Banffshire fishing village of Crovie, half the population were forced to flee to houses further up the cliff. But incomparably the worst single incident occurred in the Irish Sea – the sinking of the British Railways ferry, Princess Victoria, between Stranraer and Larne.

Thomas Frame, a former Irish international footballer, rose at 6.00am with the intention of sailing an hour later. He got as far as the pier at Stranraer before turning back: the weather just seemed too rough. An un-named local man who met the early morning boat train from London noticed that, though moored in the shelter of Loch Ryan, the ship was rising and falling at least six feet in rough seas. He was told that it would not sail in these conditions. But at 7.45am, 45 minutes late, it did. Two hours later a message was transmitted in morse code to the Portpatrick radio station: 'Urgent assistance of tugs required.' It was the first warning, followed at 10.32am by an SOS. At 1.58pm the final message reported that the ship was 'on her beam end' five miles east of the Copeland Islands, six miles from port. Of the 128 passengers and 51 crew – a total of 179 – only 34 passengers and 10 crew survived.

Not a single woman, not a single child, was among the survivors.

The coxswain of Donaghadee lifeboat, Hugh Nelson, was among the heroes of one of the grimmest days in Britain's maritime history. He went out three times in 16 hours. 'The most difficult part of the job was getting alongside a lifeboat in which a lot of people were huddled. I was afraid that a big sea would bring us crashing down on top of her, but we finally managed it.' Nelson and his crew were confronted by the pathetic sight of empty rafts, whose occupants had been unable to hold on, tossing in the sea.

A harrowing description of the ship's last minutes was given by James Carlin, manager of the Ayr employment exchange. His wife of three years, Eileen, his mother-in-law Mary Connelly and his sister-in-law Marie Connelly all perished.

I have no right to be alive. After the ship left Loch Ryan, we felt there was something wrong, but because we had no sea experience we did not know what it was. About 11 o'clock we heard over the loudspeaker system that everyone was to go to the upper deck and have their life jackets handy. We went out on to the boat deck. My wife's mother was sick by this time and went back into her cabin. My wife, her sister and I waited on the boat deck. The ship's list seemed to get worse and we were told tugs and a destroyer were on their way. About one o'clock the list was about 45 degrees to starboard and everybody was told to get as high up on the boat deck as possible. I got my wife and her sister up, and went back to the cabin to get my mother-in-law. I assisted her up the sloping deck. The list on the ship soon became about 50 or 60 degrees. I got my mother-in-law up the deck to the group of women who were sheltering beside the cabins. The men were holding on to the rails.

About 1.15pm it was announced that we were to abandon ship, but that a destroyer would be alongside in 15 minutes. I was still hanging on to the rail and could see my wife and her sister about 20 yards away. I could not get near them. I was trying to get towards them when the ship went over on its side. The siren was sounded for abandoning ship and the release of rafts and lifeboats. People were falling off the ship into the sea. With the ship lying on her side, I started to climb along in an effort to get to my womenfolk. I saw all the women slip off into the sea, but could not identify my own kin. I slipped down the side of the ship and landed almost right into a lifeboat. There were about 20 people in it. The ship shortly afterwards turned turtle. The seas were tremendous.

Robert Baillie, who had been working in Stranraer and was returning home to Belfast, gave a second detailed account.

The ship moved very slowly up Loch Ryan in a high wind. Just outside the loch it became very rough. Soon afterwards someone announced over the loudspeaker that a grave emergency had taken place and the order came to put on our lifejackets. The list seemed to get worse and everything on the ship gave way as soon as you touched it. The furniture in the saloon was rolling round the floor and knocking people down. Then there were some scenes which I shall never forget. One man was battered against the purser's office and blood spurted from his face. An old woman was trying to make her way along the deck carrying two small bags. 'All the money I have in the world is in these bags,' she told me. I helped her along for a bit. To get to the purser's office – it was about the only thing that was solid by this time – you had to cross a space where there was nothing to hold on to. We got a line across the space, but she would not come with me. 'When you get to my age you are too old for this,' she said. She pressed four cigarettes into my hand and that was the last I saw of her. I lost her in the confusion.

There was real fear. Whistles were blowing. I found myself in a lifeboat with five others. Four of them were engineers like myself, and the other was a steward. It was a terrible sight. Rafts were floating everywhere with people clinging to them. A plane was overhead and I saw a destroyer in the distance. The crew of that destroyer were wonderful. They put ladders over the side for us, but it seemed hopeless. The waves were carrying the lifeboat high above the rail of the destroyer and we were bumping into the hull. When a wave brought me down level with the destroyer's deck I jumped for it and landed safely. I can never say enough about the courage of a quiet man called McCann, one of the destroyer's crew. He got a line round his waist and jumped into the stormy sea to help the rest aboard. Then the bo'sun jumped without a line to help the people on the rafts. Everyone on that lifeboat was saved. Only the young and strong could survive in such a storm.

Baillie was close to breaking point when he described to journalists 'the most heartbreaking scene' he had ever witnessed. A man was holding on to the keel of the ship with one hand. With the other he was clinging to a little boy no more than three years old. Then something happened to him. He disappeared beneath the surface and the child was carried away by the waves.

Among the dead were 24 workers employed by Short Brothers at a branch factory in Wig Bay, near Stranraer. Every two months the workers were allowed free travel back to their homes in Northern Ireland, and on this occasion the 'free weekend' was advanced by two weeks with fateful consequences. Fourteen others from the factory who should have been on the Princess

Victoria that morning decided not to go home, but to watch Rangers play East Fife in Glasgow.

Twenty-three of the victims came from Stranraer, whose inhabitants rushed to the harbour on Sunday night, encouraged into false hope by a rumour that the ship heading into port was carrying suvivors. It was the Princess Maud, arriving to resume the regular crossing. She carried no survivors. But she did carry home the coffin of Captain James Ferguson, who was buried in a country churchyard at Inch, four miles from his house overlooking Stranraer harbour.

II

On Monday Princess Maud left on schedule at 7.00am with 133 passengers on board, 'sailing up a placid Loch Ryan, blue in the early morning sunlight'. By then difficult questions were being asked. J L Harrington of British Railways was challenged by the press to confirm or deny that Captain Ferguson, a month before the disaster, refused to sail from Stranraer because of heavy seas and that he was reprimanded for this decision. Harrington replied: 'There have been times within the past six weeks or two months that Captain Ferguson did not sail, but I should say that these were times when he had milk vehicles on board. I can assure you that he was never reprimanded. The master's word is final.' But was it? If a ship in the British Railways fleet got into trouble the master was obliged to telephone for advice to head office at London Euston. There were no port superintendents closer at hand – only an extreme form of remote control.

There was, too, a sense of shock, almost disbelief, that, even in extremely bad weather, a ship could sink in relatively safe waters on a routine crossing of 20 miles. At the port of Larne wreaths were thrown on the water as the crowd sang, 'Lord, hear us when we cry to thee, for those in peril on the sea'. Stranraer's newspaper, the *Wigtownshire Free Press*, appeared with black edging around each page.

In the midst of these expressions of grief, the questions persisted. What happened in the 14-mile stretch between Corsewall Point at the head of Loch Ryan and the position reached by the rudderless Princess Victoria when she finally sank off the

Irish coast? And why were all the survivors men? When the skipper of one of the rescue ships radioed late in the day, 'It is funny that there were no women among the survivors', he was the first to articulate what many others were thinking. Most calamitously, why was the Princess Victoria so erratic in reporting her own position? Rescue ships were directed to the wrong place, five miles too far south and one mile too far east.

Seven weeks later, on 23 March, an inquiry opened at Crumlin Road courthouse in Belfast under the chairmanship of J H Campbell, QC. Within two months it produced a report of prodigious length. The progress from first witness to final determination was impressive, but a longer perspective would have given a greater detachment to the outcome.

Members of the crew – none of the officers had survived – testified to conditions on board. Counsel put it to Able Seaman John Murdoch: 'I know this was a dreadful situation. May I take it that there was no attempt to assemble passengers in an orderly way to get them into the boats? Was it every man for himself at the last moment – every woman for herself, every child?'

'It was,' Murdoch replied. You could not assemble people on the boat deck because you could not stand on the boat deck.'

James Blair, a steward, said that, initially, the passengers remained calm. 'It was amazing, but I don't think they realised the ship was going down. Then there was a blast on the siren and I think everyone knew by this time that the ship was going. You could feel it going below you. There was pandemonium then. People tried to jump over the port side. Others were staying at the port side and were being swept away.' Blair said he got on to the hull and saw Captain Ferguson standing below him. 'The ship was then upside down and I ran the full length of her. When I got to the end I kicked off my shoes and watched for rafts or boats. I jumped into one boat and I was only seconds in it when I was pitched out with everyone else. I managed to grab a raft.'

David Brewster, master of the Fleetwood trawler East Coast, which was one of the first vessels on the scene, said he picked up seven people, six of whom were dead. Most of the victims he saw in the water had their lifebelts under their chin; he thought some were choked as they jumped in. Another witness, the skipper of an Irish coal boat, spoke of people 'hanging like flies' to the ship.

There was no doubt about the cause of the disaster. After the ship left Loch Ryan a heavy sea burst open the stern doors and a mass of solid water flooded the car deck, spreading to the lounge. If the influx of water was noticed, there was no effective attempt to stop it and no evidence that the leakage was ever reported to any officer. The inquiry decided, however, that it would be 'unfair and unworthy' to lay the main responsibility for what happened 'on people who could not answer' – the dead. It found that the stern doors were not sufficiently robust to withstand the conditions and that, following an incident in 1951 in which the doors were flooded at Larne, the owners paid insufficient heed to what should have been an obvious warning. An additional door – a 'guillotine door' – had been fitted to deal with the problem of spray and waves hitting the stern, but it was not often lowered because of the time it took. It was not lowered on 31 January 1953. Again this appeared to suggest human carelessness, but the inquiry was reluctant to acknowledge it: to have done so would have been offensive to grieving relatives so soon after the event. Instead the management took the full brunt of the inquiry's censure for the weakness of the ship's construction.

The rescue operation was ill-fated; a harsher view would have been that it was botched. At 9.45am, when the first distress signal was received, a Royal Navy destroyer, HMS Contest, went to the rescue at once, but because of the inaccuracy of the position reported by the Princess Victoria, she spent hours searching in poor visibility, only reaching the ship at 3.30pm when it was too late. The commander of the destroyer maintained that, even if she had been able to pursue a straighter line, it would still have been too late; the justification for this opinion was unclear. The inquiry heard that the stricken ship was still giving a position five miles NW of Corsewall Point when it was almost in Belfast Lough. The captain reported that he had seen a lighthouse, but it was not the lighthouse he thought he had seen. There was a perplexing contrast between the Portpatrick lifeboat, at sea within half an hour of the first SOS message, which 'played only a minor part in the rescue operation' according to the inquiry report, and the Donaghadee lifeboat, launched at a late stage, which picked up most of the survivors. And there was a suggestion of complacency on the part of the destroyer HMS Tenacious, which was still berthed in Londonderry, doing nothing of importance, as late as 5.00pm. As to the complete absence of women and children from the list of survivors, the inquiry heard that Number 4 lifeboat, which carried some of them, was seen afloat near the ship before being overturned against it and that all the occupants were thrown into the water. What happened to the others was never established.

Should the Princess Victoria have left Stranraer harbour? In the immediate wake of the disaster there were eye-witness accounts of 'phenomenal seas' or 'dangerous seas' – these were the expressions used – that the Princess Victoria had encountered on her last voyage. They fitted convincingly into a more general view of the furious weather affecting the rest of the country, and other parts of Europe, that day. Yet witness after witness at the inquiry testified that there was nothing exceptional about the weather. The harbourmaster at Stranraer gave as his view that it was 'no worse than the weather in which ships have gone out on many occasions'. Able Seaman Malcolm MacKinnon said he had 'sailed before in conditions as bad'. Commander H P Fleming of HMS Contest, asked if he would describe the sea as abnormal, replied that it was 'not out of the ordinary'. These testimonies enabled the inquiry to come to the conclusion that Captain Ferguson had been justified in sailing. It was a verdict that closed off what the inquiry report called 'the only line of retreat left open to the owners' – an error of judgement on the part of the master.

The bravery of poor Ferguson was never in question. He was observed 'standing at the salute on the bridge in the classic pose of the captain who goes down with his ship'. He was awarded the George Medal posthumously. A second posthumous honour, the George Cross, went to the ship's radio officer, David Broadfoot, for staying at his post to the very end, 'allowing passengers and crew to escape, even though by doing so he was preventing his own escape'. Two officers from HMS Contest were both awarded the George Medal for diving into the water to help survivors. Neither was called McCann.

III

On the opening day of the inquiry in Belfast there was a distraction, or series of distractions, in Scotland. Shopkeepers in Paisley and Dundee who were displaying souvenirs with the new cipher EIIR in preparation for the coronation received threatening letters in the post. The letters purported to come from the Scottish Republican Army and demanded the withdrawal of the offending items. One shopkeeper in Paisley was warned by the 'commanding officer of the Renfrewshire branch' that if he continued to stock the souvenirs 'we will be forced to destroy your shop or house at the first chance'. Another, an ironmonger, was informed that a brick would be thrown through his window if he did not remove tea caddies objectionable to the republican cause. In both Paisley and Dundee there was immediate compliance with these demands. At the same time a grocer in Pollok, one of the new Glasgow housing estates, whose window display included tins of biscuits illustrated by a photograph of the Queen, was warned that if the tins were not removed there would be no windows left in which to display them. The tins were gone before close of business.

The shopkeepers could scarcely be blamed for bowing to intimidation. Five weeks before these threats Scotland's only pillar box bearing the royal cipher was blown up by gelignite. From the moment it was erected in the Inch housing estate in Liberton, Edinburgh, in November 1952, it was a marked box. There were five attempts to damage or destroy it: twice it was daubed with paint or tar; twice explosives were dropped into it; on another occasion it was attacked with a hammer. No one had ever been seen using it to post a letter, there being a less than average chance that it would be delivered. Finally, a couple of minutes before 10 o'clock on the evening of 12 February, a young man was spotted putting something into the box; he then ran off into the estate's maze of streets. As the wireless pips sounded 10pm, there was a bang loud enough to be heard two miles away and a glare so vivid that it penetrated the curtained windows of houses in the neighbourhood; a man standing with his wife at a bus stop instinctively pushed her into the shelter of a wall. The Edinburgh CID collected the remains of the box, which had been shattered into five pieces. Until the blowing up of the pillar box, the police had dismissed the so-called army as 'small unconnected groups of irresponsible youths'; now that they had demonstrated their ability with explosives, the irresponsible youths were taken more seriously.

The perpetrator of the Inch explosion came to be known as Sky High Joe. Whoever he was, no one was ever brought to trial. Many years later Hamish Henderson, founder of the School of Scottish Studies at Edinburgh University, a legendary figure on the Scottish folk and literary scenes, wrote a song entitled *The Ballad of the Inch* which pointed the finger at himself. In the first volume of a biography of the poet, Timothy Neat confirmed that Sky High Joe was indeed none other than the revered Henderson. Ray Burnett, a reviewer of Neat's book, described the Scottish Republican Army as 'no more than a song, their bombs no more than ideas', a rather indulgent view of what happened in Inch in February 1953.

The pillar box was replaced. When the new one arrived, the local people were relieved that it no longer bore the EIIR cipher. Sky High Joe – who may or may not have been Hamish Henderson – had won. But at least it was safe to post a letter.

IV

On the day of the coronation (2 June), Wendy Wood, another nationalist on the far shores of the movement, arrived in the Castlegate, Aberdeen, and made a statement. She addressed it to 'the Scottish nation and to all freedom-loving peoples throughout the world'. The title being conferred on the Queen, said Wood, was 'a deliberate violation of the international treaty of 1707 between Scotland and England'. Meanwhile, in Largs, the contentious numerals were cut overnight from a banner hanging from the wall of the municipal buildings. Few other protests were recorded. Nothing was blown up. Sky High Joe had a quiet day.

The Scotsman detected in Edinburgh an atmosphere of 'Sabbath still', noting that most people had stayed indoors to watch the ceremony on television – except in India Street, where the New Town lawyers braved the unseasonal chill to host open-air parties. Celebrations in the north of Scotland had to contend with a 30 mph wind, temperatures of 45F, and heavy rain showers. Rockets soared into the sky on Stroma Island; out in the Atlantic the lighthouse keepers of Suleskerry, 35 miles west of Orkney, hoisted a flag; a loyal message was broadcast from the summit of Ben Nevis, which was covered in five feet of snow. A gale forced the cancellation of public events in Shetland.

'For the first time for just over 300 years,' said *The Scotsman*, 'through the excellent reception of the televison programme, Scots were able to participate in a royal coronation without leaving their native land.' But the paper's deference to the occasion was routine forelock-tugging stuff. It was a day on which forelocks were fated to be tugged.

V

'The situation in Scotland', as the Tory government put it, led to the establishment of a Royal Commission on Scottish Affairs chaired by Lord Balfour (Robert Arthur Lytton Balfour), a 51-year-old industrialist, of Bruntons' wire works in Musselburgh. As chairman of the Scottish division of the nationalised coal industry he had been prominent at Knockshinnoch during the successful rescue of the New Cumnock miners. He was not the most inspiring person to chair a commission on Scotland's constitutional future, but the Scottish Office would have regarded him as a safe pair of hands – no doubt this endorsement, or one like it, would have been used to justify his selection.

Balfour was supported by four knights of the realm, including his fellow industrialist Murray Stephen of the Glasgow shipbuilding family, and a number of other unimpeachable figures, one of whom, the military man and war hero John Spencer Muirhead, could boast of having had a poem published in the *Oxford Book of Mystical Verse*. It was entitled *Quiet*, the condition of Scotland that James Stuart, the Secretary of State, longed to achieve with the appointment of his commission. In a body numbering 15 there was a place for only one woman; and she was none other than Lady Dollan, wife of Sir Patrick.

Lady Dollan was absent from the first public hearing. She may have been unavoidably detained at home, listening to a lecture on the pressing need for fuel efficiency. But everyone else was there, including the secretary of the commission, George Pottinger, a smooth, ambitious young civil servant with an opportunity to make a name for himself. He wrote well. The Royal Commission on Scottish Affairs would be notable for silken prose, if nothing else.

The hearing took place in the upper hall of the Signet Library, 'a chamber that has much in common with the Edinburgh clubs, being lofty, austere and cool', the representative of the *Glasgow Herald* reflected. The members sat around a long horse-shoe table with few members of the public present to distract them. The academic and nationalist Douglas Young, almost as lofty as the upper hall, 'loped around as if chasing an ancient Greek'. He must have been disappointed to find only Sir David Milne, the head of the civil service in Scotland.

Milne, a son of the manse, wounded in France during the first world war, a graduate of Edinburgh University where he completed his studies after the war, entered the Scottish Office in 1921 when it was still based in London, at Dover House, and had been around long enough to witness the gradual transfer of power to Edinburgh. Two years before his retirement he published a book on the workings of the Scottish government departments. He wrote of the importance of concentrating all four departments in one building, of the informal discussions that took place in the corridors and canteen of St Andrew's House, and of the value of these impromptu meetings in the administration of the machine. He did not live to see the growth of that machine until it sprawled across several buildings, losing the immediacy of contact he thought so useful. In 1953 the combined staff of the four departments numbered only 5,200.

Was it the case, Balfour asked him, that for a long time Scotland had had a large measure of autonomy in administration?

'Yes,' Milne replied. 'Broadly that is so.'

He was keen to emphasise Scottish distinctiveness, referring first to education which, he said, had developed along different lines (from England's). He gave an honourable mention to the church, which had identified itself from the outset with 'a comprehensive system of education at all levels'.

Among the other witnesses that day, Bailie W W Gilmour of Peebles, representing the Convention of Royal Burghs, insisted that the establishment of a parliament in Scotland would not impair the unity of the United Kingdom in the least. It would promote efficiency both at Westminster and in Edinburgh because it would give MPs more time to deal with 'important matters' while measures of interest to Scotland would be dealt with by 'men on the spot'. Colin Kemp from the South of Scotland Chamber of Commerce spoke of a feeling of discontent and frustration 'so strong that a very substantial degree of decentralisation is urgently needed'. The feeling was, said Kemp, that in faraway Whitehall there was a great reluctance to admit that Scotland was a nation and that conditions in Scotland were often very different. 'Our difficulty would appear to be that we have a surfeit of advisory bodies and too few executive ones.'

The oral evidence at the first hearing, a good-natured occasion with the whiff of a positive consensus at the end of it, may have encouraged Douglas Young to believe that a Scottish parliament was just around the corner. The corner was to take a further 46 years to negotiate, by which time all those around the long horse-shoe table were dead, Douglas Young was dead, Sir David Milne was dead. The ambitious young civil servant was dead too, his career having ended in ignominy with a long prison sentence for corruption.

VI

The issue of the Queen's numerals was resolved in court when the tireless John MacCormick and his young friend Ian Hamilton launched a constitutional challenge. They contested the monarch's right to style herself Elizabeth II in Scotland, claiming that it was a breach of the Act of Union. The case came first before the Outer House of the Court of Session, where it was dismissed by Lord Guthrie with little ceremony. The pair then appealed to the Inner House presided over by Cooper of Culross, the Lord President. They had little expectation that Guthrie's judgement would be overturned, but MacCormick was hopeful that 'something would emerge which would shake the monstrous notion that the parliament of Great Britain was simply the parliament of England to which a handful of Scottish members had been added'. This hope was based mainly on MacCormick's high opinion of Cooper, who, he wrote later, had always taken 'a profound and scholarly interest in the history of the law in Scotland'.

Both the expectation and the hope proved to be justified. Cooper dismissed the appeal, ruling that the Treaty of Union had no provision concerning the numbering of the monarch's numerals. But MacCormick and Hamilton were able to celebrate Cooper's uncompromising assertion of Scotland's integrity. 'The principle of the unlimited sovereignty of parliament,' said Cooper, 'is a distinctly English principle which has no counterpart in Scottish constitutional law ... Considering that the union legislation extinguished the parliaments of Scotland and of England and replaced them with a new parliament, I have difficulty in seeing why it should have been supposed that the new parliament of Great Britain must inherit all the peculiar characteristics of the English parliament but none of the Scottish parliament as if all that happened in 1707 was that Scottish representatives were admitted to the parliament of England. That is not what was done.'

It was a significant judgement and, for the appellants, a moral victory. As MacCormick wrote: 'Scotland could never again be stated as a mere appendage of England.' But for MacCormick personally, it turned out to be a last stand. The covenant movement under his leadership had succeeded in collecting two million signatures – an overwhelming endorsement of its demand for a Scottish parliament – but the realisation of his dream seemed as far away as ever.

1954
PILLARS OF SOCIETY

I

During a visit to Turnberry Hotel shortly after new year, the 6th Duke of Montrose (James Graham) had a slight stroke. His condition deteriorated unexpectedly and he died later in January at the age of 75. He was one of the strongest supporters of home rule and the first to sign the covenant for a Scottish parliament. He dabbled inventively, experimenting with gas engines for cars, and was involved in the building of the first aircraft carrier. He was also noted for his opposition to strong drink. When he commanded the Clyde division of the RNVR in the first world war, he attempted to enforce strict control of the pubs in the area, where ships loaded with munitions were sometimes unable to put to sea because so many of the crew were drunk or hungover.

The 6th Duke of Montrose was a widely respected public figure and his funeral in Drymen, where he lived, attracted a large crowd of Scottish dignitaries including representatives of An Comunn Gaidhealach, the Arran Society of Glasgow, the Scottish Liberal Party (of which he was a member), services and war veterans' societies, the Scottish Landowners' Federation (Colonel Forbes of Callander House, Falkirk, came on its behalf), and a host of political friends from the home rule movement – John MacCormick, Andrew Dewar Gibb, Nigel Tranter, Councillor Bertie Gray and Robert McIntyre as well as John Bannerman, his own factor.

The tolling of bells gave a signal that the procession had started from Auchmar, the duke's residence about a mile from the burial ground outside Buchanan Parish Church. It was raining heavily. Twenty minutes later the cortege headed by a pipe major of the 7th Argyll and Sutherland Highlanders playing McCrimmon's lament reached the churchyard. The coffin, draped in the Graham tartan, was carried on a farm cart, the 12 pall-bearers, all estate workers, marching beside it. Immediately behind them was Robert Raeside, the duke's valet, carrying a cushion which bore the deceased's insignia and medals. The new duke, the former Marquis of Graham, who had once reminded an adjudicator at the Gaelic Mod of a piece of the Cairngorms, had flown with his wife from their home in Rhodesia, where they farmed, and where he was later to support a unilateral declaration of independence. He and the dowager duchess, heavily veiled, led the family mourners.

The coffin was placed on a table beneath the pulpit. The new duke stepped forward and received his father's baubles from the valet. Although the local minister took the service, it required two other clergymen to complete the formalities – a former Moderator of the General Assembly of the Church of Scotland and the inescapable Charles L Warr. The duke's wish that there should be no eulogy was respected, although in prayer one of the clergymen slipped in a reference to 'the head of a great Scottish house, one who loved Scotland and whom Scotland loved'. The estate workers carried the coffin to the graveside. It was still raining heavily. They lowered the coffin as the congregation sang *The Long Day Closes*, and the new duke, the dowager duchess and other members of the family then stepped forward, dropping clusters of heather into the grave. So ended the funeral of the 6th Duke of Montrose.

Such was the obsequious nature of Scottish public life, there was scarcely a mention of a notable absentee from these lamentations: the late duke's second son, Lord Ronald Graham, had not troubled himself to travel from his home in Jamaica for his father's funeral. It was many years before the truth about him was revealed through the chance discovery in a solicitor's vault of a document known as the Red Book, a record of the membership of an exclusive club founded just before the second world war. The founder of the club, Archibald Ramsay, had noted in fountain pen the names of the members (although some in code were never identified) and their membership dues. It was a distinguished list, including members of the British aristocracy, MPs, clerics, academics and civil servants. There were 235 names, each of them avowedly pro-German and virulently anti-semitic. It was the nearest thing to a Who's Who of British Nazis.

Graham was by no means the only Scot in the book. Ramsay himself, a descendant of the earls of Dalhousie, a product of Eton and Cambridge, was the Unionist MP for Peebles and South

Midlothian. In launching the Right Club he made a speech in the Wigmore Hall, London, calling for an end to Jewish control, which ended with the declaration: 'If we don't do it constitutionally we will do it by steel.' This inflammatory threat was picked up by a member of the audience, a mole from the communist newspaper, the *Daily Worker*, and reported back to his constituency, where there was consternation among local Conservatives but no formal move to sanction their MP.

Two other Scottish Tory MPs, Sir Samuel Chapman (Edinburgh South) and Thomas Hunter (Perth), were also in the Red Book, along with Lord Sempill (William Francis Forbes-Sempill), a prominent aviator, who was later exposed not only as a Nazi sympathiser in the second war but as a spy for the Japanese in the 1920s. He escaped prosecution because of his links to royalty and the potential embarrassment to MI5. Yet another Right Club member was the arch-royalist, the 12th Earl of Galloway (Randolph Algernon Ronald Stewart), who had worn black crepe over his masonic insignia following the death of King George VI. This fervent Nazi held the office of Lord Lieutenant of Kirkcudbright for 43 years, and at the time of his death in 1978 was attempting to disinherit his son, having had him lobotomised and consigned to a mental institution.

The aims of the Right Club were to 'coordinate the work of all the patriotic societies' – a euphemism for the collection of Nazi or neo-Nazi groups in Britain – and to 'oppose and expose the activities of Organised Jewry'. Its ultimate ambition, the overthrow of Churchill by a military coup, was discussed at one of its meetings in a Russian tearoom in South Kensington, a choice of venue which gave an almost comic air of conspiracy to the proceedings. But although it would be tempting to dismiss the Right Club as a bunch of far-right fanatics, evil but ineffective, its attempts to subvert the war effort and to undermine morale in London were serious enough. One of its methods was to post pro-German, anti-semitic propaganda in public places under cover of the blackout; another was to jeer in cinemas whenever Churchill appeared in newsreels.

MI5 infiltrated the club, enabling two of the ring-leaders to be sentenced to long terms of imprisonment after a secret trial. Ramsay, who disputed an allegation in the House of Lords that he would have been Hitler's gauleiter in Scotland in the event of an invasion, got off lightly: he had the dubious distinction of being the only British MP to be interned. He was fortunate not to be executed for treason, yet this odious character – allegedly personally charming and rejoicing in the matey nickname Jock – remained unrepentant despite his incarceration in Brixton Prison for almost four years. After the war, when the world learned the full extent of the atrocities in the concentration camps, he published a self-justifying autobiography still full of loathing of Jews.

His wife Ismay, the widow of Lord Ninian Crichton-Stuart, son of the Marquis of Bute, was utterly repellent in her own right. In January 1939 she gave a speech to Arbroath Business Club claiming the national press was largely under Jewish control – where this left the mightiest press baron of the time, Lord Beaverbrook, a Scots-Canadian Presbyterian, was unspecified – and defending Hitler's anti-semitism. When the local newspaper reported the speech it came to the notice of Dr Salis Daiches, the chief rabbi for Scotland, who challenged Mrs Ramsay to justify her statements. Both the Ramsays then weighed in, and the correspondence in *The Scotsman* went on for a month.

The degree of involvement by the other Scots in the Right Club is difficult to assess, but one of them, Sir Alexander Walker, supported the club with a donation of £100 (the equivalent of £5,000 at the time of writing). Walker, a whisky magnate, grandson of the founder of Johnnie Walker, lived in a grand house in Troon and dispensed largesse to local causes, including the Episcopal church and the tennis club. A municipally-owned hall in the town was named after him, and in 1946 he became the first freeman of Troon, the provost describing him at a reception in his honour as 'a man of the people'.

More than once during the war the government was asked in the House of Commons to name the members of the Right Club. Based on the information at the disposal of MI5 it could easily have unmasked some if not all of them, yet it consistently refused to do so. It claimed that it could not guarantee the accuracy of the list – it would not have taken much to authenticate every single name on it – but it is far more likely that the names were suppressed because of the damage their publication would have caused to the reputation and credibility of the Conservative Party. The cover-up allowed the various enemies of freedom to maintain their reputations as pillars of society.

II

While the British establishment kept its disgraceful secrets the small sins of common humanity were revealed in lip-smacking detail. The juicier divorces, even those which involved people of no importance, were reported at length in otherwise respectable newspapers, especially when the judges of the Court of Session mounted one of their indignant high horses.

A case in February 1954 was typical of the hypocrisy of public standards of private morality. Marie Aitken of Glasgow sued her husband John for divorce because of his adultery. Lord Birnam heard that Aitken ran two pubs in Glasgow. By 1946, after 16 years of marriage, he was keeping very late hours, sometimes staying away all night. After closing time in his pubs – which was then as early as 9.30 – he would spend several hours drinking in night clubs. The clubs closed at 1am and Aitken would then go to a hotel 'where the licensing regulations were not too strictly enforced' and continue drinking with 'one or more friends of similar tastes' until 3, 4 or 5am. The socialising took place in the room of Janet Provan, who, on days off from her work as a hotel receptionist 'in the country', indulged in what Lord Birnam called 'a perfect orgy of dissipation' – a phrase begging to be repeated in the headlines. There was abundant evidence, said Birnam, that Aitken was nearly always one of her guests, and that he was sometimes the only one. Birnam was 'not prepared to believe that drink was the sole object of his visits to her bedroom', although Aitken insisted that he was usually so intoxicated he had no memory of what passed between them.

The judge granted decree to Mrs Aitken and the case was splashed all over the newspapers, including such information as the couple's address and the fact that they had five children. No crime had been committed. A husband had behaved badly; a marriage had ended. No doubt Mrs Aitken felt that she had been betrayed. But if there was treachery it was not sponsored by the rich and powerful against the interests of democracy. It was a private matter, nicely enough soaked in booze and illicit sex to attract the attention of the ever-prurient press. Meanwhile, the treacherous Earl of Galloway maintained his position as the Queen's representative in Kirkcudbrightshire.

III

There was sordid (a Glasgow publican and his girlfriend), and there was beyond sordid, the sexual practice that dared not speak its name. In 1954 buggery between consenting males was a crime punishable by imprisonment. Some newspapers, when they reported such cases, protected the delicate sensibilities of their readers by referring obliquely to 'an offence' without specifying its nature. A sensational murder in Glasgow in the summer of that year, and the trial which followed, made it impossible to avoid discussing homosexuality in public. According to press reports the public – or those members of it who made their way early in the morning to queue outside the High Court in the Saltmarket in the hope of securing a grandstand view of the proceedings – gasped at the more lurid revelations.

George Ford McNeill, a part-time radio actor, youth worker and lay preacher, was found dead in his flat in Govan. He had been struck with an axe, probably when he was asleep. The murderer stole a cheque book and a passport as well as clothing and some household items. Some days earlier, when a fellow youth worker called at McNeill's flat, the door was answered by someone later identified as John William Gordon, 24, who described himself as a freelance journalist. Gordon explained that McNeill had gone to Paris that morning. The visitor spotted nothing out of the ordinary in his demeanour. But as soon as the police found the body and the press put the story on the front page, Gordon fled to Spain, incriminating himself further. He was picked up and went on trial charged with murder and theft.

McNeill was not exactly a household name, but his voice was familiar to listeners of *The McFlannels*, a serial of the sort that would come to be known as a soap opera, on the BBC's Scottish Home Service, in which he played a minor character, Mr McZephyr. He was a minor celebrity. It then emerged that a larger celebrity, George MacLeod, knew both the murdered man and the man on trial for his murder. Interest in the case, strong before, became feverish.

George MacLeod, born into a background of privilege as the son of a successful businessman and Unionist MP, received an education appropriate to one of his class – Winchester and Oxford – and served with gallantry as an officer in the first world war.

After the war he entered the ministry of the Church of Scotland, moving from a middle-class parish in Edinburgh (St Cuthbert's) to one of the poorest in the country, Govan, where he was profoundly affected by the devastating social and economic effects of mass unemployment. The experience converted him to socialism. He helped to conceive an inspirational scheme to rebuild Iona Abbey and liked to claim that the unemployed shipyard workers of Govan were employed in its restoration (although his son Maxwell was later to cast doubt on the degree of their involvement). An ecumenical scheme linking Iona and Glasgow was established and the Iona Community came into being. As leader of the community MacLeod continued to work tirelessly with young people. Several hundred visited Community House in Glasgow every week. Among them was the man in the dock.

His real name was Robert Gerald Weir. He was born in Rangoon, where his father was serving as a regular soldier with the Cameron Highlanders. The family moved to Scotland when Robert was a small child and they lived in Glasgow until the outbreak of the second world war, when they were evacuated to Inverness. The Iona Community had a camp-site nearby and it was there that MacLeod's association with him began. 'I was constantly amazed,' said MacLeod, 'by the extraordinary capabilities and the voracious inquisitiveness of this child of five. I had never experienced anything like it in a child of that age.' The curious boy made his first court appearance at the age of 10 on a theft charge; he went on to approved school, borstal and prison; he joined the army but was discharged with ignominy. While still a teenager, he changed his name to John William Gordon. In his early twenties he decided he was a journalist.

Through all his troubles as Robert Gerald Weir or John William Gordon he was advised and helped by George MacLeod. MacLeod corresponded with him and spoke on his behalf in various courts, once going to the trouble of championing his cause before a judge in England. At one stage he got him a job. He thought of Gordon as 'someone who wanted desperately to be good ... an exceptional person with great potentialities, who always seemed incapable of going straight, as he wanted to do'.

Gordon had at his disposal one of the greatest defence teams ever assembled for a murder trial in Scotland: Sir John Cameron, Dean of the Faculty of Advocates, later Lord Cameron, assisted by Manuel Kissen, later Lord Kissen, and Laurence Dowdall, a solicitor so respected by the criminal classes that the phrase, 'Get me Dowdall', entered popular usage. No one could have been better served than Gordon, who had the additional benefit of a glowing character reference from George MacLeod. Lord Sorn, the presiding judge, began his summing-up to the jury by praising the masterful presentation of the defence case. It was the last obliging remark uttered by Sorn.

Gordon had no obvious motive for murdering McNeill, but there was another suspect who did seem to have a motive – and a violent record. This man admitted to the court that he had once been found insane and unfit to plead to a charge of strangling a young woman. On his release from a mental institution he had been put under the joint care of McNeill and a Glasgow doctor. He was 36 years old and in love, engaged to be married, but had not told his fiancée about his past. He confided in McNeill, who insisted that he should be open with her. Was he frightened that, if he did not tell her what he had done 12 years before, McNeill would do it for him? There was also the undisputed fact that, apart from the murderer, he was the last person to see McNeill alive. Further complicating the issue, there was a third suspect. He had confessed to the murder, but his confession was disregarded because he was insane when he made it.

On the day of George MacLeod's appearance in the witness box the queue for seats formed early. The *Evening Times* noted a scene of 'great drama' as Cameron questioned MacLeod about his knowledge of the murdered man through McNeill's youth work with the Iona Community.

'Did you find in George McNeill that there had been any tendencies of a homosexual kind?'

'Yes I did.'

MacLeod turned to the bench at this point and said: 'My Lord, in the name of truth, may I make a statement?'

Sorn: 'I think you should leave yourself in your counsel's hands.'

MacLeod: 'It's just that I wanted to say McNeill was such a wonderful man.'

R S Johnston, for the prosecution, asked MacLeod how he knew McNeill had homosexual tendencies. MacLeod said it had come to his knowledge through a rumour. 'I refused to pay any attention to it until I saw a man who at that time was in the army. He said that some years previously George MacNeill had, to use his own words, "made a pass" at him. It was so serious that I saw George

McNeill. It was one of the most painful interviews of my life. He admitted that this was a tension with him. He showed every sign of being a person with a tremendous sense of morality, a tremendous guilt complex, tremendous frustration, and absolute prostration at being reminded of what happened some years previously. I tried to encourage him and got him to promise to go to a psychotherapist, and that is the only evidence I have.'

'May we take it,' asked Johnston, 'that you had no idea or thought that there would be any corruption of the morals of the young persons with whom McNeill came into contact?' MacLeod: 'One has the greatest difficulty about these matters. For the sake of society one must keep them in circulation, otherwise they go off somewhere and become real menaces.'

Gordon was not called to give evidence in his own defence, maintaining the accused's right to silence. The jury heard from others the essence of his case: that McNeill had given him permission to stay at his flat but that McNeill was expecting a guest – it seemed that McNeill was in the habit of receiving guests – and not to disturb him. Gordon arrived off the Govan ferry around 2am, went straight to the flat and to bed, rose at 10 in the morning, had a bath, ate breakfast, and stared to clean up. While he was cleaning up he decided to go into McNeill's bedroom, believing that McNeill would have gone to work. He found him dead in bed. He felt his pulse, fainted, was violently sick, panicked, and hid the body in a box room. When he was charged several weeks later Gordon replied: 'I thought George was shot.' How could he have thought that? Lord Sorn suggested to the jury that it was 'just an artistic touch'.

Sorn had to acknowledge that the evidence against Gordon was almost entirely circumstantial. But sometimes, he said, inference could be 'just as strong as eye-witness'. He described Gordon as 'a most peculiar man, the workings of whose mind are very difficult to assess' and made colourful work of his flight abroad. 'The long arm of the law reached out and took him in Spain. You may think that if ever a man by his actions proclaimed himself a murderer, it was this man. If there was nothing else to consider, I do not suppose you could have any hesitation in pronouncing him to be the guilty man. But, of course, there is much else for you to consider.' The casual 'of course' did not suggest a great deal of enthusiasm for the 'much else'. After Sorn's one-sided view of the evidence the jury took less than an hour to convict.

'A sharp push on the head by a police officer took him to his feet to receive the death sentence,' reported the *Evening Times*. After his 10-day ordeal, Gordon looked pale but betrayed little emotion. Sorn donned the black cap only when he uttered the final words of the sentence, 'which is pronounced for doom', and rested it on his head briefly before replacing it on a ledge under the bench. As Gordon left the dock and was bundled downstairs to the cells, he missed his footing, stumbling heavily. Hundreds of onlookers had gathered outside to await the final scene – the condemned man's departure for Barlinnie Prison, where he faced execution in 21 days – and the crowd grew so large that mounted police were called to disperse it.

The Gordon case was notable for several reasons: the intense public curiosity, the fragility of the prosecution case, the absence of motive, the judge's loaded charge to the jury, the extraordinary testimony of George MacLeod, and most of all the lifting of a veil on public attitudes to homosexuality and its discussion in terms of a distressing medical condition which might be cured by treatment.

A Glasgow woman, Helen Wilson, collected 14,000 signatures calling for Gordon to be reprieved and a young Congregational minister, Nelson Gray, went to St Andrew's House to support her campaign. A few days before Gordon was due to hang, the Lord Provost of Glasgow and the town clerk were conducted to the condemned cell by the prison governor. The Lord Provost read the formal notification that the Queen ('Her Majesty'), on the recommendation of the Secretary of State, had decided to exercise her clemency and commute the death sentence to one of life imprisonment.

According to a witness 'there was an illumination of Gordon's face' when the words were uttered.

The Lord Provost asked: 'Do you understand this?'

Gordon replied only: 'I do.'

IV

In the summer of 1954 there was more public interest in the murder of an actor in *The McFlannels* than in the long-awaited outcome of the Royal Commission on Scottish Affairs. When the report appeared in late July the story – such as it was – was forgotten almost at once, exceeded in popular appeal by the discovery of the body of George Ford McNeill a few days later.

The writing was elegant, the hand of George Pottinger, the commission's secretary, strongly in evidence. The commission did not doubt that Scotland continued to exist as a nation and considered the 'emotional dissatisfaction' disclosed in much of the evidence about the unbalanced relationship between the partners in the union. It believed that the roots of this dissatisfaction lay in a widespread feeling that 'national individuality is being lost' and that 'the treaty of 1707 is no longer remembered as the voluntary union of two proud peoples, each with their own distinctive national and cultural characteristics and traditions, but rather on the absorption of Scotland by England'. This discontent had been aggravated by 'needless English thoughtlessness and undue Scottish susceptibilities'.

The commission had looked at some of the more tangible manifestations: increasing London control of the day-to-day affairs of the individual; the existence in Scotland of subsidiary offices of ministries, 'giving rise to the old fear that Scotland is being degraded from a nation to a province of England'; the belief that economic recovery in Scotland had lagged behind the rest of the country, 'contributing to a suspicion that her special needs are being neglected or subordinated to those of England and Wales'. This was either a philosophical foundation for change or a nice piece of window-dressing by Pottinger. It did not take long to work out which.

The commission dismissed the movements calling for greater autonomy as products of mere frustration, and cast doubt on the authenticity of the national covenant with its two million signatures. The Scottish Covenant Association had 'admitted that it was not possible to verify individual signatures, nor to eliminate duplications or signatures by minors, athough they [the association] contended that any such irregularities would have little effect on the total number of signatures'. Did these signatures mean anything? The commission noted that the issue of parliamentary separation 'does not appear to have particularly influenced the votes cast at the few elections at which it has been given prominence'. And so, in a few bleak sentences, John MacCormick's crusade was written off.

The recommendations were so marginal, so grudging, that the

commission might as well have spared itself the bother of making any. Responsibility for the appointment of justices of the peace in Scotland, 'and certain consequential matters', should be transferred from the Lord Chancellor to the Secretary of State for Scotland; for animal health from the Ministry of Agriculture to the Secretary of State; for highway matters from the Ministry of Transport to the Secretary of State; for the allocation of factories in industrial estates to the Scottish controller of the Board of Trade. Controllers of UK departments in Scotland should normally be designated 'Scottish' rather than 'regional'. These derisory concessions to national sentiment delighted such anti-devolutionists as Arthur Woodburn, who said in the House of Commons that it was 'just the kind of report that would have been written by those who actually had the task of facing the problems with which it deals', while Sir William Darling hailed it as 'stimulating reading, a valuable piece of work for the nation'.

Several Scottish newspapers decided not to lead with the publication of this piddling verdict on the country's constitutional future. The *Glasgow Herald*, one of those which found something of more importance happening in the world, was surprised and gratified that the commission had made so few recommendations. It claimed that 'the real unity of interest in Great Britain will be grateful that a commission representing all walks of Scottish life have not deferred to a spurious national grievance based on ignorance of the facts of government'. *The Bulletin* thought it 'perhaps rather a lot to ask of busy men' that ministers and officials in London should have to think of Scotland as a nation. The irony of the comment was perhaps too subtle.

The commission had held 34 meetings in Edinburgh, six in London, one apiece in Inverness and the Western Isles. It had taken evidence from more than 200 witnesses and studied written memoranda from 75 organisations. After this extensive consultation, assisted at all times by the cultured mind of George Pottinger, it had come to the conclusion that the organisations whose evidence was opposed to parliamentary separation represented 'a broad cross-section of responsible Scottish opinion'. What, then, did the two million signatures for a Scottish parliament represent? Were they a broad cross-section of irresponsible Scottish opinion? It seemed the likeliest bet.

V

The publication of the report of the Royal Commission on Scottish Affairs was received in the Scottish press with less diligence than the enactment of a burghal tradition in Rothesay which marked the coming-of-age of the heir to the Marquisate of Bute: a ceremony conferring the freedom of the burgh on the Earl of Dumfries (John Crichton-Stuart) and his brother, Lord David Crichton-Stuart, the twin sons of the 5th Marquis of Bute, who were born 20 minutes apart (John arrived first). Fireworks were released, bonfires lit, on the heights of Bute and Cumbrae, 'proclaiming to shipping in the firth and to town and country people in island and mainland alike that the twin sons of the House of Bute had that day further strengthened the close ties with the burgh of Rothesay that their ancestors had first forged in the 16th century' (according to the *Glasgow Herald*). The town bell pealed. A 'silver-framed sporran of white baby seal' contained the Earl of Dumfries's illuminated 'ticket' to the freedom of Rothesay; the casket containing Lord David's ticket was of 'native walnut, with sycamore lining'. A house party from Mount Stuart, home of the family, attended the lighting of the bonfire on St James's Ride, one of the highest points on the island, and the brothers each received a pair of guns from their father. The notorious British Nazi, the former Lady Ninian Crichton-Stuart, was not recorded as one of the guests on this deeply respectful Rothesay occasion.

1955

CONVERSIONS

I

Early in the morning of 19 March 1955 the overnight sleeper from London stopped briefly at Dumfries. A crowd of well-wishers had gathered on the platform and were singing. Although he was still in bed he decided that if they could get up to greet him, he could get up to greet them. He put a coat over his pyjamas and spoke to them from a corridor window. Billy Graham had arrived in Scotland.

Besieged by journalists at St Enoch Station, Graham declined to take questions on the controversies of the moment – the nuclear bomb ('the H-bomb' as it was better known then) and the troubled life of the Queen's sister, Princess Margaret, who had reluctantly ended her relationship with a divorced man. Graham quoted Professor Arnold Toynbee, who had said a few days earlier that the only hope for the survival of the west was a religious revival. Otherwise he confined himself to flattery and platitude. 'Scotland,' he said, 'is a little country of only five million people, but it is an important country far beyond the statistics of the population because there are Scots all over the world. The United States owes a great spiritual debt to Scotland. My part of the country [North Carolina] is inhabited almost altogether by Scots, and we are called the Bible Belt.'

The journalists wanted to know how he preferred to style himself. He replied that, although he held several honorary doctorates, he liked to be known as Mr Graham. He agreed that his salary might appear to be excessive, but that he had many heavy expenses. He denied that he had come to Scotland to show the Scottish church what to do.

More than a thousand followers, who had been waiting for him outside St Enoch, sang the Graham anthem, 'This is my story, this is my song', and spontaneously burst into cheers. While Graham was being escorted by police to his hotel, an old woman clutched at his sleeve. Bible in hand he addressed them from a window of the hotel. The Tell Scotland crusade thus began on a note of emotional fervour which was to intensify day after day for six intoxicating weeks.

The following morning Graham made an unannounced visit to Dowanhill Church, where he joined a Sabbath congregation of the usual size – around 400. The minister, William Baxter, said that if word had got out that Graham was attending, thousands would have been there. The visitor, standing behind the communion table, spoke briefly about his home life. His wife, he said, was a Presbyterian and so were his children, while he was a Baptist. 'It makes no difference to how we get on.' He took his place among the worshippers, watching Baxter baptise a four-month-old baby, Carol Anne MacAdam.

On the same day he went to Glasgow Cathedral where 1,500 supporters – his 'missioners and counsellors' – took part in a service of self-dedication conducted by Nevile Davidson, minister of the cathedral. Graham told them that the 'beautiful hall that was called Kelvin' had been prepared. The people too had been prepared, through radio, television and the press. Now they waited for God. 'There are two symbols of God. Wind and fire. We wait for the wind and we wait for the fire. We stand and pray that the fire from heaven will fall and that the wind will scatter it across Scotland and that all Scotland will be aflame and the impact will be made on a world that desperately needs Christ.' Davidson, no match for this rhetoric, sounded appropriately awe-struck: 'God has raised up a man of consecrated personality and powerful speech to proclaim the Word.'

Graham's symbolism made its presence felt for the opening meeting of the crusade. The wind did indeed blow in Glasgow on 22 March 1955, but it was accompanied by snow rather than fire. 'The great crowds of milling, rushing people, a forever swelling torrent of humanity, middle-aged, old, and young, they poured out of tramcars, buses, taxi-cabs and private cars,' wrote one excitable eye-witness. The queue began to form as early as 3pm, was headed by 71-year-old Ann Aitken, of Ruchazie, Glasgow, and stretched for 500 yards. At frequent intervals the devout broke into lusty extracts from the Billy Graham songbook – it was the only lust permitted. Graham himself drew up in a 'small, black saloon car' at a side door, unseen by the torrent of humanity.

The disciples were finally received into a familiar setting transformed by draperies of blue and fawn fabric. Thousands of green-painted folding chairs were arranged on semi-circular scaffolding facing the stage, while half a dozen newsreel cameras and a closed-circuit TV camera were positioned on platforms above the heads of the audience. For the expected overflow a special room was equipped with six large TV screens hanging from the girders. One journalist said the scene reminded him of an American political convention and that the 1,000-strong choir on stage seemed 'transatlantic in its efficiency'.

A tall, dark-haired, shirt-sleeved young man named Cliff Barrows, Graham's master of ceremonies, led a rehearsal in a style so vigorous that onlookers feared for the microphone in front of him. 'You're not tired are you?' he demanded of the choir. As he introduced a final try-out of the *Lord's Prayer* set to music, the spectators filtered in. Once they had settled, Burrows turned and asked them to be 'real quiet', exhorting them to adopt an attitude of prayer.

II

Shortly after 7.30pm Billy Graham was brought to the rostrum by Tom Allan, leader of the Tell Scotland crusade. The evangelist was wearing a plain blue suit, a light blue shirt and a polka-dot tie with a pin which some suspected was a disguised portable microphone. Before he began his 40-minute sermon Graham asked that no one should move or walk about: 'One person moving in a great audience like this can disturb thousands. The opening night of any campaign is very difficult and we need to concentrate on prayer in the next few minutes in quietness.' The audience paid him 'close attention', according to one report, 'though it was at no time visibly moved. The final effect of his message was presumably to be gauged by the response to his invitation, spoken in a soft and appealing voice over heads bowed in prayer, to the converted to come forward'.

Making their symbolic 'act of decision' 470 men, women and children (15 of whom were under the age of 12) moved down the aisles to be met by counsellors stationed in the front row. The organ played, the choir sang gently, and the converted stood for a few minutes until Graham directed them to file out of the auditorium to a waiting room. He promised to address them there.

An anonymous Scottish journalist gave a vivid account of the spectacle: 'Mr Graham's features are mobile, his nose sharp, his jaw determined, and his eyes, with their darkish lids, glittering and faintly hawk-like. He speaks fluently and with no more than an occasional trace of Southern slurring of the consonants. He spoke of his dislike of personal publicity. He spoke without undue emphasis, though using the flexible instrument of his voice with persuasive skill. He quoted his texts from the Bible which he held in his left hand, one finger keeping the place or laid upon the desk before him. His gestures were restrained and incisive, the stubbing finger, the hands outspread and held a little away from the hips, a clenched fist crashing occasionally into an open palm. He moved freely about the rostrum, addressing himself to each corner of the audience in turn and once or twice, via the television lens, to those in the overflow room.'

His theme was faith, which he laced with the occasional joke. 'I could be born in a garage but that doesn't make me an automobile' – even this crack went down well; at the unforgiving Empire, on the other side of town, it might have been booed. 'In the main,' said the same observant journalist, 'the points were hammered home with simple words and by repetition rather than illustration.' At the end, Nevile Davidson said: 'This was Biblical preaching in the real old Scottish tradition ... There was no undue emotionalism of any kind.' Of any kind? Well, that was Davidson's opinion. Tom Allan said: 'Tonight we stand at the beginning of the greatest evangelical crusade in the history of Scotland.'

On the second night 423 converts made their way to the 'counsel rooms', as they were now being called. Graham emphasised the mortality of the body: 'One out of every four in this audience will be dead in 10 years.'

Even at this early stage subversive doubts were beginning to surface. E G S Traill, a Church of Scotland minister in Rattray, told Perthshire education committee that Graham's meetings were 'not entirely suitable' for school-children because of their tendency to mass emotionalism. Traill opposed a proposal that a teacher and 29 pupils from Breadalbane Academy in Aberfeldy should be granted leave of absence to attend. 'I don't think Mr Graham is an emotional speaker,' said Traill, 'but the whole build-up of the gatherings definitely is. That is fair enough for adults who can think things out for themselves, but psychologically it is not the correct approach for children.' Another minister, J D Craig, the provost of Pitlochry, urged members to treat Traill's opposition 'with the contempt it deserves' and the committee voted down the objection by 13 votes to five. The newspapers reported that in factories, shipyards, shops, offices and coffee rooms, Billy Graham was the chief topic of conversation: crusade-fever had taken hold of Scotland and sceptics spoke out at their peril.

A Q Morton, the minister of Fraserburgh, was one of them. He wrote: 'The Graham campaign is fundamentalist ... A supporter of the crusade said he believed the whale swallowed Jonah because the Bible said so. Indeed had the Bible said Jonah swallowed the whale it would have commanded his belief. There is no point in criticising this crusade for its beliefs are beyond the reach of reason. There remains a duty to say clearly and with conviction that this man and his beliefs are not universally accepted and that it is not necessary to surrender intelligence and integrity to become a Christian.' When another heretic, H S McClelland, minister of the posh Trinity Church in the west end of Glasgow, referred sourly in a sermon to 'Dr Graham's incredible world', he was interrupted by a member of the congregation accusing McClelland of being a blasphemer and a servant of Satan. The minister invited the protester to join him in the vestry after the service, where they discussed their differences for several hours.

In the first week 104,000 people attended the Glasgow meetings. 'It has in many ways been the greatest first week we have ever experienced,' said an official statement. 'We have never had so many respond to the invitation to receive Christ anywhere we have been.' Graham, clearly rattled by Traill's outspoken criticism, said he had read that they should not 'let little children come to Jesus. Who of us can dare to say that the Gospel is too profound for a child to understand? Jesus said it was so simple that the profoundest intellect must become as a child to get into the kingdom.'

At the fourth meeting the number of converts – 224 – so disappointed the evangelist that he made a second appeal and another 100 souls came forward. But the first weekend was remarkable: as the crowd left the Kelvin Hall from the afternoon matinee, there was already a long queue for the 7.30pm house and the approaches to the hall were packed with 150 chartered buses from many parts of Scotland. A pattern was emerging: most of the converts were women and girls and many of the girls wore school uniform. On 29 March the crusade recorded its biggest audience yet: 16,000. Preaching on the third commandant, Graham rounded on the values of popular culture. Stage plays, novels, 'even some films' were vehicles of the salacious, the vulgar and the profane; it was terrible that even women were using foul language.

III

Something of this judgemental mood leaked into the life of Scotland as a whole. There was unusually generous press coverage of a meeting in Troon of the British Women's Temperance Association which agreed to call for a complete ban on alcohol in television drama. One delegate attacked a play in which a minister's wife suggested lemonade for a wedding reception but was over-ruled by her husband, who insisted on wine. 'Mothers with young children should think twice about getting television,' she advised, 'because every other reference is to drink.' In the same spirit, or lack of it, Gourock Licensing Court refused permission for pubs to open beyond 9.30 on summer evenings, while the 'dry' burgh of Kilsyth, where no alcohol could be sold, was congratulated on limiting cases of public drunkenness to 30 a year.

A modest plan to permit Sunday play on Edinburgh Corporation's golf courses was strongly opposed. One councillor claimed that, since most 'artisans' were now on a 44-hour, five-day week, they had plenty of free time to play golf without violating the Sabbath. 'The churches have launched the Tell Scotland campaign,' he added, 'and it is up to the city to back the churches.'

A minor incidence of bad behaviour was harshly punished. James McCusker, who did no more than run on to the pitch during a Celtic-Airdrie match, was sent to prison for a month. Apart from over-zealous football supporters, there was a new threat to public order – the appearance of so-called teddy boys on the streets. Major-General D J Wilson-Haffendon, a name to be reckoned with in the Boys' Brigade, said that modern youth presented a challenge which had to be met, although he did not specify how. Dr A G Mearns, a senior lecturer in public health at Glasgow University, agreed that there were many young people who followed 'a way of life which did not give any real happiness', yet, he suggested, not all youths who dressed in a velvet collar and used a shoe lace for a tie were necessarily bad; their dress could simply be a revolt against the drabness of male attire.

A radio critic, reviewing a talk by Edwin Muir on Scottish history's 'brooding sense of waste and loss and failure', wondered how the national condition now manifested itself – 'how it should or how it does inform the behaviour of contemporary Scots at large, frenzied in the football crowd, hysterical in its welcome to screen stars'. The reviewer omitted to mention another form of mass hysteria – the one being played out nightly in the Kelvin Hall.

In an older, more joyful spirit, the bridal party and 25 guests for a two-day wedding in the Fair Isle took enough booze to last a week, having arranged accommodation in crofters' houses and in a hostel normally reserved for bird-watchers. The bride, Alice Grace Stout, 24, the only girl to have been born in Fair Isle for many years, was presented by the islanders with geese, hens and a sheep. The same weekend Newtonmore defeated Kyles Athletic to win the Camanachd Cup, the glittering prize of shinty. A pipe band led the victorious team through the village and the cup was refilled several times over. Graham, meanwhile, was having a tough time with 2,000 soldiers at Redford Barracks in Edinburgh. They listened to him 'apparently unmoved, with solemn, unchanging expressions' and when he asked who were ready to make a decision, barely a dozen hands went up.

Among other events that weekend, England defeated Scotland 7-2 at Wembley. At the beginning of the second half, when Scotland trailed by four goals to one and had, as one correspondent put it, 'as much chance of winning as Stirling Albion have of escaping relegation', the Scottish supporters began a prolonged round of cheering and hand-clapping, 'disposed to show their appreciation of the players who had caused their team's humiliation'. At the age of 41 Stanley Matthews devastated the Scottish defence with his ball control, the uncanny accuracy of his passing and crossing, and his bemusing bursts of speed. Manchester United's Duncan Edwards, not quite 19 years old, who would die in the Munich air disaster three years later, had a wonderful game too. The doomed Stirling Albion dutifully lost 4-0 to East Fife at home, while Britain's octogenarian prime minister, Winston Churchill, stepped down in favour of Anthony Eden.

IV

'The largest evangelistic meeting in history' – Billy Graham's final gig in Glasgow – was attended by a congregation of 100,000 at Hampden Park. In gathering darkness the last 2,259 converts of the crusade filed past the barriers to stand on the perimeter track and make the symbolic 'decision'. The organisers announced that two and a half million people – half the population of Scotland – had attended the meetings in Glasgow and relay meetings elsewhere, and that 50,000 'decisions for Christ' had been recorded.

Graham stepped forward, his raincoat unbuttoned, his hair ruffled by the wind – it was blowing as hard at the end as it was on the opening night – and thanked the Scots for their overwhelming response. 'We have fallen in love with you people,' he told the audience. 'We are going to carry a little bit of Scotland away with us.' To accusations that he had indulged in showmanship, he replied that showmanship did not affect 'the people in the little towns' to whom the services had been relayed and who had 'not a person to see, only a voice to hear'. Tom Allan, the chain-smoking, plain-speaking minister of St George's Tron, predicted that historians would see in the crusade 'a significant landmark in the long history of the Scottish church and people'. At a service in Glasgow Cathedral Nevile Davidson said that, whether in factories or at fashionable dinner parties, the issues of the forthcoming general election were being 'eclipsed by discussions on the meaning of conversion or the Sermon on the Mount'.

Although the crusade was over Billy Graham stayed in Scotland for a few more weeks, addressing capacity crowds wherever he went. Addressing a meeting of the Women's Jewish Mission in Edinburgh, he said it had been a strange thing to watch the Jew in history; wherever the Jew had gone, whatever he had done, he was still a Jew. He urged his audience to carry on 'with greater intensity of purpose and spirit than ever' the essential work of persuading the Jew to 'turn his face to Jesus Christ'. If Scotland's small Jewish community was dismayed by these remarks, it kept its feelings to itself. In the face of popular adulation amounting to hero-worship, opposition steadily dwindled.

Graham's star status was confirmed by his invitation to the throne gallery of the Assembly Hall, where he sat next to the Duke of Hamilton, Lord High Commissioner to the General Assembly of the Church of Scotland. The Moderator – Alexander Henderson, the minister of Leuchars – asked him to descend to the floor of the hall and speak to the fathers and brethren. As soon as Graham had finished most of the audience made for the doors, leaving the next speaker to face a rump, the exodus confirming that the only show in town was the evangelist. The assembly approved a resolution 'rejoicing in the great blessing which attended the work of the crusade and of the many relay missions held throughout the country'. The doctrinally rigid Free Church, with its preference for all things plain, was muted in its reservations. 'Whatever criticism we may make about Mr Billy Graham, his methods, and his allies, I do not think it can be doubted that the spirit of the Lord has been moving up and down our land,' said J Weir Campbell of Brora. Professor Charles Duthie, principal of the Scottish Congregational Church, said that 'as time goes on and the fruits of the crusade grow more and more apparent, more will come and offer themselves for full-time Christian service'.

Among senior churchmen George MacLeod was the only outspoken critic. He asked his fellow Scots to consider if, perhaps unconsciously, they were not being true to the Scottish tradition which went beyond personal salvation and dealt with the needs of society as a whole. His fellow Scots had little to say in response to this challenging reminder of the social gospel. From Scotland's half a million Roman Catholics reaction of any kind to the Graham crusade was negligible.

Scotland was still officially a Christian country – though only just. The membership of the Church of Scotland accounted for around 37% of the adult population, the Roman Catholic Church for a further 15% – a total of 52% excluding the adherents to smaller denominations such as the Free Church and the Scottish Episcopal Church. But the prophecy that Billy Graham's season in Glasgow would be 'a significant landmark in the long history of the Scottish church and people', proved to be over-optimistic. From a peak of around 1.3 million in the mid-1950s the membership of the Church of Scotland entered into a long and sustained decline. At the time of writing it is down to 464,000: 9% of the adult population. The crusade, for all that it gave a brief focus to a spiritual longing, failed to inspire the hoped-for revival of institutional religion. For three months the Scots lost their head to the alchemy of Billy Graham. They rediscovered it in its usual place.

V

Scotland in the spring of Billy Graham appeared to be a country enjoying unparalleled prosperity. The years of austerity were finally over and official statistics told a story of economic progress on all fronts. Scottish exports were rising sharply, the traditional industries of textiles, iron and steel were booming and the shipyards were turning out their greatest tonnage since the war. Thirty-six thousand men were employed in deep coal mining. The newer industries were thriving too. Scotland was manufacturing 30% of all the office machinery in the UK, while the output of watches and clocks jumped by 40% in 12 months. Twenty million square yards of carpet, 40 million square yards of linoleum, were being produced annually. The Board of Trade announced that it was granting certificates for the opening of 150 new factories and that capacity in many existing ones had doubled. Electricity capacity was expanding rapidly and the South of Scotland Electricity Board pushed ahead with plans for a new power station at Kincardine-on-Forth. More people were in work than at any time in Scottish history; there were persistent skills shortages in several industries. Unemployment dropped to only 59,500 out of a working population of 2.4 million.

But these impressive figures did not tell the full story. The Department of Health for Scotland said in its annual report that, to judge by hospital attendances and demands for hospital treatment, ill-health was increasing. In four years the number of in-patients passing through Scotland's NHS hospitals had grown by 30% and family doctors were calling an average of five times a year on each of their patients. The number of deaths from TB was falling, but the infant mortality rate was still causing concern and respiratory cancer had emerged as a serious killer, particularly of middle-aged men.

Much of urban Scotland continued to be afflicted by a repressive gloom. After a weekend in Glasgow, Alistair Cooke reported in the *Manchester Guardian*: 'A vast Presbyterian pall descends on the city early on Saturdays, shoos the couples out of Kelvingrove Park half an hour after sunset, closes down the pubs at 9.30, blackens out the dance halls at midnight, and leaves the world to darkness and to me, plodding along Sauchiehall Street ...' The city centre had been robbed of some of its liveliness by the dispersal of so many people to the new estates such as Drumchapel, an old village overwhelmed by council houses but which retained something of a rural feeling with its playing fields, golf course and neighbouring Kilpatrick Hills.

Glasgow's housing committee decided to erect many more multi-storey blocks in the new estates of Castlemilk, Easterhouse and Drumchapel than it had originally intended and ordered two prototype blocks of 10 storeys to be built without delay; it was estimated that without expansion into the sky, 300,000 people would have to leave the city. Some were already reconciled – or actively looking forward – to a new life in the embryonic new towns. Sir Patrick Dollan, who had moved from fuel efficiency to the chairmanship of East Kilbride Development Corporation, laid the foundation stone for the shopping centre at Glenrothes, the second of these towns, where the Rothes Colliery would bring 500 miners and their families to Fife. A few days later the Secretary of State dropped his demand that Glasgow Corporation should meet some of the cost of creating a third new town at Cumbernauld, James Stuart declaring that his sense of gravity at the city's housing problem had persuaded him to change his mind. But there was little discussion of the social and recreational infrastructure required to give a sense of community to these sprawling peripheral estates. Distracted by the charisma of Billy Graham, the General Assembly of the Church of Scotland paid little heed to a warning from its national church extension commitee that 100,000 Scots a year were moving into new housing areas where there was no church at all.

Among teachers there was a growing sense of desperation about the standards of Scottish education. Alex Russell, headmaster of Abercorn School in Paisley, wrote to the press lamenting the shortage of qualified staff, the use of retired and uncertificated teachers to plug the gaps, and the many oversized classes. The usual reply of the Scottish Office was to deny the existence of oversized classes and to draw a favourable comparison with class sizes in England. This was a shameless manipulation of the figures, since in Scotland a primary class only became oversized when it contained more than 45 pupils – an unsatisfactorily large number, according to the Educational Institute of Scotland. By this yardstick 8% of primary classes were oversized compared with 36% south of the border. But in England the threshold for an oversized class was very much lower: a fact rarely mentioned.

Adding to the problems of health, housing and education, there was the uneven distribution of Scotland's new-found prosperity, which ended in a frail, broken line somewhere north and west of Perth. Kevan McDowall told the annual meeting of the Highland Fund that the north-west presented an appalling picture. As matters stood, the crofting families were 'almost in a land without hope' and there was nothing for them but to migrate to the towns or the dominions. An initiative of five Barra crofters offered a more encouraging prospect of self-help. With the assistance of the Highland Fund they bought the Outer Hebridean islands of Pabbay, Berneray and Mingulay from an Essex farmer, intending to stock them with sheep and cattle. Their leader, Archibald Macdonald of Canisbay, said they would not make their homes on the islands, but would live on them for weeks at a time during the lambing season. The islanders reacted positively: better local men as part-time absentee landlords than Essex farmers who were never seen.

In the Inner Hebrides there seemed to be no answer to the malaise of depopulation. The islanders of Mull feared a complete evacuation of the island unless some new industry could be developed. Tourism, the most obvious possibility, was hampered by poor communications. A visitor from the United States staying in Edinburgh and wishing to reach Mull by train in a single day, had to catch the 6.50am from Princes Street, a train without food or so much as a cup of tea. With any luck he arrived in Oban at 12.25. The RMS Lochinvar, sailing at 1.15pm, landed at Tobermory at 5pm – 7pm on a Wednesday. The American visitor would have travelled 140 miles in 10 hours or 12, depending on his day of departure.

Inaccessibility in a more extreme form was revealed by a court case in Stornoway. A crofter witness, 53 years old, who spoke almost no English, was 12 before the first school was opened in his village – the most isolated on the island of Harris – where he was born and brought up. 'How do you put anyone on oath in a language he does not understand?' asked Sheriff Robert Miller. The fiscal replied that the welfare officer for Harris would act as interpreter. 'Can you not speak English?' Miller persisted. The witness, Neil Macdiarmid of Mollinginish, replied: 'Very few.' The welfare officer said there was no road to Macdiarmid's village, and that the witness had walked five miles to get the bus which took him to Stornoway for the court.

The northern isles were more remote still. After labouring for six years, a planning survey concluded that the dwindling population of Shetland could only be augmented by immigration – a finding that might have been reached in the time it took to travel from Edinburgh to Mull on a Wednesday. The survey recommended an extension of the fish processing industry and the development of an exclusive 'Shetland' brand of wool. In addition to these inspirations, it thought another survey might be helpful.

Elsewhere, progress of a sort threatened long-established ways of life. In Caithness preparatory work began on an atomic power station at Dounreay, while Uist faced the prospect of a guided missile range. The Secretary of State for Scotland, acknowledging local resentment at this intrusion into a God-fearing traditional culture, invoked what he called 'the national interest'. Crofters from 15 townships in the islands of South Uist and Benbecula were informed that a six-mile strip of their land would be taken over, but that the dirty work of building the facility would be given to the locals. The parrot cry of jobs was invariably expected to close down criticism. The politicians depended upon it. The crofters were not fools; they were not silenced. But their protests counted for nothing.

VI

Between the end of the Graham crusade and the general election of 1955 which confirmed the Conservatives in power, there was a brief interval of relative normality.

The annual exhibition of the Royal Scottish Academy opened in Edinburgh. Critics praised R H Westwater for his sketch of the snooker player Joe Davis, 'remarkable for the skilful modelling of the face', and for the same artist's portrait of Compton Mackenzie, which had the bearded author, spectacles on forehead, surrounded by the tools of the writer's trade. Joan Eardley's study of Glasgow street childen was widely commended. But most of the critical attention was devoted, as ever, to the Scottish arts establishment of Anne Redpath, William Mactaggart ('working this year in an emotion-packed range of deep, lustrous blues in landscape and still life'), William Gillies and Robin Philipson.

The theatrical event of the season brought Duncan Macrae, the foremost Scottish actor of his day, to the stage of the Glasgow Citizens', with Fulton Mackay and Andrew Keir, in *The Sell Out*, a new play by the polymath Robins Millar, critic, newspaper editor and artist as well as prolific playwright. There was perhaps a hint of professional jealousy in the review in the *Glasgow Herald*, whose critic observed acidly: 'Everyone has to keep quiet during certain, happily brief, interludes during which Mr Millar, through Mr Macrae, passes a few remarks on the glories of the individual.' The play concerned the rivalry between drapery stores in a country town. Whatever its merits – fairly slender in the *Herald's* opinion – it would prove impossible to make any retrospective judgement of it. So carelessly did Scotland guard its theatrical heritage that most of the new Scottish plays of the post-war period perished even as manuscripts.

The same newspaper gave a gratuitously cruel review, unsigned, to one of the books of the season, *The Flag in the Wind*, the autobiography of John MacCormick. It attacked his 'undergraduate contribution' to the story of the Stone of Destiny episode, noted his 'unusual agility in associating himself with each of the major political parties in turn', and claimed disgracefully that he had advocated violence in pursuit of the home rule cause. There was also a shabby insinuation that MacCormick liked to hob-nob with the titled classes, a suggestion based on nothing more than a slightly ingenuous account of a meeting with Lady Glen-Coats, the first lady of Scottish Liberalism, at her grand house in the Ayrshire countryside.

MacCormick's friend Nigel Tranter was more kindly treated by the Scottish critics for his new novel, *There Are Worse Jungles*, which was hailed as 'a story of courage and high adventure set in the steaming torrid heat deep in the rain forests of the inner Amazon'. Tranter had an unusual working method, writing his books on the hoof along the beach near his home in Aberlady, where steaming torrid heat was rarely a problem. His notebooks had plastic covers to protect them from the East Lothian drizzle.

The climax of the football season matched the mighty Celtic with the minnows Clyde ('The Bully Wee') in the Scottish Cup final before a crowd of 102,000 at Hampden Park. The annual conference of the Scottish Trades Union Congress ended in Rothesay on the morning of the game, and there was little interest in the final session as delegates impatient to reach Glasgow in time for the kick-off gave short shrift to any speaker foolhardy enough to come to the rostrum. The match itself was one of Scottish football's periodic public embarrassments; thousands of Celtic supporters, waving the flag of the Irish Republic, attempted to drown out the national anthem. One onlooker described it as an incitement to riot.

In a more harmonious competitive spirit, the first all-Scottish jazz band championships were held in the St Andrew's Hall in Glasgow. The Clyde Valley Stompers won first prize, Andy Paton's Dixielanders were runners-up, and the Nova Scotians third. The event was reported in the press as an anthropological curiosity. One critic wrote: 'Some of the young men [in the audience] wore elaborate hair styles in the Tony Curtis way and the young women wore bright-coloured sweaters, but they were a most orderly gathering, beating time silently while the numbers were being played out and then nearly blowing the walls out with their applause.'

VII

A novelty of spring 1955 was the election of Scottish representative peers to speak for Scotland in the House of Lords – the first time such a vote had taken place since the Act of Union in 1707. Thirty-one peers gathered for the ceremony round a long table in the Great Hall of Parliament House in Edinburgh; 22 others voted by post, one other by proxy. From an electorate of 115 titles, the whole list called by Sir James Fergusson, Keeper of the Records, it was a turnout of just over 50%. (The common people would do rather better a few days later.) As the one o'clock gun sounded from the castle, the voting was completed. Thirteen of the 54 voted for themselves ('It ceased to be a wonder', as one journalist cynically noted). The successful candidates were the Earls of Rothes, Caithness (who voted for himself), Perth, Haddington (who voted for himself), Lindsay, Airlie, Selkirk and Breadalbane, and Lords Forbes, Saltoun, Sinclair, Sempill (one of the Nazi sympathisers), Balfour of Burleigh, Fairfax of Cameron, Reay and Polwarth. Among the spectators 'Big Bill' Campbell, captain of the lately victorious US Walker Cup golf team, pronounced it 'mighty impressive'.

The other election, in which the people as a whole had an

opportunity to decide who would speak for Scotland, failed to generate the excitement of earlier post-war polls. The Scottish aristocracy was again accorded the greatest respect. Lord Lovat, addressing farmers in the Inverness cattle market, spoke in support of the Tory candidate, who was being strongly opposed by John Bannerman, doyen of Scottish Liberals. 'John Bannerman is a great friend of mine,' said Lovat, 'a good Highlander, and a good football [by which he meant rugby] player, but no politician. Inverness-shire has a great Liberal tradition and at heart the people are probably all Liberals, but the Highlander does not like to be pushed around. You must have the concerted action of eight forwards, and that you will not get from the Liberal Party. They did not even have a shinty team in the last parliament.' Shinty or no shinty, Bannerman came within 1,000 votes of unseating the Tory.

Among the lost deposits James Halliday of the Scottish National Party created a favourable impression in Stirling and Falkirk Burghs. One newspaper described him as 'a very likeable young man, ploughing a lonely furrow against the political machines of the two large parties'. At one campaign meeting, a worker grabbed his hand and said: 'I quite agree with all you said. But I'm not going to vote for you, for the Tory might slip in.' Another said: 'What are you, anyway, but a tartan Tory?' The 'tartan Tory' jibe – of which this was an early recorded use – haunted the SNP for many years.

The nastiest campaign of 1955 was fought in Greenock, where Ian MacArthur mounted a fierce challenge to Hector McNeil, the former Secretary of State, who had created an alternative platform for himself as a witty, provocative speaker on radio and TV, which he found more congenial than the drudgery of opposition. Attlee, disapproving of his poor attendance in the House of Commons, dropped him from the Opposition front bench, and nor was McNeil the most assiduous constituency MP. Against a smart Tory he found himself struggling for survival.

As Secretary of State from February 1950 to October 1951 McNeil had set up a scheme for 300 Scottish TB patients a year to be treated in Switzerland. Shortly before the election the Scottish Office announced that the scheme was coming to an end. McNeil's wife, in her husband's election leaflet, bitterly criticised the Tories for what she saw as an act of meanness, pointing out that in Greenock alone there were more than 1,500 people on the TB register, of whom 152 were in hospital. MacArthur retaliated equally bitterly that this misrepresented the government's position. The row then got personal with McNeil's statement: 'I cannot admire the gallantry or chivalry of my opponent in attacking a woman – in this case my wife – when a man is available for attack. I note too that the statement [ending the scheme] came from Lord Strathclyde safe in the funk hole of the House of Lords, where I cannot reach him.' The electors of Greenock were unimpressed by the spat, reducing McNeil's majority to only 1,033 – one of Labour's worst results in Scotland.

Five months later Hector McNeil died in New York at the age of 48 after suffering a brain haemorrhage on the Queen Mary. One of his obituaries claimed that the reason for his early death was to be found in the pace at which he lived: 'A man of parts, he had the ability to make a success of everything he took up and he never hesitated to spend himself to the full in doing so.' Had he lived it is unlikely that he would have returned to ministerial office. He had effectively turned his back on politics.

The near-loss of Greenock was a sign not only of personal dissatisfaction with the sitting member but of a more general swing to the right. A terrible result for Labour in Central Ayrshire, captured by the Tories with a majority of 167, gave Anthony Eden an overall majority of the Scottish seats; the Tories also won a majority of the popular vote. Particularly shocking for Labour was its failure to gain Glasgow Scotstoun despite the inclusion of the Drumchapel estate. The influx of 6,000 working-class voters should have converted a Tory marginal into a fairly solid Labour seat. 'Seldom, if ever, have Labour supporters been so sure about a polling district,' wrote a journalist covering the Scotstoun campaign. Yet the Tories held the seat. They could only have done so with the help of some of the new estate dwellers, traditional Labour voters who had been uprooted from inner-city slums. 'The great housing scheme in Drumchapel,' wrote the sitting Tory, 'shows you what we have made possible.'

And so, on a wave of full employment and religious evangelism, a Conservative Scotland came into being on 26 May 1955. One way and another, it was a year of conversions.

1956

BEFORE THE CURRY SUPPER

I

When the Suez crisis broke in the autumn of 1956 Sir Hector Hetherington, principal of Glasgow University, was conducting a graduation ceremony. Few people in Scottish public life were quoted more often, and on this occasion he was again all over the serious newspapers. Hetherington viewed the Middle East 'debate' (his euphemism of choice) as a question of public morality. 'The enemy everywhere is the mass mind,' he said. 'Thinking is difficult, painful, and liable to error ... but without it we are at the mercy of catchwords and hysteria.' He added that he could not remember any situation that had produced such a division of public opinion.

On the same page of the *Glasgow Herald* which carried these philosophical musings, there was a report of greater significance. At the age of 36 Sir Hector's son Alastair had just been appointed editor of the greatest of England's provincial newspapers, the *Manchester Guardian*. It was an unexpected promotion for the relatively inexperienced foreign editor. Young Hetherington was not a Mancunian but a Scot (although by an accident of birth he entered the world in Wales), and by the relaxed standards of the *Manchester Guardian* he was an upright citizen, even a little austere and straight-laced, a man temperamentally at home with an orange juice.

Yet, pitched into the hot seat on the eve of war in the Middle East, he responded with a dose of the hard stuff – an editorial which cost the newspaper both readers and advertising and earned Hetherington the enduring mistrust of the British establishment. In a famous editorial he described the Anglo-French intervention in the Suez canal as 'an act of folly, without justification in any terms but brief expediency'. No other British newspaper had dared to attack the government's action so boldly;

even the popular papers of the left – the *Daily Mirror*, *News Chronicle* and *Daily Herald* – hesitated to do so. The *Manchester Guardian* briefly stood alone, and with a single phrase, Alastair Hetherington cast himself into the wilderness. For a climbing man, familiar with inhospitable places, it was not the worst fate imaginable.

II

His father, the university principal, was brought up in the Hillfoots, the name given to a string of small towns and villages in the shadow of the Ochil Hills in Clackmannanshire ('the wee county'). Hector attended Tillicoultry School until the age of 13 and considered himself relatively ill-educated because he knew little of British history or of music and science and had read very little literature. But he knew thoroughly the syntax of the English language, was taught both Latin and French, had attained proficiency in arithmetic and in the basics of algebra and geometry, and had learned the catechism by heart. He said of his time at Tillicoultry that the catechism had the same status as the multiplication table and that the pupils were left in no doubt of the equal validity of both.

He went on to Dollar Academy and from there to Glasgow University, where he graduated with a double first in economic science and philosophy. It was his original intention to be a minister of the United Free Church, and had he pursued this ambition he would have brought a sharply-honed social con-science to the pulpit. As a student he chose to live in the university settlement at Possil, a deprived area of the city where he saw for himself the desperate condition of the poor. After he graduated Hetherington was appointed warden of the settlement, which aimed to provide food, shelter and clothing for those in greatest need. At weekends he and his close friends Walter Elliot and O H Mavor retreated to a sparsely furnished cottage in the Campsies, near Fintry, to walk and think. All three inhabitants of the cottage did well for themselves.

It was said of Hetherington that he was the last of the principals to know every student by name, although the name Ian Hamilton – rebellious editor of an undergraduate magazine so irreverent that it was considered necessary to suppress it – would have appealed less than most others stored in his expansive memory. Hetherington's son was to become a rebellious editor in his own right, though in a bigger way.

As a child during the depression of the 1930s Alastair Hetherington was taken by his father to Clydebank to see one of the Cunard liners. The experience left a lasting impression. 'It [the ship] was under construction,' he wrote, 'but all work on it had stopped. The grey hull towered above the shipyard, silent and desolate. But what struck me most were the drab groups of men gathered together in the streets outside, unemployed and disjointed, with nothing to do and nowhere to go. It was a profoundly sad, disturbing sight.' His radical instincts, half-formed in youth, were matured at Oxford by exposure to a gifted tutor, the Glaswegian Denis Brogan, who guided him towards a career in political journalism. His progress was spectacular.

'No editor that I can think of,' wrote the historian John Grigg, 'has faced a more searching test of his or her qualities at the very moment of assuming office.' Hetherington effectively took over from his dying predecessor, A P Wadsworth, on 17 October 1956, as the Suez crisis reached its climax. In secret collusion with Israel the British and French governments were plotting an attack on Egypt with the aim of regaining control of the Suez canal, recently nationalised by Egypt, and of removing the Egyptian president, Nasser, from power. A fortnight later they used Israel's invasion of Sinai and advance to Suez as a pretext for an ultimatum to both parties demanding their withdrawal from the canal. At that critical stage Hetherington made his move. Grigg wrote that 'although not remotely a warmonger he [Hetherington] was equally remote from pacifism. His opposition to Suez was thoroughly realistic, as well as principled'. Two big-spending advertisers cancelled their bookings, and thousands of readers stopped buying the paper in protest.

Back in Scotland the *Glasgow Herald* was uncritically mouthing the official line. It praised the resolution of Anthony Eden's government, denounced the Labour Party's opposition as irresponsible, and dismissed the objection of President Eisenhower that Britain and France had resorted to military action in defiance of the United Nations. Most newspapers took a similarly light view of Britain's moral bankruptcy.

III

The opposition in Scotland came not in the press but on the streets. Protest meetings were reported in Falkirk, Ayr, Dundee, Paisley, Kirkcaldy, Aberdeen and Glasgow. The STUC attacked the 'aggressive measures' taken by the British and French governments. Engineers at Weir's of Cathcart, one of the largest Glasgow works, staged a demonstration.

But the wildest scenes, as well as the most comical, were played out in the old quadrangle of Edinburgh University, where rival groups of students clashed. Liberals, socialists and nationalists who had formed a loose anti-war coalition attempted to organise a street procession. It was headed by an ancient car plastered with anti-Eden slogans. News of the demo reached the police, who closed off the university buildings – but not before 'a powerful black saloon car' was driven at speed into the quad and parked in front of the anti-Eden car. Its occupants removed the ignition key, locked the doors and fled, making it impossible for the enemy vehicle to move.

In this stalemate there was nothing to do but fight. Students hurled fish, fireworks and bags of flour into the air and at each other, provoking the police to warn the university authorities that anyone leaving the premises in anything resembling a procession risked immediate arrest. A compromise was agreed: the first car would be released on condition that all the anti-Eden placards were removed. As soon as it was driven away a further wave of fighting broke out, with renewed attempts by both sides to start street processions. Chanting 'We Want Eden' or 'Down With Eden', hundreds of students streamed on to the South Bridge, only to be turned back by the police. They retreated once more into the quad, where the slogan-calling and fighting continued for four hours accompanied by bursts of *Land of Hope and Glory*. The day ended with the anti-government group marching to St Andrew's House to deliver a statement to the Secretary of State for Scotland: 'We deplore Her Majesty's armed intervention in Egypt and call upon HM Government to submit to the will of the United Nations.'

The profound divisions revealed by the disturbances in Scotland and elsewhere in the UK spilled over into acrimonious exchanges on television. The most notorious occurred on a discussion programme, *Free Speech*, on 31 October in which the historian A J P Taylor and the future leader of the Labour Party, Michael Foot, almost came to blows with Bob Boothby, the Tory MP for East Aberdeenshire, who was branded a criminal by his fellow panellists for supporting his government's decision to go to war. Behind the scenes, however, Boothby was one of a small group of Tory rebels. Harold Nicolson, MP for Bournemouth, recorded in his diary that Boothby and Walter Elliot were among a small group of MPs present at a private meeting in London on the evening of 5 November at which the terms of a letter to Eden were approved.

The letter asked the Prime Minister to offer to place the British troops in Suez under the immediate command of the United Nations. Nicolson wanted to add the words 'in order to restore Britain's credit in the eyes of the world', but the others would not go that far in distancing themselves from the beleaguered Eden. Boothby, who had argued publicly in support of the war on 31 October, was thus privately opposing it five days later. This inconsistency was characteristic. Witty, socially adroit, a popular broadcaster, Boothby was as unreliable personally as he was politically. A promiscuous homosexual, he freelanced as the lover of Dorothy Macmillan, wife of the man who would succeed Eden as Prime Minister.

The Church of Scotland, which might have given a moral lead on Suez, preferred to vacillate. Ian Pitt-Watson, an articulate spokesman for its liberal wing, urged an emergency resolution on Glasgow Presbytery declaring 'with regret but conviction' that, by acting in breach of its obligations under the UN charter, Britain's authority had been seriously compromised. The presbytery rejected the resolution by 199 votes to 123 on the grounds that it would not wish to pass something which had not been fully considered. British troops were landing at Port Said, risking their own lives as well as their country's reputation; how much longer did the presbytery need? On the same day – 6 November – Ayr Presbytery decided by 45 votes to two that it would not discuss a similar resolution. When its proposer, W H Whalley, complained that a matter of public interest had been suppressed, George Anderson, the minister of Maybole, replied: 'It was not suppressed. It was the will of the presbytery.'

The commission of the General Assembly, representing the Church of Scotland as a whole, met a fortnight later. The passage of time had not improved the quality of its response to the crisis, the commission wriggling out of any condemnation of the British action by deploring the 'inability' of the United Nations to deal with it, a contortion of the facts supported by such influential figures as Nevile Davidson. In vain did Ian Pitt-Watson attempt to have the reference to the UN's 'inability' deleted.

Two days later Anthony Eden, pleading stress, left Britain on a three-week holiday in Jamaica. 'I am going because the doctors say I must,' he explained. In his absence events in the Middle East unravelled swiftly. Britain's rudderless government then found itself having to deal with a second international crisis: a popular uprising by Hungarians against their own communist government, the crushing of the revolt by Russian tanks, the mass exodus of refugees.

How, it was asked, could Britain demand Russia's withdrawal from Hungary when it was simultaneously bombing Egypt? Scotland's national church, which had made a fool of itself over Suez, fell silent in the face of this larger question.

IV

The plight of the refugees united Scotland as surely as the Suez misadventure divided it. There was widespread sympathy for a working-class people, not dissimilar in temperament to the Scots, who had been so brutally persecuted. The press reported that, on one day in mid-November, Edinburgh University students (their differences over Suez forgotten for the time being) were out on the streets with collecting cans; that a 13-year-old girl, a pupil of King's Park Secondary School in Glasgow, had given a shilling to the refugees' appeal; that canteen workers at Thomas Hinshelwood & Co Ltd, Glasgow, had raised £8; that there were collections for clothes in Lanark and Helensburgh; and that the industrialist Viscount Weir had donated £1,000.

On 19 November relatives of Alexander Angyal, a draper who had left Hungary 20 years before, came to stay with him in Glasgow; they were the first refugees to reach Scotland. Many families were offering to take children into their homes, and the Red Cross was accepting a steady stream of gifts at its Scottish headquarters. On this wave of altruism two student leaders – Ross Harper, a prominent Tory lawyer in the making, and Douglas

Alexander, who was to become a Church of Scotland minister and the father of two Labour politicians (Wendy and Douglas) – returned from a conference in Vienna with an idealistic plan for the education of Hungarian students in Scotland.

In early December the first large party of refugees was received at a transit camp near Gorebridge in Midlothian. It numbered about 250, mostly single young men and women, though some in family groups. The press reported that they were 'mostly tired travelling and not able to discuss their hardships' and that there was 'an initial atmosphere of mistrust and fear'. Small groups were observed walking the country roads near the camp. A second party of 250 arrived at West Linton in Peeblesshire, and other transit camps were set up at Meigle in Perthshire, Aberfoyle in Stirlingshire and Abington in Lanarkshire.

At all these places the refugees were sensitively interviewed before being left to decide for themselves whether to stay or emigrate. (All but a few emigrated.) Ministry of Labour officials emphasised that they should regard themselves as British citizens with the right to travel, work and live where they wished, and the refugees were offered practical assistance in finding jobs. Their welcome could not have been more sympathetic or helpful, in contrast to the reception for the several thousand asylum seekers who found themselves in a generally hostile and uncomprehending Glasgow half a century later.

Prestwick Airport became a staging post for a massive humanitarian mission, 'Project Safe Haven', organised by the United States government. On 11 December the first 50 refugees disembarked. For the next three weeks six flights a day carried a total of 10,000 homeless people. During their brief stay in Scotland, while they waited to be transferred to aircraft bound for New York and a new life, they were showered with cigarettes, coffee and sweets by local people.

Dr Katherine Schopflin, a young doctor at Ayr County Hospital, who had qualified in her native Hungary, acted as interpreter and medical advisor for the first batch of refugees. Andros, a 16-year-old schoolboy, told her that in Budapest his class left their desks and joined in the battle against the Russians. He learned how to use a machine gun, to fight in the streets, and to operate as a sniper, armed with a rifle, on the second storey of a block of apartments. Erika, a student from Budapest, who had seen her sister shot down at her side, was one of the 'freedom fighters' led by her fiancé

Niklos with whom she hoped to be reunited in America. Jeno, an apprentice engine driver, told Dr Schopflin that he had tried to assassinate the 'traitor' president of a Hungarian city council before being caught and severely beaten by the Russians. He escaped, walked 60 miles, swam a river, and bribed a Russian soldier with a wrist watch, finally managing to cross the frontier to safety.

Despite these heroic testimonies the Scottish working class was equivocal in its response to Soviet aggression in Hungary. In a national vote conducted through union branches, the miners overturned a resolution by their own communist-dominated executive 'condemning the tragic situation and the loss of life in Hungary', but agreed to send £1,000 to relieve the distress and suffering of the people. In a ludicrous exercise in proletariat semantics, the word 'condemn' was changed to 'deplore'.

The National Union of Mineworkers in Scotland was dominated by the brothers Moffat. Alex resigned from the Communist Party over Hungary, but Abe, Scottish president of the NUM since 1942, remained faithful to the cause in the face of every provocation. Born in Fife, he went down the pit at Lumphinnans at the age of 14. 'Like every other young boy in the mining village,' he wrote, 'I knew that my pit clothes with piece-box and flask were ready six weeks before I left school, as mining was the only occupation available.'

Within six weeks of starting work in 1910 he was badly hurt in an accident at work and, in the absence of an ambulance, another of his brothers (Jim) carried him home on his back. Abe recalled the grief on his mother's face at the sight of her injured son, his face unwashed, pit-black. 'My schoolmaster came to see me and put it to my father that I might return to school, but for the second oldest brother in a family of 11 children this was an impossibility. So after I recovered from the accident I resumed my occupation at the coal face with my father and eldest brother.' A Frenchman in the village, a fellow miner named Laurence Storian, an ardent communist, convinced Abe that he should join the party. He did so in 1922 and said in his autobiography more than 40 years later that he had never regretted this decision.

In a nod to scripture, Abe's only response to Alex's principled resignation from the party in 1956 was a terse: 'I am not my brother's keeper.' But the split in the family, and the popular outrage over events in Hungary, made this an awkward time for someone who had just topped the poll for the executive of the

Communist Party of Great Britain. Even in some areas of the Scottish coalfield, there was angry anti-communist feeling; in Ayrshire, miners demanded the resignation of the district secretary, Guy Stobbs, shouting: 'Get these communists out of here.' A few days later the Russian foreign minister, Dimitri Shepilov, landed in Ayrshire on his way back to Moscow from a meeting of the UN. He told James Jeffs, commandant of Prestwick Airport: 'I do not wish to speak to anyone. I wish to be alone.' He strode up and down the tarmac in front of a sign which declared: 'Welcome to Scotland, haste ye back.' When Comrade Shepilov's hat blew off he insisted on recovering it himself.

V

The natives of Scotland were not sufficiently inspired by the Hungarian patriots to instigate an uprising of their own. They celebrated their saint's day in the midst of tumultuous happenings elsewhere in the world, but did so in their customary half-hearted fashion. The Metropole Theatre in Glasgow laid on a topical entertainment optimistically entitled *Scotland the Brave*, the highlight of which was a sketch in which Gracie Clark, 'a virago with a sense of humour' sparred with her husband, Colin Murray, 'the hauden-doon but never suppressed man of the house' (according to E G Ashton, theatre critic of *The Bulletin*). The BBC's gesture to St Andrew's Day was a recital of Beethoven's rarely heard Scottish songs. 'How Scots can we get?' *The Bulletin* asked sourly.

But acts of rebellion, there were a few. As the Soviet tanks rolled into Budapest, television viewers in Perth who kept their sets on after close-down (for reasons best known to themselves), heard a voice exclaiming: 'Attention, attention, this is Radio Free Scotland calling. Do not switch off.' Accordions were heard playing *Scotland the Brave*. Was Gracie Clark about to make an appearance with her rolling pin? Apparently not. Instead a voice announced excitedly: 'This is Radio Free Scotland bringing you the truth about the home rule movement. Nationalism has been banned from the air by the London-controlled BBC.' A second voice interrupted: 'No party contesting fewer than 100 seats is permitted to make broadcasts.' There was the sound of a gong striking, followed by the jingling of money. 'That is Scottish money, pouring into England,' viewers were informed. Four more voices joined in, one shouting: 'This is Radio Free Scotland proclaiming to the nation that the fight is on in earnest.' The transmission ended with a rendering of *Scots Wha Hae*.

Whatever this was, it wasn't another Hungary. Nevertheless the authorities took a dim view of the pirate broadcast and despatched a team of experts to Perth to investigate. Dr Robert McIntyre, president of the SNP, was asked if the party had anything to do with it. 'No,' he replied, 'but I see nothing immoral in such a thing since the BBC have completely abused their monopoly. No Scotsman should help in any way in tracking the transmitter down.'

A second act of rebellion took place in Edinburgh, at the New Victoria Cinema, when the audience at a lecture started to boo the speaker, Dr H E Seller, the city's medical officer of health. The possibility that it was simply not a very good lecture and deserved to be booed had not occurred to the newspapers. Mysteriously, most of the audience consisted of teddy boys and their girlfriends, who were known as molls. Far from being given credit for attending a lecture on public health, the young spectators were ejected by the police. The Edinburgh bailies, never slow to indignation, went into their usual overdrive. 'I see no reason why any professional man should have to listen to abuse and offensive remarks,' fulminated Bailie Duncan Weatherstone. His colleague, Councillor George Hedderwick, regretted that the offenders could not be birched – 'and the girls are not much better'.

A rather older delinquent, the poet and teacher Norman MacCaig, surprised a conference of the Scottish Institute of Adult Education by recommending the burning of all copies of *Palgrave's Golden Treasury* in the possession of Scottish schools. He complained that teachers were forced to work with a curriculum which prescribed the study, year after year, of the poetry of the English romantic tradition: 'There are still teachers and compilers of anthologies who think that boys of 12, whose heads are filled with penalty goals and spaceships, still believe in fairies, and that their ultimate happiness comes when they are curled up with a good poem about elves and dewdrops. To throw that sort of claptrap down the brazen throat of a boy of 12 is the quickest way to turn him away from poetry for ever.'

There were gaps in MacCaig's reading of *Palgrave's Golden*

Treasury. His fellow Scotsman Robert Burns could be found within its pages, and Burns was no English romantic. But the speaker had little good to say about Burns either: 'He had a considerable talent for turning out humdrum little philosophical dumplings over which his admirers wag their heads like connoisseurs, savouring the profundity of *A man's a man for a' that.'*

Whatever this was, it wasn't Hungary. But, by Scotland's modest standards, it counted as a third small act of rebellion; it was almost subversive. *Palgrave's Golden Treasury* was not burned. On the contrary, it continued to be extensively stocked in Scottish schools, where boys curled up with a good poem about elves and dewdrops before trotting off with their molls to the Victoria Cinema for one of Dr Seller's improving lectures. In 1994, two years before his death, Norman MacCaig was himself represented in a new edition of *Palgrave's Golden Treasury*, along with his wild drinking friend from Milne's Bar, Christopher Grieve, who was not much of an English romantic either.

In the weeks of Suez and Hungary there was a fourth act of Scottish rebellion: the only important one in the series. Janet Mitchell became the first woman to be evicted from her house as a result of a court ruling that a deserted wife was not entitled to take over her husband's tenancy. There were an estimated 7,000 deserted wives in Scotland, so the ruling had potentially serious consequences. Janet Mitchell stood defiantly outside her house in Melrose after sheriff's officers carried her furniture down the narrow stair and past the ground-floor flat occupied by her elderly landlords. She announced that, although she had found somewhere else to live, she had allowed the eviction to go ahead in order to expose the unfairness of the law.

VI

At the end of the year, among the nominations of 'Books of the Year' in the Scottish press, new fiction by Scottish writers was not much rated. Three exceptions were *Tunes of Glory* by James Kennaway (whose promising career was cut short by a heart attack at the age of 40); George Scott-Moncrieff's *Burke Street*; and *Guests of War* (a tale of evacuees) by Robin Jenkins, who was teaching in the east end of Glasgow at the time.

The folklorist F Marian McNeill was nominated for *The Scots Cellar*, a celebration of the national traditions of hospitality and libation. Born in Orkney, a daughter of the manse, McNeill travelled as a young woman in France and Germany, worked as an organiser for the suffrage movement in London, and conducted an inquiry into the welfare of girls in English and Welsh towns. Further travels followed – to Greece, Eygpt and Palestine – before she returned to Scotland to work on the staff of the Scottish National Dictionary. She wrote a history of Iona and a semi-autobiographical novel, *The Road Home*, was closely involved in the home rule movement, and helped to revive the tradition of New Year revels at the Tron Kirk in Edinburgh: all in all, a remarkable Scotswoman.

But *The Bulletin* was less enthralled by the old Scottish traditions than by the thrill of the new: 'It's the latest novelty idea for party-giving.' Just as the sun was setting on the British empire, the curry supper arrived. With the humiliation of retreat from Suez – most of the troops were home for Christmas – the *Manchester Guardian* recovered all its lost circulation and gained many new readers. The paper dropped Manchester from its masthead and moved to London. From there it chronicled not only the decline of Britain's power and influence in the world, but a social revolution in which the curry supper was destined to play an important part – even in Scotland, home of such plain fare as the philosophical dumpling.

1957
THE PLYWOOD HILLS

I

The quote in its historical form may have been the work of some unsung sub-editor with a small talent for paraphrase. Harold Macmillan, Britain's new Prime Minister, did not actually utter the words: 'You've never had it so good.' What he did say, addressing a Conservative Party rally in Bedford on 20 July 1957, was: 'Indeed, let's be frank about it, most of the people have never had it so good. Go around the country, go to the industrial towns, go to the farms, and you will see a state of prosperity such as we have never had in my lifetime – nor, indeed, ever in the history of this country.'

The significance of the statement was missed by the press. The *Glasgow Herald*, concentrating on more prosaic aspects of the speech, buried the quote in a report headed with almost paralysing dullness: 'Premier on "worrying" problem of rising prices'. The editorial comment was dominated by a bus strike in the west of Scotland and a small rebellion in Oman; there was no mention of people never having had it so good. Yet the saying caught on as a symbol of Britain during the buoyant early years of Macmillan's premiership – minus an important qualification. He did not claim to be referring to the condition of all the people, only most of them, leaving open the possibility that the country he had in mind did not include the nation of his ancestor Daniel, a crofter on the island of Arran. How, then, stood Scotland in July 1957?

II

The month began with a heatwave. Golf correspondents in St Andrews for the Open Championship reported that the old grey town had seen little or no rain for six weeks. One wrote that the Old Course was burned to a hue lighter than brown and that the yellowhammers hopping on the fairways were distinguishable mainly by their movement. A close finish was anticipated, but the championship ended in anti-climax as Bobby Locke made it a leisurely stroll in the sunshine. The South African – 'a model of the perfectly relaxed player' – impressed spectactors by expending as little energy as possible.

In the same blazing conditions a less attractive July ritual was enacted: the annual procession of the Grand Orange Lodge of Scotland. It was estimated that 50,000 took part, mainly from lodges in the west of Scotland, and the line of marchers through Hamilton extended for miles. There were many reports of badly blistered feet and hands raw from wielding drum-sticks in the heat. In the cool of the evening bottles were thrown during disturbances at Hamilton Cross and police made 20 arrests.

On the night of Glasgow Fair Friday a quarter of a million people passed through Central Station, most on the way out. British Rail coped with the demand by borrowing 2,300 extra coaches from other regions in the network. Between seven in the evening and three in the morning a southbound train from Glasgow passed through Carlisle every nine minutes. Disappointed that they were not going on holiday with their friends, six-year-old Peter Blair and five-year-old Peter Lee, both of Glasgow, boarded a London express at St Enoch Station and hid under a table in one of the dining cars. They were found by a member of the catering staff, escorted from the train at Carlisle, and put on an express back to Glasgow.

On the same Friday 65 couples were married in the Martha Street registrar's office in Glasgow, which stayed open into the evening to deal with the holiday rush. There was the usual run on deposits at the Glasgow Savings Bank.

Rothesay – 'the Riviera of Scotland' – broke all records for holiday traffic. By then the sunshine had been succeeded by 'the usual Fair weather' as one soggy tourist put it. Among the locals there were long faces over the threat to withdraw the submarine depot ship Adamant from Rothesay Bay to the Gareloch. The island of Bute had come to depend on the spending power of 1,200 navy men, and some of Rothesay's boarding houses had been converted into married quarters.

In Glasgow the summer show, *Five Past Eight*, opened at the

Alhambra Theatre. The two stars, Jimmy Logan and Stanley Baxter, joined a skiffle group, Baxter amusing the audience with his antics on the washboard, 'absent-mindedly taking a scrub at his own pullover now and then'. Logan told members of Glasgow Rotary Club in a lunchtime speech that the Scottish theatre appealed to a family audience, 'and therefore the comedy must be kept clean'. In Rothesay the fun was as clean as fun could be: at the seaside Pavilion, holiday-makers flocked to a milk-drinking contest.

Another of the Clyde resorts, Largs, was suffering from a slight case of injured civic pride. Councillor William Reoch claimed that half the passengers on a train from Glasgow were sitting on newspapers because the seats were so dirty. 'We cannot have people coming here, the men in summer suits and the women in their summer frocks, and having their clothes spoiled.' But better to endure a squalid train to the Ayrshire coast than languish in a soot-black city of random anarchy. A resident of Maryhill complained to the press that children 'tear down the telephone lines, prise concrete facing from the walls, dig out the plaster from the masonry, and flood the place by breaking into the wash-house and turning on all the taps ... they sit and even stand on window ledges, thump on the windows, and if any are open at the bottom, spit into the room'.

Perth, of douce reputation, was scandalised by an incident on the last day of term at the academy, when senior boys acquired a full-sized skeleton and hung a makeshift gibbet from the roof; a week earlier they had imprisoned the janitor in a garret at the top of the building. John Kerr, the rector, blamed oversized classes for the misbehaviour of his pupils, but there were dark hints of a deeper malaise in Scottish education. Neville George, a professor at Glasgow University, criticised the 'barbarism' of the teachers, suggesting that some of their practices would have been 'looked into in the days of Wilberforce'; he added that many took it for granted that the child had to be driven to learn.

The teaching profession was outraged by George's candour, yet the facts supported his view that, among the consumers, there was an almost universal loathing of the system. The pupils at Perth had at least gone on to finish the course; most didn't. During a debate in the Scottish Grand Committee, John Rankin, the Labour MP for Govan, deplored the waste of talent. In his city only 10% of the boys and girls who entered secondary schools every year were still there in fifth year. The position in Scotland as a whole was only marginally better. In the year to June 1956 85% of pupils left secondary education before the age of 16. Walter Elliot wondered why. He looked in despair at the curriculum with its emphasis on subjects of little practical use. Of all the 'bilge and balderdash inflicted upon children', he put trigonometry very high indeed; he called it 'a weariness of the flesh'.

There was a more general weariness. George Lawson, the Labour MP for Motherwell, said that, among the pupils who left early, there were 'many of the highest intelligence who have no desire to go on'. Most young people preferred the alternative of work, and it was a measure of Harold Macmillan's claim to prosperity that there was plenty of it around. In Lawson's own constituency, with the opening of the Ravenscraig steel works in June 1957, the outlook had never been brighter.

III

But not all the workers left in a carefree mood for their destination of choice – to milk-drinking Rothesay, faraway Llandudno, or the more exotic Isle of Man. Dundee's 20,000 jute workers set off, if they could afford to go on holiday at all, uncertain of their future. A thousand of them were unemployed, many more on short time, and in the week of Macmillan's speech, Sir David Eccles, president of the Board of Trade, declared that protectionism was operating against the interests of customers. It was less expensive to import jute sacks – the staple product of the industry – than to buy them at home, yet users of the product were obliged to support the Dundee mills.

The commercial logic against protectionism was inescapable and had been recognised by post-war governments of both parties, but the phasing-out of so-called 'jute control' was a matter of extreme sensitivity. One of the city's Labour MPs, John Strachey, accused Eccles of 'sacrificing Dundee not to Tory principles, but to his own intense doctrinaire laissez-faire liberalism', while another, George Thomson, saw it as a breach of the undertaking given by successive governments that jute control would be preserved intact. This was not strictly true. A young Harold Wilson, when he was doing Eccles's job at the Board of Trade, had made a first tentative attempt to address the problem of jute control almost a decade earlier.

The responses of Strachey and Thomson also conveniently ignored the effective management of Dundee's transition from 'Juteopolis', the jute capital of the world, to a more mixed industrial centre less dependent on a single declining source of employment. By 1957 National Cash Registers ('The Cash' as it was known locally) had been established in the city for 11 years; another American multi-national, Timex, for 10. The policy of directing industry to Dundee was, indeed, so brilliantly accomplished that in 1949 the local jute barons, concerned about the poaching of their workers, petitioned the Board of Trade to halt any further influx. Unhappily for Dundee the Attlee government gave this self-interested appeal a sympathetic hearing and the flow of clean new jobs almost dried up.

By the early 1950s only 18% of Dundee's workforce was still employed in jute. By the late 1950s it was rather less. But the jute lobby remained so powerful that the industry continued to receive some government protection, though to a diminishing extent. Jute control finally came to an end as late as 1969, and the last mills staggered on into the 1990s. The jute barons' mansions in Broughty Ferry, a salubrious suburb overlooking the Tay, survived as monuments to the fortunes made by the few at the expense of the exploited majority. The mills themselves – as many as 131 at one time – were either pulled down or converted into smart apartments. One became a jute museum.

There was never much to celebrate about jute, although a few of its historians managed to create an aura of mercantile romance around it. The sacks, roughly fashioned out of raw material imported from the Indian sub-continent, transported many of the goods of the Victorian age, including America's vast cotton crop; they were also widely used in Europe and Asia, prompting the boast that Dundee was the world's first globalised city. But the boom was short-lived. A Calcutta newspaper reported in 1878 that Dundee had exported three million tons of jute to California one year and only 300,000 tons the next. The explanation was ominous: the Indians had promptly learned how to make these sacks – what is more, they had been taught to do so by opportunistic Dundonians – and they were making them more cheaply than the Scots. A death warrant had been signed, but protectionism ensured that it took almost a century to execute it.

Jute had a dreadful effect on the health of the people. The barons preferred to employ women because they could pay women less, and children as young as nine because they could beat them into working harder. Many of the workers went deaf from the racket of the machines and developed serious respiratory illnesses caused by the fine dust – 'stoor' – produced by the raw material, which clogged their eyes, mouths and noses. Jute changed the character of Dundee. In most households women were the main providers, an extraordinarily tough, hard-drinking breed, 'overdressed, loud and bold-eyed' as one traveller found them. The stereotype proved hard to shift, 'Juteopolis' morphing seamlessly into 'She Town'.

When the Scottish journalist James Cameron worked briefly in Dundee in the late 1920s he was repelled by its desolation, seeing it as a symbol of the depression, even despair, gripping industrial Britain. He was struck by the contrast between its intrinsic ugliness and the natural grace of its setting on a firth of breadth and grandeur and its pastoral hinterland. To Cameron it resembled Naples, though only notionally. He soon felt the impact of its brutal melancholy, the shocking paradox between the hovels of Hilltown and the opulence of Broughty Ferry, the unnatural structure of its society. The mills were idle; the many chimneys had ceased to smoke. In a community with a working population of 70,000, more than 40,000 were on the dole. Cameron witnessed a morally exhausted people and represented them in one hunchback in the Overgate, a reject of the jute industry. Dundee confirmed his instinctive socialism.

A native of the city, George Chalmers, who began writing in prison while serving a sentence for bank robbery, described his childhood experiences of Dundee in the mid-1950s. The mills were functioning again, the chimneys smoking, but otherwise the physical environment seemed little changed in 30 years; the Dundee evoked by James Cameron was recognisable still. Chalmers was brought up near the docks, sleeping under the table of a single-end. When, sometime in the year of never-had-it-so-good, he visited the house of one of Dundee's tough women, she held out a hand 'limp with gold charms'. 'What's that smell, missis?' he asked, looking over at a pot in the kitchen. 'That's the smell o' Italian coffee – when it's almost ready,' she replied. Two thimble-sized cups and tiny saucers were set out ceremoniously on a shiny, blood-red formica-topped table. The child observed that, when she moved to the sink and turned one of the taps, in a few seconds, after a splutter or two, hot water came out. He was astonished. 'You get hot water inside yir hoose?' he asked. She didn't answer, except to smile and run a red fingernail down his cheek. He never forgot her touch.

Many years later Chalmers re-visited the Dundee of his youth. The slums near his home had been flattened to make way for a multi-storey car park, 'where real horse-power once pulled laden jute carts to various mills scattered round town'. He had arrived habitually late for school, sometimes with horse sweat in his nose and dung on his shoes. 'Just a guttersnipe,' snapped Miss Moffat, as she administered four strokes of the belt to the palms of her incorrigible pupil.

IV

George Chalmers was not the only child who slept under the table in a single-end. Seven out of 10 people in Dundee in 1957 lived in houses of one or two apartments. In Scotland as a whole half the 1.4 million houses were at least 75 years old, 180,000 (13%) consisted of one room in which all the cooking, eating, living and sleeping was done, and 300,000 (21%) had no internal sanitation.

Although Dundee was very bad, Glasgow was the worst housed city in Macmillan's Britain. In a speech to the House of Commons in November 1956 John Rankin delivered a shaming indictment of conditions in his own constituency of Govan, which he likened to the slums of Kowloon:

I was in Hong Kong in the middle of September. With some Chinese friends I visited some of the houses on the waterfront at Kowloon. I saw one house where 12 or 13 people were living. The Chinese tend to live in a sort of family community. The house had three apartments and was a terrible place. There is no argument about that. It was dark and the sleeping spaces completely lacked the ordinary comforts we associate with a bed. Strangest of all, above my head there was a sort of cage in which one or two of the family were able to sleep.

When I tried to impress on those people that I did not need to come to Hong Kong or Kowloon to see housing conditions of that sort but that they were comparable with some of the homes I know in my division, they found it difficult to believe.

Three years ago on Christmas Day I was summoned to a home in Blackburn Street. Eleven people were living there, a widow with 10 children. Her husband, a docker, had been killed at his work. They were living in the top flat, a single apartment. There was a boy of 19, an apprentice on Clydeside, a girl of 17, a typist in a city office, and so on, down to a little fellow of two years of age. The gas had to be kept alight because it was almost impossible to see the way about even at two o'clock in the afternoon. There was only one bed, and I reckoned that if three slept at the top and three at the bottom that was six accounted for, and once that number was disposed of the rest of the family would find a place to lie down in the remaining part of the house. That was an example of the state of affairs in my division three years ago. At the door were four pails for the ordinary conveniences and facilities of civilised life. I did not need to go to Kowloon merely to see conditions which, though indescribable, I find at home.

This summer before I left for China and the Far East I visited certain parts of Govan division. On the first Sunday in August I went to Hoey Street and stood in houses where there were no ceilings at all except for paper, with brown paper backing, which made a sort of makeshift. In one close in Hoey Street 70 people had to use one lavatory. Of course, I know that something can be done about that, but such a feeling of despair has been created in many parts of Glasgow because of the inaction of the government that folk simply sit and complain among themselves instead of going to their member of parliament.

Official statistics gave a sobering perspective to Rankin's depiction of life in Govan in the middle years of the 20th century. The Westwood report on Scottish housing, published in 1943, had stated that Scotland needed half a million new houses. By 1957 a quarter of a million had been built. But the existing stock had deteriorated so badly in the interim that the target was now 400,000, only 20% less than it had been 14 years earlier.

The Earl of Dundee, speaking in a House of Lords debate in July 1957, expressed his frustration at the slow rate of progress, particularly in clearing Glasgow's slums. He urged on Glasgow Corporation a policy of building high-rise flats as an alternative to removing large numbers of people to other parts of the country. He could not believe that an ambitious programme of high-rise building would cost more than dispersal. 'I hope we are not going to sit back and say that these horrible housing conditions which have disgraced Scotland for so long must go on,' he declared.

Glasgow Corporation had not done badly. Since housing

became a municipal responsibility after the war, it had built 100,000 new homes for rent. The nature of the problem was one of immense scale, overcrowding being officially 20 times worse in Glasgow than it was in comparable English cities such as Birmingham and Manchester. The hangover from the Industrial Revolution remained severe and the Earl of Dundee's proposed cure overlooked some obvious dangers. The concentration of population in areas dominated by high-rise was startling: 700 people to the acre, a density without parallel in any other civilised city in the world. Yet no one in power seemed to have grasped the potential social consequences of replacing one form of overcrowding in intimate tenement closes with another in anonymous tower blocks.

In Edinburgh, where the housing shortage was less acute, the municipal addiction to multi-storey flats went unquestioned. They were even championed on aesthetic grounds – as a pleasing alternative to the 'monotony of cottage-type dwellings and their mostly indifferent gardens'. Occasionally simple humanity did prevail. Dunbarton County Council decided against the installation of windowless bathrooms in their houses on the Kildrum estate in the new town of Cumbernauld.

As the public sector struggled for answers to the continuing housing crisis, the Macmillan government, in the face of fierce opposition, pushed through one of the most controversial pieces of post-war legislation – the 1957 Rent Act. The law was designed ostensibly to stimulate the availability of privately rented property by removing statutory restrictions on rents which had been in place since the first world war. In practice it became a charter for unscrupulous landlords; a term unknown in 1957, Rachmanism, would enter the language as a result. In Glasgow the symptoms of the new free for all were swiftly apparent. When a firm of chartered surveyors advertised 12 houses to let in various parts of the city, the first on the market since the passing of the act, the telephone rang every 10 seconds. Inquirers were informed that they should think about offering double the advertised rent.

Little boys would continue to sleep under the table for a while yet, and sometimes they were safer there. The High Court heard that, when the lights went out at a wedding reception in a house in Castlemilk, one of Glasgow's peripheral estates, a guest realised that he was 'the marked man in the company' and had his face slashed with a razor.

V

In the absence of external distractions in such places as Castlemilk, they made their own amusements. Scotland's relatively primitive quality of life was cannily noted by a Canadian businessman, Roy Thomson, before he set up his latest venture, a commercial television station. He did not see it as a problem: quite the opposite. The founder of Scottish Television prophesied that TV would have a greater impact in Scotland than in the United States, where there was a greater choice of amenities competing for a viewer's time. He was wrong: prosperous Americans got just as hooked on the box as the poor people, and, being American, they had more channels for the satisfaction of their addiction.

Thomson, the son of a hard-boozing barber with Scottish roots, had interests in publishing, oil and travel, expanding his empire mostly with borrowed money. He had not heard of the adage that no one on their death bed ever wished they had spent more time at the office; or, if he had, he scorned it. He positively longed to die at work, in London, Toronto, or wherever else he happened to be tending his many enterprises. In old age he complained of the infirmities which occasionally kept him from his desk; in the end he cut his prodigiously long working week, but only slightly.

When he bought *The Scotsman*, a national newspaper though an enfeebled one, in 1956, he made an inspired appointment as editor. Alastair Dunnett, a man of flair and passion, appealed to Thomson's instincts. Dunnett had an unhappy time at school and, as soon as he could, left to make his way in the world. He got a job in the Commercial Bank of Scotland, not a natural home for a 15-year-old of his spirit and ambition. With a friend, Seamus Adam, he founded a magazine for boys, *The Claymore*, persuading the bank to buy advertising space. He entered full-time journalism, first with *The Bulletin*, then with the *Daily Record* (to which he returned as editor after the war).

He had the good fortune during the war to work as one of Tom Johnston's inner circle at the Scottish Office, helping Johnston to shape his practical vision of developing hydro-electricity and tourism in a Scotland at peace. The riches of oil had not been dreamt of, but when they were, Dunnett was Thomson's man to manage the Claymore field, commemorating the little magazine of his youth. So Alastair Dunnett ended his career not as a journalist but as an oil mogul.

Thomson went into television to make money, diverting to his papers such profits as he cared to release. He had an unsentimental view of both media. He described the editorial matter in newspapers as 'the stuff you separate the ads with' and politically he was straightforward: 'I've got money, so I'm a Conservative.' He was, however, a fairly admirable press magnate as press magnates go: Dunnett enjoyed editorial freedom during his 16-year reign at *The Scotsman* and used it to promote policies generally unfriendly to Conservatism. Thomson never hired anyone of comparable quality at Scottish Television. He made do with second-raters, with predictable results. But, in his own words, it was 'a licence to print money'. He printed a lot of it.

The launch in Glasgow, on 31 August 1957, may have given the wrong impression. A variety show from the stage of the Theatre Royal, big and glossy, a gala occasion, it drew to the pavements of Hope Street crowds 'searching hopefully for personalities'. The audience – 700 of them – arrived in evening dress, but the heat in the auditorium, aggravated by arc lamps, was intense. Fur wraps were removed as soon as decently possible; souvenir programmes served as fans. Andrew Hood, the Lord Provost of Glasgow, described it as 'a national occasion of historic importance to Scotland as a whole, the inauguration of a development of supreme significance in which we are all proud and privileged to participate'. Even by the standards of civic speeches, this was fruity. There is no record of Roy Thomson wincing.

Sir Kenneth Clark, patrician chairman of the Independent Television Authority, delivered a more realistic appraisal of the prospects for Scottish viewers: 'Athough the worst of the variety programmes which will reach you on the network will be rather foolish and rather vulgar, they will be no worse than those to which you have been accustomed by our august rival.' Such programmes, said Clark, posed 'in an acute form the old problem of democracy: to what extent ought one to give people exactly what they want?' Clark himself went on to present a much-lauded series entitled *Civilisation* on a channel of the august rival and was henceforth known to *Private Eye*, the satirical magazine, as Lord Clark of Civilisation.

The opening production at the Theatre Royal was a version of civilisation in Scotland. It included a film about the glories of the country, 'mellifluously spoken when he could remember the words' by the actor James Robertson Justice. 'The whole thing culminated as might have been prophesied,' said one critic, 'with a pipe band marching down the plywood hills.' Colin Maclean in *The Bulletin* praised the production as 'slick and skilful' and said that the kilted tenor Kenneth McKellar had been given 'the predominance he deserved'. He was less impressed by the 'lush lugubrieties' of James Robertson Justice, the use of the word lugubrieties almost justifying the expense of hiring the mellifluous thespian in the first place.

The inaugural evening also included *Wyatt Earp* and *Val Parnell's Saturday Spectacular* as well as ads for 'Rael-Brook Toplin, the shirt you don't iron' and Duncan's chocolates. Sunday brought, among other delights, a sermon from George MacLeod on 'Doubt and the Damned' – the title perhaps a premonition of Monday lunchtime and the first edition of the *One O'Clock Gang*, a daily live entertainment from the Theatre Royal, which Thomson had acquired as the headquarters of his station.

The *One O'Clock Gang* appears to have been Thomson's personal inspiration, his cunning response to a demand from the Independent Television Authority that the station must make eight hours of local programmes a week. A dismayed Thomson, confronted with the alarming possibility that this would cost serious money, worked out that 40 minutes of variety each weekday would not only fill some of the yawning airtime, but would dispense with the need to pay crews overtime. He gave an instruction that only the cheapest comics should be hired, and when he heard that the producer had employed a five-piece band, his response was to fire four of them and buy a Wurlitzer organ. Several years later when Charles Hill, Clark's successor as chairman of the ITA, came to Glasgow and bore witness to the *One O'Clock Gang*, he asked ('for God's sake') how long this rubbish had been going on. The long-running confection came to an end, but not before Kenneth Clark had had an answer to his question about the old problem of democracy.

The BBC in Scotland reacted to the brash newcomer with a mixture of complacency and distaste. Melville Dinwiddie, in a farewell broadcast after 23 years as regional director, made no attempt to disguise his disenchantment. He predicted that the extension of the BBC's television service, and the coming of commercial TV, would 'increase the problem of family discipline and give parents the difficult task of deciding when to have their sets on for family listening and viewing and when to shut them off and give time for other home occupations'.

His successor, Andrew Stewart, cautiously welcomed a new transmitter at Rosemarkie, 'a quite extraordinary place, nothing between you and Siberia', but dismissed any idea of giving Thomson a run for his money: 'If the BBC were to throw away their standards by wholesale competition, they would be better to be put out of business.' On the opening night of Scottish Television Stewart refused to distract BBC viewers with some enticing alternative. Gordon Gildard, one of his deputies, contented himself with the thought that 'natural curiosity will make them switch channels, but they'll be back soon enough to rejoin the familiar, once the fuss is over'.

The BBC's only concession was the introduction of a Scottish news summary on television. It closely resembled the radio bulletins on the Scottish Home Service, lasted five minutes, and was read in a formal way by staff announcers. Two reporters, John Lindsay and Maurice Lindsay (no relation), lent some journalistic credibility to the modest enterprise. But the only serious creativity came from the drama department, whose producers Pharic Maclaren, James Mactaggart and Finlay J Macdonald were men of skill and originality, a brilliant trio scattering seeds in a barren landscape. Unchallenged, Roy Thomson went on printing money with his licence. He at least had never had it so good.

1958

A GIFTED SPEAKER

I

The smartly dressed young man entered the dock of the High Court in Glasgow, yawned, flicked dust off his blazer and folded his arms. It was the first appearance of Peter Manuel, the central figure in a case billed by the press as the 'trial of the century'. He stood accused of eight murders.

There were only 60 seats in the public benches, and the queue for places started to form around 7.30 the night before. William Perryman, 42, unemployed, the first to arrive, wearing a thin overcoat and scarf to protect him from the chill wind of a Scottish spring, had brought a slice of toast to sustain him through his all-night vigil. Sitting on the stone ledge of the court building, Perryman told reporters that he knew Manuel and was determined to be present on the opening day of his trial. Other spectators were interviewed as they arrived, bit-part players in the soon to be unfolding drama.

Before a word of evidence was spoken the newspapers were anticipating the trial with barely suppressed excitement. They printed artists' impressions of how the court would look, with arrows pointing to places of interest around the room, accompanied by a mass of detail about such matters as the functionaries who would accompany Manuel in the dock ('two constables wearing hats and white gloves and carrying batons'), how many witnesses had been cited (280), how long the trial would last ('several weeks'), the number of journalists who had been accredited to cover it (68 'from all over the world'), the number of steps the prisoner would climb from the cells to the dock (17), and the melodramatic ritual – a fanfare of trumpets, if you please – which would herald the appearance of the judge every morning. Most papers carried potted biographies of the leading actors – Lord Cameron (Jock to his friends, who in a previous incarnation as Dean of the Faculty of Advocates had supported John MacCormick's home rule campaign); M G Gillies, the advocate depute who would lead the Crown case; Manuel's counsel, Harald Leslie, an Orcadian of booming voice, and his assistant W R Grieve.

There was no mention of the past life of Manuel himself, Scots law prohibiting any mention of an accused's previous convictions until his trial was over; nor could mug-shots of the prisoner be published. But there was no restriction on the obsessive chronicling of his every twitch in the dock. On the first day *The Bulletin* reported that he 'took frequent notes in a large notebook, and glanced occasionally at documents relating to the case'. The following day he 'stepped smartly into the dock looking fresh and again wearing his black blazer' [although it had been 'navy blue' in the same newspaper 24 hours earlier] ... he nodded and smiled to Mr W R Grieve QC, one of his counsel. A minute later he said "Good morning" when his leading counsel, Mr Harald Leslie QC, walked into court. Then the trumpets sounded, and the judge, Lord Cameron, took his seat at 10.14am'.

On day five, when Manuel turned up in 'a new checked shirt and a red tie', the snappy outfit made front-page news. This form of journalism was known in the trade as 'scene setting': it was reserved for events of the highest importance and derived some of its impact from the use of precisely recorded minutiae. Had Lord Cameron sat down at 10.15am, it would have sounded too approximate to be dramatically effective. Fortunately his bottom landed on the bench a minute earlier, giving the moment of contact a sense of theatre.

The breathless coverage, far from exaggerating the interest in the case, reflected it faithfully. No single event in Scotland's post-war history came close to stimulating the intense curiosity provoked by the trial of Peter Manuel. Serial killing (the term itself had still to be invented) was a new phenomenon in Scotland; all eight murders were committed within a small radius of Lanarkshire; one of the victims was a child, two of the others were scarcely more than children; the random nature of the murders, and their extreme violence, had instilled fear in the population. Cameron, in his summing-up, fairly described them as 'crimes whose gravity had not been equalled in this country for very many years'; he might have added, 'if ever'.

But the depravity at the centre of the case was only part of its fascination. The trial would reveal a dark sub-stratum of Scottish life, a world of seedy pubs and clubs, gangsters and guns; the ambiguity of the relationship between criminal lawyers and their clients; the incompetence of the police; the unexamined lives of the suburbs; the fragility of young people wandering the streets; the distinction between the psychopathic and the certifiably mad. For all these reasons, to say nothing of the bizarre oddities the case threw up, this was more than a trial; it was an episode in social history that continued to resonate long after the young man in the blazer was hanging from a rope. It chilled and thrilled in equally potent measure.

II

The first of the victims was 17-year-old Anne Kneilands – 'this poor, unfortunate, wretched girl, murdered most brutally and savagely' as Cameron put it – whose body was found near the fifth tee of East Kilbride golf course on 4 January 1956. Anne lived with her parents in East Kilbride and had a job as a machinist. On 2 January she left the house around 5pm. Her parents went out later to visit friends in Glasgow, and when they returned between 11pm and midnight, Anne was not at home. They were unconcerned. Anne was on holiday; they assumed she had gone to stay with relatives, though without a telephone in the house there was no way of checking. By the morning of the third day, when there was still no word, her father reported Anne's disappearance in person at Blantyre police station. A few hours later her body was discovered along with a few pathetic belongings – a pair of shoes, an ear-ring, a watch and a French coin.

George Gribbon, who made the discovery, saw that her head was open and that her right arm lay across her face. William Woods, a police inspector, said that Anne's shoes gave the appearance of having been sucked from her feet as she ran. There were scrapes and scratches which suggested that she had crashed over a barbed wire fence. David Mullen, a doctor who examined the body, found pieces of bone and brain tissue scattered on the grass; he described her head injury as 'very severe'.

Manuel was working in the area as a gas fitter at a new housing development. He was characteristically bold, even having a conversation with James Marr, a young policeman near the crime scene, who noticed that he had several scratches on his face. Richard Corrins, a Gas Board foreman in charge of Manuel's squad, challenged him about the scratches, asking him where he had got them. Manuel replied that he had been in a fight. Another of the squad said it seemed to him that the scratches had been inflicted by fingernails. A week later, when Manuel returned from work to the home of his parents, with whom he lived, he was told that the police had visited the house and taken away some clothes. James Hendry, a superintendent with Lanarkshire CID, asked him to account for his movements. Manuel said he had spent New Year's Day drinking heavily and that on 2 January he had watched television.

A few days earlier, at a post-Christmas party, Anne Kneilands had met Andrew Murnin, a young man home from the army, and arranged to meet him again at six o'clock on the evening of 2 January, at Capelrig Farm in East Kilbride, 'where the bus turned'.

Gillies (for the Crown): 'Did you keep that appointment?'

Murnin: 'No, sir.'

Gillies asked him why. Murnin paused, then said quietly: 'I went to a party on the Monday and met some friends.'

What happened to Anne Kneilands after she was stood up? She was never seen alive again – in Manuel's company or anyone else's. In a confession to the murder more than two years later, a confession subsequently denied, Manuel got the date wrong: he gave it as New Year's Day. He said that he arrived in East Kilbride around seven in the evening. 'At about 7.30, I was walking towards the Cross when I met a girl. She spoke to me and addressed me as Tommy. I told her my name was not Tommy, and she said she thought she knew me. We got talking, and she told me that she had to meet someone, but she did not think they were turning up for the meeting. After a while I asked her if she would like some tea or coffee … we went into the Willow Café.'

In the absence of any witness, the visit to the café may have been one of the many inventions of a professional liar. But the confession was more convincing in its account of what happened next: 'When we came out [of the café], she said she was going home, and I offered to see her home. She said she lived miles away, and I would probably get lost after I took her home. I insisted, and she said "All right". We walked along the road up to Maxwellton

Road. From there we went along a curving country road which I couldn't name. About halfway along this road I pulled her into a field gate. She struggled, and ran away, and I chased her across a field and over a ditch. When I got up to her I dragged her into a wood. In the wood she started screaming, and I hit her on the head with a piece of iron I picked up.'

Hugh Marshall, a local man who was out with his dogs, heard a sound from the golf course. 'It was a scream or a yell, a voice crying "Oh oh". Then I heard it again.'

Despite the police's suspicions at the time, Manuel continued to walk the streets.

III

Nine months later, on the morning of 17 September 1956, Helen Collison, the housekeeper of the Watt family in High Burnside, Lanarkshire, went to the back door of her employers' home, expecting to find it open. Unusually, it was locked.

'When I got no answer to my knocking,' she said, 'I chapped on Vivienne's bedroom.' Vivienne was the 16-year-old daughter of the Watts. 'There was no answer. I didn't want to disturb Mrs Watt, so I tried to ease up the window to call Vivienne. I got the window up two or three inches and looked into the bedroom. I could see a little table on the bedside which always bore a lamp and clock, and sometimes a glass of water. The table was completely bare. I could see the bed and what I thought was a figure at the foot. At the top of the bed all the clothes were turned down.' She fetched a neighbour. They went on knocking without response. Then the postman arrived. He put his hand through a broken panel in the front door and turned the handle. The door opened; Helen Collison entered the house alone.

'I went into Mrs Watt's bedroom. I could see they were both dead, Mrs Watt and Mrs Brown [Marion Watt's sister].' She said that daylight filtering through the curtains enabled her to identify them. She went from there into Vivienne's bedroom.

'Vivienne was covered up with bedclothes. The pillow was covered with blood. I heard three or four big snores from the bed. I went straight out.'

'You are quite clear you heard snores?' asked Gillies.

'Yes, sir.'

When Arthur Nelson, a doctor, arrived at the house he was told that one woman was still alive. He went straight to Vivienne's room and saw that she was not long dead. She had a bullet wound close to her left eye, and her face was still warm. Nelson went from there to the front bedroom and saw that both women had been shot near the eyes. They were lying 'very peacefully, as if they were asleep'. Nelson concluded that they had been dead for a number of hours.

A next-door neighbour and friend of Vivienne, Deanna Maria Valente, described by the press as 'a 19-year-old attractive brunette', visited the Watts' bungalow the night before the murders. While Marion Watt and Margaret Brown listened to records in the living room, the two girls chatted in Vivienne's bedroom. Around 10.30pm the phone rang. It was William Watt, Vivienne's father. He asked to speak to his daughter. After Vivienne took the call she was annoyed. She told Deanna that he had just cut off her allowance.

Deanna left the house 20 minutes before midnight. Vivienne's last words to her were: 'I'll see you tomorrow.' The women were still listening to music and when Deanna got back to her own house she said it took her 'rather a long time to get to sleep' because of the racket from next door.

Marion Watt suffered from a heart complaint and often stayed in bed until three in the afternoon. But that night she was not only cheerful but appeared to be well. Deanna said that she had never seen Mrs Watt looking so well. She was dressed in a blue sweater and a black pleated skirt. 'She looked very happy,' Deanna recalled. At least one of the women was drinking.

Gillies asked if she and Vivienne ever discussed what Vivienne wore in bed. Deanna said that she wore 'a jersey and things' to keep her warm.

'Did Vivienne ever say to you that she wore a brassiere in bed?'

'That is not a nice thing to say to anyone,' Deanna replied sharply, and the question of Vivienne's bra was not pursued.

At 1.26am the local telephone exchange received a call from Stonelaw 4055 – the number of the Watt house. It requested an alarm call for 7am. Manuel is believed to have broken into the house around 6am. He wrote in his confession: 'I went in and opened a bedroom door. There were two people in bed. I went into the other room and there was a girl in bed. She woke up and sat up. I hit her on the chin and knocked her out. I tied her hands and went back to the other room. I shot the two people in the room and then heard someone making a noise in the other room. I went in and the girl had got loose. We struggled around for a while and then I flung her on the bed and shot her too.'

The police arrived at the house at 9.20am. Andrew McLure, a superintendent, found a watch under Vivienne's pillow which had stopped at 2.52am. Cameron wanted to know if there was anything to indicate whether the two women were asleep or awake when they were shot. McLure thought from the position of the bodies that they had been asleep. But he formed a different impression of Vivienne. Clothing was scattered round a wicker chair, and he found a broken lamp base and pieces of a light bulb. These details supported Manuel's subsequent account.

A few nights before he murdered the women, Manuel was drinking in the aptly named Crook Inn in Uddingston. He pulled a gun out of his waistband and showed it to a customer in the pub. With his other hand he pulled out some bullets. On the eve of the murders, while music blared from the front room of the Watts' house, Manuel was boasting to a customer in another pub that he had recently put a gun against the head of a cow, pulled the trigger at the cow's nostril, and shot it.

IV

William Watt was on a fishing holiday in Argyll, staying at the Cairnbaan Hotel in Lochgilphead, when his wife, daughter and sister-in-law were killed. He had been there for several days and was a well-known visitor at the Cairnbaan. Ruby Leitch, the proprietor, said that Watt had told her that he wanted to go out fishing at 6am because 'the river was in good order and he wanted to get at it before breakfast'. If Watt did as he intended, then he was out fishing while Peter Manuel was breaking into his house 85 miles away. There was, however, some suggestion that he slept in that morning. Ruby Leitch woke around 7.30am and an hour later she heard a car pulling into the hotel grounds. It was Watt.

The timing was critical. Although, as Ruby Leitch pointed out, the Loch Lomond road was 'very bad, very twisty' and the journey from Lochgilphead took at least two and a quarter hours, Watt had more than enough time to drive from the hotel to his home, commit three murders, and get back to the Cairnbaan for breakfast. This macabre theory was not wholly implausible. John Taylor, night ferryman on the Renfrew ferry, insisted that William Watt was a passenger on his boat around 3am. Taylor was inconsistent about the make of Watt's car, but his evidence impressed the police, particularly when a second witness came forward. Roderick Morrison, an engineer, said he encountered a car being driven at high speed between Luss and Inverbeg around 2.30am. 'I saw the driver of the car smoking,' said Morrison. 'He was sitting smoking with his hand level with the dash and his other hand across his face. I had never seen anyone smoking a cigarette in the way that man did.'

The police organised an ID parade and asked the men taking part in it to put their hands to their mouths in the singular manner of the smoker. Morrison picked out William Watt. He had seen the reckless driver at a distance of 25 feet for a few moments in the middle of the night, but the testimonies of these witnesses were together enough to persuade Lanarkshire CID that they had the killer. They charged Watt with the three murders and he spent 67 days in Barlinnie Prison, where he had a tough time from fellow inmates before being released. He was still regarded as the prime suspect.

Where was the motive? Watt was the part-owner of a successful bakery business in Glasgow. The shops were being refurbished and he was short of ready cash. Mrs Collison, the housekeeper, remembered that, a day or two after the bodies were found, Watt asked her for the keys of the bureau. He wanted to get hold of the 'society books' – the insurance policies. Mrs Collison, perhaps suspicious, asked him if he thought it had been a robbery. He thought not. A little piece of jewellery had been taken – Mrs Watt's watch. Then Mrs Collison said: 'Have they any idea who did it?', and Watt replied mysteriously that, if it was who he thought it was, he knew them. But financial gain had to be ruled out: when the police examined the 'society books' they discovered that the insurance policies on Marion Watt's life amounted to no more than £70 ('nowhere near providing a motive for a crime of this nature', as the judge observed).

There was another obstacle from the police's point of view. Why would Watt have chosen to kill his wife and daughter when he knew his sister-in-law was staying in the house? That left the familiar motive. Even it was slow off the starting block. Watt admitted that he had been unfaithful to his wife on several occasions, but Ruby Leitch of the Cairnbaan Hotel wasn't giving much away.

Grieve (for the defence): 'Have there ever been ladies staying in the hotel when Mrs Watt was not?'

'Yes, Mrs Milligan.'

'He knew her very well?'

'I do not know how well.'

At this point Ruby Leitch asked for a glass of water. Grieve, developing the innuendo, suggested that Watt, when he was told about the murders, had acted with surprising composure. Ruby Leitch replied: 'I am afraid I could not give an impression, as I was upset myelf.' This was not hugely supportive of Watt. A policeman who met him later in the day was actively incriminating. He claimed he told Watt: 'I thought I was going to bring back a broken-hearted man and I found a man with a smirk on his face and without a tear.' He claimed that Watt replied: 'I believe you are right, sergeant.' Watt denied this.

Manuel's counsel probed the relationship between the Watts. Grieve asked Helen Collison: 'Did you ever see them going out together on pleasure bent in the morning?'

On pleasure bent. Even the horrors of mass murder failed to disturb the arch prose of the Scottish Bar.

She replied coolly: 'A few times they went out, but I don't know whether it was on business or pleasure.'

Grieve persisted: 'Did Mr Watt go away quite frequently and stay away from the house?'

'When he was away fishing or shooting, he'd stay the night or a weekend, but not very often during my time there.'

If anyone needed a good lawyer it was William Watt. He had hired the most celebrated in Scotland, Laurence Dowdall. Some time after Watt's release from Barlinnie but before Manuel's arrest, Dowdall received a letter from Manuel. 'I would like you to come and see me on Wednesday,' he wrote. 'The proposals I have outlined are to our mutual advantage, mainly due to the fact that I have some information for you concerning a recently acquired client of yours who has been described as an all-round athlete – Yours sincerely, P. Manuel.' The all-round athlete was William Watt. Dowdall agreed to meet Manuel.

Manuel began by telling him that William Watt was innocent

and that he, Manuel, knew who murdered his family. Dowdall responded: 'If you know who did it, why don't you go to the police?' Manuel indicated that he didn't approve of the police. Dowdall asked for the name of the killer. When Manuel wouldn't give it, Dowdall said: 'You had better tell me something about it.' Manuel described the position of certain articles in the Watts' house, including a wardrobe in the hall, and the position of doors, including the door of what he called 'the girl's bedroom'. Later that day, Dowdall arranged with the police to see inside the house. He found that it fitted Manuel's description exactly.

Dowdall decided that Watt and Manuel should meet face to face. Watt understood that Dowdall would be present, but when Watt arrived at the Whitehall Restaurant in Glasgow city centre there was no sign of his solicitor. A barman came over and said that Dowdall had gone and that the man Watt had come to see was sitting in a corner. Watt went over and said: 'I suppose you are Manuel?', to which Manuel replied, 'Yes. Mr Watt?'

Early in the encounter Watt told Manuel that if he had anything to do with 'the Burnside affair' he would pull Manuel to bits.

The Burnside affair. It was an odd phrase for a victim to use about the murders of his wife and daughter.

'What is it you want to tell me?' Watt demanded. Manuel replied that he was suspicious of two men sitting at the next table and that he wanted to go somewhere else. They continued their conversation in the Crown Street Bar, where they drank heavily; Manuel later accused Watt of getting him drunk. Manuel repeated what he had told Dowdall but there were few new revelations about the murders of the Watts. There was, however, a reference to a murder earlier the same year. 'He [Manuel] put his hand in his pocket and took a photograph out. I recognised it. It was a photograph of Anne Kneilands which I had seen in the newspapers. She appeared to be paddling at the seaside, and was holding her skirt above her knees. I handed it back to him, and he tore it up into little pieces and put them in our ashtray.'

Dowdall did nothing to discourage further contact between his client and Manuel, who developed a friendship of sorts. In September 1957 the two men were close enough for Watt to invite Manuel to visit the house of his brother and business partner. John Watt was impressed by Manuel's familiarity with 'practically every stick of furniture' in William's house and by the easy relationship between his brother and Manuel – 'the Peter Manuel we have been hearing all about', as William introduced him. William told John that Manuel had given him 'a new slant on the matter'. The new slant, whatever it was, turned horribly sour in the High Court when Manuel accused William Watt of triple murder.

V

The social gathering in John Watt's house took place close to the first anniversary of the shootings. Manuel marked another notable milestone – the bludgeoning to death of Anne Kneilands in early January 1956 – with a second killing during the festive season.

On 28 December 1957 William Cooke and his wife left their house in Mount Vernon around 4pm. When they returned four hours later their 16-year-old daughter Isabelle had gone out to a dance. Unlike Anne Kneilands' friend who never showed up at the bus stop, Isabelle's date, Douglas Bryden, 17, faithfully waited 45 minutes at a pre-arranged meeting place in Uddingston. He remembered it as a windy, dry night. Eventually he gave up hope of Isabelle appearing. When her body was discovered she was wearing only a cardigan, a suspender belt, and a pair of nylon stockings. A bra was tied round her neck, a headsquare round her mouth. She was buried in a shallow grave in heavy soil. She had been strangled.

Manuel wrote in his confession that he had gone to Mount Vernon by bus. 'Just over the bridge I met a girl walking. I grabbed her and dragged her into a field ... I took her handbag and filled it with stones from the railway ... I flung it in a pond in the middle of a field ... I then made her come with me along towards the dog track. When we got near the dog track she started to scream. I tore off her clothes and tied something round her neck and choked her. I then carried her up the line into a field and dug a hole with a shovel.'

A shovel when it was needed. An iron bar when it was needed. Manuel always had an implement to hand at the critical moment.

When he was arrested 15 months later Manuel invited the senior policemen in charge of the case, Robert McNeill and Tom Goodall, to accompany him on a midnight trek to the site of the body. The three men were handcuffed together, Manuel in the middle, as the suspect stopped abruptly in a ploughed field and pointed to the ground. Manuel said: 'I think she is in there – I think I am standing on her.' The policemen started digging, without success at first, and the prisoner grew impatient. He said he would take them to a spot where they would find one of Isabelle's shoes. Manuel bent down, removed a brick, and unearthed a silver dancing shoe. They continued walking. Manuel stopped, pushed aside some ashes, and exposed the other shoe. Goodall said they should return to police headquarters, but Manuel insisted that they wait until Isabelle's body was discovered. At 2.15am it was.

Nine months elapsed between the death of Anne Kneilands and the triple murder in the Watt household; a further 15 months before Isabelle Cooke was killed. But there was only the briefest interlude before Manuel killed again, in the first hours of 1958.

The Smarts – Peter, 45, and Doris, 42 – were undecided about staying up for the New Year and half-thought of having an early night. They had originally intended to spend Hogmanay with Peter's parents in Jedburgh, but the weather broke and they didn't relish the prospect of travelling to the Borders on bad roads. Their neighbours in Uddingston, Stanley Jackman and his wife, went first-footing, returning around 2am. Jackman saw lights in the front room and kitchen – kitchenette as he called it – of the Smarts' bungalow. A little later, while he was seeing friends away, he noticed that only the kitchen light was still on. Within a few minutes it too was switched off. The Smarts had indeed gone to bed, though later than expected.

Meanwhile, in the Manuel household in Birkenshaw, just over a mile from Uddingston, a party continued through the night. Manuel's parents were there, his sister Teresa (a nurse at the Southern General Hospital), his brother James, and a cousin from America. Members of the family testified that they brought in the New Year watching TV, singing songs and drinking. Teresa was among the last to go to bed at 4.30am, leaving the two brothers. James said that when he turned in at 5.45am Peter was still up. Manuel claimed at his trial that he went to bed at 6am. An hour or so later 'everyone was getting ready to go to church. The place was like Central Station. I couldn't get to sleep'.

It was a poor alibi. It would have taken Manuel only 15 minutes to walk from his parents' house to the Smarts'. He maintained in his subsequent confession that he arrived at the Smarts' bungalow around 6am, got in through the kitchen window, went into a bedroom and took £38 in new notes from Peter Smart's wallet, which was in his jacket hanging over a chair. 'I shot the man first, and then the woman, and I then shot the boy [Michael, their 11-year-old son]. At first I thought it was a man in the bed. I then went into the living room and ate a handful of wee biscuits from a tray, and I got about 18 shillings from a red purse in the woman's handbag.'

Four hours later, at 10am on New Year's Day, when John Buchanan opened his shop in Birkenshaw, his first customer was Peter Manuel.

'Did you notice anything about his appearance?' asked Gillies.

'He was very well groomed.'

'More so than usual?'

'No, he generally was.'

'Was there anything unusual about his appearance?'

'The only unusual thing was that anyone at that time on New Year's morning was so well groomed.'

Manuel bought cigarettes – not his usual brand, Capstan, but five Woodbine. Manuel explained to the shopkeeper that he was short of money. He wasn't: he had stolen change in his pocket. There was no logical explanation for his pretence of poverty. But later that day he reverted to his usual reckless form, using some of the new notes from Peter Smart's wallet to buy drink in a local pub.

The following day, the second anniversary of Anne Kneilands' murder, he was bold enough to give a lift to a young policeman who had been assigned to search a river for clues to the murder of Isabelle Cooke. He and Manuel talked casually about the weather.

Several days passed in the suburbs of Uddingston. The sociability of Hogmanay had dissolved into the somnolence of the Scottish hangover season. On 6 January Smart's firm phoned his brother to say that he had not turned up for work after the Christmas and New Year holiday and that his car had been found abandoned. (Manuel had taken it to a car park the night after the murders.) Frank Hogg, a police sergeant, was sent to the house to investigate. All the windows and doors of the bungalow were locked and the curtains in the front room were drawn. Hogg got into the house by charging at the front door with his shoulder. He discovered the Smarts dead in bed in one room and Michael dead in bed in another. They had been shot through the head at close range, probably while they were asleep.

Manuel's revised story was that he had known Peter Smart for several years and had laid the flooring in his bungalow. Just before

Christmas Smart asked him if he could get a gun. Manuel asked him what it was for and Smart replied that he wanted to have it 'about the house'. Manuel said he could get a gun but that it was not up to much. On Hogmanay Smart phoned him and asked if he could get the gun that night. They arranged to meet in a pub. He and Smart had a discussion in the lavatory of the pub, where Manuel showed him how to load the gun and gave him bullets. Smart handed him money, refused a drink, and left. Smart also gave Manuel a key to his house, saying that the family were going on holiday on New Year's Day and that he wanted Manuel to go to the house because there was a man coming to see him and he had been unable to contact the man to put him off. When Manuel arrived at the Smart household he discovered the bodies.

'There was no doubt in my mind. I thought he had done his son in and then done his wife in, and then himself.' He took the gun, which he claimed was in Smart's hand. To this fanciful narrative he added the story of a cat, 'growling and squealing', who had bolted into the house when he opened the front door. The kindly visitor gave it a drink of water and some salmon; it was one of the few survivors of Manuel's homicidal adventures. Later he slung the gun into the Clyde.

Since Anne Kneilands' murder Lanarkshire CID's handling of events had been inept. They had charged one man, William Watt, with three murders then released him; they had suspected a second man, Peter Manuel, but pinned nothing on him; they had been slow to make connections between the murders; they had watched helplessly as the bodies piled up. Now, reluctantly, they involved their colleagues from Glasgow CID in the multiple investigation; Tom Goodall, an experienced detective, was put on the case. The new notes spent by Manuel in the pub were promptly traced back to Peter Smart; Manuel's extended run of luck was finally over. When the police arrested him at his parents' house, he told them: 'You can't take me, you haven't found anything yet.' Cameron, in his address to the jury, made much of the word 'yet'. He called it an 'unfortunate' choice. Its use inched Manuel closer to the condemned cell.

VI

On the tenth day of the trial there was an unexpected development. Cameron had just taken his seat on the bench when Manuel stood up. 'My Lord, before the examination of this witness [Goodall] begins, I would like to have an opportunity to confer with my counsel.' The court was adjourned. When it reconvened 45 minutes later Harald Leslie addressed Cameron in his usual orotund fashion: 'I have to inform your Lordship that I am no longer in a position, with my colleagues, to continue in this case. The panel is desirous of conducting the remainder of the trial.'

The judge turned to the accused: 'Manuel, do you now wish to conduct your own defence or would you like an adjournment of the case to enable you to instruct other counsel to proceed?'

In a firm voice Manuel replied: 'I will conduct my own defence for the remainder of the case.' He then launched into a ferocious cross-examination of his tormentor from the Glasgow CID. A court reporter noted: 'There was no sign of diffidence, no shyness, no fumbling of questions as he peppered Inspector Goodall with questions relating to the few days following his arrest.'

In the battle of wits Manuel was more than once a winner on points. He teased Goodall with the recollection of the midnight visit to the field in search of Isabelle Cooke's body.

'You contend that, in the dark, I just stopped, shoved aside a brick, and pulled out a shoe?'

'You did.'

'Why didn't you pick it up?'

'Because you beat me to it.'

'I could not beat you to it for I was handcuffed to you.'

'I think you reached down with the hand by which you were not handcuffed to me.'

The following day Manuel looked completely at ease as his own advocate, his left hand resting on his hip in the theatrical manner of the courtroom lawyer. He began by requesting the recall of William Watt, who had already been in the witness box for more than four hours. Cameron wanted a reason for bringing him back. 'I strongly object to the manner in which my counsel cross-examined … he left a great deal unsaid,' said Manuel. Cameron: 'Do you think it is going to do you any good?' – 'Yes, my Lord.'

Manuel, facing Watt from a distance of three yards, cruelly baited him about one of their meetings.

'Do you remember the part of the discussion wherein you described how you had carefully planned for months to kill your wife?'

'That is atrocious and a lie.'

'Do you remember the part of the discussion wherein you stated that, so carefully had you laid your plans, they had even involved changing your address?'

'That is a lie.'

'Do you remember describing to me that you could drive a car faster than Stirling Moss?'

'That is also a lie.'

'Do you remember that you said to me that when you shot your little girl Vivienne it would have required very little for you to turn the gun on yourself?'

'No.'

'Do you remember describing to me the manner in which you killed your wife?'

'I never did.'

Watt had been badly injured in a car accident and gave his evidence from a couch. As he was being wheeled out of the court at the end of his ordeal by accusation, he gave Manuel what one journalist described as 'a long, piercing look'.

Manuel then entered the witness box and, according to *The Bulletin*'s sketch-writer Malcolm Nicolson, 'enthralled the packed courtroom' and 'emerged in a new role – that of a persuasive, gifted speaker'. For six hours he gave a radically different account of his actions from the one contained in the confession, which he claimed was 'full of details that were absolutely idiotic – murdering people and burying them'. He agreed that the statements were in his own handwriting, but insisted that he had written them under duress after being informed by a policeman that his father had been arrested and taken to prison and would only be released if he confessed. He claimed that Goodall had told him: 'I know all about you, Peter – you are crazy. You definitely killed these people, but you didn't know what you were doing. You just go around the country killing people and then sort of forget about it. You need treatment. You're barmy. You're crackers.'

Goodall's version of how the confession came to be written in Bellshill police station was this: 'Manuel deliberated what he was going to write. After some minutes he wrote a little and stopped, considering what he was going to write. Then he completed the document. He read it over and then said, "This won't do. I'll write you another". Manuel took a fresh piece of paper and made a second statement.' When Gillies, for the Crown, put this to Manuel in cross-examination, Manuel replied that he had explained as carefully as he could his alternative version of events. He added testily: 'If it cannot penetrate I feel sorry for you.' Gillies murmured 'Very well, you feel sorry for me' and pressed on with his cross-examination. It was a revealing vignette: Manuel had momentarily lost his composure.

During Gillies's summing-up on the 14th day of the trial, the prisoner gave another of his yawns. The prosecutor's speech was methodical rather than inspired, not a match for Manuel's flashy rhetoric, and when Cameron came to address the jury he praised the remarkable skill with which the accused had presented his own case. But it seemed that this remarkable skill was not necessarily incompatible with madness. The judge noted that there was one plea that was not open to the jury to consider because it had not been entered – the plea of insanity. 'I say that for this reason, that the catalogue of crime is so formidable, and presents so many curious features, that it might be very easy to infer that, if the conclusion was reached that the hand responsible was that of the accused, that was the hand of a man who was not responsible for his actions.'

Before he sent the jury out Cameron directed it to find Manuel not guilty of the murder of Anne Kneilands. There was the confession, but he ruled that there was no corroborative support for it: there was nothing to link Manuel to the crime with the possible exception of the scratches on his face, for which there could have been an innocent explanation. Cameron clearly placed little weight on a witness's view that the scratches had been caused by fingernails, or the fact that the injuries inflicted on Anne were consistent with the chase described by Manuel, or the production of Anne's photograph in the company of William Watt. To this day the murder of Anne Kneilands formally remains an unsolved crime.

The requirement for corroboration, a distinctive feature of Scottish criminal justice, was an issue throughout a case in which the Crown depended heavily on the authenticity of a confession. Paradoxically the most striking corroboration placed William Watt southbound on the Loch Lomond road and shortly afterwards on the Renfrew ferry in a plausible chronology.

The jury returned at 4.45pm on 29 May after deliberating for two and a half hours: not guilty of the murder of Anne Kneilands, but guilty of all the others. Barely quarter of an hour later Cameron placed the black tricorn on his head and pronounced the death sentence, giving the date of execution as 19 June between 8 and 10am. A flushed Manuel turned and walked briskly down the steps to the cells. He left for Barlinnie Prison with the boos and jeers of the crowd in his ears. But it was not much of a crowd – about 100, mostly women – and there was almost a sense of anti-climax about the press coverage.

VII

From the condemned cell close to the execution chamber, Manuel planned an appeal which would prolong his life by a few weeks. The grounds were unsurprising: misdirection of the jury and a confession made under duress. The prison governor said that Manuel had 'taken to the verdict and sentence with equanimity and remained self-assured and jaunty'. But on 20 June, five days before the appeal was to be heard, prison staff noted a change. Manuel appeared to be 'feigning madness by acting strangely and adopting peculiar habits'. The doctors decided that his behaviour was 'a hysterical reaction' to his extreme predicament. On 25 June the Scottish Criminal Appeal Court threw out both grounds of appeal and set a new date for execution. Lord Clyde said there was no evidence of threat or pressure by the policemen who took his confession and that he had 'deliberately made up his own mind to unburden his soul of the dark deeds which he narrated with such convincing detail in statement number 142'.

Manuel, who was not present in court, had the news broken to him by his solicitor, John Ferns, who said that his client sat at the end of his bunk, 'showing no emotion whatever'. On 30 June a further report from psychiatrists cleared the way for execution. They decided that Manuel's behaviour was consciously motivated rather than a manifestation of insanity. He spent his last days listening to the radio. Rubber silencers were placed on the trapdoor in the execution chamber so that the prisoner would not be disturbed by the sound of rehearsals.

On the day of his death he rose at 6am and had a glass of whisky with breakfast; it was said that he walked calmly and unaided the 12 steps from his cell. A white hood was placed over his head seconds before he was hanged. At 8.01am on 11 July 1958 – two months to the day since he had stepped into the dock of the High Court, yawned, and flicked dust off his blazer – he was pronounced dead. John MacDougall, a Glasgow magistrate who attended the execution, said that Manuel said nothing, 'made no reference to anything'. Only 12 people gathered outside the prison and no notice of the execution was posted at the gates. He was buried in the grounds. Later that day his brother came with flowers for the grave. He was 31 years old.

VIII

Emilio Coia, a notable Scottish caricaturist who attended the trial, described Manuel as 'a small dark man with a big personality attractive to women, a thrusting dominating profile, fleshy nose, restless sensuous mouth and deep-set black eyes that are the coldest I have ever seen. He had the short stubby hand of the super-confident and the vanity which is found in most lacking stature'. Was this object of demonology, so vividly evoked through the perception of an artist, mad or bad?

Born in 1927 to Scottish parents in New York, he moved with his family to Britain at the age of five. He soon became a petty thief and went to approved school and borstal for a succession of offences. In 1946 he was sentenced to eight years' penal servitude for rape. When he murdered the Watts he was out on bail for burglary. A shocking record, though not markedly worse than many others – and, as he demonstrated at his trial, he was not without a raw adversarial ability.

Manuel dismissed the idea of pleading insanity when this was suggested to him by his defence team. He told Harald Leslie that he wanted to hear 'no more of that'. He may have been correct in his evaluation of his own clinical condition. Angus MacNiven, a doctor who examined him before the trial, wrote: 'The accused is quick and alert and appears to have a remarkable memory and gives what appears to be a lucid and connected narrative of events leading to his arrest. He never hesitates in his speech and is never at a loss to remember a detail. He tells a story in a remarkably detached manner, never showing any emotion and speaking as if the experiences he is describing were someone else's and not his own.' MacNiven concluded that Manuel was a psychopath, sane and fit to plead.

Manuel's sister, a certified mental nurse, told a second specialist who examined her brother that she had always thought he was a psychopath. But when the loyal Teresa entered the witness box, smiling warmly at the figure in the dock, she was careful to conceal her professional opinion. Invited by Cameron to say whether she had noticed anything unusual about his behaviour during the years of the Lanarkshire murders, she replied: 'I would not say any more unusual. To me it was usual behaviour. I have always known him the same.'

It was inevitable that many myths should develop around a case so riddled with ambiguities and unanswered questions. Among the more fanciful were that Manuel stayed in the Smarts' house for a week after the murders – he didn't; that Anne and Vivienne were both raped – he didn't touch them sexually; that his mother Bridget had confronted him angrily at the police station – she didn't; that Teresa was a hospital matron – she wasn't; and that Manuel was 'unable to convince the jury of an insanity plea' – such a plea had been specifically rejected. But in the many resurrections of the case there was one immutable feature – the face of Peter Manuel with its deep-set black eyes, the coldest Emilio Coia had ever seen, and its power to go on haunting the darker recesses of the national imagination.

1959

THE PLUTO CRATER

I

The Russian space rocket Lunik II hit the moon in September 1959 after travelling 236,160 miles from the earth in 33 hours 26 minutes. Tass, a news agency renowned for its slavish devotion to the communist cause, announced: 'The Soviet coat of arms has landed on the surface of the moon. It cannot be destroyed because it has been constructed so that it will not break up.' There was disappointment in the United States that the Americans had not got there first, followed by sour grapes when the New York Society of Engineers declared that it was not at all convinced that the claims from Moscow were genuine.

The American president, Dwight D Eisenhower, was sunnily unconcerned by the latest Soviet oneupmanship. As Lunik II prepared for take-off he 'returned for relaxation' to Culzean Castle in Ayrshire, where the National Trust for Scotland maintained a spacious apartment – nine rooms on the top floor – for his exclusive use. Cordially greeted by spectators at Prestwick Airport, he lifted his hat and shouted 'Hi-ya, folks' before being driven off in an open-topped limousine (USA1) down the coast road, past the fishing village of Dunure. Crowds lining the route continued to cheer, and several times he stood up in the car to give them a wave.

Within three hours of stepping off his flight Ike (as he was affectionately nicknamed) was changing into golf shoes in the clubhouse at Turnberry for his first game of golf in Britain. He played the Ailsa, the tougher of the courses overlooked by the Victorian railway hotel, and was caddied by 'Sunch' (Tom Mulhall), a legendary local bag-carrier with half a century's experience of these links. 'When are we coming to the easy holes?' Eisenhower cheerfully demanded of the local professional, Ian Marchbank, at the eighth. The president had resorted to an electrically driven caddy car, a contraption never seen before at Turnberry. Despite Sunch's expert advice he managed no better than an 89, not quite 24-handicap golf, but close.

After dinner at Culzean the president was reported to have 'played a little bridge'. Two days later he joined a congregation of 450 in the village church at Kirkoswald, built 12 years before the inauguration of the first president of the United States, where Souter Johnnie, a friend of Robert Burns, was buried in the kirkyard.

Fresh from his Scottish holiday Eisenhower was back in the White House only days before the Russian leader, Nikita Krushchev, took the UN General Assembly by storm, demanding complete world disarmament within four years: the abolition of all armies, navies and air forces, the closing down of all foreign military bases and war ministries, the destruction of all nuclear bombs. When these proposals were not at once enthusiastially endorsed, the volatile leader went off like a Soviet rocket into a huff of cosmic proportions, threatening to abandon his American tour unless he was taken seriously. His relaxed American counterpart may have been pining for the eighth hole at Turnberry and a little post-dinner bridge at Culzean Castle.

II

Lunik II's exploits and the imminent launch of Lunik III – there was a Lunik I, but it missed the target – generated universal interest. In Scotland, however, these events took second place to the so-called Maybole tawse trial, a curiosity almost as fascinating to the Scots as the Manuel case a year earlier. Lunik II got an incidental mention during the trial, when the solicitor for the defence, in his summing-up, expressed astonishment that his client had displaced the moon mission from the front pages of Scottish newspapers.

The client was Elizabeth Gallacher, head mistress of Lumsden Roman Catholic School, a residential institution of Glasgow Corporation, where girls with behavioural problems were billeted far from the distractions of the city. It was close enough to Culzean Castle to have allowed its pupils a glimpse of an American president on his way south. But nothing was known of the school, or what went on inside it, until Gallacher appeared in the dock of Ayr Sheriff Court charged with assaulting seven of her pupils.

Corporal punishment was widely practised in Scottish schools. The Lochgelly, named after the Fife town which supplied the product to a thriving home and export market, was a leather strap of two or three thongs (three in this case), typically 24 inches long and an inch and a half wide, and came in various densities up to the half-inch thickness of the XH (extra heavy). Almost all Scottish teachers possessed one. They were empowered to belt pupils over the hand, the number of strokes up to a notional maximum of six varying according to the nature of the offence or the mood of the teacher. Children were not allowed to be belted for poor work (although they often were); in theory the Lochgelly was the ultimate sanction for breaches of discipline.

Boys could be belted by women, girls by men, yet parents were either unaware of the psycho-sexual sub-text of these classroom rituals or simply chose to overlook the darker agenda. Whatever the explanation, there was a popular consensus behind corporal punishment and periodic demands that its use should be extended to borstal and prisons. All this made the prosecution of Elizabeth Gallacher – 61 years old, a teacher for 40 years, with an unblemished record – highly unusual.

Gallacher gave evidence in her own defence. She described how 'the villagers' – she seemed to be unaware that Maybole was a town – had complained of the ringing of door bells by seven girls in her charge – Catherine (11), Sarah (10), Susan (9), Theresa (8), Anne Marie (8), Catherine (7) and Mary (6). Gallacher claimed that other children in the school had objected to their fighting. Two days before they were belted she warned the seven about their behaviour in the dormitory, which included jumping out of bed, banging doors and laughing loudly. The girls paid no heed and Gallacher decided that the production of 'the famous strap' – her description – had become unavoidable.

She ordered the girls to stand outside her office. One by one they were summoned inside, told to bend over, and strapped across the bottom. Asked why she did not belt them over the palms of their hands as the rules prescribed, Gallacher replied that 'the other method' was more humane and that the natural place for the punishment of girls was 'the posterior' – she preferred this genteel alternative to the coarse word 'buttocks' which appeared in the charge. The impact was severe enough to inflict weals still visible when Dr James Ewen, principal medical officer for school health services, inspected them. Gallacher maintained that she had acted *in loco parentis* and felt quite justified in doing what she did.

Her solicitor said his client sincerely believed that she was properly executing her duty to the children. 'They were completely out of control and the question became: who was running the school – the teacher or the pupils?' The sheriff found her guilty of punishing six of the children excessively and unreasonably but acquitted her of assaulting the six-year-old because, in that case, she had administered only one stroke. He fined Gallacher £10. The accused was wearing 'a three-quarter length jacket and gaily striped sweater' – the newspapers did love their fashion notes – when this lenient sentence was imposed. She responded by thanking the bench.

The girls, who had endured the indignity of punishment and the further indignity of being examined by a male doctor, had their full names published in the newspapers. Press comment was sympathetic to their teacher. Alastair Phillips, a columnist with the *Glasgow Herald*, suggested that the girls had got off lightly with Gallacher's regulation belt and were lucky not to have been at the receiving end of 'one of the over-cooked sjamboks, as hard and wrinkled as rhinocerous hide' which were routinely applied to pupils' hands in schools of his acquaintance.

III

The Maybole case failed to shake the favourable public opinion of corporal punishment, which continued to be daily practised in most Scottish schools for a further quarter of a century until it was forbidden by European human rights legislation. Indeed the actions of Elizabeth Gallacher were mild compared with the institutionalised brutality at a Roman Catholic home for girls, the disclosure of which a year earlier had produced no outcry.

The Irish state was profoundly shaken when the full truth of the physical, sexual and emotional abuse which occurred in the country's Magdalene asylums was finally revealed in 2009 in the report of a commission of inquiry. But Ireland was not alone in hosting these malign institutions. They existed worldwide and one of them was long established in Glasgow. Latterly known as the

Lochburn Home and Laundry, it was originally (as far back as 1815) the 'Glasgow Magdalene Institution for the Repression of Vice and the Reformation of Penitent Females'. It existed to rehabilitate 'fallen' young women with the aim of redeeming them from a life of supposed immorality. Few of these women were 'fallen' in the sense of being prostitutes. Unmarried mothers, the mentally retarded, even flirts who dressed loudly could end up in the laundry.

Formally at least, the regime was voluntary: the inmates, many referred by inadequate parents, had to be willing to submit to discipline, to undergo industrial training and to devote themselves to a life of Christian piety and observance. But these places were in effect prisons. The work was laborious, the regime harsh and unyielding, the atmosphere oppressively evangelical, and for many of the women there seemed to be no hope of escape.

One night in the autumn of 1958, however, escape somehow became possible. Twenty-six teenagers – about half the number incarcerated in Lochburn Home and Laundry – broke out by climbing a ladder and dropping from a wall. Newspapers reported that they had made 'a dash for freedom', that police all over the city were hunting for them, and that the citizens of Glasgow should be on the lookout for girls wandering the streets in a uniform of blue frock and white apron. None of the escapees had been convicted of a criminal offence, yet they were being stereotyped as dangers to the public.

Another 18 inmates escaped the following night by climbing down the fire escape, smashing a glass pane in the process; all were 'recaptured', but not before one told reporters: 'If they force us to go back, we will break out every night.' A third exodus within 72 hours occurred as two inspectors from the Scottish Home Department were inside the home conducting the first stages of an inquiry into the events of the week. Three girls ran along the banks of the Forth and Clyde Canal at Maryhill, one of them managing to pass a note to reporters that they had been locked in the linen room but had managed to force the lock. The writer, who signed herself Margaret McColl, said she had been in the home for two years. 'I want out because if I don't get out I will keep on running away. We refuse to work in a home like this.' Ten other girls then appeared on the roof. One of them slipped, damaging a foot. Her companions knelt beside her as she lay against the chimney head on a steeply sloping roof. Journalists reported that she looked frightened.

The father of a girl who had been in the home for six months told the press that she had been reduced to a bundle of nerves by the experience. When he visited his daughter he was allowed to see her in the presence of a member of staff, but never alone. He understood that the matron censored the girls' letters. The girls themselves claimed that they were thrashed and drenched with cold water. These allegations were subsequently corroborated by the similar testimony of Magdalene victims in Ireland, but in the Glasgow of 1958 there was no public sympathy for the victims of Lochburn.

At first the management of the home categorically denied the use of corporal punishment. They then reluctantly conceded that thrashings were administered, but only when girls had been 'fighting among themselves'. They did admit drenching, but an official added: 'If any girls have water thrown at them, it is only when they become hysterical.' By the end of 1958 Lochburn Home and Laundry had closed down as a result of the Scottish Home Department inquiry, the conclusions of which were never made public. But the ill-treatment of children and young people in schools and homes continued; a year later Elizabeth Gallacher still felt justified in wielding her famous strap over the buttocks of her pupils.

IV

The Russians declared that the moon had no magnetic field. They said that, when Lunik II hit the surface, it was travelling at 7,200 miles an hour and that the container with the Soviet coat of arms landed east of the Sea of Serenity after its journey of 33 hours 26 minutes. While these lunar announcements were broadcast to the world, 48 miners were caged in a bogie going down to the foot of Auchengeich Colliery, in Chryston, Lanarkshire, at the start of the dayshift. This journey took only eight minutes.

As soon as they stepped out the men were enveloped in a blanket of smoke. They re-boarded the bogie in a desperate attempt to reach the safety of the pit head, but were overcome. Only one survived. The full moon – the one newly colonised by the Russians – illuminated a crowd of several hundred people who held on to hope all night but knew there was none. The television arc lights cast a stronger, harsher light. Men who ran out of cigarettes were reduced to borrowing. The village shop, which could have sold all its stock, had closed for fear of being thought to be cashing-in on the tragedy. 'There was a sense of unreality,' wrote one reporter, 'that 47 men who had gone to work in the morning were no longer alive.'

The deadly combination of an intense underground fire and poisonous fumes ruled out any immediate attempt to recover the bodies. Myer Galpern, the Lord Provost of Glasgow, made a solemn declaration of the statistics: 76 dependent children; 41 widows. Three days later 44 of the bodies were located and a large crowd stood motionless in a high wind and driving rain as rescue teams gathered at the pithead. Their first task was to set up a temporary mortuary.

V

Dirty, dangerous coal, although still a major employer, was barely above ground in a glittering exhibition which drew 375,000 people to the Kelvin Hall in Glasgow in the month of the tawse trial, the moon landing and the Lanarkshire pit disaster. The Scottish Industries Exhibition was proudly advertised as a showcase for goods made in Scotland. Its chairman, Sir Robert Maclean, said there had been so many applications for space that the hall could have been filled twice over.

The Queen's sister, Princess Margaret, stepped from the royal train at Glasgow Central and was greeted by George Smith, the station master, resplendent in full morning dress and top hat. Large crowds rivalling Eisenhower's lined the route of her procession to the Kelvin Hall where, before she formally opened the exhibition, she was introduced to a 16-year-old apprentice at Colvilles' steel works. She asked him if he liked his job. George Hutchison replied that he liked it 'fine' – which, in Scotland, could mean almost anything.

From an official programme alphabetically listing the exhibits by category, one journalist picked out the letter B, which stood for beer and belting – the famous strap? perhaps not – and Bibles – the Ayrshire family of Collins turned out the holy book in phenomenal numbers – and binnacles – though, from Kelvin and Hughes, it was 'a binnacle with a difference' – and biscuits and boats and boilers and other Bs too numerous to mention. 'Perhaps,' he mused, jumping swiftly from B to S, 'the most important exhibit, in relation to the future of Scotland, is the model on the Colvilles stand of the strip mill which is to be built at Ravenscraig.'

He also admired the 'eye-catching avenue of windows and portholes for ships' in the corridor of the Carron Company, the oldest firm in the exhibition, which was celebrating its 200th anniversary. The princess was moved to describe all this as 'spectacular', but there was an element of the spectacle that would have impressed the more vigilant onlookers: the traditional products of Scotland were almost outmatched by those of branch factories. Since the last such exhibition only five years earlier, 500 new factories or factory extensions had been established in Scotland, many of them by companies owned in the United States.

It took a London newspaper, *The Times*, to spot the potential significance of this phenomenon and to point out its risks. In a leading article the paper acknowledged Scotland's success in attracting new industries from the United States and England but asked why the impetus for Scottish progress was now coming mainly from outside Scotland. Why should it be necessary to rely so much on foreign enterprise and initiative? *The Times*'s verdict was that Scotland's indigenous industries had not made much of the long periods of high activity and demand since the end of the war. It cited shipbuilding as an oustanding example: the Scots had moved only slowly forward while the techniques of the industry in the rest of the world had been transformed. 'To whatever extent the Scottish industry has changed, it has done so under pressure.' In steel, too, essential changes had been delayed, while the history of the Scottish coal industry had been 'a continuous disappointment'. *The Times* detected 'Scots caution at its worst' as the root of the problem and concluded: 'What is needed is more imagination and initiative to create more new indigenous Scots enterprises.'

The Scottish press reacted indignantly to this accurate analysis, no more welcome for originating in a distant metropolis, but the *Glasgow Herald* did admit that one of Scotland's most harmful characteristics was 'a dour complacency which in our industrial life has too often resulted in a lack of drive and imagination'. The paper believed that there had been too much reliance on traditional heavy industries. Who could reasonably quarrel with this statement of the obvious? But there was no acknowledgement that the drivers of Scotland's economic progress – the Scottish Council (Development and Industry) among others – had pursued the creation of a branch factory economy, that this remote-controlled economy was vulnerable to the vagaries of trade winds and the whims of foreign owners, and that there had been a damaging neglect of such native entrepreneurship as Scotland possessed.

Politically none of this mattered. The Scottish Industries Exhibition, which promoted a record of success without too close an examination of its underlying fragility, could not have been timed more opportunely from the point of view of the Scottish Tories. In the middle of it, as crowds flocked to the Kelvin Hall, Harold Macmillan called a general election.

VI

Hugh Gaitskell, the Labour leader, put a brave face on it. When he addressed a rally of the faithful – 2,600 of them in the St Andrew's Hall in Glasgow – he insisted that the spirit of Labour had been restored, that it was '1945 all over again', that people were 'alive as they have never been before'. The meeting closed with the audience on its feet cheering, Gaitskell acknowledging the ovation with his right hand raised high above his head. But on the same night the Conservatives drew an audience of almost double that number to Green's Playhouse, where Super Mac delivered a version of his familiar 'Never had it so good' turn.

The old master gave a contemporary account of what life had been like in what he called 'the sixth winter of the Socialist Utopia': February 1951. 'Life is unnecessarily hard for old folk especially, housewives in particular, everybody in general, and this could be altered by our own government without much upset. I have been short of tea, short of sugar, short of butter, short of eggs, short of butcher meat and I am sure so is everybody else.' Macmillan paused; he was adept at this sort of trick. 'A pretty good description,' he reflected thoughtfully. And then the killer blow: 'The writer was that very outspoken socialist, whom you know so well in Scotland, Mrs Jean Mann.' The housewives' champion, the Labour MP for Coatbridge and Airdrie, had come to the aid of the party – the wrong party. Green's Playhouse erupted.

Esmond Wright, Tory academic and writer, saw many signs

favourable to the prospects of the ruling party: the slight drop in unemployment, the stability in the cost of living index, the appearance of more cars on the roads than ever before, the finest summer weather for 200 years. Even the astronomical aspect – 'Apollo visible, Mars in retreat' – Wright regarded as friendly to the Tory interest. He stopped short of giving Macmillan credit for the moon landing. But there was something about the crowds spilling on to the streets of Glasgow after those mass rallies that convinced Wright, if he needed convincing, that the Tories were on course for a famous victory. As they dispersed from the political meetings they had been swamped by bigger crowds leaving dance halls and cinemas. 'And as they moved homewards,' he wrote, 'their gaze was caught by the succession of brightly lit windows of radio and car sale rooms that have mushroomed with the current prosperity.'

Wright thought these people would be impressed by a Tory leader with 'old-fashioned manners, who publishes books and hails – three generations ago – from a croft on Arran'. But he sensed that they would be more impressed by shop windows bursting with the promise of a new materialism. He called it the bread-and-butter election, neglecting to add that Macmillan was promising jam on top.

Understandably the Scottish Tories felt secure enough to have some fun at Labour's expense. Ian MacArthur, the tormentor of Hector McNeil in Greenock in 1955, was now ensconced in the Tory stronghold of Perth and East Perthshire. Addressing a women's meeting in Perth, he imitated Macmillan by recalling what shopping had been like under the socialists in 1951. But MacArthur went one better than his leader, producing from his jacket and waistcoat pockets – even from the pouch of his leather sporran – items from the weekly ration, including one egg hard-boiled for the occasion. Finally he held up the one-and-a-half-ounce cheese ration – 'a man-sized meal for a mouse'. The Tory ladies of Perth were delighted by these amateur theatricals.

The Tory ladies of North Lanarkshire, a rare breed, may have been just as delighted by their 28-year-old candidate, George Younger, who was described as 'a member of the sales staff in the family firm of George Younger and Son, the Alloa brewers', and whose dedication to the campaign, according to one press report, 'can be readily seen in his attempt to cram every scrap of propaganda, every favourable fact and figure, into his regular 40-minute platform speeches'. Another promising young Tory candidate, Robert Kernohan, a *Glasgow Herald* journalist, supported the view of the late Walter Elliot that there was 'a Tory household in every close in Glasgow, even in the most blighted districts', and predicted that Labour would fail to win the marginal seat of Cathcart despite the addition of 18,000 municipal tenants to the constituency.

By comparison Labour sounded glum and defensive. The party's industrious Scottish secretary, Willie Marshall, complained that the BBC in Scotland was broadcasting a daily review of the newspapers. 'The practice is to quote extensively from editorials, and since the majority of these editorials favour the Tory Party, it looks as if the BBC are not honouring their much-vaunted claim of providing impartiality,' he said. His grouse demonstrated the growing influence of television.

The choice of Esmond Wright to present the BBC's hustings programme from Scotland confirmed Marshall's suspicions. John S (Jack) Maclay, who had succeeded James Stuart as Secretary of State, defended the Tories' record on Scottish unemployment: no easy task considering that, despite the buoyancy of the propaganda around the Kelvin Hall exhibition, 83,391 people were unemployed in Scotland, 3.9% of the working population, compared with 1.9% in the UK as a whole. George Thomson represented Labour on the programme, Sir Andrew Murray appeared for the Liberals. The Scottish National Party, angry that it had been denied a place on the panel, used a pirate radio transmitter to broadcast its own election message from David Rollo, its national treasurer. Rollo claimed that the BBC was 'completely in the hands of the big political organisations' and showed no independence of mind. Since the range of his 'Radio Scotland' transmitter was no more than four miles in and around Hamilton, where Rollo was standing, its effect was negligible except as a PR stunt.

When a decisive Tory majority became more and more likely, the sideshows were of more interest than the serious campaigning. 'A bitter contest' – invariably a euphemism for some shameless entertainment – was taking place in the Western Isles, where Labour's Malcolm Macmillan, who had held the seat for 24 years, faced a 27-year-old Liberal-Unionist, Donald MacLeod. Macmillan attacked MacLeod in a letter to the local newspaper as 'toffee-nosed', which MacLeod took as a thinly veiled attack on his father, 'a respected confectioner in Stornoway when Mr Macmillan was in short pants (perish the thought)'. Each candidate accused the other of favouring the desecration of the Sabbath – always a touchy subject in the Hebrides – and of supporting easy divorce and more relaxed liquor laws.

A provoked MacLeod said he would have 'no alternative but to act as an islesman or any real man anywhere would in the circumstances'. What he meant by this threat was revealed a few nights later when he attended one of Macmillan's election meetings and daringly presented the Labour candidate with a box of liquorice allsorts. MacLeod told one of his own meetings that hearing his opponent speak reminded him of a bag of oatmeal which had burst and was dribbling quietly on the floor. He added that his opponent was no more than a 'traughan', Gaelic for a miserable wretch; Macmillan retaliated by dismissing MacLeod as 'a wilting narcissus' (for which there seemed to be no Gaelic translation immediately to hand). The press were bemused but delighted by this trade in insults.

Another exotic feature of the 1955 election was the appearance of the Fife Socialist League candidate, 34-year-old Lawrence Daly, in pit clothes, steel-capped boots and protective helmet when he handed in his nomination papers to a wigged and gowned Sheriff Ronald Kydd. Daly, a former communist who had resigned from the party over Hungary, was hailed by journalists as 'a born speaker, a man of strong personality' and probably the only candidate in Britain who went down the pit every morning, worked a shift in the hardest job in coal-mining ('bursting'), and then went out campaigning. Daly called for the abolition of nuclear weapons, a policy also favoured by Nikita Krushchev. John Boyd Orr sent him £2 towards his election costs.

The Liberals, led by Jo Grimond as 'the party for the individual in modern society', boasted two large personalities, if not quite in the Daly class: George Y Mackie, a farmer of Ballinshore, Kirriemuir, 6 feet 4 inches tall, massively built, 'a forthright and able debater', who was standing in South Angus; and Elma Dangerfield, its candidate in South Aberdeen, who lived up to her name. Dangerfield's determination to canvass the workers knew no bounds: she addressed fishermen on board a trawler, went to the bottom of a granite quarry to speak to the labourers, and gatecrashed a wedding to distribute Liberal leaflets to the guests. The only obstacle she seemed unlikely to surmount was the indomitable Lady Tweedsmuir, her Tory opponent.

The SNP fielded only six candidates. Mary Stuart MacPhail Holt had intended standing in Argyll as a Scots Independent. While she drove from her home in Appin she was delayed by a flock of sheep on the road by Loch Eck and arrived 11 minutes too late with her nomination papers at the sheriff clerk's office in Dunoon. On a previous electoral outing, in Argyll in 1950, she had polled only 490 votes and lost her deposit. On this occasion the obliging sheep saved her further needless expense.

In Glasgow the press lamented the absence of unorthodox candidates, who tended to make better copy. There was no A E Pickard, who had once stood as an Independent Millionaire, and no Guy Aldred, the Independent Socialist who held the record as the most unsuccessful candidate in Scottish electoral history. He contested six elections between the 1920s and 1950s, lost his deposit every time, and polled a total of 2,416 votes in 30 years. One of the few moments of hilarity in the Glasgow campaign came when Myer Galpern, the Labour candidate for Shettleston, addressed a crowd of supporters as 'fellow lunatics' – a reference to Field-Marshal Montgomery's claim that anybody who voted Labour was barmy.

The result of the election was worse than Labour had feared. It was not '1945 all over again'; it was 1955 all over again, but with a doubling of the Conservative majority from 54 to 107. Scotland bucked the national trend, though not spectacularly. Labour gained four seats – Lanark, Central Ayrshire, Craigton (won by Bruce Millan), and Scotstoun, which the new township of Drumchapel had finally converted into a Labour seat. It lost Kelvingrove, which it had taken in a by-election after the death of Walter Elliot, and, as Robert Kernohan had predicted, it failed to win Cathcart, stronghold of working-class Tories. In the Western Isles the traughan beat the wilting narcissus with a much-reduced majority; in Aberdeen South Elma Dangerfield polled 20,000 votes fewer than Lady Tweedsmuir; and in West Fife Lawrence Daly languished in third place behind Labour's Willie Hamilton and an able young Tory, Alick Buchanan-Smith. George Younger, who had been thrown to the wolves in North Lanarkshire, returned to his humble vocation as a beer salesman.

VII

The Russians sent another rocket to the moon. Professor Tikhov of the Kazakh Science Academy said that Lunik III would study the possibility that lower forms of life existed near the fringe of the lunar disc in the Pluto Crater. But it was not necessary to go all the way to the Pluto Crater in search of lower forms of life; they were discernible to the naked eye in the hostile environment of the Saltmarket in Glasgow, where the defence was opening in a High Court trial of three men and a woman charged with cracking the safe of a bank in Shettleston and removing the sum of £38,789.

The case featured several of the leading Scottish personalities of the day, including Detective Inspector Thomas Goodall, fresh from his triumph in the Manuel case; Lionel Daiches, QC; and the gangster Dandy McKay, who was there only in spirit, having absconded three months earlier from the hospital wing of Barlinnie Prison to avoid the inconvenience of a court appearance. Lord Wheatley, the presiding judge, had to make do with Dandy's brother John in the dock. The trial was thus a Glaswegian version of *Hamlet* without the prince. Among the supporting players in the picaresque tale was the mysterious 'limping man' who visited a left luggage office in St Enoch Station and lifted a case containing some of the stash.

Although the crime was executed in Shettleston, because that was where the money was, it was planned in the Gordon Bridge Club near Central Station. Although its name suggested a genial establishment where President Dwight D Eisenhower might have felt at home, playing a little bridge after dinner, appearances in this case were deceptive. Bridge was the last thing on anyone's mind in the Gordon Bridge Club. The punters preferred a game called faro. It was played twice a day, afternoon and evening, and between 50 and 100 gamblers took part in each session. Serious money changed hands.

Peter Manuel was a regular in the Gordon Bridge Club and it was there that he met the club's owner, Dandy McKay, and acquired the Beretta pistol and ammunition with which he shot three of his victims. No doubt he would also have met brother John, who claimed to be employed in the club as a clerk of sorts, when he was not disposing of the proceeds of bank robberies. An exasperated Wheatley freed two of the accused, including the woman, in view of the state of the evidence, but jailed brother John for three years and sent down a Glasgow bookmaker, Alexander Gray, for 10.

The trial induced a moral froth in the Scottish press and the club closed its doors. How, the papers asked, could such a den of ill-repute have been tolerated in the business centre of the city, particularly after the Manuel trial? Gambling clubs were not exactly a new addition to the seedy under-belly of Glasgow's night life. Half a century earlier, in May 1909, the Grant Street Club, the West End Club, the Sloper Club and the Motor Club had all received unflattering notices during the trial of Oscar Slater. But the glory days were over; Dandy McKay and his friend Peter Manuel had seen to that.

In a sequel to these events, travellers arriving at Renfrew one morning in June 1960 were dismayed to find the airport cordoned off. As soon as the flight from Dublin landed, three carloads of police and security men raced across the runway to apprehend a handcuffed passenger who was being escorted off the plane by detectives. He was wearing a sports jacket and flannels with an open-neck shirt. He looked fit and tanned after his extended holiday in Ireland. But the tan would soon vanish – to be replaced by the pallor of the long-sentence prisoner. Dandy McKay had come home.

VIII

Professor Tikhov, if he was still of a mind to seek out lower forms of life, could have gone equally profitably to the city of Edinburgh, where the same Lord Wheatley interrupted his weekend for an emergency hearing in the Court of Session. The Duchess of Argyll, a promiscuous socialite otherwise known as Margaret Whigham, sought to persuade Wheatley to recall an interim interdict banning her from Inveraray Castle, the ancestral home of her husband. The duke alleged that a fortnight before the hearing she had secretly entered the castle, broken into his study with the help of a locksmith, and removed an oil painting, some photograph albums and two boomerangs. Among the many unusual features of the case, the seductive appeal of the boomerangs was never explained. The duke further alleged that, out of spite, she broke some gramophone records of which he was 'particularly fond'.

Twelve days later the duchess sent the duke a telegram: 'Arriving castle for lunch Saturday 19 with my father and Donald Nicoll. Another couple arriving for dinner and weekend. Please inform staff and tell MacDonald to make sure my bedroom is ready. Give my fondest love and a big kiss to Colin. – Margaret.' The duke at once sent a reply, also by telegram: 'I confirm that you are forbidden to enter Inveraray Castle.' The duchess, who was billeted in an Edinburgh hotel with her father, George Hay Whigham, a textiles magnate, was so perturbed by this response that she engaged the services of W I R Fraser, QC, Dean of the Faculty of Advocates, claiming that she required to visit the castle to collect her personal possessions. So that is how the Court of Session came to meet on a Saturday, the day that MacDonald was expected to have her ladyship's bed ready. But Wheatley refused to lift the ban. He said it seemed to him that, rather than turn up in person, the duchess should simply write to her husband and request the return of her property.

The restless Professor Tikhov could have confined his investigations to a small country in his own planet. Instead he went on insisting that lower forms of life might be had in the Pluto Crater. If the Russians succeeded in finding any, they would be doing well.

1960

A SLIGHT HAZE

I

In the early evening of 28 March 1960 the foreman of a bonded warehouse in Cheapside Street, Glasgow, near the Clyde, was locking up when he noticed 'a slight haze hanging around'. He thought it was coming from the tobacco warehouse next door, did nothing about it and went home. Earlier that day the manager had carried out a routine inspection of the bonded warehouse, leaving the top floor unvisited; when he was asked about this omission, he could not explain why he had not finished the job. In the parts of the building he did inspect, he found nothing untoward. None of the casks seemed to be leaking, although it was beyond the scope of a routine inspection to look at all 21,000, which contained in total more than a million gallons of whisky. The smell of the liquor was 'no more than usual'. At 5.20pm the manager left the premises. Almost two hours later, at 7.15pm, someone in a nearby ice cream factory dialled 999 after spotting smoke coming from a window of the warehouse. A fire crew responded promptly at 7.21pm.

One of the first officers on the scene, Robert Herbert, sent a fireman to fetch a 14lb hammer to force a door which was bolted from the inside. As the man moved off Herbert heard two muffled explosions in the centre of the building followed by a cracking sound and saw what looked to him 'like a tracery of ivy on the walls illuminated by blue flame'. Immediately there was 'a tremendous roar and a whoosh, and the whole thing came out like a dam bursting, cascading across the street'.

The word 'whoosh' was used by several witnesses. George Pinkstone, deputy manager of the ice cream factory, was walking along Cheapside Street when he heard 'a dull whoosh'. The wall bulged and fell 'right on top of the fire engine, which went up like a torch'. John Swanson, an assistant firemaster, heard 'a rumble and a whoosh' and then saw 'the whole frontage of the building coming out on to the street'. It was 7.49pm – only 34 minutes since the original alert.

Robert Herbert had started to run. 'I was hit by masonry on the right leg, which caused severe bruising. I ran towards Broomielaw, alongside the wall. As I was going down the street, I was conscious of pressure on my right shoulder, forcing me into the wall. I whipped off my helmet, and was struck on the shoulder by small pieces of masonry, and one particularly heavy bit struck my right shoulder. I cannot account for the fact that I escaped. The only thing I can suggest is that I was so close to the wall that it fell out over me.'

In the words of fireman-driver James Frew 'blazing whisky was coming down like rain'. Flames bursting through the warehouse roof were visible all over the city. Passengers at the Broomielaw boarding the Royal Scotsman for Ireland were showered with red-hot embers blown from the burning building; at Springfield Quay the MV Yoma had to be tugged to safety. In Cheapside Street itself the heat was so intense that it was impossible to reach the dead and dying. One fireman was being raised on an extending ladder when the force of the blast hit him; he died clinging to the tip of the ladder, flames licking around him. 'It was like some ghastly Guy Fawkes' night,' said one reporter. 'Showers of sparks were flying hundreds of feet up into the air over the warehouses and storage sheds on the wharfs.'

Fourteen firemen and five members of the Glasgow Salvage Corps lost their lives. Most of their bodies were unidentifiable. It was – and remains at the time of writing – Britain's worst fire services disaster in peacetime.

The following morning police cordoned off thousands of sightseers. Children played in the surrounding streets. Hoses were playing too – on the smouldering wreckage of the warehouse. A man was observed talking to his horse – there were many horses on the streets of Glasgow in 1960 – above the whine of a fire pump and the roar of lorries carrying off hundreds of tons of rubble. Sodden heaps of orange-coloured leaf littered the remains of the tobacco warehouse. In Stobwell Street a china bowl was placed outside a café with an appeal to passers-by to contribute to a fund for the dependants. Thirty children were fatherless. But one family had cause to be thankful. Joseph McGhee, a fireman listed as presumed dead, was found alive suffering from shock, but not before a minister of religion had called on his wife to break the news that he was missing.

Cheapside Street was uniquely bad, yet it could easily have been worse. Martin Chadwick, the Glasgow firemaster, believed that the city was on the verge of 'a very serious disaster' that night and that he had not expected his men to be able to control it from spreading as successfully as they did. The swiftness of the calamity was astounding – from an unremarkable 999 call to men buried half an hour later. The *Glasgow Herald* commented that the danger of fire in the city's many bonded warehouses was 'as obvious as the high export value to Scotland of the goods they contain' and demanded a searching inquiry into conditions at the warehouse.

II

Three months later almost to the day M G Gillies, QC, last heard of as Crown counsel in the Manuel trial, who had been elevated to the bench as Sheriff of Glasgow, opened a fatal accident inquiry in which more than 90 witnesses were cited to give evidence.

One of the first was Ronald Johnston, managing director of Arbuckle Smith & Co, owners of the warehouse. He acknowledged that there had been no automatic fire alarm system and no sprinkler system in the building. Gordon Stott, QC, appearing for some of the dependants, asked if there was any reason for not having sprinkler devices. 'Yes,' Johnston replied. 'First, it was believed and known that they tend to go off when they are not supposed to and, thereby, as we do not own the commodities, they can be damaging. Secondly, we understand they might not be, and are not, effective. Thirdly, there would be the presence of water in the bond.' The formality of this statement suggested careful preparation.

'Is there any reason,' persisted Stott, 'why a whisky bond should be situated in the heart of a built-up area?'

'Only that it is part of the commerce of Glasgow that has grown up over the past 100 years. It requires a central point to which whisky from all over Scotland must ultimately come.'

Martin Chadwick, when he gave evidence, took a dim view of Johnston's explanation. The firemaster said that whisky warehouses in built-up areas were a major hazard because of the danger of fire spreading from one building to another.

Stott: 'Have you expressed the opinion that whisky should not be stored in this type of building at all?'

Chadwick: 'I should say that whisky should be stored in types of buildings designed specifically for the purpose.'

John Evans, the city's fire prevention officer, told the inquiry that he had examined the wreckage the day after the fire, but there had been 'very little to be learned'. The devastation was so 'fantastic' that the debris gave no clues to the origin. But he offered a theory. 'There was no ignition source in the building other than the lighting. I was shocked to find that fluorescent lighting should be used in a bonded warehouse.' William Macnab, the depute procurator fiscal, asked Evans why this form of lighting would provide a source of ignition. 'If you have a vapour which is inflammable,' the witness replied, 'it has access into this lighting because there is no protection of the electric element.'

Macnab: 'Of course, it is impossible to say that that did cause the fire?'

Evans: 'Oh, quite impossible.'

He agreed with Alexander Thomson, QC, counsel for Arbuckle Smith, that nearly all the bonded warehouses in Glasgow were in built-up areas and that most of them had wooden floors. But he echoed the criticism of the firemaster about the close proximity of the warehouses and said that, if they were storing large quantities of whisky, they should have reinforced concrete walls and floors.

Thomson: 'Can you say how many bonded warehouses in Glasgow have sprinklers or automatic devices?'

Evans: 'There are quite a number and the number has increased over recent years.'

Thomson: 'But there are equally a considerable number that don't have them?'

Evans: 'Unfortunately, yes.'

Thomson: 'Do you consider that the use of fluorescent lighting adds appreciably to fire risk in a building?'

Evans: 'The whole answer to that question depends on what you are using the building for. Obviously in a building which can be filled with whisky vapour, I should say yes.'

James McLellan, a detective superintendent who headed the police investigation, said there were two probable causes. Either it was an accident due to the carelessness of an employee – the unspoken innuendo being that it was something as simple as a cigarette thoughtlessly dropped – or it was due to some electrical fault. He said he did not know what happened. He was not alone: no one knew, then or ever. But McLellan discounted the theory that fluorescent lighting may have been to blame. In his opinion 'and in the opinion of persons consulted', that was extremely unlikely.

In his summing-up to the jury Gordon Stott did not conceal his frustration that whisky had been stored 'in these quantities and in this type of building in a built-up area, and yet it appeared in evidence that this is nobody's business. It is an extraordinary situation when we have witnesses tell us this is nobody's business. The fire service say: It is not our business, it is for Town Planning. Town Planning say: We have nothing to do with it. The Dean of Guild say the same. You can see how hazardous it is. Millions of gallons of this stuff in built-up areas and nobody has the power to say: This should not be there.'

Thomson, for the company, excused his clients: 'There is no suggestion that the accident would not have happened in the same way if the warehouse had been in the middle of Rannoch moor.' This was logical up to a point. On Rannoch moor there were smokers who, if anyone cared to build a bonded warehouse in the middle of it, would just as likely drop a lit cigarette and have the entire wall fall into the wilderness. But the fire service would not have been on the scene within six minutes of the non-existent Rannoch moor ice cream factory dialling 999; the wall would have collapsed into the nearest burn long before there was any possibility of 14 firemen and five members of the Salvage Corps losing their lives because of a smoker's negligence; and there would have been no risk of the fire spreading to densely populated areas since no one lived on Rannoch moor.

This ludicrous defence nonetheless impressed Sheriff Gillies, who found it possible to inform the jury that there had been 'a remarkable absence of fault on anyone's part'. It seemed clear from the evidence that Arbuckle Smith & Co had carried out 'such duties as they had to do under statute from a common-sense angle'. He thought there was 'a great deal of force in what Mr Thomson said – that it would not have mattered where the warehouse was sited had the same set of circumstances existed'. Gillies said there was no evidence that a sprinkler system would have made any difference, and he doubted that an automatic fire alarm would have prevented the disaster. On the question of design and dispersal of whisky bonds, he said he was sure that the authorities concerned would study the evidence that had been laid before the inquiry.

What was the jury to do? Its powers in a fatal accident inquiry were in any case severely limited; and it had just listened to a judicial address of astonishing complacency. Its first responsibility was to the facts. It found that the firemen died from multiple injuries sustained when the walls of the bonded warehouse fell into the street and they were struck by falling debris. In an implied rebuke to Gillies it added a rider to this formal verdict, recommending that an automatic fire alarm system should be fitted in all bonded warehouses used for storing alcohol. Even if Gillies had dismissed the usefulness of such an elementary precaution, the jury clearly thought otherwise and had the independence of mind to say so.

III

Was this the searching inquiry that the *Glasgow Herald* had demanded the morning after the disaster? The paper was non-committal. It published no comment on the unsatisfactory outcome of the inquiry, instead devoting its first leader to a House of Commons debate on the Wolfenden report, which had recommended that homosexual acts between consenting adults in private should no longer be a criminal offence.

It was worth recalling, said the *Herald*, that James Adair, the former procurator fiscal of Glasgow, had differed from the majority of his colleagues on the Wolfenden Committee. This was disingenuous: as the paper knew or should have known, Adair's was the only dissenting voice on that committee. He went on to deliver an inflammatory speech to the General Assembly of the Church of Scotland in which he said that it would no longer be unlawful for 'perverts to practise sinning for the sake of sinning' and prophesied that homosexuals would be soliciting people on the streets. The Kirk, having listened to this poisonous outburst, voted against the Wolfenden reform by a large majority. The *Glasgow Herald*'s own stance on homosexuality was unambiguous: 'The dividing line between socially abhorrent behaviour as a sin and as a crime is exceptionally hard to draw ... It is much more important that medical and psychiatric research should be intensively directed towards discovering a cure for or a socially acceptable palliative of homosexuality than that public order and decency should be risked, even to a minor degree, by premature changes in the law.'

On questions of private and public morality there was indeed 'a slight haze hanging around' – and it often smelled of hypocrisy. In the Scotland of 1960 two men who consented to have sex together were classified as criminally depraved. But a firm of Glasgow warehousemen employing a foreman who went home without investigating the possible symptom of a fire and a manager whose idea of an inspection was to ignore the top floor, which housed a million gallons of whisky in a building with wooden floors and fluorescent lighting, which did not consider it necessary to have a fire alarm and which neglected to install sprinklers for no better reason than that they occasionally went off at the wrong time – this firm was behaving within the law and in a manner regarded by Sheriff M G Gillies as common-sensical.

IV

A slight haze – another one – was hanging around Auchengeich Colliery in Lanarkshire on the morning of the fire which killed 47 miners. This was the subject of the second major inquiry of 1960. It too raised troubling questions about the value placed on human life, and the inadequacy of the measures taken to protect it by those in positions of responsibility.

As an investigation it was far superior; the press would have been entitled to call it searching. It was not a fatal accident inquiry presided over by a member of the Scottish Bar, but a public inquiry ordered by the government and chaired by T A Rogers, HM inspector of mines and quarries. The dock was removed from one of the courtrooms of the High Court in Glasgow to make way for a long table of exhibits. Floodlit plans of the colliery, scene of Scotland's worst pit disaster of the 20th century, occupied much of the wall space. Day after day miners crowded into the public benches, their mood often charged with barely controlled anger.

Eight hundred miners were employed at Auchengeich, producing 700 tons of coal a day round the clock. It was an unhappy pit. Absenteeism was exceptionally bad, there was a disruptive element among the workers, the management was poor, industrial relations were dreadful. In many ways Auchengeich was a disaster waiting to happen.

The first person to notice the slight haze, James Dickson, an assistant oversman, went down the pit around 6.30am to investigate. Soon the belt of a ventilator fan in the return airway – the route to the surface and safety – was ablaze. He tried a fire extinguisher but it failed to work. He then phoned the pithead for hoses to be brought down. Dickson made no attempt to prevent men from entering the bogies at the pit head; he was 'not unduly alarmed' by the fire and wanted to 'find out what was happening first'. Alexander Pettigrew, the under-manager, heard about the trouble with the ventilator fan when he arrived at the colliery around 6.15am, but an hour elapsed before he learned that smoke was coming from the return airway.

Henry Hyde, divisional inspector of mines for Scotland, who was leading the evidence, asked Pettigrew: 'Up to that time had you any suspicions that there were some men in the return?' Pettigrew replied: 'None whatever.' He agreed that he gave no instructions to stop the movement of men. The next member of the management team to arrive was James Smellie, the colliery manager, around 6.40am – his usual time. Pettigrew told him that a fan seemed to be on fire. Smellie claimed that it had not occurred to him that there might be men in danger. Abe Moffat, representing the NUM, put it to him: 'You know, as a responsible man, what should be done when there is any smoke or indication of fire?' Smellie replied: 'Withdraw the men.' But the men were not withdrawn. When Moffat asked him why he did not immediately call the fire brigade, Smellie said: 'A fire is not always accompanied by loss of life nor is it always necessary to phone for the brigade.' By 6.50am, when 48 men stepped into a bogie to go down to the bottom of the pit at the start of their shift, the management had already torn up the rule book.

Thomas Green, 51, well-known locally for his great height (6 feet 5 inches), was aware of a slight smell of smoke and burning. He told the inquiry that he had been a long time in the pit and had never smelled burning of that kind before. But he was given no instruction not to go down. The bogie started its run and the atmosphere thickened. Green described what happened next:

When we got to the terminus, the smoke became blinding. It was pure black. We got out of the bogie and started to walk in towards our work. We walked only about two or three yards. We were all grouped in the narrowest part of the area in an absolute blanket of smoke. We saw that we couldn't go on and there was a general urge to get back to the bogie. We climbed back in and someone belled the train away. We started without delay and proceeded right up the one-in-five gradient and got on to the level part. I had the collar of my jacket over my mouth to protect myself from the smoke and I tried to shout to those sitting next to me to do the same. We had been going through this smoky atmosphere all the way from the terminus but I am not sure how far we got. Pat Harvey was sitting next to me and I heard him say, Tammy, Tammy, for God's sake give me a hand with Mulholland. When I turned round I saw Mulholland hanging over the side of the bogie and Pat Harvey trying to hold him up. I shouted to the train guard to stop the bogie for a minute. I thought Mulholland was going to fall out or hit some object in the passing. The train guard brought the train to a halt so that we could give assistance to my mate. I don't know how long we were stopped, we started up again and things were getting rather difficult for us. I am not very clear what happened thereafter. How I got out of the bogie I just don't know.

Green was the only survivor of the 48 men in the bogie. Forty-three were overcome by carbon monoxide fumes where they sat. James Imrie, chief medical officer to Glasgow city police, said they would have died quickly and painlessly. One fell from the train. Three others attempted to escape but quickly succumbed. Pat Harvey, who tried to help Mulholland, died at the age of 33, Mulholland himself at the age of 50. The youngest victim was 20-year-old George McEwan, the oldest 62-year-old Henry Clayton. Among the roll-call of the dead many of the occupations of the industry were represented: there were roadsmen and beltmen, cuttermen and shotfirers, strippers and back brushers.

At 7.20am Robert Boyd, a day-shift oversman, having been told that the ventilator fan was on fire, went straight to the scene and got 'the shock of my life'. The pit was ablaze for 30 feet beyond the fan. The walls and roof were on fire and the roof timbers were falling down; there was no one fighting the blaze. Forty minutes later Boyd was told that the hoses were 'on the road in'. He heard then for the first time that men on a bogie had been trapped. But nothing could be done about the fire until the hoses arrived. Boyd admitted that, when the full extent of the disaster became clear, they – management – 'didn't know what [they] were doing'. Abe Moffat suggested that the plight of the miners was forgotten. 'I wouldn't say it was forgotten,' Boyd replied. He paused. Then he added: 'Maybe momentarily.'

In the depths of the pit Dickson, the assistant oversman, had ordered men to try to smother the blaze with sand and stone dust. John Campbell, one of the coal-face workers, told the inquiry that he and another man carried three bags of stone dust to the fire – 'it was useless'. Campbell then went in search of fire hydrants and found none. Another of the men, James Donaldson, said that when he got to the fire at 7.15pm, 'everything that was burnable was burning'. Donaldson was told to go to the pit bottom for fire-fighting equipment. On the way there he met someone – 'a chap' – who asked him if he had seen four of his mates. 'They went in there,' the man said, pointing to the inferno. Donaldson and others found that the extinguishers were of no use. At this stage only hoses would do the job and there were no hoses underground.

Robert Harvey, the safety officer, turned up at 7.50am after receiving a message about events at the colliery. When the mine rescue team arrived he accompanied them down into the pit and waited as they entered the return airway. 'They were gone about 10 minutes. When they returned they said they couldn't stand it – that it was nipping the eyes out of their heads. They reported that they had found a body.'

William Adams, one of the rescuers, said the smoke was the worst he had ever experienced. His colleague Alan Bridges said he was ordered to take a canary through the doors into the return airway. 'My mate took off his helmet and safety lamp and held it up to the cage and I held the cage in front of my eyes. The bird was immediately distressed, and fell down in the cage unconscious.' Shortly after 8am, an hour and a half after the discovery of the fire, the first water was at last applied to it, but by then it was too late.

In this catalogue of inexcusable delays there was yet another. It was not until 12.30pm that the safety officer began a roll-call of the day shift to identify the names of the missing men. Had anyone else checked? he was asked at the inquiry. Harvey replied that he didn't know. By 6pm, when the colliery manager escorted a party of officials into the pit, the fire was out.

One mystery was never satisfactorily explained. Several hours after the 47 men died, and the only survivor had been rescued, a bell started ringing underground. A chilling sound, almost supernatural in its eeriness. There was an immediate investigation, but it yielded nothing. No one else was found alive. The ringing stopped.

V

The cause of the disaster was not in dispute. William Williams, mechanical inspector of mines for Scotland, said that as the ventilator fan was a fairly small one and running at its maximum speed, a new set of blades should have been fitted at least four years earlier. Williams carried out tests on pieces cut from the fan which showed that it was sub-standard. He speculated that a blade may have been missing. That would have caused vibration and metal fatigue, and the machine would have steadily deteriorated. The National Coal Board, owner of the nationalised colliery, blamed the fan's defects on the manufacturers, which had failed to supply belting of the specification needed to drive it. But the board could not deny that, according to mine regulations, the fan should have been checked every half hour. It wasn't.

Nor was there any mystery about the absence of effective fire-fighting equipment underground. The hoses had been withdrawn. Why? Pettigrew, the under-manager, said in reply to cross-examination by Abe Moffat: 'It is better that they should be kept down there. But if hoses were kept down the pit, the brass pieces were cut off and, I presume, sold for scrap. That is why the hoses were kept on the surface.' (Though not in sufficient numbers to cope with a serious fire – most had to be imported.)

Moffat: 'It takes a disaster of this kind to convince you that this is wrong?'

Pettigrew: 'If whoever is doing this was to refrain from doing it, I would say the best place is underground.'

Moffat: 'Do you consider it right to penalise and jeopardise a whole pitful of men through the action of one or two people?'

Pettigrew: 'I know it is not right.'

Harvey, the safety officer, said it was impossible to keep fire-fighting equipment in working order down the mine. He claimed that extinguishers were tampered with and emptied of water and that, since the disaster, about 30 had been discharged; days before the inquiry one had been pulled off the wall of the pit baths. He complained that his job was regarded as 'the lowest of the low', that he was sick of it, that he would not be in the mining industry for much longer.

If Harvey was defeated and self-pitying, Michael Lynch, a deputy at the pit and a part-time member of the local fire brigade, was combative. He said that when he tried to tackle the fire he was handed two extinguishers neither of which worked. He knew why.

Moffat: 'What makes you say that the fire extinguishers had been tampered with?'

Lynch: 'Because there was so much of that going on in the colliery.'

Moffat: 'But you didn't investigate this fully? This is only supposition on your part?'

Lynch: 'It is.'

Moffat: 'There has been some criticism of hoses not being kept underground?'

Lynch: 'I don't see any reason to keep hoses underground when they are going to get wasted. They can stand a certain amount of abuse, but not that.'

Abe Moffat, the communist leader of the Scottish miners, was a skilful examiner. He wasted no opportunity to commend the bravery of his own members who came before the hearing, and invited Rogers, the inquiry chairman, to join him in several formal expressions of gratitude. Rogers was seldom if ever drawn. But when Coal Board managers, senior or junior, came to the surface, Moffat went for the jugular, supported by the Greek chorus in the public benches. No confrontation was more bruising than his cross-examination of Dickson, the assistant oversman who was first down the pit and made a fatal misjudgement in not stopping the flow of human traffic as soon as the fire started.

Harald Leslie, the QC fired by Peter Manuel, represented Nacods, the union of the colliery managers. During Moffat's inquisition of Dickson, Leslie rose to protest that Moffat was not allowing the witness to complete his answers. When Rogers diplomatically pointed out to Moffat that he was frequently talking at the same time as the witness, Moffat replied that he was finding it difficult to accept Dickson's answers, that he was asking direct questions and not getting direct answers. Dickson intervened: 'I think, Mr Moffat, I am giving direct answers and you are trying to confuse me.'

The bitterness was palpable. If a fight for the truth was being conducted in the dockless High Court, so was a version of the class war, the boundaries of which had not shifted much since the mines had been taken into public ownership. Leslie exacerbated a tense situation with a needlessly provocative summing-up in which, having pointed out that seven Nacods members died in the disaster, he berated Moffat for insulting their memory. 'It is a slander to say that [the deceased officials] didn't do anything and it is against the evidence to utter that slander,' he contended. He acknowledged that most of the miners were responsible people. 'But you have a few who are so insane and inane that they will wreck the very lifebelt that will save human life. No matter what has been said about extinguishers or hoses, can anyone imagine how Dickson felt when he first saw the fire at the belt? He says to himself, Here's an extinguisher. All's well. But it has been sabotaged. Get another – same state. Never mind, he'll get the hoses. Huh, someone has sold the brass nozzles for pieces of silver.'

At this there were murmurs from the public benches of 'terrible'. Leslie: 'It is not terrible, it is fact.' But the future Lord Birsay, prosperous and privileged, had gone too far with his reference to pieces of silver in relation to men doing filthy, dangerous, ill-paid work.

Four months later Rogers produced a report of admirable concision and clarity. He said it was difficult to understand why the haze observed at the pit bottom, and by the men on the first bogie, was not recognised as a symptom of an outbreak of fire. 'But it was not so recognised by anybody.' The reaction to the outbreak was 'an example of an unfortunate tendency on the part of persons faced with an emergency to concentrate their attention on establishing the cause of the danger rather than first safeguarding against its possible effects.' Rogers said that anything in the nature of smoke underground, 'however faint it may be', constituted a potential danger to life, which had to be met by the immediate withdrawal of men to a place of safety. He criticised the long delay in applying water to the blaze and said that the fire would probably have been prevented if the ventilator fan had been under constant supervision. He condemned the malpractices in the pit, the reckless tampering with fire extinguishers and hoses, but added firmly that these did not absolve the management from its legal obligations.

Although the report amounted to an indictment, no one was prosecuted for the negligence at Auchengeich Colliery, and the reasons for the disaffection within the workforce were left unexplored. The bell which broke the long silence of the afternoon might have been tolling for an industry.

VI

In this year of inquiries, the most personal was ordered by the Secretary of State for Scotland into the dismissal of Dr George Trapp as rector of the Gordon Schools in Huntly, Aberdeenshire. A glittering cast was assembled for the occasion. One leading member of the Scottish Bar, Manuel Kissen, who was to become Scotland's first Jewish judge, conducted the inquiry while another, George Emslie, a future Lord President of the Court of Session, represented Trapp. Half a million words of testimony were spilled over 15 days; the dismissed teacher himself gave evidence for 19 hours; the newspapers devoted acres of space to a series of extreme claims and counter-claims. Seventeen years later echoes of the case continued to reverberate through the law courts.

Who was this curious character? Born in Falkirk in 1906 he began his teaching career at the town's High School, where he had been a pupil, and rose rapidly in the profession. He was rated highly enough as a botanist to be elected a Fellow of the Royal Society of Edinburgh at the age of 35. By all accounts he was affable and courteous at that early stage in his career, and noted for his 'grand sense of humour' – a compliment often attached to people with no discernible sense of humour whatever. His promotion to the rectorship of Huntly's high-achieving state school (despite the plural there was just the one) came as no surprise to anyone who knew of his outstanding abilities. He was 42 when he got the job in 1948.

Alexander Young, the director of education for Aberdeenshire, agreed that Trapp had 'exceptional breadth of academic qualifications and a variety of educational experience' – although that was the extent of any testimonial he was prepared to offer. At first, according to Young's version, their relationship was amiable enough, but 'matters underwent a gradual change' and came to a head over a number of incidents involving a harmonica band, salt in the rector's coffee, and a stink bomb.

Two girls, members of the harmonica band, sought leave of absence for their last four days at school to allow them to go on a musical tour of Orkney. They had the consent of their parents and the support of the director of education when he came to hear of the case. So far as Young was concerned 'four days at the end was a very small part of a course lasting five years'. The rector would have none of it; the girls would stay at school and complete the course. The girls defied their rector and went to Orkney. Trapp then attempted to withhold their leaving certificates, as well as the certificate of a boy who, he claimed, had put salt in his coffee on the last day of the 1955 summer term.

The director of education thought all this 'troublesome'. Trapp, however, insisted on writing to the Scottish Education Department asking it to support his decision to withhold the three leaving certificates on the grounds of 'the grossest misconduct'. The department informed him that he had no right to deny the pupils their certificates and instructed the rector to issue them. He refused and eventually they were posted from the Education Department's offices.

End of term tended to be a difficult time for the rector. On the final day of the 1953-54 session a pupil brought stink bombs into the school. Trapp was furious. But it was only after the school had broken up for the summer that he discovered the identity of the culprit. It was none other than the head girl and dux, who had just left garlanded with honours. Any remnant of the rector's renowned sense of humour deserted him. He retaliated by delivering to the head girl a box containing one of the unexploded stink bombs with a letter.

George Emslie put the best possible construction on this behaviour: 'Having regard to the girl's position in the school, the prizes she won, and the reasons given for these awards, did you think it was right for this girl to go out into life without knowing of your displeasure?' Trapp replied: 'I thought I had to let her know that it just didn't make sense to me that she should accept these prizes and at the same time do an irresponsible act like this.' The rector heard nothing more about the embarrassing episode. Five years later, however, the provost of Huntly, one of the town's many Gordons, produced the box containing the unexploded stink bomb, with the rector's letter, at a meeting of the local education committee. Emslie asked why he thought the provost had done this. Trapp said: 'I presume to influence them in thinking I had done something wrong.'

The evidence against him was piling up, but some of it was petty. The inquiry spent a long time poring over his rejection – admittedly pompous in tone – of a request that organised football should be available for boys who preferred it to rugby. His use of a room not officially designated as the rector's, and the apparent irregularity of a telephone extension from the school to his house, exercised the bureaucrats more than was reasonable. Trapp had a deputy who admited to despising him – the deputy objected to being put in charge of the boys' lavatories, a humble duty which he considered beneath his dignity – and a maths teacher who sent abusive letters about him to the director of education; yet neither was reprimanded or transferred.

By the end there was the whiff of a witch hunt. Nine hundred parents and former pupils in the small town signed a petition opposing his dismissal; for all Trapp's faults – his autocratic style, his intellectual arrogance, his occasional want of judgement – the support for him in Huntly was impressive. But he stayed sacked. Manuel Kissen ruled that Aberdeenshire education committee was justified in dismissing him.

Trapp, who was married with two daughters, would not let go. He went on pursuing the case – attempting first to take out a private prosecution against one of the witnesses at the public inquiry and, when that failed, suing Maitland Mackie, former convener of the education commitee, for allegedly making defamatory statements about him at the inquiry. Lord Ross held that, since Mackie's evidence was protected by privilege, Trapp's action was hopelessly irrelevant. He awarded his opponent's costs against Trapp, who had conducted the case himself. The stress of his dismissal, the humiliating personal revelations at the public inquiry and the subsequent legal misadventures would have destroyed many men, but Trapp survived to the age of 96, convinced to the end that he had been the victim of an injustice engineered by his enemies. He maintained that he had enjoyed 'little support from the powers-that-be' and stood alone and isolated.

George Trapp took a high-minded view of his vocation. He said he believed passionately in the power of education as a remedy for 'the confusion of motives and directions in the life of mankind'. In the fulfilment of this ideal he was clear about the role of a head teacher: it was to develop his school 'into a beacon of good order and discipline, a shining example to the community'. In 1959 the Gordon Schools won the BBC's general knowledge quiz *Top of the Form*. A shining example indeed, even if the rector was soon to be exposed as the sender of a stink bomb.

He lived long enough to witness a steady decline in the status of the teacher. When her old rector died the owner of the stink bomb, who had at some stage dropped it into the grateful hands of the provost, who in turn had found it expedient to take it to the education committee, would herself have been approaching old age, if she was still alive. The confusion of motives and directions in the life of mankind had proved to be beyond remedy. There always seemed to be a slight haze hanging around.

1961

THE GLOOMIER ASPECTS OF THINGS

I

October 1961 was a significant month in Scottish politics. As one John died another entered public life. MacCormick and Smith had much in common. They practised their debating skills at Glasgow University, they combined eloquence with personal warmth, they touched the hearts of the Scottish people. Both died young – MacCormick at 56, Smith at 55. It was said that they failed to realise their full potential, Smith because he was cut down in his prime by a weak heart. Had he lived he would probably have led Labour to victory in the 1997 general election, though not by the landslide achieved by Tony Blair, his successor as leader of the party. But the case of MacCormick was sadder and more complex. While John Smith died at the peak of his powers, John MacCormick was worn out; a spent force.

His obituaries were long enough by the modest standards of the time to include the essential facts of his early life: born in Glasgow in 1904, the son of a Mull sea captain; his mother, a MacDonald from Glenurquhart, the first Queen's district nurse in the Western Isles; young John, at the age of 17, walking up the hill from Woodside School to the university, where he graduated in arts and law; active in student politics as a member of the Labour Club and the ILP; emerging in the Union as a speaker of natural flair; so fervent in the home rule cause that he provoked a heckler to ask whether Scotland would have not only independence but her own 'King John'. The title stuck. It was dutifully recorded that he deserted Labour to join the National Party of Scotland, precursor of the modern SNP, but that his attachment to the UK pulled him closer to the Liberals. There, however, the consensus in the tributes to MacCormick broke down.

There was little agreement about the reasons for the extraordinary success of the covenant movement inspired and organised by King John. Did the two million signatures gathered with astonishing speed for a devolved administration in Edinburgh represent a genuine groundswell in favour of a Scottish parliament? Or were they, as some newspapers suggested, largely a revolt against the centralisation and austerity of post-war Britain, which MacCormick himself made the rallying cry of his ill-fated campaign in Paisley? He had, as one of his more critical admirers put it, 'briefly caught the ear of a great part of Scotland', but having got the signatures he seemed unsure what to do with them. His insistence that the covenant movement should transcend party politics invited criticism that it was simply a pressure group with vague aspirations led by a man of no settled political loyalties. Before the funeral his critics resurfaced to accuse him of sentimentality, of glorying in a country which belonged to his imagination rather to the reality of modern Scotland.

In the wake of his death there was an unedifying spat between the opposing sides in the nationalist schism of 1942. Douglas Young wrote to the press correcting an impression given by some of the obituaries that the faction of the National Party in favour of a neutralist stance at the start of the second world war had succeeded in electing him (Young) chairman of the party. Young claimed that neutralism was not an issue: MacCormick had been secretary of the party in 1937 when its annual conference passed a resolution calling on members of military age to resist conscription by a non-Scottish government. In 1939, when Chamberlain's government was preparing to introduce the call-up, MacCormick and the rest of the executive had published a leaflet calling on Scots to resist it. 'Our position,' wrote Young, 'was that a Scottish government should control whatever war effort the Scots people thought fit to make.' His fellow activist Bertie Gray took issue with Young's version of SNP history. He maintained that, two days after the start of the war, the executive of the party put its organisation and premises at the government's disposal to assist the war effort and that the party 'received the thanks of the government'. By the time of the divisive conference of 1942, MacCormick, Gray and others 'were in uniform' - a barbed reference to Young's status as a conscientious objector.

These stale battles, which were being re-fought in the week of MacCormick's funeral, had the immediate effect of obscuring his personal achievement. He got Scotland talking about its own purpose and destiny and, once the conversation had started, it proved impossible to shut it up completely. He wielded no power – unlike many of the pygmies who did and whose names were quickly forgotten. What he did wield was influence. It continued to be felt and expressed so long after his death that John MacCormick, who believed instinctively in the United Kingdom, became a potent symbol of nationalist aspiration. Although this was not foreseen by the obituarists in October 1961 it may have been sensed by Andrew Dewar Gibb, who delivered the eulogy in the chapel of Glasgow University. 'Of this I am sure,' Gibb said, 'if in time to come a new and different Scotland comes to be erected, the work of John MacCormick will be on the headstone in the corner.'

Gibb touched in his address on the high personal cost of MacCormick's idealism: 'He sacrificed worldly advancement, wealth, and high promise, giving himself unstintingly to his task.' It was a tactful way of acknowledging that John MacCormick was starved by the neglect of his country – a not uncommon fate of the Scot in history.

II

What might King John have made of the passing events of Scotland in the month of his death? He would have been interested in the rebellious condition of the people of Mull, the birthplace of his father, where the population was declining sharply. As MacCormick lay dying in the Western Infirmary in Glasgow, his supporter Lord Cameron, chairman of the Advisory Panel on the Highlands and Islands, was addressing a public meeting in Salen Hall attended by 300 people. There was a rowdy reception for Viscount Massereene and Ferrard, the owner of one of the main estates, when he rose to explain the afflictions of the landed class, claiming that it had cost him £6,200 to renovate a single farmhouse. Duncan Campbell, a crofter, was loudly applauded when he described the state of one of the viscount's farms as a disgrace. Above the uproar Massereene could be heard shouting: 'It would cost me £30,000 to put that farm in order if the farmer left. Where the hell do you think the money's coming from?' Island hearts failed to bleed.

On the Friday before MacCormick's death – a Friday the 13th – the first truck was driven off the assembly line at the Bathgate factory of the British Motor Corporation. 'With a happy disregard for superstition' (one newspaper hopefully speculated), the vehicle emerged bearing the slogan 'The first of the many' to the cheers of the 350 workers.

III

While the dispute about the political reputation of MacCormick continued, someone of no public reputation – the Labour candidate in the East Fife by-election – made his first reported speech of the campaign. He spoke at a meeting in Newport about the plight of salmon fishermen: 'The fishermen have as much right to the fish in the sea as the river proprietors have to the fish in the rivers,' he said. It was not much of a quote, but for John Smith it was a start.

'Mr Smith is 23 but already has seven years of activity in the movement behind him,' reported a journalist covering the campaign. 'He has had as little as two and at the most 70 electors at his meetings. He bustles about the division from 7am to late at night, hardening the pockets of support in Leven and Kennoway and going for the government policy with everything but the 50-megaton bomb. Mr Smith speaks with a smile of the Liberals taking many votes from the Tories and sending him as the youngest MP to parliament.'

John Smith, the son of a West Highland schoolmaster, was a product of Dunoon Grammar School, where he boarded. One of his teachers was the novelist Robin Jenkins. It was there that he joined the Young Socialists – 'I knew that was my side, somehow' – and the notion of political activity entered his head for the first time. He did a history degree at Glasgow before studying law; even as a child he had wanted to be an advocate. But it was as a brilliant university debater – one of a team which also included his fellow socialist James Gordon, who went on to pursue a career in broadcasting – that Smith achieved wider notice. He was spotted by Douglas Young, the same lanky, scholarly figure whose election as leader of the nationalists had prompted the angry resignation of John MacCormick but who had himself subsequently deserted the

National Party. Young, who lived in Tayport and ran what there was of the East Fife Labour Party, invited Smith to fight the seat. Smith recalled: 'Half of Glasgow University decamped to the constituency. Some of them weren't even members of the Labour Party, but there was this tremendous sense of being their man.'

Despite his tireless energy the by-election came to life only fitfully. The churches convened a meeting of all three candidates – Sir John Gilmour, the Tory, and Donald Leach, the Liberal, were the others – to debate three issues worrying the Christian folk of East Fife: the hydrogen bomb, 'the racial question' and capital punishment. The meeting got out of hand. 'Imported questioners with no constituency or church connections turned it into just another hustings,' wrote a local reporter. 'Many vitally concerned with the three questions they expected to hear debated left halfway through.'

The candidates were then summoned by the St Andrews Women Citizens' Association to give separate addresses. Each was asked to explain his policy on the law of intestate succession – not the most pressing topic at a time when the Russians were threatening the peace of the world, but clearly of some interest to the women citizens of St Andrews. Smith prefaced his answer by admitting that he was a law student at Glasgow University but that he 'hadn't got that length yet' – the length of intestate succession. He marshalled some frank thoughts on this obscure subject: 'I don't think male heirs should have any greater rights of succession than female heirs, but I don't think it is a great issue. These things loom large in the minds of women who think they are oppressed but not in the minds of those who actually are oppressed.'

By the end of the campaign John Smith's bravura about the possibility of a sensational victory had evaporated and he was 'speaking thoughtfully of the embarrassment which Labour would be caused if they were lowered to third place'. The outcome was never in doubt. As one journalist observed with an eye to local history: 'If Sir John Gilmour is not elected, it will be the biggest surprise since the ancient and royal burgh of Auchtermuchty went bankrupt.' Auchtermuchty had indeed gone bankrupt. In 1818 the council decided to build four bridges over the burgh water, a scheme it could ill afford. For this fiscal recklessness the councillors were thrown into the town jail and creditors seized such assets as they could lay their hands on, including most of the common land, two mills, even the pews in the parish church. It took many years for the town to recover. Auchtermuchty then faced a further blow in its informal adoption by John Junor.

There was no shock to equal the bankruptcy of Auchtermuchty. The Conservatives won the seat with a reduced majority and young Smith spared his party the embarrassment of coming third – though only just. He finished 96 votes ahead of the Liberal. It was not a brilliant result, but nor was it a bad one considering that East Fife subsequently became a Liberal stronghold. He waited 10 years to be given a winnable seat in Lanarkshire, and then there was no stopping him. By the late 1980s he was shadow chancellor of the exchequer, deploying his forensic ability in opposition to Margaret Thatcher, a Prime Minister for whose ideology Smith expressed a strong distaste.

IV

Their paths did not cross for many years. In 1961, while John Smith was failing to enter parliament as Britain's youngest MP, Thatcher was already installed in the House of Commons and defying her party by voting for the restoration of birching. It did her no harm politically. Later in the year she was rewarded with her first junior appointment as parliamentary under secretary of state in the Ministry of Pensions and National Insurance. Few outside her constituency of Finchley had heard of her and it would be a long time before her surname became synonymous with a distinctive brand of free market economics. But as the future iron lady, no more than an iron maiden at the time, took her first step on the greasy pole, there appeared in Scotland a whiff of what was to come. A bluff Englishman, John Toothill, general manager in Edinburgh of Ferranti Ltd, the weapons manufacturers, published a much-heralded report on the Scottish economy.

His grandly styled 'Committee of Inquiry', commissioned by the Scottish Council (Development and Industry), consisted of himself, Professor Thomas Wilson of the chair of political economy at Glasgow University, and five businessmen: Norman Best, managing director of Rance Ltd of Columbus, Ohio; James Gammell, a partner in the Edinburgh merchant bankers Ivory and Sime; A J C Hoskyns-Abrahall, a director of Unilever Ltd; John Russell Laing, chairman of Weir Ltd; and Willis Roxburgh, managing director of Morphy Richards, a household name in vacuum cleaners. If the Scottish Council (Development and Industry) had consciously set out to create a committee perversely unrepresentative of the people of Scotland, it could not have done a better job. Half the population – women – were ignored, and it seemed that the trade unions had no contribution to make either. A committee of seven was struggling to achieve a bare majority of Scots in its composition. But although it was produced by a group distinguished by its own mediocrity, the Toothill report was widely acclaimed as the nearest thing to the holy grail. The press and the Conservative political establishment received it with the utmost respect.

The report began with the seemingly unpromising statement: 'If there is a panacea for Scotland's economic problems we have not found it.' After this admission of defeat it continued for a further 200 pages, offering a variety of small panaceas, 81 of them, including the formation of a new department to deal with economic planning. When the Scottish Development Department came into being as part of a reorganisation of the St Andrew's House bureaucracy the following year, Toothill was credited as the daddy. But his personal obsession was the poor state of air communications between Scotland and England. He said at a press conference launching his report that businessmen visiting the UK rang him from London to complain that they could not get a seat on a flight for three weeks: 'What the hell goes on in your country?' they would demand to know – in an American accent more often than not. The train must have been too ridiculous an idea to recommend as an alternative; Toothill had little to say about the potential of railways.

The report called for 'a vigorous and purposeful demonstration of initiative and enterprise by Scotland's own people' and wondered in its mangled prose 'how our young men [there was no mention of women] can find scope to exercise responsibility, to expend their energies and to create from their ideas, to try and to fail and to succeed'. It proposed that pupils in senior secondary schools should specialise more in scientific and technical subjects and that a stronger vocational bias should be introduced towards the end of junior secondary courses. And it predated the public relations industry with its emphasis on image, Toothill viewing the national preoccupation with 'the gloomier aspects of things' as a turn-off for potential investors.

On the face of it there was not much cause for gloom. Shortly before Toothill unleashed his anatomy of the Scottish economy, there was an upbeat assessment from St Andrew's House rating the country's industrial prospects 'very high'. In 1961 Scotland was producing almost three million tons of steel a year; the Rolls-Royce factories in Hillington, Blantyre and East Kilbride were booming; industrial output was at an all-time high. In a single year 1,493 industrial building projects were completed, providing 80,000 new jobs, and 32 American firms were employing 23,000 people. Employment at the Bathgate vehicle plant was expected to grow to 5,000 within three years, while at Ravenscraig in Lanarkshire 3,000 men were employed in the building of the steel strip mill, which would be in full operation by the end of 1962.

Despite these symptoms of economic progress, unemployment was still stubbornly twice the UK average. Toothill's panacea – or non-panacea since he claimed not to have found any – was to increase council house rents to 'a sensible level' – how this was supposed to assist economic recovery was never satisfactorily explained – and to end the policy of 'propping up dying areas and the undue concentration on looking to others for help'. A few weeks later he revealed his true colours, not that they were ever in much doubt, with a speech to the British Institute of Management in which he attacked the STUC for convening a conference on the future of coal mining. He proposed that uneconomic pits should be closed as soon as possible, and accused the unions of 'being up to their old games' by calling too many strikes. The iron maiden, if she had worked out a coherent political philosophy at that stage, would have purred with approval at this early manifestation of Thatcherite principles, paid for and endorsed by the ostensibly non-political Scottish Council (Development and Industry). The Scottish press did not purr; it roared its endorsement of Toothill. The *Glasgow Herald* applauded the report's 'common sense' approach, a phrase with an echo of the common sense approach of Messrs Arbuckle Smith to industrial safety in the warehouses of Glasgow.

There were few dissenters, but one of them was an influential voice in the far north, the outspoken Sir Robert Urquhart, chairman of the Crofters' Commission. He said that the report had alarmed and angered the Highlands and north-east by virtually ignoring them. He described Toothill as a man who 'if given his way, would finish off the job that the Duke of Cumberland began' and ridiculed the idea that the Highlands should 'get itself a growth industry'. Urquhart maintained that the report's main themes, its emphasis on growth industries and air travel, were not original but borrowed from America and that, 'even with its imported talent', the committee had failed to produce anything of value for Scotland as a whole. Although Urquhart's polemic exposed the phonyness of Toothill, his was a lone voice.

V

There was a larger distraction, a cloud no bigger than a man's hand. Would anyone live to see the embodiment of all that Toothill stood for, and much more, in the person of Margaret Thatcher? Or would the 'gloomier aspects of things' prevail in some all-too-foreseeable nuclear catastrophe? Such an eventuality would no doubt be embraced in the final edition of the *Glasgow Herald* as a common sense approach to the annoying problem of human existence.

In October 1961 Russia exploded two nuclear devices in the atmosphere. The Medical Research Council studied the radioactive contamination of milk as a result and found that Scotland recorded by far the highest concentration of iodine 131 in the UK. Once inside the body it was concentrated in the thyroid gland and presented a particular danger to babies under the age of one. The General Assembly of the Church of Scotland responded by deploring the testing of atomic weapons. Ian Pitt-Watson condemned the resumption of atmospheric testing as 'a quite appalling example of human ruthlessness, cynicism and duplicity', while John R Gray summed up as convener of the church and nation committee with a judicious evaluation of God's position. Gray said he could not accept that the death of children from leukemia was a matter with which the Lord was unconcerned.

In the Western Isles, where the needs of a rocket range had deprived crofters of their land, the Free Church of Scotland reacted with horror to the latest 'nefarious project' – the proposal to site a NATO base on the islands, near the spot where Bonnie Prince Charlie and Flora MacDonald set sail on their bonny boat. Noting that there was no word of any provision for the defence of the people against enemy air attacks, the Free Presbytery of Lewis decreed that it should be repeated from every pulpit that the plan was 'an act of brutal callousness which may well cover with lasting shame the leaders of the present government responsible for it'.

But the opposition to the rampant militarisation of Scotland was mainly focussed on the Holy Loch, home of the recently arrived Polaris submarine fleet. Wretched weather almost ruined the first major demonstration against the American presence, which had been arranged for a September weekend in 1961. Gales and an unusually high tide disrupted Clyde ferry services and the protesters were put ashore at Hunter's Quay, some distance from their destination. Police escorted them on an unscheduled march to the base at Ardnadam, chatting amicably with four clergymen at the head of it. The demonstrators – most of whom were under the age of 40 – carried placards with such messages as 'Macmillan has an H-bomb shelter – have you?' and 'Where shall I run to, mummy?'

At Ardnadam, where sailors of the United States came and went unimpeded, the protesters lay down on the road, 'limply passive' according to one onlooker, before a police van reversed towards them and the first was 'carefully lifted by two solemn policemen and placed in the van'. Over a four-hour period 278 people were arrested and taken to a local church hall where they were kept in custody. Three others, Anglican vicars, were incarcerated within the precincts of a Roman Catholic church. Dunoon Sheriff Court was packed when Sheriff D J MacDiarmid took his seat at seven o'clock on Saturday evening. During a sitting which ended around 10.30pm, fines of £10 were imposed on most of the 91 prisoners who appeared from the church hall. Two Church of Scotland ministers, Walter Fyfe of the Gorbals and Albert Goodheir of Tayvallich in Kintyre, each received a fine of £15.

The sheriff twice threatened to clear the court after bursts of applause from the public benches. Half a dozen of the accused pleaded not guilty to the charge of breach of the peace, objecting with majestic pedantry to the words 'did conduct yourself in a disorderly manner' which were part of the formal wording of such a charge. They insisted that there was nothing disorderly about their manner.

A few weeks later more of the protesters appeared in court. They were offered an admonition if they gave an undertaking that they would not return to the county of Argyll to commit a similar offence. Not one was prepared to do so, and they were fined instead. The court was told that 185 uniformed police were on duty during the demonstration and that, although most of it was good-humoured, three protesters had jumped over the barrier into a no-go area. The sheriff clerk admitted that he was 'snowed under' with work collecting 291 fines totalling £2,542, most of which was eventually paid. A clue to the feelings of the submarine crews came during a student demonstration through the streets of Glasgow organised by Keith Bovey, chairman of Glasgow CND. An American sailor, looking on from the steps of a dance hall, drew cries of 'Yank go home', to which he responded: 'Just wish I could.'

VI

The serviceman who longed to go home was adrift in an alien world. 'What the hell goes on in your country?' bemused Americans would ask Sir John Toothill. The intending visitor had to wait three weeks for a flight, and once he got to Scotland he might have the misfortune to arrive on a Sunday when it was almost impossible to buy strong drink.

The pubs were shut all day, and the arcane laws of the land dictated that hotels were permitted to sell alcohol only to a strange breed known as *bona-fide* travellers who had to prove that they had journeyed a distance of at least three miles. These Sunday pilgrims tended not to travel much further than the required mileage; if, say, they lived in Oban, it was their custom to take the one o'clock bus to the village of Connel, just beyond the mandatory distance, where the landlord of the Ferryman's Hotel, known locally as the Glue Pot, would be obliged to serve them drink on production of their bus ticket. Since the returning bus left as late as four in the afternoon, the *bona-fide* travellers often got back to Oban in an advanced state of inebriation.

The system was a hypocritical farce, yet it had been a characteristic of Scottish licensing law for more than a century. It was finally blown apart by the government-appointed Guest committee, which recommended the abolition of the *bona-fide* rule, the Sunday opening of pubs, and a general extension of licensing hours. There was widespread astonishment when John S Maclay, the Secretary of State for Scotland, declined to accept Guest's package of reforms in full. Instead he bowed to the pressure of the

Sabbatarian lobby and the representations of such pillars of the community as Nevile Davidson, the Moderator-designate of the General Assembly, who opposed Sunday opening on the grounds that it was 'contrary to the Scottish tradition of observing the Lord's Day'. Maclay's objections were paternalistic rather than theological. He declared that 'it might be a bad thing if the only possible social centre on Sundays was to be the local pub'. Many pubs were indeed spit and sawdust dens, but the circumscribed nature of the Scottish Sunday, a day on which nothing moved, drove many a Scot to drink whether the bleak house was open or not.

The government produced a compromise hostile to the interests of the working class. The pubs would stay shut, the *bona-fide* traveller would make an unlamented outing to his final resting place, and hotels would be entitled to serve alcohol to all comers between the hours of 12.30 and 2.30pm on Sunday afternoon and 6 and 9pm on Sunday evening. This policy favoured rural areas where hotels outnumbered pubs. Urban Scotland, which had more pubs than hotels, was less hospitably placed. In Glasgow there was one hotel for every 42,000 people. Clydebank's 50,000 inhabitants, Coatbridge's 54,000, each had only one hotel in which to drink on a Sunday. Five other towns possessed only one – Renfrew, Port Glasgow, Johnstone, Barrhead and Milngavie. Paisley, with a population of 90,000, had two. The deserted county of Sutherland, on the other hand, boasted 47 hotels (22 more than Scotland's largest city), one per 260 of the population. Guest had warned that, such was the uneven distribution of licences, confining Sunday drinking to hotels 'would not help appreciably in reducing the amount of travelling for the primary purpose of obtaining liquor'. Maclay ignored the warning.

The other provisons of the 1961 Licensing (Scotland) Bill were more widely welcomed. Permitted weekday hours were standardised and slightly lengthened – 11am to 3pm, 5pm to 10pm, with 10 minutes' 'drinking-up' time after each session. It was felt that the small relaxation at the end of the drinking day would create a more civilised atmosphere and bring to an end what one newspaper called 'the desperate scramble'. The scramble continued regardless of this tinkering at the edges of Scotland's relationship with alcohol. But some small progress had been accomplished: it was now possible to drink in one's own town on a Sunday.

VII

If the weary, footsore *bona-fide* travellers had reached the end of the road, the Scots as a whole continued to stumble towards an uncertain destination. At the end of 1961 Jo Grimond speculated at length on the nature of this national journey. What was it for? Where were the Scots heading? 'The Scots have got to make up their minds why they think Scotland is worth keeping,' said Grimond, 'for what purpose they want to keep it, and if it is worth keeping they have got to realise it is because it is different.' He acknowledged the argument that the Scots should have self-government because they were badly treated, because they did not believe that Scotland got a fair share. 'But it is something much subtler than that. The fundamental reason why Scotland should have a degree of self-government is that it still has something to contribute to the world as a nation.' Were they listening in the newly liberated hotel bars? Were they listening in the grim little pubs? It was difficult to tell. The impulse behind two million signatures for a self-governing Scotland seemed to have dissipated without so much as a farewell toast.

1962

VOWS OF SILENCE

I

There was rarely a quieter start to a year in Scotland. Fewer than 200 souls braved ice and snow to bring in the New Year at Glasgow Cross, and the poor atmosphere was not enhanced by the ominous failure of the Tolbooth clock to strike midnight. The chimes began to play *A Guid New Year Tae Ane An' A'* five minutes before the end of 1961, but they were still playing at 10 minutes into 1962 without any acknowledgement that one year had ended and another begun. When the hand of the clock reached the hour, some in the crowd tentatively exchanged greetings, while others waited patiently for the official sound which never came. An entrepreneur – Sir John Toothill would have been proud of him – fetched jolly paper hats from a cardboard box and made a forlorn attempt to flog them. 'In another year or two,' said a policeman, 'there won't be anyone here on Hogmanay at all. They're all going for Christmas now.'

In George Square a few dozen gathered in front of the City Chambers before setting off on the traditional first-foot. A second despondent police officer was on hand to assist the inquiring press: 'Three things have gone to make it such a quiet New Year: the bad weather, the special television programmes, and the amount of money people are now spending on Christmas.'

In Edinburgh 1962 was greeted 'more decorously than at any time in living memory'. Since Edinburgh was the last word in decorum at any time of the year, the overhanging Calvinist gloom must have been oppressive. 'Fewer first-footers than ever appeared to be around,' a journalist noted with melancholy relish. Yet in Dundee a crowd of 6,000, most of them in their teens, gathered in the city square to hear the customary civic greeting from the steps of the Caird Hall, where Maurice McManus, the

Lord Provost, wished the citizens happiness and prosperity, the latter a word seldom whispered in Dundee.

The rest of Scotland, arranged around their television sets, had a choice of 'genial Jack House' – a cultivated Glasgow journalist not especially well cast for Hogmanay celebrations – introducing one of Roy Thomson's low-budget numbers headed by Calum Kennedy, a honeyed vocalist from the far west, or the BBC's starrier line-up of Andy Stewart, Duncan Macrae, Roddy McMillan and the kilted dancers of the White Heather Club. It was not much of a contest; Macrae's recitation of *A Wee Cock Sparra* in the first minutes of the year had become a well-loved ritual.

The critic Robert Kemp was impressed by the predominance of comics and Church of Scotland ministers in the output of both channels. He wrote: 'Hogmanay and New Year's Day are two such times when they seem to take charge completely, the ministers supplying us with a dram of spiritual uplift, the comics adding a diluting dash of entertainment.' The juxtaposition was misplaced: a dram of entertainment from the comics, followed by a diluting dash of spiritual uplift from the ministers, would have more faithfully reflected the Sabbatarian spirit of a country which still kept its pubs bolted whenever possible. But it was true that ministers had a lot to say for themselves, and did not lack the vehicles in which to say it.

II

The influence of the Kirk in the life of Scotland was so pervasive that the visit of Archie Craig, the Moderator of the General Assembly, to Rome in the spring of 1962 repeatedly made front-page news. The questions exercising the country, or that small part of it obsessed with such matters, were whether Craig would see the Pope, whether he should see the Pope, and whether the Pope would see him. The laboured preliminaries to any such meeting were the subject of intense speculation. As one ecclesiastical correspondent noted: 'Papal protocol demands a first approach from the party seeking an audience, and the Moderator has no authority for such an approach. He is empowered only to accept an invitation from the Vatican to see the Pope, and so far no invitation has been received. It has been suggested as a possibility that a visit might be arranged through an informal contact while Dr Craig is in Rome.' The niceties would have done credit to one of Jane Austen's drawing rooms. How could an introduction be facilitated with propriety intact on both sides of the barrier? The best to be hoped for, perhaps, was a fraternal peck on the cheek rather than a full-blown embrace.

A few days before Craig was to preach at the centenary service of St Andrew's Kirk in Rome, the Church of Scotland press office could barely conceal its pleasure at the successful outcome: 'The Moderator of the General Assembly has received a cordial communication from the Vatican. On learning that the Church of Scotland had decided that a courtesy visit to His Holiness Pope John XXIII would manifest Christian charity, foster good will, and be a step to friendlier relations between Protestants and Roman Catholics in Scotland and elsewhere, His Holiness has indicated that he would, for his part, warmly welcome such a visit.' Stuart Louden, convener of the colonial and continental committee, for it was true that a committee of that name existed in 1962, emphasised that the meeting 'had in fact come from the RC side ... they knew he was to be in Rome and wrote to him ... he virtually received an invitation'.

This triumph of elaborate diplomacy did nothing to appease the critics of the meeting. John Walker, minister of Girvan Old, wrote to the press: 'The Church of Rome has not changed its fundamental attitude towards so-called heretics such as the Church of Scotland. Don't let us fool ourselves. We shall be made welcome, but only on the Church of Rome's terms.' The Free Church of Scotland called the meeting 'a virtual betrayal of the historical Protestant faith'. But only one of the critics went to the trouble of pursuing Craig all the way to his destination. The Moderator was asked if he had had any contact from one Matthew Arnold Perkins, 'General Director of the National Union of Protestants', who had flown to Rome in order to dissuade him from meeting the Pope. Craig replied dryly: 'He has not yet called on me.' In a move intended to disarm opponents, he added that the meeting had no religious significance and that hostile Scottish reaction was 'very small'.

Earlier in the day there had been a loud cry of 'Amen' in St Andrew's Church when the Moderator made a passing reference to Calvin and Knox. It was not believed to have come from Matthew Arnold Perkins, but the general director made his feelings plain soon enough. He claimed that, although the world was kept guessing about the meeting, it had been organised secretly for some time. 'It is a tragedy and a disgusting thing,' said Perkins, 'that he [Craig] should fraternise and shake hands with this man. He would not cross Princes Street to have fellowship with non-conformist churches but he would cross a continent to shake hands with the Pope.' Members of the Congregational Church repudiated the allegation, insisting that Craig had indeed crossed Princes Street to meet them.

The much-anticipated encounter finally took place. The Pope greeted the Moderator on the threshold of the private library of the Vatican with the words: 'Dr Archibald Craig, out of the simplicity of the heart I thank you for your visit.' Craig said that, in their 38 minutes together, John had spoken often about 'unity among brethren in Christ'. Craig added: 'The Pope said he needed cardinals around him for advice on running the church because his job was for life and not temporary like mine.' (The Moderator, whose status was that of a first among equals, held office for a year.) The Vatican newspaper *Osservatore Romano* reported that His Holiness had been 'pleased to underline the great gifts of religiousness, tenacity and intelligent activity of the Scottish people', that the meeting had been 'marked by a spirit of extreme cordiality' and that it had 'touched on various subjects as well as personal episodes and memories of a spiritual nature' – a phrase of masterly elusiveness.

Archie Craig, whose experiences in the first world war earned him the Military Cross and converted him to pacifism, was a lecturer in Biblical studies at Glasgow University from 1947 to 1957. Some of his friends felt that his implacable opposition to war cost him a professorship in practical theology. He was a brilliant preacher who had a rule about sermons that 'every minute over 20 requires double justification'. He was also one of the Scottish church's more attractive personalities, always happy to share stories against himself. When he was general secretary of the British Council of Churches – the job he got in the absence of any offer of a chair at his university – he was sitting opposite a woman on a train. She observed that he was reading a book of theology but not wearing a dog collar, and inquired why. 'I am ordained as a minister,' Craig replied, 'but I am not now in a parish.' The woman nodded sympathetically and asked: 'Was it the drink?' It was not the drink, nor the pacifism, but Craig had other problems. His commitment to Christian unity – he was suspected of favouring bishops in the Kirk, a prospect anathema to the *Scottish Daily Express* – made him an unpopular figure among many of the faithful, yet he was so liked and respected that, despite the rejection of his 1957 report supporting closer links with the Anglicans, he was elected Moderator in 1961–62.

A Roman Catholic with whom Craig found common cause was responsible for a second ecumenical initiative in the closing months of the moderatorial year. Dom Columban Mulcahy, the abbot of Nunraw, a community of Cistercian monks in the Lammermuir Hills near Haddington, offered to arrange a meeting between 30 priests and laymen of the RC Church and a similar number of representatives of the Church of Scotland. It was promoted as a simple gesture of reconciliation – no more if no less than the hand of Christian friendship – but the modest proposal was an overnight sensation in the Scottish press, which gave prominence to the Free Church's refrain that an acceptance of the invitation would confirm that the Kirk was being led by men who were 'serving the interests of Rome'.

Kirk leaders danced nervously around the offer. Andrew Herron, the clerk to Glasgow Presbytery and one of the Kirk's supreme insiders, welcomed it tentatively as 'evidence of a change in the intransigent attitude which has been taken by the Roman Catholic Church and their refusal to admit that those outside their church are in the body of Christ'. While the Kirk's evangelical wing sharpened its claws, John R Gray – a man inseparable from his middle initial – retreated deep into the defence: 'One must not think that this is the Church of Scotland entering into negotiations with the Roman Catholic Church', and Herron sounded more dismissive than before: 'I am sorry that so much is being made of what I consider a very small event'. Tom Torrance, the Kirk's most distinguished academic thinker, was less inclined to beat about the burning bush: 'We must learn to talk with one another face to face, as those who have profound agreements and yet profound disagreements, and as those who have genuine respect for the conscience of each other.'

The very small event, to which the press were excluded, took place in Dowanhill Convent in Glasgow. Outside the gates a group of Protestant objectors shouted 'No popery' and 'Scotland for Protestantism' as the deputation entered and left. Two of the more boisterous protesters were removed in a police van. Inside the convent the Duke of Hamilton and the other Church of Scotland delegates were welcomed by James Ward, a senior priest representing the Archbishop of Glasgow, with the greeting, 'Friends, Romans, countrymen', and Mulcahy gave a speech quoting Francois Mauriac: 'Intelligence is but an insignificant thing on the surface of our nature; deep down we are emotional beings.' The abbot of Nunraw said the point of the quotation was that 'we must solve our psychological differences before we solve our theological ones'. John Kent, moderator of Glasgow Presbytery, declared afterwards: 'We have not come closer to one another's beliefs, but we have certainly come closer to friendships.'

There had been a tentative acceptance of the value of inter-church meetings. Beyond that nothing came of the enterprise. But there was an intriguing side-effect – an insight into the world of Cistercian monks in Scotland. The newspapers started to take an interest in Dom Columban Mulcahy and the monastery he had led since 1948, when he presided over its foundation. It was claimed that his slight speech impediment may have influenced his decision to join the Cistercian order. He was ordained a priest, taught philosophy and directed young student monks; he was then appointed to the order's office in Rome, a vocation cut short by his election to Nunraw. He took seriously the rallying call of Pope John XXIII for the churches to be 'open to the signs of the times'. He was a realist; he did not delude himself that his own church or the Church of Scotland was likely to make any hasty moves towards unity. But he was idealistic enough to believe that 'the future belongs to those who see it first'. He thought he saw a future in closer relationships between Christians, and worked devotedly towards them.

He was open to the inquisitive nature of journalists and welcomed them to Nunraw. They were impressed by what they found. Sixty-four monks worked and prayed in silence. Their day began at 2.15am and ended at 7pm. Dinner at noon consisted of bread, soup and vegetables; only invalids were allowed meat and fish. Milk was the only beverage. The monks took turns of waiting on the community and reading aloud improving texts during meals, the one daily relief from the vow of silence. Part of the day was spent working their farm, but most of it in prayer and contemplation. Conversation was not permitted; such communication as was necessary – 'business only' – was made by signs. The abbot said with a smile: 'There are those who think that Cistercians are a pretty clod-hopping order – good at looking after cattle, but not much else.' In 1967 the talky controversialist

Malcolm Muggeridge made a television documentary about Nunraw, finding in Mulcahy a kindred spirit. The abbot died almost as soon as he reached the age of three score years and 10.

III

A vow of silence would have been helpful in the case of another clergyman in the news in the spring of 1962. William Kenny, minister of St Andrew's Church, Dumbarton, scandalised the Glasgow middle class with accusations of misconduct against pupils of the city's High School for Girls, a fee-paying establishment of previously unimpeachable reputation. Kenny claimed to have overheard 15-year-old girls, wearing the uniform of the school, in frank conversation in a Sauchiehall Street café. The vigilant Kenny was so perturbed that he felt compelled to investigate further and on that occasion – or a later one; the exact circumstances were almost as muddy as inter-church relations – questioned the girls about their social and sexual habits. He further claimed to have been accompanied on one of his fact-finding missions by a police inspector and that the girls had admitted frequenting city centre cafés, smoking, drinking and going to wild parties 'with coloured men'.

James Robertson, the chief constable, sent a report on Kenny's allegations to the education committee. Leonard Small, convener of the Kirk's temperance and morals committee, thought there was 'something there to be carefully investigated' adding that the allegation of loose morality was 'only a symptom of something much deeper, not purely a Scottish thing, something of which we have been hearing suggestions from quite a lot of other places'. Two Sunday newspapers splashed the story across their front pages and the correspondence columns of the *Glasgow Herald* bulged with angry letters from parents. One suggested that Kenny 'ought to serve an apprenticeship in the cafés of Dumbarton, where there is vice in minor forms, before attempting to graduate into the big-time Glasgow league' while another commented: 'It is gratifying to know that the girls in Dumbarton are morally so far beyond reproach and are such devout Christians that Mr William Kenny can find sufficient time to investigate matters in Glasgow, and as a result blacken the name of a good school.'

Glasgow Presbytery ('the biggest in the world' as it sometimes styled itself) came down on the side of the school, throwing its own man to the wolves. 'The parents of the girls are confident that they know their daughters very much better than does Mr Kenny, and they have complete confidence in them and in their school,' was its official verdict – a statement with the hand of Herron all over it. Kenny furiously dissociated himself from this note of surrender, which he told the press he had been asked several times to sign, but refused. 'I have not withdrawn my allegations,' he declared. The affair fizzled out, though not before the Church of Scotland had made itself look clumsy and personally disloyal in its handling of it.

IV

Were the girls of Glasgow High School in the vanguard of the sexual revolution – as Leonard Small darkly hinted – or were they simply bragging to a young man in a dog collar who then passed on everything they said to the papers? Kenny retired bruised to his manse in Dumbarton; the girls vanished into the swinging sixties; Leonard Small rose to become Moderator of the General Assembly; and the identity of the 'coloured men' at the wild parties was destined to remain a mystery. But, in the midst of this minor scandal, no one challenged Kenny to explain why the ethnicity of the party-goers was so significant. Was he suggesting that coloured men were more likely to corrupt the morals of posh girls from Bearsden? Would the girls perhaps have been safer going to parties with white ones?

A second question of ethnicity arose on Lewis, an island invariably bubbling with outrage, when Kenneth MacRae, minister of Stornoway Free Church, condemned 'a stranger of Eastern blood' who was preparing to open a betting shop in the town, although Macrae preferred to call it 'a centre for the gambling vice'. The stranger of Eastern blood was revealed as Kaftan Kamal Arif, 24, a native of Thurso, the son of an Iraqi doctor. Arif had successfully established three centres for the gambling vice in Caithness and proposed to expand into God-fearing Stornoway. The Free Kirk Presbytery of Lewis issued a decree that any communicants known to have used the betting office would have all the privileges of church membership withdrawn; they would no longer be able to take communion, or be married in church, or have their children baptised. There was no mention of what would happen to punters who died clutching a slip for the three o'clock at Sandown Park – no definitive statement on their prospect of a Christian burial. Forty customers risked eternal damnation by visiting Arif's premises as soon as the shop opened.

V

But if Hell was the ultimate sanction in authoritarian Scotland, there was never a shortage of shorter-term earthly alternatives. Young offenders between the ages of 17 and 21 could end up in the South Inch detention centre, Perth. The idea of the 'short, sharp shock' (as it came to be known and adored by right-wing politicians) was to expose inmates to a brisk regime of strict discipline. When the centre was opened, the Scottish Home Department advised the courts that the programme would involve 'a full working day and regular daily sessions of physical training with emphasis on general alertness of response, high standards of personal conduct, cleanliness and good manners'. The PE instructors interpreted this brief with sadistic zeal. The authorities admitted to seven serious incidents of attempted suicide by inmates who would rather have cut their wrists and bled to death than submit to the brutality. There was also an implicit admission that prisoners who were ill and unfit were forced to undergo physical training regardless of their condition.

The Secretary of State ordered an inquiry. Six former prisoners who had complained of ill-treatment gave evidence along with 19 other ex-inmates selected at random. The hearings were held in private and, in accordance with the usual standards of institutional secrecy, the report was kept under wraps. In such situations the political establishment invariably took a vow of silence. The obsequious Scottish media raised no complaint, being content to report meekly that the Scottish Office had issued an edict that the PE should be less arduous in future.

VI

On April Fool's Day 1962 John S Maclay achieved the distinction of becoming the longest-serving Secretary of State for Scotland. He took office on 14 January 1957 and was still there five years, three months and 18 days later. He possessed neither the sense of mission of a Tom Johnston nor the political intelligence of a Hector McNeil; he was fortunate that nationalism never gave him a moment's trouble; he was not a gifted public speaker. But he decided early on what needed to be done to revive the Scottish economy and stuck to his guns. Recognising that an industrial structure based on coal-mining and shipbuilding was in terminal decline, he did what he could to create a new one. Opinions varied on his degree of success. His friends pointed to the strip mill, the vehicle plants and three prosperous new towns; his opponents to rising emigration, relatively high unemployment and the decay of rural Scotland.

Between 1951 and 1961 more than a quarter of a million people left Scotland. Had it not been for the loss of these emigrants, unemployment would have been considerably worse: there was that to be said for the grievous loss of talent. But the number out of work remained stubbornly high – 79,000 in the spring of 1962 compared to 69,000 a year earlier. *The Scotsman* saw the nature of the problem as essentially political: 'Present methods, in fact, are not the right ones for bringing about an industrial renaissance. Those working to bring new industry are much in the position of a branch office, free to determine details, but not to take any big initiatives.'

The lack of political direction was painfully transparent in the far north despite the valiant efforts of the Advisory Panel for the Highlands and Islands, chaired by the patriotic Lord Cameron, most of whose suggestions for improvement were ignored. The destruction of the social and economic fabric drove John Bannerman, chairman of the Scottish Liberal Party, to despair: 'Basic communications are second-rate or entirely absent; arterial highways are so narrow that tourists have second thoughts about risking their cars on them or are impatient at delays occasioned by having to stop at every second passing place. Township roads, the lifeline of many crofting areas, are in a terrible state, causing these areas to become depopulated. High freight costs make a loaf of bread 4d dearer than in any other area of Scotland.'

But in many remote communities there were defects more basic than terrible roads and punitive food bills. In 1962 the 1,000 inhabitants of the Shetland island of Yell were still lighting their houses by paraffin lamp. 'How can we persuade the younger generation to stay in a place where such things as water mains and electricity are unknown?' they asked. Campaigners drew attention to their plight by distributing black postcards with the words 'Yell for Light' in brilliant yellow. The islanders complained that 46% of the houses were officially no longer fit for habitation and that it cost £4 to 'send a bullock to Scotland' – prompting the question of which country the people of Yell believed they belonged to if it was not Scotland. Moved by their protestations, Sir Robert Urquhart, chairman of the Crofters' Commission, and Jo Grimond, MP for Orkney and Shetland, led a delegation.

Urquhart and company left Lerwick by ferry for Fetlar, the main settlement in Yell, at six o'clock on an April morning. Grimond had gone the night before and was waiting to help the two boatloads of strangers on to the slippery pier at Ulsta four hours later. Buses took them north to such Nordic-sounding places as Cullivoe and Gloup and south and west to Burravoe and Gossabraugh. 'They drove past deserted school houses, derelict crofts and the whirring windmills which bring electricity of a sort to the occasional fortunate household,' wrote a journalist who accompanied the party. Two hundred people – a fifth of the population – crowded into Mid Yell Village Hall to air their grievances. Fraser Jamieson, chairman of Yell Development Council as well as the island registrar, denied that the people were lazy; he agreed there was apathy but insisted that this was due to years of neglect. At midnight rain and wind swept up Yell Sound while the visitors were ferried back to the Shetland mainland after 16 hours in the second most northerly parish in Britain. Coffee and sandwiches awaited them in their hotel in Lerwick, where the discussions about Yell, and what could be done about it, continued into the wee sma' hours.

None of this mattered in St Andrew's House. The Secretary of State, two days after the muted celebrations of his record-breaking run, was faced with a double blow compared to which the paraffin lamps of Yell were a small matter.

VII

Two major industries closed on the same calamitous day. In West Lothian 1,000 men were made idle by the decision of Scottish Oils Ltd to shut down what remained of the shale oil industry. Its founder, James Young, would have been intrigued by the continuing use of paraffin on the island of Yell, for it was Young who found that it was possible to distil paraffin from coal, a discovery that launched the world's first commercial oil industry in Bathgate in the middle of the 19th century. He acquired the nickname Paraffin Young.

At its peak shale oil employed 10,000 people in the area around Bathgate, bringing prosperity to such outposts as Pumpherston, Addiewell and Uphall. The wages were always better than average, and apart from one dispute in 1925 the industry had a strike-free record. But the process was laborious, productivity correspondingly low, and younger men were discouraged from working in it by the increasingly uncertain prospects. 'The winding up,' wrote an authority on the industry, 'will not be important in the context of British oil needs, but it will be missed as a large-scale training laboratory producing the experienced men who gave Britain a strong footing in overseas oilfields.'

For most of the workers laid off, the outlook was bleak. 'There may be work at Bathgate at the British Motor Corporation factory,' wrote one commentator, 'but the older men know it is not for them. The young shale miners will go and help dig ditches and foundations at Livingston New Town when the civil engineering work gets under way. The older men cannot move away from the district. What is there for them to do? Will new industries come to this quarter? Amenity is as important a factor as many others in determining site desirability, and this barren place of shale bings [he was referring to Addiewell] has none to offer.'

On the same day a legendary name in railway engineering, the North British Locomotive Company, closed its Springburn works in Glasgow, putting 1,500 men out of work. Jean Roberts, the city's Lord Provost, whose father had worked for the company, described this as 'a social as well as an economic disaster'; the STUC called forlornly for a renewed effort to direct new industry to Scotland; the Scottish Council (Development and Industry), sponsor of Toothill's empty rhetoric about council house rents and air communications, added the qualification that this was 'the classic example of an old-fashioned industry not having moved with the times', its chairman, Lord Polwarth, blaming the labour force for its reluctance to accept that the glorious age of steam was coming to an end.

Springburn, which had made engines of power, beauty and utility for the world, and which had boasted a lively intellectual and cultural life with a Caledonian Railway Debating Society and regular concerts in its park, was left a desert overnight. Forty years later it was officially the poorest constituency in Scotland. The number of school leavers with no qualifications was 300% higher than the Scottish average, teenage pregnancies 60% higher, deaths from lung cancer 94% higher, the incidence of heart disease 40% higher, the number of people on income support 130% higher, unemployment 140% higher. This state of affairs could be traced back to a single day in 1962. But 40 years later, when visitors to the local public library asked to see books about the social and industrial history of Springburn, they were informed that such books were no longer kept in stock. The past had been expunged with impressive brutality; in its place there was the usual vow of silence.

VIII

The world almost came to an explosive end in October 1962 over the Cuban missile crisis. In the same week a terrorist known as the Black Pimpernel (Nelson Mandela) appeared in court in Pretoria charged with organising a strike, and a second leader of the African National Congress, Albert Lutuli, was elected rector of Glasgow University in his absence. He could not be there because he was being held under house arrest near Durban. The nationalist Robert McIntyre was a distant second behind Lutuli in a rectorial campaign which ended in a near-riot or the customary exhibition of high spirits (interpretations varied). Several thousand supporters of the rival candidates, who also included Edward Heath and the Earl of Rosebery, blocked University Avenue. As the police over-reacted by arresting 32 students, the crowd cheerfully whistled the theme tune of *Z Cars*, a police procedural series on BBC Television.

In this jaunty atmosphere there was no hint of an impending nuclear holocaust. Uptown it was business as usual at the Glasgow Empire, graveyard of English comedians, where Dickie Valentine and Winifred Atwell topped the bill. On this occasion no one died at the Empire. The curtain came down and the audience went home to their beds uncertain that they would still be in one piece in the morning. Mr Krushchev blinked first, the world was saved, and the 32 students appeared in the Central Police Court charged with something or other.

In the same eventful month the first James Bond film, *Dr No*, hit Scottish screens. Glasgow's *Evening Times* was underwhelmed: 'You would hardly expect an actor called Sean Connery to be a Scotsman. But Connery, starring in *Dr No* at the Odeon, was born in Edinburgh, and began his working life as a milk delivery boy.' Connery's performance was not thought remarkable enough to be mentioned, but the paper's critic, Tom Goldie, described the film as 'fine, harmless fun for the family, though you see the same sort of thing any night on television'. He was more enthusiastic about *Dr Finlay's Casebook*, a BBC drama series in which another promising young Scottish actor, Bill Simpson, played a rural GP. Fifty years later it was Connery who was the elderly international superstar and Simpson who was dead and forgotten.

1963

WIDE EYED

I

At three hours 20 minutes it was the longest judgement in the Court of Session that anyone could remember. It was not only approaching the length of a small novel; in places it read like one. It was dark and comic with touches of absurdity, narrated by a man whose view of sexuality hinted at a Presbyterian prudishness. John Wheatley was, however, that comparatively rare specimen, a Roman Catholic on the bench, and rarer still, one who grew up in a Glasgow tenement. But in some ways he was a figure of Kirk-like rectitude, punishing sex offenders with unusual severity. In background and temperament he could not have been more alien from the two protagonists in the most salacious case of his long career – the Argyll divorce.

In the blue corner: the 11th Duke of Argyll, chief of the Clan Campbell, hereditary master of the royal household in Scotland, three times married, with a casual interest in pornography. In the red corner: his wife Margaret, daughter of a millionaire Scottish businessman, spoiled, vain, sexually rampant, whose 'melting eyes and pale magnolia skin' made her irresistible to men. She was said to have had 88 lovers; it seemed she had been counting. Her friend Barbara Cartland said after her death: 'Every man wanted to go to bed with her and she wanted to go to bed with every man. And why not? I think men found her rather boring after a while.'

Cole Porter wrote a song called *You're the Top* which included the lines 'You're an O'Neill drama/You're Whistler's mama.' For the English version, P G Wodehouse changed them to 'You're Mussolini/You're Mrs Sweeny' – Mrs Sweeny being a much-photographed beauty of her age, the wife of Charles Sweeny, an American golfer. The marriage ended in divorce and Mrs Sweeny re-married Ian Campbell, Duke of Argyll, in 1951. The honeymoon was short-lived. The duke grew tired of her sexual recklessness; the duchess complained of his excessive drinking and sadism.

After a hearing lasting 11 days Wheatley found that all four allegations against the duchess had been proved. He decided that she had committed adultery with Sigismund von Braun, a diplomat; with Harvey Combe, the PR director of the Savoy Hotel; with John Cohane, an American businessman; and with an un-named man or men depicted in a series of nude photographs. He said he was forced to the conclusion that the duchess was a promiscuous woman whose desires were not limited to 'normal sexual relations'.

Picking his way distastefully through the various lovers, Wheatley reserved his strongest censure for Cohane, who had 'appeared to display the morals of a tom cat'. He decided that he and Margaret had gone to bed together between 9 and 10am on 13 January 1956 and dismissed the notion that this was an unlikely time to have sex. He said that, since his elevation to the bench, he had reached the conclusion that there were no prescribed or proscribed hours for 'the act'. Letters addressed by Cohane to the duchess had been addressed 'Dearest Margaret' or 'Darling Margaret' – 'a common form of address in America', noted Wheatley, but not one he regarded as acceptable. The phrase in one letter, 'You are an incredibly exciting woman', struck him as incriminating. Wheatley had less to say about von Braun, but only because the purple patches concerning this relationship were in his view too disgusting to repeat in detail.

About her adultery with the PR man, he said that Combe had spent an hour and a half in her flat in London on the night of 13-14 July 1960 in circumstances which could not be explained away by Combe's testimony, supported by the duchess, that they were cleaning up the mess made by his dogs while the two of them were out together. Wheatley denounced this as 'a false story to cover up the real fact, namely that they were having a sexual relationship on the occasion in question'. By the time of this affair, the duke had started divorce proceedings and had fixed a bolt on his bedroom door to prevent his wife from getting into bed with him. Combe had admitted that he was very fond of Margaret. But Wheatley was unconvinced by his suggestion that it was a platonic relationship; the role Combe played in this 'sordid and sinister transaction' indicated that he and the duchess were 'closer and more intimate than either was prepared to admit'.

Having disposed of the three named, Wheatley was left with the unidentified figure or figures in the nude photographs. The judge said he would spare the duchess the indignity of describing the photographs; he would say only that they showed 'persons indulging themselves in a gross form of sexual relationship'. Wheatley said that the duke himself was not averse to carrying pornographic photographs on his person. A woman from America had testified that he showed off a collection of such pictures at a party in New York and had seemed to treat them as something of a joke.

But the photographs kept by the duchess, which the duke claimed to have found in a cupboard, were more personal. They were a series of Polaroid photographs, all showing either a nude male or a nude male and a nude female. The nude female was the duchess. But who was the nude male? Might there have been more than one? It was difficult to tell since the photographs showed the guilty parties from the neck down. 'The headless man', as the press branded him, was soon the talk of the town.

Enter John Profumo, the minister for war. He had assured the House of Commons in March that there was no impropriety whatever in his relationship with Christine Keeler, who was routinely described as a prostitute although there was little or no evidence that she accepted payment for her services to older men. In early June Profumo resigned after admitting that he had lied about the nature of his friendship with Keeler. Harold Macmillan's government was now in terminal trouble, made worse by a cabinet meeting at which Duncan Sandys, minister of defence and son-in-law of Winston Churchill, acknowledged that he was rumoured to be the headless man. Macmillan promptly appointed Lord Denning, England's senior law lord, to conduct an inquiry into the non-existent 'security risks' of the two scandals involving ministers.

Denning, with a lascivious dedication to the fine detail of the brief, invited the main suspects in the Argyll case – von Braun, Cohane, Combe, Sandys and the film actor Douglas Fairbanks jnr – to the Treasury to assist him with 'a very delicate matter'. As they arrived, they were asked to sign in. This ruse enabled Denning to compare their signatures with the handwriting on the captions of some of the photographs. A nude man was masturbating in various states of arousal – 'gratifying himself' as the *New York Times* was still delicately putting it 37 years later. Under these images were the captions 'Before', 'Thinking of you', 'During – oh', and 'Finished'. Denning sent the samples to a handwriting analyst, and then asked a Harley Street doctor to examine Sandys' pubic hair with a view to establishing if it corresponded with the pubic hair of the headless man. In another set of photographs the duchess, who was wearing three strings of pearls though nothing else, was 'performing a sex act' – a euphemism for fellatio still commonly in use in the early years of the 21st century – on either the same nude man or a different one.

When Denning's report was published the Stationery Office in Castle Street, Edinburgh, opened at half past midnight to cope with the anticipated demand for copies. An egalitarian queue of 50, some wearing evening dress, others in the uniform of bus drivers, waited in heavy rain for the premises to open. In the first 15 minutes 200 copies were shifted.

The report was a masterpiece of titillation. Denning said that 'a certain minister' – a reference to Sandys – had brought to his attention claims that he (the minister) was the unknown man in the Argyll divorce case and had paid money to prevent himself being cited in the case. A medical man 'of the highest eminence' had examined the minister – an oblique allusion to Sandys dropping his pants in the national interest – and the results had demonstrated to Denning's satisfaction that the unknown man in the photographs was not the minister. The *Glasgow Herald* was relieved to hear it. 'The serious and widespread rumours of immorality in high places have been shown to be without foundation,' said the paper. 'He [Denning] has shown that British public life is no worse in its standards, and perhaps a little better, than much British private life.'

The *Herald* did not say how it had come about this remarkable fact about the sexual habits of the majority. Profumo, whose immorality had cost him his career and reputation, sought refuge with his wife, the actress Valerie Hobson, in the House of Tongue, a shooting lodge in Sutherland. Ian Mackay, a student who worked as a ghillie at the house, recalled that the Profumos were so well liked there that the locals 'discouraged the press pack as much as they could, mainly by not offering accommodation and by leading them on wild goose chases'. After a few nights of sleeping in their cars, with no reported sightings of the disgraced politician and no stories worth sending back, most of them left.

II

The scandals of 1963 finished Supermac. In October, while in hospital for a prostate operation, he announced his resignation. The choice of successor seemed to rest squarely between Rab Butler, the deputy prime minister, and Reginald Maudling, the Chancellor of the Exchequer. Long before the Conservative Party decided such matters with some semblance of democracy, it was the party's grandees who called the shots.

As they deliberated, a small paragraph in the newspapers went almost unnoticed. It announced that 'Mr George Younger, Easter Leckie, Gargunnock, Stirlingshire, was yesterday adopted as Unionist candidate for the by-election in Kinross and West Perthshire'. Inheriting a majority of 12,248, the young brewer was guaranteed a parliamentary seat for life; he could look forward to giving up selling Alloa ale for a living. But a few astute political observers wondered mischievously if the comfortable seat – which was more of an easy chair – might soon be occupied by someone other than Mr George Younger of Easter Leckie. The rumours forced Major D Maitland Graham, chairman of the local Tory association, to issue a disclaimer: 'There is no question of Mr Younger being asked to stand down in favour of anyone else.' The following day Younger earned the everlasting gratitude of his party by gallantly standing down in favour of the new Prime Minister, the Earl of Home.

There was general consternation that a peer should have been chosen to lead the government. George Brown, Labour's deputy leader, said during a visit to Ayr that it was 'an insult to the nation, the most staggering development'. Jo Grimond, the Liberal leader, was more measured: 'I like and respect Lord Home very much and wish him every success. He has many admirable qualities but it is not these qualities that seem to have got him the job but the fact he was believed not to want it. This is carrying the cult of the amateur too far.'

Among the Scottish Tories loyalty was severely tested. John Henderson, the Cathcart MP, said he was dreadfully sorry that Butler, after his long years of 'magnificent service to the nation' should have been passed over for a second time (he had been rejected in favour of Macmillan in 1957). Robert Kernohan, the party's candidate in Pollok, admitted to being distressed by the treatment of Butler, adding: 'I am sorry that if there had to be a compromise, we didn't turn to the Macleod-Maudling generation.' The paper for which Kernohan worked, the *Glasgow Herald*, bit its editorial tongue with limited success: 'Lord Home has made a mistake in yielding to the pressure which has been put on him. Now we hope to be proved wrong.'

In Coldstream, the Borders town of Home's ancestral residence, The Hirsel, no such doubts were entertained. Only Lady Caroline, his eldest daughter, was at home. She told a reporter: 'I was out hunting this morning and the first we heard about it was on the radio. It is a great honour for the family, but a most difficult job to tackle.' The local Burns Club, of which the Prime Minister was president, promptly sent their man a telegram with lines from the poet's *Epistle to a Young Friend*:

Conceal yoursel' as weel's ye can
Frae critical dissection;
But keek thro' ev'ry other man,
Wi' sharpen'd sly inspection

In his first hours in the job Sir Alec (as he was known after renouncing his title) failed to conceal himself frae critical dissection. It was more or less open season on the laird. James Jack of the STUC observed that he was 'simply not of this world, but belonged to the 19th century', while John Bannerman of the Scottish Liberals said that 'the selection of a peer by private auction merely serves to emphasise the breadth of the chasm between the Tory hierarchy and the ordinary people'. The Prime Minister denied that he had no knowledge of how the other half lived. He thought this allegation a case of inverted snobbery. He was a farmer; he knew 'all about the work on the farms'.

All attention was focussed on Kinross and West Perthshire, where extra telephone lines were installed between Crieff and Whitehall to enable the Conservative candidate to go on running Britain while he attempted to become a member of the House of Commons. There was little gratitude for W Gilmour Leburn, the MP whose death had conveniently left the seat vacant. Leburn had been parliamentary under secretary of state at the Scottish Office, for what that was worth, but his main achievement in politics was to die at strategically the right moment.

William Rushton, a mimic of Supermac on the BBC satirical programme *That Was The Week That Was*, declared his intention to stand as an independent. Andrew Forrester, the Labour candidate, hoped to conduct his campaign while on honeymoon, an ambition which threw up several satirical possibilities. Arthur Donaldson represented the SNP. Ian Smith, the owner of a garage in Callander, came forward as an Independent Unionist. Richard Wort, a mathematics teacher from Wimbledon, was a late entry for the Light and Dark Blue Conservative Party, whose chief policy was to oppose the disclaiming of peerages in order to achieve the office of Prime Minister. In such a diverse field it was supposed that the main opposition would come from the Liberals, whose candidate, Alasdair Millar, a 49-year-old farmer from Aberfeldy, was a veteran of the 1945 election.

The Prime Minister began his campaign at a remote school in Glen Lyon, travelling by narrow, twisting roads. He was enthusiastically received by crowds unprecedented in the village halls – 300 each at Fortingall and Grandtully. But at one of them he made an early mistake which revealed his lack of political acuity. Answering a question on Forth Road Bridge tolls, he appeared to accept as true a suggestion that there were no tolls on the Mersey tunnel (there were).

In the evening he and his wife returned to the home of Major and Mrs Andrew Drummond-Moray, and their daughters (Vicki, Xandra and Georgina) at Easter House, Comrie, where they were billeted for the campaign. The following morning, the hosts were reported to be 'wide eyed' with astonishment at the invasion of their house by an army of journalists and photographers. With a screech of tyres the Prime Minister embarked on another tour of the villages, smartly followed by a procession of 35 cars full of Fleet Street's finest.

The press reported that his young opponent Rushton wore crimson socks and a pocket handkerchief – the former considered a mark of dandyish eccentricity, the latter worthy of note even in 1963. He said he hoped for 2,000 votes. Asked what he knew about winter keep, the farmer's worry, Rushton replied with disarming candour: 'Translate, please.' He added that it would be hyprocrisy for him to say any more about winter keep: 'Everyone would know the information had been planted.' He said he had voted Tory in 1959, but would not do so again. So how would he vote if he were an elector of Kinross and West Perthshire? 'Labour,' he said, 'especially with their man's devotion to duty, electioneering on his honeymoon.'

At Amulree the people of the glens came to the hotel to drink sherry and meet the Prime Minister. Shepherds, 'their faces tickled purple by wind and sun and framed with granite grey hair', shook hands with Home, applauded, and heard improving talk about the modernisation of Britain. In the evening the candidate ventured into the brooding hills and spoke at packed meetings about the dangers of automation's rapid advance: 'We do not want to live in a card-index and push-button society that forgets the supreme value of the individual. Let it be clear that the machine is the servant and that what matters in the age of science, as in the age of faith, is that the individual under God shall remain supreme.'

As Sir Alec pondered the role of the Almighty in the future of the Conservative Party, George West, a Glasgow comedian who started his career as a clog dancer, died at the age of 73. An obituarist wrote that, in private life, he was an imposing figure in 'a strikingly well-cut overcoat and a good hat' and that he carried a silver-headed malacca cane – 'his whole appearance that of a man of position and influence'. He would have been a convincing fringe candidate in the Kinross and West Perthshire by-election, his good hat an electoral asset.

It was dripping wet on 30 October, and the Prime Minister had to be escorted from the house under a gaudy golf umbrella. 'Lady Home and the Drummond-Moray ladies pursued him in a battledress of suede, scarf and boot, like brave female followers of rugby football,' wrote one journalist. At Muthill, the last stop before lunch, he was given a horseshoe for luck and adjourned to the local pub. By the afternoon he had retreated, red-slippered, into the drawing room of the Drummond-Morays for a press conference.

That evening ITN broadcast a nine-minute item on the by-election despite the Liberals' refusal to cooperate. The time allocated to the party was filled in meaningless fashion by shots of the candidate leaving his car and, when this was no longer bearable, by still pictures of him, while a disembodied voice read extracts from the manifesto.

On Halloween, a thousand women 'in heather tweed, woolly stockings and functional headgear' stood to applaud the first British Prime Minister to visit Crieff. He had started the day climbing the shoulder of Ben More escorted by Ewan Cameron, a champion caber-tosser and Highland cattle breeder from Lochearnhead, whose chest measured 53 inches, his biceps 16 inches, his thighs 36 inches and who stood, all 22 stones of him, six feet five inches in height. Never was a new Prime Minister more impregnable to attack. Home paused to look at one of Rob Roy Macgregor's alleged graves before prodding a sheep. An observer wrote that, as he talked to the shepherds, he looked in his knickerbockers, with crags and narrow lochs behind him, 'as if he were posing for some Scottish pictorial calendar'. Fleet Street was touched by the 'wide-eyed children of the glen' – you did not have to be wide eyed to live in this constituency, but it helped. They clustered shyly around Home, producing grubby scraps of paper from their pockets for signing, and they laughed at the journalists, 'floundering about in printed suede boots and drainpipe trousers'.

The Glasgow Empire had closed earlier in the year. On the last night a demolition gang of Duncan Macrae, John Mulvaney and Albert Finney came on the stage like the gravediggers from *Hamlet*, Jack Radcliffe read messages of condolence, and among the many others who put in an appearance were the world ballroom dancing champions, the pipes and drums of the City of Glasgow and Ayrshire Regiment and May Moxon's high-kicking dancing girls. When the curtain fell on the Empire to the strains of *Auld Lang Syne* and *God Save the Queen*, there were lamentations for the death of the music hall in Scotland. But the obituaries were premature. They had not reckoned with the Kinross and West Perthshire by-election.

For belly laughs there was Rushton, portly scourge of the establishment, opening his campaign in subversive Killin before a crowd of 200. He admitted that, beyond his scorn for Home, he had no policy worth discussing.'A vote for me,' he declared, 'means one thing – that the electors of Kinross and West Perthshire refuse to have Home, of all people, foisted upon them.' It was the first public meeting Rushton had ever addressed. He spent the rest of the day dishing out copies of *Private Eye* magazine.

Sir Alec was not amused. He told the villagers of Kenmore: 'Mr Rushton has been going about spreading the rumour that I shall not be here at the general election. I don't mind him being a funny man but I don't like him debasing our political currency and using dirty tricks like that when our politics in Kinross and West Perthshire are always kept clean. If he wants to conduct that kind of funny business, he had better go back on the stage.'

At Kinloch Rannoch – the constituency was groaning with memorable place names – the Prime Minister, 'speaking as the father of four children under 30', turned to the place of youth in today's society. They did not want to be thought of as a problem, they did not need to be preached at (etc). Here the Empire Loyalists – no connection to the late lamented Glasgow theatre – 'made their presence felt with wild and weird interruptions'. In the shopping centre at Auchterarder he was 'mildly harassed' by Young Socialists and then the anti-nuclear Committee of 100 arrived with 'bizarre banners that raised eyebrows in Crieff'. (It took a lot to raise an eyebrow in Crieff.)

On Sunday, 'a day of peculiar quiet', it was noted that the Labour Party was playing 'a strangely unobtrusive, unostentatious role' with its honeymooning candidate Forrester 'not easily available to the press'. Possible explanations were tactfully left unexplored. The newspapers fell to wondering if a record might be broken in the by-election for the lowest poll ever achieved by a candidate in Scotland, evidently the record being held by a suffragette candidate in Glasgow Camlachie who polled 35 votes in the 1910 general election.

The only piece of mildly diverting Sabbath news was that the son and three daughters of Sir Alec had given up their titles. Lord Dunglass would be known as David Douglas-Home Esquire, the unmarried daughters as Miss Caroline and Miss Meriel Douglas-Home, the married daughter as Mrs James Wolfe-Murray. The four signed a petition to the Lord Lyon King of Arms stating that they were forgoing their titles because of 'the love and favour and affection which they bear towards their parents'. Were these gestures necessary? The Peers Act, giving members of the House of Lords the right to disclaim their titles, had been passed in July, only four months before these events, and the constitutional position of disclaiming peers' children was still being disputed. Home attempted a little joke about it all: 'My daughters have been calling themselves near-misses for days.'

Smith, the garage man from Callander, introduced a late whiff of grapeshot, attacking the organised planting of crosses by candidates at Crieff war memorial. The former wing commander and fighter pilot, who had been decorated for bravery, told the press: 'I lost many friends in the war and I just can't do this sort of thing.' Millar, the Liberal, who had fought at Dunkirk and held the Military Cross, also boycotted the ceremony. But Home and Forrester, as well as the SNP candidate and the mysterious Wort, all went up with their tributes. The locals were unmoved by the row, reserving their outrage for a BBC TV *Panorama* profile of the constituency entitled 'Sheep and Retired Colonels'.

The retired colonels were furious. As for the non-voting sheep, there was no denying their influential role in the campaign. The 'persuasive and charming' Liberal, when he claimed that the hill-farming country which embraced Blair Atholl, Pitlochry and Aberfeldy was solidly behind him, made a heavy point of assuring the bemused foreign press that 'I know where the people are, and I know their sheep, and they know me and they know my sheep'.

After travelling 1,500 miles and making 60 speeches in nine days the Prime Minister ended his campaign by 'offering the nation the happy life'. He said in his closing speech: 'There is no cause for the British people in 1963 to live colourless, drab and uniform lives. We can be a happy people, enjoying prosperity, and using it morally and well.' His Liberal opponent drew 600 people to an eve-of-poll rally, while younger voters flocked to the 11.30pm meeting of Rushton, who had contrived to have the last word.

TV crews colonised the area around the County Buildings in Perth for the declaration, at noon on Friday 8 November, by George Emslie, the Sheriff of Perthshire. In a high poll Home took 57% of the votes – 11% less than Leburn at the general election – with the Liberals second, Labour third, the SNP a distant fourth. Wort created a new Scottish all-comers' record with 23 votes. Rushton got 45, only 1,955 short of his personal target. Asked if he would buy a house in the constituency, Sir Alec replied: 'I have too many houses to live in already.' He was also asked if he would drop Macmillan's slogan, 'You've never had it so good'. He said he saw nothing wrong about spreading prosperity: 'We should get away from the idea that there is a moral stigma attached to prosperity.'

There was no danger of a moral stigma in East Kilbride where 800 workers at Holyrood Knitwear had just been fired, or in Glasgow where Harland and Wolff had closed its yard with the loss of 1,300 jobs, or in Stornoway where 21% of the workforce were unemployed. 'I am quite confident we will win the general election,' Sir Alec announced before he left the constituency for London. As one of the perkier adornments of the Profumo scandal said in another context: 'He would say that, wouldn't he?'

III

Far away on the island of Rousay, Orkney, John Flett, grieve at the farm of Westness, was digging a hole to bury a cow when he stumbled upon a grave. It contained jewels as well as bones. Among the finds was a silver and gold filigree brooch, mid-eighth-century in origin, of exceptional beauty and archaeological importance. But the grave itself belonged to the mid-19th century. So why was the brooch there? And whose bones were buried with it – were they of a Viking or a Victorian? Among remains of more recent provenance, Duncan Sandys was awarded a life peerage in recognition of his services to the state; John Profumo devoted the rest of his life to the poor; the Duke of Argyll married a fourth time; the duke's former wife Margaret died in penury in a nursing home in Pimlico; and, although Margaret hinted that it was Sandys, no one ever owned up to being the headless man.

IV

It was one of the small ironies of the by-election that the temporary seat of government in Britain for 10 days was Strathearn, at the end of a single-track branch railway from Gleneagles which had recently been earmarked for closure by Dr Richard Beeching – Lord Beeching as Home prematurely referred to him. The Beeching report on the future of the railways recommended a reduction in the number of stations and halts in Scotland from 669 to 230, the withdrawal of 51 passenger services, and the closure of two mainline stations in Glasgow (St Enoch and Buchanan Street) and one in Edinburgh (Princes Street). There would be no passenger trains north or west of Inverness, north-east of Aberdeen, south of Ayr, or through the Borders from Edinburgh. About 1,350 route miles would be closed, a reduction of 41%.

The list of little stations which were closed in this act of anti-social insanity read like an elegy for a vanishing Scotland. They included, among many others, Kitty Brewster, Lonmay, Maud Junction, and Udny in Aberdeenshire; Ballachulish and Benderloch in Argyll; Hollybush, Kilkerran, and Pinmore in Ayrshire; Findochty, Ladysbridge, and Tillynaught in Banffshire; Grantshouse and Reston in Berwickshire; Tillycoultry in Clackmannan-shire; Back o'Loch Halt and Rhu in Dunbartonshire; Pittenweem in Fife; Boat o' Garten (later anglicised as Boat of Garten), Culloden Moor, Daviot, and Nethy Bridge in Inverness-shire; Laurencekirk in Kincardineshire; Crook of Devon and Rumbling Bridge in Kinross-shire; Southwick in Kirkcudbrightshire; Douglas West and Elvanfoot in Lanarkshire; Heriot in Midlothian; Knockando and Spey Bay in Morayshire; Comrie and Tullibardine in Perthshire; Uplawmoor ('for Caldwell') in Renfrewshire; Hassenden in Roxburghshire; Greenhill and Manuel in Stirlingshire; Glenluce and Glenwhilly in Wigtownshire.

Voices of protest were heard throughout the land. William MacLeod, convener of Sutherland County Council, said that if the closures went ahead there would be a clearance in the Highlands worse than any in history. John Rollo said that the government might as well write off the north of Scotland: 'We shall fight this plan, as every Scot must fight it.' Bill Nicolson, director of the Scottish Tourist Board, said the proposals were 'disastrous not only for the Scottish tourist industry but for the Scottish economy'. But opinion was far from unanimous. Lord Polwarth, chairman of the Scottish Council (Development and Industry), felt that Beeching had done 'a thorough-going piece of work and one could not help admire it', while the *Glasgow Herald* praised it for soundness of conception: 'Perhaps it should be conceded that Dr Beeching could have been still more ruthless in pursuit of economy and operating effficiency … There should certainly be no blanket condemnation of the report.' Even this drivel was outdone by Jean Roberts, Lord Provost of Glasgow, the same Jean Roberts who had objected to the mess left by the VE night celebrations, who saw the rail closures as a wonderful opportunity to build car parks.

After a campaign of fierce resistance, some of the threatened lines did survive – the trains continued to run north of Inverness to Thurso and Wick, west of Inverness to Kyle, and south of Ayr. But most of them were lost, including the branch line to the station of the Drummond-Moray ladies. Jean Roberts got her car parks, Beeching his peerage.

V

The Earl of Mansfield, Lord High Commissioner to the General Assembly of the Church of Scotland (1961 and 1962), called for the re-introduction of the treadmill. He may have felt that an extreme remedy was required to deal with the declining standards in public life. Even in Tomintoul things were not what they were. Francis Walsh, Roman Catholic Bishop of Aberdeen, went to live there with his housekeeper, Ruby Mackenzie, the divorced wife of a Church of Scotland minister. It was an excellent choice for a runaway couple, since Tomintoul was the end of a famous road beginning at Cockbridge, a road blocked by snow for much of the year and so not easily negotiated by inquiring journalists.

Such were the hypocritical niceties of the age, it was possible for a bishop to start a new life with a mistress in Tomintoul but out of the question for Kenneth Tynan, theatre critic of *The Observer*, to register a mistress at the George Hotel in Edinburgh for the festival. Fortunately there was an annexe not routinely monitored by the guardians of morality. Ken smuggled Kathleen up the back stairs to his room, where he introduced her to two of his greatest interests, the Communist manifesto and spanking, not necessarily in that order.

When Tynan was not in bed with Kathleen he was helping to organise a drama conference at the McEwan Hall involving many distinguished personalities from the theatre world. Christopher Small, Scotland's leading critic, noted that Tynan was 'clearly looking forward to a week of storm and chaos', but that the first session was not only decorous but rather dull. However, on the last day of the conference, things perked up unexpectedly. A 'happening' took place. It started with a planted heckler rebuking the director Charles Marowitz for inviting the audience to suggest the deeper meaning of *Waiting for Godot*. After organ music and taped extracts from the week's debates, a nude woman on a BBC camera trolley was wheeled across the balcony.

Kenneth Dewey, the American organiser of the spectacle, explained that 'we are trying to give back to you, the audience, the responsibility of theatre, performing with your own thoughts, building your own aesthetics'. Duncan Macrae, the craggy Scottish thespian, shouted at Dewey from the floor: 'I think, mister, you're talking a lot of baloney.' Few paid much attention to this exchange.

The audience was transfixed by the vision of a naked woman, in public, in Edinburgh, at the festival.

The city was scandalised. Duncan Weatherstone, the Lord Provost, said it was 'a great pity – indeed a tragedy – that the glorious festival should have been smeared by a piece of pointless vulgarity'. He wrote to Sir Edward Appleton, the principal of Edinburgh University, formally apologising on behalf of the city fathers – Edinburgh didn't go in much for city mothers – 'that such an exhibition occurred in academic buildings so kindly placed at our disposal'. Tynan said sheepishly that he had not much liked the happening, 'but we had condemned censorship earlier in the conference, so we could hardly censor this'. A rising star of Scottish journalism, Magnus Magnusson, asked in *The Scotsman*: 'Was this theatre in any recognisable form? Or was it merely a mischievous prank to stimulate reaction – any reaction?'

The nude, an 18-year-old student and single mother named Anna Kesselaar, recalling the incident half a century later, said she had done it for art and a fee of £4. 'I went to the McEwan Hall at a given time and just took my clothes off. There were splutterings from the audience and then I just got out the other side and there was somebody there with my coat. All of a sudden, a man said "There she is", and it was me they were after.' Kesselaar suffered many humiliations. She was charged with indecency (although the ludicrous prosecution was dismissed), lost her job at Basil Spence's architectural practice ('I have to think of the other girls,' Spence told her), and was denounced from the pulpit of St Giles as someone who was morally unfit to bring up her child. She was so terrified that her son would be taken from her that she fled Scotland. 'It was absolutely huge,' said Kesselaar, 'completely loony stuff.' The critic Bernard Levin preferred to think of it as the beginning of the permissive society.

VI

In the third week of November 1963 there were complaints about a less than flattering portrait of Scotland on *Panorama*. The programme had deserted the retired colonels of Perthshire and was now exposing vandalism on trains and buses. Lord Ferrier suggested in the House of Lords that some of the scenes had been fabricated by actors. In the same week it was announced that New Lanark, the model industrial village built by David Dale and Robert Owen, would be restored as a living community. And so it was, with sensitivity and success. Glasgow was preparing for the foundation of Scotland's fifth university, Strathclyde, the first to be established north of the border since 1583 and Britain's first technological university, guided into creation by Samuel Curran, a physicist and inventor. That week too, in the Ayrshire town of Darvel, Marie Hamilton, aged seven, was killed on her way home from school when the gable wall of a Nissen hut, part of a lace factory, collapsed during a gale.

And then, on the 22nd of the month, John F Kennedy, the president of the United States, was shot in Dallas. BBC TV persisted with its schedule except for interruptions for news flashes followed by a minute or so of solemn music; STV continued its normal transmissions of anodyne pap. At the United States air base at Prestwick the news was greeted with disbelief. 'When I heard the announcement on television,' said a captain at the base, 'I just sat and stared.' At Glasgow Central Station people on their way home from pubs and cinemas were stunned into silence by the front pages of the early editions. Everything else that week was forgotten suddenly.

1964

THE COLD MEAT COUNTER

I

Rosaria, a town in Argentina with a population of 600,000, was an unhealthy place to live. In the country as a whole the number of deaths from typhoid each year, averaging between 106 and 130, suggested that the disease was endemic. Rosaria was likely to have had more than its share of carriers. It discharged its sewage into the river Parana untreated: every day, 66 tons of human excrement and a quarter of a million gallons of urine were disposed of in this way. Many of the people drew their water supplies from wells contaminated by the sewage, making them vulnerable to infection.

The sewage left the outfall pipes only half a mile from the town's meat-packing plant, where almost one in 10 of the workforce suffered from amoebic dysentery because of poor sanitary hygiene in their own homes. This heavily polluted water, which carried all sorts of deadly stuff, including the typhoid bacillus, then flowed past the plant. The conditions presented an obvious risk to public health, and the irresponsibility of the management made it worse. In 1955, after a can of tongue produced there was suspected of being the source of an infection at Pickering in Yorkshire, they stopped using untreated river water in the cooling process and introduced chlorinated water. But from December 1962 until March 1964, unknown to the Ministry of Agriculture in Britain, the chlorination system was out of action and the plant reverted to the use of polluted water from the Parana.

The meat canned at this appalling establishment continued to be exported in large quantities, and in May 1964 a consignment from Rosaria was delivered to a branch of the William Low supermarket chain in Union Street, Aberdeen. Although it could never be proved, it is almost certain that the typhoid infection which crippled the city that month was contained in a single 6lb can of corned beef, that it was there when it arrived in the shop, and that it was the result of pollution from a river 7,000 miles away.

After its journey from South America the product was opened by an Aberdeen shop assistant using a can opener fixed to the wall of the supermarket and its contents were divided, some put on a display shelf behind the cold meat counter and the rest in a south-facing window exposed to the warm spring sunshine. As soon as the can was opened, the corned beef became a perfect medium for the growth of bacteria. In the heat of the shop window between 7 and 9 May, the period during which the first customers were infected, it would have taken only hours for a few typhoid bacilli to multiply into several million.

When the corned beef on the shelf behind the counter was sold, it was replaced by the meat from the window. The infected portion again contaminated the hands of the staff who touched it and spread to the other cold meats being sold from the unrefrigerated shelf. At the end of the working day all the unsold meats were placed on a tray and stored overnight in the fridge – an ideal environment for cross-infection. Yet there was nothing unusual about the hygiene standards in the shop. It had only recently been opened; inspectors judged it modern in design, clean, well-run.

On 14 May a GP was called to a house in the city where four members of a family of five were ill. The doctor was disturbed by the symptoms and took blood samples; they came back positive – salmonella typhi. A woman admitted to the City Hospital with suspected gastro enteritis turned out to have typhoid, which went on to infect her husband and two children. On 19 May two students were transferred from Aberdeen Royal Infirmary to the City Hospital as suspected cases; these too were confirmed after bacteriological tests. By the evening of 20 May two more victims had been diagnosed and 12 patients were in hospital with typhoid either confirmed or suspected. Ian MacQueen, the city's medical officer of health, quickly identified a vital link between the patients. They had all eaten canned meat from the same shop about 10 days earlier.

No time was lost. On 21 May MacQueen arranged to have samples of blood, faeces and urine taken from the staff in the shop. At the same time samples of cold meats were sent for testing to the regional laboratory. From the evidence of the patients MacQueen deduced that the probable source of the infection was corned beef; the tests confirmed his suspicion. It was now 23 May. Had the infection been limited to the cold meat counter or was there a risk of a more general infection? It was MacQueen's professional judgement that there was no longer typhoid in the supermarket. But how could he have known for sure? He would have been entitled under the Public Health (Scotland) Act to close the shop and have it thoroughly disinfected. He decided against this precaution. When the full facts were revealed months later it left him open to the accusation that he had continued to expose customers to infection, that some bought contaminated meat for a few days after the original discovery, and that an unknown number, probably very small, contracted typhoid as a result.

The events in Aberdeen were slow to surface in the national press. But by 25 May, after a weekend in which the number of confirmed cases rose to 48, the outbreak was front-page news. Twenty-four hours later there were 82 victims, including a prominent local councillor, Frank Magee, and his two daughters. An urgent appeal went out to nurses who had left the profession to volunteer their services at the City Hospital. The city entered the grip of a crisis from which there was only momentary relief from the Pangloss of the hour, one H Webber, the city's director of publicity, who insisted that inquiries from prospective tourists were coming in as plentifully as ever.

Rumours spread as rapidly as the infection itself. One had it that passports would be necessary for Aberdonians to leave the city, and there were tales of visitors getting as far as Stonehaven before turning back in fear. The wildest of the speculation – easily disproved, yet somehow it caught hold – was that dead bodies were being piled high on the beach at Aberdeen, awaiting burial. Although 487 people ended up in hospital, some of whom were found not to have typhoid, no one died.

Ian MacQueen felt at the outset that the city was doubly threatened – not only by a spread of the infection through neglect of personal hygiene but by mass hysteria. His response was to launch an intensive campaign harnessing the power of modern communications; for the first time in a health crisis, television played a critical role in educating the public. It was a brilliant strategy. If the medical officer of health had neglected to cleanse the shop, he was never in danger of neglecting to massage the media. He took personal charge of the PR offensive, staging a twice-daily press conference and making innumerable appearances before the cameras. This was something new. Public officials in Scotland were not renowned for their adroitness in handling the press or for their candour. MacQueen was accessible and emotionally frank to a fault.

On 27 May he announced that, although the first wave was over, there could be a second one. He claimed that his department could do nothing to stop it because its victims would have been incubating the disease before it was known that there was typhoid in the city. On 28 May he declared cheerfully that he had just eaten food bought from the infected supermarket. It was an ill-timed attempt at *sang-froid*, for this was the last day of relative normality. On 29 May the second wave struck and there were 37 new admissions to the City Hospital, the largest for any single day. MacQueen decided to close all the city's schools until further notice, advising parents to keep their children as close to home as possible. He said it was impossible to forecast how big the second wave would be.

Aberdeen was bleeding to death. Fruiterers and grocers had lost half their trade. Restaurants were empty. Aberdeen Chamber of Commerce said that people were not moving about and that money had ceased to circulate. Sporting fixtures were cancelled.

On the last day of the month the number of confirmed cases passed 200, each of the patients facing the prospect of at least a month in hospital with no visitors. The outbreak was so severe that the city imposed a voluntary quarantine on itself. 'One must think of Aberdeen at the moment as a sort of beleaguered city,' MacQueen told the press. Visitors were advised to stay away and residents were asked not to leave. Swimming pools were shut down along with ballrooms, bingo halls and cinemas; church attendances fell sharply; hotels might as well have closed their doors. These drastic measures raised the temperature of the media coverage. Apocalyptic allusions to 'plague city' and 'ghost town' forced the medical officer to change tack: 'I do not think the situation, serious as it is, is enough to convert the city into a monastery or an isolation ward.' That was not what he had been saying a day or two earlier.

Two weeks into the epidemic the government announced an independent inquiry. Labour's Willie Ross demanded to know why it had taken so long for an authoritative statement on the epidemic to be made to parliament. Michael Noble, the Secretary of State of Scotland (his predecessor Jack Maclay having been a victim of Harold Macmillan's 'night of the long knives'), replied that the delay had been caused by the need to investigate all the possible leads. He added pointedly that 'up to date [MacQueen] has turned down any offer of extra help'.

This high-level implied criticism introduced a new dimension to the crisis: the personality of MacQueen himself. Robert Kemp, the critic, wrote in his defence: 'He makes good television, coming across as a man of clear opinions, who obviously doesn't care to judge, and those citizens who have been interviewed over the past week or two have, in general, done credit to the city's reputation for articulate good sense.' Letters in the press were also supportive; one stated that MacQueen had 'a record in preventive medicine unequalled in any comparable British city'. But his credibility had been dented by Noble's Commons statement, and the Secretary of State's subsequent endorsement, 'He is doing jolly well', lacked conviction. The appointment of an insider, Sir David Milne, the former head of the civil service in Scotland, to chair the 'independent' inquiry was seen as another sign of the government's willingness to undermine MacQueen's efforts. Dickson Mabon, Labour MP for Greenock and a medical man himself, claimed that Milne was not independent enough.

In what had the makings of a political as well as a medical crisis the Scottish Office hurriedly denied that it was trying to foist help from outside on MacQueen. He claimed that he had asked the public health department in Edinburgh to release the deputy medical officer of health to help him, but they had proposed someone more junior, a compromise which did not suit the strong-willed MacQueen: 'Thinking it over, and without having anything against him, I have decided that probably we will manage to struggle through.' It transpired that no fewer than eight medical officers in Edinburgh, not just 'someone more junior', had offered to go to Aberdeen but had been rebuffed. The strain was telling on MacQueen. He admitted that he had been working 20 hours a day for the last fortnight and that he might crack unless he got 'a bit of a breather', yet he was reluctant to accept expert back-up when it was offered. Civil servants in Edinburgh muttered privately about his 'ridiculous antics'.

On 6 June he gave a measured performance at his press conference. Asked about Aberdonians being treated like outcasts in some parts of the country, he said there was more fear outside Aberdeen than in the city itself and that the locals shared a sober recognition of what they faced. But for the first time he had to deal with personal criticism of his handling of the crisis and the suggestion that drastic action at an early stage would have checked the outbreak. MacQueen replied that he simply did not know what drastic action could have been taken, omitting to mention that he had failed to have the shop disinfected. He said he had not named the shop for several days because he wanted to avoid the panic that might have resulted if the community had known that thousands of people were at risk. What he did not acknowledge was that this policy created a larger window of opportunity for the infection to spread.

On 14 June Aberdeen had its first good news for almost a month: a drop in the number of confirmed cases. 'It is the kind of thing that makes you want to go out and split a bottle of champagne,' said MacQueen. The city's recovery was symbolically confirmed at the end of June with an unexpected announcement from the royal yacht Britannia, anchored in the Moray Firth: 'The Queen will call on the Lord Provost of Aberdeen tomorrow at 10.30pm.' No-one could remember an official royal engagement so late in the day. On a balmy mid-summer evening thousands cheered the Queen as she drove from the station to the Town Hall and on the return journey the royal car was forced to a standstill several times as huge crowds closed in.

But for MacQueen the ordeal was not quite over; he still had to fight for his reputation. Sir David Milne's report, published in December, gave the medical officer credit for the speed with which he traced the source of the infection, but the rest was damning. The publicity methods he employed, through the press and TV, had 'resulted in the outbreak being given the status of a national disaster, a degree of gravity which it never attained'. Fearing a rapid and alarming spread of the disease he had embarked on a full-scale health campaign which in Milne's view was unnecessary. In short: MacQueen had over-reacted.

But Milne betrayed a surprising naivety about how the media operated when he wrote: 'We readily accept that it was the medical officer of health's original intention that his exhortations relating to personal hygiene should be directed solely at the population of Aberdeen and its immediate vicinity. However, to drive home the message he took further steps which, although in themselves entirely justifiable, caught the attention of the national press, television and radio … These measures had a serious effect not only on Aberdeen but to some extent on Scotland as a whole.'

What did Milne expect? Did he imagine that, when it became known that a city had been virtually isolated from the rest of the world, the reporting of such a drama could be limited to the circulation area of the Aberdeen *Press and Journal*? His belief that the medical officer of health could somehow have 'toned down' the coverage was unrealistic.

Michael Noble, who had praised MacQueen for the 'jolly good job' he was doing, decided in retrospect that it had not been jolly good after all. Echoing Milne's unreasonable criticisms, he lamented the 'tremendous slump' in the Scottish tourist trade, accusing MacQueen of having been prepared to 'throw Scotland to the winds' in order to safeguard Aberdeen. MacQueen, in a typically robust counter-attack, reminded his critics that the all-clear was given in 28 days, 'a remarkably short period', and maintained that the use of health education techniques and the cooperation of the media had shortened the duration of an epidemic which could have lasted months. The Scottish press agreed with this assessment, dismissing Milne's report as a typical product of establishment thinking. Hector Hughes, one of Aberdeen's Labour MPs, told the House of Commons that in future such inquiries should be headed by a High Court judge and not by someone with a civil service background.

MacQueen's knockout victory in the propaganda war was partly deserved. His no-holds-barred campaign created a prototype for public health crisis planning; there would be no repetition of Milne's negative perception of the value of the media in tackling such a crisis. But the journalists MacQueen had so assiduously courted were reluctant to admit the merits of some of Milne's more justified misgivings. Little was said about MacQueen's cavalier methods: his failure to alert GPs in Aberdeen to the outbreak (they learned about it from the press and television), his casual attitude to cooperation with other agencies, his unwillingness to accept help, his poor judgement in not having the shop disinfected.

Elizabeth Russell, a young house doctor, was on duty in the City Hospital when the first typhoid victims arrived. 'We expected people to die and they didn't,' she recalled. 'It was a mild organism. We were lucky. But it is apparently true that Aberdonians still wash their hands after going to the loo more than people anywhere else in the country.'

II

As the crisis in Aberdeen unfolded, other events in the spring of 1964 were in danger of being overlooked. Even the General Assembly of the Church of Scotland took second place to typhoid. But it was impossible to ignore the year's most impassioned public discussion, when the assembly was asked to grant the petition of Mary Lusk for ordination to the ministry. The panel on doctrine was split. In a typical piece of Kirk fudge, its report recommended that Lusk's petition should be refused pending further consideration. The Presbyterian hell might freeze before the church came to a decision on anything of importance.

As Johnston McKay observed many years later in his obituary of Lusk, she was 'far better qualified and intellectually far superior to the vast majority of the then ministry of the church'. She graduated at Oxford University with first-class honours in philosophy, politics and economics, studied divinity at New College in Edinburgh, represented the Church of Scotland at the Assembly of the World Council of Churches and in the early 1960s was appointed assistant chaplain of Edinburgh University. She was in every way an admirable candidate for the ministry – except that she happened to be the wrong sex.

McKay wrote of the General Assembly debate: 'One of the galleries was filled with students and supporters. Occasionally they boisterously cheered those who spoke in favour of the petition, and twice the Moderator, Professor James S Stewart, had to threaten to have the gallery cleared.' One of those in the gallery recalled that 'while some of the arguments against granting the petition made an attempt at theology, some bordered on the insulting. Clearly there were those who feared the church would change forever.'

Lusk was permitted to address the assembly from 'the bar', a witness stand or dock (it could function as either) from which testimony was given in a legal manner much adored by the aficionados. It was an eloquent speech driven by controlled anger. 'I am not sure,' she said, 'that I can convey to an all-male assembly the pain which the whole attitude and the very title of the report [which referred to the 'place' of women in the Kirk] give to me as a woman. For it assumes that there is a certain definite and limited "place" which is to be given to women in the church. Whereas the truth is that we, together with you, fathers and brethren, are the church, and there can be no question of your prescribing for us an appropriate sphere. Perhaps the point can best be brought home by suggesting that you substitute the word "men" for the word "women" in the title of the report, and ask presbyteries to consider the sphere of ministry appropriate to men in the church. Ludicrous, of course, but not more so than the proposal before you.'

Her parish minister, Leonard Small, issued a challenge to the assembly: 'On what grounds are we to exclude a woman of Miss Lusk's undoubted distinction from the ministry?' As a long Saturday afternoon wore on, in a hall packed with delegates who had hoped to be attending a royal garden party at Holyroodhouse, Roy Sanderson, convener of the panel on doctrine, would not be budged and Lusk's petition was narrowly defeated. The Church of Scotland prevaricated for a further five years before it bowed to the inevitable and admitted women to its ministry. Mary Lusk – Levison as she had become on her marriage – was finally ordained in 1978 as assistant minister at St Andrew's and St George's in Edinburgh, with special responsibility for outreach to the offices and shops of her city centre parish. 'Mrs Levison always told you what she thought,' said one of the shop workers, 'but she was always interested in what I thought. I wasn't used to that in ministers.'

III

While the Kirk feebly resisted one necessary reform, the Kilbrandon inquiry bravely tackled another. This government-appointed committee chaired by Lord Kilbrandon, a High Court judge, recommended the abolition of juvenile courts and their replacement by lay panels – 'children's hearings' as they came to be known – with the power to order special forms of education and training for delinquents under the age of 16. It was radical stuff and, given the conservative nature of Scottish society, ahead of its time. It was also ahead of the rest of the world. Kilbrandon proposed scrapping a system of juvenile justice predicated on the establishment of guilt or innocence and the punishment of the guilty, removing children from the jurisdiction of the criminal courts except in special cases, and transferring responsibility for child offenders to the social services. With its proposal for a dedicated department in every local authority headed by a 'director of social education', the report inspired the creation of social work in its modern professional form.

'The committee recognise,' said Kilbrandon, 'that their proposals may be felt by some to represent a degree of interference into personal and family life which is unacceptable to society. If that view were to be accepted, the practical alternatives would have to be faced. A return to a purer form of the "crime-punishment" concept is in the committee's view altogether unacceptable.'

Kilbrandon's holistic remedy received mixed notices in the Scottish press. The *Glasgow Herald* commented favourably that few departmental inquiries had 'left so convincing an impression of having said the last word on their subject'. The *Evening Times* was less persuaded: 'Those who hold that to spare the rod is to spoil the child will not be enthusiastic.' The unreconstructed rod continued to be exercised despite Kilbrandon's vision of a new enlightenment, but corporal punishment in schools was no longer attracting the rave reviews it once did.

The Appeal Court in Edinburgh, hearing an appeal by David Gray, headmaster of Lennoxtown Public School, against a conviction of assaulting an 11-year-old pupil, said there was no doubt that a schoolteacher was vested with disciplinary powers, but the question in every case was whether there was dole. Dole was an old-fashioned term denoting evil intent. According to the law of Scotland, dole had to be proved. Such matters as the nature and the violence of the punishment inflicted on the boy, his age and health, his conduct, all these had to be taken into account, said Lord Guthrie. Was there dole? Gray had given the boy eight strokes with the school belt within two hours. Counsel for the headmaster found it inconceivable that any court would hold that eight strokes in two hours was excessive. But Lords Guthrie, Wheatley and Kissen decided otherwise, upholding the sheriff's original verdict and the fine of £10 imposed on the headmaster. The teachers' union, the Educational Institute of Scotland, said it was deeply perturbed by this outcome, 'which could have far-reaching repercussions for teacher-pupil relations and school discipline'. After the Lennoxtown case teachers could not belt without the fear of prosecution – 'persecution' as the EIS called it –

but they nevertheless went on belting day after day, year after year, perhaps calculating that the slight threat of dole over their heads was worth the risk.

IV

The youth of Scotland, caught between the devil of juvenile courts and the deep blue sea of children's hearings, consoled themselves with an ear-splitting scream. It greeted the first appearance of the Beatles in Scotland, at the ABC Cinema in Lothian Road, Edinburgh, when 5,000 adolescent fans showered the stage with jelly babies. Such was the din, the new sensations from Merseyside were seen but not heard. Afterwards, close to midnight, 300 policemen struggled to control the crowd outside the cinema. 'It was impossible to get a car within 100 yards of the exit,' reported one newspaper. 'Inside the cinema after the final curtain, the audience remained in their places for several minutes chanting "We want Paul", "We want the Beatles", but there were no curtain calls. The group were smuggled out unnoticed.'

The following night they performed at the Odeon Cinema in Renfield Street, Glasgow. Two hundred and fifty people, mostly teenage girls, had to be treated for shock or hysteria, a reaction far in excess of anything encountered in Aberdeen at the height of the typhoid epidemic. Some were carried into the foyer, where they lay prostrate on the carpet being revived by hard-pressed ambulance-men and nurses. According to one paramedic, by the end of the second house the auditorium resembed a battlefield clearing station. Even the usherettes were overcome. The Beatles rushed out by a side door, were bundled into a waiting car which drove off at high speed down West Nile Street, and boarded their chartered aircraft within half an hour of leaving the stage.

Between their Edinburgh and Glasgow dates the group stayed the night in the Roman Camp Hotel in Callander. When word got out that they were there, the children of the town besieged the hotel, chanting the usual refrains, 'We want Paul', 'We want the Beatles' – the repertoire was never in danger of straying into originality. A brief appearance by Paul McCartney satisfied them, and they went to their classrooms an hour late, risking the belt for lack of punctuality.

On the same day, when the headmaster of Gateside Junior Secondary School in Cambuslang gave several boys six strokes each for hitting a prefect over the head, a teacher in the room interrupted the ceremony, shouting, 'Stop it! Stop it!, I'll call the police!' This small act of rebellion against the harsh culture of Scottish education was considered so remarkable that it got into the newspapers.

The headmaster of Braehead Junior Secondary School in the Fife pit town of Buckhaven would have appreciated the gesture. R F Mackenzie was a lone voice in the teaching establishment, a man who subscribed to the unfashionable belief that a child was a sacrosanct being to be loved and cared for rather than disciplined and punished. He was able to develop some of his experimental ideas at Braehead with the help of such kindred spirits as Hamish Brown, introducing the children of a socially deprived community to the Scottish wilderness. He fell foul of his local authority employers because of his resistance to the use of corporal punishment and his disdain for conventional notions of educational success, yet he won unexpected promotion as head of Summerhill School in Aberdeen, where he was less successful in managing the opposition to his humane principles. His peremptory banning of the belting of girls precipitated a staff rebellion, followed by his suspension and eventual dismissal, but this prophet without honour had the last word in *A Search for Scotland*, a deeply thoughtful evocation of his native country.

V

There was no difficulty in assembling 2,500 well-behaved children from the schools of Fife to line the northern approaches of the new Forth Road Bridge for the official opening by the Queen on 4 September 1964. But the weather was not on its best behaviour. Before the formalities were due to be observed an impenetrable mist descended, making the bridge invisible.

Brigadier Alasdair Maclean, organiser of the festivities, announced that the fly-past by fighters and helicopters would have to be cancelled in the interests of safety. There would be no symbolic final crossing of the ferry from South to North Queensferry, which had linked Edinburgh with the kingdom of

Fife ever since Queen Margaret of Scotland established the facility for pilgrims to Dunfermline Abbey and St Andrews. Nine centuries on, a crowd estimated at 100,000 could see nothing. Meanwhile the historian of the crossing, John Mason, collapsed on North Queensferry pier a few minutes before the arrival of the royal party.

As the Queen delivered her speech, a pale sun broke through the gloom and the south tower made a tentative appearance. Along the route nationalist posters ('2s 6d toll – it's time we voted SNP') were suddenly visible too. Warships still shrouded in mist thundered a royal salute which was followed by a chorus of foghorns and bells. Mason recovered sufficiently to present the monarch with a copy of his scholarly work. All in all it could have been worse; perhaps not much.

Most newspapers ran 'souvenir' editions. The *Evening Times* captured the patriotic mood: 'The bridge's simple, slender elegance contrasts strikingly with the noise and fumes of the motor age it is to serve and to which it will be a memorial ... At one time there was bitterness, and threats of a bridge boycott, because tolls were to be charged, while England's motorways remained free. Now the bad feeling is forgotten in the pride of achievement, which all Scots share.' At a total length of 8,241 feet, including the approach viaducts, it was the longest suspension bridge outside the United States at the time of its construction. In its first year it carried 2.5 million vehicles; 40 years later it was carrying almost 12 million.

Hew Lorimer, the National Trust for Scotland's representative in Fife, designed a commemorative plaque which was unveiled by the Queen. It made no mention of the seven men who died building the bridge. Michael Noble, trailing dutifully in the royal wake, wore a kilt for the grand occasion, his last important one as Secretary of State for Scotland.

VI

Josephine Collins, leader of the Hutchesontown-Gorbals Tenants' Association, urged the people of the Gorbals to vote Tory in the 1964 general election. The Conservatives had been in power nationally since 1951, but she blamed the Labour-controlled Glasgow Corporation for the continued existence of the slums. The tenants crowded into Wolseley Street School to protest against the 'foul sanitary conditions, like something out of the Middle Ages' – or, they might have added, a 20th-century Argentinian meat-packing plant.

A reporter was impressed by the passion of the local women, 'angry with husky, bronchial voices', who spoke of rats – 'hungry and, aye, impiddent tae' – biting babies in their cradles, water supplies being abruptly cut off ('Somebody stole the water pipe'), chimneyheads being dismantled and never re-erected over lived-in houses. A Glasgow doctor in the audience challenged the public health authorities to take the slum landlords to court, claiming that a patient of his had been bitten on the face by one of the impiddent rats.

But the people of the Gorbals did not vote Tory. They did what they always did and elected a Labour MP, Alice Cullen. Much of the rest of Scotland also voted Labour in October 1964, the party ending the night with 43 of the 71 seats, the Tories 24, and the Liberals holding the remaining four, all of them north of the Great Glen.

West Renfrewshire, the constituency vacated by Jack Maclay (who had been pushed upstairs as Viscount Muirshiel), fell to the cerebral Norman Buchan, an authority on Scottish folk song, but a number of other Labour men of promise failed to get themselves elected: John Smith was again trailing in East Fife, Donald Dewar finished second behind Lady Tweedsmuir in Aberdeen South, and John P Mackintosh narrowly failed in Berwick and East Lothian. David Steel, a young son of the manse, came within 1,700 votes of converting Roxburgh, Selkirk and Peebles into a Liberal seat.

Among the Tory losers Nicholas Fairbairn was described by one commentator as 'the flamboyant advocate with the Beau Brummel costumes'. The less flamboyant Robert Kernohan, who would not have been seen dead in Beau Brummel costumes, surrendered a 7,200 majority in Glasgow Pollok and returned to journalism. The virtue of George Younger, who had stepped aside in Kinross and West Perthshire a year earlier, was rewarded with victory in Ayr; Hector Monro, a popular local farmer, increased his majority in Dumfries; Angus North and Mearns elected the able Alick Buchanan-Smith. Otherwise it was a dreadful night for the Conservatives in Scotland. It was to become more dreadful still.

Home ended the campaign, and his short premiership, in the Masonic Hall, Crieff. Earlier, on eve of poll, he had arrived to a 'great cheer' at Prestwick Airport and gone on to Ayr railway station where he was greeted by 'incoherent cries from the maroon blazers of Ayr Academy' and a man yelling 'Home rule for Irvine'. But election fever was barely detectable elsewhere. In Glasgow the occasional balloon exploded in the face of Cathcart's resident populist, Teddy Taylor, but the biggest crowds flocked not to election meetings, as they had once done, but to the Modern Homes Exhibition in the Kelvin Hall.

Home came within a whisker of denying Harold Wilson an overall majority, but the years of Conservative rule – the '13 wasted years' as Labour repeatedly called them until the label stuck – were over, and Willie Ross, a competent but stereotypically dour Kilmarnock dominie, succeeded Noble as Secretary of State for Scotland. On polling day Dr William Horne, Glasgow's medical officer of health, the MacQueen of the south, reported a marked increase in the incidence of rickets because of the poor nutrition of babies. In Glasgow in 1964 32 children out of 1,000 died before their fifth birthday.

1965

THE DIGNITY OF THE LAW

I

Andrew Quinn, a 44-year-old labourer at a brickworks in Shotts, Lanarkshire, owed his life to a Labour politician he had never met. Quinn was working a night shift when he got involved in a bitter dispute with the foreman, apparently about some safety issue. It was so bad that the manager had to be called in to settle it. He did so by firing Quinn on the spot. Quinn went home, returned with a shotgun and killed the manager. It was a straightforward case of capital murder and there was no attempt on the accused's part to deny it. His only defence was that he had been asked to do a dangerous job; it was not much of a defence.

Sydney Silverman had few friends in the Labour Party. It was half-expected that, when the party won the 1964 election, he would have been given a junior office in the new government. He wasn't. No one doubted his ability, or his own high opinion of that ability, but Richard Crossman spoke for most of his parliamentary colleagues when he described Silverman as 'vain, difficult and uncooperative' and impossible to work with in any kind of group. This quintessential loner refused to join the British army during the first world war, registered as a conscientious objector, and went to prison for his pacifist beliefs (which he abandoned during the second war when he realised what the Germans were doing to the Jews).

He qualified as a solicitor, working for the poor in his native city, and helped to found the Campaign for Nuclear Disarmament. But his main causes, influenced by his experiences in prison, were penal reform and the abolition of the death penalty. In 1956 his first abolitionist bill was defeated in the Lords, but with Labour's return to office, and Harold Wilson's personal hostility to capital punishment, there was a safe passage for his private member's bill – which became The Murder (Abolition of Death Penalty) Act 1965 – replacing hanging with a mandatory sentence of life imprisonment.

For Andrew Quinn the timing of Silverman's bill was critical. The case came to the High Court in Glasgow as the new law was on the brink of receiving the royal assent. The Crown refused to accept his plea of guilty, and the prisoner was told that he would return to court 24 hours later, when it would be possible for the prosecution – represented by Ian Hamilton of Stone of Destiny fame – to amend the indictment from a capital charge incurring the death penalty to one of simple murder.

Fifteen men were hanged in Scotland between the end of the second world war and the passing of the Silverman bill. The youngest, Anthony Miller, was 19 when he was hanged three days before Christmas 1960 after a trial which Wheatley, the trial judge, painted in lurid colours for its revelations of 'vice and depravity' in the Queen's Park district of Glasgow; the condemned youth's father was gathering signatures for a reprieve even at the 11th hour. Seven others were in their twenties; three (including Peter Manuel) in their thirties; four in their forties; the oldest, a double murderer, was 45. The execution of the sentence on the last of them, 21-year-old Henry John Burnett, at Aberdeen Prison on 15 August 1963, generated so little public interest that not all the Scottish newspapers troubled themselves to report it. Yet, if there was any murder trial which justified the abolition of capital punishment, it was Burnett's.

II

Burnett denied murdering Thomas Guyan, a merchant seaman, by shooting him in the head at a house in Aberdeen. He also denied assaulting Guyan's wife Margaret by taking a knife to her and seizing her by the throat, and a further charge of assaulting James Irvine by pointing a shotgun at him and robbing him of his car. That Burnett committed these acts was not in dispute. But what was his state of mind at the time? His lawyers lodged a special defence of insanity and would have been entitled to do so with some confidence.

Thomas and Margaret Guyan were married in 1957. Five years later Margaret met a new admirer – Burnett – and went to live with him. They discussed going to see Guyan together to ask him for a divorce, but it seems nothing came of this idea. Twenty years old, emotionally immature and obsessively jealous, Burnett took to locking Margaret in the house. On one of the rare occasions she was allowed out alone she met her estranged husband, apparently by chance, and agreed to go back to him. She returned to the house she shared with Burnett to collect her son, taking a friend for moral support. When she announced her intentions Burnett shouted 'Margaret, Margaret, you are not going to leave me' and drew a knife to her throat. The friend, who was waiting outside, banged repeatedly on the front door until Burnett finally opened it and ran off. Shaken but uninjured, the two women left at once for the house of Margaret's grandmother, where Guyan was waiting for her. Burnett, meanwhile, went to his brother Frank's house, forced open a cabinet, and stole a gun and some cartridges. He then boarded a bus.

Margaret described to the jury at the High Court in Aberdeen what happened next. She said she was sitting with her husband, her grandmother and her son when they heard a commotion outside. 'My husband got up and opened the door and Harry Burnett was standing there with a gun. My husband asked who he was and Harry Burnett said, "I've got you now". The gun went off and my husband fell. Then he reloaded the gun and threatened to shoot everybody else. I told him I would go with him if he did not shoot everybody else.' He took her to a nearby garage where he threatened Irvine, a complete stranger, with the gun, stole his car and drove off at high speed towards Peterhead with Margaret in the passenger seat. Burnett asked her to marry him. 'I said I would.' When they were stopped by the police, 'he did not look in his right mind ... his eyes were staring out of his head'.

In his summing-up to the jury W R Grieve, QC, the Solicitor General, gave a one-dimensional view of the case with its 'sordid background of a sailor's wife being unfaithful to her husband when he was at sea' and of 'the lover with whom she consorted being unable to bear seeing his mistress's favours being given elsewhere'. But the evidence of mental instability was extremely strong. Burnett's mother, Matilda, testified that her son had tried to commit suicide some years earlier when his then girlfriend deserted him, and that her brother and father were both in mental hospitals. When she broke down and wept in the witness box at her own account of this family history, Burnett struggled with his police escort in the dock, shouting 'She's had enough, hasn't she? Take her out'. Mrs Burnett turned to him with the words: 'Henry, it's ok, my loon, I'm ok.'

Ian Lowit, a consultant psychiatrist who had first treated Burnett after his attempted suicide, gave expert evidence for the defence. He said that an electric brain-testing machine had been used on Burnett and that the results showed 'a definite abnormality': there were times when he was incapable of rational decisions or of assessing the consequences of his actions. Lowit believed that Burnett fell into the category of a psychopathic personality as defined in recent mental health legislation and that he should be detained for compulsory treatment in a secure hospital.

In an interview with the BBC many years later, Bob Middleton, a senior local councillor who exercised his privilege to sit alongside Lord Wheatley as an observer, recalled having been disturbed by the attitude in court to Lowit's evidence. Middleton said the body language of court officials suggested they were pooh-poohing the psychiatric testimony. He was also unimpressed by Wheatley's insistence on interposing himself into the cross-examination of the witness more than was necessary.

Lowit himself confessed to being devastated by the experience. 'I was completely torn to bits by the prosecution,' he said. 'I wasn't at all prepared for the onslaught I was subjected to. I was completely inexperienced in such matters ... I thought I would be examined on medical psychiatric evidence in medical psychiatric terms, not in adversarial terms. I felt they were trying to ridicule and minimise my evidence.' Lowit believed that he had let Harry Burnett down and continued to be troubled by this belief into his old age, long after Burnett was dead.

It was expected that, in so difficult a case, with a man's life at stake, the jury's deliberations would be protracted. Rooms were booked in a hotel in anticipation of an overnight stay. There was no need: the jury returned after just 25 minutes with a majority verdict – 13 votes to 2 – convicting Harry Burnett of capital murder. The familiar figure of Lord Wheatley promptly donned the black cap and, for the last time in Scotland, pronounced the death sentence 'for doom'.

As Burnett returned to Craiginches Prison to spend his first night in the condemned cell, the two prosecutors – Grieve and his junior Robert Henderson – joined the queue at the ticket office of

Aberdeen railway station and discovered that they were standing next to the foreman of the jury. Henderson recalled: 'We offered platitudes to him about how difficult it must have been, but he said: "No, not at all. The choice was whether this man was mad or bad. I see boys like this every day who are just bad." I think he had been a headmaster.' The foreman added that 'quite a few of the women on the jury didn't want to see a conviction recorded' but that he had reminded them of their duty, 'and we did our duty'.

In the immediate aftermath of the trial there was a flurry of official activity. The Secretary of State (still Michael Noble at the time) called for the court papers and Wheatley prepared his own report on the case. He wrote: 'As Burnett did not give evidence I was not able to form any definite opinion of him.' He did acknowledge that Burnett's family background was 'not a happy one', adding that he doubted if all the facts had been presented to the court.

Three psychiatrists examined Burnett in prison to determine if he was sane enough to be hanged. 'We confirm,' they wrote, 'that Burnett is of a psychopathic personality. The psychopathic personality may reasonably be considered to be of such a degree as to mitigate his responsibility for the crime he committed.' This verdict, supporting Ian Lowit's expert testimony, should have led to a reprieve, particularly as there was some head of steam behind a petition for clemency signed by both the family of the condemned man and, unusually, the family of his victim. Burnett did not assist his own cause by allegedly telling prison officers that he knew exactly what he was doing when he shot Guyan – a remark noted in an 'occurrences book' at Craiginches Prison – and by instructing his solicitors not to appeal against the sentence. To the end Burnett believed that he stood a better chance of a reprieve through the petition than through legal process. The occurrences book noted his confidence throughout that he would be reprieved.

The final nail was applied to his coffin by Lord Avonside, the Lord Advocate, who urged Michael Noble to stand firm: 'I consider any slack use of the power to reprieve is merely giving way to the theory of abolition. Easy reprieves undermine the whole force and dignity of the administration of law by the courts, as the attitude of this particular murderer illustrates.' Avonside was effectively opposing a reprieve on political grounds: that it would have played into the hands of the abolitionists. And what was it about the administration of the law in this case that supported his use of the word 'dignity'? Robert Henderson, barely a week at the Scottish Bar when he went to Aberdeen for the trial, was profoundly affected by the experience: 'In those days when the High Court went out on circuit, the event was accompanied by considerable panoply. The Gordon Highlanders put on a guard of honour outside the court, complete with fixed bayonets. Union Street was closed while the judge went out and inspected the guard of honour before starting the trial. There was a vast crowd of onlookers … It made you feel you were taking part in something historic, as a capital trial undoubtedly was.' But Henderson felt also a sense of sickening inevitability … 'like the beginning of a funeral'.

Lord Wheatley's low opinion of psychiatric evidence in general was confirmed by his autobiography. He wrote of the importance of maintaining Scotland's 'great legal tradition', adding that if he had on occasions appeared over-strict 'it was simply because I felt that standards were not being preserved'. He made no comment on the trial of Henry John Burnett. He may even have deluded himself that it lived up to those high standards that he so jealously protected.

III

Burnett was unlucky. In contrast Walter Scott Ellis, one of the most dangerous men in Scotland, led a charmed life with juries. In 1960 Ellis was brought to the High Court in Glasgow to face a charge of capital murder – the fatal shooting of John Walkinshaw, a taxi driver, for which, if he had been convicted, he would have been hanged. No weapon was discovered despite an intensive search by the police, there was no evidence to prove that the taxi which took Ellis from Bridgeton on the night of the shooting was driven by Walkinshaw, and the fingerprints in the taxi did not match those of Ellis. The only thing going for the prosecution was the admission by the defence that Ellis lied to the police when he said that he was not out of the house after 11 o'clock on the night of the murder.

His counsel, R A Bennett, QC, suggested to the jury that there were many reasons why men did not tell the truth 'but the fact that Ellis lied to the police when first approached in connection with the murder does not prove his guilt'. Bennett reminded the jury that William Watt had been sent to prison on suspicion of three murders and that it was only when Peter Manuel was later convicted of these murders that Watt was finally cleared. It was a dubious comparison. Watt, unlike Ellis, had always been consistent about his movements on the night of the murders. But it may have been effective in implanting the idea that the police were not always to be trusted. Ellis maintained his right not to give evidence on his own behalf and the jury took only 43 minutes to bring in a unanimous verdict of not proven, releasing a pathological gangster back on to the streets.

The not proven verdict, a peculiarity of the Scottish system, was widely disliked. Its many critics believed that, in returning this verdict, a jury was saying in effect: 'We think you're guilty but the prosecution hasn't been able to prove it.' Francis Middleton, an outspoken Glasgow sheriff, said that if the guilt of a person was not established beyond the required yardstick of reasonable doubt, 'then it is the duty of the jury to return a verdict of not guilty; that is their duty as citizens'.

Whatever the rights or wrongs of the verdict Ellis was free to continue with his career as a professional hard man until he was caught for a routine crime by his standards, or framed by the police as he preferred to claim, and taken out of circulation for a while, giving Glasgow a break.

But even in prison Ellis was a menace. In February 1965 he made the latest of his many appearances in the High Court charged with sending letters to Lionel Daiches, the sheriff who had sent him down, which threatened him and the procurator fiscal with bodily harm. On this occasion, as on others, he was represented by the clever young advocate Nicholas Fairbairn, he of the Beau Brummel costumes.

Ewen Stewart, the advocate depute, pursued Ellis's suggestion that someone in the prison had advised him to send threatening letters to Daiches. Who was it? Ellis prevaricated. Stewart turned to the judge, Lord Grant: 'He is refusing to say.' Grant: 'Ellis, I have to direct you that this is a proper question which you are bound to answer.' Ellis would not be budged: 'I have two years of my sentence yet, and I am liable to get a knife in my back. There have been 13 men stabbed in Barlinnie this year already. I don't want to be classed as a prison informer.' Grant: 'Are you going to answer or not?' Ellis: 'I don't want to be assaulted or maybe stabbed.' Grant: 'Are you going to answer the question or not?' Ellis: 'No.'

Grant: 'I have to warn you that this is contempt of court and that I may have to deal with you when the case is finished.'

Stewart went on to quote from one of the letters: 'I am rotting here for four years through the perjured evidence of two policemen.' The letter complained also of the 'rotten, lying, perjured, biased address to the jury' by Daiches. Stewart asked Ellis if he still believed that the sheriff had lied. 'He made a few mistakes which may have been intentional,' Ellis replied carefully.

In the absence of any satisfactory handwriting analysis the jury found the charge not proven, the same verdict which had rescued him from the capital murder charge in the Walkinshaw case. Grant said he would take no action on the contempt of court, and Ellis was sent back to Barlinnie to complete his sentence. And that was that – until an intriguing sequel, which will be dealt with in a later chapter, ended the short career of Lionel Daiches on the bench. The judge in this ill-starred case, Lord Grant, a notoriously fast driver, was killed in an accident on the A9 in 1971. By then Walter Scott Ellis had run out of luck and was serving a long sentence for something else.

IV

Although Ellis lied routinely he may not have been over-estimating the risks of being incarcerated in Barlinnie Prison. Later in the year Alexander Malcolmson, a 24-year-old prisoner in the first few days of a six-month sentence for theft, was stabbed to death in A Hall. On the same day that a fellow prisoner, Joseph Cairns, also 24, appeared in court charged with his murder, James Shields, 21, from a Glasgow estate, Blackhill, notorious for gang warfare, was jailed at the High Court for 10 years for attempting to murder a police constable with a sawn-off shotgun. When two other policemen went in pursuit Shields aimed shots at their car, shattering its rear window. It made little difference if it was inside prison or out: Glasgow in the 1960s was a city with an international reputation for violence.

The city magistrates deplored the effect of each new outrage on 'the good name of Glasgow', an overworked phrase which made a large assumption about Glasgow's name, and when the outrage in question involved misbehaviour abroad the civic leaders feigned shock as well as dismay. Fortunately the bad boys did not tend to venture far in 1965 – the phenomenon of mass tourism had not yet arrived – and so the opportunities for disgracing the good name of Glasgow were limited.

'Abroad' during the Glasgow Fair Fortnight often meant nowhere more adventurous than the Isle of Man. This was the holiday destination of four 19-year-old youths who used bottles and a deck-chair as weapons in an assault on visitors on Douglas promenade which put one man in hospital with a broken jaw. The magistrate, Tom Radcliffe, sentenced each of them to the birch, a form of retribution long outlawed on the British mainland but still eagerly retained on the Isle of Man and the Channel Islands. The youths were taken to the cells, ordered to remove their trousers and pants and bent over a table. Each received nine strokes from a policeman.

The popular reaction in Glasgow was not to condemn the magistrate for the severity of the punishment, but to applaud him for giving the teenagers a dose of their own medicine. 'Birching may be medieval, inhuman and sadistic,' commented the *Evening Times*, 'but in the Isle of Man's experience it works and it is no more inhuman and sadistic than smashing a bottle over a man's head and booting him … There will be no sympathy at all for the youths who were given nine strokes of the birch.' Nor was there. Even the father of one of them agreed that the punishment was merited. 'My son is definitely not a thug,' he assured the newspapers. 'He does not drink and has never been in any kind of trouble in his life, but if I thought for one minute that he was guilty of using a bottle on a man then he deserves everything he got – and more.' Maurice Shinwell, the city's senior magistrate, said that it appeared from comments in the press by the youths themselves that birching was 'more salutary and effective than the imposition of fines'.

When the violence was not random (as it appeared to be in the Isle of Man incident), it was associated with gangs; and when it was not associated with gangs it was often provoked by sectarianism in football. In October 1965 the so-called 'Old Firm' – a term conferring on Protestant Rangers and Catholic Celtic a deceptive air of solidarity – met in the Scottish League Cup final at Hampden Park. It was a rough game which Celtic won 2-1. But then the real contest began. The Celtic players attempted a lap of honour, holding the trophy aloft; this was seen by the Rangers supporters as an act of provocation, a rubbing of their noses in defeat, and some ran on to the field and attacked the victorious team. Shinwell, who was present at the game, said that the good work of the police in controlling the disturbance prevented a disaster. There were only 16 arrests in the stadium, but the trouble persisted in the streets. Bricks and bottles were hurled at a Rangers supporters' bus while it passed through the Gorbals, smashing several windows and injuring two men on the bus. Later that night James Robertson, the chief constable, was called from a dinner to take charge of violent scenes at the Broomielaw, when fighting broke out between rival supporters on a Burns and Laird steamer which was about to sail for Belfast. The Royal Ulsterman eventually set off with 19 Glasgow policemen on board.

Raymond Jacobs, a sports journalist, said he doubted that people like him should be covering the Old Firm clashes and that such violent encounters would be better reported by war correspondents. Perhaps Jacobs had never covered a real war. He blamed the players for setting a bad example: 'Men went for men, tripping, kicking, hacking and jersey-pulling were rife. Two penalties were scored and five players had their names taken.' Jacobs felt that the lap of honour was a mistake: 'There is no doubt that the loathing of one camp for the other breeds on these occasions an atmosphere so explosive as to be combustible when victory by one is flaunted in the face of the other.' He noted with distaste how even the formal playing of the national anthem before the match was subverted into an expression of mutual hatred, the Celtic fans drowning out the words with prolonged jeering while the 'loyal' opposition retaliated by singing them more aggressively than ever – 'which one suspects had little connection with sentiments of loyalty to the Crown'. The magistrates' response to these events, apart from the normal lament about the good name of Glasgow, was to enforce a ticket-only rule for admission to all future Old Firm fixtures.

A few weeks later, when Italy played Scotland in a World Cup qualifying game in the same stadium, Italian newspapers branded the Scottish fans in advance as the 'Beasts of Glasgow' and advised their travelling supporters to beware of 'a ferocious, menacing crowd who behave like madmen'. Although this was often not far from the truth, the night ended well for Scotland, John Greig's 'goal of a lifetime' giving the home team an unexpected victory, and the supporters went home in a sunny mood for once. But the Glaswegians resented the unflattering character reference from the Italians. It seemed that the natives were allowed to denounce the behaviour of their own; from outsiders it was regarded as a gratuitous affront to civic pride.

There were not many attempts to inquire into the psychological and cultural roots of violence in Glasgow beyond the tribally obvious, but the urban poverty still prevalent after 20 years of peace, and which seemed beyond the power or will of the political establishment to remedy, continued to be a major source of disaffection.

A movement of radical clergymen known as Christian Action produced, towards the end of 1965, the most outspoken diagnosis yet of the city's malaise. Its report was based on conditions in the Gorbals, 'the worst slum in Britain and rapidly deteriorating', and was heavily informed by the observations of an Episcopalian vicar, Richard Holloway, who lived and worked there. 'Waste in the Gorbals is everywhere, from the decaying houses and the rubbish to the malnutrition of its inhabitants,' said the report. Diseases, infant mortality, overcrowding – five or more living in a single room – and infestation by vermin (recalling 'the impiddent rats' of the general election campaign) were particularly bad in the Gorbals. The report castigated the inadequacy of parents, the public authorities, the schools, the landlords and the churches. The condemnation was sweeping though not quite comprehensive; it exempted the children of the ghetto from any responsibility for its wretched state. 'A city like Glasgow,' the report concluded, 'cannot begin to talk about redevelopment until it attends to the education of its society.' But the impact of this well-researched polemic was diminished by the choice of London for the news conference to launch it. Its authors had to deal with distracting suggestions that they were out to 'knock' Glasgow from the safety of the metropolis and that they lacked the courage to say what they had to say in the Gorbals itself.

In the same month Nelson Gray, a Congregational minister, evoked in a magazine article the reality of life among the backcourt ashpits of the city, describing the recent discovery of a new-born baby abandoned in one of them. 'The children who found him are the real victims, condemned to grow up in Glasgow's shadowland,' he wrote. The article ended on a note of despair – 'Why is it that these open ashpits are still tolerated in 1965?' – and with a demand for practical action to solve 'Glasgow's tragic housing situation'.

Since the focus of attention was almost always on the Gorbals or the well-named Blackhill, the potential for social disorder elsewhere in the city tended to be overlooked. The Labour government inherited not only a disintegrating inner city from which much of the life had been drained with the departure of ambitious young families to the new towns, but a number of soulless peripheral estates, isolated miles from the centre, which lacked many of the civilising amenities.

V

The near-collapse of the shipbuilding industry on the upper Clyde contributed to the perception of a city in crisis. In the autumn of 1965 Labour felt compelled to bail out the bankrupt Fairfield yard in Govan with a loan of £1 million. But the rescue deal came with tough love attached.

Roy Mason, the minister for shipping, fired some unpalatable truths at the workforce. In Japan one million man hours were required to build a 60,000-ton tanker; in Britain it took one and three quarter million man hours to build the same ship. In 1950 the UK produced 37% of the world's tonnage and Japan only 9%; in 1964 the position was almost exactly reversed, the UK turning out 9%, the Japanese 39%. He pointed out that shipbuilding was no longer Glasgow's basic industry: 60,000 were employed in engineering, 34,000 in food and allied trades, only 23,000 in shipbuilding.

Six years earlier the centenary of Fairfield had marked a hundred years of shipbuilding on the Clyde. The sense of continuity was impressive. 'It is quite usual,' said a newspaper report, 'to find men there with more than 50 years' service and without thought of retiring.' The 'father of the Fairfield family', 76-year-old John Lipton, had been a draughtsman with the firm since 1898. His knowledge of the internal pipe work on the submarine K13, which sank in the Gareloch during trials in 1917, saved many lives. Lipton managed to pinpoint the spot at which the hull should be pierced to connect an air supply for the men trapped inside. 'His friends say that John Lipton was able to guide the rescuers by the rivet heads as though they were reading Braille,' said the report. In the end they got a food pipeline, as well as an air supply, through the hull of the submarine. When he was asked to name the biggest change he had seen in his lifetime, Lipton replied: 'The lighting of the shipyard and the ships.' In his youth the drawing office in Govan had been lit by gas, the ships by lamps, and he recalled how workmen on board sometimes used candles to see their way.

In 1960 Fairfield employed a full-time wood carver, John McLay, 'a slight active little man of 78', who had been one of 150 carvers employed in the building of the Lusitania at Clydebank as long ago as 1907. He retained some hope for the future of his craft and was busy initiating a young apprentice into the trade. The apprentice wood carver was lost to history. Fairfield itself was becoming lost to history.

Who was responsible for the precipitous decline and fall of the Clyde-built tradition? Roy Mason, a blunt Yorkshireman on the right of his party, concentrated the bulk of his attack on the workforce. He described industrial relations as appalling, reminding union leaders that, in the first half of 1965, the Scottish yards accounted for half the days lost in the UK shipbuilding industry as a whole. His barrage of statistics proved indigestible for many attending a meeting in Glasgow convened by the STUC. One delegate responded that it was time for Mason to put on his bowler hat and join the management.

Finlay Hart, a communist shop steward, lambasted the minister in the press, claiming that his assault on the workforce revealed his ignorance of the problems facing the industry. 'I have never been consulted by any shipping company when it placed an order or by any shipbuilder when it was accepted,' he wrote. For Hart it was 'the most natural thing in the world' for a man to resist a new working practice which might eventually put him out of a job, while the wide pay differentials between men doing the same job in different yards inevitably stoked resentment: 'All the statistics that Mr Mason can throw at us will not make a man happy if he is receiving less than his mates.' Mason used hard facts as his ammunition; the workers hit back with hard experience. There was little hope of reconciling these positions. But a life-saving cheque for £1 million – £16 million at current prices – guaranteed the immediate future of the yard.

Fairfield's position was desperate. For years the management had been willing to sign contracts with a profit margin so narrow that even a routine problem could put the operation into loss. It was a multi-purpose yard in a world of specialists; it had failed to adapt;

it was uncompetitive. It was also too late for blame, yet the old battlegrounds, fought in the language of class war, were far from deserted; they were still bristling with warriors, one side simplistically distinguished by its bowler hats, the other by its cloth caps. John Craig, secretary of Colvilles, the Motherwell steel makers, saw the Fairfield crisis in symbolic terms as the dramatic symptom of a more general sickness. 'There has been a serious failure in our industrial development since the war,' he wrote, 'the failure to modernise the men at the same time as modernising the machines.' He had no ideas for modernising the men; he was content to lash them verbally for their 'lethargy, buck-passing and reluctance to accept change'. But when he deplored the first strike of steel-melters since 1886 it was not the absence of industrial strife for 79 years that impressed him, nor the admirable industrial relations that this long period of stability implied, but the eruption of unrest on his own watch. It did not seem to have occurred to him that it took two sides to go to war and that the management was partly responsible.

A receiver was appointed at Fairfield and the government appointed a committee of three Board of Trade officials to work with him, none of whom was based in Scotland. The modernisation of men had its limits, and for the civil servants these limits were reached at Potters Bar, Hertfordshire, beyond which no Board of Trade official could reasonably be expected to go.

VI

The Labour government threw exactly the same amount – £1 million – at the new Highlands and Islands Development Board in its first year, but with more hope of a return on the investment.

The demographic context of Labour's leap of faith in the Highlands was salutary. The population statistics published by the Registrar General drew a portrait of an overwhelmingly urban Scotland in which 36% of the population lived in the four cities – Glasgow with 1,018,582 inhabitants, Edinburgh with 473,270, Dundee with 185,228 and Aberdeen with 185,034 – and most of the rest in the towns. The largest of the burghs in 1965 were Paisley (96,637), Motherwell and Wishaw (76,249) and Greenock (74,492); the smallest Culross (527), Inveraray (511) and New Galloway

(337). The total population of the seven crofting counties, the area covered by the new board, was 276,328, just over half that of the small capital city.

The Toothill report on the Scottish economy had dismissed the Highlands, its author muttering unconvincingly about new towns as a means to their regeneration. But there had long been a marked absence of more sympathetic remedies for the twin curses of depopulation and decline. A census report on Sutherland reported that, in 1965, a third of its households were without a bath, 29% without hot water, 15% without any water. James Jack, general secretary of the STUC, liked to remind his members that the 5,000 people unemployed in the Highlands represented a percentage higher than the figure for Scotland as a whole.

There was the aggravation of absentee landlords, who were mainly interested in the commercial possibilities of mass slaughter for summer pleasure. While the Highlands Board was being set up a Dutchman, Jan de Vries, bought two-thirds of the inner Hebridean island of Coll with the intention of developing it as a sporting estate. His acquisition included six tenanted farms and six crofts amounting to 12,000 acres, most of which had been in the hands of the local lairds, the Stewarts, for more than a century. Alastair Oliphant, the owner of the Coll Hotel, resisted all blandishments from Amsterdam and refused to sell up, a local hero of the hour but the only one.

'Perhaps there is nothing left for the Highlands,' mused the *Evening Times*. 'Decades of decline, depopulation and talk have resulted in a situation requiring drastic measures, and the government have certainly provided them.' Willie Ross had promised that the new board would be given 'staggering powers'. He was not exaggerating. The law setting it up conferred on the board the right to acquire land and property by compulsion and to inspect business records – almost anything that would 'advance the economic and social well-being of the Highlands'. Anyone obstructing its wishes would be guilty of an offence, and there was no machinery for appeal against the board's actions.

The *Glasgow Herald*, disturbed by the scope of these measures, complained that the region was being turned into 'a laboratory of socialist experiment' and that the government's real agenda was to gun down the landlords. In any case, asked the paper, what could such an organisation usefully do? What was the point of 'another board'? In the Highlands, however, the arrival of the laboratory of socialist experiment, headed by a respected Scottish planner, Professor Robert Grieve, was widely welcomed. A lobby group which had successfully campaigned for a reprieve of the railway services north and west of Inverness claimed to detect a new mood of hope and activity in place of the familiar deep resentments.

The board began its work on 1 November 1965. Grieve and his fellow directors met in Inverness to discuss how to interpret their sweeping terms of reference on the sort of budget that might take the pressure off an ailing Clyde shipyard but would do no more than make a modest contribution to solving the long-term problems of the Highlands. They were met at the front door by their first potential client, David Ross, a crofter from Garve, Ross-shire, who explained that he was seeking a loan to build a workshop, a filling station, a tearoom and a caravan site. John Rollo, Grieve's deputy, interviewed him on the spot and said afterwards that this was a project the board should support. What could such an organisation usefully do? the *Herald* had asked. The informal meeting on the board's doorstep, in the first minutes of its existence, gave the beginnings of an answer.

1966

GAMBLERS

I

The sudden death of Lord Fraser of Allander from a heart attack at his grand house, Mugdock in Stirlingshire, which he bought from James Graham, Duke of Montrose, inspired the sort of tributes reserved for national heroes. Nevile Davidson, delivering the eulogy at his funeral in Glasgow Cathedral, described him as a man of principle, simple and modest, who loved people, loved being among people, and had friends in every walk of life. 'He touched the life of Scotland at so many different points,' said Davidson, 'that his name had become a household word.' Michael Noble went further: 'Scotland has lost a great man.'

The *Glasgow Herald*, in a long and fulsome editorial, hailed him as 'an inspiring symbol of free enterprise at its best' who was known and respected for his liberality in the service of many charitable causes; the piece concluded that Scotland had lost 'one of her best-loved sons'. But these were not the sentiments of a disinterested party. Two years before his death Fraser had fought off a hostile bid, or series of bids, for the *Herald* from Lord Thomson of Fleet, proprietor of the rival *Scotsman*. It was a battle royal in which Fraser, starting as the underdog, needed all his financial acumen and native cunning to thwart a determined campaign by the Canadian press magnate.

Fraser played the patriotic card with his customary determination; it became 'a fight to keep the paper in Scottish hands'. Five weeks into the struggle Thomson had his latest offer rejected and a spokesman for Fraser issued a statement calculated to galvanise native sentiment: 'He has had, if I called it a torrent I would not be exaggerating, of letters, telephone calls, telegrams and messages of all kinds from people he has never heard of, saying "We are Scots. We have had these shares for two generations and we are supporting him through thick and thin".' Two weeks later Thomson capitulated. Fraser now owned a majority of the shares in George Outram and Company and the company's prize possession, the *Glasgow Herald*, had been saved. But saved from what?

There was an assumption among the journalists that if Thomson had got his hands on the paper he would have merged it with *The Scotsman* to create a single broadsheet daily, the Scottish equivalent of the *Irish Times*. If this was indeed Thomson's intention, it would have been anathema to Fraser. For him the *Glasgow Herald* was 'a newspaper of the informed, educated person upon whose initiative, professional skills and leadership the way and standard of life of our people must surely depend' and for that reason it had to continue to be 'owned and controlled by Scotsmen in Scotland – the only Scottish national newspaper not controlled from London'.

But if Fraser was a patriot he was no nationalist. He was a Tory businessman to the tip of his immaculately polished shoes. Having inherited the family drapery business from his father at the age of 23, he had built it into a retail empire through a policy of bold acquisitions, culminating in his takeover of Harrods, London's flagship department store, in 1959. He had always had a head for figures. 'I could get answers to my sums quicker than the others,' he explained, 'and very often by unorthodox methods which I could not explain to the teacher.' He combined an exceptional understanding of money with managerial skill, the energy of a workaholic and sheer force of character. In his well-tailored suit, an orchid often to be found in its buttonhole, he could look deceptively jaunty. The reality was that Fraser was a nervy, intense 60-cigarettes-a-day man who sought relaxation in gambling, an addiction he passed on to his son. He looked 10 years older than his 63 years – his age when he died.

The funeral was a state occasion Glasgow-style, the cortege making its way along Buchanan Street past the offices of his newspaper and the headquarters of his business. The 'who's who' of the Scottish establishment which packed the cathedral was so glittering that the *Herald*'s list of the principal mourners ran to hundreds of names. They included two former Secretaries of State for Scotland (Rosebery and Stuart), the civil servant George Pottinger representing Willie Ross, the shipbuilding magnate Sir Eric Yarrow, such ornaments of the Scottish funeral as Tom Honeyman, Andrew Dewar Gibb and the cinema magnate Alex B King, and many important people from the Scottish media – Ian

McColl, editor of the *Scottish Daily Express*, Andrew Stewart, the controller of BBC Scotland, Willie Ballantyne, the official mouthpiece of the Scottish Office, Alasdair Warren, the *Herald*'s editor, and his deputy George Fraser, who subsequently interjected the middle name MacDonald and fled to the tax haven and birching paradise of the Isle of Man to write popular novels about Flashman, a character from *Tom Brown's Schooldays*. But there was no Lord Thomson of Fleet. The arch enemy sent his managing director Alastair Dunnett.

Most of the organisations which Fraser patronised with his vast wealth were represented, among them the Scottish Conservative and Unionist Party, of which he was honorary treasurer at the time of his death. But there was no mention in the *Herald*'s extensive list, nor was there any mention in the many adulatory obituaries, of a body close to the patriot's heart, so close that he was its Scottish president. Its name was the Economic League, which had been founded in 1919 as National Propaganda. Ostensibly non-party and non-sectarian it dedicated itself to spying on people it suspected of being 'agitators' in the trade unions, industry, politics and journalism. Its secret blacklist of 22,000 names – a silent British version of the McCarthy witch hunt – amounted to a huge database of alleged subversives which, unknown to the individuals concerned, was regularly accessed by employers who subscribed to its beliefs. In its ideology and methods it was as close to fascist as made no difference, yet it continued without public scrutiny until the early 1990s when its activities were finally exposed by Maria Fyfe, a Glasgow Labour MP, in the House of Commons and such impeccable democrats as Gordon Brown, the then Chancellor of the Exchequer, were discovered to be on its list of undesirables.

Fraser's close association with the Economic League should have been known to the *Glasgow Herald*'s editorial hierarchy, which had eagerly supported his successful bid for the newspaper; they were journalists after all. Yet the sober suits in Glasgow Cathedral went on perpetuating the myth of Fraser as a lovable man of the people, a saviour of press freedom, an inspiring symbol of enterprise, when the truth was that the proprietor of the *Glasgow Herald* was giving his name to an extreme right-wing organisation which blacklisted journalists. They did more than turn a blind eye to Fraser's active endorsement of its mass snooping; when he died they tactfully expunged it from the record of his life.

As a gambler the old man knew when to stop. The same could not be said of young Hugh, who inherited the *Glasgow Herald* and more than 100 department stores. The Kelvinside Academy boy did not go on to university, but instead began work in his father's shops at the age of 17. Before long he was being described in the newspapers as Scotland's most eligible bachelor. He was twice married and twice divorced. Both his marriages (to Patricia Bowie, an heiress, and the show-jumper Aileen Ross who died in an air crash) were alleged to have collapsed because of his obsessive dedication to work, but he was equally addicted to roulette. His favourite number was 32. It brought him no luck; he was a colossal loser in the London gaming clubs, habitually returning to his luxury hotel suite in Park Lane at four in the morning. In one memorable session he played two tables back to back at Ladbroke's in Mayfair at a personal cost of £250,000 – the equivalent of £4 million in 2013. He was also a frequent visitor to Monte Carlo – he once drove there non-stop from Glasgow to see how fast he could get to the casino of his choice – but the change of air made no difference to his performance at the tables.

The increasingly desperate tycoon resorted to selling shares in his own company to help settle his mounting gambling debts. These transactions were so suspect that the Stock Exchange ordered an inquiry. The subsequent report dealt lightly with Fraser, accusing him of nothing more culpable than an ignorance of financial matters – perhaps not the ideal qualification for running a major company – but clearing him of insider trading for which he might have gone to prison. He died of cancer in 1987 at the age of 50 and, like his father, was praised for his philanthropy, including his purchase of Iona, which was later gifted to the National Trust for Scotland. By the time of his death he had ceded control of the *Glasgow Herald* (as well as everything else) and the newspaper for which his father battled so tenaciously had been absorbed into Lonhro, a global conglomerate later described by Edward Heath as 'the unacceptable face of capitalism'.

II

There was no need for Fraser, after he bought the *Glasgow Herald*, to impose his own views on the newspaper even if he had been minded to do so; it was already a paper espousing more or less a full set of his political doctrines. Short of outright promotion of the Economic League the *Herald* could not have been more conservative in its instincts and sympathies. In February 1966, for example, the House of Commons gave a second reading to the Sexual Offences Bill, which sought to legalise homosexual acts committed in private by consenting adults. The paper noted with approval that the bill did not apply to Scotland (or Northern Ireland), but wondered how long that happy state of affairs would continue. 'Can anyone imagine,' it asked, 'that homosexual "emancipation" in England will not settle the matter in Scotland? Those Scottish MPs who would rather keep the law as it is should now do their best to ensure that the Bill is mangled or strangled in committee.'

On social and economic issues *The Scotsman* was more liberal in its thinking – no great achievement given the absence of any serious competition for liberal credentials in the Scottish press – and articulated Scottish feeling more faithfully. Alastair Dunnett, its editor, would tell the people around him that the paper should speak for Scotland and be heard where it counted – 'because if we don't do it, no one else will'. Certainly not the *Herald*, which had even found a way of supporting the Beeching plan for emasculating the railways. But *The Scotsman* was a weaker newspaper. Arnold Kemp, when he joined it as a sub-editor, was dismayed by its grey pages with 'the repressed and fluting tone of pan-loaf Edinburgh speech' and taken aback by the deference of some of the journalists. He recalled that the reporter based in St Andrew's House adopted the mannerisms of a mandarin, once telling Kemp that 'we were very upset' about a story in the paper – 'we' being the senior civil servants.

Since neither of the national broadsheets was synonymous with vigorous journalism until *The Scotsman* created an investigative unit headed by Magnus Magnusson, there was a gap at the top end of the market, and a larger gap in the life of intelligent Scotland. The obvious place to look for an inquiring alternative was Queen Margaret Drive. But the policy at BBC Scotland was to avoid controversy and play it safe. James Williams, one of the few critics who dared to pop his head above the parapet with an outspoken attack on the broadcasting establishment, accused the BBC in Scotland of 'failing the public miserably'. He gave some credit to the drama department for *The Vital Spark*, an engaging adaptation of Neil Munro's novels about a Clyde puffer crew, and *This Man Craig*, a series addressing contemporary issues in a moralising tone, in which John Cairney was well cast as an idealistic, good-looking young teacher. But news and current affairs, headed by the autocratic James Kemp, showed little flair or sense of adventure. Williams pointed out that the superficiality of the output was summed up by the dreadfully apt title given to the evening news magazine: *A Quick Look Round*. That was what BBC Scotland did: it had a quick look round. But that was all it ever did.

Yet, as Williams said, there were many issues which 'cried out for treatment in depth'. He gave as an outstanding current example the difficulties facing Fairfield shipyard.

III

A week before Christmas 1985 the Scottish businessman Sir Iain Stewart was found dead of shotgun wounds in the dressing room of his mansion near Gatwick Airport in Sussex. The house commanded magnificent views across the north and south Downs, and Stewart, who had remarried a few years earlier, had the money to run it fully staffed under a butler. But, despite these outward appearances of material and personal well-being, he was a man who believed he had nothing left to live for. He had been ill, and there were suggestions that he feared he was dying. Whatever the explanation, there were 'no suspicious circumstances' – the police's euphemism for suicide. Chain-smoking Fraser was gone at 63, dissolute son Hugh at 50, and now Stewart had put a gun to his head at 69.

Of the three Stewart was the most attractive personality. He was a Tory who was prepared to think radically about Scotland's disfigured industrial relations, who longed for an opportunity to bring management and workers together in a spirit of conciliation, and who saw a compromise between capitalism and socialism as a way of saving the bankrupt Fairfield yard. His views would have been subversive enough to qualify him for Fraser's Economic League blacklist, but they appealed to the Labour government and in particular to the volatile George Brown, who headed up the newly-formed (and short-lived) Department for Economic Affairs.

A scheme revolutionary by Scottish standards came into being: the formation of a new company, Fairfield (Glasgow) Ltd in which the government controlled half the equity and the other half was held partly by a consortium of Iain Stewart and such rich friends as Sir Isaac Wolfson and Lord Thomson of Fleet and partly by the trade unions. This mixture of private enterprise, government and the workers was a new concept in British industry, inspiring Sean Connery to come to Glasgow and make the only film he ever directed, *The Bowler and The Bunnet*. But the grand experiment was not universally popular. The *Glasgow Herald*, which had nothing to say about its proprietor's links with the far right, heaped disdain on the idea of Fairfield as a proving ground for Stewart's suspiciously leftish ideas.

One of the paper's younger journalists, R E (Ronnie) Dundas, a Conservative parliamentary candidate, took the unusual step of writing a letter to his own paper to attack a fellow journalist, John Hossack of Scottish Television, who had presented a programme sympathetic to Stewart and his ambitions for the yard. Dundas complained that Hossack had failed to reflect the views of shipyard employers and other industrialists who opposed government intervention in the form it was taking. The accusation was one of bias – although Dundas left unarticulated any thought in his mind that it was bias on the part of a television company whose chairman, Roy Thomson, was not only the proprietor of a rival newspaper but a partner in Stewart's new enterprise. Stewart took care in his reply to avoid a slanging match: 'My ideals are simply an adaptation of those which have been utilised successfully elsewhere. Indeed, almost every civilised industrial nation except Britain applies them to their system of employment.'

But not every civilised industrial nation had to cope with the deep-seated problems confronting Fairfield (Glasgow) Ltd. The demarcations in the Clyde shipyards were far from straight-forward. They existed rancorously between management and workers, but were complicated by inter-union rivalries and friction. The new company made a number of imaginative moves to break down the traditional barriers and lighten the confrontational atmosphere. Apprentices, who had always been designated according to their trades, became known simply as shipyard workers. A joint council of management and unions was established to negotiate everything of consequence.

Stewart's warmth and straight talking endeared him to the shop stewards, including the two Jimmys, Reid and Airlie, whose opinions carried considerable weight. As a result of all this patient work and no little goodwill, there were fewer strikes, but it was not long before a familiar problem resurfaced. In November 1966 Stewart delivered a blunt warning that, unless there was a significant improvement in productivity by the end of the following year, the shipyard would close. He told the 2,000 workers that Fairfield had lost a lucrative contract for a guided missile destroyer because it could not guarantee delivery in four and a half years; the yard's best offer was five.

Ten months later Stewart's baby was killed off. A new and more conventional company, Upper Clyde Shipbuilders (UCS), inherited both the assets and the problems. According to one school of thought, the one attended by such critics as Ronnie Dundas, Stewart's proving ground was doomed from the start. It simply 'failed'. According to another, Stewart was not given enough time to develop his ideas. He accepted a senior board appointment with UCS but did not stick around long. He said in retrospect that he had not gone into Fairfield 'to make fancy profits' – there was never much danger of that – but in order to demonstrate the benefits of improved industrial relations. In that aspiration he was partially successful.

Away from the limelight he returned to his portfolio of non-executive appointments, retreating from public view. 'I had the utmost respect for his basic humanity,' said Jimmy Reid when he heard of Iain Stewart's death. It was a sentiment shared by many others who knew him.

IV

The 'socialist laboratory' in Inverness, as the *Glasgow Herald* viewed it, was doing rather better than its equivalent in Govan. Willie Ross fought hard in the cabinet for Dounreay as the site of the prototype fast reactor, the new prize of the nuclear industry, against stiff competition from Winfrith in Dorset. Professor Robert Grieve, chairman of the Highlands and Islands Development Board, backed the Secretary of State, putting a persuasive case for Dounreay to Frank Cousins, the minister for technology. When Cousins announced in the Commons that Dounreay had won there were cheers from all sides of the House and Grieve was singled out for praise.

James Jack, general secretary of the STUC, called it 'the most exhilarating news which has come to Scotland for a very long time'. Without the prototype the atomic energy establishment in the far north, employing 2,300 skilled workers on a six-year research programme, would have been progressively run down. Caithness was now guaranteed at least a further 10 years of full-scale research and an expansion of the permanent workforce, as well as 700 temporary jobs during the building of the reactor. Cousins admitted that the choice was not justified on economic grounds and that such a remote location would add considerably to the cost of transmission lines. The underlying message was unmistakable: this was a political decision for which Willie Ross was entitled to take much of the credit.

A few weeks later Grieve presented a cheerful progress report on the work of his board, even if one of its main proposals, for a chain of hotels throughout the Outer Hebrides aimed at 'the medium-income family man', seemed almost deranged in its impracticability. The season was short, the weather unreliable, and there was a limit to the number of medium-income family men who might be persuaded to go on holiday to Lochmaddy in any circumstances. Was there, anyway, no better way of creating employment for the people of the Western Isles? But the Scottish press reported the scheme as if it were the epitome of commercial sanity. Nothing came of it.

A more realistic scheme for developing tourism was already semi-completed. The Aviemore Centre, a complex of hotel and leisure facilities handily placed for the ski slopes of the Cairngorms, had been instigated by old man Fraser with some help from his friend the brewer, Sir William McEwan Younger, and the cooperation of the Scottish Office. St Andrew's House was so keen on the project that it seconded one of its favourite sons, George Pottinger, to assist the development company and work with the architect John Poulson. In the absence of its late founder the opening of the first phase of the centre was conducted by his widow, Lady Fraser of Allander, in front of 700 guests. At the end of the extravagant bash Poulson presented Lady Fraser with a silver salver. More would be heard of this gift; it would re-emerge years later as a supporting player in a criminal trial in Leeds. For the moment, however, there seemed to be nothing wrong with the Aviemore Centre apart from its brutal architecture.

But there was something wrong at the Highlands Board. The

Prime Minister, Harold Wilson, called a general election in the expectation of bolstering his parliamentary majority, and almost as soon as he did Russell Johnston, the Liberal member for Inverness, demanded a ruling from Willie Ross on the political activities of a part-time member of the board, Frank Thomson, managing director of Invergordon Distillery. Thomson had made no secret of his allegiance to the Labour Party and of his intention to support the party's candidate in Johnston's seat, the novelist Allan Campbell McLean. 'Considering that I have always been known as a socialist, being a part-time member of the board does not mean I cannot express myself politically,' he argued. The spat was forgotten in the heat of the election campaign, but the name Frank Thomson would return to haunt the Highlands Board, just as Lady Fraser's silver salver would return to haunt the creators of the Aviemore Centre.

V

Harold Wilson celebrated his 50th birthday with a visit to Glasgow. An audience of 2,500 supporters in Green's Playhouse cheered his arrival on the platform along with his wife Mary, Willie Ross and Manny Shinwell. When the ovation died down some women at the back began to sing 'Happy birthday to you', and the chant was taken up until it became a roar filling the hall.

The reception for his Conservative opponent Edward Heath (Sir Alec having stepped down as leader of the party) was muted by comparison. When he came to the city a week later Heath called on police headquarters as a signal that he regarded crime and punishment as major issues. His party's candidate in Springburn said that three-quarters of all the questions on the doorstep were crime-related; he was one of several Glasgow candidates clamouring for the return of both corporal and capital punishment.

The contest in Woodside was spectacularly nasty. Neil Carmichael, defending the seat for Labour, claimed that the Tories had 'reached the depths of degradation by bringing the birch issue into the campaign'. Michael Hirst, a Tory worker (and future MP), accused Carmichael of complacency, challenging him to speak to the constituents who were afraid to leave their houses after dark 'for fear of being beaten up and robbed by the numerous gangs whose names are indelibly chalked on walls and doors'. Hirst alleged that 'a young lady of Conservative sympathies' had been manhandled after she left one of Labour's public meetings; Labour retaliated with an allegation that Tory campaigners had hurled eggs at its committee rooms.

Of the hangers and floggers only Cathcart's Teddy Taylor, a right-winger with the popular touch, was elected. But there was no denying the strength of civic feeling on the subject. The Glasgow police committee heard that half a million stair lights had been destroyed by vandalism in the past five years, provoking Councillor Isa Carter, the convener, to recommend 'a right good skelping' for the culprits. The full council was informed that in the past 12 months there had been 2,000 slashings and 250 stabbings in the city, and that most of the victims were terrified of intimidation.

George MacKintosh, a member of the group known as the Progressives (a pet name for Conservatives), lambasted 'the intellectuals, the long-haired thinkers, and the university dons, who have experimented too long with their wishy-washy thinking on crime'. MacKintosh proposed, as well as corporal punishment for young offenders, the opening of detention centres 'in isolated parts of the north of Scotland, where prisoners would be placed in complete solitude'. The council voted against the reintroduction of the birch, though by the narrow majority of 49 votes to 41, and the north of Scotland was spared a network of detention centres full of Glasgow miscreants condemned to a view of the moors and a period of enforced silence.

Labour's John P Mackintosh, professor of politics at Strathclyde University, would have pleaded guilty to being an intellectual, a thinker and a university don, only confounding the stereotype with his short hair. 'We are all against crime,' he said, 'but it is not a party issue.' This was wishful thinking. Clearly it was a party issue, in effect if not in theory, but Mackintosh's liberal stance did him no harm. He unseated the chairman of the Tory 1922 Committee to take see-saw Berwick and East Lothian, while Lady Tweedsmuir, in the biggest shock of the night, went down to defeat in Aberdeen South after holding the seat for 20 years. Donald Dewar, her 28-year-old successor, impressed the press as 'quickfire of speech and confident of manner'. With the recruitment of Mackintosh and Dewar, Labour's Scottish contingent did not lack intelligent firepower.

Among the Communist Party candidates, Honor Arundel,

'poetess and authoress', wife of the actor Alex McCrindle and 'mother of three', received 279 votes in Leith, while Govan shop steward Jimmy Reid saw his vote in Dunbartonshire East fall to 1,548, a couple of hundred down on his 1964 result. Russell Johnston, who had been attacked by the churches for supporting the abolition of capital punishment, did well to retain Inverness and his fellow Liberal, David Steel, who 'combined honest appraisal with classical circumspection' according to one evaluation in the press, kept the Borders seat he had won in a 1965 by-election, going on to present his bill for liberalising the law on abortion. Ronnie Dundas, scourge of the Fairfield rescue plan, came third in the shipbuilding town of Greenock.

The SNP put up candidates in 23 constituencies, failed to win any of them, but doubled its vote and saved more deposits than it lost, the party's first decent performance in a general election. It should have been a warning to the established parties. Harold Wilson gained a majority large enough to enable him to govern for a full term, and that was the predictable outcome of the 1966 general election, after a campaign in Scotland almost bereft of serious ideas about the afflictions of society.

VI

The communities, if they could be called communities, which bred many of the smashers of stair lights, gatherers in gangs and disturbers of the peace, had as many as 50,000 inhabitants. A Castlemilk or an Easterhouse was as large as the city of Perth, yet possessed neither cinema nor pub, neither bowling alley nor bingo hall, neither tearoom nor café. Bets were collected round the doors. A journalist who went on an expedition to these peripheral half-towns compared the self-containment of the houses with the social intimacy of the tenement closes from which most of the people had migrated.

Even the common privy on the stairs, for all its primitive indignity, had provided a meeting place of sorts. What was there here? A social worker explained: 'You cannot have a community unless you have public houses, because the men will not put their roots down, particularly the younger men. I am not making a case for drinking, but their tendency is to go to pubs outside the district instead of going home to their tea, and on Saturday after the match they go into the pubs and many miss the last bus home.' One young wife said: 'It was great in Govan. He didn't go out till eight o'clock and he came home at 10, and we knew where he was.' There was an aching loneliness, especially among women.

James Currie, a local Church of Scotland minister, deplored the council's philistinism in destroying physical links with the past which would have given a sense of historical continuity to such outlying settlements as Drumchapel. In Castlemilk an action group criticised the council for long delays in repairing property and for its harsh attitude to tenants, and there were regular complaints about the lack of police on the beat. In the name of improvement the people in power had created deserts in the suburbs and then affected an air of astonished outrage at the inevitable consequences. The detention centres and young offenders' institutions were so overcrowded that the Secretary of State advised the juvenile courts that there was not a single place left in any of them.

Lord Kilbrandon, chairman of the Scottish Law Commission, whose proposals for the treatment of child offenders had earned him a reputation as an enlightened reformer, proved to be less enlightened about the criminal justice system as a whole. Declaring that the time might be ripe for 'revolutionary change', he proposed that before a trial it should be possible for the accused to be brought before a duty magistrate, in the middle of the night if necessary, to answer questions; that during a trial the accused should be forced to give evidence for the Crown, losing his right to silence; and that the life history, family circumstances and personal character of the accused, including his previous convictions, should be laid before the judge and jury before a verdict. These proposals, on which the Labour government sensibly declined to act, would certainly have put more people in prison, the innocent as well as the guilty.

There were occasional glimpses of the inadequacy of Scottish prisons. Witnesses at a fatal accident inquiry described the final hours of Rose Adam, 45, who had been remanded to Saughton Prison in Edinburgh pending a court appearance on a charge of shoplifting. A fellow prisoner, Mary McClements, testified that when Adam was moved into a dormitory at 3.30am, she was clearly distressed. She became hysterical, getting out of bed, praying, speaking to people who were not there. McClements tried to summon help by pressing a bell and banging on the door, but no one appeared. By the time a prison officer arrived at 7.30am Adam was dead. The court heard that the dormitory bell had a defective spring and did not always work. Adam, who had got the bell on a bad night, was suffering from congested lungs and died of an acute pulmonary condition which the prison staff had failed to notice. Sheriff Sinclair Shaw, returning a formal verdict, was not prepared to add a rider suggested by the deceased's advocate that her death might have been prevented by the exercise of greater care on the part of Margaret Nisbet, the wardress (as female prison officers were known) who was on dormitory duty that night. Rose Adam, being a person of no importance, was accorded as little respect in death as she had been in the final hours of her short life.

VII

Very few works of fiction attempted to give meaning or dignity to the circumscribed existence of the urban poor. In 1966 the critics welcomed *The Dear Green Place*, a first semi-autobiographical novel set among the working class of Glasgow. Its author, Archie Hind, was introduced with a hint of condescension by the literary press – 'a Glaswegian who, we are told, has gone through a series of jobs from clerking and labouring to data processing. We gather also that his higher education consisted of a year at Newbattle Abbey and a course of WEA lectures'.

In its willingness to tackle urban themes *The Dear Green Place* was exceptional. A few years earlier J M Reid, former editor of *The Bulletin*, had lamented the absence of Scottish novels about industrial communities: 'It is still true, as it always has been, that the background to most Scottish writing is the countryside or the country town.' Reid's list of urban novelists consisted of Guy McCrone and George Blake, to which he could now add Archie Hind. 'Do we as a people instinctively turn our backs on what we and our immediate forebears have made of Scotland?' he wondered.

When the Caithness novelist and poet Neil Gunn was interviewed on his 75th birthday in November 1966, he was reluctant to talk about himself but eager to praise his contemporaries George Mackay Brown, Iain Crichton Smith and Sorley

Maclean, all of whom came from non-urban backgrounds and drew heavily on their own cultures and experiences – Brown's Orkney, Crichton Smith's Lewis, Maclean's Raasay. 'When we talk about literature blossoming,' he said, 'we imply roots.' If Gunn was correct, the wandering tribes of post-war urban Scotland – a people 'decanted' according to the dehumanising jargon of the housing bureaucrats – had no roots or roots so shallow that they were as yet unimaginable in fiction.

Just as documentary realism eluded the writers of Scotland, so the potential for satire was largely unexplored. As good a starting point as any for a satirist of Scottish life would have been 30 November, always a day fraught with blush-inducing embarrassments. Lord Polwarth of the Scottish Council (Development and Industry), friend of the Beeching cuts, delivered a BBC St Andrew's Day lecture groaning with platitudes about the wonderful state of the Scottish economy. On the same night in Edinburgh 1,000 freemasons 'celebrated the festival of Saint Andrew' with a dinner at which Sir Ronald Orr Ewing, the grand master mason, thanked the many ministers of the Church of Scotland who gave up their time to attend lodge meetings. One of them, Tom Scott, chaplain of the new Heriot Watt University, delivered the principal toast, but it was the reply that caught the media's attention. James McHarg, a visitor from Rhodesia, was received as an honoured guest despite his country's recent unilateral declaration of independence. He joked about being a rebel, but of not feeling like one in this company. 'We are facing a world today,' said McHarg, 'that somehow seems to be smitten with the idea that if you find a white man in Africa, you have found an anomaly.'

The satirical novelist might then have turned his attention to a St Andrew's Day session of the House of Commons in which Russell Johnston introduced a private member's bill for Scottish self-government. The anonymous parliamentary sketch-writer of the *Glasgow Herald* was unable to restrain himself, jesting mercilessly at Johnston's expense. The member had come 'red of face and white of knee, wearing yellow woollen hose, a worried expression, and a kilt in the family tartan'. When the MP for Inverness, warming to his theme, quoted Hugh MacDiarmid's evocation of 'the small, white rose of Scotland that smells sharp and sweet and breaks the heart', the House erupted in derisive mirth. 'Where's your pipes?' bellowed the Labour back benches, while the Tories 'nearly split the seams of their dark blue suits with glee', one of them shouting: 'Build a wall!' The *Herald*'s headline of choice was 'Guffaws greet Bill on Home Rule'. Journalists were still attached to the guffaw, a Scottish word of early 18th-century origin denoting coarse laughter, but were less sensitive to the chilling subtleties of Hubris, a much older word, Greek in origin.

1967

A SENSIBLE MODICUM OF WHISKY

I

Lionel Daiches wished he had been a contemporary of Boswell and Hume. For someone of his flamboyance the 18th century would have been more congenial. Regrettably his entrance was delayed for 200 years and he was born into a century in which his glittering qualities were not always appreciated. He was the older son of Salis, chief rabbi of Scotland, and the brother of David, a prominent academic and literary critic. When he was asked how it felt to be the brother of a famous man, Lionel replied: 'I don't know. You had better ask him.' Lionel was as celebrated in the law as David was in literature.

Daiches enjoyed a reputation as the advocate with the golden tongue, a natural defender, good with juries, although such was the transparent guilt of many of his clients he lost many more times than he won; even Daiches's eloquence, unmatched at the Scottish Bar, could not save some of the monstrous individuals whose innocence he pleaded. They carried guns and knives; the most unusual item Daiches ever carried was a snuffbox. He was adored for his anecdotes and conviviality. But as a sheriff in Glasgow, a post he unaccountably decided to take up in 1962, he was miscast. He found the work dull. Later he confessed that his years on the bench were the most miserable of his life.

Daiches, in this more respectable incarnation, was unable to resist introducing incongruous theatrical touches from his extensive repertoire. Summing up in the case of a Glasgow underworld figure, Arthur Thompson, he used the phrase 'hotter than a red-hot poker'. When the conviction was referred to the Appeal Court in Edinburgh, Ewan Stewart, the advocate depute, explained to Lord Clyde, the Lord Justice General, that a 'red-hot poker' was a slang expression meaning that the more recent the theft the hotter the stolen property.

357

Nicholas Fairbairn, who was almost as colourful as Daiches though without the latter's endearing qualities, contended on Thompson's behalf that the sheriff's charge to the jury was 'prejudiced, superlative and unfair'. He claimed that Daiches had taken the facts of the Crown case, dealt with them at length, and then excused himself for not dealing with the defence case. Clyde was not amused; Clyde was rarely amused. He rebuked Daiches for 'unduly flowery and extravagant language quite out of place in a charge to a jury by a Scottish judge'. Lord Guthrie, who was sitting with him, said he agreed that highly coloured language was inappropriate, but failed to see where it took the appeal. Thompson's conviction was upheld; the gangster went down for four years.

As reported in an earlier chapter, Daiches had got into trouble with another Glasgow criminal, Walter Scott Ellis, for a charge to the jury which Ellis considered prejudicial. He was intimidated by Ellis's threatening letters from prison and partly blamed them for a deterioration in his health. In the early part of 1967 he went to his doctor complaining of stress. He was certainly in poor shape when he was stopped by the police and breathalysed after a visit to the theatre. The incident resulted in the indignity of an appearance in the dock of his own court, facing a charge of driving while under the influence of drink or drugs. The case was heard by a man he knew well, M G Gillies, the Sheriff Principal of Glasgow. There would have been more integrity in the outcome if the case had been heard by a judge Daiches did not know well. Perhaps such a person did not exist.

Daiches was represented by Laurence Dowdall, solicitor to the criminal classes, who opened with an admission that he had had 'hot and furious arguments' with his client about Daiches's decision to plead guilty. 'Normally,' confided Dowdall, 'when a client does not accept my advice, like Pontius Pilate I wash my hands of him and leave him to go his own course.' But Daiches had insisted that higher standards should apply to him than to a layman. 'I think it is my duty and I know it is my privilege to tender a plea, not so much, I feel, in mitigation as in explanation,' Dowdall continued ponderously. He then made an oblique reference to 'the unpleasant aftermath of a case which your lordship will know about' – Ellis – and said that Daiches had been prescribed barbiturate tablets to cope with the tensions of his work.

Daiches listened intently from the dock, his hands clasped under his chin, as Dowdall gave an account of the ill-fated night out. 'After the theatre, when his stomach was behaving queasily, he took an extra tablet. Thereafter, in a discussion with some friends, he took some black coffee and in the last black coffee he put a sensible modicum of whisky.' He quickly developed 'an unusual headache' and decided to go home. Two taxi drivers saw him driving erratically and, after a near collision, they called the police.

None of this justified any other plea than guilty as charged. But, had it come to trial, Dowdall would have argued a defence worthy of Daiches on an off day. Dowdall asked the court to believe that his client, whose professional life routinely involved the hearing of driving offences, had no knowledge of the effect of taking alcohol on top of barbiturates, adding that his GP had not specifically warned him against drinking. Dowdall said he had spoken to Dr Imrie, the police surgeon, who had told him that if a person took a drug not knowing the effect, then drove a car while impaired by the drug, he could not be held at fault. A lawyer seemed to be deferring here to a doctor's knowledge of the law of Scotland. Imrie had in any case failed to mention the possible influence of a 'sensible modicum of whisky', whatever that meant, on a driver's ability behind the wheel.

Gillies addressed his colleague: 'Sheriff Daiches, I do not think it would be proper for me to treat your case any differently from any other person in this position. In view of the certificates from your doctor to the effect he did not warn you of the danger of taking alcohol with the drug, I think I can proceed on the basis that you did not have sufficient warning of the consequences, and accordingly I can treat this case as being one where the breach was undoubtedly involuntary.' He gave Daiches an absolute discharge. Despite a plea of guilty the accused left the court without a conviction to his name or a stain on his character. Gillies's undertaking that Daiches was being treated no differently was immediately disproved. On the same day in the same court four men charged with the same offence were fined and banned from driving for between one and four years.

There was a furious popular reaction to the case and its exposure of judicial double standards; the letters columns of the Scottish newspapers were full of it. 'I think it is appalling that he should be given an absolute discharge,' said one. 'In my opinion a man of his learning should know that drink and drugs do not mix.' Another asked: 'Would Sheriff Daiches, or Dr Imrie, or the notable

Mr Dowdall, care to tell us what is a sensible modicum of whisky?'

Into this melting pot of indignation tiptoed Winifred M Ewing, secretary of the Glasgow Bar Association, with a brief letter in support of the beleaguered QC: 'The Glasgow Bar Association hold Sheriff Daiches in the greatest possible esteem as an impartial judge, a brilliant lawyer, and an excellent sheriff, at all times fair and courteous in his dealings.' If this was intended to assuage public feeling, it had the opposite effect. 'So what?' began one bilious missive. 'The Glasgow Bar Association should know that the attributes referred to by them ought to be expected of any judge.' John McNamara of Glasgow wrote with feeling: 'If Sheriff Daiches is as fair and courteous as Miss [sic] Ewing would have us believe, I only wish he had judged my trial for a speeding offence, when I suffered the abominable penalty of being fined £20 and banned for a month.'

There was no way back for Daiches. He resigned from the bench and resumed his career as a barnstorming performer in the various halls of the High Court. Restored to full health, he profited from the introduction of legal aid and went on working into his eighties, dying a few months before the end of the century into which it had been his unhappy fate to be consigned. When his friends in Edinburgh came to write appreciations of his life, his appearance in the dock was brushed off as an episode of no consequence. But the memorable phrase associated with the scandal, 'a sensible modicum of whisky', lingered like a good malt, much savoured by students of the euphemism. As for the secretary of the Glasgow Bar Association – well, she was about to become a Scottish celebrity in her own right.

II

Esmond Wright, academic and commentator, won the Glasgow Pollok by-election in March 1967 with a majority for the Conservatives of 2,200, taking the seat from Labour. Wright should have been the man of the hour, but his triumph was eclipsed by the performance of the candidate in third place, George Leslie, whose 28% of the poll represented the SNP's best-ever performance in Glasgow and put the party just behind Labour. The nationalists' strong showing could have been predicted; they had done well in the general election without coming close to winning a seat. But there was a sense of shock among its opponents that a party long regarded as an electoral joke had somehow persuaded 10,884 electors in Pollok to vote for it.

Leslie, a Glasgow dentist, was scarcely a beacon of liberal-left enlightenment. In a televised debate during the campaign he argued for the retention of fee-paying schools and against David Steel's abortion reform bill. The party as a whole had an attitude to Britain's proposed membership of the European Economic Community (EEC) that would later be called 'Eurosceptic', a misleading term routinely used to describe opponents of the project rather than genuine sceptics. At its annual conference not long after Pollok, the SNP approved a resolution refusing to countenance Scotland's inclusion in the EEC without the approval of the Scottish people.

Strains of anglophobia resurfaced in a resolution deploring the 'increasing number of executive and teaching positions in Scottish universities being given to Englishmen [no mention of women] to the exclusion of Scots'. John Gair of Eskdale, moving the resolution, asserted that 'excess numbers of English lecturers and professors may change the character and tradition of Scottish universities'. The party chairman, Arthur Donaldson, whose brief imprisonment during the war on suspicion of Nazi sympathies still rankled with the party faithful, proposed a new slogan based on a Bannockburn battle cry: 'On them! They fail!' According to Donaldson, the Glasgow bus conductress was in no mood to exchange her familiar greeting, 'hen' for the English 'duckie'. It was an embarrassing performance. They did this stuff rather better in the low music halls.

Although there was no attempt to conceal the xenophobic tendencies of the party, the SNP's march through 1967 continued unimpeded. An avalanche of articles in the press attempted to grapple with the nature and causes of the phenomenon and to suggest possible cures. Sir William McEwan Younger, the Tory brewer, was laughed out of town for proposing as an alternative tipple 'administrative devolution', a brand the Scots had sampled and found too weak for their taste. Fyfe Robertson, the Scottish-born broadcaster, replied that administrative devolution was no more than 'political shandy with too much ginger beer'; Robertson sounded like a man who would have preferred a sensible modicum of whisky.

David Steel laid his hands on an SNP policy document which anticipated a Scottish army 'sufficient to make any invasion or physical occupation a very difficult undertaking'; there would also be a Scottish navy and a Scottish air force. The same pamphlet proposed legislation to banish from an independent Scotland all chain stores under 'alien control' – i.e. English. Steel denounced these ideas as 'quite unsupportable' and speculated that the nationalists would not be enjoying such success if the electors were aware of their true colours. The SNP's insistence that the document no longer represented its official thinking was a weak response to Steel's probing of the party's more extreme elements.

Christopher Grieve, undaunted by John MacCormick's view of him as a liability to the cause, entered the discussion with a recitation of the glories of romantic nationalism, laced with his customary invective. He wrote that 'in all the countries I know of where independence has been gained or regained the necessary impulse came from poets and artists', and went on to lament the influences of anglicisation on Scottish life. Why, he asked, were Burns, Allan Ramsay and Robert Ferguson so loved by the people? He suggested that they 'emboldened thoughts and emotions most rife in the national bosom' – a bosom no longer swelling with pride. English language and literature, even English history, enjoyed 'a virtual monopoly' in the schools and colleges to the almost complete exclusion of Scottish literature, the Scottish languages (Scots and Gaelic) and Scottish history.

On these questions of cultural identity he had company. Lord Reith, in his rectorial address at Glasgow University, and Harry Whitley, the successor to Warr as minister of St Giles, had recently said much the same. But there had been few votes in it. Were there any votes in it now, or were the Scots turning to the SNP for other reasons?

Robert Kemp, whose adaptation for Tyrone Guthrie of the Scots classic *The Three Estates* had been the hit of the 1948 Edinburgh Festival, contributed a balanced perspective to the debate. He was old enough to remember 'the romantic period of nationalism' led by MacDiarmid with assistance from Lewis Spence, Moray McLaren and others. One of two things was true, said Kemp. Either the poets and intellectuals could start a movement or they had some prophetic sense of what was on the way – but they would never be trusted by the public. The nationalists of the new generation tended to be young men (still no mention of women) well up in the latest speech by William Wolfe, the party's vice chairman, rather than the kilted figures of the past.

Kemp was on to something with his reference to the pragmatic, level-headed Wolfe, an accountant who spoke the new language of economics. He expected Wolfe to be 'a very important person in Scotland one day'. But Robert Kemp did not live to see it. Nor did he live to celebrate the defeat of a plan for an Edinburgh inner-ring road, which would have lopped off part of the graceful New Town crescent in which he lived. Later that year he died of a stroke at the age of 59, his life having been cut short, so his family believed, by the stresses of his choleric opposition to the proposed scheme. His son Arnold wrote of him: 'His cultural nationalism remained dominant. He believed passionately that the distinctive traditions of Scotland should be celebrated, sustained and, if possible, renewed.'

III

Willie Ross also believed passionately in the distinctive cultural traditions of Scotland. He was an authority on the life and work of Robert Burns, delivering thunderous toasts to the poet's immortal memory. But there was nothing of the romantic nationalist about the Secretary of State. He refused to admit the growing likelihood that the SNP would become a credible political force and continued to regard it with lofty disdain.

In the first half of 1967 he may have felt that there were more pressing questions than the nationalist threat, real or imagined. Freezes and squeezes were making the Wilson government unpopular nationally, on top of which Ross faced problems specific to Scotland. A government inquiry chaired by J B Cullingworth, of the Department of Social and Economic Research at Glasgow University, published a damning analysis of Scotland's housing stock. It estimated that at least 273,000 houses should be demolished rapidly and that 193,000 more should go within 30 years. These figures stood in shaming contrast to the official claim that only 100,000 houses were unfit for habitation. In many rural areas, particularly in the Highlands, there were housing conditions as bad as Glasgow's if not worse: 'We have seen families inhabiting rural cottages in unbelievably squalid conditions – without water, electricity or sanitation.'

It was the dense concentration of slum housing that made Glasgow's situation so unusual – unique in Britain according to Cullingworth. He wrote: 'Even the Glaswegian who sees only the often imposing, yet on closer inspection often crumbling, front exterior seldom appreciates how revolting and inhumane are the conditions inside in the closes, on the common staircases, and in the back courts, and even if he does occasionally glimpse the physical squalor which is out of sight to the passer-by, he can have no conception of the extent of the problem.' Cullingworth reported with dismay that as recently as May 1966 Glasgow Corporation had declared that 41% of the city's housing stock was below standard, yet the city persisted in demolishing houses of reasonable quality. While he was finalising his report, 249 decent homes were pulled down to make way for the approach roads to the new Clyde tunnel.

Labour could blame the 13 'wasted years' of Tory rule for the wretched living conditions of many Scots. But in the far north there was nowhere for Willie Ross to run. The Highlands and Islands Development Board, one of the first initiatives of the new government, was unravelling over allegations that members were personally profiting from their association with it. Two, including the Labour activist Frank Thomson, were both closely involved in a projected petro-chemical complex at Invergordon. Russell Johnston, who had been the first to raise concerns about Thomson's non-executive appointment, told the House of Commons that no board member should be vulnerable to suspicion of having made private gain out of public money.

Ross at first attempted to head off the crisis with bluster, denouncing the 'rumour, innuendo and speculation' which were damaging the board's reputation. Two days later, with Thomson's abrupt resignation in the face of new revelations, the Secretary of State was left looking shifty. He admitted to parliament that £38,000 had been advanced to business interests of board members and that most of the money had gone to Thomson's companies. But Ross promptly dug a deeper hole for himself, hinting that there was a sinister vendetta against the board. His young colleague Donald Dewar spoke of 'a stupid witch hunt' against Thomson, while the entrepreneur issued a statement bemoaning 'the dark period of anguish, despair and misery' which all those 'who truly love the Highlands' were going through. His personal misery was undeniably acute: not only had his group, Polyscot, received

£25,000 from the board; a subsidiary had applied for a further cheque for the same amount, which now stood no hope of approval. By October most of Thomson's business was in liquidation.

The board's naivety was cruelly exposed by the scandal. Robert Grieve, its chairman, had been warned about the risks attached to the appointment but had chosen to ignore them. Few in the Highlands were disposed, however, to attack the character of an honourable public servant. When Campbell Finlay, chairman of Mull and Iona Council of Social Service, said at the height of the crisis that Grieve was held in the highest respect, there were murmurs of approval. Personally he was. But the failings for which he was ultimately responsible were not confined to misjudgements about the people around him; they were symptomatic of a more general myopia.

The prescription for economic revival was brutal. Rather than encourage a patient, holistic approach, which had seemed to be its policy in the beginning, the board decided to create a new city of half a million people in the Moray Firth based around and beyond the proposed petro-chemical complex. Alastair Mackenzie, the Liberal MP for Ross and Cromarty, pointed out the obvious pitfall of the scheme: centralisation on so extreme a scale would draw people away from the outlying areas, particularly of the west and north, making it more difficult to sustain viable communities. The board had overlooked the basic flaw in a strategy all too obviously influenced by the over-rated Toothill report. The city of half a million people was a non-starter, reinforcing the impression that Willie Ross's Inverness baby, after a promising start, had lost its way.

The launch of the new Cunard liner at John Brown's Clydebank yard should have offered a respite to a government beset with so many difficulties. But all was not plain sailing. First there was the question of what to call the ship. John Banks, a Glasgow bookmaker, invited bets. Sir Winston Churchill was the favourite at 8-1, followed by Prince Charles, Princess Margaret, Prince of Wales, John F Kennedy, and Queen Elizabeth II. The choice of the last-named was a propaganda gift to the SNP, reigniting the ill-feeling in Scotland about the double numerals after the monarch's name. Gordon Wilson, the party's national organiser, called the decision insulting and ignorant and said it would be resented north of the border. He was supported by Labour's John Johnston, the Lord Provost of Glasgow, who claimed to have heard many expressions of regret.

Next there were logistical difficulties at the launch itself. Queen Elizabeth II – or, more accurately in Scotland, Queen Elizabeth I – had to repeat her 'God speed' message when her first attempt was drowned out by the cheers of 30,000 shipyard workers and their families. Despite the personal blessing of the Almighty, the ship was reluctant to move. 'Gie it a shove' rose a voice from the crowd. According to one newspaper report the liner finally 'slipped gracefully into the Clyde with a deep curtsy to the Queen after whom she had just been named'. Either the ship was such a loyal subject that she had already learned to curtsy, or the journalist who claimed to have seen her curtsy had availed himself of a sensible modicum of whisky.

IV

On the morning of the Hamilton by-election in November 1967 a seasoned political commentator wrote: 'At Westminster, only a belief in the incredible allows a win for Mrs Ewing, although she is expected to beat the Conservative for second place.' The SNP candidate had just addressed the biggest audience of the campaign – 900 in the Town Hall for her eve-of-poll rally. But the star turn was not Winifred M Ewing – Winnie as she was now generally known, giving her a warmer appeal than she had enjoyed during the Daiches debacle – but Ludovic Kennedy, patrician broadcaster, penal reformer and disillusioned Liberal. Kennedy said that the people of Hamilton had nothing to lose by supporting Ewing and that the freedom and dignity of Scotland could best be served by voluntarily restoring to her the powers she had surrendered 200 years before. (Like ships, countries were generally assumed to be female – except perhaps when they needed a shove.) Kennedy's speech was punctuated by loud applause, which turned to cheers when he declared: 'This movement [Scottish nationalism] may not come to fruition now, but nothing in the world is going to stop it.'

A few days earlier Ewing had tickled the press corps by likening Scotland's emigration rate to 'a big hole in the bucket', emphasising her point by singing a self-composed series of verses to an old tune. 'There's a hole in the bucket, dear Willie', it began.

There was no need to ask who the Willie was. Her Labour opponent, Alex Wilson, a 50-year-old Lanarkshire miner, had no answer to this winning folksiness. But the two protagonists had more in common than they were prepared to concede. Both came from ILP backgrounds, Ewing as the daughter of a cabinet maker, George Woodburn, who lost his right hand, and his trade, in an accident. With the money he received in compensation he started in business as a wholesale paper merchant.

Both his daughers went to Glasgow University, but while the elder was active in the socialist club, Winnie was influenced by the speeches of John MacCormick, the rector of the university, and joined the National Party. When her father heard, he accused her of being a traitor to the working class. Eventually he relented, joining the SNP a few months before his death. Despite their differences father and daughter were agreed on their basic socialist principles. Winnie was at that stage on the left of the SNP, a party without any settled political ideology beyond independence.

Willie Ross's immediate reaction to Ewing's victory, and the loss of a Labour stronghold, showed how little he understood the symbolism of the result. At a news conference in Aberdeen (where he happened to be the morning after) he lamented the success of 'this phony political party'. Later in the day, at a lunchtime meeting, he was evidently in jovial form but no more emollient: 'This is not politics, it is emotion and when it comes to a general election reason will take over.' Unapologetic about this implicit insult to the electors of Hamilton, the Secretary of State betrayed no hint of contrition: 'If I thought for a minute that this was a real political party and not a political mood, then there would be much greater cause for concern.'

An influential constituent of Hamilton, James Jack of the STUC, expressed a different view of the SNP's victory: 'Mrs Ewing's talent and vivacity have not been without significance ... one doubts whether the Labour Party will even now be prepared to learn that the Scottish National Party can no longer be brushed aside.' Jack was impressed by the active involvement of young people in the SNP's campaign, rightly interpreting this as a worrying sign for Labour. The newspapers were unanimous in their view that Ross was paying a heavy price for under-rating the nationalists. Was this stubborn and divisive character really the man for the job? they asked. But Harold Wilson stuck by him.

On the morning of her triumph Ewing told the press that she

expected a great deal of activity from Scottish MPs, if only because 'they all have draughty seats'. She said she would be pressing for a debate on the emigration of Scots and another about the desperate housing situation revealed by Cullingworth. But it was not a day for policy statements; it was a day for flourishing telegrams of congratulations. Ludovic Kennedy declared in one of them that he was 'very proud to have been with you on the last lap'. The new MP said she intended to go ahead with a planned holiday to Orkney and Shetland, via Larkhall – 'the cradle of socialism' – where her confident supporters had printed tickets for a victory ball several days ahead of the result.

A British Railways sleeper was chartered to take Ewing and 400 supporters to London for her first day in the House of Commons. The media were ecstatic. 'It was a right royal welcome for Winnie, who looks the most splendid product Scotland has exported for a long time,' enthused the *Evening Times*. 'After the all-night journey she was as fresh as paint, her coiffure in perfect order as if she had just come from under the hairdryer. As her train drew into King's Cross, a huge SNP sign on the front of the engine, the photographers rushed forward expectantly to the first coach. Sure enough, Mrs Ewing was there. She popped her head out and turned on a smile that lit up the whole station.' Such fawning was not quite in the class of Queen Elizabeth II's curtsy to a monarch of the same name, but it was getting close.

An American reporter asked her: 'Is it true to say that Scots don't really want an independent Scotland?' Reply: 'I wouldn't have been elected in Hamilton if that was the case.' He persisted: 'Would you really like to see Scotland independent with its own seat in the United Nations?' Reply: 'What do you think I'm doing here?'

A crowd of several hundred started to gather outside the Palace of Westminster around one o'clock. An hour and a half later the member for Hamilton, surrounded by jostling supporters, turned up in a Scottish-made Hillman Imp. Her husband Stewart and her three children Fergus (10), Annabelle (7) and Terry (4) had come along for the ride.

'Thoroughly modern Winnie,' enthused the press, 'working mother and white hope of the Scottish nationalists.' She was wearing a quilted purple coat ('because it is a ceremonial colour and the colour of the thistle' she explained). Sir Gerald Nabarro, a moustachioed Tory of the old school, cried out 'Scotland the brave' as she entered the chamber. Lord Boyd Orr, who supported her from the peers' gallery, had taken his seat in the Commons (representing the Scottish Universities) on the same April day in 1945 as Dr Robert McIntyre, Ewing's only predecessor.

'She is clearly in her prime,' noted a shrewd old bird in the press gallery. 'Whether she will turn out to be in her element as well, only time will tell.' Time did: Winnie Ewing was not in her element. 'Catcalls every time I went in,' she recalled. 'Interruptions every time I spoke. Personal insults. Abuse. It's all there in Hansard. That's the beauty of it. It's all recorded for posterity. I was attacked in a way that the Speaker, Horace King, told me no one had been attacked in the history of the House of Commons. It was a daily crucifixion scene.' She claimed that the Tories sat and watched while most of the crucifying was done by embittered Labour members – the ones memorably evoked by Oliver Brown, one of the wittier nationalists, who said that after Hamilton 'you could feel a chill along the Labour backbenches looking for a spine to run up'.

The only exception was Emrys Hughes, the veteran Labour MP for South Ayrshire, who told Ewing that he had no reputation left to lose and gallantly proffered the hand of friendship, inviting her to tea most days. The Liberal group was hospitable too, but for lunch she mostly sat alone at a table for two, under a portrait of Benjamin Disraeli. She found the place 'disgusting and obscene', and her loneliness intensified when her patron Hughes died. By then the euphoria had died too.

V

But it was slow to evaporate in Glasgow after the singular triumph of one of its football clubs. Celtic became the first British team to win the European Cup with a 2-1 victory over some hotly fancied but, in the event, petulant and ill-tempered Italians. 'Mair fouls than you'd see in a hen hoose' was the verdict of one Glasgow fan on the famed Inter Milan. The Celtic manager, Jock Stein, got it wrong with his pre-match prophecy that the team which scored first would win. On a Lisbon night 'hot enough to roast an ox' Inter Milan scored from a disputed penalty after only eight minutes. In the end a terrific Celtic side could and should have won by four or five goals. Stein was so overcome that he left the scene 30 seconds before the final whistle, disappearing down the tunnel. 'We won and we won on merit' was his laconic response.

A man of humble origins, a socialist, a coal miner before he took up football full-time, Stein could be ruthless. His thrift and austerity were legendary. He paid his players poorly and insisted on short back and side haircuts. He was not renowned as one of the game's innovators. But as the sports writer Kevin McCarra wrote after his death in 1985, Stein 'had a senior civil servant's gift for cunning and strategy' and, in his management of the players before an important match, he possessed the gift of tongues, 'knowing the perfect words and tone for each individual'. Perfection was achieved in Lisbon. At the end some of the 12,000 supporters who had travelled from Scotland leapt over a moat six feet wide and eight feet deep which separated the crowd from the playing field, almost strangling the players in an overwhelming communal embrace.

Success for the 'Lisbon Lions' was all the sweeter for being deep, almost familial, in its roots. All 11 heroes – goalkeeper Ronnie Simpson, Jim Craig, Tommy Gemmell, Bobby Murdoch, captain Billy McNeill, John Clark, Jimmy Johnstone, Willie Wallace, Stevie Chalmers (who scored the winning goal), Bertie Auld and Bobby Lennox – were born within a narrow radius of the city of Glasgow, belonging to the same identifiable community as their fans. When the team returned home with the cup, Paradise – otherwise known as Parkhead, home of Celtic – was regained. A modicum of whisky flowed. But no one pretended that it was sensible.

1968

ROADS TO PARADISE

I

The resignation sermon of the broadcaster Malcolm Muggeridge in January 1968 was rated so highly that the BBC broadcast it live on radio. He was the first rector of Edinburgh University ever to resign from the job, and perhaps the only rector of any university ever to resign because of the contraceptive pill. A congregation of 2,000, the Edinburgh establishment at prayer, gathered in St Giles Cathedral to witness St Mugg's last stand against the permissive society. In the olden days he would have been an Old Testament prophet. Now he had to settle for being a television personality.

The storm over Muggeridge's majestic exodus would normally have rumbled on for days. Instead it was swept away by a proper storm. For 48 hours the Met Office had been unobtrusively charting the progress of a secondary depression heading towards the British Isles. The weather experts had expected it to pass over St Kilda and the Faroe Islands. It didn't. It turned east and kept deepening, its radius widening, the force of its wind gathering. By midnight it was centred north of Benbecula. For the next six hours it tore across Scotland, hitting parts of the country with devastating ferocity.

Hurricane Low Q peaked between 4 and 5am. Gusts reached 125 mph, radio masts collapsed on Lowther Hill in Dumfriesshire, telephone lines blew down on Tiree, and a 60-foot-high crane weighing 600 tons fell to the concrete bottom of the Scott Lithgow dry dock on the Clyde. Five people died in Greenock. Three were trapped when a dredger capsized and sank off Princes Pier; a chimney head fell into a room in Margaret Street, killing a young woman as she lay in bed; an employee of the town's sugar works was suffocated in the rubble of her house, also as the result of a collapsing chimney head.

Glasgow, unfamiliar with a natural phenomenon of such

violence, suffered greater damage than other cities because of the dangerous vulnerability of so many of its older properties; Cullingworth's warnings had come too late. The bodies of four of the nine people who died in the city were recovered after a 12-hour search in the basement of a three-storey tenement in Dumbarton Road. One of the victims, Anne Best, lived in England but had come north to attend her mother's funeral. She was staying with her sister in the top flat, but because of the storm she and her three-year-old daughter moved down one storey to the flat occupied by Janet Gowran and her 10-year-old daughter. Both mothers and both children were killed by falling masonry. One of the survivors from the same block said that he and his wife had just moved bedrooms after a fall of soot when the chimney head came down, the ceiling caved in, and they leapt for their lives into a close full of screaming women.

A shortage of materials and incessant rain compounded Glasgow's misery. Two thousand houses in the city were damaged by the hurricane and many of their occupants pleaded unsuccessfully with factors, the police and the army for tarpaulins to cover the roofs. Creeping damp seeped into houses which had escaped the worst of the havoc. A Glasgow journalist, Edna Robertson, wrote: 'One room was affected and I camped out in another. But when I got up this morning the bathroom was like a miniature Niagara.' Scotland's most destructive storm for more than 40 years left 20 dead and hundreds homeless, with the incidental result of denying the resigning rector the prominence to which he was accustomed. No sooner had Muggeridge finished his rant against the swinging sixties than his words were cast to the unforgiving winds. The prophet would not have slept soundly that night. Few slept at all.

II

The decade had so far failed to swing for Scotland. Its liberating qualities were experienced mostly vicariously, through occasional reports from London of expatriate Scots indulging themselves in reckless pleasures.

In the summer of 1966 'the Maryhill-born folk singer' Donovan (Donovan Philip Leitch) was fined £250 after pleading guilty to being in possession of cannabis – 'Indian hemp' as the Scottish newspapers felt obliged to add. His girlfriend Donreen Fabienne Samuel, 20, was put on probation for 12 months. She and Donovan were found naked in his London flat when the police forced their way in. Screaming 'I am too young to read a warrant, you cannot nick me', Donovan jumped on the back of a sergeant and told the officers that they were not to go into the bedroom because he was having sex with a woman in it. The police found Donreen 'staring straight ahead and blinking her eyes as if the light hurt them'. While they were being escorted from the premises Donovan said: 'I don't know why it's against the law. It's not like beer. At least you don't have a head in the morning.'

The most scornful critic of such excesses was elected rector of Edinburgh University a few months before the 'summer of love' in 1967, but in his rectorial address Muggeridge avoided sex and pot, concentrating instead on the evils of modern education: 'In our society, the belief that the road to paradise is paved with A-levels is held at least as tenaciously as any article of Christian dogma in the days of Torquemada. No doubt we will go on raising the school age, enlarging our universities, increasing expenditure on education until illiteracy multiplies so alarmingly that the whole process will be called into question.' He had little to say at that stage about the possibility that the road to paradise was paved with discarded condoms as well as useless A-levels. He contented himself with the 'near-certainty' that his successor as rector would be one of the Beatles 'or one of those extraordinary young ladies that get married from time to time in diaphanous short costumes'.

Eleven months later, as a secondary depression moved towards Benbecula, he was no longer exercised by the futility of modern education. He spoke instead of free love, its causes and consequences. *Student*, the Edinburgh University newspaper edited by Anna Coote, a *Guardian* columnist of the future, had challenged him to support a motion of the Students' Representative Council that the university health service should provide information about the contraceptive pill and make the pill available to students who wanted it. Either the rector should back the motion, said the SRC, or the rector should resign. Muggeridge's answer was uncompromising. He described the request as highly distasteful and wondered how representative of student opinion a rector must be. 'Whatever life is about,' he said, 'it is not to be expressed in terms of drugged stupefaction and casual sexual relationships.' Considering his own record of infidelity to his long-suffering wife Kitty, he was something of an authority on casual sexual relationships. But the speech was not attacked for its delicious hypocrisy. By many of those who left St Giles in an ever-stiffening wind one January night in 1968, it was regarded as an affirmation of traditional values.

Peace was not quickly restored to the fractious Edinburgh University student community. Later in the year Yvonne Baginsky, a 21-year-old law undergraduate from Boston, who had succeeded Anna Coote as editor of *Student*, was fired over her coverage of the campaign to elect Muggeridge's successor. Kenneth Cargill, chairman of the publication board, said that Baginsky had failed to observe the right of fair comment by refusing to publish a letter from one of the candidates, the broadcaster Kenneth Allsop. Baginsky's point of view was that only Stephen Morrison, the student candidate, was worth taking seriously.

Allsop arrived at Turnhouse Airport, piped off the plane by his supporters. 'In a personal sense, one is sorry,' he told reporters. 'It is rather sad for the young lady. But it seems to me an absolutely proper measure that the publication board has taken.' A photograph of a defiant Baginsky in hot pants and long black boots appeared in the newspapers. Allsop won the rectorial election, confounding Muggeridge's prediction about his successor (Allsop was not one of the Beatles, nor did he wear diaphanous short costumes). Both the other men at the centre of the row went on to successful careers in broadcasting, Cargill as head of news and current affairs at BBC Scotland, Morrison as chief executive of Granada TV. Suddenly the media had emerged as the first choice of ambitious students who would once have aimed for the law or teaching.

III

The young women who did still go into teaching bore little resemblance to the disciplinarian spinsters of the immediate post-war era with their strict regard for the formalities of punctuation and arithmetic – 'the dragons' as James Docherty, a leader of one of the teaching unions, indelicately stereotyped them. The new generation would not have appreciated being called young ladies by such dinosaurs as Muggeridge or Allsop, and many looked favourably on the bold style of Yvonne Baginksy and other dedicated followers of fashion.

The traditionalists of the profession reacted with horror or sexist condescension, or both, to the disturbing new trends in the classroom. 'Should young women teachers be allowed to wear mini-skirts to school?' was the big question at a weekend conference of the Educational Institute of Scotland. Donald Maclean, assistant director of education for Ayrshire, said he was repelled by the idea of teachers as 'swinging chicks' while the formidable Ethel Rennie, principal of Craigie College of Education in Ayr, said that if women flaunted their personality in this way it suggested that they had no inner resources. But, she added mischievously, a great deal depended on the length of the mini-skirt and the shape of the girl inside it. Robert McClement, general secretary of the Scottish Schoolmasters' Association – an organisation in which there seemed to be no place for schoolmistresses – titillated the delegates with the story of his 10-year-old daughter who came home from school one day and said: 'Mummy, we have a new teacher. She is young and nice and she wears a mini-skirt. Every time she stretches to the top of the blackboard, the boys whistle.'

Coincidentally, as skirt lengths shortened, the queue of pupils volunteering to stay on until fifth or sixth year lengthened. 'All through' comprehensives were replacing the four-year junior high schools and the discredited junior secondaries. Almost half of all the secondary pupils in Scotland were now attending fully comprehensive schools, and the Scottish Education Department noted with approval in its annual report that schools were looking 'more and more beyond the confines of the classroom and narrow traditional concepts of the curriculum'. It commended such initiatives as Wick High School's expedition to the uninhabited island of Stroma, a journey across eastern Turkey by a party from Port Glasgow High School, and the various initiatives of pupils of Kingussie High School who had written and published a history of the school, formed their own mountain rescue team and won a trophy for skiing, 'a sport hitherto the monopoly of English public schools'.

Muggeridge would have scoffed at these developments, seeing them as proof of the impending collapse of civilisation and adding that since he hoped soon to be going to 'another place' – by which he meant the House of Our Lord rather than the House of Lords – he would be spared the inevitable downfall of western man. But even he might have applauded the innovating spirit of the young people who were making their way in journalism and the arts. An Edinburgh undergraduate, Bob Cuddihy, a 'voluble, long-haired American' who had been a pupil of Kilquhanity, John Aitkenhead's progressive school in Galloway, turned up one night at Robert McLellan's cottage in High Corrie, Arran. 'Hullo, my name's Bob Cuddihy and I'm starting a magazine,' he introduced himself. 'You're mad,' replied McLellan. But the playwright gave Cuddihy a bed for the night and a poem to print, and *The Islander* was born. Paul Harris, another of the enterprising students, founded a publishing company in Aberdeen while Bob Tait launched *Scottish International*, a literary quarterly backed by the Scottish Arts Council. These and similar enterprises were short-lived, but it was remarkable that they were happening in Scotland at all.

The autonomy awarded to the former Scottish Committee of the Arts Council of Great Britain was symptomatic of a new, still fragile but perceptible mood of national self-confidence. Now a public body in its own right, with its own budget and Ronald Mavor (Bridie's son) as its first director, the Scottish Arts Council was more adventurous than its predecessor. It even gave a little money to the notoriously difficult Ian Hamilton Finlay, the 'concrete poet', who fashioned his work as physical artefacts in stone and glass as well as concrete. The journalist Douglas Eadie, who made a pilgrimage to Stonypath, Finlay's farmhouse-cum-studio 1,000 feet up a Lanarkshire hillside, found at the top a 'tallish, angularly stooping, heron-like man with a sad faraway expression and gentle, but sometimes abrasive speech'. Finlay had endured not only poverty and ill-health but the blank incomprehension of the Scottish cultural establishment, making him 'deeply suspicious of any Scottish goodwill shown to him'. When Eadie asked him about his work the poet replied: 'It belongs in Scotland. It's as Scottish as you can get.'

The arrival of Magnus Magnusson at BBC Scotland, an institution not noted for the fearlessness of its current affairs output, was another sign of the times. His investigative unit at *The Scotsman*, where he had Gus MacDonald and David Kemp assisting him, had broken stories embarrassing to the people in power, notably the scandal at the Highlands and Islands Development Board. But Magnusson, a man in a hurry, keen to make his name in broadcasting, decided to abandon prospects of advancement at North Bridge and take his chances at Queen Margaret Drive.

He was soon at the centre of a row. He claimed in *Checkpoint*, a weekly programme under his chairmanship, that, of the 71 Scottish MPs it had canvassed for their views on devolution, 43 were in favour of a Scottish parliament. 'For so many to make an admission which would have been unthinkable for all except the Liberals a short time ago is something of a landmark,' admitted the *Glasgow Herald*. But the authenticity of the poll was contested by a number of Labour MPs. Willie Hamilton insisted that there had been a BBC plot to mislead the participants. His colleague Hugh Brown walked out of the studio in disgust, protesting that the statistics were a gross distortion of MPs' views and that 'Mr Magnus Magnusson can no longer be regarded as an impartial chairman in these matters'.

James Kemp, head of news and current affairs, defended the BBC's integrity, explaining that the MPs were invited by telephone to answer what he called a simple question: 'Would you be in favour of the kind of devolution that would mean creating some form of Scottish parliament?' Although it was not the most elegantly phrased question, its meaning was plain enough. 'No one whom we telephoned objected to the question,' said Kemp, 'and we made it clear that we would repeat it as often as they wished if they had any doubts.' After Kemp's statement the politicians who claimed not to have understood the question were accused in the press of being disingenuous, while Magnusson, who would have played little if any part in the organisation of the disputed poll, was hailed as a new tribune.

IV

This diverting interlude highlighted the extreme sensitivities about devolution since the Hamilton by-election, particularly in a Labour Party still vacillating over the issue. Sensing a gap in the market, Edward Heath made his so-called 'Declaration of Perth', pledging to introduce a Scottish assembly or senate or convention (he avoided the word parliament – a term too far for the Scottish Tories in the audience). His promise went further than most of the faithful were prepared for and further than Michael Noble, the shadow secretary of state for Scotland, would have wished. The declaration was strong on specifics. The assembly, or whatever it was to be called, would consist of 50 or 60 elected members linked territorially to local government areas – a new regional structure was being actively considered – rather than to parliamentary constituencies. The Speaker of the House of Commons would refer bills relating explicitly to Scotland for the consideration of the assembly. The Secretary of State would divide his time between Scotland and Westminster. A minister of state (perhaps a peer) would be the resident minister at the assembly, introducing legislation, otherwise acting as the voice of the UK government.

The shadow cabinet had decided to live with the probability that the political complexion of the devolved body would be different, if not actively hostile, but reckoned that if the majority party in Scotland employed wrecking tactics it would risk being branded by the electorate as irresponsible. Esmond Wright was among the first to welcome the scheme. The MP for Pollok said that Heath's speech 'could well mark a turning point in Scottish history ... it is a political testament, a reply to the over-centralisation and frustrations of life at Westminster, an indication that the Conservative Party is thinking hard about government in fresh and original terms'.

But when Heath announced the setting up of a Scottish Constitutional Committee to prepare detailed plans, the hazards of the project emerged in an unexpected way. The 11-member committee, chaired by Sir Alec Douglas-Home, included Lord Avonside (Ian Shearer), the Court of Session judge who, as Lord Advocate, had undermined the campaign to save Henry John Burnett from the gallows. Scotland's senior law officers – Henry Wilson, the Lord Advocate, and Ewan Stewart, the Solicitor General – publicly dissociated themselves from Avonside's appointment. Wilson said that members of the judiciary should stand aloof from participation in political activities; Stewart claimed that the appointment was constitutionally objectionable. Lord Clyde, the Lord Justice General, who bristled at any challenges to his authority, maintained that the purpose of the committee was not to formulate policy for a political party but to carry out a policy which had already been formulated. He neglected to add 'by a political party'.

Arthur Donaldson, chairman of the SNP, wrote a cheeky letter to Clyde inviting him to nominate a judge of similar rank as advisor and assessor to the nationalists' own committee on a prospective written constitution for Scotland. Clyde replied: 'I have just received your letter of 29th July which has been forwarded to me. As you yourself recognise in the second paragraph of your letter, membership of your committee would involve political activity. If so it would in my view be objectionable for a judge to act as assessor for such a body. I do not therefore feel able to comply with your request. J L Clyde.' But did not Avonside's membership of a committee set up by the Conservative Party also involve 'political activity'? Or was political activity only really political when it involved a party other than the Conservatives?

Backed into a corner by the condemnation of the law officers and the SNP's clever opportunism, Avonside and Clyde looked ridiculous. Avonside was left with no option but to resign from the Tory committee, and that should have been the end of the matter. But his churlish statement in doing so only succeeded in converting a mini-crisis into a full-blown one. 'If the political spleen and venom of the past 10 days have taught me one thing,' he said, 'it is that in the past I have paid far too little attention to what is happening in this country and the actions of those among us who attempt to arrogate to themselves a monopoly of speech. In the future, I will exercise to the full my undoubted right to comment on those happenings and those people.' It was a thinly disguised personal attack on Wilson, the Lord Advocate.

Wilson hit back with a public statement:

I gather that we differ about the constitutional position of judges. I respect Lord Avonside's views, but I do not share them. I am sorry that he should see fit to question the motives which inspired my intervention. I do not think it would be fitting for me to indulge in an interchange of jibes of a personal and political nature with a judge. No doubt Lord Avonside has been under a little strain during the past 10 days – as indeed I have. I am prepared to make allowances. I get the impression from one passage in his statement that Lord Avonside threatens in the future to indulge publicly in political controversy. Perhaps I misunderstand, but if that impression is correct I sincerely hope that he will not carry out his threat. If, unhappily, he does, he will just have to take the consequences.

The reference to 'taking the consequences' was combustible. Senior members of the legal hierarchy had not simply fallen out; they had declared war. The newspapers loved it, relishing the opportunity to embarrass Clyde, no friend of the Scottish press. A leader in the *Evening Times* summed up the mood of the moment: 'Lord Avonside has done a wise thing … It is unfortunate that his resignation should be phrased in such intemperate language. Logic has been lacking in the attitudes of Lords Clyde and Avonside. Lord Clyde, mightily powerful as Lord President of the Court of Session, feels it is suitable for Lord Avonside to join a Tory committee, but unsuitably political for him to join an SNP committee. This is nonsense.' The leader rounded on all the guilty men, castigating Sir Alec for involving a judge in his committee, Clyde for thinking that he could 'bulldoze his way through public life', and Avonside for not keeping his thoughts to himself.

The obituaries for Avonside, who died in 1996, omitted this episode, while acknowledging that he had 'little patience with fools and did not attempt to conceal his opinions'. If he was something of a fool himself, no one was prepared to admit it publicly. But he missed very little by not being a member of the Scottish Constitutional Committee. The 'Declaration of Perth', far from being a turning point in Scottish history as Esmond Wright had predicted, came to be revealed as a false dawn.

Henry Wilson resigned as Lord Advocate in 1970. In common with most former holders of that post, he may reasonably have expected elevation to the bench of the Court of Session. The call never came. Revenge for Clyde was a dish best served cold: Wilson, having crossed him, went no higher than director of the Scottish Courts Administration and Sheriff Principal of Lanarkshire.

V

The life of a Glasgow sheriff could be dull (as Lionel Daiches discovered to his cost), but there were occasional consolations. It fell to Sheriff William Bryden to hear the civil case of the year, a thespian melodrama in which Katy Gardner, an actress, raised an action to prevent the BBC from repeating a TV drama series written by her estranged husband, Edward Boyd.

When the series was originally shown on BBC2, Gardner claimed to detect in a character called Julia a resemblance to herself. Julia was an immoral woman, a bad mother, a drug addict and a lesbian. Ian Kirkwood, counsel for the BBC, asked: 'If Julia is depicted as immoral, is that defamatory of you?' She replied: 'I dare say I am immoral. I live with someone to whom I am not married and have done for six years. I don't consider myself promiscuously immoral, which is the way the character Julia is depicted in the plays.' A bemused sheriff intervened: 'If your husband wanted to poison people's minds against you, surely he only needed to tell them directly or lie about you rather than do it in this oblique way?' Gardner: 'He has told a lot of lies about me ... I have told people the truth about how our marriage broke up. This is something he would prefer not to have come out.'

The hearing took a bizarre twist when Keith Bovey, Gardner's solicitor, told the court that his client had received menacing telephone calls in the night. They had continued at regular intervals. In one of them the caller said: 'You're an actress, aren't you? How would you like to act in a murder play?' The case had a predictable outcome: Julia was soon all over BBC1, leaving viewers to ponder why Katy Gardner, if she saw a resemblance to herself in such an odious character, would ever have wanted to make it public.

VI

But the fictional (or semi-fictional) Julia was a model of old-fashioned virtue compared with the main protagonists in a sensational trial which scandalised the city and district of Aberdeen towards the end of 1968. If Scotland had missed out on the headier excitements of the swinging sixties, events in the north-east showed that it was not too late to catch up. The case somehow managed to encompass group sex, murder and the SNP. If Edward Boyd had written it as a script, it would have been rejected as too implausible.

In the dock of the High Court in Aberdeen, Sheila Garvie, 34, her lover Brian Tevendale, 12 years her junior, and Tevendale's associate, 20-year-old Alan Peters, denied murdering Maxwell Garvie, Sheila's husband, at the family farm, West Cairnbeg, Laurencekirk, by striking him on the head with the butt of a rifle or iron bar, and shooting him.

When Max Garvie went missing the official reputation of a well-respected local farmer, speaker on agricultural topics, and SNP activist was shattered by a lurid profile in the *Scottish Police Gazette*: ' ... spends freely; is a heavy spirit drinker; consumes tranquillisers and tablets when drinking; is fond of female company; has strong homosexual tendencies and is often in the company of young men; is a man of considerable wealth and until four years ago was completely rational; deals in pornographic material; and is an active member of nudist camps.' It was claimed at the trial that much of the information for this testimonial came from Sheila and Tevendale.

Tevendale met Garvie at an SNP 'outing' in Bannockburn and was invited to the farm. The social niceties on this first visit did not amount to much; Garvie pushed his wife into Tevendale's bedroom and shut the door. Sheila broke it to Tevendale that she had been told to spend the night with him 'or else'. Her young visitor had no objections to this ultimatum. A few weekends later Garvie made homosexual advances, assuring Tevendale that he loved him more than he loved his wife. By then Sheila was smitten by Tevendale emotionally as well as sexually. It was getting complicated.

Repelled by her husband's 'sexual aberrations', she confided in the parish minister. The minister told the court that Sheila's mother, Edith Watson, spoke to him of orgies in a cottage at Alford in Aberdeenshire, which Garvie had set up as a nudist colony and which was known locally as 'the kinky cottage'. Sheila claimed that Garvie insisted that she and their three children should take part in nudism, that he asked her to perform the opening ceremony at the kinky cottage, and that she agreed on condition that she was fully clothed. Her mother likened Garvie to Dr Jekyll and Mr Hyde – one moment the decent husband, the next transformed into a darker personality. Garvie informed her that he was determined to get kicks out of life.

The kicks often involved a family foursome. While Sheila had sex with Tevendale, Garvie had sex with Trudy Birse, Tevendale's sister. Trudy admitted that she was immediately attracted to Garvie and that the four of them stayed at various hotels, Max picking up the bills. On at least one occasion he tossed a coin to determine who would sleep with Sheila first. 'If you were in his company you could almost feel the electricity?' she was asked in court. 'If you care to put it that way,' Trudy replied.

Trudy's story was that Garvie actively promoted the

relationship between her brother and Sheila. 'He told me Sheila was frigid and didn't respond to his love-making the way he wanted. He said he was encouraging the friendship between Sheila and Brian so that Sheila would become a better lover for him.' A 6am ritual was established: in an explosive climax to the night's sexual entertainment Garvie would push Trudy out of bed and summon Sheila to join him in the hope that, whatever Tevendale had taught her about the techniques of love-making in the preceding hours, she would pass on to him. Edith Watson said that this way of life had changed her daughter completely. Before all this she had been a decent girl, an assistant housekeeper at Balmoral, well thought of at the royal residence.

One evening Max Garvie attended an SNP meeting in Stonehaven. When Trudy met Sheila the next morning she realised that something had happened. 'She was shaking a bit and I asked her to sit down and made a cup of coffee. Then Sheila said: "It had to be done. I couldn't take any more. There was no other way".' Trudy decided that the apparent confession was not worth reporting to the police. Three months later Garvie's body was found in a culvert on a farm at St Cyrus, Kincardineshire.

Sheila, in a statement to the police, said that her husband arrived home from the SNP meeting around 11pm, had a drink and watched TV. They went to bed together and had sex. Sheila fell asleep. She was wakened by the sound of her lover Tevendale's voice in the dark. He was with another man (Peters) who was unknown to her; Tevendale was carrying a gun. Sheila claimed she was hustled through to the bathroom and told to stay there. 'I heard our bedroom door closing and terrible thumping noises.' Later Tevendale said something like: 'You won't have any more of him to put up with.' The two men then pulled the dead man out of the house.

In a barely audible whisper she explained to the court how she felt after Tevendale and Peters drove off with the body. 'I sat and thought about what had happened and the longer I thought about it the more guilty I felt. I blamed myself terribly. I felt morally responsible for what had happened because I had allowed Brian to fall in love with me ... I took a decision that night that whatever happened I would protect Brian because he had done this for me.' She admitted that, after the murder, she slept with Tevendale regularly.

'The elimination of your husband gave you what you wanted,'

suggested counsel for Peters. 'It enabled you to meet your lover, isn't that true?'

'The way you are putting it, that is not right.'

'You were sharing the bed of this man whom you knew had murdered your husband.'

'Yes.'

Peters was depicted by his defence team as a reluctant participant, someone who lived in such fear of Tevendale that he would not have dared to intervene: 'I might have got the same so far as I knew.' Yet, two months after the murder, he was best man at Tevendale's wedding. Was this duty, like the removal of a body, only undertaken because he was afraid of the consequences of refusal? Was there anything that Peters would not do for Tevendale?

While his dutiful accomplice remained a slightly elusive figure, Tevendale incriminated himself at every turn. The police found in a room which he occupied in Aberdeen live bullets, spent bullets, and a book called *The Death Trap*, some pages of which had been cut out to form a container. In the container there were two hypodermic syringes and a bottle of liquid. The police also recovered from the room a jacket with 'SNP – Free Scotland' on the back. If the murderer and his victim had little else in common (apart from Sheila, of course), they did share a devotion to Scottish nationalism.

On the second day of the trial the dead man's skull was produced from a cardboard box, an unusual occurrence even in Aberdeen, home in the recent past of such unsettling events as the last hanging in Scotland and a typhoid epidemic. The skull was held up by an expert witness who was anxious to display to the jury the bullet hole in Max Garvie's head, although the fatal wound might just as well have been described in the absence of the head itself. Its sudden appearance was too much for Sheila, who fell forward in a near-faint and had to be removed to the cells, where she received medical attention before the trial could resume.

In his summing-up Ewan Stewart, the Solicitor General, clinically deconstructed Sheila's carefully phrased protestation of innocence: 'I did not shoot, kill, or cause any injury to my husband.' Well, said Stewart, that might be true. But even if it was, she was still guilty if she acted with others in the knowledge that a murder was to be committed. The jury had to choose between two Sheila Garvies. There was the prosecution's view of her as 'a skilled liar', 'hard as nails', 'a resourceful, cool, business-like woman'. There was the defence's contrary opinion – vintage Lionel Daiches – of an innocent woman brought down by her husband 'into the valley of the shadow'. The jury, having looked into the valley of the shadow, preferred to go with the more mundane skilled liar theory.

The case against Peters was found not proven. Sheila and her lover were sentenced to life imprisonment, leaving the dock 'white-faced' according to the press. Trudy Birse walked hand in hand with her husband out of the courtroom and into Union Street, where they were besieged by a crowd which consisted mostly of jeering women. Some surged across the street in pursuit and blows were aimed at Trudy.

Sheila was depicted by the newspapers as a homicidal fashion victim with a taste for mini-skirts and racy tops. Released at the age of 44 after 10 years in prison, she married twice more, ran a B&B in Stonehaven, and was often seen walking her dog along the beach. After his release Tevendale also entered the catering trade as the landlord of a pub in Perthshire. 'I was stupid and naive,' he said shortly before his early death, 'and I probably thought I was in love.' They never saw each other again. Among the colourful cast of characters only a supporting player flourished: the Scottish National Party.

VII

There were two morbid cases of fast living that year: the fast living in the Mearns which led to the death of one farmer; and the fast living on the world's race-tracks which led to the death of another. Jim Clark was killed during a race at Hockenheim in West Germany when his car skidded on a wet surface at 170 miles an hour, failed to take a right-hand bend, somersaulted several times, and hit a tree. A doctor who examined the body said that Clark died instantly from a broken neck and a double fracture of the skull. The race continued and several hours passed before a crowd of 100,000 was informed of his death.

Three years earlier, after winning the world motor racing championship for the second time, Clark had processed in triumph on an open-topped double-decker bus through his native village, Chirnside in Berwickshire. *Time* magazine described him as the most famous Scot since Robert Burns: 'Today, at 29, he is the man to beat in any kind of race, in any kind of car, on any kind of track anywhere.' The mystery was why, rather than retire in one piece at the top of his game and financially secure, he went on in a sport notorious for its mortality. 'The truth appears to be,' said one observer of the grand prix scene, 'that he had become a compulsive driver with the challenge of the most gruelling circuits the main consideration.' He was an intelligent man and painfully aware of the dangers. In 1961 he was involved in a crash on the Italian track at Monza in which the German driver Wolfgang von Trips and 10 spectators were killed. Clark was suspected of negligence at the wheel and for three years competed with a shadow over his reputation. Finally the Italian authorities exonerated him, declaring that the accident had been a complete mischance.

Clark was born to be a Borders sheep farmer, and had he quit motor-racing he would have inherited a thriving business. 'I think he intended returning,' said William Campbell, the farm steward. 'His heart was still in it.' His parents were uneasy about Jim's dedication to speed. 'I was never keen,' said his father, 'but we had to accept it, and we were proud of him.' More than 3,000 people, including his fellow drivers Jackie Stewart, Graham Hill and Innes Ireland, attended the funeral service in Chirnside, where 'The Flying Scotsman' was laid to rest at the age of 32.

1969

THE EXECISE OF POWER

I

When it was proposed to erect fences in the gardens of Easterhouse, a Glasgow council estate notorious for gang warfare and other anti-social behaviour, Bailie James Anderson, the convener of Glasgow Corporation's police committee, said it was the most outrageous thing he had ever heard, a comment which suggested that Anderson's life had been formerly lacking in outrage. The daring idea of garden fences, even on an experimental basis, was rejected by the council after Anderson assured his colleagues that they would be torn down and used as weapons. The majority were not disposed to respect the view of Tom Fulton, the Labour councillor for Easterhouse, that the people would welcome such an amenity and take care that their precious fences came to no harm.

Ronald Nicholl, professor of urban planning at Strathclyde University, confused the issue by producing statistics which appeared to show that the estate's crime figures were not dramatically different from the average. 'It is significant,' he wrote, 'that, in Easterhouse, which was developed on the basis of four neighbourhoods, a strong territorial element has been attached to the gang set-up. One gang has been developed in each, and it cannot be denied that many members are ready, willing and able to defend their territory from invasion from outside.' Nicholl saw this as a hopeful sign, if the energies of the gang members could somehow be constructively re-directed. He was also encouraged by his discovery that they were not gangs 'in the old Gorbals sense'. They were younger, scarcely more than children. 'Many of these teenagers are in their first jobs and have money to spend, but with no café or chip shop, no cinema or dance hall, they cannot even buy the entertainment they seek. They are bored and frustrated. The police break up any large gathering of teenagers. It must be bewildering for many of these boys to be picked up for loitering when there is little alternative.'

An occasional visitor to the city, the high-kicking crooner Frankie Vaughan, materialised as the unlikely catalyst of change in Easterhouse. Vaughan had been familiar with the most challenging audience in Britain – second house on a Saturday night at the Glasgow Empire – and may have felt that the gangs of Easterhouse were tame by comparison. In the summer of 1968 when he launched an initiative to reconcile the warring parties, his initial idea of a weapons amnesty was taken up immediately. He then pursued a more ambitious plan: a youth centre which would bring together the rival gangs on neutral territory. At first Bailie Anderson was sceptical. But as the gangs started to wipe their slogans off the walls of Easterhouse, even the tough guy police convener had to concede that positive changes were in the air. He hinted that, if the youth centre idea came to anything, he might be prepared to become a trustee.

Vaughan invited the four gang leaders to a 'peace conference' in Blackpool, where he was appearing for the summer season. Three revealed themselves as George McDyre, 18, of the Rebels; Gerry Neil, 16, of the Pak; and Isaac Macrae, 17, of the Toi. The leader of the Drummy refused to be named. They travelled together from Glasgow, shared rooms in a seaside boarding house and travelled back together. Of the three who were prepared to be photographed for the newspapers, all wore sun-glasses, two sported ties, one a smart jacket; only the camera-shy representative of the Drummy declined to take part in the photo-call. Graham Noble, a social worker who accompanied the quartet, told the press: 'They are friends. They got on very well together and are in perfect agreement about the future.' Anderson was impressed: 'I am giving this venture my complete support.' A few days later he visited the estate to apologise for doubting the gangs' sincerity about ending hostilities. Isaac Macrae confirmed the new mood of harmony: 'We are sick of fighting each other and getting charged by the police. We don't want to be called gangs. We are teams. The gangs are scrubbed.'

As a physical entity the youth centre amounted to no more than a double Nissen hut staffed by Graham Noble and Archie Hind – the same Archie Hind who had recently made his mark as a novelist – with modest financial support from the council. But as an optimistic symbol of what a high-profile, celebrity-backed scheme could achieve in unpromising terrain, it attracted national attention. Six nights a week several hundred teenagers from the four neighbourhoods flocked to it. Bill Williams, a Glasgow journalist, wrote that the occupants of the hut were taking part in 'the most worthwhile social experiment being undertaken anywhere in Great Britain'. Williams, having made this large claim, went on to qualify it with an acknowledgement that a small undertaking on a shoestring budget could not hope 'to eradicate completely all lawlessness from a community the size of Greenock'.

Events soon proved him right. After a long trouble-free spell, there was a sudden outbreak of weekend violence in which five young men were slashed. One of the former gang members was sent to approved school after assaulting a ballroom attendant with an axe at an Easter dance in Millport on the Clyde island of Cumbrae; he told the sheriff that he had been carrying the weapon for his own protection. At the High Court in Glasgow four Easterhouse youths were accused of murdering a young man by threatening him with a knife and forcing him through a window into the backcourt, where they dragged him unconscious and dumped him in a bin to die. The victim's crime was to be English and 'queer'. He was neither.

Bailie Anderson's patience, never on the longest fuse, was severely tested by Graham Noble's liberal policies, particularly when Noble admitted sanctioning the use of £20 from the project's funds to provide bail for two youths charged with a breach of the peace in the youth centre. Noble claimed that it was a proper use of limited resources and that, anyway, the bail was returnable with interest. But the project paid a high price for the leader's 'unconditional love' – his own phrase – for the gang boys of Easterhouse. The fragile local support evaporated and by the summer of 1970, barely 18 months after it opened, the centre had run out of money and goodwill. A last-ditch fund-raising lunch for business leaders, which Noble hoped would raise £30,000, fetched £300. The centre was heavily in debt and there was nothing left to pay the staff.

When it finally closed in 1971 an unforgiving Bailie Anderson, who had resigned as a trustee in disgust, declared that he did not think it had contributed 'one solitary thing to the community of Easterhouse'. He was mistaken: many of the older boys had opted out of the gang structure as a direct result of their involvement in the centre and the territorial apartheids, fostered in the first place by Glasgow Corporation's poor planning of the estate, had to some extent broken down.

Graham Noble took a philosophical view: 'Most of the young people who have gone through the project have had very little sense of the world around them. Their school education appears to have equipped them for very little, and most of them have long decided – and are being constantly reminded by society – that they are failures.' Noble saw most of the violence in Glasgow as naive, ultimately directed against itself. He quoted the case of 'a highly intelligent boy from a good home' who was serving a sentence for serious assault. A few weeks before he committed the crime he said to Noble: 'How can you criticise me for being anti-social or violent when the so-called leaders of the world make wars and use official violence the whole time? What a lot of fucking hypocrites you are.'

II

Unlike the critic of global hypocrisy, Jimmy Boyle had not worked out a philosophy of violence. As a teenager in the Gorbals, a member of a gang in what Professor Nicoll would have called 'the old sense', he simply became aware that violence or the threat of it was not only essential for survival in his world but addictive. He first recognised its allure as a small child when another boy was chasing him. He stopped and threw a brick at his pursuer. The boy ran away. He remembered the feeling of power the experience gave him.

He lived in a community which, far from disapproving of crime, respected such figures as Jimmy Boyle's father, a professional safe-blower. The son embarked on a career of petty thieving which quickly spilled over into more serious offending; approved school was followed by borstal. In 1965, at the age of 21, he faced his first murder trial. He was acquitted, and acquitted again later the same year when a second charge of murder was reduced to one of assault. Towards the end of 1967 he returned to the High Court in Glasgow for a third murder trial in as many years, possibly a Scottish record. The victim, stabbed to death in his own home, was Babs (William) Rooney, a Glasgow hard man known to Boyle though prison. There was no third acquittal; the jury came back after 45 minutes with a unanimous conviction. Boyle protested his innocence, continuing to do so long after his eventual release from prison.

The case was heard against a background of intimidation. Rooney's girlfriend, Sadie Cairney, fled Glasgow after the murder and when the police tracked her down to an address in Manchester she told them that 'a team from Glasgow' was out to get her. Neighbours, too, were forced to leave the city and relocate in other parts of the country. Lord Cameron, the trial judge, told the jury: 'It is perhaps surprising to you that such drastic action had to be taken to protect persons whose only offence was that they might tell the truth.' He described Boyle as 'a dangerous menace to society' and said he would recommend to the Secretary of State for Scotland that he should not be released on licence until he had served a minimum of 15 years in prison.

Boyle had taught himself not to show any emotion when a jury found him guilty of a crime. He showed no emotion that day. But when the foreman uttered the word 'guilty' he observed that the court usher raised his two thumbs in a victory sign to the police. Some months later, as he contemplated killing himself with a razor blade, he was dissuaded by the sudden thought of the pleasure his suicide would give to the usher.

Boyle resurfaced briefly early in 1968 when he had 18 months added to his life sentence for assaulting a prison officer. Nine months later he was back in court charged with assaulting an officer at Peterhead, the grim establishment on the Buchan coast where he was being held. Boyle did not deny attacking the man, but claimed that he acted in self-defence after five or six officers had lashed him with batons in his cell in the punishment block. His next-door neighbour in the block explained that there was a ventilation shaft connecting the cells which enabled prisoners to talk to each other. He shouted down the vent 'Jimmy Boyle' and asked him if he was all right. 'They've battered me,' came the reply. Another prisoner said he heard shouts and screams from Boyle's cell after the officers went in. He heard one of them say, 'Watch you don't kill him.' The jury believed the testimony of the prisoners, adding a rider to its guilty verdict that Boyle had committed the offence under provocation. This appeal for mercy had no effect on the sentence: four years. Boyle was then transferred to Porterfield Prison in Inverness.

In the early weeks of 1969 Boyle was one of seven inmates of

Porterfield who signed a letter to the Scottish press calling for an inquiry into conditions at Peterhead. Boyle wrote: 'In Peterhead at the moment the air is electrified by tension and it is such that a man endeavouring to do his sentence quietly is finding it very hard.' The Scottish Office rejected the prisoners' demand and a spokesman for the prison officers at Peterhead said that the atmosphere had improved since the worst trouble-makers – meaning the signatories of the letter – had gone elsewhere. 'Talk of rehabilitating men like that is just nonsense,' he added.

It was not nonsense in Boyle's case. He spent five and a half years in solitary confinement, and for long periods was kept in a cage three feet by 11 feet where he lay naked, claiming that he covered himself in his own excrement to discourage his minders from beating him up. Then, to his astonishment and dismay, he was sent from the cage to the recently established special unit, a therapeutic experiment in Barlinnie for the treatment of a handful of difficult long-term prisoners. Boyle hated the idea: he preferred to be alone; he rather liked solitary confinement. Instead he was expected to participate in the rough democracy of a unit where he was no longer treated as sub-human and where the prisoners had a say in the running of their affairs. The prison officers wore white coats, confirming in Boyle's mind that he had become part of some sinister laboratory experiment and that they were out to have him certified as clinically insane.

Ken Murray, a prison officer, was opening some parcels in the special unit one day when he handed Jimmy Boyle a weapon. He gave him a pair of scissors and invited him to help with the parcels. 'We're all in the dark here,' Murray told him. 'We've got to try to make this place work.' With such simple gestures trust was slowly established.

Boyle remained in the special unit for eight years and was befriended by several influential visitors, including Kay Carmichael, a social worker who had been a member of Harold Wilson's 'kitchen cabinet' in the 1964-70 Labour government. He wrote an autobiography, *A Sense of Freedom*, married one of his visitors – Sarah Trevelyan, a psychiatrist – and began to produce muscular works of sculpture – all this while he was still serving the 15-year minimum imposed by Cameron in 1967. He served every day of that sentence and when he was finally released despite the misgivings of Jean Morris, the chairman of the Parole Board for Scotland, he went on to lead a blameless life. John Mortimer, writer and lawyer, said after meeting him: 'Jimmy Boyle's story shows what a creative penal system might do for the whole of our society in reforming criminals.' But the creativity was of relatively short duration: the special unit did not long survive the departure of its most celebrated guest.

III

In the dark city of Glasgow there was no set night of the week for gang violence; it could erupt at any time. The sport of adultery, and the serial killing supposedly associated with it in the late 1960s, had a more prescribed ritual. Over-25s' night in the city's ballrooms – the Barrowland, the Plaza, the Albert, the Locarno and the Majestic – was a euphemism for late-night groping in tenement closes followed by illicit mating. On Thursday – over-25s' night did tend to be a Thursday – the married people came out to play, though not often with their spouses.

On the last Thursday in October 1969 Helen Puttock and her older sister Jeannie headed for the Barrowland. Helen was the more physically attractive. She was 29 years old, married to a serviceman who was stationed in Germany (although he happened to be at home on leave that night). She was slim, brunette, good company, sexually active, a young woman of strong will. Helen, said Jeannie, 'always said that no one could get the better of her'. But on 30 October 1969 someone did.

Helen refused to be deterred by the notoriety of one of the city's more downmarket dance halls. Before they went out their mother reminded them that two young women – Pat Docker and Mima MacDonald – had been strangled after nights out at the Barrowland and that both crimes were unsolved. She pleaded with her daughters not to go. Helen flashed her long nails. 'Can you imagine anyone trying anything on me?' was her response.

The two women left Helen's flat in Earl Street around 8.30pm, got a bus into the city centre and by nine o'clock were installed in the Trader's Tavern at Glasgow Cross, a short walk from the dance hall. In the absence of any licence at the Barrowland, many of the punters fortified themselves for the night ahead. Jeannie had certainly been drinking, and the popular notion repeated in many articles and books that she had an exceptionally sharp memory of what happened that night was exaggerated. Her recollections were so dulled by alcohol that the police despaired of ever obtaining a full and coherent account of events – until a young officer suggested to his superiors that she should be asked to undergo hypnosis. This did reveal some interesting details about the man who was to enter Scottish mythology as Bible John.

Jeannie's description of her sister's dancing partner was of a tall man of between 25 and 35, with sandy hair and a fresh complexion, wearing a well-cut brown suit, a blue shirt and a dark tie with thin red stripes, and short suede boots. When Jeannie spoke to him her eyes came only to the level of his mouth, so she had a good view of his teeth. Two of his front teeth overlapped and one back tooth was missing. The police regarded this as a vital clue and interviewed several people with dental peculiarities of that sort, but their oral inpections took the investigation nowhere.

Jeannie said that the man was unusually well-spoken, polite and attentive, in marked contrast to the usual Barrowland crowd. But, in an incident outside the cloakroom around 11.30pm, his good manners deserted him. Jeannie was trying to buy cigarettes from a machine when the coins stuck and could not be dislodged. Helen's John made a tremendous fuss, calling imperiously for the manager, threatening the Barrowland with the licensing authority. It was then, according to Jeannie, that he referred to the dance hall as 'a den of iniquity', a common enough phrase at the time, although the police chose to imbue it with dark significance. She remembered a second remark suggestive of some personal religious hinterland; Jeannie could never recall the words, only that 'it was something from the Bible', but it was enough for the over-excited press. The legend of Bible John was born.

Four of them came out of the Barrowland together: Helen and John, Jeannie and a second man called John, who had chatted her up in the dance hall. The second John told them he was going to George Square to catch a bus to Castlemilk. Despite many police appeals over the years nothing more was ever heard of 'Castlemilk John', a key witness whose attendance at the over-25s' night would not have been appreciated by his wife, if he had one. That left Jeannie to share a taxi back to Scotstoun with Helen and the first John, a journey of about 20 minutes. Jeannie got out first. Seven hours later a neighbour found Helen's half-naked body crouched against a drainpipe in one of the back courts close to her home. She had put up a fight and attempted to escape by scrambling up a railway embankment, but was knocked unconscious with a heavy instrument and strangled with one of her stockings. 'The Dance Hall Don Juan With Murder On His Mind' and 'Hunt For The Lady Killer' were among the front-page headlines.

There was an immediate assumption that a serial killer was at large in Glasgow and that the killer of Helen Puttock had also murdered Pat Docker and Mima MacDonald. The similarities were striking enough: all three victims had been at the Barrowland; all three had been sexually assaulted; all three had been menstruating. But these common factors did not exclude the more prosaic possibility that, in a city known for random violence, the Barrowland had attracted more than one killer and that the second and third murders were copycat.

If a serial killer was indeed at large he was not a serial killer in much of a hurry. He murdered his first victim, Pat Docker, in February 1968 and waited 18 months before he struck again. He was also a serial killer who was prepared to make himself vulnerable. When he picked up Helen Puttock there was a notice in the foyer of the Barrowland with a drawing of the man the police were looking for. Yet he proceeded to create a scene outside the cloakroom, challenging the manager and the bouncers to their faces. Psychologists suggested plausible theories not only for the long interval between the first and second murders but for the apparently perverse decision to draw attention to himself; they also attempted to justify the police's view that he was pathologically disgusted by menstruating women.

But not all the officers engaged in the long and fruitless search subscribed to the majority opinion of their superiors. There was an alternative opinion at a high level within the Glasgow police: that had all the evidence in the police's possession been made public, it would have undermined the official version of a single killer.

It was a bungled inquiry from the outset. On the night she was murdered Pat Docker told her mother that she was going to the Majestic. Either this was a lie or she changed her mind at the last minute. But the police accepted that the Majestic was her destination and concentrated their inquiries there, overlooking other obvious possibilities. When it emerged eight weeks later that she had never been at the Majestic, that she had gone to the Barrowland instead, memories of the night had faded. The trail, never warm, finally went cold 21 months later, at 2am on Friday 31 October 1969, when a man with a dishevelled appearance who had boarded a bus near Earl Street, scene of Helen Puttock's murder, was dropped off at the junction of Dumbarton Road and Gray Street. Was this Helen's murderer? If it was, it was the last sighting of him.

IV

Glasgow knew where it was with girls who came to sticky ends, dance hall murderers and gangsters such as Jimmy Boyle. The city found it harder to understand criminality which operated behind a veneer of middle-class respectability. The young man in Easterhouse, the friend of Graham Noble, who deplored the hypocrisy of the 'so-called leaders of the world', would not have been surprised by the hypocrisy of the so-called leaders of his own city.

The council which starved the Easterhouse project to death was the same council which, by its penny-pinching in the original building of the post-war estates, had created new and expensive social problems. Rather than address these problems in a serious way, the council called for tough measures against young delinquents. But this was the same council which for years had turned a blind eye to outrageous abuse of power by some of its own members. The chief hypocrite, the daddy of them all, was exposed in 1969. By the time James F Reilly, solicitor, Labour councillor and pillar of society, finally exchanged his trademark bowler hat and pinstripe trousers for a prison uniform, he had helped to make his party and his city synonymous with corruption.

Reilly denied at his trial in the High Court in Glasgow that he took a bribe from a taxi driver for the transfer of a council house tenancy. John Lough, an accountant, testified that the driver, a friend of his, told him that he was having difficulty getting a larger council house and asked Lough if he knew anybody on the council who could help. Lough suggested Reilly – the best-known fixer in town – and arranged a meeting. Reilly took a £100 note from the taxi driver, Francis Hynd, but then Hynd decided to buy a house and wanted his money back. 'I told Reilly this,' said Lough, 'and he said that I should not have brought a client like that to him.'

Hynd's evidence was that two months after his meeting with

Reilly he had heard nothing and was becoming impatient. 'I went to see Reilly. He told me there were staffing changes being made in the city factor's office and I was to hold on. When I went to see him later he told me the same thing, but gave me a letter to take to the city factor's office. They were rude to me there, and I got a letter from them telling me I would have to wait my turn.' It was then that, inconveniently for Reilly, a frustrated Hynd decided that he no longer wanted to live in a council house. The corruption started to unravel.

Lionel Daiches, a master of the crocodile tear, asked Lord Cameron to impose a fine. In a selective version of Reilly's shameful record in local government, Daiches pleaded: 'His career has come to an end, and I think I am justified in saying it has been on the whole an honourable one. He was tempted and he fell.' He added that Reilly was a happily married man with 11 children. Cameron sent him down for 18 months.

After a week in prison Reilly won an application for release pending an appeal; at the bail hearing he was represented by John Smith, who had been admitted to the Scottish Bar on the day of the SNP's triumph in the Hamilton by-election. The successful pleading of the future Labour leader gave Reilly a further five weeks of freedom before his case was unceremoniously dismissed. The Appeal Court judges were unimpressed by the production of a medical certificate disclosing that Reilly's health had deteriorated because of his ordeal, and did not find it necessary to leave the bench before announcing their verdict.

Reilly, who was waiting in a side room, apparently too unwell to attend in person, was returned to Barlinnie to serve his time. A few months later he was joined there by a former colleague on the Labour benches in the City Chambers, John Paterson, who got 12 months for corruptly receiving £290 from a businessman to use his influence to obtain planning permission for a car showroom, and £640 from another businessman to use his influence to obtain a lease of land. The best that Lionel Daiches could say about the septuagenarian Paterson was that he had been a devoted supporter of youth clubs.

In Reilly's case the single bribe for which he went to prison was a representative sample. As the accountant Lough hinted at his trial, Reilly was 'the man to see' in Glasgow if you wanted a better council house or had a problem getting a pub licence. It was racketeering on an almost industrial scale: for many years Reilly employed a gang of underlings who were despatched with wads of cash to negotiate favours of various kinds. A Labour councillor, James Cannell, said that when he was elected in Reilly's former patch and held his first surgery, a publican threw 'a very thick envelope on the table'. Cannell responded by asking the publican if this was what he thought it was. 'I got the impression,' said Cannell, 'that he believed this to be normal behaviour.' The offer was rejected.

Reilly made a full recovery from the mysterious illness which afflicted him while the prison gates were closing. When he died in 2003 at the age of 90 he was surrounded by members of his large family in the house in Bishopbriggs which had been partly financed by his many bribes.

V

According to one obituary the fall of James F Reilly 'heralded the dawn of higher standards in public life'. Two events in 1969 made corruption less likely anyway – Labour lost control of Glasgow and Lord Wheatley produced a report on the reorganisation of Scottish local government. So reduced were the statutory duties of Glasgow City Council that according to Donald Liddle, the new (Conservative) Lord Provost, 'what is left to us could pretty well be done by our paid officials'. The power of Scotland's Tammany Hall politicians – the Reillys and Patersons who operated cash in hand – was not destroyed at a stroke by the Wheatley reforms, but it became more difficult to manipulate. The lazy, arrogant Labour fiefdoms were disappearing as local government in its traditional form was itself disappearing.

Wheatley could not have been accused of a lack of boldness. His commission proposed sweeping away a creaking 19th-century structure of 430 councils and replacing them with seven regional authorities and 37 district authorities, a reduction of 88% in the number of councils. He proposed that the regions should be responsible for strategic planning and for such major services as housing, police, fire, education, social work and health. The districts (including Glasgow) would be given the crumbs of planning, housing improvement, libraries and licensing courts – not the most stimulating snack.

The regions, where matters of importance would be settled, were identified as West based in Glasgow; Central in Falkirk or Stirling; South-west in Dumfries; South-east in Edinburgh; East in Dundee or Perth; North-east in Aberdeen; and Highlands and Islands in Inverness, the latter serving an area stretching from the tip of Shetland to the Mull of Kintyre.

Wheatley explained his thinking: 'What we wanted was to give local government a chance to be something bigger in the life of the nation. It is not that local authorities have broken down or that services have stopped functioning. The trouble is not so obvious as that. It is rather that the local government system as a whole is not working properly – it is not doing the job that it ought to be doing.' His indictment was extensive. He said that the areas were wrong and the functions badly assigned, that the structure was too complicated and the financial set-up too weak, that central government was too dominant and that the level of public interest in local government was too low. He concluded that the answer lay with a concentration rather than a proliferation of authorities, and with full-time councillors who would be paid substantial salaries.

It was the end of local democracy in Scotland in any sense that could be called genuinely local. The people would be detached from the centres of power and from their own elected representatives. Wheatley's solution to the loss of accountability was a sop – the establishment of community councils which would 'give expression to local opinion' and maintain ceremonial functions; he suggested that they should be permitted to appoint provosts and other dignitaries. But these councils would not be local authorities: no powers were proposed for them. They were irrelevant.

Two members of the commission, Betty Harvie Anderson and Russell Johnston, published notes of dissent. They opposed community councils and pointed out that the second-tier authorities were so big that their democratic viability was questionable. Both favoured the creation of 101 second-tier 'localities' with a responsibility for such matters as the environment and local amenities, and they recommended all-purpose authorities for Orkney, Shetland and the Western Isles. A third member, Hugh MacCalman, published a note of reservation rather than dissent, expressing concern that, if top-tier functions were conducted from Inverness for Orkney and Shetland, island services would suffer from remote control. Wheatley's reply was that 'a Highlands and Islands Region offers the chance for the first time of having questions affecting the Highlands as a whole dealt with democratically by the inhabitants of the Highlands themselves'.

Another contentious issue was the decision to split the kingdom of Fife, giving to the East region the burghs of Auchtermuchty, Crail, Cupar, Elie and Earlsferry, Falkland, Kilrenny, Ladybank, Newburgh, Newport-on-Tay, Pittenweem, St Andrews, St Monance and Tayport while the Edinburgh-based South-east region would swallow up the burghs of Buckhaven and Methil, Burntisland, Cowdenbeath, Culross, Dunfermline, Inverkeithing, Kinghorn, Kirkcaldy, Leslie, Leven, Lochgelly and Markinch. Although the logic was clear enough – the rural burghs in the north of the county were to be sacrificed to Perth or Dundee, the industrial burghs in the south to Edinburgh – it was an insensitive carve-up of a county rich in historical associations and with a strong sense of identity. Wheatley conceded that his proposal would seem like sacrilege to the people of Fife. He was not exaggerating.

Scottish opinion on the proposals as a whole was sharply divided. The SNP growled its disapproval: 'Despite much hypocritical mumbo-jumbo about helping local democracy, the ordinary voter will be even more isolated than at present.' The Association of County Councils doubted that seven regions would provide a sufficiently democratic system. Predictably the provosts of the wee burghs, all of which would be abolished, were aghast. But the STUC endorsed the plan, and James McGrandle, assistant Scottish secretary of the Labour Party, predicted that it would form the basis of local government in Scotland for a hundred years. The Scottish Chambers of Commerce also welcomed the report: 'Inevitably this is the day of large-scale organisations, and the proposed streamlining can do nothing but good, especially when room is still left for pride in the neighbourhood.'

The *Glasgow Herald* adopted a similar line, asserting that Wheatley would 'go a long way to increasing public respect for local government and developing a proper sense of regional pride'. Such breezy assurances overlooked a vital reality of Scottish life – that Scots did not naturally identify with amorphous regions artificially constructed by High Court judges, but preferred to give their allegiance to a homelier construct – a town or city or, if they lived in Fife, a county. The idea that 'a proper sense of regional pride' could be developed from the many distinctive communities and cultures of the Highlands and Islands was plainly absurd.

Some of the more ludicrous features of the blueprint were corrected when it came to be enacted. The government approved the minority recommendation of single-purpose authorities for Orkney, Shetland and the Western Isles. After enormous pressure Fife was saved as a regional entity. It was decreed that West would be known as Strathclyde, South-west as Dumfries and Galloway, South-east as Lothian, East as Tayside, North-east as Grampian. No more imaginative name than Central could be found for the area encompassing the old droving burgh of Falkirk and castellated Stirling. Highlands and Islands, shorn of the latter, became plain Highlands. The burgh title of provost was appropriated by some of the district authorities, denying the community councils even that small dignity.

The facts did not strongly support Wheatley's notion that there was a low level of public interest in local government – one of the stated reasons for reorganisation. In the local elections in May 1969 many of the small burghs ran lively contests – 11 candidates for three seats in Denny and Dunipace, eight for three in Darvel, 11 for five in Campbeltown, eight for three in Elie, among many examples of vigorous local democracy. The following May the turnouts for the doomed councils, though far from spectacular, were fairly decent – in such diverse burghs as Gatehouse and Girvan, Darvel and Tillicoultry, more than 60% of the electorate voted and in many others more than half. Likewise, the idea that the reforms would reinvigorate public interest proved to be mistaken; turnouts steadily dwindled to the derisory in some areas. A second reorganisation became necessary in 1996, confounding the prophecy of the Labour Party's James McGrandle. But there was this much to be said for the changes: since most people ceased to know the names of their councillors, or where to find them, or what their functions were, the opportunities for suspiciously thick brown envelopes to be thrown across surgery tables diminished.

VI

Far from the brutality of urban life with its dodgy dance halls, its Boyles and Reillys, its gangs, its wads of cash, largely indifferent to the illogicalities of local government reorganisation, barely part of Scotland at all, the few inhabitants of Longhope, a huddled settlement of 30 houses on the island of Hoy, boasted a lifeboat crew. Its coxswain was a local legend, 59-year-old Daniel Kirkwood, who had three times won the silver medal of the Royal National Lifeboat Institution for his rescue work. In 1968, when he was asked if he would consider retiring, Kirkwood replied: 'I'll go on for a wee while yet.' His sons, Raymond, 28, and Jack, 26, were members of the crew along with the second coxswain John Johnston, 62, and his sons James, 34, and Robbie, 31. From these two families the lifeboat drew six of its crew. A seventh, James Swanson, 58, was a married man with no children.

On a Monday night in March 1969 the Longhope lifeboat went to the rescue of a Liberian freighter, Irene, which was aground on South Ronaldsay having been overturned by mountainous seas. There was an eighth man on board that night: 24-year-old Eric MacFadyen, a merchant seaman home on leave, who, having seen the maroons go up, volunteered at the last minute. Coastguards described the weather as 'absolutely atrocious' with 60-knot winds whipping the seas into a 'white hell of swirling fury'. Half an hour after the lifeboat set off from its red corrugated shed in Longhope, contact was lost. At first there was no alarm; Daniel Kirkwood had reported having trouble with the radio.

The cause of the disaster would never be known. A freak pillar of water – tons of it – could have crashed down on the boat, capsizing it. 'You would not have seen the water until it was on top of you,' said Captain Denis Wickstead, an inspector with the RNLI. There was a theory that Swanson, whose body was not recovered, could have been next to the cockpit door when the sea swept him away. But all this would remain speculation. There were no survivors.

The bodies of the seven other crewmen were recovered after the upturned vessel was towed into Scrabster by the Thurso lifeboat. A crowd of several hundred stood in silence behind barriers as two frogmen dived beneath the stricken boat and reported back that there were bodies inside. One was in the wheelhouse, the others below decks. In Longhope all the houses were shuttered and silent, the two roads through the village were motionless, and the empty lifeboat shed was battered by a ceaseless wind.

Bill Rodgers, minister of state at the Board of Trade, said: 'It was an act of singular courage by the lifeboat crew to put out in the conditions which prevailed last night.' It was, however, what such men did. In 1953 six lifeboat men at Arbroath and six at Fraserburgh were lost; in 1958 eight at Broughty Ferry; and now eight more at Longhope. The bodies of Daniel Kirkwood and his two sons, of John Johnston and his two sons, and of Eric MacFadyen, the last-minute volunteer, were taken across the Pentland Firth on a fishing boat. There was no question of a lifeboat being used for the last voyage back to Longhope: a superstition of the sea forbade it.

1970
THE JUDAS CARD

I

In the first week of the third full decade of peace, tour operators advertised an unprecedented number of summer flights from Scottish airports to the Mediterranean. One said there was no denying the attractions of the package holiday, often at prices lower than the cost of a holiday at home. Why, he asked, would the Scots want to stay in Britain when they could have a week in the Spanish or Italian sunshine? The people who held the key to a new and better way of life for the majority were no longer politicians but travel agents.

In the same week Tam Dalyell, the Labour MP for West Lothian, called for Christmas Day to be recognised as a public holiday throughout Britain. What did the Scottish Vigilantes, a society of censorious patriots, make of a country which now preferred the Costa Brava to the Kyles of Bute and Christmas to New Year? The Scottish Vigilantes printed calling cards called 'Judas cards' and distributed them to Scots who fell short of their own high standards. The many treacherous natives who had abandoned Rothesay and embraced Christmas would surely have merited a Judas card if only the printing presses of the Scottish Vigilantes had been able to cope. But the new age of sex, drugs and rock 'n' roll provided no shortage of alternative targets.

The Scottish Vigilantes had a supporting role in one of the first court cases of the decade. A 21-year-old laboratory assistant was accused at Glasgow Sheriff Court of 'lewd and libidinous practices' – a legal term unequalled in its evocative associations. Detectives who raided his flat in Hillhead found the accused and a 'well-educated schoolgirl of 14' naked in bed in a room lit by a dim blue lamp. There were 'about 18 young people' in the flat – the Glasgow police had not found it necessary to count the exact number – and cannabis was freely available.

On another visit they discovered schoolgirls 'who should have been at hockey practice' listening to records. The accused's solicitor, Len Murray, told Sheriff John Bayne that his client, between court appearances, had received one of the Scottish Vigilantes' cards, informing him that he would be dealt with 'for letting Scotland down'. Bayne was untroubled by this unusual development. 'I don't suppose you are going to pay much attention to the Judas card,' he told the accused, 'but it is interesting that there are people concerned to see that this city does not become a sin city like London.' How the Scottish Vigilantes must have rejoiced at this endorsement from the bench.

Impressed by the young man's ambition – he claimed he wished to go to university, where the girls were safely above the age of consent – Bayne spared him a prison sentence and gave him probation instead.

The exercise of such leniency was comparatively rare. The Scottish Home and Health Department, in its annual report, chronicled a 25% increase in the number of under-21s being sent to prisons, young offenders' institutions, borstal, and detention centres. Hundreds of cells built for one were regularly holding three. 'Overcrowding must be regarded as the chief cause of high and rising disease rates,' said the report. In Barlinnie the 22 showers could just manage to give each prisoner a shower once a week.

The prisoner was fed regularly: that much could be said in favour of Scotland's penal establishments. But at the start of the decade a prominent doctor claimed that too many elderly people were going without food in their own homes. A few days before Harold Wilson called a general election, two elderly sisters were discovered in a house in Glasgow. A neighbour noticed a burst pipe, went to investigate, and found the door of the house open. One of the women, Margaret Mellon, was seriously ill and died later in hospital. Her sister Mary lay dead on a bed beside her. The building was condemned; the sisters, who shared a flat on the top floor, were among the last people still living in it. There was no food in the house; there was no sign that the fire had been recently lit; the neighbour could not recall having seen either of them for many months. A post-mortem determined the cause of their deaths as starvation.

The man known in the press as 'the old folks' champion', Dr Arnold Cowan, the son of a rabbi, recently anointed Citizen of the Year by a Scottish newspaper, said that the same thing was happening all over the country, a scandalous state of affairs if true. But by the end of the year the Citizen of the Year was no longer in a position to advise the press on these matters. He was starting a three-year prison sentence for, among other things, issuing a false medical certificate to one of his patients with a view to excusing him from a court appearance. The doctor considered this an act of kindness. The Lord Advocate saw it less charitably as a perversion of the course of justice.

II

In mid-May an opinion poll gave Labour a national lead of 8%. It was enough for Wilson: 24 hours later the Prime Minister announced the date of the general election. The omens for the party north of the border were not especially propitious: Labour entered the campaign with 86,000 of the Scottish workforce unemployed, a rate of 4% compared with 2.5% in the country as a whole. The gap between north and south had narrowed only slightly despite the efforts of successive governments since 1945.

In the far north, where the number of jobs had continued to fall despite a massive investment in new industries by the Highlands and Islands Development Board, unemployment stood at five times the UK average. The industrialised central belt was more prosperous, but rarely with any sense of long-term security. The juxtapositions were brutal. The black asbestos towers of the Cameron Iron Works dominated the entrance to the new town of Livingston, symbolising the power of an American industrial giant and the importance of inward investment to post-war Scotland. Next door in Bathgate 5,000 employees of Leyland Motors were being warned of the danger of closure because of strikes and restrictive practices. On the upper Clyde the agonies were unrelenting; UCS declared that 3,000 jobs must go, and quickly, if liquidation was to be avoided.

Yet the state of the economy was not the overwhelming theme of the election in Scotland. The populists of the Scottish National Party and of Teddy Taylor's Cathcart Conservatives introduced a number of diversions. The SNP's manifesto was a strange concoction, shrilly right-wing in proclaiming individual freedom, encouraging the active and enterprising, and scorning the growth of bureaucracy. Teddy Taylor, who complained of the number of civil service jobs created since Labour gained office, would have applauded all of that. Likewise the SNP opposed Britain's imminent entry into the Common Market as strongly as the far right of the Tory Party, and its blueprint for a Scottish parliament included a provision for crowd-pleasing referendums on such issues as capital punishment. Few of these policies, short of the ultimate aim of separation, would have repelled Teddy Taylor. But even he might have stopped short of endorsing the SNP's plan for the compulsory direction of the work-shy into public sector labour, and he would have certainly opposed its proposed removal of nuclear bases from an independent Scotland The manifesto was a masterwork of political schizophrenia.

The Cathcart Conservatives were led and inspired by a former *Glasgow Herald* journalist of whom Brian Wilson, founder of the admirable *West Highland Free Press*, said that calling him by the cuddly name Teddy was 'like calling the Hound of the Baskervilles Rover'. Taylor was popular with journalists, whose availability for comment earned him the nickname 'Dial a Quote'. His only visible outward sign of weakness was an addiction to cigarettes. He smoked particularly heavily during election night counts, when he habitually convinced himself that he was about to lose.

Taylor espoused a coherent if simplistic world view. The 'good things' were small traders, hanging, Rhodesia and national referendums. The 'bad things' were monopolies, North Vietnam (his supporters could never understand why the Americans had not bombed it to bits), the Common Market, immigration, foreign aid and – worst of all – the weakening of respect for authority. He and his loyal army saw law and order as the first responsibility of government. They believed in 'the Dunkirk spirit'. They demanded the repatriation of immigrants who were unemployed for more than four months, and the withdrawal of benefits from claimants who had 'made it clear' that they were not willing to work. They wanted to see more people standing up for the national anthem in cinemas.

In council house Castlemilk, which should have been solidly Labour, this radical brand went down a treat. 'I could not have won in 1966 without the support I received in Castlemilk,' Taylor admitted. 'All right, I had to tell them we would be putting up their rents, but I told them why. And I told them a lot of other things which no other politicians were telling them.'

For the battle of Cathcart Taylor could count on the support of 2,000 warriors. No other Scottish Tory had the same pulling power or charisma. In his ability to exploit the darker instincts of the urban working-class voter, Taylor was a one-off.

But the toughest contest in 1970 was fought not in Cathcart but in the Borders seat of David Steel, whose private member's bill liberalising the law on abortion had passed into statute and was not expected to appeal to the socially conservative voters of Roxburgh, Selkirk and Peebles. William Cassell, a company secretary from Sheerness, announced that he was standing against Steel 'to defend unborn babies from extermination'. If the intervention of a single-issue fringe candidate was no more than a minor irritation, the sitting member's support of the anti-apartheid movement was potentially anything but. Earlier in the year, when the South African rugby tourists played at Galashiels, Steel had joined demonstrators outside the ground. This gesture was exploited by his Tory opponent, Russell Fairgrieve, who claimed that, of all the Scottish constituencies, Roxburgh, Selkirk and Peebles had most to lose from a boycott of South African goods, since South Africa had become a growth market for Borders knitwear and tweed.

Fairgrieve then twisted the knife, claiming that Steel should be 'standing for Johannesburg West, not the Borders'. He told a visiting political correspondent: 'The person elected should not be someone who can bring unemployment to the constituency. Are we going to see demonstrators outside our Border mills?' The note of local patriotism was reinforced by Fairgrieve's slogan, 'A Borderer for the Borders'. But the Boy David (as Steel was known on account of his youthful appearance) was not averse to rough tackling in retaliation. He pointed out a curious omission from Fairgrieve's official CV – his major shareholding in (and directorship of) Dawson Holdings, one of the largest employers in the constituency. Steel wanted to know if its 6,000 employees in the Borders were aware that the company had made a sizeable contribution to the Scottish Conservative Party.

The social and moral questions on which David Steel had fought, at considerable risk to his political future, surfaced in other Scottish seats. The Tory candidate in Glasgow Kelvingrove, Ronnie Dundas, chief leader writer of the *Glasgow Herald*, declared that he was opposed to legalised homosexuality and to Steel's abortion act. He told a public meeting: 'If a woman does not want to have a child because she is living in bad housing, it is much better to try and get her a new house than have her going through an abortion operation. It offends both moral and natural law.' Labour's Maurice Miller replied from a position of authority: 'I am a doctor and Mr Dundas is not. I have seen women die through having to go to a back street abortionist. Over 80% of the women in the country wanted a change in the abortion law and that includes 60% of Roman Catholics. Two out of three doctors also support the act.' Undaunted, Dundas continued to preach his anti-abortion message in what his own paper, apparently indifferent to possible allegations of partiality, singled out as 'a strong door-to-door campaign'.

Just before the election, when a proposed tour of Britain by an all-white South African cricket team was called off in the face of political pressure, Sir Herbert Brechin, chairman of the organising committee of the 1970 Commonwealth Games in Edinburgh, was observed by the Scottish press 'beaming with relief'. The decision meant that the threatened boycott of the games by other African countries would no longer go ahead.

Brechin's pleasure in the anticipation of a multi-racial gathering in the Scottish capital was not universally shared. Gerald Warner, a young Tory compared with whom Ronnie Dundas was the soul of moderation, wrote to the newspapers objecting to the participation in the games of 'such genocidal states as Tanzania and Nigeria', to the 'warped sense of values' that had 'inflated the importance' of the slaughter of 68 black South Africans at Sharpeville, and to the 'sinister erosion of democracy represented by the forced cancellation of this cricket tour'. Warner proved to have staying power. Forty years later he had a regular berth in a Scottish Sunday newspaper in which to articulate his bracing political philosophy.

III

Not for the first time, a general election coincided with the General Assembly of the Church of Scotland, a conjunction of events which brought out grandstanders both spiritual and temporal. The minister of Burdiehouse, J E M Baikie, leapt from the traps as eagerly as the top dog at Powderhall. On the same day as Sir

Herbert Brechin celebrated the saving of the Commonwealth Games, Baikie declared himself a racialist and called for an end to all immigration into Britain.

But, as ever, it was sex that drew the crowds. A liberal report on the pill had incurred the wrath of that Presbyterian guardian of virtue, the *Scottish Daily Express*, which suggested that at this rate the permissive churchmen in the moral welfare committee would soon be abolishing marriage. A hundred commissioners were marooned in corridors unable to find a seat, and the lucky ones inside the hall were urged to 'squeeze up a bit' so that as many as possible could be present for the big debate on the popular topic of bad girls.

John Peat of Ayton, the committee's convenor, defended its view that 'in certain circumstances it is the lesser of two evils not to deny the unmarried promiscuous woman the pill'. There were several attempts to have the offending phrase expunged from the record, not as a rebuke for its circuitous use of language but because, according to James Philip of Holyrood Abbey, it stirred feelings of 'deep distress, shock and even outrage'. Peat replied: 'Here is a lass who, God help us, is going to be promiscuous whatever you say – perhaps she honestly can't help herself. Who knows?'

A few days later James Scott, a young minister from Denbeath in Fife, did a Muggeridge, resigning his charge over the committee's qualified acceptance of contraception. When Hugh Douglas, the Moderator, announced that the business was being adjourned for lunch, Scott addressed himself to 'the people of the Church of Scotland' from his spectator's seat in the gallery. Douglas vacated his chair and most of the fathers and brethren followed him out. Scott went on talking to the emptying hall, denouncing 'the corrupt and corrupting church ... This Sodom which has trampled the Lord underfoot, and his Gospel'. By the time the dissenter was finished, the Moderator would have been half-way through his first course.

Jack Glass, pastor of a sect known as the Zion Church of Sovereign Grace, was not so easily brushed off. The assembly erupted when Scotland's evangelical arch-Protestant, his wife Margaret and a dozen or so of his supporters rose in protest at the welcome extended by the Moderator to a delegation from the Greek Orthodox Church. While eight men and women stood in the south gallery brandishing placards which spelled out the words 'No Popery', Glass and his wife shouted from the east gallery and others from the west, in a performance of well-orchestrated discord. One of the demonstrators then showered the ministers and elders with pamphlets, forcing Douglas to abandon the moderatorial chair and lead the Greek delegation to the safety of the wings. The disturbance was reignited a few minutes later by the return of the official party. Delegates stamped their feet and began a slow handclap. 'You won't clap in Hell,' yelled a woman's voice from one of the galleries. It might have been Mrs Glass, advancing the theory of Hell as an applause-free zone. Douglas ploughed on with his introduction to Nicolaus the Sixth, Pope and Patriarch of Alexandria and All Africa, 'a representative of one of the most ancient seats in Christendom and the 105th incumbent of the office'. Nicolaus the Sixth was able to utter only a few words in response before Margaret, first incumbent of the wifely office of Glass, rose with arms outstretched, loudly proclaiming: 'Save us from Popery'.

She and two others, though not the man of the house, were charged with breach of the peace. After a preliminary appearance at Edinburgh Sheriff Court the accused and their supporters marched straight back to the Assembly Hall, fortuitously arriving there just as Harold Wilson was leaving. The Prime Minister smiled and waved cheerfully at the agitators, who were unfurling a banner in protest at the Kirk's support of the permissive society: 'The pill for fallen women. The Church of Scotland says – Go and sin some more.'

Glass was refused permission to represent his wife at her trial, a decision from the bench that left all three accused representing themselves. They testified that they had been 'prompted by the Holy Spirit to defend Protestantism', Mrs Glass adding – on oath – 'I was not making a protest, I was saying a prayer'. The sheriff did not believe her and all three were found guilty of breach of the peace and admonished (warned as to their future conduct). But Jack Glass could claim a victory of sorts. He had arranged for the defence to cite as witnesses two of the Kirk's bigwigs – Douglas the Moderator and J B Longmuir, the principal clerk to the assembly, with no serious intention of calling them. Glass had succeeded in inconveniencing the Kirk establishment, and with no fine to pay, and no solicitors' bills to meet, the trial was a cheap date for the pastor.

Later he widened the scope of his attacks, picketing the concerts of his fellow Glaswegian, the comedian Billy Connolly, for their allegedly blasphemous content. At the height of their careers both were remarkable for their beards – Glass's short and pointed, giving him a devilish air – but the resemblance ended with their shared liking for facial hair. Connolly gave as good as he got, introducing into his act a song to the tune of *Jumping Jack Flash* which included the refrain: 'Pastor Jack Glass is an ass, ass ass'. Not everyone in the Church of Scotland thought him an ass, ass, ass; he had a few secret admirers on the Kirk's wilder evangelical shores.

He was the journalist's friend, a source of easy copy in the class of Teddy Taylor or the Edinburgh councillor John S Kidd, who wanted an end to filth at the Edinburgh Festival and its substitution by such inoffensive warblers as Kenneth McKellar and Moira Anderson. Kidd, once flattered with many column inches for his reactionary opinions, was quickly forgotten. But the reputation of Pastor Jack lingered beyond his death in 2004 at the age of 68, from a cancer which he believed had been visited on him by Satan – an extreme version of the Judas card. He looked forward to joining his maker in a heaven mercifully free of Papists, blasphemers and fallen women.

If this unreconstructed zealot amounted to anything in this life, it counted for little in the Protestant enclave of Glasgow Bridgeton, where he stood as an independent in the 1970 general election. He complained of the press's description of him as a former shop assistant, insisting that he had been a commercial traveller 'before entering the ministry'. His 1,180 votes put him bottom of the poll, a position in political purgatory from which there was seldom any hope of salvation.

IV

BBC Scotland's star presenter, Mary Marquis, a former actress, told an interviewer, Alison Downie, that she regretted not attending RADA, the metropolitan school for thespians. 'Let's face it,' she said, 'you have to go to London at some point.' She did not say why. Perhaps it was implicitly understood. But were the Scottish Vigilantes twitching at the thought?

In her next interview Alison Downie was struck by the 'shoulder-length fair hair, large wide-set eyes, and full, sensitive mouth' of the SNP's candidate in Paisley. This may have been the first media profile of Margo MacDonald, wife of the licensee of the Hoolet's Nest pub in High Blantyre. 'There was a time,' she told Downie, 'when I thought it was possible to retain a sense of nationhood in Scotland while not being involved politically. It took me some time to realise this wasn't possible, and although I joined the SNP five years ago, I still feel it's more of a cause than just a party – that's why it has this appeal to young people, who are not on the whole politically conscious.' Downie wrote that Margo was remembered at Hamilton Academy as 'a big girl with a powerful personality' and that she had gone on to be teacher of physical education at East Kilbride High School when it was still a junior secondary. The interviewer did not have to ask Margo MacDonald about going to London. In her case the question was superfluous.

At the age of 27 'Big Margo' was not the youngest woman candidate in Scotland. Susan Bell, 23, caught the jaundiced eye of political journalists with her 'trendy fur coat, long brown hair and large sunglasses', a daring look in Motherwell and Wishaw. Among the young men 24-year-old Malcolm Rifkind, (advocate), was standing for the Conservatives in Edinburgh Central, 24-year-old Robin Cook (teacher) for Labour in Edinburgh North, 28-year-old George Foulkes (youth worker) for Labour in Edinburgh West, 27-year-old Vincent Cable (university lecturer) for Labour in Glasgow Hillhead, 29-year-old Ian Lang (insurance broker) for the Conservatives in Central Ayrshire. Of that talented and ambitious group none was elected in the 1970 election, but Peggy Herbison's retirement gave John Smith a safe berth in Lanarkshire from which to launch his parliamentary career.

In Hamilton, the temporary residence of Winnie Ewing, the Tory candidate stole the SNP's thunder with his campaign stunts. There was not a chance of the party winning the seat, so Ross Harper could afford to enjoy himself. He produced, to the delight of the local paper, a Tory dog which barked and growled whenever it heard the names Harold Wilson or Alex Wilson (the Labour candidate). Harper then announced that he intended to make the longest speech in British political history, a 10-hour marathon delivered in Hamilton's new shopping centre with a five-minute break at the end of each hour. Although the newspapers were impressed by his energy and enthusiasm the electors of Hamilton were less impressed. Harper, nursing a lost deposit and a sore throat, was free to develop a successful career in the law.

His fellow solicitor Winnie Ewing was not enjoying herself. She and her party decided to make the evils of European integration one of the key themes of her campaign: 'Workers in Scotland would, if Scotland were forced into the Common Market, have their wage rates and their conditions of work fixed for them, whether they liked it or not, in Brussels or Paris or anywhere else in the Common Market. Decisions affecting working men and women would be taken in Brussels with no reference to those working men and women.' The evils of European integration, some of which existed only in the candidate's imagination, failed to catch on as an issue in Hamilton, and a few days before the poll a disconsolate Ewing admitted that the local Labour machine was pulling out all the stops. Even she could not have anticipated a Labour majority of 8,582.

In Scotland as a whole the SNP had a bad night, a just reward for its manifesto. William Wolfe, the national chairman, in one of his unsuccessful bids to unseat Tam Dalyell in West Lothian, railed against Europe even more virulently than Ewing. In his major speech of the campaign he claimed that opposition to the Common Market sprang 'from all that is best in the Scottish character, its individuality, its love of country, and its hatred of centralisation' – a statement which may have come as a surprise to the miners of West Lothian, who prized a sense of community, even solidarity, above any expression of individuality.

The chairman's trouncing by Dalyell was almost as embarrassing as Ewing's exit from Hamilton after three years as the constituency's MP. But the SNP's performance said more about the ineptness of its campaign than about public interest in its core policy. According to an opinion poll in the week of the election 86% of Scots supported a referendum on what form of government Scotland should have; 34% favoured a devolved Scottish parliament; a striking 23% supported complete independence.

In the circumstances a more effective target than the Common Market would have been the Labour Party for its failure to respond to public feeling on devolution. John P Mackintosh, the party's resident intellectual, managed to write a 1,200-word critique of the election issues without once mentioning devolution or the constitutional question, and a month before the election, the STUC produced an insulting blueprint for a Scottish assembly. The talking shop would have no power to enact legislation and no budget of its own. The 142 members – two from each of the Westminster constituencies – would be part-time, fulfilling a brief to 'initiate discussion' on the work of the Scottish Office.

Presented with this open goal, and with the Scottish Conservative Party's far from overwhelming endorsement of its leadership's plan for a more meaningful assembly (a quarter of the faithful had voted against the plan at their conference in Perth in May 1970), the SNP was unable to score. It preferred to chase imaginary bogeymen in Brussels than bogeymen on its own doorstep, with all too predictable results. But it did take the Western Isles with a popular local candidate, Donald Stewart, and the feisty Elizabeth Whitley, journalist and ecclesiastical historian, came second behind Sir Alec in Kinross and West Perthshire. These should have been warnings to the established parties that the SNP even at its worst could not be written off. But the warnings continued to be ignored.

V

The day before the election the opinion polls fluctuated wildly, one predicting a 150-seat Labour majority, another putting a Tory win within the range of statistical error. But only the last poll, which appeared in the London *Evening Standard* on election day itself, predicted a Conservative victory, though not by the comfortable margin that Edward Heath achieved. It was the first election in which 18-year-olds were able to vote, and one of the first to do so, at 8.09am, the exact moment of her birth in 1952, was Janis Weir, an Edinburgh typist, who told journalists that she had put her cross against the name Malcolm Rifkind, a candidate only six years older than herself.

In a mixed night for the Scottish Tories Esmond Wright lost Pollok and Ronnie Dundas failed to win Kelvingrove, but George Younger celebrated a hefty increase in his majority in Ayr, Teddy Taylor swept to a brilliant victory in Cathcart, Hamish Gray ousted the Liberals in Ross and Cromarty, and young Susan Bell, who had so dazzled the press pack, did well to persuade 12,509 people in the Labour stronghold of Motherwell and Wishaw to vote for her. In the battle for South Aberdeen 'clean-cut, polished' Iain Sproat took the seat from 'angular, fast talking' Donald Dewar. David Steel held on grimly in the Borders, his majority cut to 550 after two recounts. He called it the dirtiest campaign he had ever experienced – not that he had much of a background in dirt to draw on – and claimed that the Tory agent had distributed a letter to supporters instructing them to remove Steel posters on sight. His opponent Fairgrieve, an ardent European and an unflinching supporter of devolution, rather like Steel himself, went on to be MP for West Aberdeenshire in 1974 and was regarded as the elder statesman of the party in Scotland when he died in 1999. By then his foe Steel was an elder statesman himself.

In an assessment of the election result in Scotland, Robert McLaughlan, a Labour-supporting commentator, welcomed the arrival of John Smith – 'an outstanding recruit' – but regretted the loss of Winnie Ewing. 'It seems hard to imagine,' he wrote, 'that Scotland will benefit from her political demise when her successor at Hamilton has no special commendation.' But reports of that demise were exaggerated. Within a few years she was being hailed as 'Madame Ecosse' in the parliament of the European project she had berated so roundly at Hamilton. Donald Dewar would likewise return from the political dead – so successfully that, by 1999, he was first minister of Scotland and 'father of the nation' no less.

VI

With the election out of the way, the nation could turn from bread to circuses. Kilted pipers and drummers introduced the Commonwealth Games, free of boycott, at the new Meadowbank Stadium in Edinburgh. The Jamaicans, 'brilliant in mustard jackets', led the parade of the 42 teams. The Gambian women appeared in white trouser suits, the Bermudans in shorts, the Mauritian standard-bearer in Black Watch kilt and Highland doublet, the Nigerians in sky-blue robes, the Swaziland leader in a tribal cloak hung from one shoulder. Miss K G Badra was the single representative of the Sinhalese, while the gloriously named Barrymore Scotland carried all the hopes of Dominica.

The only downbeat nation was the host one. Lachie Stewart, the spokesman for the Scottish team, took his annual holidays during the games rather than ask for time off from the Glasgow Dental Hospital where he was employed as a technician. He said that a cloud of boredom had settled on the home camp. 'It's all right for the overseas countries,' he explained. 'They can go sightseeing and shopping, but most of the Scots have seen it before. The worst time is between lunch and dinner. You train in the morning and evening, but the time certainly drags in the middle of the day.' Frank Dick, the national coach, agreed: 'What we need are some amusement machines to give them something to occupy their minds.' Sorely provoked as they must have been, there was no word from the Scottish Vigilantes.

1971

A YEAR IN GOVAN

I

In the late afternoon of Saturday 2 January 1971 Maureen Oswell was standing at the window of her top-storey house in Cairnlea Drive, Glasgow, overlooking stairway 13 at Ibrox Stadium. Her husband was listening to the match on the radio. In the 89th minute Celtic broke the deadlock, scoring the first goal in the traditional New Year fixture between the 'Old Firm' of Scottish football. The Rangers fans, supposing that the game was lost, started to make their way home. But in the last seconds their team equalised and pandemonium erupted on the terraces.

Maureen Oswell saw two men – teenagers, she was reported as calling them – one squatting on the shoulders of the other, waving scarves at the top of the steps. 'Something's going to happen,' she said to her husband in a moment of premonition. He had no opportunity to reply before something did. 'The teenagers seemed to disappear completely and the rest of the crowd behind them caved in like a pack of cards. It was as if all of them were falling into a huge hole.' Her husband Robert said: 'The rescuers pulled scores of trapped people out of the mass of bodies and lifted them over a fence into bushes. One young boy managed to stagger down the embankment holding his stomach and I thought he had escaped, but he just flopped down at the foot of the embankment and later I learned that he had died.'

In the press box high above the ground Andrew Young, a Glasgow journalist, was chatting to colleagues about the excellent behaviour of the crowd when he noticed four or five policemen in the north-east corner standing on the track looking up into the terracing. 'Fighting must have started,' someone said. To Young this seemed inexplicable. Almost at once, across the floodlit mist, he could hear distant sounds of shouts and screams. He and a colleague hurried down the spiral staircase from the top of the stand and across a frost-hardened pitch. There was now a numb silence, interrupted only by calls for stretcher-bearers. 'Half a dozen lifeless forms were lying on the ground,' wrote Young. 'Rescuers were tripping over the dead and injured as they struggled back with more victims.'

The disaster occurred at 4.46pm. Sixteen minutes elapsed before the ambulance service received the first emergency call, and ambulances were further delayed in getting to the stadium because of the density of the crowds in the streets.

One of the survivors had gone to the match with his teenage cousin. 'We were trying to get down the steps when everybody started falling. My cousin and I were separated and then I was caught in the crowd. I felt sick and began to choke, but just then two men pulled me out of the heap. I am sure I would have been killed if it had not been for them.' The cousin died.

Among the other eye-witness testimonies, William Burns described the pressure on the stairs as unbearable. 'I could hear those in front of me shouting and kids screaming. Then the people in front started falling. Next thing I knew I was lying on the steps and the barriers were twisted about me. I must have lost conscious-ness because the next thing I remember is being brought round with smelling salts by an ambulance man.'

'There was a rush of people,' said Desmond O'Donnell, 'and I was pushed down on top of others ahead of me. As I fell flat out, I felt someone grabbing me and pulling me aside to safety. I've no idea who did that, but whoever he was, I'm quite sure he saved my life.'

Such was the crush of bodies, the last of the victims died upright. 'They were standing up perfectly straight,' recalled John Williamson. I saw the colour of their eyes change to purple. They were standing looking at you. They were speaking to you with their eyes but there was nothing in them.'

Donald Liddle, the Lord Provost of Glasgow, walked across the pitch, climbed over the wall into the terracing and knelt beside a man who had had a pillow of beer cans made for his head. 'He was dead,' wrote Andrew Young. 'The Lord Provost was in tears. Occasionally one could hear the noise of coins falling from the victims' pockets as they were lifted away.' Young noted the absence of footwear on the bodies: the sheer pressure of the crowd had pulled the shoes from all of them.

Professor Gilbert Forbes, a forensic specialist at Glasgow University, examined the bodies of the 66 victims. He found that 60 of them died of asphyxiation by external pressure and the remaining six from suffocation caused by obstruction to their air passages. The youngest victim, eight-year-old Nigel McPherson, was on holiday from his home in Canada; his father Donald, a migrant Scot, died with him. Twenty-eight of the dead were in their teens. When five of them failed to return to the Markinch supporters' bus, the organisers, unaware of the carnage inside the ground, assumed that they they had been delayed in the huge exodus. The only woman who died, 18-year-old Margaret Ferguson from Falkirk, was such a keen Rangers supporter that a few weeks earlier she had made a doll as a Christmas present for the baby daughter of the club's centre-forward Colin Stein and delivered it personally to Stein's home in Linlithgow.

It was the worst disaster in British footballing history and among the greatest misfortunes ever inflicted on Glasgow. The following morning an emotional Lord Provost found it almost impossible to express its enormity in words. The flags in the city flew at half-mast, briefly fluttering above the corrosive sectarian rivalries which divided Protestant Rangers, who were notorious for not signing Catholic players, and Catholic Celtic. Yet there was something in the theory that football was more important than life or death. Some newspapers found space for a report of the match itself. It had been a good one, up to a point.

II

During a week of deep mourning which appeared to unite the city, the religious laments were nonetheless observed separately – a requiem mass in St Andrew's Roman Catholic Cathedral followed by a memorial service in Glasgow Cathedral, a place of Presbyterian worship. At the mass players and officials of both clubs sat by side to hear James Donald Scanlan, the Archbishop of Glasgow, speak feelingly of the tragic repercussions of so many lost in the flower of youth. Robert Crampsey, a BBC sports commentator, read the lesson from the Old Testament and Jim Craig, the Celtic full-back, the lesson from the New.

The service in Glasgow Cathedral was televised live throughout

Britain by the BBC. 'The poignant silences between prayers and hymns,' wrote one journalist, 'were often rent with the sobbing of women, several of whom were overcome by emotion and had to be led outside.' William Morris, minister of the cathedral, derived comfort from his belief that, as in a war, the suffering at Ibrox Stadium had 'taught men of different faiths and of rival prejudices that they were brothers', while Robert Bone, minister of Ibrox Parish Church, paid tribute to 'the ordinary man in the crowd who, despite danger, turned back to help the man he did not know'. Bone struck an affecting note of human sympathy when he referred to the players: 'They have seen in a week as much sorrow as many do in a lifetime.'

In the case of the Rangers players this was certainly true. Every bereaved family was contacted personally. On 7 January a shuttle service of limousines came and went from Ibrox throughout the day, enabling members of the team and club officials to pay their respects at 40 funerals taking place as far apart as Selkirk and Dunoon. In the village of Slamannan near Falkirk three players were among the mourners when the brothers Richard and John McLeay were buried together.

The following day Lance-Corporal John James McGovern of the Royal Engineers was laid to rest with military honours in a cemetery overlooking the Firth of Forth. Eight pall-bearers from his regiment carried the coffin into Tranent Parish Church for a funeral service attended by his commanding officer and by the Rangers captain John Greig and his team-mates Alfie Conn and Sandy Jardine. A piper playing a lament led the cortege from the church to the cemetery along a half-mile route lined by the villagers. Seven hundred people crowded round the graveside, where a buglar played the Last Post and a party of 10 soldiers fired a salute. McGovern, 24, had been in the army for six years. He was spending his New Year leave with his wife Ellen, 20, and his sons aged three and two, and decided to go to the game on a local supporters' bus organised by Ormiston Rangers.

Elsewhere in Scotland that day 17 other victims of the disaster were buried in the presence of Rangers players. *They have seen in a week as much sorrow as many do in a lifetime.* But despite the heartfelt response of the team to so concentrated an exhibition of raw grief, it took indecently little time for normal service to be resumed in Scottish football. In a week of funerals the football journalists reverted to their usual coloured prose, one alluding to Celtic's 'ruthless pursuit' of the championship with no mention of the context and no second thoughts about the use of the word ruthless. Bailie James Anderson, the councillor who had dished the Easterhouse youth project, announced that he was organising an 'all-star variety show' in the King's Theatre, followed by a champagne buffet supper in aid of the fund for dependants. Not all the victims were in their graves, and Anderson talked of champagne.

III

Two inquiries were set up in the immediate aftermath: a fatal accident inquiry, which began with admirable promptness only five weeks after the disaster, and a longer-term review of safety at football grounds chaired by the man for all seasons, Lord Wheatley.

The fatal accident inquiry opened in Pollokshaws Burgh Hall with a statement by Sir Allan Walker, Sheriff of Lanarkshire, that the task of the jury of four men and three women was to ascertain the causes of death. Maureen Oswell, one of the first witnesses, repeated her account of the two figures she saw from the window of her house, although with a variation from the original press reports which had them as teenagers. In court Mrs Oswell indicated that a youth was sitting on the shoulders of an older man. 'He [the youth] was swinging his body about and his arms were in the air. I felt that something was going to happen and I remarked to my husband that it was a stupid thing to do … All of a sudden it seemed as if everyone was going forward in a kind of chain reaction.'

A second witness, James Lowrie, supported her theory with additional evidence. He said he saw 'two boys [a term in Glasgow commonly used for men of any age] throwing their scarves and jackets in the air … When they bent down to pick up the articles they had thrown, they were pushed down the stairs with the crowd going on top of them. Everyone piled on top of them.'

Robert Duncan, a neighbour of the Oswells, likewise watched the events on stairway 13 from his house. 'The whole thing happened with the Rangers equaliser,' he told the court. 'Everyone had got what they wanted. They came down the stairs full of beans.'

Although beer cans supported one dead man's head, it was official policy that fans were not allowed to drink in the ground. Instead they did so before entering it. In the days following the disaster some challenged the wisdom of this policy, claiming that young men unable to hold their drink were incapable by the time they got to the match. The Celtic club doctor testified, however, that 'the absence of drink [in the dead] was marked. I noticed no drink.' What, then? Did 66 people die because of a single act of human folly caused by exuberance? Not quite.

The inquiry heard that this was the fourth accident at Ibrox Stadium within 10 years and that all of them had occurred on stairway 13. In the first incident, in November 1961, two men were trampled to death. In September 1967 eight men were injured. In January 1969 a further 29 were injured. It was a shocking record. What did it say about the club's regard for the safety of supporters?

The evidence given to the inquiry by the directors of Rangers Football Club was notable for its evasiveness and prevarication. David Hope, one of the directors, was asked repeatedly for details of a meeting to discuss crowd safety on stairway 13 between himself and two senior police officers following the 1969 accident. The meeting was clearly recalled by David White, the club's former manager, and by John Nicholson, a chief superintendent of police, both of whom were present. Nicholson said that he made a specific proposal on the spot – to alter the railings so that the crowd, after going a certain distance down the stairway, could 'fan out'. Hope agreed with this idea and undertook to propose it to his fellow directors. Nicholson heard no more about it, and the police's recommendation for improving crowd safety was never implemented.

Hope, a man of 66, seemed to be having great difficulty remembering the occasion. The most he was able to tell the court was that such a meeting 'could have taken place' and that he 'could have been present'.

David Brand, QC, the Solicitor General: 'I presume as a director of Rangers FC, the occurrence of a third serious accident in the stairway might have been of some interest to you?'

'Yes.'

'Do you still say that you can't remember whether you had any meeting at which the safety of the stairway was discussed?'

'No, I can't remember anything definite.'

Was the witness suffering from a clinical loss of memory? Or may there have been another explanation for his unimpressive performance in the witness box – the possibility that he would be accused of personal negligence?

Closely questioned by Charles Macarthur, QC, counsel for some of the bereaved families, Hope volunteered that after the 1969 accident the directors had discussed stairway 13 and that they were 'quite satisfied they had done all they were told to do for the safety of the stairway'. This answer failed to satisfy Macarthur: 'Did they not consider that as there had been three serious accidents on the same stairway, there seemed to be something unusual?'

'No, I don't think I can recollect them saying anything about the previous disasters.' The witness could not distinguish between a serious accident and a disaster.

A similar case of amnesia was afflicting the club chairman, 77-year-old John Lawrence, a West of Scotland house-builder, when he gave evidence to the inquiry. Lawrence could not remember if the board had discussed safety after the 1969 incident, 'but commonsense would tell me that we did have some discussion'. In a well-ordered company the minutes of board meetings would have provided a record of any such discussion. Lawrence was asked if Rangers Football Club kept minutes. Evidently yes. But the chairman was not sure that the discussion, 'if it took place', would have been recorded in the minutes. It seemed he had not checked them before his appearance at the inquiry.

Lawrence was also hazy about a meeting of the directors held less than 24 hours before he gave evidence. The timing of the meeting intrigued Macarthur: a Sunday in the middle of the inquiry, after Hope's far from satisfactory testimony. He wanted to know the purpose of this meeting. 'It was just to discuss the questions, that is all' was Lawrence's ambiguous reply. Why was Hope not present? 'That is his business, not mine,' said Lawrence. He admitted that he had met Hope on Sunday evening, at Anderson's champagne reception in the King's Theatre, but maintained that he had not discussed the inquiry with him. Later in his evidence Lawrence changed his mind about the reason for Hope's non-appearance at the Sunday meeting. He said it would not have been right for Hope to be there, since he had already given his evidence.

If the purpose of the meeting was to agree a narrative for the rest of the inquiry, it failed miserably. A third director of the club,

Ian McLaren, at the age of 62 almost a boy on the Rangers board, then gave evidence which undermined Lawrence's. He told Charles Macarthur that the meeting had been called, not to discuss questions arising from the inquiry as Lawrence had implied, but 'to discuss the match at Aberdeen on Saturday'.

'Do you usually meet on a Sunday to discuss a match that has taken place?'

'Sometimes.'

'Was that the purpose of the meeting yesterday?'

'It was just to chat generally.'

In his address to the jury Macarthur criticised the quality of the directors' evidence and said he would not shirk from claiming that 'some blame [for the disaster] must lie clearly at the door of Rangers Football Club'. The Solicitor General, whose presence underlined the public importance of the inquiry, was more circumspect in his language but left an unmistakable impression: 'It may be unfair to apportion blame at this stage, but you will have to bear in mind that this was the fourth accident on this stairway ... Mr Lawrence and Mr McLaren are builders. You will consider whether they applied their minds properly to the safety of the crowd, particularly in relation to the stairway, and it is for you to consider what weight if any you attach to the evidence given by the three directors.'

What weight if any ... One of Scotland's senior law officers had come close to challenging the integrity of the board. But Sheriff Walker urged caution on the jury: 'All I can say is that if you have not heard evidence which enables you to say that some specific thing which might have been done was not done – and I don't think you have – you are not in a position to say there was fault or negligence on the part of the club.' Walker had chosen to disregard the evidence of a key witness, Nicholson, who had indeed proposed a 'specific thing' which might have been done to improve the safety of stairway 13 but which was not done. How could the sheriff then tell the jury that it had heard no such damning evidence? Not for the first time a Glasgow jury was being invited to protect powerful business interests in the city. It had happened at the inquiry into the Cheapside fire. It was happening again.

The jury found that the accident occurred because 'one or more persons fell or collapsed on the stairway at a time when those descending were packed closely together and were being pushed downwards by the pressure of others above and behind them'. It avoided direct criticism of the board, but added a rider to its verdict that deaths or injuries 'would always be liable to occur on stairway 13 in its present state if such a densely packed mass of people were allowed to descend'. The jury recommended that expert advice should be sought on reducing the number of people using the stairway.

At the end of an inquiry which cast so unflattering a light on the Rangers board, exposing the directors as unreliable witnesses at best and downright untruthful at worst, the city's only serious newspaper, the arch-unionist *Glasgow Herald*, had nothing to say about the conduct of those who gave evidence or about the inquiry in general. The paper ran three leaders the morning after the verdict: on the iniquities of David Steel's abortion law, the situation in the Middle East, and traffic flows in the west end of Glasgow. But about the official verdict on the Ibrox disaster, in which so many died and which had such a profound impact on the life of Scotland – not a word.

IV

A year later the Stage Company (Scotland) – a group of travelling players dedicated to new Scottish writing – went on tour with a short play inspired by the Ibrox disaster. It was written by Joan Ure, a Glasgow dramatist whose real name was Elizabeth (Betty) Clark; she adopted a pseudonym because of family sensitivities about her work. The critic Christopher Small thought highly of the piece and of Ure's writing in general, admiring its insight, honesty and delicacy of touch.

The Hard Case took the form of a court plea in mitigation by a Glasgow citizen so overcome by the disaster that on the Sunday morning – 3 January 1971 – he took his umbrella and banged so hard on the windows of an abandoned department store that he shattered the glass. He had been at the match.

'I was sitting there in the stand,' he explained to the sheriff. 'Safe because I had a few bob more for a seat. As simple as that, the difference. At the end of the game. A draw. No hurry. Take my time. Not really watching the terracing. Not really watching. Then … the shambles. And because I paid more for my seat, I was … spared! Folk died a park's width away. And it isn't the same on TV.

It bloody isn't. I couldn't get it out of my mind. You see ... I couldn't help feeling I'd pushed them.'

The play included the line: 'We don't have yer actual wailing wall in Glasgow. I think it's about time it was built.' The Everyman of the title was bound over to keep the peace by a sympathetic judge who declared that football had been 'carrying something foreign to it as a sport. It raised the gate money – but at what cost'. They didn't build the wailing wall in Glasgow, and football went on carrying something foreign to it. Eighteen months later John Lawrence was ousted from the Rangers board in a power struggle over the choice of his successor as chairman. He wanted it to be his friend David Hope, but the fact that in 1930 Hope had married a Roman Catholic was held against him. The intense suffering on stairway 13 had changed nothing.

V

Govan, the home of Rangers Football Club, became the focus of international attention for a second time in 1971 when Edward Heath's administration, with its decision to destroy a proud tradition of shipbuilding on the upper Clyde, precipitated the greatest crisis in Scottish industrial life since the 1930s. John Davies, the trade and industry secretary, announced that the Conservative government would no longer support UCS (Upper Clyde Shipbuilders).

The year had begun promisingly for the company. In the final weeks of 1970 management and unions had negotiated a pay and productivity deal which provided, according to one union official, 'a base for peace and stability in the Clyde yards'. James Murray of the Boilermakers' Society predicted that it would restore the government's confidence in the yards. The management agreed: 'We can go ahead and improve the efficiency of our yards. Generally this will help us in the whole operation of the business.' That was January. By the middle of June the government was pulling all the plugs. Confidence, far from being restored, had evaporated.

Yet the moderately bullish forecasts early in the year were well founded. Between the beginning of 1970 and the middle of 1971 UCS's weekly production rose from 867 tons a week to 1,300. The output of ships increased from a paltry three in 1968 to 12 in 1970. The order book for all four divisons – Govan, Scotstoun, Linthouse and Clydebank – was full until the end of 1972. The decision to concentrate on unsophisticated ships – cargo vessels – had involved the loss of 3,500 jobs, but the exceptional cooperation of the unions had allowed this painful transition to be accomplished. Seven and a half thousand people were still in work. The small shops and businesses which depended on the yards, employing as many as 17,500 people, had cause for modest optimism. Morale in the shipbuilding communities was slowly reviving.

The hard-won progress came to a shattering end in a late-night exchange of telephone calls between Anthony Hepper, UCS's chairman, and ministers. Hepper made it clear that the company had been under-capitalised at the start, that it continued to face liquidity problems as a result, and that it required an immediate injection of £6 million. The ministers made it equally clear that there would be no more cash and that the £22 million thrown at the company by the Labour government of 1964-70 had been money down the drain. John Davies repeated his insistence that the Conservatives would no longer prop up 'lame duck industries', of which, in his view, there were few limping more badly than shipbuilding on the Upper Clyde. Lobby correspondents reported the perception in government that 'UCS must either solve its own financial problems or face the consequences of failure'. No one was left in any doubt about the immediate consequence – the liquidation of the company.

Ken Douglas, UCS's managing director, warned in advance of a cabinet meeting that, unless the money was forthcoming, all 7,500 jobs in the yards would go at once. Jimmy Airlie, convener of the joint shop stewards committee, issued his own statement: 'We will continue working normally in our determination to resist any closure of this key, basic industry. The liquidator may have a problem getting in.' It was the first indication of the union strategy, and it came within hours. But the newspapers gave Airlie's unusual response little prominence. They concentrated instead on the 'moment of truth' facing John Davies: to yield to pressure and pump further money into the company would not only compromise his own philosophy of shooting the lame ducks, but compound what the Tories saw as Labour extravagance and waste. Despite the potentially lethal electoral price and the risk of giving a push to the nationalist bandwagon which had been halted by the

1970 election, the outcome of the cabinet meeting was a foregone conclusion.

Davies told the Commons: 'The government have decided that nobody's interest will be served by making the injection of funds into the company as it now stands.' Nobody's interest? Had Davies forgotten the workers and their families? Whatever the logic of the decision, the use of language was offensively loose. He said that a liquidator would be appointed to explore which parts of the business might be saved. Davies maintained that he was given only five days' warning that the company had hit the rocks and that, until then, he had been assured that UCS was moving gradually towards profitability. Ken Douglas did not demur, but explained that a variety of things had gone wrong – suppliers were demanding money more quickly; ships were still not being built fast enough. Davies bluntly confided to colleagues that he had no faith in the management.

UCS IN LIQUIDATION screamed the headlines across the front pages of the Scottish newspapers. Even the Conservatives' closest media friend in Scotland, the *Glasgow Herald*, was moved to describe the decision as a tragedy. It ran a front-page editorial which reflected the gravity of the situation facing the west of Scotland: 'The economical and social cost – never mind the political cost – of allowing UCS to go to the wall could be vastly greater than £6 million. And to do so at a time when great strides are being made in the yards would be a cruel blow to the morale of the management and workpeople throughout the region.' This radical departure from the paper's hard-right ideology reflected the depth of feeling in Scotland.

The blow struck hardest in Clydebank, which had suffered grievously in the blitz of 1941. Robert Fleming, its provost, said that the British government was trying to do to his town what the Germans had failed to do in the second world war. It was widely believed that Clydebank's yard – large, old-fashioned and unprofitable – would be the first to go and that its record of craftsmanship as the builder of magnificent liners would soon be consigned to history. Con Higgins, one of the shop stewards, said he had heard that tugs had been ordered to stand by: 'This can only mean that they are ready to take UCS boats out of the yards to be finished elsewhere. It could be the next high tide and must be resisted.' The high tide passed without incident, but such melodramatic rumours were breeding in an atmosphere of fear and mistrust.

Labour's Anthony Wedgwood Benn – who had yet to be reborn as plain Tony Benn – claimed after a meeting of the Clydebank shop stewards that the government had secretly plotted the butchery of UCS for many months; he chose to disregard his own party's unwillingness, during its years in power, to go on bankrolling UCS to the extent that the management believed was necessary for the company's long-term viability. But the next part of his statement was more enlightening; it showed the extent to which the workers' thinking and planning had progressed. Turning to the shop stewards, he said they would be 'absolutely justified' in taking over the yards: 'It is my view that you should not evacuate, you should not go away.' There was no longer any doubt what the unions had in mind. Again, however, the newspapers attached no significance to the clue; it was regarded as an idle boast and reported without comment.

Davies's announcement in the Commons was greeted by 'a gasp of dismay, followed instantly by a surge of bitter abuse from the opposition'. Willie Ross thundered from Labour's front bench that it was 'one of the blackest days in the history of Scottish industry'. The noise in the chamber was so deafening that John Rankin, the Labour MP for Govan, had to ask John Davies to repeat part of the statement. Jo Grimond said that Davies should acknowledge that UCS's 'crisis of liquidity' was down to liabilities taken on at an early stage in the company's short history. When Hugh McCartney, the Labour MP for East Dunbartonshire, estimated that 100,000 human beings were affected by 'this disaster on the Clyde', Davies was stung into a denial: 'There is a grave risk of escalating the problem beyond reason ... I do not anticipate the kind of figures which have been mentioned.'

These words were scarcely dry on Hansard's page before Courtney Smith, the liquidator, delivered a stark evaluation of UCS's prospects: 'I was unaware that this was a company with a total liability of £28 million, assets of doubtful value, and a problematic value of partly completed ships.' Anthony Hepper was not around to hear any of that: he had gone on holiday. Smith remarked dryly: 'He was going anyway.'

The workers were not going on holiday. They were going to London on business, confirming Mary Marquis's opinion that one had to go to London at some point. After more than 400 had travelled through the night, Provost Fleming headed a deputation to see Heath. The Prime Minister gave them an undertaking that shipbuilding on the upper Clyde would continue in some form, but he would not commit to the scale of the redundancies.

Another of the deputation was a Clydebank councillor and shop steward known to the newspapers as James Reid – although it was not long before the formalities were dispensed with and he was generally known as Jimmy. 'I got the impression,' he said, 'that we were talking to men who did not know what it means to stand in the dole queue, or what it will mean to working-class families – and, worse, who don't appear to care.' The other Jimmy – Airlie – added in his usual combative fashion: 'We will mobilise a political movement in Scotland to fight this decision.' Airlie possessed great organisational ability, while Reid's facility for avoiding the stilted dogma of union pronouncements gave a human dimension to the crisis. He had not been visible to the media until the London confrontation with Heath. Suddenly he was. Once in the spotlight he never left it. But although Reid overshadowed Airlie as a public figure, theirs was essentially a partnership of complementary skills.

The newspapers speculated on the choice of scapegoats. Hepper's tactical departure was accurately interpreted as a prelude to resignation. Davies, who had not yet gone on holiday, cut an even less impressive figure, a poor speaker, a far from persuasive defender of his cause, a transparent mediocrity. But events were moving too quickly to allow much time for reflection on personalities, or the woeful absence of them on the government side.

Although the company had 32 contracts on its books and work had not started on 18 of them, the liquidator decided to proceed only with those contracts which would convert quickly into cash. He was right to be sceptical about the value of some of the orders. Sir Iain Stewart accused the board of 'going off round the world to get a very attractive looking order book for business which was profitless'. Smith announced that workers who were not required for the remaining work would be kept on temporary paid leave. The shop stewards replied that, if the men were being paid, they would work for their wages.

After a few weeks of limbo late July brought a sensational Commons statement. Six thousand jobs were going: most UCS workers were to lose their jobs. As part of this nightmarish resolution of the crisis, far worse than many had foreseen, the Clydebank and Scotstoun yards were doomed, and there could be no guarantee of a future for even the remnant of the group. Davies got through the early part of his statement without interruption, but when it dawned that only 2,500 of the huge workforce would be left in work, Norman Buchan broke the stunned silence with the words: 'God Almighty'. The chamber then broke into scenes which one seasoned Westminster commentator described as unprecedented since Suez. Benn was among the first on his feet, noting angrily that Davies had made the announcement without a single word of regret.

Willie Ross was reported to be trembling with fury. The former army major told his fellow MPs that one of the saddest moments of his life had been going through Clydebank in his HLI uniform the day after its bombing by the Germans. 'The blow delivered by the government is even worse than that. They should be ashamed of themselves.'

Later that day the Prime Minister shared with the 1922 committee of Tory back-benchers his perception that 'the problem of Scotland' was the decline of the three basic industries of shipbuilding, coal-mining and agriculture. His frontline minister in the dispute had had enough of the problem of Scotland. John Davies decided to go on holiday – the south of France in his case. In the traditional manner of ministerial vacations he would be 'kept informed of developments'.

Meanwhile the liquidator had embarked on his doomsday strategy, applying to the Court of Session for a winding-up order which would give him the authority to complete only the profitable orders and to make all 7,500 workers redundant; he would then re-employ enough to complete the orders. The *Glasgow Herald* commented: 'The present crash has coincided with the worst underlying rate of unemployment in post-war Scotland. Moreover, in Clydebank, the demise of shipbuilding in the town is a calamity.' Alex Ferry of the Amalgamated Union of Engineering Workers articulated popular sentiment when he said that the government should be 'tried in public for the attempted murder of an industry'.

VI

All the clues to the workers' intentions, heavily dropped over many weeks but comprehensively ignored, suddenly fitted into place. The shop stewards declared that they were taking over the yards and instructed the liquidator to carry out his duties in his own office in central Glasgow and not in the yards. The stewards were adamant: 'These are our yards and our assets. Nobody goes in or out without our permission.' The business was symbolically renamed Upper Clyde Shipbuilders Workers Unlimited.

Jimmy Reid emerged from a 75-minute meeting between the shop stewards and the liquidator. 'We have totally rejected his statements,' he began. 'We have told him we will try to keep him out. There will be no violence, but he can do his business from his business office, not here. Nothing has been accepted. Nothing has been discussed. This is a new era in British history. The stewards will decide what will be built and whether it will go out of the Clyde when it is built – everything.'

Smith declined to comment on the takeover, but when he was asked if he would be going into any of the yards, he said that he would do so if he felt it necessary. Benn, after a tour of the yards, proclaimed the significance of the moment: 'No one should make any mistake about this. This is something which will be recorded when the history of the Labour movement comes to be written.' He called it 'the birth of industrial democracy' and predicted that the power demonstrated by the workers would not be snuffed out. The rhetoric was eye-catching, but Benn was never completely trusted by the shop stewards.

The first test of the workers' resolve was confronted a few hours later when their representatives called a press conference at Linthouse. Smith moved to assert his authority by letting it be known that journalists and TV cameras were forbidden from entering the yard. In their first act of positive defiance the stewards allowed them in anyway. A delegation manned the entrance to each yard and no one was permitted to come or go without the stewards' permission. The work-in had begun, although the phrase itself had still to be coined.

Jimmy Reid, addressing not only the workers but a much larger audience on television, emphasised the positive nature of the action. And then he said: 'There will be no hooliganism, no vandalism. There will be no bevying. Because the world is watching us and it will be up to us to conduct ourselves with responsibility and maturity.' Although the Scottish press was slow to seize on their significance, these few sentences resonated across the world, the meaning of the word 'bevying' having to be explained in many languages. The speech established Reid as a forceful orator and as the face of the campaign, its natural leader. It did not escape the notice of the right-wing press that he was also a member of the Communist Party.

The stewards were asked how the men would survive financially. They replied that shipyard workers, who were used to living from week to week on their wages, were also accustomed to prolonged strikes. The only difference was that, instead of being out on the streets, they would be inside the yards working. The simple audacity of the coup, and the decisiveness of its execution, caught Heath and his colleagues off guard. James McKillop, an industrial correspondent, neatly summarised the state of play after day one: 'The government are faced with an unprecedented dilemma over Upper Clyde Shipbuilders with the takeover of the yards by the workers. They must decide whether to turn a blind eye and hope that the workers will soon tire of their new role or try somehow to return control to the liquidator. The men say they are staying put.'

The *Glasgow Herald* turned on the union leadership: 'There is nothing necessarily wrong with the idea that workers should participate in industrial management [but] workers' control is another matter ... It is not too much to say that in the west of Scotland orthodox union leadership has been very poor. But at least it has nothing to gain from anarchy and industrial dislocation. Can the same be said of the Communist movement among shop stewards? The present occupation smacks too much of Jacobitism, a phenomenon tinged with nostalgia and doomed to defeat.'

The first weekend of the occupation allowed all sides a breathing space to group or regroup for the inevitable conflict. Reid, in his new role as Bonnie Prince Jimmie, used the term 'work-in' for the first time, but in the same interview positioned himself more pragmatically. His earlier talk of a new era in British history had gone. Challenged to say that UCS was the start of a socialist revolution he replied cannily that it was a fight for jobs. 'If this new form of protest opens the way to a new form of socialism,' he added, 'it will be a by-product and not the fundamental objective.'

The shop stewards were displaying a sound instinct for public relations. They invited the newspapers to Scotstoun to see Sammy Barr of the boilermakers arrive for weekend gate-watching duty with his wife and two young sons. The boys, Paul and Samuel, were reported to be fascinated by the shipyard cats. 'There was a time when I would have liked them to follow me into the yards, but not now,' said Barr. 'There just isn't the security.' The government issued a hard-nosed briefing to Scottish political correspondents at Westminster that the 'hostile reaction' to the collapse of UCS was 'dimming hopes that even one of the bankrupt yards can be saved'. But the shop stewards were more than holding their own in the early stages of the propaganda war, and they were winning friends in unexpected places. Robin McLellan, a respected figure in the Scottish business community, was among the first to offer moral support: 'The situation at UCS is the human reaction of men who are hurt, despondent and frightened, and should be viewed with human understanding.' It was an understanding lacking in the Heath government.

On Monday morning, at the start of the first full week of the work-in, the ritual at the gates was unchallenged: visitors entering and leaving were asked to identify themselves; the shop stewards were demonstrably in charge; and there was no attempt by the police to intervene.

A fighting fund was established. One of the first donations came from two children in Aberdeen, John McConnachie, 13, and his sister, Elaine, 10, who sent £2 from the proceeds of a jumble sale. This was followed by a donation of £1,000 from Kathleen Rutherford, a doctor in Harrogate, who had graduated from Glasgow University in 1921 – half a century before these stirring events. 'I trust these men,' she said. 'They are not sitting back doing nothing. They are trying their best. I think they are good lads, and I don't think we should say things are hopeless. It must be depressing to have the whole world against them, and if there was a bit more industrial democracy we might get somewhere.' The stewards said they had been overwhelmed by the initial response to the appeal, with offers of financial help from trade unions in many parts of the world. But Dr Rutherford's cheque, and the touching gesture of the children in Aberdeen, hinted at a more general support. The stewards were astonished a few days later by the arrival at the Clydebank yard of a bouquet of red roses with a message of good wishes, and a donation, from John Lennon and Yoko Ono.

The truculent Edward Heath did what key figures in the UCS crisis tended to do at awkward moments: he went on holiday; a yachting one for him. Reginald Maudling was left in charge of the government, and Gordon Campbell, the ineffectual Secretary of State for Scotland, was rarely seen or heard, in marked contrast to his voluble predecessor, Willie Ross.

Despite the workers' assurances that they were prepared to work without wages and to react with force to any attempt to remove them from the yards, and despite the far from convincing handling of the crisis by the government, there was a great deal of scepticism about the outcome of the work-in. Even journalists close to the union leadership agreed with the *Glasgow Herald*'s judgement that the experiment was doomed; one wrote that more people knew it was a lost cause than were prepared to admit it. Yet productivity at the yards remained high, the disciplined workforce did nothing to erode public trust, the donations continued to flood in.

On 18 August 50,000 demonstrators were warmly received by the people of Glasgow as they marched through the streets in support of the UCS workers. They linked arms in solidarity, waving to the office workers who watched and applauded from windows along the route. As they approached Glasgow Green the marchers were singing a new version of an old favourite: 'John Brown's shipyard [Clydebank] is rising from the grave'. But when the platform party for the mass rally was made aware of the front-page of the *Evening Times*, high spirits were dampened by the headline 'Lord Provost attacks UCS demo'. Donald Liddle had criticised the decision to stage the march on a working day, describing the loss of productivity as 'not clever'. Jimmy Airlie was visibly angry. On the same day the liquidator did his best to spoil the party by posting the first 167 redundancies. But the enormous show of support from all over Britain was a clear sign to the government that it had underestimated the strength of public feeling.

Potential buyers for the yards came and went without encouragement and by the early autumn the leaders of the work-in were struggling to sustain momentum and to give the media the fresh angles they demanded. The story disappeared from the front pages for a while, as other events took precedence.

VII

Boxer Ken Buchanan returned to Edinburgh, cheered by a crowd of 100,000 in his native city after a points victory in New York made him lightweight champion of the world. Harry Ewing, a Leven postman, held Stirling and Falkirk in a by-election, but the SNP, bouncing back from its humiliation in the 1970 general election, took 35% of the vote. Two boys aged 15 and 16 were found guilty of murdering a 42-year-old man in Inverness. Four other youths, one of whom said he had been on a LSD trip, stood by as the man was savagely kicked and left to die in the early hours of a Sunday morning. Lord Cameron suggested to William Smith, the provost of Inverness, that he 'may have been struck by the insensitive and callous character of some Crown witnesses who were content to watch' and by the availability of dangerous drugs on the streets of his town.

But the most significant news of autumn 1971 was the announcement by BP that it had discovered in the North Sea one of the world's biggest oilfields. By 1976 the Forties field would be producing a third of Britain's oil consumption, and the company was on the verge of investing up to £100m to bring it ashore. The plan would involve the building of a 110-mile underground pipeline from the oilfield to a site near Cruden Bay and a second pipeline 140 miles in length from there to the BP refinery at Grangemouth; the building of two production platforms; and the creation of an island terminal in the Firth of Forth to accommodate tankers of up to 200,000 tons. The scale of the discovery and its potential benefits to an ailing Scottish economy were without parallel, yet the media at first evinced little interest in the project. Did it simply sound too good to be true?

But perhaps the rekindling of the UCS saga was more immediately compelling. From the ashes of UCS the government established Govan Shipbuilders Ltd, appointed as its chairman Hugh Stenhouse, a millionaire industrialist and former treasurer of the Scottish Conservative Party, and declared that the new company would employ 2,500 people at no more than two yards. Neither side had budged in any meaningful way; the shop stewards continued to insist that all four yards must be protected. The non-negotiability of this core demand provoked Sir John Eden, a junior minister for industry, into a warning that the government was losing patience with the workers – which erroneously presupposed that the government had had much patience with them in the first place.

The shop stewards reacted angrily to the government's initiative. Jimmy Reid labelled Stenhouse a quisling and ridiculed the board's lack of shipbuilding knowledge. He was prepared to acknowledge that Archie Gilchrist, the chief executive, had some experience of the industry, 'though minimal'. Jimmy Airlie gave notice that the directors would have to clamber over the men guarding the entrance to the yards.

Some of this hostility was swiftly defused by Stenhouse's unexpected success in persuading Ken Douglas, managing director of UCS, who was respected by the shop stewards, to stay on as deputy chairman of the new company. In an extraordinary turn of events, they came to respect even the quisling. Within a few days the chairman achieved a transformation in attitudes. After a meeting of unexpected cordiality described in the press as 'back-slapping', the shop stewards greeted the media with the news that Stenhouse, previously barred, would now be welcome in the yards.

The stewards believed that in Stenhouse they had found a man with whom they could do business. Jimmy Reid responded to Davies's repetition of the familiar prognosis (Clydebank could not be saved) with a statement revealing the basis of the new-found trust: 'Mr Stenhouse has indicated to us his preparedness to consider taking over all four units on the upper reaches. There had to be workers' support and government assistance. Well, he's got the cooperation of the workers.' Impressed by this concord the *Glasgow Herald* decided that it was not a doomed Jacobite enterprise after all: 'No one can deny the determination of the shop stewards' fight and the influence they now hold in the yards.' The government had again been outwitted.

A wounded Davies returned to the attack with a warning that the embryo company was on the verge of collapse because of the shop stewards' intransigence; Jimmy Reid, sensing a minister on the run, brushed this off as blackmail. Finally, on 11 October, four months to the day since the UCS crisis began, an agreement was reached allowing Govan Shipbuilders to become operational within a fortnight. The agreement respected the integrity of the work-in, which would continue until the shop stewards were satisfied that all four divisions were safe.

Six weeks later, with no final solution in sight, Hugh Stenhouse was killed in a car accident in Leicestershire at the age of 56. It was a cruel setback as well as a personal tragedy. Of his native Scotland, to which he was passionately devoted, he had once said: 'I am fed up with everyone saying we are living on charity. I am also fed up with everyone saying we are finished.' In the final weeks of his life he did his finest work as a skilful and humane negotiator in a conflict which had seemed beyond reconciliation. It was one of the many ironies of the UCS drama that he did not live to see that work completed.

VIII

The year came to a dark end with Stenhouse's death and Jimmy Reid in hospital suffering from exhaustion. Although the work-in had survived far longer than anyone had believed possible, the men of the Upper Clyde would enter 1972 with their future still undetermined; serious discussions between the shop stewards and the management had been suspended and there was the looming threat of a showdown with the government. But an unexpected development was reported in the Hogmanay edition of the *Evening Times*: Dan McGarvey, president of the Confederation of Shipbuilding and Engineering Unions, was flying to Texas in the first days of the new year for talks with a company which seemed to be interested in building ships at Clydebank.

1972

ALIENATION

I

Fate decreed a fortuitous conjunction of events. On the day that Heath's government and the Marathon Manufacturing Company of Texas agreed terms for the takeover of UCS's Clydebank yard – 28 April 1972 – Jimmy Reid delivered his rectorial address at Glasgow University.

He had been elected to the post in October 1971, receiving 1,458 votes, well ahead of his two rivals, Teddy Taylor and Peggy Herbison. Martin Caldwell, the student president, greeted the result as 'a victory for the ordinary people of Clydeside against paternalism, academic snobbery, and the present government ... it shows that the students are concerned about the people of Clydeside and their plight'. The *Glasgow Herald*, displaying all the zeal of a convert, was effusive about his election: 'Since the UCS crisis began, Jimmy Reid's shock of hair with generous sideburns and his singular face has become as widely known throughout Scotland as any top entertainer ... His repertoire of oratory knows no bounds.'

Jimmy Reid was born into the depression of the 1930s in Glasgow, a city with the highest infant mortality rate in the western world. Of his six siblings three died within 18 months. He recalled: 'My mother told me that one of the kids died over Hogmanay. My father had the dying kid in his arms, praying to God, while all around people were singing *Auld Lang Syne*.' The boy sensed from an early age that there was something profoundly wrong with society; many years later he spoke with intense feeling about his lost sisters. He said that, whatever it said on the death certificate, they had been murdered by social conditions – what he preferred to call the capitalist system. Having 'imbibed the socialist creed with my mother's milk', he did not have to think hard about which side he was on politically. But his beliefs were not purely instinctive; they were supported by serious study. From the age of 12 he was reading Marx – 'Karl, not Groucho'.

Deprived of books at home, he was a regular visitor to Elderpark public library, which he claimed was where he received his education. But he was so keen to acquire his own copy of Tom Johnston's *History of the Working Class* that he borrowed money from an older sibling to buy it. He attended debates in Govan at the Iona Community, listening with admiration to its radical leader, George MacLeod, although Reid remained an atheist to the end ('a genial one, not one of your hard-nut atheists', he would add). He became chancellor of the exchequer in MacLeod's youth parliament and, a quarter of a century later, it was MacLeod he succeeded as rector of Glasgow University. He was not quite 40.

His rectorial address in Bute Hall was free of the rowdy noises-off synonymous with such occasions. Apart from a vain attempt by a pink pantomime horse to enter the hall, there were no disturbances. Reid spoke for 30 minutes interrupted only by bursts of applause. When he sat down he received a standing ovation.

Clearly Glasgow had heard something exceptional, but there was no immediate signal from the local press that Reid had just delivered one of the outstanding speeches of the 20th century. The address merited 57 lines in the *Evening Times* under the heading: 'I have a dream by Rector Jim Reid'. No one called him Jim. On the same page the paper gave greater prominence to a proposal by William S Gray, the city treasurer, that Glasgow Corporation should invest in local radio and to a bus crash which uprooted a tree in Mosspark Drive. (The bus driver was unhurt.)

By the following morning the rhetorical power of the address was being widely acknowledged. The *Glasgow Herald* devoted a generous editorial to its new hero: 'It was from the chaos of the UCS collapse that James Reid emerged as a public figure. This newspaper condemned the work-in he promoted, but what could have become an anarchical situation was wielded with discipline and order mainly by his responsible leadership. Reid is a Scot who, in this milk and water age, is something of a throwback to the bonny fechters of the past, representing the true spirit of the Scottish working man. Deprived of the higher education that his intelligence justified, he nevertheless gave Glasgow University and Scotland an address which few great academics or theologians would excel. It was a profound analysis of the human predicament today.'

Choosing alienation as his theme, Reid explained what he

meant by the word: 'It is the cry of men who feel themselves the victims of blind economic forces beyond their control. It is the frustration of ordinary people excluded from the processes of decision-making.' He described how alienation expressed itself in anti-social behaviour and in a desire by young people to opt out of conventional society through drink and drugs. He examined too, in a torrent of blistering images, the unappealing alternative – 'the scurrying around scrambling for position, trampling on others, back-stabbing, all in pursuit of success'.

He appealed to the students directly:

Reject these attitudes. Reject the values and false morality that underlie these attitudes. A rat race is for rats. We're not rats. We're human beings. Reject the insidious pressures in society that would blunt your critical faculties to all that is happening around you, that would caution silence in the face of injustice lest you jeopardise your chances of promotion and self-advancement. This is how it starts and before you know where you are, you're a fully paid-up member of the rat-pack. The price is too high. It entails the loss of your dignity and human spirit.

Jimmy Reid had not forgotten those debates at the Iona Community or the social gospel preached by his predecessor as rector. The atheist and New Testament student went on to quote Christ: 'What does it profit a man if he gain the whole world and suffer the loss of his soul?'

'A rat race is for rats' became the most celebrated phrase of the rectorial address; it was still being widely quoted when he died 38 years later. Less often quoted was this piece of social criticism wrapped in metaphor:

Everything that is proposed from the establishment seems almost calculated to minimise the role of people, to miniaturise man. I can understand how attractive this prospect must be to those at the top. Those of us who refuse to be pawns in their power game can be picked up by their bureaucratic tweezers and dropped in a filing cabinet under 'M' for malcontent or maladjusted. When you think of some of the high flats around us it can hardly be an accident that they are as near as one could get to an architectural representation of a filing cabinet.

The newspapers were full of letters about the speech, most in praise. James Currie, a Church of Scotland minister serving a Glasgow working-class parish, wrote that Reid had delivered a rebuke to many professed Christians who, by their silence or submission, had condoned the evils of society. Some correspondents wondered, however, why the rector had avoided any mention of the iniquities of the Communist Party, which he represented as a councillor in Clydebank. Reid did eventually renounce the party, joining Labour, before a further defection late in life to the Scottish National Party, and was sometimes written down as a political chameleon.

He attracted further criticism for his second career as a journalist and broadcaster, which included a spell as a columnist with Rupert Murdoch's shrill right-wing tabloid, *The Sun*. He insisted that he had the freedom to write as he pleased and it is true that he never wavered in his commitment to socialist principles. He died a working-class hero.

Jimmy Reid should have received an honorary doctorate from Glasgow University and the possibility of awarding him one was belatedly being discussed not long before his death in 2010 at the age of 78. When his family asked about the possibility of a posthumous honour, they were informed that it was not the policy of the university to make posthumous awards, an illustration of institutional Scotland at its most inflexible. He was a man of humanitarian achievement, oratorical brilliance and personal warmth, one of the few compelling personalities in Scottish post-war life.

II

As the world reflected on the Glasgow rectorial address, which was reprinted in full by the *New York Times*, the pgymies of Scottish political life sounded shabbier than ever.

Gordon Campbell was audacious enough to let his government take the credit for 'efforts to reconstruct the basis of shipbuilding on the Upper Clyde' when the whole country knew that the impetus for saving the Clydebank yard had come from the workers and that the Heath government had repeatedly maintained that it had no future. Jimmy Airlie gave a measured response to the news that Marathon was taking over the yard to produce off-shore drilling platforms and ships for oil exploration. 'We have got the retention of the four yards which we were after,' he said simply. Later in the year the work-in came to an end after 16 months, its founders vindicated by its impeccable conduct and successful outcome.

But Edward Heath was graceless to the end. In an interview with the political correspondent John Warden a few days after Jimmy Reid's rectorial address, he said: 'My own belief is that the imposition of a work-in in any yard or factory damages the image of good industrial relations so necessary to Scotland and only makes it harder to persuade industrialists to invest in the area. I am glad that despite these difficulties we have been successful in our attempts to save shipbuilding on the Clyde.' Warden failed to challenge this re-writing of recent history; nor did he ask the Prime Minister to explain why, given the damage done to industrial relations, an American company had just decided to invest in the upper Clyde.

The UCS crisis accelerated the ebbing of Conservative support from the high tide of 1955 when the party held a majority of the Scottish seats. Through the events of 1971-72 there was a loss of trust and credibility from which the party north of the border never recovered.

III

The students of Scotland's newest university, Stirling, a manifestion of the explosion in higher education, had learned nothing from the workers of the upper Clyde about the importance of self-discipline in the pursuit of a cause. They were not fighting for their livelihoods or for the future of their communities. They were campaigning in a self-interested way for nothing more glorious than higher student grants, and they had forgotten the first rule of the crusade: no bevying.

When the Queen emerged from a tour of Murray Hall, a student residence, she found herself in the thick of a protest directed mainly against a heavy-handed police presence. The bars of the university had been open all morning, and many of the protesters were drunk. One mature student was photographed drinking from a bottle of wine in front of the monarch. He claimed that all he said to her was 'slàinte mhath' (Gaelic for good health) and that he meant her no harm. Nevertheless he became a national symbol of undergraduate anarchy, receiving threats in the post so serious that his wife and two children left home for their own safety.

The student activists were left with few friends after an incident which attracted international media coverage. Sir William McEwan Younger, chairman of the Conservative Party in Scotland, a brewer to trade, said the protesters had done 'incalculable damage to Scotland's image abroad'. William Baxter, the local Labour MP, deplored 'the law of the lout', adding that young men and women had not been taught the basic rudiments of good manners. He blamed the university authorities for the easy availability of alcohol. His colleague Tam Dalyell said that the actions of a small number had made it harder to argue for the unpopular cause of higher student grants.

For a few days some shopkeepers in Bridge of Allan, the small town close to the campus, refused to serve students. The newspapers were hostile, the *Evening Times* noting that the Queen had been in danger of being manhandled. The paper commented: 'Many of the public would like to protest too – about the cash being spent on privilege, the privilege of people who are allowed to absent themselves from earning a living for three or four years, who study in modern, comfortable universities, and accept grants as a matter of right – then show themselves to be totally unfitted to be in positions of such privilege.'

Ronald Don, a fourth-year student, put the protest in a more realistic perspective: 'About 50 militants led about 400 little sheep to the slaughter.' A diplomatic response from the authorities would have gone a long way. Instead the university over-reacted, announcing that 15 members of the students' association, including its president Linda Quinn, as well as nine other students, would face internal disciplinary charges. This extreme action provoked a mass demonstration on the campus by 3,000 students, including many from other UK universities. They reserved most of their abuse for Tom Cottrell, Stirling's first principal and effectively its creator, who at the time of his appointment at the age of 42 was one of the youngest men to have held such a senior appointment in British academia.

The innovating Cottrell, a research chemist, had introduced new subjects and new ways of teaching them, and had a personal role in the design of a campus more aesthetically pleasing than most. His semester system – two terms instead of the traditional three – was designed to encourage study in depth. But these achievements were forgotten in the face of the student revolt. 'Cottrell out' they chanted. 'Support the 24'. One of the platform speakers saw the rally in terms of 1970s' agitprop as 'a mobilisation force in preparation for war, if war comes'. Brian Gill, a young advocate (and future Lord Justice General), was hired to defend the 24, reduced to 23 when one of the students, Jack Carter, was killed in a car accident.

The first to face a disciplinary hearing, 19-year-old Martin Beever, was found guilty of unauthorised entry to a reception in honour of the Queen and reprimanded. His solicitor complained that every defence objection was over-ruled, every prosecution objection upheld, and that the defence was not allowed to call all its witnesses. It was impossible to judge the fairness of these criticisms since Cottrell, in the first of several bad moves, had decided to hold the proceedings in private.

The principal compounded this folly by instructing the warden of Murray Hall to compile 'a personality profile' of troublesome students with a view to introducing a stricter selection process for admission to halls of residence. William Kidd, the warden, eagerly backed this divisive scheme, claiming that 'a small, but not negligible' number of students had 'little interest in the civilised functioning of the university community'. Cottrell accused the student leaders of being opposed to the policies of the university and opposed to society in general. This confrontational stance was unhelpful, particularly as the 'trials' of these same student leaders were continuing.

Catherine Gillie, a second-year history and sociology student, who was alleged to have worn a paper crown during the Queen's visit, was fined £10 for conducting herself in a drunken and disorderly manner, while Linda Quinn was suspended for four months for taking part in meetings 'at which ways to disrupt the Queen's visit were discussed'. But Jackie McKie, proposer of the Gaelic toast, was acquitted of 'an act abusive and discourteous to the Queen' after the committee decided that his intentions were not malign. William Macfarlane Gray, a former provost of Stirling, resigned from the university court in protest at the leniency shown to McKie. The verdicts were riddled with inconsistencies and there was a widespread belief that the students who had been charged were not the main culprits.

As the hearings dragged on into the new year, staff morale plummeted and Cottrell was openly attacked by members of his own staff. Ian Macfarlane, a psychology lecturer, suggested that his vetting plans for admission to the halls would create a race of young conformists, while Max Marwick, the head of the sociology department, followed Gray out of the university court though for different reasons. 'The hearings are achieving nothing but the destruction of student relations and the needless dislocation of academic work,' he said. Twelve lecturers called for the abandonment of the disciplinary proceedings, expressing their dismay over the harsh treatment of Linda Quinn and the explicit threat to the rights of assembly, free speech and peaceful protest.

By March 1973 the university was disastrously split. Students occupied the main administrative building in several days of protest and almost half the teaching staff supported their call for an inquiry. The principal refused to meet any of their demands, which he said ranged from 'the absurd to the possible' and also refused to address the students who were blockading the building. Yet Cottrell was not some drab, grey-suited bureaucrat. He disdained the conventional, sporting a lurid orange tie and driving a fast sports car. He had promised, when he became principal, that the new university would be 'there for the students, not the other way round'. But he proved incapable of handling the protests. He was out of his depth.

His friend Alastair Hetherington believed that the troubles tormented Cottrell. 'In retrospect,' Hetherington wrote, 'what happened that day [of the Queen's visit] may come to seem insignificant, but it did not seem so to many people outside the university at the time. It gravely harmed what he had worked for … it was too much for him.' A fellow principal, Edinburgh's Michael Swann, said that only those closest to Cottrell knew how much he had been hurt by the intense criticism of his leadership. In June 1973 Tom Cottrell died at his home on the campus at the age of 49.

IV

While students had to work at alienating the wider community, to many football supporters it came naturally. Within 18 months of the Ibrox disaster, the fans of Rangers Football Club travelled to Barcelona to see their team play Moscow Dynamo in the final of the 1972 European Cup-Winners Cup. Rangers won 3-2. The second the final whistle blew, hordes of ecstatic supporters, fuelled by drink, invaded the pitch. Ninety-seven Scots were arrested and

33 Spanish policemen were injured. The Spanish government complained formally to the British Embassy about the behaviour of Scottish spectators and about the perceived anti-Spanish bias of the BBC's coverage of the riots.

The excuses were all too familiar. John Lawrence, the club chairman, whose lapses of memory had been such a deplorable feature of the 1971 fatal accident inquiry, told the chief constable of Barcelona (through an interpreter) that the 'unfortunate circumstances' arose when, two minutes before full-time, the referee gave a foul and went to pick up the ball. 'Our people thought this was the finish of the game and ran on to the field,' he explained. Willie Waddell, the churlish manager, refused to accept any responsibility for the supporters' conduct and the fans themselves were unrepentant, blaming the police for violent over-reaction. 'I saw them lashing out with their batons at anyone within range – men, women and children,' said one. 'Bottles and cans were thrown at the police, but only after they started splitting people's heads.' Another claimed that while a man lay on the ground, having been struck down by batons, policemen continued to attack him.

Although the disturbances on the pitch were the focal point for most of the bad publicity, it was the trouble in the city before the match that soured the mood and alienated the police. Charles Gillies, a Glasgow journalist, said that in many years of covering events of all kinds he had never seen worse behaviour than that of Rangers supporters in Barcelona. In his hotel on the eve of the match, guests had been lucky to get more than three hours' sleep because of boisterous singing and shouting. 'I had occasion,' he wrote, 'to seek help to eject four drunk supporters who fell into my bedroom while fighting among themselves in the corridor, in which they had urinated.'

Some of the worst scenes took place at Barcelona Airport late on the evening of the game as supporters waited for chartered flights back to Prestwick. The pilots were reluctant to fly because of the danger to crews; the police were equally adamant that the Rangers fans would not be allowed to stay in Spain. The police finally prevailed. One of the flights was cancelled because more than half the passengers were incapably drunk, but the others took off. 'The result for the sober majority,' reported one journalist, 'was a flight more in keeping with a nightmare.'

Back in Glasgow there was little sympathy for the fans. Lord

Provost John Mains sent his counterpart in Barcelona an abject apology, assuring him that the behaviour of the Rangers supporters was 'not typical of the sport-loving football public of Glasgow and Scotland'. The newspapers pointed out that every harmful stereotype of Glasgow had been reinforced, not only south of the border but now on the continent too. The city had recently appointed a public relations officer – one of the first in the new breed of official propagandists – and it was reckoned that Harry Dutch, a former journalist, would have to work hard to restore the city's reputation.

The damage to that precious flower, 'the good name of Glasgow', mattered not a jot to the supporters. Still intoxicated by victory in Europe they gave their team a rapturous reception when they arrived home. At the end of a touring holiday in Scotland John Orr, a visitor from Carlisle, decided to join the huge crowd at Ibrox Stadium for the parade of the trophy. He was so dismayed by the experience that he wrote to the press: 'The evening was spoiled by the bands striking up anti-Catholic airs. These were eagerly bellowed forth by the majority of the spectators who apparently did not know any better; but what left a sour note was the manner in which the players enthusiastically supported the "choir" … Why did Rangers Football Club allow such hymns of hate on such an important occasion?'

Coincidentally, a few days later the General Assembly of the Church of Scotland called for the abolition of segregated schooling. While the majority of children attended non-denominational schools sometimes erroneously called Protestant, Roman Catholic pupils were (and continue to be) educated in their own schools. One of the minority who opposed integration was George Reid, a future Moderator. He acknowledged 'a kind of nastiness in Glasgow between Catholics and Protestants' but added: 'Whether it is because of segregation in schools or the rivalry between Rangers and Celtic is a deeply debatable question.' It was also destined to remain a theoretical one, since the possibility of the RC hierarchy in Scotland agreeing to integrated education was as remote as the Pope ceasing to be a Catholic.

V

In Edinburgh the week of the General Assembly was one of the busiest of the year at 17 Danube Street, home of Dora Noyce, the most notorious brothel-keeper in Scotland. At the age of 72 she was nearing the end of her long career. When she appeared in Edinburgh Sheriff Court in May 1972 shortly after the Kirk's annual meeting, she recorded her 26th conviction in an association with the criminal law dating back to 1934.

A visitor to the premises, who claimed that he had not availed himself of the service, remembered it as a scruffy establishment with a large television set in the living room. Madam served dry white wine while her girls sat around on sofas waiting to be called. Noyce had 15 prostitutes in residence, but was able to draw on 25 temps as the need arose. The need did arise on such occasions as the docking of an American warship at Leith, when hundreds of sex-deprived sailors hastened to Danube Street, forming a long queue outside her door, an unusual sight in the otherwise respectable Georgian New Town. But for most of the year Noyce depended on her regular trade. In May she could count on the support of the fathers and brethren. In August and September she earned enough during the Edinburgh Festival to see her through the leaner winter months.

Noyce was a staunch Conservative and displayed posters for the party in her windows at election time. She abhorred the term brothel, thinking of herself as the provider of a social service and of her house as 'the YMCA with extras'. Ever the entrepreneur, she seldom missed an opportunity to promote the product. When the police came on a raid she would open the door with the familiar greeting: 'Business or pleasure, gentlemen?' She implored journalists, who were the sort of people who got their facts wrong, to print her correct address, adding that in her line there was no such thing as bad publicity. In 1972 she was sent to prison for six months, serving four. It was her last conviction. Dora Noyce died five years later and was discreetly missed by her many admirers. Her departure created a gap in the market.

Another New Town favourite – although there is no suggestion that he and Dora Noyce ever met, professionally or otherwise – was Sir Compton Mackenzie, prolific novelist and ardent supporter of the nationalist cause. The SNP's Robert McIntyre flattered him with the title 'The Grand Old Man of Scotland'. Mackenzie claimed to be descended from an Episcopal vicar of Cromarty, but he himself was born in West Hartlepool, the son of an actor with the surname Compton. These facts of genealogy were overlooked in the service of the Grand Old Man of Scotland myth.

Mackenzie, who held court in his house in Drummond Place, was a genial host with a gift for mimicry, although some found his fund of self-aggrandising anecdotes tiresome. He died in 1972 a few hours after he was interviewed by Mary Marquis for her BBC series, *First Person Singular*. David Martin, the producer, said he was devastated by the news since Mackenzie had appeared to be in excellent spirits. But his death at the age of 89 was observed in the same theatrical manner as his life. As his biographer noted, he 'created around him a stage on which he could represent himself'. The thought of expiring in the arms of the lovely Mary Marquis would have delighted him. He almost succeeded.

Mackenzie would have been the first to applaud the fictional qualities of his funeral on Barra, where he lived for 10 years and which provided the inspiration for his whimsical comic novel, *Whisky Galore*. The aircraft bringing his body to the island was 40 minutes late because of poor weather and had difficulty landing in wind and driving rain. The piper for the occasion, Mackenzie's old friend, Calum Johnston, gamely walked out to the airstrip (part of the beach) and played a lament as the coffin was carried from the plane. The mourners then made their way to Eoligarry cemetery for the service. Johnston, at the age of 82, marched with his pipes up a steep hill to the burial ground, a distance of around 200 yards, where Father Angus MacQueen, the Roman Catholic priest of Castlebay, conducted a brief service. As soon as it was over Johnston collapsed. He was carried back to his house, where he died.

A third adornment of the Edinburgh scene, Sir Duncan Weatherstone, outraged the douce burghers – never too arduous a task – during his term as Lord Provost by asking the Beatles for £100,000 to help the Edinburgh Festival. When they replied with a suggestion that he should pawn the Lord Provost's chain instead, 3,000 ratepayers signed a petition objecting to his 'begging' and demanding a public apology. Revelling in his reputation for extrovert gestures he once presided over a civic dinner in honour of Russian academicians none of whom could speak English. Weatherstone cut short his speech and burst into song with a rendition of *My Bonny Lies Over the Ocean*, claiming that it was the only tune he knew. He campaigned unsuccessfully for the demolition of Waverley railway station; he wanted the bus station in St Andrew Square removed too; he demanded roads everywhere. Some found him endearing.

In 1966 there were two important events in Weatherstone's life: his eventful reign as Lord Provost came to an end and his wife died. Two years later, at the age of 70, he re-married Elizabeth Evans, a 29-year-old hospital secretary. He dismissed the difference in their ages: 'The best basis for a marriage is mutual understanding and respect – and that presents us with no difficulty.' Evans described her husband as 'understanding, humorous and a wonderful companion'. She might have added to this list of attributes a reckless generosity. Keen to impress his young wife, Weatherstone began spending beyond his modest means as a retired insurance manager. Edinburgh was scandalised when Beatrice Kay, a dress shop in George Street, raised an action against him for a debt of £1,400.

A warrant was granted in the Sheriff Court for the sale of household furniture, jewellery and furs and a date for the auction was advertised in the press. Weatherstone pretended that it was the result of a misunderstanding and that the debt would be paid. It wasn't. On the morning of the sale in January 1972 three sheriff's officers, an auctioneer, and 20 members of the public gathered in the doorway of the couple's flat in Buckingham Terrace, in the west end. The sheriff's officers knocked on the door. When they got no response they broke a pane of glass and went in. Seconds later one of them addressed the crowd through a gap in the door: 'I think there has been a tragedy. The sale will not go on. Is there a doctor here?' Rather than face public humiliation in a city where appearances counted for so much – the capital once crudely stereotyped as 'all fur coats and no knickers' – the Weatherstones had taken their own lives.

VI

A fourth Edinburgh celebrity, Wendy Wood, began another of her fasts unto death in December 1972 in protest at the government's tardiness in fulfilling its promise to set up a Scottish assembly or convention. She stopped eating at 11.45pm one night after Gordon Campbell refused to meet her or to give a firm date for a Green Paper on the subject. Campbell, when he was informed of her fast, said only that it did not seem a very sensible thing to do. He added that the government would carry out the Wheatley reforms of local government before putting forward its plans for devolution.

In the face of this rejection Wood drank a little water to sustain herself. Winnie Ewing and William Wolfe called at her house, urging her to take milk or fruit juice every day in order to give Campbell more time to see sense. She refused.

A leader in *The Scotsman* which bore the mark of its deputy editor Arnold Kemp expressed sympathy for Wood: 'Many will share her sense of impatience and frustration. The tempo is decidedly *andante* ... But she must not rob us of her presence with a gesture that is almost certain to be futile.' On the sixth day Gwynfor Evans, president of Plaid Cymru, sent a telegram to the octogenarian hunger striker assuring her that the Welsh people were greatly moved by her 'heroic self-sacrifice for the Scottish cause'. Wood replied that she was now 'past being hungry'.

The blackmail worked. Campbell, in an unexpected *volte face*, announced in the Commons that he was concerned about Wood's health and gave an undertaking that the government's proposals for a Scottish assembly would be introduced 'during the life of the present parliament'. Jim Sillars, the Labour MP for South Ayrshire, made a personal appeal on television, begging her to start eating. After the broadcast she took a quarter of a cupful of milk. The fast had lasted 138 hours 45 minutes.

Wendy Wood lived for another nine years and died a Scottish heroine, a dotty and by many accounts personally disagreeable one, but a heroine nonetheless. Many years later, however, there were rumours that she had not been all she seemed. The SNP's Robert McIntyre, shortly before his death in 1998, told how Wood had once left a suitcase in a student flat in Edinburgh and asked Calum Maclean (brother of the poet Sorley) to look after it for her. Maclean was horrified to discover that it contained gelignite and contacted McIntyre, who arranged for it to be dumped in the Firth of Forth. The police promptly raided the flat. Had Maclean been compromised by Wood?

In a second allegation reported by Arnold Kemp in *The Observer* in 1998, the widow of Arthur Donaldson, the SNP leader briefly imprisoned during the second world war on suspicion of being a

German spy, claimed that Wood had framed her husband and that she was a British government agent. A paranoid fancy? There is no evidence to support the theory, and it is hard to square the allegation with her extreme devotion to Scottish independence. But if Compton Mackenzie was not The Grand Old Man of Scotland, neither was Wendy Wood The Grand Old Woman. With Dora Noyce at least you knew where you were.

1973

NORMAL BEHAVIOUR

I

On 1 January 1973 Britain joined the European Economic Community. Gordon Campbell saw it as 'the beginning of a great enterprise, the restoration and strengthening of Scotland's ties with Europe – not only that well-known link with France but also with the nations of northern Europe'. George Thomson, the Scottish-born UK commissioner to the EEC, called it 'a historic new year' offering Scotland the opportunity to attract modern science-based industries, while journalists went on ward alert for the arrival of the first 'new European'. A son for Ian and Carol Portland was born in Paisley Maternity Hospital 60 seconds after Britain's entry, 'enthusiastically yelling' as befitted a child of the new Europe. He was named David and the newspapers faithfully recorded that he weighed 3.74 kilogrammes. But the press's fascination with metric was short-lived, as was its enthusiasm for the EEC in general. Soon babies of 3.74 kilogrammes had reverted to being babies of 8lb 2oz.

As David Portland came into the world another David – the comedian Dave Willis – left it at the age of 78. The obituaries lauded him as one of the funniest comedians Scotland had ever produced, but Willis had a wretched time after his retirement from the boards when he was still in his mid-fifties. He bought a hotel in Rothesay, confident that it would support him into a comfortable old age. It was a ruinous venture and he died broke.

Between the departure of a popular entertainer and the fabricated delirium over Europe, a third new year event was in danger of being overlooked. George Pottinger, who had been tipped as a future head of the civil service in Scotland, was suspended over allegations of corruption. Although 'Gorgeous George', so nicknamed because of his impeccable taste in clothes, would not have recognised any personal connection with a broken-down music

455

hall comic, he and Dave Willis had this much in common: they both lived to regret having anything to do with Scottish tourism.

II

Later in January the first public disclosure of Pottinger's folly emerged at bankruptcy proceedings in Yorkshire against his erstwhile friend John Poulson. Ten years earlier Pottinger had been seconded from the Scottish Office to help Sir Hugh Fraser (as he then was) to fulfil his vision of a major tourist development at Aviemore. It was on Pottinger's recommendation that Poulson won the contract to design the complex. That was the civil servant's first poor decision. Everything else in his fall from grace flowed from it.

A decade later, with his architectural practice in ruins, Poulson appeared before his examiners with a command of memory which would have done credit to the board of Rangers Football Club. Could he remember paying the mortgage instalments on George Pottinger's splendid new house, The Pelicans, overlooking Muirfield golf course? No, he couldn't. Could he remember receiving a letter from the building society, of which he was a board member, informing him that Pottinger's instalments were in arrears? No, he couldn't. Could he remember the general manager of the society warning him that they might have to get tough with Pottinger? This too seemed to be news to Poulson.

Muir Hunter, QC, representing the trustees in bankruptcy, reminded Poulson that, when Pottinger took out the mortgage, he assumed a liability to pay £163 a month, four times the rent he had been paying on his previous house. Could Pottinger afford to service such a debt? 'I do not know anything of Mr Pottinger's financial affairs,' Poulson replied, 'you are talking about things I know nothing about.' Hunter, rebuking Poulson for 'a foolish answer', produced a letter from Pottinger to Poulson dated 1 April 1967 in which Pottinger admitted that he could not afford the mortgage repayments. Surprise surprise, Poulson denied any knowledge of the letter.

Hunter challenged Poulson: 'The only possible inference is that you undertook to provide for Mr Pottinger the purchase price of the land, the whole of the construction cost, the whole of the architects' fees, and the whole of the mortgage instalments and that Mr Pottinger did not pay a penny of his own.' Poulson replied lamely: 'That is not correct.'

The architect also had to be prodded hard about the gift of a gold cigarette lighter to Pottinger's wife, May. Memory again failed him. Lighter? What lighter? Only when incriminating letters were read out did he admit that he had given Mrs Pottinger a gift of that sort after she had lost her own lighter on a cruise – a holiday that the Poulsons and Pottingers had taken together. In a moment of unintentional hilarity he added that he didn't think it was gold.

Back in Edinburgh the suspended permanent secretary of the Department of Agriculture and Fisheries issued a statement deploring a procedure 'under which allegations could be made with no warnings or opportunity for reply in court'. George Pottinger, despite the embarrassing revelations in Wakefield, continued to enjoy the fraternity of the all-male Honourable Company of Edinburgh Golfers, the embodiment of the Scottish establishment, who played and socialised at Muirfield, evidently never pausing between shots to marvel at the opulent lifestyle of one of their own members, a moderately remunerated public servant.

The case briefly disappeared from view. As soon as it did another establishment scandal took its place, confirming that scandals were like buses: after a long wait two often turned up at the same time.

III

One evening a week before Christmas 1972 two teenage girls were walking home in the dark in the Ayrshire coastal town of Prestwick when they were approached by someone they described as 'a polite man', who had stepped out of a car. His first words were 'Excuse me'. He then asked for directions to Troon. He told the girls that he lived in Edinburgh but was staying in a hotel in Troon for a few days.

His next words changed the character of what had seemed a routine encounter: he asked the girls to help him with judo practice. 'Right here?' asked one of the astonished girls. The man said: 'No, if we could get into the car and go somewhere quiet.' He offered them £1 each if they would walk on him, jump on him and kick him, all ostensibly to win a bet with a woman at Edinburgh University. The girls refused the money and thought it was 'a funny request'.

The man asked them if they were students. The girls explained that they were only 14 and still at school. 'I suppose,' said the man, 'that is a type of student.' He added that it was really older students he wanted. The girls repeated that they would not go with him and walked away, but not before the man asked them to forget the conversation and say nothing about it. When they got home they told their parents and the police were called. The girls were escorted on a tour of car parks and asked if they could spot the man's car. Outside a small hotel they did spot it.

A strange incident in Ayr Road, Prestwick, instantly became a *cause célèbre*. The car belonged to David Anderson, QC, a former Solicitor General, once a Tory MP, who had recently taken up a new job as chief reporter for Scottish public inquiries. He was staying in the hotel during the hearing of his first major inquiry, into a plan by Ayr County Council to rezone 2,000 acres of agricultural land for industry. Anderson was charged with breach of the peace and the case came to trial at Ayr Sheriff Court five months later, in May 1973.

The first of the girls had difficulty identifying Anderson. Asked if she could see him in the courtroom she indicated one of the reporters in the press box. It was only when the procurator fiscal asked her to have a more thorough look that she pointed to the figure in the dock. The second girl recalled in evidence that her mother had made her write down the make and number of the car. She said it was a bright blue Chrysler with a 4 and a 5 in the number. Anderson's car was a Triumph estate with a number which was fairly easy to remember (DSC 5551).

There was a further inconsistency. Both girls insisted that the man who spoke to them was wearing a flat cap and checked tweed overcoat. But the accused's wife, Juliet Anderson, testified on oath that she had helped her husband to pack and that he took with him a raincoat and a soft hat, not a tweed overcoat and a flat cap.

Irving Garrett, the proprietor of the hotel, told the court that, as far as he knew, Anderson's car was parked in the grounds all night. He had been watching to see if his distinguished guest left the hotel because on a previous evening Anderson had gone out and returned very late. Elizabeth Garrett, the proprietor's wife, said she served Anderson high tea early that evening and that she thought she would have seen him if he had left the hotel at any time before 10 o'clock. Anderson maintained in evidence that he spent the evening in his room working on a backlog of documents concerning another inquiry, went out for a few minutes about 11pm for a breather, and then turned in for the night. The prosecution argued that these accounts of Anderson's movements (or lack of movements) fell far short of an alibi.

Anderson was represented by James Mackay, QC, vice-dean of the Faculty of Advocates, whose subsequent incarnation as Lord Mackay of Clashfern included a spell as Lord Chancellor in Margaret Thatcher's government. The accused's wife told Mackay that the day after the alleged offence her husband seemed completely normal at a cocktail party in Edinburgh. How could this be? He had just been arrested by the police in Ayrshire; his career and reputation were potentially in ruins; yet here he was at a cocktail party behaving as if nothing had happened.

Mackay pressed on. 'Do you know of any interest in judo of your husband?'

'Absolutely none.'

'How would you describe your relationship?'

'We are a very devoted couple and have been married for 25 years.'

'Do you know of any unusual desires of his in relation to your life with him?'

'Absolutely not. Our marriage is completely normal.'

The notion of David Anderson's normality was, however, severely tested by his own statements to the court. Instead of claiming that he had been the victim of a simple case of mistaken identity, which would have been the sensible strategy, he suggested that he had been impersonated as part of a conspiracy against Edward Heath's government. He addressed the sheriff: 'Unfortunately, in this country, there are bodies dedicated to embarrassing a right-wing government. I have a letter from the Prime Minister to men in public life warning of this serious possibility and I do not wish to depart – especially in my position – without making this clear. It is not an irresponsible or fanciful suggestion. I know only too well from documents which it would be breaking the Official Secrets Act to disclose, except in general terms, that this is a serious danger which has in the past happened to men in public life.'

Anderson was no longer a law officer in Heath's administration, nor had he been promoted to the bench, as law officers often were; instead he had been shuffled off into a backwater. The idea that the enemies of the Conservative Party would despatch a man in a flat cap to Ayr Road, Prestwick, on a winter's night with a mission to accost teenage girls, in order to discredit the chief reporter for public inquiries while he went about his lawful business after an early tea, was not one that the sheriff, George Reid, was prepared to regard seriously. After an adjournment of 20 minutes he found Anderson guilty and fined him £50. The accused had the last word: 'With the greatest respect to your lordship, I am completely innocent as charged.'

There were grounds for reviewing the verdict: although the girls had impressed the bench as credible witnesses, the prosecution case was from far from watertight. But in December 1973, a year after the episode in Ayr Road, the Appeal Court in Edinburgh rejected David Anderson's contention that there had been a miscarriage of justice and refused his petition to have the conviction re-examined. The case rumbled on for years, and was the subject of a play, produced in London, which was sympathetic to Anderson's position.

In an intriguing coda some years after his death, Judy Steel, wife of the former Liberal leader, said that, when she was a student at Edinburgh University, a man asked her to do what the Prestwick schoolgirls had been asked to do. She concluded in retrospect that the man was David Anderson. This did not quite settle the matter, though it came close.

IV

As a devoted husband and former Solicitor General was asserting his normality to one Scottish criminal court, the comedian Chic Murray was anxious to confirm his abnormality to another.

Unlike David Anderson, Murray often wore a flat cap – or, as he would have called it, a bunnet. He was much admired for his droll commentary on the absurdities of life, including such overlooked hazards as the act of opening a door. But no one ever thought he was normal, least of all Murray himself. By 1973 he had parted from his wife and stage partner, the diminutive Maidie, his popularity had faded, and he was drinking heavily. He would regularly take his hangover to the BBC canteen in Queen Margaret Drive, Glasgow, where he was a dejected fixture, mostly ignored. Chic Murray required to die before he was elevated to the status of national treasure.

He did, however, succeed in turning his appearance in the dock of Glasgow Sheriff Court, where he pleaded not guilty to being drunk in charge of his car, into a virtuoso performance. His supporting cast included police officers – the straight men of the production – who testified in the customary deadpan fashion to his behaviour on the night in question.

The court heard that, after his arrest, he remained silent, staring straight ahead. But when he was asked who owned the vehicle, he broke into a sentence characteristic of his laconic style. 'I stole it in Edinburgh yesterday,' he said. When he was charged and asked if he had anything to say, he replied: 'I was terribly obstreperous.' Murray explained to the court that he was pleased to have been able to enunciate such a word at that time of night.

PC John Bone testified that when Murray was asked several times to get out of the car he did not respond. 'Eventually,' said Bone, 'he opened the door and almost fell on to the pavement.' But he was not obstreperous: the court had Bone's word for that. The constable asked him if he wished to see a lawyer, and Murray uttered the words 'Joseph Beltrami' (a latter-day Laurence Dowdall). Another of the straight men, PC Andrew McKenna, said that Murray told him that he had assaulted 'a vast number of people'.

Alone at the top of the bill, Chic Murray entered the witness box in his own defence. He said that he had parked the car near his flat. The car was like an office to him – one of the policemen had said that it was strewn with papers and boxes, so there was no dispute about that. He said he had gone down to the car to fetch some scripts. 'I would say I had a fair amount to drink,' he admitted. So far this was holding up as a goodish Chic Murray sketch. It became funnier still when he was asked why the ignition key had been in position when the police arrived. He explained that the car was small and that there was not enough room to put the key in his pocket while he was sitting in the driver's seat. He swore that he had no intention of driving and that, anyway, he could think of nowhere in Glasgow he would want to go at that hour of the night. He described the remark about the car being stolen as 'a quip'. He was acquitted.

V

On the summer evening of his arrest George Pottinger was dining in the clubhouse at Muirfield with a High Court judge and two sheriffs. His companions were either indifferent to the serious criminal charges looming over Pottinger or recklessly loyal – or possibly both.

During the evening he was called away to answer an urgent telephone call from The Pelicans. It was his wife, possessor of the infamous cigarette lighter. 'We've got visitors, you have to come home at once,' she told him. He did not have far to walk to the house that Poulson had built and paid for him – with its walk-in drinks cupboard and its grand piano set on a marble plinth, a monument to 1970s' tastelessness. The police were waiting. He was driven to police headquarters in the High Street of Edinburgh, where he was detained in a cell overnight before a longer morning drive to Leeds. There he and John Poulson were reunited, sitting side by side in the dock for a preliminary hearing.

The joke, though it was not really a joke, was that Pottinger knew so many of the judges that there would have been no one left to try him impartially in Scotland. Instead the case was set for trial in the city of the bankrupt architect.

VI

Twenty years had passed since George Pottinger, then a hot property in the Scottish Office, had elegantly penned the report of the Balfour commission, dismissing the idea of meaningful devolution for Scotland. If, as he kicked his heels in The Pelicans awaiting trial, he had any inclination to consider the state of Scottish politics, he might have reflected on the missed opportunity of 1954. The clamour for meaningful devolution had not disappeared. Despite Pottinger's way with words, the commission had settled nothing.

But the big parties continued to make a hash of it. The Scottish Tories, at their annual conference in Perth, in the same hall where three years earlier they had reluctantly endorsed Heath's plan for a Scottish assembly, overwhelmingly rejected a resolution calling on the government to hasten its plans for the elusive legislature. This was a serious setback for Gordon Campbell, who had persuaded Wendy Wood to end her fast only by promising her a Green Paper within the lifetime of the present parliament. Wood herself was not best pleased when she was ejected from the press bench at the conference, having failed to satisfy the organisers that she was a *bona fide* journalist. The vote was equally embarrassing for Edward Heath, whose speech at the conference contained a rebuke to the faithful for their about-turn and a feeble reiteration of his 'Declaration of Perth' of 1971.

Nicholas Fairbairn, backing the Prime Minister, said that the party was in danger of breaking its word to the electorate. But the delegates were keener to heed Iain Sproat, the right-winger who had displaced Donald Dewar in Aberdeen, when he predicted that an assembly would create serious frictions and 'provide a platform for an irresponsible element, publicity-seekers, and extremists like James Reid'. Ronnie Dundas, the failed parliamentary candidate from the leader writers' room at the *Glasgow Herald*, added that there was no place for an assembly between Westminster and the new regional authorities.

The *Herald*, in a leader which might have been written by Dundas himself, embraced the party's change of mind, asserting that the Scottish Conservatives had 'at last come to their senses' and that opinion at Westminster must now 'harden against an assembly, leaving the Secretary of State little choice but to bring out a Green Paper which takes account of the impossibility of getting legislation on an assembly through parliament'. Lobby journalists were briefed that the government was more likely than ever to water-down its proposals, leaving Gordon Campbell's authority as Secretary of State damaged beyond repair.

Labour's position on devolution was scarcely more credible. There were rumblings that the party most resistant to home rule was reluctantly drifting towards it. But the plan, if it was a plan, involved nothing bolder than a strengthening of the Scottish Grand Committee, allowing it to meet in Edinburgh several times a year to complete the progress of parliamentary bills initiated at Westminster. It was a mouse that posed no challenge to the supremacy of the House of Commons and no threat whatever to the union.

With both the main parties in disarray over the issue, the death of John Rankin, the devolutionist-minded Labour MP for Govan, could not have come at a more opportune time for the Scottish National Party. Labour's choice of candidate for the by-election, Harry Selby, a 61-year-old barber, was uninspiring. The suspicion that it smacked of arrogance was confirmed when a party manager exuded confidence over the outcome. 'We are certainly out in front, with the Tory a poor second,' he announced early in the campaign. Selby had inherited a majority of 7,142 in one of those impregnable Glasgow seats from which, it seemed, Labour would only be dislodged by a political earthquake high on the Richter scale. The seismologists failed to spot the SNP's Margo MacDonald, 'an ex-schoolmistress from Blantyre', who was widely dismissed as a plucky ingénue.

The SNP was handed a gift: the half-forgotten inquiry of the Kilbrandon commission on the constitution finally reported after four years of study. Kilbrandon, true to the form of his earlier report on children and young people, proposed a prescription for change more radical than anyone had expected: an assembly of 100 members in Edinburgh elected by a system of proportional representation and with the power to legislate, a reduction in the number of Scottish MPs at Westminster from 71 to 57, the removal of the Secretary of State for Scotland from the cabinet, and his replacement by a Scottish prime minister heading a Scottish government.

Margo MacDonald seized on the report, inviting the people of Govan to 'serve notice on London that it should be put into operation without delay'. Outside the SNP, however, there were not many enthusiasts for Kilbrandon. Allan Campbell McLean, chairman of the Scottish Council of the Labour Party, betrayed a disturbing lack of judgement when he drew a parallel with Northern Ireland which managed to insult both the people of the province and the people of Scotland in the same sentence: 'When one considers the calibre of members of the Ulster Stormont for the past 50 years, it is hardly likely to inspire great confidence.' Maclean was more successful as a novelist than as a political operator: it would not have been difficult.

When devolution was eventually granted, the resemblance between the constitutional settlement of 1999 and the Kilbrandon proposals of 26 years earlier was striking (although the Secretary of State did retain a seat in cabinet). The immediate political reaction in 1973 was that Kilbrandon, by going too far, had made home rule a more distant project. But the celebrated dictum of Harold Wilson

– not that Wilson could remember when, or even if, he had uttered it – confounded the pundits almost at once. A week was indeed a long time in politics, certainly in Govan.

Eight days after Kilbrandon 29-year-old Margo MacDonald, 'amid scenes of near-hysteria', took the seat with a majority of 571. Her husband Peter was not in Govan Town Hall for the count; he was behind the bar in the Hoolet's Nest, where Mary Queen of Scots stayed after the Battle of Langside, so the newspapers claimed. Home for the MacDonalds and their two young daughters was a flat above the pub, and it was there that she returned as the new MP for Govan, her sensible head not in the least turned by her unexpected triumph and a teetotaller's first tentative sip of champagne. 'It's never been my life's ambition to become an MP,' she said. 'My main ambition is to become a member of the Scottish parliament. The sooner this happens, the better.' Margo MacDonald fulfilled her ambition, but not for another 26 years.

Geoff Shaw, a Church of Scotland minister who combined intelligence and idealism as Labour's group leader on Glasgow Corporation, and was soon to head the new Strathclyde Regional Council, correctly identified complacency as one of the reasons for Labour's defeat in a heartland seat. Even Allan Campbell McLean was chastened by the result, promising a period of serious heart-searching.

It was unfortunate that some of Labour's new generation were otherwise engaged – Donald Dewar in the wilderness, Shaw in local government – or, in the case of John Smith, too inexperienced to be established. The fiercely ambitious Gordon Brown had not yet entered real politics. He was student rector of Edinburgh University, and falling out badly with Sir Michael Swann, the principal, over what Swann saw as Brown's determination to exceed the rector's authority. Brown countered by alleging a plot to remove him as chairman of the university court. It was a playground rehearsal of much to follow in the career of Gordon Brown.

In 1973, however, the young politician of the moment was not a member of the Labour Party nor was she a star of the university debating societies. She was a publican's wife. What was to be done about her and her cause? For all their posturing the established parties were as clueless as ever.

VII

Margo MacDonald delivered her maiden speech – an unusually short one – in the House of Commons in December 1973. It was an opportunity for the honourable members – on this occasion the few present for the debate on the Clyde Port Authority (Hunterston Ore Terminal) Order Confirmation Bill – to set political differences aside and congratulate the new boy or, in this case, girl, on her debut; it was the last such flattery a member could expect.

After the loss of Govan the reaction of some on the Labour side was understandably muted, even a little chilly. One of the party's rising stars, Jim Sillars, confined himself to 'welcoming the conversion of at least one member – I put it no higher – of the Scottish National Party to the campaign for the development of Hunterston'. Relations between MacDonald and Sillars thawed sufficiently for them to marry some years later. But the warmer testimonials provided an illuminating commentary on the sexism of the age. Tam Galbraith, Tory MP for Glasgow Hillhead, said that if all he had heard from the honourable lady 'did not please my ears, everything that my eye saw was a delight', while Labour's Dick Mabon observed that in a choice between beauty and the beast – the beast being Hunterston nuclear power station – Mrs MacDonald was certainly the beauty.

A succession of West of Scotland MPs of both the main parties rushed to agree with her proposition that there had been enough talk about an ore terminal and that it was time to get on with it. The business case seemed inescapable: ore was needed to make steel; the town of Motherwell ('Steelopolis') depended on steel; the General Terminus Quay in Glasgow was no longer equipped to take the larger ore carriers; the waters off Hunterston were some of the deepest in Europe.

An alternative site at Ardrossan less harmful to the environment was rejected. Only Hunterston offered the scope for related developments such as an oil refinery, a petro-chemical plant and a steel works. To the people of Fairlie, the village next door, these proposals were anathema. A deputation of 17 chained themselves to the railings outside parliament. 'We have been ground down,' said one of the group, Elizabeth Pearson, 'and in a democracy this should not happen.'

But there were few dissenting voices. Only Sir Fitzroy Maclean, the local Tory MP, spoke for the protesters: 'The project will blight and pollute one of Scotland's greatest beauty spots. Industrial Scotland will be deprived of one of its principal playgrounds. It will strike a severe blow at our vitally important tourist industry. It will eat up some of the best agricultural land in the country and utterly destroy the amenities of a considerable residential area.' He added: 'Matters are made worse because the chances are that the usefulness of the projects will be of short duration. In 10 or 20 years from now there will no longer be any need for them.'

Maclean's intervention was dismissed as last-ditch special pleading. As Margo MacDonald put it: 'I fully sympathise with the people of Ayrshire who fear that industrial development at Hunterston will irreversibly damage their environment. Indeed, they are to be complimented on the way in which they have highlighted the dangers of unsuitable development. But the social and physical environment of all the communities in West Central Scotland will be better served by industrial regeneration than by industrial decay.'

The ore terminal was approved. It was one of the few projects on which the ruling Conservatives and the Labour opposition, as well as the two SNP members (the other being Donald Stewart), could agree. Two former Secretaries of State for Scotland, William Ross and George Younger, were among its strongest supporters. Yet it was followed, not by the widely anticipated industrial regeneration, but by continuing industrial decay. The British Steel Corporation chaired by Monty Finniston, a Glasgow-born industrialist with a low opinion of the Scottish workforce ('a lazy set of bastards, to be quite frank'), went on cutting production at Ravenscraig until Steelopolis packed up completely in 1992. For a few years, but a few years only, platforms for the North Sea oil industry were built at Hunterston. But there was no oil refinery, no petro-chemical plant, no steel works: none of these projects ever materialised. There was, however, a second nuclear power station, just as ugly as the first one, though Teddy Taylor had somehow managed to convince himself that Hunterston 'A' had 'added to the beauty of the area'.

Remarkably, there was no mention in the Commons debate of uncontrolled land-grabbing at Hunterston involving a variety of competing private and public enterprises; no mention of the role of the Hunterston Development Company which laid claim to ownership of the peninsula and which included on its board the two main landowners in the area – the Montgomeries and the Cochran-Patricks – as well as the shipbuilder William Lithgow and the housebuilder William McAlpine; little concern for safety and the potential hazards of placing an oil refinery next to a nuclear power station; and only a token nod to the inevitable destruction of the natural environment. In short there was no socially responsible vision.

The prophet of the night, Fitzroy Maclean, proved to be broadly correct in his evaluation of the short-term benefits of the grandiose scheme. Most of his parliamentary colleagues were too blinded by its superficial merits to acknowledge that large-scale industrial development at Hunterston, brutalising and polluting everything around it, was not a solution to the endemic problems of the Scottish economy. Yet the consensus behind it was almost unanimous: it united the political parties, the STUC, the Scottish Council (Development and Industry) and the Church of Scotland.

John McGrath's 7:84 Theatre Company (a name inspired by the claim that 7% of the population owned 84% of the wealth) toured Scotland that autumn with *The Cheviot, The Stag and the Black Black Oil*, a superb piece of theatrical polemic, staged in the style of a ceilidh, which took a hard look at land speculation and its relationship to the depopulation of the Highlands. The villain of the piece was an entrepreneur by the self-explanatory name of McChuckemup, a natural successor to the unsentimental 19th-century 'improvers'. But such disciples of progress were not confined to the Highlands. They were now to be found as far south as Ayrshire, jealously appraising the lands of Hunterston with the eager assistance of the politicians. Soon, in oil-rich Scotland, they would be everywhere, paying little heed to the preservation of precious landscapes or to the social fabric of fragile communities.

In 2011 the Scottish Wildlife Trust and other environmental groups, backed by a well-organised local campaign, successfully resisted plans for a third power station at Hunterston. The age of McChukemup was finally over. But it had taken 38 years to see him off the premises.

1974
BLIND SPOTS

I

In the first days of January 1974 an oil rig foundered in Scottish waters off the North Sea. Transocean 3 had only just taken up its station 140 miles north-east of Orkney when structural faults were detected in one of its legs and the 53 men on board had to be winched off by helicopter. Twelve hours later the rig capsized. It was an early warning of the hazards of extracting Britain's newly-discovered oil wealth.

But for the time being the country was preoccupied by the hazards attached to an older source of energy. A work-to-rule by the miners, which had begun in the final weeks of 1973, had so rapidly diminished stocks of coal at power stations that Britain entered the new year in semi-darkness. Industry was reduced to a three-day week, the government ordered a 10pm shutdown of television, and domestic consumers shivered in unheated living rooms as electricity was cut off to conserve fuel.

Edward Heath had come to view the prolonged dispute over the workers' latest pay claim as a struggle not only between the government and the miners but between order and anarchy. In this near-apocalyptic atmosphere, the powers of darkness had to be symbolised and personified, if only to allow rotten eggs – a product relatively unaffected by the various restrictions – to be thrown at the target. The person destined to fulfil this vital role was the dentally challenged Mick McGahey. Virtually unknown before the 1974 confrontation, the national vice-president of the miners' union, with his gravel voice and combative platform manner, was a gift to the right-wing press, which instantly labelled him 'Britain's most militant militant'.

It helped that everything about McGahey conformed to the required stereotype. He was born of mining stock in the

Lanarkshire village of Shotts, home of the world's best pipe band; his father was an activist in the 1926 general strike; Mick himself went down the pit (Gateside in Cambuslang) at the age of 14 two days after leaving school. 'A pony driver when I started. Hard, brutal work. Pick and shovel.' His family experienced poverty, 'not the grinding poverty of colonial peoples, or anything like that, but poverty all the same. The north ward in Cambuslang had the highest tuberculosis rate in western Europe – including Franco's Spain, as we always used to emphasise.'

McGahey joined the Communist Party at the age of 18, just as his father and two brothers had done before him, and was soon active in the Young Communist League. He was sacked for organising an unofficial strike during the second world war and came to regret his action: 'The war against fascism was the most important thing at that stage, in the interests not only of Britain but of the international working class. But I was young, immature, not well-developed politically.' It taught him to be more realistic in the pursuit of objectives.

The hard-left Scots on the union executive – McGahey, Bill McLean and Lawrence Daly (the ex-communist general secretary who had signed his nomination papers for the 1955 general election wearing his pit boots) – exercised an influence out of all proportion to their number. Several months before the dispute began, Daly had set an uncompromising agenda for what was to follow: 'So long as the economy requires coal, the miners will be determined that those who dig it from the bowels of the earth will be the highest-paid industrial workers in Britain.'

But it was neither Daly, nor the relatively emollient national president Joe Gormley, who emerged as the voice of the conflict. From his power base in Edinburgh McGahey drew a metropolitan media circus to his daily press conference, ratcheting up the crisis with the language of the class war. Challenged to say what he would do if the government called in the troops to move coal supplies, McGahey replied that he would appeal personally to the soldiers: 'The troops are not all anti-working class. Many of them are sons of miners. Sons of the working class.' In response to questions about the high stocks at two Scottish power stations, Longannet and Cockenzie, he implied a readiness to mobilise support: 'It takes more than coal to work power stations ... It is surprising what steps we can take. However, we shall always use peaceful persuasion.'

The threat was no less clear for being expressed in menacing hints. Ministers briefed the Westminster press lobby that they could find themselves dealing with 'nothing less than organised sabotage against the state' and that no action was ruled out 'including the withdrawal of social security payments to miners' families'.

Through several weeks of negotiations which ended predictably in mutual recrimination, Heath hesitated to call a general election. He went on dithering until the point of no return. In early February the miners voted overwhelmingly for a strike and three days later the Prime Minister addressed the nation on television: 'The election will give you the chance to make it clear to these people how you feel.' The phrase 'these people' was needlessly offensive. It risked alienating many voters who may have felt that 'these people' were not paid enough for doing dangerous work at considerable cost to their health. John Warden, political editor of the *Glasgow Herald*, was not alone in praising Heath's 'unequalled display of political leadership' and the bookmakers made the Tories odds-on favourites to win the 'Who governs Britain?' election.

II

In the parallel universe of Leeds Crown Court the trial of George Pottinger and John Poulson was still pulling the crowds long after the pantomime season. On the 49th day of the run there was a moment of unexpected drama when the judge abruptly withdrew the bail of the two men in the dock. Mr Justice Waller said he was acting in accordance with 'the normal procedure on reaching the late stage in a trial'. The accused posed no danger to society and there was no indication that they were about to flee the country; Waller could have exercised his discretion and allowed them the dignity of freedom for the few remaining days of the case. His decision sent an unavoidable message to the jury.

One of Scotland's highest-ranking civil servants, who was more accustomed to the luxury of the Dorchester Hotel, returned to a cell in the remand wing of Armley Prison on the night that Edward Heath called a general election. Whether he would be free to vote in that election was still to be determined.

The trial, now in its fourth month, was as long-established as the miners' dispute and almost as bitterly fought. It was a curiosity of the English jurisdiction that, before a word of testimony was heard, the prosecution presented a summary of its case. Back in November 1973 John Cobb, QC, had taken full advantage of this opportunity to excite the jury with a grandstand view of bribery and corruption in high places.

Unveiling the plot, he introduced Poulson as a businessman thirsty for fame and honour who 'cascaded Pottinger with gifts', including Savile Row suits, a house, holidays and a Rover car ('taxed and insured': Cobb believed in laying it on thick). He introduced Pottinger as a public servant with 'an overriding duty to act with impartiality and integrity and above all to safeguard the interests of the state', yet who allowed himself to be intoxicated by Poulson's criminal extravagance. In return he 'showed favour to Poulson in relation to government contracts' (for the Aviemore winter sports complex) and tried to secure the businessman a knighthood.

Poulson paid for Pottinger and his family to have holidays in Scandinavia and Italy. After one of them Pottinger wrote: 'I need not say again that we are quite overwhelmed by your kindness. Having said that, I have set out a note of what we would really like.' He appended a list of dates, places, hotels. It was shameless greed. The jury would have to decide if it was also corrupt.

The prosecution claimed that Pottinger doctored files in the Scottish Office in an attempt to conceal his true relationship with Poulson: that he removed letters between himself and Poulson and altered file numbers. Pottinger tried to dispose of this damaging allegation by joking that, if he had doctored the files, he would have made a better job of it.

Cobb put a sinister spin on apparent coincidences. He described how Poulson enlisted Pottinger's help when he got into difficulties with the Aviemore project, once prevailing on Pottinger to draft a letter to Lord Fraser, the prime mover in the development. Cobb could not reasonably claim that this was corrupt; it was not even improper. Pottinger had been seconded as a fixer; he was there to sort out problems. But Cobb asked the jury to note the timing: while the letter was being drafted Pottinger's bank account received a welcome injection of capital to cover the purchase price of a plot of land at Muirfield – the land on which Pottinger built his house.

According to the prosecution Poulson was under the

impression that Pottinger had been responsible for Fraser getting his knighthood and baronetcy and hoped for the same favour. But Poulson 'hoping' for an honour was not enough to convict Pottinger unless the prosecution could prove that Pottinger had actively sought an honour on Poulson's behalf.

Cobb's opening statement, though formidable in its detail and powerful in its impact, was not without flaws. One of them surfaced on the first day of evidence when Colonel Ian Grant, a Highland landowner, testified that Pottinger put pressure on him to sell land near Aviemore to Fraser's consortium. He said that Pottinger had informed him during a telephone conversation that ministers would take a serious view if he sold it to the Rank organisation for a rival hotel development, as Grant was proposing. This might have been an example of Pottinger's corrupt intentions. But it could equally well have been a genuine attempt to defend the integrity of his master's pet project, a quarter of the cost of which was being met by the government.

The bloody-minded laird did sell to Rank. He claimed there was then an undue delay in receiving planning permission for the rival development. Did the delay show that a compromised Pottinger obstructed the plans of the colonel's purchaser? For this theory to stand up, Pottinger would have had to influence officials in a branch of the civil service, the Scottish Development Department, for which he had no responsibility, and there was no evidence that he did.

Whether or not Pottinger was guilty of corruption, the Scottish Office connived in a stitch-up at Aviemore. There was no written contract for a multi-million-pound project involving a significant investment of public money and the building of the centre was never put out to tender. The work was simply awarded to a company, Bovis, whose chairman, Harry Vincent, was also a director of Fraser's outfit. These decisions were Fraser's and Fraser's alone. They should have been challenged by his backers at St Andrew's House – if not by Pottinger then by his superior Sir Douglas Haddow, the head of the civil service in Scotland, and if not by Haddow then by his political masters. But Fraser was the richest and most powerful man in Scotland, proprietor of one of its principal newspapers, a man who was accustomed to getting his own way. Even by the lower standards of transparency and accountability which prevailed at the time, the deal stank.

Haddow's relaxed view of the arrangements extended to an

implicit trust in the conduct of George Pottinger. If it had been left to Haddow there would have been no criminal proceedings against Pottinger even when the Poulson bankruptcy proceedings revealed the extent of the largesse he had received. Haddow did not accept that Pottinger had exercised 'undue influence' in exchange for the gifts lavished on him. He recalled to the court what he said during a telephone conversation with Pottinger: 'I have consulted your colleagues individually and collectively about the recent publicity and you will be glad to know that there is no one who does not believe you will live it down.' A few months later the police arrived at The Pelicans and there was no more talk at St Andrew's House of Pottinger living it down – or up.

Lord Fraser, the master builder of Aviemore, had been dead for seven years. He had not lived to see the official opening of the complex and the presentation of Poulson's gift to his widow, which the prosecution gratuitously cited as yet another example of the architect's wickedness. It was left to Fraser's son and heir, the playboy and SNP supporter Hugh, to enlighten the court about Pottinger's relationship with his father. Fraser said that Pottinger had seemed 'rather fed up at the Scottish Office', that he was having difficulty funding his son's education at an expensive private school and that he had requested and been paid £2,500 to write a biography of Lord Fraser. Pottinger approached young Hugh about the possibility of a highly-paid job at the House of Fraser as the firm's public relations officer. Fraser rejected the idea. He said he found Pottinger 'humorous and witty' but that Pottinger talked above his head.

A disillusioned civil servant strapped for cash – how the prosecution must have lapped it up. But by the Christmas break, with Haddow's evidence in his favour, Pottinger may have calculated that if the opposition was ahead, it was only narrowly on points.

III

When the trial resumed in the first week of January 1974, John Poulson walked slowly from the dock to give evidence in his own defence. 'He looks old and ill,' wrote William Hunter, one of the Scottish journalists in attendance. 'Throughout the long day he seldom moves except gently to caress the walking stick he always now needs. His eyes do not often lift from the floor.' But appearances were deceptive. His counsel doubted that he would survive a prison sentence. He survived another 19 years, only three of which were spent in prison, and died at the age of 82.

Subjected to a gruelling cross-examination during his nine days in the witness box, Poulson perfected the role of the broken man. He agreed that he had been 'foolishly generous' in bankrolling Pottinger's house. He agreed that Pottinger had been 'a shade greedy' in expecting him to pay for such indulgences as a mosaic, trees and shrubs for its garden at a time when his architectural practice was in financial trouble. But he rejected the prosecution's suggestion that he had pinned his hopes on Pottinger facilitating work for him which would help him to rebuild his business. 'No,' said Poulson flatly. As to an honour, and Pottinger's possible usefulness in securing one, Poulson said he had found while abroad that an honour would have been an advantage in dealing with 'coloured people and the Arabs'. Did he have a knighthood in mind? Poulson lied that he didn't know.

When the judge asked him why he had given so many gifts to his friend at the Scottish Office, Poulson invoked the values of his childhood: 'I was brought up in the creed that it was a greater pleasure to give than to receive. I was in a position to do so and it was a pleasure to do so.' After the trial those who knew Poulson took a more cynical view: Poulson, they insisted, was a ruthless operator who knew that every man had a price and usually knew what it was. The prosecution wrung from him the admission that all his gifts to Pottinger, including the car, had been put down as business expenses, and damned this as 'a swindle on the state', a fraud against the Inland Revenue. Yet, to the end, Poulson pursued the myth that he was more sinned against than sinning.

After the sad old man with the walking stick, the next actor into the witness box was in a different class. William Hunter noted Pottinger's coolness: 'He makes much play with his spectacles. He crooks an elbow on the ledge of the witness box. He looks relaxed.' But under cross-examination day after day from Peter Taylor, QC, Pottinger slowly hanged himself. It was odd that a man with so high an opinion of his own intelligence seemed to be unaware of the noose tightening.

His stage presentation was more polished than Poulson's. He put the same gloss on his relationship with Poulson as Poulson had done earlier but he did it more elegantly: 'I know it is often said and perhaps rightly that after 40 one does not make new friends readily. This may be true. I don't know. But when one does make friends at a late age the friendship becomes lasting.' Taylor refused to buy this testimonial to the enduring value of friendship just as he had dismissed Poulson's self-righteous hypocrisy about the pleasure of giving. He suggested to Pottinger that he had once told Colonel Ian Grant, during negotiations over Aviemore, that 'Poulson is not one of us' – the implication being that Poulson was of a lower social class. Pottinger replied: 'That is a self-condemning phrase which I think would much more likely come from the lips of an arrogant Highland laird than from myself.' It may have started to occur to a Yorkshire jury that if there was anyone in Scotland more arrogant than a Highland laird, it was a senior civil servant.

When Taylor ventured that Pottinger was 'a highly educated and literate man of sophisticated tastes', the recipient of the barbed compliment did not demur. Taylor mischievously pushed his luck: 'Are you also a bon viveur?', stinging Pottinger into the response: 'I think that is snide.'

Taylor: 'Bon viveur is a straightforward description of someone who enjoys the good things of life.'

Pottinger: 'In moderation.'

The contrast in styles between the two accused was striking. During the mid-day adjournment, while the bon viveur headed briskly to lunch at a Leeds hotel, the architect retreated to the police canteen below the court and opened a small packet of sandwiches. At the height of his career Pottinger had preferred to lunch with important friends in the New Club rather than with colleagues in the staff canteen at St Andrew's House. Even now, humiliation staring him in the face, there were standards to maintain.

In one of their many spiky exchanges Taylor finally got Pottinger to agree that the three qualities a civil servant should possess were integrity, impartiality and independence.

Taylor: 'In other words, or to put it a simpler way, like Caesar's wife you should be above suspicion?'

Pottinger: 'Yes, it is a well-known cliché in that situation.'

Taylor: 'I am sorry, Mr Pottinger, if I resort to clichés.'

Taylor had a habit of resorting to literary allusions as well as clichés. With a nod to Oscar Wilde he remarked that 'to receive one free holiday may be accorded good fortune, to receive two sounds like recklessness'. About the gift of three suits and an overcoat on three separate visits to a Savile Row tailor, he floored Pottinger by again employing wit as a weapon: 'Is it the case that some have greatcoats thrust upon them?' Pottinger snapped, accusing Taylor of having 'a warped mind incapable of conceiving any kind of friendship without some sinister motive'. Taylor retorted that Pottinger should keep personalities out of it.

Pottinger was then tormented with the recollection of a second friendship. It so happened that this other friend also had bags of money. His name was Johnny Mancha. 'A very nice man', Pottinger recalled. Nice indeed. When Pottinger was faced with a bill for £13,500 from the official receiver handling Poulson's bankruptcy, he persuaded Mancha, a fellow member at Muirfield, to pay £14,000 into his bank account, making a profit of £500 on the transaction – a rather Pottinger outcome. A letter from Poulson advising him to take what he could from Mancha because 'he will never miss it' was produced in court (Poulson had retained all the relevant correspondence for the proverbial rainy day). Pottinger claimed that taking all he could from Mancha was a reference to a golf match. If the jury believed that, the jury would believe anything.

Taylor: 'Is one to understand that there are people lurking about the clubhouse at Muirfield when Mr Mancha plays, waiting to take money from him?'

Pottinger: 'Yes, there are.'

Taylor: 'This is the Honourable Company of Edinburgh Golfers, is it not?'

Pottinger: 'You must not be disrespectful. It happens at many clubs.'

In the closing stages of the trial Pottinger remained supremely confident of acquittal. Privately he continued to refer to the gifts from Poulson as 'baubles'. In January he had attended a hunt ball, regretting that the case was still hanging over him. But now the self-delusion was complete: a man who would soon be slopping out in Armley Prison objected to this slur on the good name of the Edinburgh establishment.

Taylor went for the kill: 'You are now living in a house almost exclusively built by Poulson, driving a motor car supplied by Poulson, which was taxed and insured by Poulson. You were wearing a variety of suitings provided by Poulson and when you were not following your employment with the Scottish Office and had a holiday or a weekend off, you were having your travel and accommodation and that of your family paid for by Poulson.'

It was a rhetorical question, if it was a question at all. What could Pottinger find to say to this withering summary of his life?

'Yes' was all he said.

Late in the interrogation Taylor produced from his conjuror's hat another of Poulson's letters, this one dated October 1963, which enclosed rail tickets for a weekend at Pontefract for Pottinger and his wife and son.

Taylor: 'Have you ever heard of a relationship between friends where one sends another railway tickets to visit his house for a weekend?'

He got another monosyllabic answer: 'No.' The mask was slipping.

The disintegrating defence called Lord Craigton, a junior minister in the Tory government and a former colleague of Pottinger. Craigton said he had first met Pottinger in 1952 when the two of them shared a room in the Scottish Office. Pottinger, who was in his thirties at the time, was private secretary to James Stuart, the Secretary of State for Scotland. Stuart thought highly of the young man. So did Craigton: 'George Pottinger had a more positive mind than the average civil servant, and was unusual in that he had a mind of his own.' But he agreed that it was wrong – 'highly improper' though he stopped short of using the word 'corrupt' – for Pottinger to accept gifts. Craigton was critical of the offer of a Hellenic cruise at Poulson's expense, following which Pottinger advised Poulson how to go about getting an honour. The judge cut in: 'The receipt of a large gift just about the same time makes it worse.' There was a difference between advising Poulson how to go about getting an honour and actually soliciting for one on his behalf, but Mr Justice Waller had lost any appetite he may have possessed for such nuances.

The jury took four hours to reach a unanimous verdict against both men. Waller was in no mood to temper justice with mercy. He informed them that he would not be taking into account their age – Pottinger 57, Poulson 64 – or their state of health. 'It is my unpleasant duty to have to pass a long sentence of imprisonment on two such men as you, but the evil nature of what was done was such that I cannot do otherwise.' Both were sent down for five years. Poulson, weeping as he left the dock, faced a second corruption trial with T Dan Smith, a fallen godfather in the Labour Party's north of England cosa nostra, and had two years added to his sentence; Pottinger, who took his leave dry-eyed, appealed and had a year deducted from his. The establishment looked after its own. While Poulson languished in one closed prison after another, Pottinger was transferred within six months to a single room in an open prison in Sussex, where he served the rest of his sentence in relative comfort.

In the immediate aftermath of the trial Pottinger's boss, Sir Douglas Haddow, gave a candid assessment of his disgraced colleague: 'George was a brilliant civil servant and an excellent worker. He could do in half a day what others would have taken a week to accomplish. He appears, however, to have had a very large blind spot about accepting gifts from Poulson.' A blind spot – was that all it had been?

Pottinger, the son of an Orkney manse, had acquired 'a taste for the good life', said Haddow, mainly through his memberships of Muirfield and the New Club: 'He is certainly a snob, and he would have little to do with those under him, although he was good company with superiors and equals. He was not particularly well liked.' But if Pottinger had so many ideas above his station and so many airs and graces, why was his lifestyle never queried by his superiors? The retired permanent secretary explained feebly that he had been content to accept the popular rumour that Pottinger's mentor, Lord Fraser, had shown him how to invest successfully in the stock market.

Poulson, too, was accepted uncritically by the Scottish Office, though he was never much good at what he did. When he set up his architectural practice his former employer remarked that Poulson was not fit to design a brick shithouse. For all the many gifts he lavished on others there was none he could call his own. His essential attributes were those of an oily PR man and for a long time he was ably assisted by another of the breed, the chairman of two of his companies, Reginald Maudling, the man who had been left in charge of the country during the UCS crisis. The former Chancellor of the Exchequer was fortunate not to join Pottinger and Poulson in prison.

Unlike Poulson, George Pottinger did possess genuine gifts. He threw them away for a grand piano on a marble plinth, a walk-in drinks cupboard, a Rover car, and a succession of meaningless holidays. When he was released from prison he achieved a partial rehabilitation as a writer of books and died in 1998 at the age of 81.

The scandal left several questions unanswered. Why were the files in St Andrew's House not sealed off pending the police investigation? Why was a civil servant lower in rank than Pottinger put in charge of them? Why did the mandarins not offer the police more help with their inquiries? Jim Sillars accused the Scottish Office of closing ranks over the affair and imposing 'a code of silence'. In some of the circles in which Pottinger mixed, this would have been considered good form.

IV

Fortuitously for all those concerned, any discussion there might have been about standards in Scottish public life in the light of Pottinger's behaviour, and the hinterland of official complacency which made it possible, was closed down by the 'Who governs Britain?' election. Heath was quickly disabused of any notion that he could sustain a three-week campaign around the single issue of trade union power. In Scotland the talk was not about the striking miners, who had the instinctive sympathy of most of the electorate north of the border anyway. Nor was it about George Pottinger, a person of no public profile, an obscure pig in a trough. The talk was mostly about a very much larger trough – the one soon to be overflowing with oil.

The Scottish National Party called it 'Scotland's oil'. It was a seductive slogan. Heath himself, when BP discovered the Forties field, sensed the potential for a nationalist upsurge on the back of it. In 1972 he had attempted to head off the SNP threat with a bold proposal that Scotland should be allowed to benefit directly from the North Sea revenues. He instructed Robert Armstrong, the head of the civil service in London, to prepare a paper on how this was to be achieved. The Treasury, which risked losing direct control over some of the spoils, was determined to thwart Heath's ingenious scheme. No surprises there. But the covetous exchequer found an unlikely ally in Gordon Campbell, the Secretary of State for Scotland, who opposed the proposal because it seemed to him to present insuperable practical difficulties. Heath reluctantly dropped the idea and the SNP surge that he had prophesied and feared duly materialised.

It was only in 2002, with the release of cabinet papers under the 30-year rule, that these facts became public knowledge. If they had been known at the time they would have ignited the SNP's February 1974 campaign, which opened with Margo MacDonald's demand that the oil revenues should be used to develop the infrastructure of Scotland. She was not to know that Heath had proposed more or less exactly that, only to be rebuffed by the Scottish Office which had most to gain from the plan.

There was no hint of the once dominant romantic nationalism in the party's manifesto, a pragmatic document which appealed to economic self-interest with the question: 'Do you wish to be rich Scots or poor British?' The SNP promised increased pensions and family allowances, the abolition of income tax for poorer families, a freeze on rents and a five-year holiday from domestic rates – but only if it could lay its hands on the oil money. 'North Sea oil,' said William Wolfe, the party chairman, 'has destroyed for ever the myth that Scotland is too poor to be a self-governing country.' Murdo Ewan Macdonald, a prominent theologian, attacked the 'simplistic naivety' of the SNP's slogans and what he saw as their inherent racism. But the propaganda, expertly backed by Donald Bain's research at party HQ, was playing well with the electorate: all the polls pointed to nationalist gains.

In its chief target seat, Moray and Nairn, the SNP pitched its star performer, Winnie Ewing, against Gordon Campbell. The *Glasgow Herald*'s William Hunter, reporting from the constituency, depicted it as a contest between unevenly matched personalities: Ewing 'waspish and witty' with 'a highly mobilised bandwagon', Campbell 'warm, honourable, straight', but with an orotund accent and a slightly pompous delivery, unsure how to deal with his opponent. Hunter observed that, at her well-attended meetings, Ewing would return to the same narrow themes: small was beautiful; Norway was the nearest thing to heaven on earth; it was undignified for a country not to make its own decisions. Ewing was playing on greed, he wrote, and without oil the nationalists would have nothing to talk about. But the economist in Hunter had to admit that nationalism was beginning to make financial sense.

If Moray and Nairn was fierce, Govan was plain dirty. Margo MacDonald complained of Labour slander: 'They're going about asking people if they want a part-time barmaid representing them. They're trying to suggest that I pull pints instead of working as an MP.' The newspapers would not print what they called 'stronger and more serious allegations', but predicted an increase in her majority.

Elsewhere in Scotland Labour MPs who had sat on massive majorities for years were shaken by the proliferation of SNP posters and stickers and by the professionalism of the nationalist campaign. A few days before the poll the press sensed a political upheaval: the possibility that many of the 71 seats would change hands was seriously discussed. The result was less spectacular. The SNP, as well as ousting Gordon Campbell, gained Argyll, Banff and East Aberdeenshire from the Tories and ejected Labour from one of its strongholds in the central belt. George Reid, a current affairs broadcaster, had agreed to stand in East Stirling and Clackmannan at the last minute mainly to ensure that the SNP had a candidate in the field. 'It was difficult to know who was more surprised about the result – himself or the defeated Labour candidate Dick Douglas,' marvelled one onlooker. Labour also surrendered Dundee East – to Gordon Wilson, the SNP's oil spokesman – and failed to recapture the Western Isles from Donald Stewart. The only setbacks for the SNP were the loss of Govan, bringing to a temporary halt Margo MacDonald's career in politics, and Wolfe's inability, yet again, to seize the winnable West Lothian seat from Tam Dalyell.

Wolfe overcame personal disappointment as he surveyed the impressive performance of his party: the SNP, by taking 22% of the popular vote, had achieved what he called 'the breakthrough point'. Winnie Ewing offered a less rational analysis of the outcome, claiming mysteriously that 'the millennium God' was on the SNP's side. History vindicated her when the millennium God, assisted by the Scottish people, produced a parliament in Edinburgh 12 months ahead of schedule, confirming the lady's powers as a soothsayer.

Across the UK the electorate gave an inconclusive reply to Edward Heath's question: the result was a dead heat. But Labour held the largest number of seats, enabling Harold Wilson to exercise a moral advantage over a demoralised Heath, whose only hope of clinging to power – some arrangement with the Liberals – foundered. While the miners returned to work, Wilson returned to Downing Street and promptly reappointed Willie Ross as Secretary of State for Scotland. It was a provocative move. 'Looks like someone is giving the nationalists a couple of venticled fingers,' mused an un-named Tory spokesman. Bill MacKenzie, political director of the Scottish Liberals, guessed that Wilson might decide to transfer meetings of the Scottish Grand Committee to Edinburgh, 'but that's about the extent of it'. The SNP's official response was restrained: 'It implies an indifference to the changing mood in Scotland.' Ross himself seemed to be undergoing a small conversion on the road to Dundonald. 'I have never been a hard liner on devolution,' he claimed with a straight face.

A great deal of modern Scottish history had to be hastily revised. The political commentator Robert McLaughlan admitted that his assessment after the 1970 general election that the SNP would be consigned to a footnote in the history books had been proved wrong. He now veered in the opposite direction, foreseeing 'a major constitutional crisis' within 10 years as the SNP exploited its capacity to 'reach emotional depths which liberal rationality can never tap'. McLaughlan identified the essential strain of the nationalist appeal as anglophobia: 'Scottish oil allows us to indulge the feeling which has distinguished us as a nation. It is not surprising.' The SNP's Oliver Brown responded: 'We are aware of the latent anglophobia of the Scot and of its possibly dangerous consequences, but far from exploiting it we have discouraged it.' He didn't say how.

V

The patriotic spirit rekindled by the prospect of the oil bonanza soon infected the national game. Scotland's footballers qualified for the World Cup finals in Germany, inspiring a discussion in the press about the merits of replacing *God Save the Queen* as the official team anthem. Both the Jocks – Stein, the Celtic manager, and his Rangers counterpart Wallace – favoured *Scotland the Brave*, which was also the choice of Cliff Hanley, a popular broadcaster and writer. Hanley was not exactly a disinterested party: he had written the lyrics of *Scotland the Brave*.

'Scotland go into the World Cup with a good shout,' thought the *Glasgow Herald*'s William Hunter, who had installed himself in Frankfurt for the football after sojourns in Leeds for the fall of George Pottinger and Elgin for the fall of Gordon Campbell. The portents were far from encouraging. Would the fall of Scotland be next on his busy schedule?

Goals by Lorimer and Jordan in a 2-0 victory over Zaire in the first game produced a moment hailed by the Scottish press as 'historic': the country's first-ever victory in the final stages of the tournament. Hunter found Scotland 'standing here on the edge of a possible new era in football … the life, sense of liberty, and pursuit of happiness of a proud, poor and ancient people might also benefit'. Other commentators drew parallels with Bannockburn in the build-up to the meeting with the world champions, Brazil.

The 10,000 Scottish fans in the stadium booed and whistled during the playing of *God Save the Queen* before the match. Willie Ormond, the team manager, confessed to a feeling of embarrassment but no shame; he too thought a proud, poor and ancient people should have their own anthem. The game ended in the anti-climax of a goal-less draw – an excellent result for the underdogs.

The team was now delicately poised in its group; Scotland needed victory against Yugoslavia to qualify for the knock-out stages. William Hunter detected 'a dour and cussed optimism' gripping the home support as they anticipated the showdown. There was cause for dourness apart from the natural Scottish tendency to that condition. Bar prices were prohibitively high, bawbees were running out, and British Consular officials reported anxiously that several hundred Scots were sleeping rough and that many others were close to privation. They had been in Germany all of eight days.

Ian Archer, one of the leading Scottish commentators, donning tartan bunnet and scarf, spurned his free pass to the press box and paid money to stand and roar from the terraces with the rest of the Scottish contingent. Another draw; Scotland were undefeated, yet out. At the end, wrote Archer, the supporters 'sang defiantly, proudly, and with such intensity that one's mind turned back the centuries to forefathers in the glens, even on the eve of Bannockburn … Yes, I cried for my beloved country'.

Narrowly avoiding being drawn into a European effluent of purple prose, William Hunter spotted in the absolute discharge of the Scottish football team a neat parallel with an earlier absolute discharge, that of Lionel Daiches, QC, after driving while under the influence. The day of Scotland's exit had been 'a kind of Ne'erday in June' in which 'more than a modicum of alcohol was taken, but sensibly'.

VI

In October Harold Wilson called a second general election of the year with the aim of winning an overall majority to enable him to govern for a full term. He succeeded, though only just.

As in February, Scotland fought its own election. Since the arrival of 'The Magnificent Seven' at Westminster, there had been no stopping the SNP bandwagon. How many more seats could the party take? The message from the polls was that there were few constituencies safe from the nationalist advance. William Clark, a Scottish political correspondent, speculated that the SNP could win a majority of the 71 seats: 'It would be a phenomenon in European politics, and all the more astonishing for the fact that most people do not support the break-up of the UK.'

None of the opinion polls supported Clark's scenario, the last of them giving the SNP 18 seats. But a statement by the general council of the STUC on the eve of the election showed how roughly the cage of the political establishment had been rattled. The SNP had 'waged a campaign with a blend of hot air and mendacity and in some constituencies its supporters vary between extreme nationalism and fascism'. James Jack, the STUC's general secretary, disputed the party's claim that it was on the side of the working class: 'There is no basic difference that I can see between the Conservative Party and the SNP.'

The 'Tartan Tories', as their enemies delighted in calling them, were drawing support from the Conservatives in such seats as Perth and East Perthshire, where the business journalist Douglas Crawford demolished Ian MacArthur's 9,000 majority, and Galloway and South Angus, which also fell to the SNP. In every election since 1955 the Tories had been pushed further out of urban Scotland, but October 1974 marked another watershed for the party – its hold on rural Scotland was loosening too. In the two elections of 1974 the Conservatives' share of the vote slumped from 33% to 24%. It had further still to fall.

But there was a flaw in the widely-held view that the SNP was simply an alternative home for the lost tribe of disillusioned Tories. Despite the flirtations with nationalism at Govan and Hamilton, Labour held on in the West of Scotland in both the 1974 elections. But most of the post-election commentary either failed to spot that the SNP had installed itself in second place in nine of the 13

Glasgow constituencies or attached no significance to this ominous fact.

The SNP stopped far short of achieving a majority of the seats, but its share of the vote leapt from 22% to 31% between February and October; not only did it retain in October all the seats it had won in February, it added four. The parliamentary squad had grown to the size of a football team and included two women: the indomitable Winnie Ewing and her future daughter-in-law, Margaret Bain. The team assembled for a celebratory press conference in a room commanding a splendid view of Princes Street. On a morning heady with promise, the promised land seemed within sight at last. Who would have dared to predict that 25 years would pass before it was reached?

1975
THE LAST COMMA

I

When the Scottish car industry was reborn in 1963 in the 18th-century village of Linwood, Renfrewshire, pedants argued that the manufacturing plant was actually situated in Elderslie, birthplace of Sir Malcolm Wallace, father of the patriot. This was the least of the disputes which dogged the enterprise, and one of the few which did not necessitate an urgent union meeting.

Twelve years later the industry hovered on the brink of collapse. Early in 1975 the media swooped on Linwood when the plant's American owners, Chrysler, announced that it intended to build a new small car for the European market but that it would be made in France, 'where the labour picture is more stable'. Despite this rejection of Linwood because of its wretched industrial relations, BBC Scotland broadcast in its *Current Account* series a sympathetic portrayal of the community. 'Through the programme,' wrote a critic, 'one theme ran. Men and women are desperate to know the truth about the future, even if that truth is to be the closure of the plant. At present the company are still insisting in a far from convincing voice that they have no plans to close, but the facts point otherwise.'

The obituaries turned out to be premature, but the outlook was certainly poor. Men who were once assured of a five-day week plus overtime were lucky to work three days. In a town with a population of 16,000, of whom a higher than average proportion were school age, Chrysler's intake of apprentices had dropped from 120 a year to 12 against a background of declining world car sales. Now, as the BBC Scotland programme pointed out, the fate of a community rested on a decision which would be made in another country. How could it have come to this in scarcely more than a decade?

When the Duke of Edinburgh formally opened the plant in May

1963, the mood in the press was one of near-euphoria. 'A Scottish car right down to its hub-caps, and it's Scots who will build it,' trumpeted the ultra-patriotic *Scottish Daily Express*. 'Now, isn't that refreshing?' Norman Buchan, the local Labour MP, was suitably refreshed. 'The factory will be a growth centre of immense significance to the whole Clyde,' he predicted.

For Linwood to become a growth centre, it would require to attract components suppliers and ancillary industries. Greenfield sites were prepared but never occupied; Linwood was simply too far removed from the rest of the UK car industry to draw supporting investment. But the social benefits were apparent at once. Two thousand new houses were provided for the car workers, many of whom had been recruited from the declining shipyards and coal mines. For these men and their families, the spring of 1963 should have marked a point of departure from spent industries and barbarous slums. But the monarch's husband had been gone barely three weeks when Linwood went on strike for the first time. Shop stewards complained that the men's wages compared unfavourably with rates of pay at the main plant of the then owners, Rootes, in the West Midlands. Although the strike lasted only 36 hours, it was a discouraging start.

By October 1964, the month that Harold Wilson became Prime Minister, the first Scottish-made car since the 1920s was 'rolling off the production line at the rate of one a minute' – a headline-grabbing statistic, if not always true. The Imp, Scotland's very own Volkswagen of the glens, was somewhat comical in appearance and experts claimed to have detected a fundamental design fault. Nevertheless it began to be exported to England in fairly large numbers – though never enough to make a profit.

Lord Rootes had wanted to expand into the volume car business in Coventry, where he had offices, technical know-how, engine-shops, the lot. Harold Macmillan's administration lured him away by stick and carrot. Vigilantly applying its regional development policy, it steered growing industries not to the places they necessarily wanted to be, but to the places of greatest need. It did so by withholding industrial development certificates for existing locations, effectively forcing the car industry to move to the north of England or Scotland. Only Rootes, flattered by various financial inducements, was persuaded to gamble on Scotland.

The prototype of the Imp was capable of a top speed of 100mph. The proprietor, given half a chance, would have quit Linwood even faster. Peak production of 72,000 cars, achieved in the first year of manufacture, was less than 50% of theoretical capacity. Eighteen months after it opened the plant was already reduced to a four-day week. Industrial relations, never good, deteriorated sharply.

'Sure, there were a few stupid strikes,' acknowledged one of the shop stewards in hindsight, 'but we were never as black as we were painted. The management hadn't a clue. No consultation. Once we started to make real money, the first bonus was 12 quid a month. Very good money. Then it went down to 11, then 10. By the finish it was 30 bob. They included everybody in this bonus, down to the shithouse clerk.'

In 1968 Rootes sold out to Chrysler, but the change of ownership failed to improve the rancorous atmosphere. The local management, which was forbidden from spending more than petty cash without authorisation from head office 4,000 miles away, alienated the workforce on a scale impressive even by Linwood standards. The men went on strike for a month over a disputed productivity plan. Even *The Scotsman*, a paper of moderate temper, grew restive. 'The rights and wrongs of the present dispute have become almost impenetrable,' it acknowledged in an editorial. 'But the details are less important than the persisting lack of responsibility shown by the workers towards their industry, which in Scotland is a frail plant. If the growing spirit of nationalism is to have a positive content and lead to political self-government, it must include a realisation that industrial democracy (and profitability) are as important as a parliament in Edinburgh. Opposition for the sake of disruption, a refusal to attend a meeting because it involves crossing a road in the rain – that kind of destructive obtuseness widely shown would put Scotland beyond redemption by its own parliament or anything else.'

In April 1969, on a day of brilliant sunshine, Barbara Castle, Labour's secretary of state for employment, arrived in Linwood by helicopter to defend her government's unpopular policies for trade union reform. The management, fearful of a rough reception, waved her to a waiting car, but the minister turned and walked towards the crowd. A young apprentice leant over the wire and yelled: 'Give us a kiss, Barbara.' 'Of course,' she replied and held up her face. A roar of delight went up. There were only a few boos.

The newspapers had developed a lazy habit of referring to

Linwood as a symbol of Scottish industrial regeneration, a handy shorthand which disguised an unpalatable truth. Although 8,000 people (half the town's population) were employed at the plant, losses were running at £2.5 million a year, sales were sluggish, the local managers were inept and the workers volatile and unhappy despite wages far higher than they once earned in the yards or mines. But the underlying reality was glimpsed only when yet another dispute erupted, as it did with depressing frequency.

The deep pockets and political will of successive governments, increasingly motivated by the fear of nationalism, kept Linwood open. 'Give us a kiss.' 'Of course.' And every time a UK government blew a kiss in the direction of Linwood it blew another few million in subsidy until, by the end of Scotland's love affair with car production, a total of £100 million of public money had been invested – or squandered – in a single plant. This was not industrial regeneration in any meaningful sense. It was an illusion of progress.

There was a more profound dimension to the illusion. It concerned the faith of the lowland Scot in the power of the machine, which was akin to a form of worship. It took an Englishman, Rudyard Kipling, to understand the nature of this machine idolatry. He wrote a poem about a Glasgow engineer, MacAndrew, a monologue in which the Calvinist Scot welded his engine to his God in a perfect union of the physical and the spiritual:

From coupler-flange to spindle guide I see Thy Hand, O God –
Predestination in the stride o' yon connectin' rod
John Calvin might ha' forged the same – enorrmous, certain, slow –
Ay, wrought it in the furnace-flame – my 'Institutio'

History is disorderly: the small car did not neatly succeed the great ship. There was a period of overlap during the history of Linwood in which the last of the great liners was launched from Clydebank: hail and farewell, baptism and funeral, in a single day. Then there were no more connectin' rods. Nothing connected any more. But the significance of the occasion took a while to penetrate the national consciousness. The lowland Scot went on pretending that there was a machine left to love.

What died that day in Clydebank, and could never be re-created in Linwood, was the pride of the craftsman in his individual skill, and a fascination with the world of ships and engines which by his own hand he had helped to fashion. Kipling appreciated that it was not enough for these men to make something of little or ephemeral value. It must be a thing of beauty and nobility. It must be built to last. And it must pay. Calvin might have forged it personally.

When these same men were asked to stand on an assembly line and turn out a silly little car at the rate of one a minute, only then – at the point of mass production – did the lowland Scot finally fall out of love with the machine. He decided he might as well be a waiter.

II

Linwood did not collapse in 1975. It acquired a third owner, Peugeot, and staggered on for another six years. But a political development in the early weeks of 1975 guaranteed its eventual demise: the election of Margaret Thatcher as leader of the Conservative Party. Her first visit to Scotland, soon after she toppled Edward Heath, was a spectacular triumph. A piper playing *A man's a man for a' that* – an ironical choice in more ways than one – greeted her at Edinburgh Airport and when a shopping centre in the city was besieged by 3,000 supporters, a planned walkabout had to be cancelled. On the same day there was a crowd of 1,000 in George Square – an impressive turnout for a Tory in socialist Glasgow. 'Something almost messianic seemed to be happening,' wrote a journalist who covered her Scottish trip. By 1981 Margaret Thatcher had gained power and her hard-nosed government made no serious attempt to save the Linwood plant when its losses spiralled out of control. Suddenly the gravy train didn't stop there any more.

The closure falls outside the timescale of this book, but it is worth recalling the final scenes on 22 May 1981 if only to complete a lamentable story. To the dismay of the STUC, the workers rejected their shop stewards' advice to oppose the closure. As one union leader put it: 'Few people here have any experience of winning.' One of the workers recalled what happened then: 'The senior foreman came round and said, "Right, that's it, lads". We were told to congregate over in the west area, where we used to eat our piece. Then everybody was told to go across to the south side, and then you got your cheque, and that was it. I got £7,500. I think the average was about £4,000. They actually did me a favour. I was 52, my family were grown up, my wife was ill. I looked after her for 10 years till she passed away. I never worked again.'

In the House of Commons Alex Fletcher, a junior minister in Thatcher's government, dismissed the Scottish car industry as a relic which had to be swept away. It was indeed swept away, brutally, in a 'sale of the century' supervised by an auctioneer named Mr Butcher, who disposed of 14,000 lots of plant and machinery worth millions of pounds. Scholars were free to exhume the remains. Most agreed that a new, ill-trained labour force should never have been expected to make a new car; that it had been a failure of commercial sense, a misadventure, and that it should have been foreseen.

In the knacker's yard of the Imp they went on to open a shopping centre called the Phoenix retail park. A supermarket was built on the site of the paint shop; a burger joint arose from the ashes of the press shop; and, where the boilerhouse used to be, the redundant workers of Linwood whiled away the afternoon playing bingo.

III

Just as the fear of nationalism kept Linwood in business long after it ceased to be sustainable, the same phenomenon forced an abrupt change of policy on the Labour Party. But it was one thing to rush into a White Paper on devolution a few weeks before the October 1974 general election, another to deliver the project. In February 1975, when the Commons had its first opportunity to debate the White Paper, the opening speech by Edward Short, leader of the Commons, was pitiful. It was clear that little intelligent thinking had been done on the plans for elected assemblies in Scotland and Wales, even less on the half-baked proposition that the English regions should have their own mini-assemblies.

Gwynfor Evans called it a historic debate. For two days the main, almost only, business of the House was to consider the constitutional futures of Scotland and Wales. Evans wondered when this had happened before. Had it happened this century? Had it ever happened? But the quality of the debate failed to match the promise of the occasion. If Short was woeful, most of the contributions from the floor were little better. The lofty Jo Grimond dignified the proceedings with an elegant speech championing the cause of Scottish home rule. It had no equals for literacy or for the maturity of its thinking, but was little noticed amid the rabble. The man of the moment, though certainly not for outstanding oratory, was Tam Dalyell, chairman of the Scottish group of Labour MPs, who exposed the divisions in the governing party's ranks.

Dalyell was an unlikely socialist, an Old Etonian whose wife was the daughter of a High Court judge (Lord Wheatley, no less) and whose grand house, the Binns near Edinburgh, had been the ancestral home of the Dalyell family for more than 300 years. He began his working life as a teacher at Bo'ness Academy, managing the school football team so successfully that the grandfather of one of the players rewarded him with the nomination of his trade union for the vacant parliamentary seat of West Lothian. By this unorthodox route the young man with the top-drawer accent, originally a Tory, emerged as a standard-bearer of the Scottish working class.

Dalyell admitted early in the debate that, in the interests of party unity in the run-up to the second of the 1974 elections, he had gone along with Labour's abrupt conversion to the merits of devolution, but claimed that giving an assembly responsibility for the Scottish economy, as the government proposed, went much further than the party in Scotland, or the STUC, had been prepared to contemplate in the past.

'If we were right not to go further and to say that it [economic power] would be the smash-up of the United Kingdom, how is it that the same is not true today?'

David Lambie, the MP for Central Ayrshire, intervened from the Labour benches: 'What is wrong with it?'

Dalyell: 'There may be nothing wrong with it, but let us face the issue for what it is. The issue is the break-up of the United Kingdom.'

The 'reactionary villain', Dalyell's defiant assessment of his own standing in the party, said that no Linwood worker in his right mind would want separation from England and ridiculed Scottish claims to the oil revenues from the North Sea. 'Do you imagine,' he asked, 'that an English government would meekly doff the cap and say, "Yes, you can take all the oil in the North Sea, we shall forget about the money we have put into it, and we shall forget about the past 250 years of history"? Would an English government do that?

For heaven's sake, let us face reality.' The reality was, said Dalyell, that if the Scots divorced their English neighbours, they would end up 'a very lonely people'. He visualised an independent Scotland as 'the north European Albania'.

Jim Sillars disputed Dalyell's ultra-pessimistic take on the state of the union: 'What I find remarkable is that those who argue in favour of [it] are quite certain that it is a fragile flower – that, put under too much pressure, the petals will fly off in different directions. Is it really the case that, after 270 years of all these peoples being together – with the social intercourse, the financial and political mix, giving one another a great deal of strength and benefit and learning from one another – the union is so fragile it will break up almost overnight?' It was not long before the able Sillars himself lost faith in the union and in the Labour Party and flew off with his own petal, dedicating himself to the break-up of the UK. When the petal failed to fly, he explored what was left in the flower garden and joined the SNP.

The nationalist group performed poorly in the debate of February 1975. One of them, Douglas Crawford, decided that he had something better to do on the first day. Another, his fellow journalist George Reid, got so bogged down that the Speaker interrupted his speech and implored him to give others a chance. Reid then did himself no favours by invoking James Maxton in support of his vision of a social democratic Scotland.

Robin Cook, who spoke next, said it was 'a bit much to hear the Dick Taverne of Clackmannanshire' (Taverne, a right-wing Labour MP, had recently deserted the party) quoting a socialist hero in support of a political creed to which Maxton would not have put his name. Norman Buchan, too, was repelled by the appropriation of Maxton 'in advocating this peculiar right-wing social democracy'. He could not resist an acid personal reference: it was to Buchan's wife Janey that George Reid had written resigning from the Labour Party only six months after joining it, whereupon he had promptly signed up with the Scottish National Party.

Crawford was roundly abused when he turned up on the second day. Alick Buchanan-Smith, the shadow secretary of state for Scotland, wondered aloud what sort of example his failure to attend had set to his 'party of demagogues'; Norman Buchan accused him of misrepresenting his former employer, the Scottish Council (Development and Industry), by ascribing to it a claim that, before oil, Scotland was running a balance of payments surplus when the truth was that the council had made no such claim; and Willie Ross, closing the debate, brushed off with rough humour an interjection from Crawford about the current high level of Scottish unemployment.

Ross: 'We had more than that when the honourable member was a Tory.'

Crawford: 'On a point of order, Mr Speaker, I have never been a member of the Tory Party.'

Ross: 'I did not realise that the honourable gentleman had not even paid his dues.'

A debate distinguished mainly by petty wrangling and the settling of private scores left most questions of substance unresolved. Would Westminster have power to over-ride a Scottish Assembly if a conflict arose? Would the assembly be able to levy its own taxes? How many members should it have and how should they be elected? After two days of heat precious little light had been cast on any of these questions.

The Scottish press, unimpressed by the 'historic' debate, concluded that the cabinet had no idea how to deal with the constitutional problems posed by devolved assemblies. Tam Dalyell gave notice that, if the legislation conferred economic power on a Scottish assembly, he would fight it to 'the last comma'. His was the only reputation that emerged from the debate enhanced. The SNP members, who were accused by Norman Buchan of 'giggling their way through two days of debate on their own nation', emerged with theirs diminished.

A few weeks later there was a diverting interlude in the Commons during a debate on some industry bill. Winifred Ewing started to barrack Alick Buchanan-Smith who was sitting inoffensively on the opposition front bench: 'Get up on your feet. Where is he? Get up on your feet. You have nothing to say. Come on Alick.' Buchanan-Smith blushed as the minister, Eric Heffer, ploughed on with his speech. The interruptions of Ewing became so insistent that Selwyn Lloyd, the Speaker, felt moved to intervene. 'Is the honourable lady quite well?' he inquired. Ewing assured Lloyd that she was very well and that it was Buchanan-Smith who was not quite well.

Four years later, at the 1979 general election, only two of the 11 SNP MPs retained their seats after the party had contributed to the fall of James Callaghan's government. But the London exile of the patriots was convivial enough while it lasted. Alan Watkins, *The*

Observer's political columnist, wrote of the nationalist contingent that they 'celebrated Hogmanay at least once a week'. The mother of parliaments was a duller place without them.

IV

While the SNP ebbed and flowed as a political force, Tam Dalyell of the last comma was invariably to be found in the same awkward place. He remained for years a persistent thorn in the flesh of his party over devolution, which he regarded as an unworkable half-way house.

He was tenacious in exploiting a fundamental design fault rivalling the Imp's: that while Scottish MPs at Westminster would continue to be able to exert influence on English legislation, English MPs would be denied an equivalent say in Scottish matters once the assembly was established. How, Dalyell demanded to know, could such a state of affairs be justified? At every conceivable opportunity on every available platform, he raised the accursed question. He went on and on raising it, wearing down resistance, exhausting all around him, until it entered the language as the West Lothian Question.

Dalyell was once asked whether his personal opposition to the devolution bill had been a significant factor in the outcome of the 1979 referendum, when the Scots voted narrowly in favour of an assembly but not by the required majority. 'Yes,' he replied, 'because if one Scot hadn't opposed it, the others wouldn't have felt they could have played their part, and the whole thing would have gone through. Jim Callaghan privately agreed with me. When I went to see him, he used to say, "Don't waste my time on that nonsense. Tell me what the party's thinking about Cyprus".'

V

In a cabinet not exactly brimming with enthusiasm for a Scottish assembly, the minister responsible for bringing it about, Willie Ross, was decidedly lacking in missionary zeal. Alastair Hetherington, editor of *The Guardian*, obtained an insight into the

Secretary of State's lukewarm opinion of the project during a private meeting with him in the early part of 1975. Hetherington found Ross in cheerful mood, but on the subject of a Scottish assembly he was caustic. He told Hetherington that it would be 'full of Edinburgh lawyers and nabobs', though he seemed to have no doubts that it would happen.

Hetherington had wanted to see Ross to let him know that he intended to leave *The Guardian* to take up the post of controller of BBC Scotland which had been offered to him by Sir Michael Swann, chairman of the BBC governors. Ross's reaction to this news was not recorded, but Hetherington's colleagues in journalism were sceptical. 'You're mad,' said David English, editor of the *Daily Mail*. 'It will destroy you.' It was a prescient judgement. Hetherington, however, had edited *The Guardian* for almost 20 years, yearned for a new professional challenge before it was too late, and fancied living closer to his beloved mountains. He sensed that, politically as well as personally, the timing was perfect. 'In Scotland,' he wrote, '1975 was a fascinating time. A new dynamism had come to Scottish politics.'

Swann feared that, with a degree of self-government in prospect, there was a chance that broadcasting north of the border would be removed from the BBC's control; he believed that, in order to fight off such a challenge, the BBC needed someone with high-level political experience to run the Scottish operation. A restless Alastair Hetherington seemed to Swann to be the obvious choice, but Charles Curran, the director-general, was less keen about an outsider with no BBC pedigree. Although Curran failed to block the appointment, Hetherington's feet were only just under the table at Queen Margaret Drive when the director-general set out to make trouble for him. Hetherington had begun a meeting with Kirk leaders in Edinburgh when he received a peremptory summons to return to Glasgow for a meeting with Curran by radio link. It was a hint of the humiliations to come. One of London's next moves was to despatch a trusted lieutenant, Andrew Boyle, to Glasgow, ostensibly to oversee news and current affairs though his main function was to spy on the new boy, a task for which he was eminently qualified.

Hetherington found much to admire in the output of BBC Scotland, particularly in the quirky programmes of Ian Mackenzie, the maverick head of religious broadcasting, and in the excellent work of the drama department, whose senior producer, Pharic

Maclaren, had adapted Lewis Grassic Gibbon's *Sunset Song* for the small screen. He recognised the BBC Scottish Symphony Orchestra's important contribution to the arts, and even managed to see some good in what passed for light entertainment. The editor in him was less satisfied with BBC Scotland's journalism, and he made determined efforts to improve it by appointing several specialist correspondents, including Chris Baur and Helen Liddell.

Hetherington was not cut out by temperament or experience for the back-stabbing world of the BBC's higher echelons. It wore him down and forced him into some clumsy moves. He offended not only Curran but his successor, Ian Trethowan, with his constant demands for more money, more autonomy, and more network exposure for Scottish-made programmes. But even if his handling of the BBC's bureaucracy had been more adroit, he would not have lasted long. There was no genuine will on the part of the London hierarchy to concede meaningful devolution to its Scottish management. By the end of the 1970s the unhappy fate of Alastair Hetherington at BBC Scotland had begun to feel like an early symptom of a more general malaise.

VI

As Hetherington, a young officer during the second world war, looked forward to a late new career at the BBC, Scotland marked the 30th anniversary of VE Day with little ceremony. The *Glasgow Herald* remarked that, whereas the basic stability of British society had not been in doubt in May 1945, an outsider looking at Britain in May 1975 would conclude that the country was on the verge of dissolution. 'Appeals to the heroic spirit of 1940 will not help,' said the paper, 'since the threat is by no means as clear-cut now as it was then.'

On 8 May 1975, the 30th anniversary of VE Day, a House of Commons select committee met in Glasgow City Chambers to hear testimony from battered wives. A mother of four told MPs: 'I had a baby kicked out of me. My husband kicked me on the body when I was pregnant and I had a miscarriage.'

On the same day Patrick Meehan, serving a life sentence for the murder of an elderly woman in Ayr in 1969, failed for the second time to obtain leave to prosecute three police witnesses who testified at his trial. Meehan languished in prison for several years before a determined campaign on his behalf enabled him to prove his innocence.

On the same day a 70-year-old woman and her mentally retarded son, aged 40, were discovered sleeping on the floorboards of an empty house in Paisley. The woman had gone into hospital for an operation and her son had been taken into temporary care. While they were away, their house was wrecked by vandals and they were allocated another flat. They turned the key to find the place unfurnished, with no heat or light, no means of cooking or keeping warm. Despite appeals to the Paisley social work department, they spent six nights huddled together with only an old jacket covering them.

On the same day the Third Eye Centre in Glasgow announced its opening programme under the direction of Tom McGrath, including an exhibition of the work of Joan Eardley and a poetry reading by Sorley Maclean. That night, at the Royal Lyceum Theatre in Edinburgh, John Grieve, Roddy McMillan, Lennox Milne and Morag Hood headed a cast of Scottish actors in Bill Bryden's production of Robert McLellan's classic, *The Flouers o' Edinburgh*. Christopher Small hailed it as 'a spikily brilliant comedy which hoists the Saltire resolutely to the mast'. Small thought it might be a sign of the times.

On the same day there was another sign of the times. The SNP launched its campaign for a 'no' vote in the referendum on Britain's membership of the Common Market. The party described the EEC as 'not a market but a political super power' and Winnie Ewing, hoisting her own Saltire to the mast, said that if the poll was less than 50% it should not be taken seriously. The poll was 64% and Scotland voted by a majority of 3-2 to stay in, only Shetland and the Western Isles voting against.

But the main event on the 30th anniversary of VE Day was the continuing trial of leading members of the so-called Tartan Army (Army of the Provisional Government or APG) on a formidable indictment which included charges of conspiring to rob banks, break into Ministry of Defence establishments, destroy dams, power supplies and labour exchanges, and of taking part in a bank robbery in Springburn, Glasgow, to raise funds for their cause. Colin Boyd, secretary of the APG, spent months as a mole within the organisation, supplying the police with information. He agreed that it was possible he had suggested that blowing up oil pipelines would be a dramatic way of bringing public attention to 'Scotland's plight'. He told the court that he liked the members he had informed on – they were 'nice' – and that he had 'tried to stop them killing people'.

William Murray, 'a passionate Scottish nationalist', eloquent and intelligent, was jailed for eight years. William Anderson, the most violent of the group, managed to get himself on an oil rig; the police seriously thought he might be planning to blow it up. When he was arrested he maintained that he was a prisoner of war; he had plenty of time to get used to the idea when Lord Keith sent him down for 10 years. William Bell, the APG's 'admin officer', who got one year, was seldom seen in anything but a kilt and a glengarry, took the oath in Gaelic, and told journalists: 'I am very anti-English. I object strongly to the way foreigners are taking over my country to get this oil.' A former lay preacher, Bell had studied architecture while detained in a psychiatric hospital. The quartet was rounded off by a deranged eccentric, Major Frederick Boothby, 'one of the most informed diehards on the Scottish home rule scene' according to a newspaper profile, who was jailed for three years. Boothby had chaired meetings in his house in Biggar to discuss the enforcement of order within the APG and considered shooting through the kneecaps as a punishment for breaches of discipline.

It was 30 years to the day since a Dutch serviceman in Glasgow had climbed the statue of the Duke of Wellington in Exchange Square and entertained the crowd with his burlesque of Hitler. Thirty years since a way had been found through the throng in George Square for a young mother pushing a pram, whose occupant would come to be known as one of the baby boomers. Thirty years since the joyous hooting of ships' horns in the Clyde. Thirty years since Tom Johnston had delivered his stirring victory oration in the Usher Hall. Nothing of this was remembered publicly.

In May 1975 Scotland's 430 local authorities convened for the last time before regionalisation in a series of 'greetin' meetings'. John F Smith, Lord Provost of Aberdeen, buried a casket containing such items as a piece of Rubislaw granite, plans of the Town House extension and minutes of the council's last meeting. Culross, one of the smallest authorities, led itself out behind two pipers playing a slow march. But reports of their deaths were much exaggerated. Although Culross lost its local authority status, it was not 'wiped from the map' as some newspaper reports suggested, and the full powers of the cities were restored after a second reorganisation. *Plus ça change* ...

VII

What was the state of Scotland now? Tom Johnston had been shrewd in identifying tourism as a potential source of post-war prosperity. Its prospects were enhanced by a new concern for the natural and built environment, fostered by such charities as the Scottish Civic Trust. A plan to create a 96-mile cross-country footpath from Milngavie to Fort William was taking shape; opened in 1980 and named the West Highland Way, it did more than any other single initiative to extend access to the Scottish countryside.

The arts in Scotland were livelier and more soundly financed than at any time in their history. Scottish Opera, having acquired the Theatre Royal in Glasgow as its home in 1974, enjoyed critical acclaim under the leadership of its founder, Alexander Gibson, but absorbed a disproportionate share of the resources of the Scottish Arts Council. In the less generously supported professional theatre, the Glasgow Citizens' had all but abandoned indigenous drama but was making a wider mark with Giles Havergal's bold reworkings of the classics; Clive Perry had revived the fortunes of the civic theatre in Edinburgh, the Royal Lyceum, after Tom Fleming's brave but unsuccessful attempt at a European repertoire; the kilted Kenneth Ireland continued to host an eclectic summer season at Pitlochry, in his romantic 'theatre in the hills', where it was possible to 'stay six days and see six plays', usually including something by Barrie or the otherwise forgotten Bridie; Dundee Rep was experimenting with drama documentary, and the tiny Traverse in Edinburgh with new plays.

The leading Scottish dramatist of the 1970s, C P (Cecil) Taylor, who was much influenced by his Glasgow Jewish background, preferred to live just over the border in Northumberland, claiming that he could breathe more easily outside his native country. His contemporary Stewart Conn, senior producer of radio drama at BBC Scotland, was not only an accomplished playwright himself, but a major promoter of others' work.

Literature and broadcasting were both more representative of the lives of the urban majority. In the vanguard of the new generation of writers, William McIlvanney, a Kilmarnock school-teacher, tackled challenging themes far from the traditional kailyard, while the launch in 1973 of Radio Clyde, skilfully managed by James Gordon, 'scooped the patter off the streets and put it on the air', as one critic put it.

The baby boomers enjoyed unparalleled access to higher education, the arts and physical recreation. They enjoyed more robust health than their parents and could expect to live longer. They were more decently housed. Yet, after 30 years of peace and growing relative prosperity, some of the problems at the heart of Scotland felt as intractable as ever.

In the spring of 1975 more than 35,000 secondary school pupils were condemned to part-time education because of a chronic shortage of teachers which had been the subject of protests from the educational unions for the whole of the post-war period.

Despite the oil boom and the new jobs generated by it, the number of people unemployed in Scotland rose that spring to 101,000. Such were the inequalities of Scottish society, there was an acute shortage of labour in the oil-rich north-east. But in the central belt, it was not only the car workers of Linwood who felt insecure. The steel workers of Lanarkshire faced the threat of large-scale redundancies and the British Steel Corporation was attacked for reneging on its commitment to build a new plant at Hunterston.

Scottish fishermen feared for their future. They demanded urgent measures to conserve declining stocks off Shetland and the west coast, insisting that only a 50-mile limit would protect the industry from the raiding parties of foreign fleets. Peter Duthie, one of 120 skippers and mates who flew to London to lobby government ministers, articulated their feeling for the young people entering the industry: 'There's nothing can stop a laddie who's determined, but you can't help wondering what sort of a future there is for someone coming in now. It's not just a job, it's a whole life, and it's in our blood. Whole communities live by it, so we have to make sure the industry stays alive.'

Harold Wilson convened a meeting in Scotland. Although it was talked up in the press as a 'summit', it amounted to little more than a working dinner with the STUC. Wilson's deputation included the hapless Edward Short; Michael Foot, secretary of state for employment, sporting his familiar donkey jacket; John Smith, on the first rungs of the greasy pole as a junior minister in the Department of Energy, with his boss Eric Varley; and the Scottish Office team of Willie Ross and Bruce Millan. Jimmy Dollan, son of the late Patrick, led the STUC delegation.

The summit was booked for Suite 815 on the eighth floor of the Excelsior Hotel at Glasgow Airport. The London contingent intended to fly into Glasgow and drive – or be driven – the short distance to the hotel without having to see anything of the problematic semi-nation. But then the electricians at Glasgow Airport decided to go on strike – a piquant touch – and the party found it politically expedient to touch down at Prestwick and travel the 30 miles to Glasgow by limousine.

It was 12.20am before Harold Wilson finally emerged from Suite 815 to face the press. He announced that there had been a considerable discussion about the possibility of expanding the coal industry in Scotland. It seemed that this was not some obscure joke and that the Prime Minister was seriously proposing a leap into the industrial past as a solution to Scotland's economic problems. Nothing more was heard of the idea. But perhaps it had been a very good dinner.

VIII

On 2 November 1975 the *Evening Times* named the 'toggle-fastened duffel coat' as the cult fashion of the winter. William Pattullo, a Glasgow sheriff whose wife was one of 21 people killed in a gas explosion at Clarkston, near Glasgow, in 1971, died at the age of 54. Among the arrivals that day in Paisley Maternity Hospital, a daughter, Elaine Margaret, was born to Ian and Margaret Cox. Nicholas Fairbairn delivered a tirade against 'the air-conditioned, centrally heated, lush-salaried, inflation-proof life of the bureaucrat', but had nothing to say about the cushy number of people like himself who lived in castles (his own being Fordell in Fife). Ally McLeod, leader of a future Tartan Army, a generally peaceable one which was to follow the unsuccessful national team around the world, was appointed manager of Aberdeen Football Club. Norman Buchan called for a referendum on devolution. Billy Connolly initiated legal action to stop a Glasgow shop calling itself 'The Big Yin', the nickname by which he was known, claiming that it was a blatant attempt to cash in on his popularity. It was another day in the life of Scotland. According to the Queen or her speech writer, however, it was 'a day of outstanding significance in the history of the United Kingdom': the arrival of an economic miracle. Just before noon the first oil to be piped ashore from the North Sea entered BP's Grangemouth refinery.

At Dyce, the control centre of the pipeline between the Forties field and the refinery, the Queen formally switched on the supply. Pictures of the oil passing through a transparent section of the line at Grangemouth appeared on TV screens and were applauded by guests. 'Auspiciousness and mutual congratulations hung over the aristocratic event like cigar smoke,' wrote a journalist struggling for a metaphor. It was one of Harold Wilson's last major engagements before his unexpected resignation in March 1976. In a speech big on hyperbole – he predicted that North Sea oil would lead a new industrial revolution – Wilson made a statistical error. He said that the reserves so far proved in the British sector had been valued at £2,000 million (£2 billion). The true figure was £200 billion. It was put down to a typing mistake.

The event took place, according to newspaper reports, 'amid the strictest security precautions ever arranged for a royal visit'. A threatened protest by the Scottish National Party failed to materialise, and the ring-leaders of the Tartan Army were behind bars. Still, no chances were taken. When a parcel was found taped to the Forth Road Bridge on the morning of auspiciousness, the bridge was closed to traffic for 80 minutes until an army bomb disposal unit shot the parcel off the superstructure from a height of 180 feet. The suspect floated for three minutes before sinking without trace.

Far out in the North Sea 1,300 workers on the first of the Forties platforms looked forward to a celebration lunch. But at Grangemouth there was little sign of 'one of the biggest public relations festivals of modern times'. A BBC reporter – who went on to write this book – stood outside the refinery on a late autumn day for a live outside broadcast, trying to sound excited about the first tiny container of North Sea oil which had been thrust into his hands. He was able to report a statement from BP that, in two and a half hours, Scottish motorists would be filling up with petrol from the North Sea.

The reporter was not asked to return the oil. He kept it in its container and it moved with him from house to house for many years. After one such move he noted without close examination that its contents had vanished. He wrote to that effect in a newspaper, thinking it a neat metaphor, but was corrected by a scientific reader who assured him that, in his expert opinion, a residue remained. What was true of the contents of the bottle may also have been true of the life of post-war Scotland: that the spirit of the nation, though invisible to the naked eye, never quite evaporated.

THE SUMMING-UP

I

John Lawrence, the chairman of Rangers Football Club, had a problem with minutes – not the minutes marking the passage of time, but those that translate events and decisions into a formal record and help to write the history of a society. When he gave evidence at the fatal accident inquiry into the deaths of 66 supporters on stairway 13 at Ibrox Stadium, he could not remember whether a previous accident on the same stairway only two years earlier had been discussed by the club's directors or whether a minute had been taken of any such discussion. Knowing that he would be giving evidence at the inquiry, he had not troubled himself to check the minutes. Although his friend and co-director David Hope had attended a meeting on stairway 13 with the police and others, Hope had no clear recollection of having been there. He too could have consulted the minutes as an aid to memory, but chose not to do so.

The testimonies of Lawrence and Hope lacked both candour and credibility. But the problem with minutes in the fragmented narrative of post-war Scotland is a more general one.

Where, for example, is the official record of the ill-treatment of young women in the Magdalene institution in Maryhill, Glasgow? These unfortunate souls had committed no crime, yet they were imprisoned, coerced into hard labour, and punished by beatings and drenchings. It was only when some managed to escape, shouting their desperate protests from rooftops, that the Scottish Home Department was moved to investigate. A few months later, as a result of that investigation, the malign institution closed and the ill-treatment of its 'inmates' came to an end. Yet the department did not consider it necessary to release its findings into the public domain. Its report, if there was one, remained confidential and the victims were not given what would later be called 'closure': the state failed to explain its long turning of a blind eye to abuse, while the Roman Catholic Church offered no public apology. Victims of Magdalene institutions in Ireland were ultimately treated with more dignity, though perhaps only because there were more of them and their many cries of anguish could no longer be ignored.

Likewise, when the right-wing notion of 'a short, sharp shock' for young offenders was corrupted at a recently opened detention centre in Perth into a regime of physical abuse, and a disturbing number of prisoners attempted suicide rather than submit to it, the Secretary of State for Scotland (John S Maclay) ordered an inquiry. The abuse was promptly stopped, but there was no indication that disciplinary action had been or would be taken against the prison officers responsible for it. The report of that inquiry was kept under wraps for many years (although it is now belatedly available for inspection, by prior appointment, at the National Records of Scotland).

The state protected the perpetrators of these offences against young people in Glasgow and Perth. There was no duty of transparency or public accountability as these terms came to be understood, but nor was there any popular will to challenge institutionalised secrecy.

The requirement for an open record, unavoidable in the case of public inquiries, was not always a guarantee of integrity; there were occasions when the minutes were a disgrace. The judicial view of the Ibrox disaster was that the jury could not apportion blame because there was no evidence that the directors of the football club had failed to do what they should have done to protect human life. This was a scandalous misrepresentation of what the jury had in fact heard: that the police had proposed a specific measure for improving crowd safety on stairway 13 and that the club had failed to act on it. That failure, with its tragic consequences, could and should have led to the prosecution of the directors. Instead Sheriff Allan Walker ensured by his distorted summary of the facts that Lawrence and Hope emerged with their standing in the community no worse than dented by the proof of their own prevarication in the witness box.

Another Glasgow sheriff, M G Gillies, took a similarly indulgent view of the management of the bonded warehouse near the Clyde where a million gallons of whisky were stored in conditions condemned by the city firemaster and others. His judgement that the management had acted responsibly, that it could not be blamed in any way for 19 deaths, was so perverse that some challenge to it by the city's main newspaper, the *Glasgow Herald*, might have been expected. But the *Herald* at that time was the organ of the West of Scotland business class. It made no criticism of the directors of the warehouse, just as, a decade later, it had nothing to say about the whitewashing of the board of Rangers Football Club.

The deference of the Scottish press, which often bordered on the obsequious, safeguarded the interests of the powerful even when the powerful were enemies of freedom. Four months before the start of the second world war, a communist newspaper, the *Daily Worker*, smuggled a mole into a meeting of the fascist Right Club in the Wigmore Hall, London, and reported the threat of the club's founder to end 'Jewish control' by force. When the speaker was named as Archibald Ramsay, the Unionist MP for Peebles and South Midlothian, there was no immediate campaign for his removal. It was many years before the names of the other Scottish supporters of this odious organisation were finally revealed, though not as a result of any investigative work by the Scottish press. Such unimpeachable subjects as the Queen's representative in Kirkcudbright, the then Earl of Galloway, who combined his duties as Lord Lieutenant with a devotion to the Nazi cause, escaped prosecution.

But then so did the abusers of young women in the Magdalene institution, the sadists on the staff of Perth detention centre and the directors of both Rangers Football Club and the Cheapside Street warehouse. The establishment looked after its own, and the press meekly went along with it. In such a cosy relationship, there was no need for minutes.

II

Occasionally, however, these minutes meant the difference between life and death. When the judge in a capital murder trial pronounced sentence, he did so 'for doom' and the prisoner in the dock could expect to die in 21 days. An appeal postponed the execution of the sentence for a few more weeks. It was seldom successful.

There was no royal prerogative of mercy for James Smith, aged 21, who was hanged in 1952, or Henry John Burnett, aged 21, who was hanged in 1963. The conduct of both cases was reprehensible, though for different reasons. Smith's trial, after a fatal stabbing in a dance hall brawl, was notable for the casual reference by a prosecution witness to the discovery of a second knife in the dance hall. It had not been examined, it had not been lodged as a production, it had not been made available to the defence, yet it might have helped to show that Smith acted in self-defence. Was the failure of the police to produce it not an attempt to pervert the course of justice? Did it not cast some doubt – a reasonable one – on the guilt of the accused? Despite a direction from the bench nudging the jury towards acquittal, the jury convicted. But it was ultimately open to James Stuart, the Secretary of State for Scotland, to recommend clemency in a case so obviously flawed. The future Viscount Stuart of Findhorn let Smith hang. The press in its usual acquiescent fashion raised no objection, the execution was scarcely noted, and the possibility that there had been police corruption was never mentioned publicly. Better in such a case to have no minute than a minute potentially embarrassing to the Crown Office.

The trial of Henry John Burnett cast an equally unflattering light on the standards of Scottish criminal justice. A psychiatrist who gave an expert evaluation of Burnett's state of mind was treated as a hostile witness, there was little inclination by the trial judge, Lord Wheatley, to respect his evidence, and the body language in the courtroom during his ordeal by cross-examination went unchecked. Burnett was convicted and sentenced to death. While Michael Noble, the Secretary of State for Scotland, considered the case papers, Ian Shearer, the Lord Advocate, urged him not to recommend clemency. Clemency, Shearer argued, would play into the hands of the abolitionists. It is unclear whether Noble was impressed by Shearer's gratuitous pleading, but in the end he refused to lift a finger to save a man who had not been responsible for his actions.

Shearer went on to become a judge – an office dignified by the title Senator of the College of Justice – and chose to be known as Lord Avonside when his own surname would have done. Having successfully politicised the application of the death penalty, he thought nothing of politicising his own bench by accepting membership of a committee set up by the Conservative Party to inquire into Scotland's constitutional future. For unintentional hilarity, Shearer's indignation when he was confronted with this blatant partiality was matched only by the granting of an absolute discharge – by the same Sheriff Gillies who had presided over the Cheapside Street charade – to Lionel Daiches after 'a sensible modicum of whisky', and a quantity of barbiturates, had rendered Sheriff Daiches unfit to drive a car.

Wheatley delivered the judgement in the Argyll divorce. That too was unintentionally funny. Only Wheatley, its author, failed to appreciate it. As a public servant – the chairman of this committee of inquiry and that – his masterwork was a report demolishing local government so comprehensively that Orkney, Shetland and the Western Isles were all to be ruled from Inverness. Even the Labour government, with its fetish for centralisation, thought Wheatley had gone too far and diluted or expunged the wilder absurdities of the scheme.

III

The reason for re-assembling in this final chapter some of the more deplorable features of Scottish public life is not only to expose by example the poor quality of so much of it. It is to make the general though perhaps rather obvious point that the people of Scotland were on the whole badly served by their masters – and by what passed for a free press. The subsequent erosion of trust in institutions had its roots in the arrogance and incompetence of so many who held positions of power and influence in the post-war era. How did they get away with it? Why did no one notice that the pillars of society had already begun to crumble? The honourable exceptions showed what might have been possible, but they also laid bare the shabbiness of so much else.

Among these exceptions, Tom Johnston's pragmatic vision stimulated Scottish tourism and brought electricity and amenity to many remote communities in the far north. The Labour government of 1964-70 created the Highlands and Islands Development Board (but then mishandled it). Lord Kilbrandon's report decriminalising juvenile delinquency, introducing the children's hearing system and paving the way for a modern social work service, was a model of enlightenment of which Scotland could be proud. Professor J B Cullingworth, in drawing attention to the living conditions of the urban and rural poor, gave a moral dimension to the extended crisis of Scottish housing and a renewed urgency to the imperative task of dealing with it. The official report into the Auchengeich Colliery disaster was scrupulous and unsparing, though it may have been significant that it was conducted not by a member of the Scottish Bar but by an inspector of mines and quarries. The superbly disciplined UCS work-in and the leadership of the two Jimmies – Airlie and Reid – was an outstanding illustration of what 'ordinary people' could achieve in the face of political hostility. Although UCS could be seen in retrospect as the last stand of the Scottish working class, it was a deeply impressive one.

Such exceptions were rare and too often overwhelmed by mediocrity and self-interest. Sometimes the folly was so staggering that it remains a marvel that it was so warmly embraced at the time. The simplistic approach to the problem of an economy based on declining traditional industries was to throw enormous sums of money at branch factories owned by Americans, but very little at indigenous enterprise. Encouraged by governments of both parties, the Scottish Council (Development and Industry) pursued this short-sighted policy with fanatical zeal, promising the unsuspecting inward investor a land of championship golf courses and clean air with a well-trained, adaptable workforce. These were the actual phrases used; it was no more representative of reality than Brigadoon.

It then commissioned a group of corporate nonentities to bring forth, in the Toothill report, an ill-written prescription for economic revival, anticipating Thatcherism. The same Scottish Council even found something positive to say about the Beeching plan for the butchery of Scotland's railways. Lord Polwarth, its figurehead, confessed to 'admiring' a report which proposed the withdrawal of all rail services to the Borders, north and west of Inverness, and south of Ayr.

But the supposedly politically neutral Scottish Council was not alone in its admiration of Beeching's savagery. Jean Roberts, the Glasgow municipal leader who was so outraged by the rubbish left in George Square after the VE night celebrations that she banned Churchill from using the square during the 1945 election campaign, thought Beeching an excellent opportunity to build car parks on the site of abandoned stations. For her contribution to civic Scotland, she was appointed a Dame of the British Empire. Dame Jean could claim to be something of a visionary. There were indeed to be many car parks.

IV

While rich American industrialists, lured by Scotland's championship golf courses and clean air, to say nothing of its well-trained, adaptable workforce, were accorded the greatest respect, there was less tolerance of other minorities. In 1962 it was socially acceptable for the Free Church of Scotland to use the phrase 'a stranger of Eastern blood' to describe someone born in Thurso, the son of an Iraqi doctor; and the following year it was socially acceptable for young Anna Kesselaar, who had been wheeled naked across a platform of the Edinburgh drama conference, to be hounded out of her home for immorality and for the Lord Provost of Edinburgh, who some years later committed suicide because of his reckless spending, to describe her exhibition of nudity as a tragedy for the festival. The man must have known little of tragedy, until his own.

In 1955 it was socially acceptable for homosexuality to be discussed in a High Court murder trial as a medical condition curable by treatment; and when the Wolfenden Committee subsequently proposed the legalisation of homosexual acts between consenting adults, the sole dissenting voice on the committee was a Scot, James Adair. It was socially acceptable for this man to inform the General Assembly of the Church of Scotland that it would no longer be unlawful for 'perverts to practise sinning for the sake of sinning'. The General Assembly, having listened to his poisonous rant, decisively rejected the Wolfenden proposals.

The Kirk wielded enormous influence in Scottish life, to a degree almost inconceivable to the modern mind. It was an institution with a mass membership; its leading figures were household names; and the Scottish press dutifully chronicled its annual deliberations in what was called 'the nearest thing to a Scottish parliament'. But its generosity of Christian spirit did not bear close examination. If it disapproved of homosexuals, it was not much keener on women. The war had not quite ended when it voted against allowing them to become elders. In 1964 Mary Lusk's magnificent speech appealing for the ordination of her gender fell on the usual deaf ears. And in the same week that it collapsed gratefully at the feet of the new saviour in its midst, Billy Graham, it paid scant regard to a report pointing out the inhumanity of creating new townships in the suburbs – the Drumchapels and Easterhouses – without also providing the civilised amenities of life.

V

The Kirk's reluctance to accept reforms that would come to be seen as inevitable was mirrored by the crippling timidity of the political establishment. It would be an insult to the humble truism to deny that some progress was made in improving the condition of the Scottish people between 1945 and 1975, but it was achieved painfully slowly. There was no great leap in longevity – the core test of national well-being – from the wretched expectation that a boy born in Glasgow in 1948 would live to the age of 51. At the time of writing, there is a district of that city where the average life expectancy is still only 51. Although slum clearance, one of the keys to a longer life for the urban poor, was the declared priority of post-war governments, it was so badly managed that an indictment of Scotland's housing stock was possible 23 years after the war had ended.

We should not be surprised by any of this, for the quality of political leadership was low. Joseph Westwood, Arthur Woodburn, James Stuart and Michael Noble were not impressive figures, yet each of them was considered fit to be Secretary of State for Scotland. Of the 10 men who held the office in the 31 years covered by this book, Hector McNeil was the smartest intellectually, but decided he would rather be a writer and broadcaster than a politician. The positive qualities of William Ross, one of his successors, were overshadowed by his disastrous misreading of the rise of the SNP.

Were the people of Scotland any brighter than their leaders? If they were, it would not have been saying a great deal. But most were denied a proper education by the disciplinarian culture of secondary schools which drove children out of the classroom as soon as legally possible. There were repeated warnings about the alienating effect of using fear as a method of educating young minds, but such warnings were resented by the teaching profession. When the one lonely reformer, R F Mackenzie, committed the ultimate sacrilege of forbidding the corporal punishment of girls, he was cast into the wilderness – giving him time to write a great book.

The children of Scotland were doomed to endure a curriculum so rigid that Walter Elliot was moved to describe part of it as a weariness of the flesh. But there was one subject that most children would be spared – a thorough history of their own country. Lord Cooper delivered one of his magisterial rebukes when he said of Scottish education that it was calculated to condition the Scottish mind to turn instinctively towards London. The exclusion from the curriculum of all but a tokenistic smattering of Scottish history – a policy pursued by governments of both political persuasions – could not have been other than wilful, in the same way that the proscription of Gaelic in the schools of the Western Isles had been wilful. In denying children an adequate knowledge of their own culture and identity, it asserted the relative insignificance of Scotland.

VI

The Britishing of the Scots did not wholly quash a national yearning for something better or, at any rate, different. It found expression in the national covenant, which called for a Scottish parliament within the union and was signed by two million people. The unionist political parties responded to this extraordinary result in a predictably low fashion, by casting doubt on its authenticity. The enigmatic John MacCormick, the leader of the covenant, marched his two million troops – give or take a few duplicates – to the top of the hill and, knowing not what to do with them, marched them all the way down again. The bewildered troops dispersed.

Nothing happened – or very little. Labour lost power and the dreadful George Pottinger was drafted by St Andrew's House to facilitate James Stuart's Royal Commission on Scottish Affairs. It produced a number of recommendations so derisory that they might as well have saved the forest. The same Lord Cooper had delivered another of his magisterial rebukes on the subject of the Queen's numerals, declaring that although he could do nothing about the Queen's numerals, their adoption was a sign of contempt for the integrity of Scotland within the union. But still nothing happened – or very little – despite the support for the home rule cause of such prominent Scots as the scientist John Boyd Orr, the dramatist O H Mavor and the lawyer John Cameron (Dean of the Faculty of Advocates).

Scotland reverted to the place ascribed for it in the union as an unthreatening backwater distinguished by the poor education, poor health and poor housing of its people. The more ambitious got out, some to London, many to the talent-hungry countries of the Commonwealth. Their departure had a beneficial effect on the unemployment figures; there was that to be said for the exodus of talent.

The Scottish National Party had long been a joke, though not one amusing enough to qualify as a music hall sketch. In 1950 – the year of the Stone of Destiny episode – the party put up four candidates in the general election. Five years earlier Dr Robert McIntyre had unsuccessfully attempted to defend his Motherwell seat with the slogan 'Scotland for the Scots'. He was not expelled for racism; on the contrary he remained a hero of the SNP until his death half a century later. Nor was Arthur Donaldson run out of town when he suggested in his chairman's speech to the annual conference in 1967 that the party should have a new slogan based on a Bannockburn battle-cry. But the people seemed not to mind such xenophobic aberrations. They had grown so tired of the alternatives, so cynical about the routine indifference and betrayals of the ruling political classes, that they were ready for a mystery tour.

The unexpected victory of a socialist, Winnie Ewing, in the Hamilton by-election of 1967, followed by Margo MacDonald's triumph in Govan six years later, made it more difficult for the Labour Party to ridicule the nationalists as Tartan Tories. But they were still capable of own goals scored from the right wing. Their 1970 manifesto was a mess. By 1974 they had pulled themselves together, sending a squad the size of a football team to Westminster after the second of that year's general elections, but it was a squad short on political maturity, short on coherent policy, and short on leadership. The manager came later – so much later that it is here, on the penultimate page, that his name, Alex Salmond, appears for the first and only time.

VII

The period encompassed by this book – a half-decade, two full decades, and another half-decade – is a mere fragment of the experience of an old country. It is a minute of what is no more than a second in the long stretch of Scottish history, and it would be futile to pretend that it describes a prosperous and well-governed people. Between the end of the narrative and the time of publication, however, there was an interval of 38 years. Much changed during the interval; most of it for the better.

Scotland is now more competently administered (largely by a parliament in Edinburgh), more sympathetic to sexual minorities and less tolerant of abuses of power, more humane in its treatment of children and young people, and less respectful of authority. Inconveniently for any latter-day Pottinger, there is greater scrutiny of those in public life. The judiciary is perhaps a little less pompous than it was; the trumpets have gone, along with the power to kill people. Among the obvious downsides, there is the loss of manufacturing industry and the stubbornly poor health of many urban Scots despite a succession of well-meaning attempts to improve it. But for most of the progress made in the post-post-war era, we should be profoundly grateful. When the next minute comes to be written, I hope and expect that it will tell a happier story.

Afterword

The writing of *The Invisible Spirit* coincided with the start of the referendum campaign on Scottish independence. We have just had the result: a decisive though far from overwhelming vote for the union after an unprecedented turnout of almost 85% of the electorate.

The question, 'Should Scotland be an independent country?', was loaded in favour of the Yes side and put the pro-union opposition on the back foot from the outset. This may have been responsible for the negativity of the No campaign, which concentrated almost exclusively on the risks of Scotland going it alone.

The more positive question of dual nationality – the wish of many Scots to be both Scottish and British, usually in that order – was never discussed in any depth, although it was always a powerful sub-text in the post-war Scotland charted by this book and continued to be so as recently as referendum day (18 September 2014).

Likewise, the nature of modern British identity, as exemplified by such rocky institutions as the BBC and the National Health Service, was seldom celebrated, perhaps because there was so little left to celebrate; indeed the BBC became a focus of nationalist anger over unsubstantiated suggestions of biased reporting.

The Yes side, with its passion and flair, engaged many people, including the young and the poor, but alienated others with its intolerance of contrary opinions. In the last stages of the campaign there was a good deal of intimidation and abuse, much of it generated on social media.

The outcome revealed a country divided between the areas of middle-class prosperity and growth, all of which voted heavily against independence, and the former centres of traditional heavy industry which either voted emphatically in favour (Glasgow, Dundee, North Lanarkshire, West Dunbartonshire) or came close to doing so.

It was interesting how many of the themes of this book were strongly represented in the campaign: a detachment from centres of power, the social isolation of peripheral urban estates, the consequences of post-industrialism, the failure of the political class to deal with the sources of popular discontent, the general collapse of trust in institutions.

The fact that at least a third of Labour voters opted for independence, despite dire warnings from business leaders about the effect on their pockets, spoke eloquently of their sense of betrayal and an instinctive feeling that life in a self-governing Scotland could scarcely be worse than it had been under Westminster rule. That would not have come as a surprise to anyone who had read this book, with its many accounts of the party's post-war complacency and corruption. Labour was indeed fortunate to escape from the referendum in one piece. Yet, strangely, the campaign was conducted without any close examination of the record of the devolved parliament or the quality of its elected representatives; it was almost as if Scotland had no devolved powers or that it had never used them.

The heavy vote for independence – 1.6 million – reflected, too, a fairly widespread satisfaction with the Scottish National Party's competence as the governing party in the Edinburgh parliament since 2007 and, most hopefully, it symbolised the idealism of young people, including 16 and 17 year olds who voted for the first time, most of them for home rule. But the cause failed to ignite as a national and unifying one; only four of the 32 local authorities registered a victory for independence and the No vote in places as diverse as the Borders, the northern isles and the well-heeled capital city was strikingly high.

It is difficult to avoid the conclusion that the referendum came much too early to produce any other outcome than the conservative one it did. There was an interval of 18 years between the first referendum on devolution (1979) and the second (1997), but an interval of only 13 years between the re-establishment of the parliament and the calling of the referendum. Instead of steady progress, there was a rush to the ultimate destination of the nationalists, for which most of the country was unprepared – even in propitious circumstances which may never be repeated.

As I write this in the immediate aftermath of the vote, the invisible spirit of the post-war era has been replaced by a more astringent cocktail of disharmony.

September 2014

References

Many of the quotations most personally revealing were drawn from meetings with their sources.

Over tea in the House of Lords, Alec Douglas-Home recalled his impressions of Hitler at the fateful last meeting in Munich (p 30) and surprised me with the warmth of his affection for James Maxton (p 53).

From a number of conversations with Ena Lamont Stewart I learned that her masterpiece *Men Should Weep* was not ideologically driven as some of her admirers wanted to believe, and that she was astonished as well as amused to have been branded a communist (p 57).

John Junor's denunciation of stay-at-home Scots as 'whingeing third-raters' (p 122) came during a bruising encounter at Gatwick Airport. Monty Finniston provided an equally unflattering national character reference (p 467), but in a more congenial mood.

The story of John Smith's first campaign in East Fife (p 271) was related by the candidate himself during an entertaining afternoon in his house. Winnie Ewing was at home too, but less relaxed, particularly when I probed her unhappy introduction to the House of Commons (p 369). A convivial meeting with Mick McGahey in which he explained the roots of his political faith (p 470) took place over a succession of whiskies in a trade union social club. The recollection of James Callaghan's withering dismissal of Scottish devolution (p 496) I obtained from a long interview with Tam Dalyell in the House of Commons.

Jimmy Reid's eloquent remembrance of his dead siblings and of his political development (pp 440–1) emerged from an extended dialogue with a group of young people. Another such group heard James Black discuss the importance of the happy accident in scientific discovery and the impact of adrenaline on the human body (pp 139–40).

The statement that Jean Morris, the then chairman of the Parole

Board for Scotland, agreed to the release of Jimmy Boyle with some reluctance (p 392) was based on something she said to me at the time. Boyle's autobiography, *A Sense of Freedom*, is alluded to on page 392.

Among my many references to Hugh MacDiarmid, most of which are unflattering, I should have included a qualifying note that, when I spent an afternoon with him at Brownsbank near the end of his long life, he was delightful company. I would have liked to ask George MacLeod if unemployed shipyard workers really were involved in the restoration of Iona Abbey, as he often claimed, but by the time I finally interviewed him on his beloved Iona he was almost deaf; and, anyway, I continued to swallow the story about the shipyard workers until his son cast doubt on it in an article in the *Scottish Review* a few months before the publication of this book.

My scepticism about the Bible John case (p 395) was inspired by the shrewd hunches of a senior figure in the Glasgow police, long retired, who worked on the case and whose testimony when I met him seemed credible.

Long after the Linwood car plant closed, I gathered the reminiscences of a few of the workers; the brief extracts on p 489 and pp 491–92 show the depth of their resentment and how long that resentment endured.

The *Scottish Review*, which I have edited since its launch in 1995, was the source of a great deal of other material, including Bet Low's evocation of post-war Glasgow (pp 56–7), Ian Hamilton's memoir of his father (pp 112–3), the portrait of John Boyd Orr by members of his family (p 98), Ian Lockerbie's assessment of John Grierson (p 102) and Kevin McCarra's of Jock Stein (p 370), George Chalmers' unsentimental journey back to his childhood in Juteopolis (pp 206–7), and Ian Mackay's anecdote about Profumo seeking refuge in Sutherland (p 297).

Among the many books which occupied me, two political biographies were particularly helpful. From Tom Johnston's *Memories*, I included the tale of how the chairman of the North of Scotland Hydro Electric Board stole a war-time camp (p 45) and his rueful thoughts on the distractions of public service (p 33). John MacCormick's *The Flag in the Wind* offered valuable insights into the formation of Scottish Convention (pp 78–80) and the signing of the national covenant (pp 94–6), though fewer on the Paisley by-election (pp 80–3). The book was consistently illuminating of the character and motivations of that remarkable Scot.

From Sir David Milne's study of St Andrew's House, *The Scottish Office and Other Scottish Government Departments*, I selected a few perceptive observations (p 156).

Within the Fringe by James Stuart, a former Secretary of State for Scotland, though a slight work, did yield an engaging sketch of his appointment by Churchill (p 127) and a couple of fragments involving Geordie Buchanan, a forgotten House of Commons character (pp 72 and 128). Keith Aitken's *The Bairns o' Adam: the Story of the STUC* conjured up in a single phrase another Scottish character, George Middleton (p 140). Abe Moffat's testimony of his early life and first day at work (p 196) was extracted from his autobiography, *My Life with the Miners*.

For Orwell's experiences on Jura, and his treatment in Hairmyres Hospital (pp 73–75), I relied mainly on Jeffrey Meyers' biography, *George Orwell: Wintry Conscience of a Generation*, but drew also on a touching pamphlet, *Reminiscences of Eric Blair*, by a local woman, Mrs Nelson of Ardlussa.

Ivor Brown sweltering in the heat during an early Edinburgh Festival (p 67) I came across in his book of seasonal wanderings, *Summer in Scotland*. Kathleen Tynan's *The Life of Kenneth Tynan* I quoted (p 307) for its exposure of Calvinist hypocrisy at a later Edinburgh Festival.

In considering the possible role of Hamish Henderson in the blowing up of a pillar box (p 154), the first instalment of Timothy Neat's biography, *The Making of the Poet*, was enlightening. In considering the role of Ian Hamilton in the taking of the Stone of Destiny, his book *The Taking of the Stone of Destiny* was equally enlightening.

I am grateful to John Forsyth for recovering from his papers a number of interviews on the case of Henry John Burnett, extracts from which are used on pp 328–9. The trial judge Lord Wheatley's poor opinion of psychiatric evidence and his reflections on the quality of Scottish justice (p 330), I read first in his autobiography, *One Man's Judgment*.

The account of Alastair Hetherington's tenure as controller of BBC Scotland (pp 496–8) was informed by his book, *Inside BBC Scotland 1976–80*. The comments by John Grigg on Hetherington's role in the Suez affair appeared in *Alastair Hetherington: A Man of His Word*, a book edited by myself. Bob Boothby's more ambiguous role in the crisis I stumbled on by accident in Harold Nicolson's *Diaries and Letters 1945–62*.

Confusion to Our Enemies, a collection of the journalism of Arnold Kemp edited by his daughter Jackie, produced not only an insider's insight into the sycophantic nature of Scottish journalism (p 345), but a revisionist view of the nationalist heroine Wendy Wood (pp 453-4). The biography referred to on p 451 is Andro Linklater's excellent *Compton Mackenzie: A Life*. On pp 117–9, I deal with the hostile reception in the Hebrides for *The Western Isles* by Alasdair Alpin MacGregor.

Jean Rook's autobiography, in which she described Auchtermuchty as an invention of John Junor (p 122), is *The Cowardly Lioness*. James Cameron's autobiography, which I re-visited for his experiences with D C Thomson as a young journalist and for his memories of Dundee in general (p 85), is *Point of Departure*. Gilbert McAllister's biography mentioned on p 52 is *James Maxton: Portrait of a Rebel* and Lauchlan Weir's on p 25 is *The Tragedy of Ramsay MacDonald*.

Douglas Young's last book, *Scotland*, published in 1971 and briefly referred to on p 78, contained many well-informed perspectives on the state of the nation at that interesting time, and was accomplished with a light yet scholarly touch. I also recommend R F Mackenzie's *In Search of Scotland* (p 321), an emotional voyage loosely disguised as a travel book, which should be considered in the same class as the earlier *Scottish Journey* by Edwin Muir (p 16).

Some vignettes in the book were born of personal experience: the shocked silence in Glasgow Central Station on the night of John F Kennedy's assassination (p 309); the loneliness of Chic Murray (p 461); Nigel Tranter writing a novel on the hoof (p 185); Mick McGahey's mastery of his daily press conference in the showdown with the Heath government (p 470); and, most memorably, the heady atmosphere in an upstairs room of the Caledonian Hotel the morning after the SNP's triumph in the October 1974 general election (p 486).

Index